The Cubs on Catalina

*A Scrapbookful of Memories
About a 30-Year Love Affair
Between One of Baseball's Classic Teams...
& California's Most Fanciful Isle*

Jim Vitti

Lennie Merullo, Bobby Sturgeon, Billy Rogell, & Bobby Mattick, 1940.

Settefrati Press

DARIEN, CONNECTICUT   SAN JOSE, CALIFORNIA   ATLANTA, GEORGIA   FROSINONE, ITALIA

The Cubs on Catalina
Copyright ©2003 by Jim Vitti
All rights reserved.

Published by Settefrati Press / *www.SettefratiPress.com*

Distributed by PBS/Pathway Book Service, an Ingram / Baker & Taylor Vendor-of-Record, 1-800-345-6665 / *www.pathwaybook.com*

Library of Congress Cataloging-in-Publication Data:

Vitti, Jim, 1961-
    The Cubs on Catalina: *A Scrapbookful of Memories About a 30-Year Love Affair Between One of Baseball's Classic Teams . . . & California's Most Fanciful Isle* / by Jim Vitti
        p. cm.
    Includes bibliographic references & index.
    ISBN 0-9742424-0-3

1. Chicago Cubs (baseball team) — Pictorial Works. I. Vitti, Jim II. Title.
2. Spring training (baseball). I. Vitti, Jim II. Title.
3. Santa Catalina Island (Calif.) — History. I. Vitti, Jim II. Title.

GV875 2003
796.357'64—dc21

Book design by Jim Allyn, Allyn Advertising.
Printed in the United States of America by Bang Printing, Minnesota, 1-800-328-0450 / *www.bangprinting.com*

First Edition

07 06 05 04 03   5 4 3 2 1

On the cover: 1934 team picture . . . The key to Room 227 at the Hotel St. Catherine in Avalon . . . 1930s postcard.

Front endsheets: Stan Hack swinging away, 1936 -- with newsreels & WHO-radio announcer Dutch Reagan (leaning over to adjust his equipment) lining up along the 1st-base line.

Back endsheets: Wrigley Field on Catalina Island (from the old grandstand) -- Avalon, California.

Contents

The Gulls-Eye View *A magical place, a magical time, a magical team* 7

The Magic Isle *A Rookie's Guide to Santa Catalina Island* 11

The Cubbies *A quick look at one of baseball's oldest, most beloved, legendary teams* 16

Springs Before Catalina *Boiling off the winter's remnants* 21

1921-1951 *A 30-year relationship — sort of* 24

Getting There *Trains, planes, buses, steamships, streetcars, cabs, & the occasional thumb* 35

Hack Miller, Hack Wilson, Stan Hack, & Warren Hacker
An assortment of colorful Cubs just kept hacking away... 46

Practice, practice, practice *Goat trails, medicine balls, & a dash of pepper* 73

After practice *Snipe hunts, a friendly game of cards, & putt perfection: What's a boy (on an island) to do?* 88

The natives are *female!* *Dames, skirts, & even an occasional broad* 112

Dutch
How a plucky young radio man parlayed his Catalina trip into a career in Hollywood ...& another in Washington.. .118

Lefty Carnett, Lefty Chambers, Lefty Minner, Lefty O'Doul, & Lefty Sloat
Where's a good southpaw when you need one? 128

Norma Jeane *The stars really came out...while the Cubs played on Catalina* 174

The great quake of '33 *California rolled out more than just the red carpet one March afternoon* 187

Jolly Cholly, Gabby, Old Flash, Cavy, & other managerial types
A collection of colorful coaches & skippers came over to keep the boys in line 194

Doc *They don't make 'em like Andy Lotshaw...or Yosh Kawano...any more* 218

Chuck Connors, the Branded Rifleman
After Dutch, another strapping visitor from the East hopped over to Hollywood from the Catalina diamond 230

Onto the Summer & into the Fall: Back to the Friendly Confines
Once the boys broke camp, they spent a little time at Wrigley Field, too 235

What I did during my winter non-vacation
In those days, most ballplayers slogged through blue-collar wintertime jobs...after making it back home at season's end 240

More Contents

The other Channel Islands — & isles further out to sea
There were a few other ports around the deep blue oceans... 250

Mr. Wrigley, PK, & the executive team
Meanwhile, back at the tower...they made a lot of chewing gum, a few good baseball decisions, & way too many bad ones 255

The War, & the dreary front at a place called French Lick
Spring Training in the snow, while the others had traded their bats for bayonets 268

The press   *Jimmy the Cork, T-Bone Otto, Gentleman Jim, & a variety of others with ink in their veins* 277

Overtown to the other Wrigley Field
Before anybody found a diamond at Chavez Ravine, a beautiful ballpark (or two) graced Los Angeles 286

Roy Hobbs: the greatest hitter there ever wasn't
*An Iowa farm kid missed his tryout with the Cubs . . . but came back
to bust up the Wrigley Field scoreboard with the New York Knights* 290

Marcelino, Lolo, & lots of other locals
Hang around the Avalon barbershop long enough, & you'll hear plenty of baseball tales that're sure to curl your hair 293

Where have you gone, Conrad Lopez?
A Catalina kid had all the tools — but would he ever make it to the Show with his beloved Cubbies? 307

Great trades (in the Cub tradition)
Some Catalina Cub alums made baseball history (& legend) by taking part in some of the most notable swaps of all time ... 311

On to Mesa   *A great thing comes to an end* 316

Baseball on Catalina today
*The diamond remains virtually unchanged — a time capsule to a glorious
past — but is there still any baseball to be found on Catalina Island?* 320

The Cubs today   *The flannels & the colorful characters are all gone now...or are they?* 326

Appendix   *Statistics & such* 329

Author's afterthoughts   *Randomized musings, now that the game is over* 337

Sponsors   *Avalon's favorite merchants & fans* 344

Index   *An alphabetical list of players & places* 358

This book is dedicated to The Boys of Spring — all the greatest-generation guys who played ball on Catalina Island.

Larry French & Larry French, 1940.

"For 26 years between 1921 & 1951, the Chicago Cubs held their annual Spring Training at this field in Catalina…"

-- *A small, unobtrusive bronze marker in Avalon, California*

The Gull's-Eye View
A Magical Place, a Magical Time, a Magical Team

*"I was playing baseball, on Catalina Island!
What more could you want?"*

Hal Jeffcoat

The Spring of '34.

What more, indeed? What could anybody want, besides getting to play big-league baseball...on a sunsplashed island...when wintertime was getting old?

Santa Catalina Island is about as far from a Chicago February as you can possibly get. Yet each year, for a time, a small group of Chicago's most famous local heroes spent a little while here — and the whole world got to read all about their exploits over breakfast in the next morning's paper.

The time was 1921 through 1951, for the most part. The reason was William Wrigley, a visionary chewing gum businessgenius who happened to own a baseball team and the part of a mountain range that raised up from the Pacific Ocean floor off the coast of Los Angeles.

It started out as a golden era of the Chicago Cubs, when they seemed to win the National League pennant every 3 years or so...although the World Championship always eluded their grasp. It spanned decades of Americana: the carefree, youthful roaring '20s...the hard, heavy years of the Great Depression...the resolute seriousness of World War II...and it finally all ended with a whimper — as the dull thud of modern, economics-driven ball crept over to Catalina's shores.

In all, a few hundred ballplayers suited up here. *Sixteen* Hall-of-Famers practiced on this diamond, carved out of a canyon, and a few others visited for exhibition games. Names that stir the imagination, like Grover Cleveland Alexander and Dizzy Dean, Gabby Hartnett and Jolly Cholly Grimm.

Movie stars came over, and sometimes worked out with the team. Starlets flirted with the ballplayers — Betty Grable, Olivia de Havilland, and Marilyn Monroe spent time here. A future TV star, Chuck Connors, actually played for the Cubs one Spring. The biggest of the Big Bands joined the party, too.

And a young radio broadcaster, destined to become a movie man and then the president of the United States, came over for a couple of Springtimes and made his mark.

There were rainstorms and earthquakes, binges and brawls, careers made and careers ended. Some of the young hopefuls never made a major league roster; others are still active in professional baseball, more than 50 years after the last bag of Cub equipment got thrown onto a freighter.

There are goats and great fish and wild boar and even buffalo in this yarn — visitors you might not expect in a story about baseball. And a lot of the guys golfed at the course adjacent to the ballpark — so you can be certain legends emerged there, as well.

It's about great steamships, now sunk to the bottom of the sea, and massive puffing old railcars, chugging their way out of an icy downtown Chicago station to the screaming-to-hoarseness cheers of devoted Cubbie fans, hundreds of them, braving the wind chills — as the Pullmans headed on to a 3-day journey through farms and fields that would end amidst orange groves on an 80-degree day in a long-lost Southern California that most people wouldn't recognize today.

It's about balls and bats and tiny leather gloves and heavy, scratchy grey flannel uniforms, grouchy reporters armed with sometimes-poetic yet often-poison pens...plus a colorful cast of supporting side characters that are straight out of the cartoons and the movies.

Catching strategy session, 1937.

Getting started, 1930.

At the Bird Park, early '30s.

And it's about little boys in a small town that happened to be out in the Pacific Ocean, getting to worship the heroes who arrived, right on time, by boat — each and every February.

Truly, this was a magical place. A magical time. A magical team.

It can't happen again, the way baseball has changed, the way the world has changed. But the old baseball diamond remains — marked only by a small bronze plaque beside the road. Yet ironically, Catalina remains virtually unchanged — somewhat of a living, breathing time capsule, forever memorializing a vision William Wrigley had some 80 years ago.

Gabby Hartnett, 1939.

"Charlie Grimm was a pretty good man. I liked him, all the kids liked him. I say kids — well, we *were* kids then — this was 50 years ago, back then!"

Ox Miller

Practice, 1920s.

The Great One, Dizzy Dean -- 1940.

About 60 of the old ballplayers are still alive... not to mention a variety of locals and others who still can taste those glory days as though they happened last Saturday afternoon. Their memories and their stories live on — and, fortunately, a lot of other Catalina Cub happenings, great and small, have been recorded here-n-there. A lot of the tales are lost forever, sadly — but enough remain to make for some poignant, funny, fascinating remembrances.

Arriving, 1937.

And that's what this scrapbook is all about. Things that happened to a grizzled old veteran on a particular Tuesday afternoon in 1934, things that happened to a fresh-faced, hopeful young kid on a day in 1950 that he'd rather forget. The veteran may have passed away, but the kid is still kicking, maybe living in a small town in Wisconsin or some such place, just a little old man now who slowly shuffles along at the mall — alongside a new generation of kids who'd give anything to play in the major leagues, but have no idea that this man, this slow-moving white-headed old fella who's kind of meandering in their way, once did.

And he did it on Catalina Island.

So here are the tales and the fading photographs, sometimes serious and sometimes a riot — sumptuous stories that are too good to have been made up. Wonderful truths, many stranger than fiction, many never published before.

As Phil Cavarretta often says, quoting every good Italian grandmother at the dinner table, *"Mangia, mangia"* — eat, feast, and most of all — *enjoy.*

Medicine Ball exercise, 1930s.

Rookie hopeful Bobby Mattick, 1938.

The Magic Isle
A Rookie's Guide to Santa Catalina Island

"Say, Mr. Grimm. I thought we were going to Catalina Island. Isn't this place Mexico?"

Teenage rookie Johnny Hutchings, minutes after stepping off the boat in 1936

While most of us aren't quite as geographically challenged as greenhorn Hutchings, a lot of people *would* have a hard time drawing Catalina onto a map of the U.S. — or telling someone much about the place, even on a game show with high stakes.

Fortunately, we offer this primer to initiate the uninitiated...the basics of a place so magical, you'd think Walt Disney imagined the whole thing from scratch. Fortunately for us, Walt didn't have to — because God Himself (with a little help from deep-pocketed William Wrigley) *did*.

Santa Catalina Island lies 20-some miles off the coast of Los Angeles. It's shaped roughly like the side view of a goose in flight, and it's about 21 miles long from stem to stern — 8 miles across at the widest point, less than half a mile at the narrowest (which is called the Isthmus). 'Santa Catalina Island' is the official name, but for the non-cartographers of the world it's simply 'Catalina.'

There are two towns: Avalon, population just over 3,000...and Two Harbors (at the Isthmus), population a few dozen. There's not a single stoplight, and most of the island is completely undeveloped.

*Johnny Hutchings finally **did** discover where he was. Years later, still rattled by the whole thing, he served up Mel Ott's 500th career home run.*

Native Americans found a way to navigate the channel in wooden canoe-like-things thousands of years ago. Europeans first came along in 1542, when Cabrillo claimed the spot for Spain. Mexico eventually took over, and finally the U.S. in 1846.

William Wrigley bought Catalina in 1919 for about 3 million smackers, and then poured several times that much into making it a world-class resort. In 1975, the family gave most of it away (for tax purposes) — so nearly 90% is now forever preserved in the wild.

Catalina is one of 8 Channel Islands...and the only one with any towns. Of the rest, 5 make up the Channel Islands National Park...and 2 are used by the Navy for target practice.

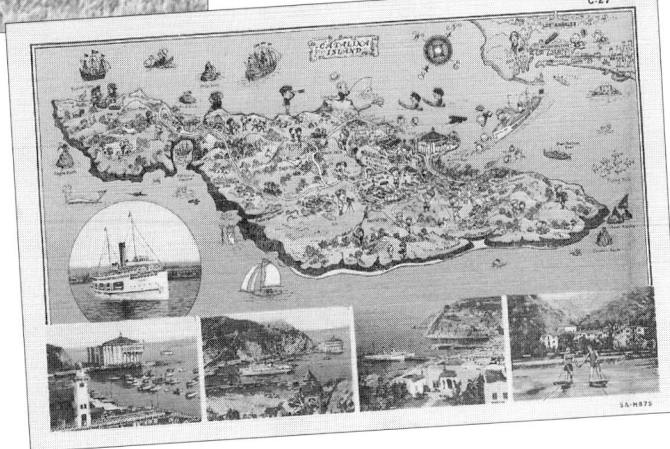

Avalon rests around the edge of a perfectly-shaped crescent harbor.

Despite the name, the Casino opened in 1929 as a dance hall & theater — not an offshore prohibition gambling hideout.

Since Mr. Wrigley made it into a resort...and since it was so close to Hollywood...Catalina quickly became a playground for stars and other celebs. In the '30s, CBS radio broadcast Big Band shows from the Island's landmark Casino, live from coast-to-coast.

And the place is beautiful beyond sensibility.

"There always is a spot just a little bit better than any you have seen," Harry Neily of the *Chicago American* wrote for the *Catalina Islander* in 1921, "but none of us has found the place that excells Avalon and Santa Catalina Island. The infielders and outfielders who reported to Pasadena and were not fetched here were certainly out of luck."

"An island — I didn't know!"
Bill Voiselle

"My first experience was 1948," smiles Bob Kelly. "That was my rookie year, so my first Spring Training ever was on Catalina — it's a long way back down to earth from there!"

Johnny Klippstein felt the same way: "You'd wake up in the morning and think, 'This must be a dream, being out here on an island.' Of course, it's every kid's dream to get to play baseball."

In fact, the lure of Catalina actually extended Billy Rogell's career. After being traded from Detroit to the Cubs, "I was ready to quit in 1939," he says, "but my wife wanted to go to Catalina!" Even when camp ended and Billy hit the road, his family decided to stay behind. "After I left, Mum — I called her Mum — she spent a month there. We took our 2 boys out."

"I had never been to any place like that before," Woody English said in *Wrigleyville*. "It seemed like I had always heard about Honolulu, Hawaii, and that's the first thing that entered my mind. The water was so clear and blue, and it really struck me. I thought, I must be in heaven."

"Stan Hack...was roosting in one of the easy chairs outside the St. Catherine Hotel, absorbing the sun," 'Jimmy the Cork' Corcoran wrote for the *Chicago American* in 1936. "His eyes roamed over the blue Pacific. 'You know, sometimes I'm afraid I'll wake up and find that this whole thing isn't true. A kid like me. Didn't have a thing a few years ago. And now, I'm on top of the world.'"

"It was a great set-up," Phil Cavarretta recalls, "one of the best places to have Spring Training."

"Boy, it sure was great out on Catalina," agrees Turk Lown. "We really enjoyed it. There was a lot of solitude — we didn't have to worry about anything." Apparently, players could make what they wanted of the locale — whether they liked peace and quiet, or whether they liked a little action. Grace Bradley Boyd (a film star in the '30s who married Hopalong Cassidy after dating a few of the Cubs) preferred the night life. "Catalina was a great place — very alive, things going on," she says. "There were beautiful little places there; it was a great little getaway."

"Mother always had a twinkle in her eye when she talked about that place."

Charlie Owen (Mickey's son)

The weather was tough to beat, especially compared to wintertime Chicago. "I reported in February in the middle of a big snowstorm with the temperature 3 below zero," Kirby Higbe wrote in his autobiography. "I got off the train with just my suit on. People looked at me like I was nuts. There was no use saying I forgot my overcoat. I never had one. Two days later we were on the train for the 4-day trip to Southern California and on to Catalina Island, where a boy from South Carolina can get along just fine without an overcoat."

"It was a lotta fun," Carmen Mauro says, "to be in Chicago, in that snowy environment, then to step off the train in that sunshine in Los Angeles, then to Catalina — I thought I'd died and gone to paradise."

But then again, we're all necessary, aren't we? Lonny Frey: "I didn't like it. You're tied up, you can't do anything. I just wouldn't like to ever live on an island. I went to Hawaii — and I couldn't wait to get home. Did I ever go back to Catalina? Are you kidding? I'm a city boy."

"My first time to Catalina was in 1927 — I was 8 years old," says Della Root Arnold (Charlie's daughter), who went over during 14 different Springtimes. "These were things I'd never dreamed would happen; I thought everyone lived like this!

"The pitchers and catchers went out the 2nd week in February, and the others came out the next week," she says. "We'd get an extra week!"

But then again...

"It was a real boring place — one of the coldest places I've ever tried to train," Ben Wade recalls differently. "It was really foggy, especially in the mornings."

Nine-to-five

Okay, so most of the Cubs agree that Catalina is a pretty nifty vacation spot. But what about the reason Mr. Wrigley called this meeting — *baseball*? Was Catalina really a very good Spring Training site?

"This is a good place to start the Spring Training," Harry Williams wrote for the *Los Angeles Times* in 1921. "If any of the bushers fail to suit Evers, he can simply tell them to go jump in the ocean. Looks like a royal feast of rookies for the sharks. The bait question also has been settled. Leaping tuna also love to snap the ears off a fat rookie."

Eleven seasons later, Williams was still having fun with the whole thing. "The submarines nosing around flushed all the flying fish in the channel. Some of them flew into my room just now and are very bothersome...Only way you can get rid of them is to smoke stogies in your sleep."

In 1936, the *Times*' Bob Ray featured Gabby Hartnett. In the piece, he recounted Gabby's early years as a steelworker — rising at 5:30 a.m. in the Massachusetts cold. "One wintry morning when the thermometer was below zero," Ray wrote, "Gabby discovered when he reached the mill that his ears had been frozen. 'I thought they were going to explode or drop off,' says Gabby. 'Right then I decided I'd renounce work in all its branches. I vowed I'd never work again and I never have. So I turned to baseball. And when I look at the sunshine and the green grass at Catalina while it's ear-freezing weather back home, I think I made a brilliant move.'"

Rookie hopefuls Duncan Grant & Al 'Pard' Epperly (along with their new best friend) took advantage of Island amenities when they needed a post-practice snack in the Spring of 1937.

Gabby's longtime pal, Charlie Grimm, liked it too. "The year 1925 wasn't a complete blank," Jolly Cholly recorded in his autobiography. "I discovered Catalina Island, that magical little spot across the channel from the Southern California mainland."

"Wrigley was able to see in it a vast playground to which untold thousands would one day come on pleasure bent."

Warren Brown, describing William Wrigley's 1st reaction to the pretty-much-undeveloped Catalina in 1919

In 1923, the *Chicago Tribune* reported: "Jack Doyle and Bobby Wallace, veteran players who are now helping coach Oscar Dugey, admit it adds 10 years to their lives to be allowed to come to Catalina. 'How long has this been going on?' asked Wallace. 'If this is part of the Cub ball club treatment to players, then a pennant should be forthcoming ere long. You know I was in organized ball in the big leagues for some 24 periods, and I have yet to see the equal of a Cub training trip.'"

Did Catalina indeed add 10 years to Bobby Wallace's life, as claimed? The stunning fact: Hall-of-Famer Bobby lived to be 86, despite doing all those nasty things ballplayers did in those roughneck years.

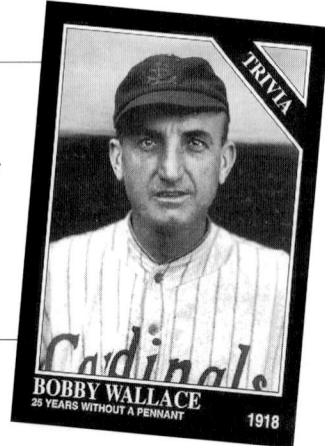

"You must be aware of the fact," Edward Cochrane wrote for his *Chicago American* column in 1937, "that when the Cubs are on the Island, the headlines carry many a fine piece of publicity for the resort, and that's one of the ideas."

Mr. Wrigley's slogan for Catalina was, "In All the World, No Trip Like This." All-inclusive trips were heavily advertised — in 1922, for instance, you could enjoy 2 days on the Magic Isle, with steamship transportation to-and-from the mainland, a room overnight at the lavish Hotel St. Catherine, 4 meals at the hotel dining room, and a ride on the glass bottom boat — all for just 10 bucks.

"We stayed at the Hotel St. Catherine," Della recalls. "It was beautiful. They had a great big lobby with oriental rugs and big, soft furniture. They had a jewelry store and a little curio shop. The dining room was all glass, overlooking the ocean. Off to the left, they had this little room where the guests could play pool.

"The Island itself hasn't changed much, but it's sad to see where the St. Catherine was — it was such a beautiful hotel. It was a time that will never happen again."

And the Cubs kept coming to this lovely little Isle. In 1950 — after the bumps and bruises inflicted by World War II and the decline of the late '40s — the *Catalina Islander* quoted manager Frankie Frisch: "Catalina is an ideal training base, and as far as I'm concerned, we'll be returning here for many years to come. And even after we leave Los Angeles, I'll be sending ball players back here for workouts at the ball park."

What a difference a year can make...

Strike up the band

Catalina's had a few semi-well-known songs written about her. Most notably: *26 Miles (Santa Catalina)* was a #2 *Billboard* hit in 1958 for the Four Preps, a harmonizing groups who influenced Brian Wilson into creating the Beach Boys hits you can sing in your sleep. You may've heard *26 Miles* at some point, and until audio technology equals scratch-n-sniff, we regret that we cannot play it for you here. As a consolation, we present the chorus:

Twenty-six miles across the sea
Santa Catalina is a-waitin' for me
Santa Catalina, the island of romance,
romance, romance, romance...

Charlie & Dorothy Root dance 'til dawn at the Casino.

Ironic that the view out the window of the Hotel St. Catherine dining room is pretty much the same today...although the window isn't there any more!

The Country Club clubhouse & locker rooms, where the Cubs dressed (Still used for golf & dining)

The Atwater Hotel, where they sometimes stayed (Still open for business)

The Airport in the Sky (Opened in the late '40s) ⟶

Wrigley Field

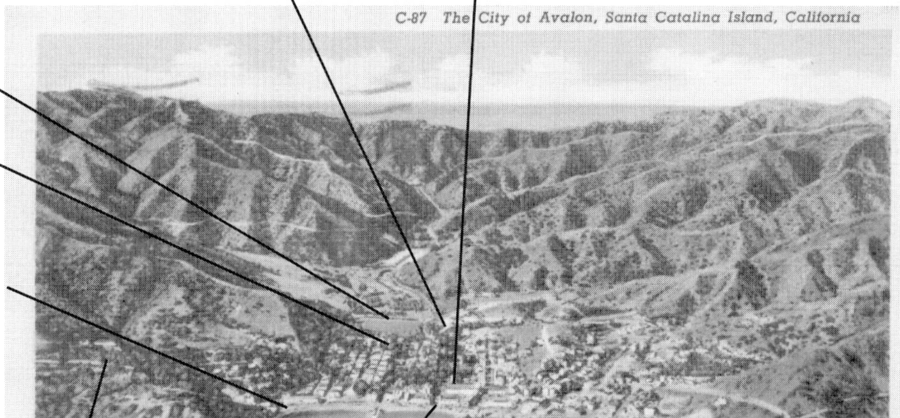

Las Casitas, just beyond right field, where players who came with their families usually stayed (Private homes now)

Seaplane turnaround — the planes landed & alighted in Avalon Bay (Removed; the spot is now part of the Hamilton Cove condo subdivision) ↘

The Bath House, used in the early '20s as the Cub locker room (Burned down a few times, not replaced the last time)

The Hotel St. Catherine, where the team usually stayed (Demolished in the '60s)

⟵ *The Tile & Pottery Works (now a helipad)*

The William Wrigley mansion (Now a bed-n-breakfast, The Inn at Mt. Ada)

The Steamer Pier (Dismantled)

Sportland Arcade (Replaced by the Pavilion Lodge)

The Casino (Still used for dances & movies, though not as often)

The Cubbies

A Quick Look at one of Baseball's Oldest, Most Beloved, Legendary Teams

"We'll get 'em next year!"

Hack Wilson's son Bobby, after Hack missed a ball in the sun during a 1929 World Series loss to the A's

Everybody loves the Cubs.

I mean, they're a part of our culture. Our history. An American icon.

"Since I was a kid, I was always a Cubs fan — even growing up in Boston," Lennie Merullo says. "The most popular Cub at that time, Gabby Hartnett, was from here...so I fell in love with the team. One of the local sportswriters was from Chicago, so it was easy to follow them."

People have been writing histories of the Cubs since the 1800s — so this section will just provide a brief recap. (If ya want details, there's an appendixful of volumes to peruse.) We're gonna stay on Catalina, but a bit of background might be helpful...to put some things into context.

There really are 2 Cubs teams: the legendary champions of yesteryear, and the lovable losers of today. Let's start with the old days.

The Cubs were charter members of the National League in 1876 — but they've been around since 1869, barnstorming about against other clubs. Over the first few decades, the team's name changed a few times. Here's the nickname history:

1869-1889	***White Stockings*** (Yep, the current White Sox were named after the original Cubs!)
1890-1897	***Colts***
1898-1901	***Orphans***
1902-	***Cubs***

"Yaah, Cubbies!" -- Lennie Merullo

16

The pioneers were legendary baseballers, like Al Spalding (whose name still appears on balls, gloves, and uniform labels)...and player-manager Cap Anson.

The team dominated the N.L. in those days — league champs in 6 of their first 10 seasons, including 3 in a row.

There are about 3 dozen Cubs in the Hall of Fame. And baseball fables surround the Cubs, like the legendary double-play combination of Tinker-to-Evers-to-Chance.

The Cubs appeared in the World Series 3 straight seasons, from 1906-1908, and again in 1910 — 4 times in 5 years. They won in 1908 — the last time they were ever World Champs. Over the next 37 seasons, they appeared in 7 more World Series — including an 'every-3-year' run in the '30s (1929, 1932, 1935, 1938).

Talk about tough characters. These guys got into brawls on the field — and beat up reporters at train stations. They got shot at by female admirers. They caroused with mobsters. They drank all night, then swatted game-winning home runs while playing both halves of a double-header. They growled and grunted and spit and scratched...and won ballgames.

As well as the hearts & souls of their faithful fans.

Before he became a brand of baseballs, Mr. Spalding guided the early Cubs to glory.

Yet the winning brought a double-edged sword: Competitors hate to lose, so losing was tough. Take the tight 1937 race, for instance. "We should've won the pennant that year," Lonny Frey recalls. "We had a 6 or 7-game lead going down the stretch, but we had an accident — one of our best pitchers had his wrist broken, and that just seemed to take the wind out of us. We had some other injuries: Herman was hurt, he had a bad finger, and that put me at 2nd. I played short too, and even a few games at 3rd that year. Those were tough days, a different era. I was really upset we didn't win the pennant — we had a 6-game lead going into September, and everybody was spending their World Series money before they had it! All the wives were out shopping already."

"Whatever their dietary or monetary standards, these Cubs were a ripsnorting team which played baseball for all it was worth."

Warren Brown, in his
1946 team history

The last World Series appearance: 1945.

That's a lotta Hall-of-Famers in one Bird Park: Rogers Hornsby, Hack Wilson, Charlie Grimm (the only one besides the birds who's not in the Hall, but he oughta be), & KiKi Cuyler, 1929.

Charlie Grimm unfurls the championship banner for Mr. PK Wrigley, Charlie Root, Larry French, Carl Reynolds, Joe Marty, & Frank Demaree to kick off 1938's festivities.

The mid-60s Cubbies. The Topps caption is quite telling, when you consider the fact that there weren't a lot more than 8 teams in the league back then.

But after all those glory years, something happened.

That something was Philip K. Wrigley, son of William. When Bill passed away in 1932, PK took over the reins. The firm foundation kept things going for a while, but by the time World War II came, it was time to rebuild. Alas, PK never rebuilt — and thus began the slump.

"I have lots of good memories," Carmen Mauro says, "but also some frustrations — because the Cubs were never contenders. I was just one player, called up from the minors, how much could I do? So I had to be a team player, and contribute what I could."

To put things into perspective, let's get back to the Hall of Fame. Of the 36 Cubs enshrined in Cooperstown, 27 played before 1950. And of the 9 who suited up since then, it's a stretch to consider most of 'em as Cubs — since they played the vast majority of their careers elsewhere. For example, Lou Brock's on the list...but the Cubs lost him in a really dumb trade before he did much...and while Hoyt Wilhelm's technically on the list, he only played for the Cubs 1 season of his 21-year career.

Realistically, then — Ernie Banks, Ferguson Jenkins, and Billy Williams are the only Cub Hall-of-Famers from the past 50 years. (Compare this to the recent Atlanta Braves, for instance, when there were probably 3 future Hall-of-Famers in the bullpen alone on any given afternoon...)

After the War, players had to go elsewhere to win. "I got a phone call in December of 1955," Randy Jackson says. "It was a sportswriter asking if I knew I'd been traded. No, I didn't. I asked who — Pittsburgh? He told me it was the Dodgers, and I didn't believe him. You've gotta be teasing. They had just won the World Series. This was fantastic — I was going from a 6th or 7th-place team to a winner."

Yet still, the Cubs were known for being good people. Even though baseball wasn't as cut-throat a business then as it was now...some teams weren't as highly regarded by the players. "Chicago had a good reputation as an organization," Paul Schramka says. "They'd never had any holdouts. All the old ballplayers said everybody should play at least one year with the Cubs before they retire — they treated the players well, they only had day games..."

These days, Cubs who make it to the Hall of Fame generally only spend a few minutes with the team & perform their heroics elsewhere. Consider Hoyt Wilhelm, who pitched 3 of his 1,070 games for the Cubbies!

Part of the extended Cub family: Cub Larry French, kid Larry French, & Gabby Hartnett, late '30s.

"My memory of the players on that team was, they were a heck of a bunch of nice guys," Red Adams says. "You couldn't meet a nicer bunch of guys. They treated us rookies like we were one of them. I remember going to New York, on a Sunday, after a day game — somebody knew an Italian restaurant, and 10 or 12 guys would go. These were the front-line guys — there was no dividing line with them."

The family feel extended beyond the ballplayers to the staff, too. "After I got out of the Service," 60-year equipment manager Yosh Kawano remembers, "the General Manager wouldn't let me work — he said, 'You should go to school with the GI Bill.' But I didn't want to. So he said, 'Yosh, you'll always have a job here if you want to work.'"

A most familiar pose for Cub fans: the catcher (here, Bob Scheffing, 1947) watching an opponent perform the home-run trot around the bags.

Talk about loyal — Charlie Grimm insisted that his ashes be sprinkled over Wrigley Field. They were.

Then again, there were lapses. "Every year since I've been out of baseball, I received a Christmas card," Randy Jackson told Carrie Muskat in *Banks to Sandberg to Grace*. "Guess from who? The Baltimore Orioles. And I only played 30 days with them. The Brooklyn Dodgers sent me cards the last 5, 6, 7 years. The Chicago Cubs? Never."

Losing became an art form. Book titles even addressed the subject. *Banks to Sandberg to Grace* was subtitled, "Five Decades of Love and Frustration with the Chicago Cubs." And *Take Me Out to the Cubs Game* was followed with, "35 Former Ballplayers Speak of Losing at Wrigley."

"There was never a dull moment with the Cubs, win or lose."

Charlie Grimm, in his autobiography

In his 1946 team history, Warren Brown told of an unwavering fan's grumbling:

"The way things are going," he explained, "I am afraid (Manager Jimmie) Wilson would have me in the line-up one of these days if he happened to see me standing around."

This recalled a caustic utterance by another and earlier critic of the Cubs in the Bill Killefer days. He refused to go to Spring Training to cover the story, lest he might make the team.

(How odd, that some Cub fans thought they had it bad *then*!)

"Let's play two," Ernie was famous for saying. Of course, the cynical fan might reply, "Yeah, so we can lose two!"

We close this chapter with a 1947 Catalina dispatch from Edgar 'the Mouse' Munzel to *Chicago Sun* readers:

AVALON, Calif. — Manager Charlie Grimm of the Cubs had just teed off on the first hole of the Catalina course today, joining in the holiday he had declared for the squad, when one of his heckling opponents in the match yelled —

"Why, your shortstops can hit better than that."

But don't worry, Cub faithfuls. Because after all...
...we'll get 'em next year!

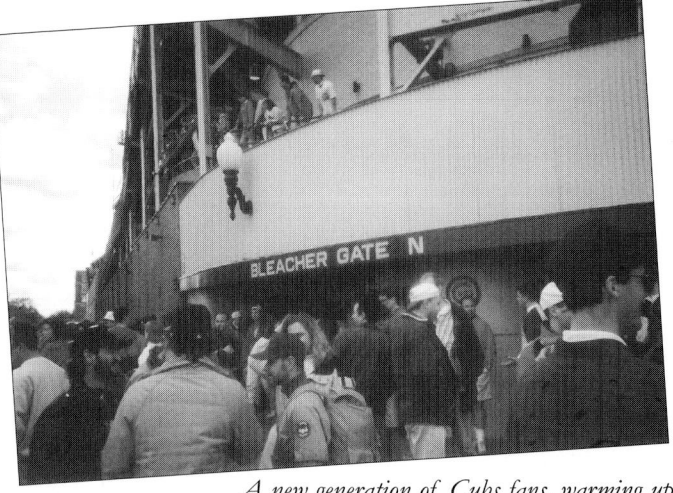

A new generation of Cubs fans, warming up to take in today's defeat at Wrigley Field.

News from the Isle -- April 15, 1950.

20

Springs Before Catalina
Boiling Off the Winter's Remnants

"The highly congested conditions of this winter have made the local hotel folks regret the contract they made with the Chicago club a year ago. If there is no other way, William Wrigley Jr. threatens to build training quarters for the Cubs on the Catalina islands..."

I. E. Sandborn, writing for the *Chicago Tribune*, 1920

Before Catalina, the Cubs tried a variety of Spring Training sites.

In fact, here's some nifty trivia: The Cubs actually invented Spring Training!

'Tis true. There are actually 2 differing accounts of how and when, but either way...the Cubs were the team.

(By the way, keep in mind that the 19th-century Cubs were called the White Stockings, then the Colts — but it's still your beloved Cubbies we're talking about, kinda like the Seattle Pilots became the Milwaukee Brewers or the Kansas City A's became the Oakland A's.)

The traditional story:

None other than Hall-of-Famer Cap Anson came up with the idea, way back in 1886. Consider this tidbit, written by Daniel M. Daniel* for *Baseball* magazine in April, 1935, in his article called, *Fifty Years of Spring Training*:

This year marks the fiftieth anniversary of Spring Training. My authority for this statement is Billy Sunday, the famous evangelist.

In 1886, Sunday was an outfielder with Cap Anson's Chicago Colts. Cap was not only a great player and manager, but he was quite a showman. Anson conceived the idea of Spring Training away from home. It had never been done before. In fact, the idea did not catch on at once, and Anson and his Colts were left pioneering all alone.

Anson took his players to Hot Springs, Arkansas. And today ballplayers still go to Hot Springs, to boil out.

Boil out, indeed: Daniel (or Daniél, depending on whether we're being formal or not) continued,

The innovation certainly was justified, for the Chicago club kept the National League championship and set a new record with 90 victories and only 34 defeats, for .726.

Hall-of-Fame Chicago Cub/Colt/White Stocking Cap Anson, illustrated nicely on an 1887 baseball card.

Cub historian extraordinaire, Ed Hartig, provides some additional detail on this 'boiling' business — Ed points out that the roughnecks of yesteryear intended to "boil off the alcoholic microbes," quoting Anson in his autobiography. Ed suggests there's evidence supporting earlier Southern jaunts, away from the Chicago cold. As early as 1870 — when the Cincinnati Red Stockings were barnstorming through the South — the Chicago White Stockings (now Cubs), traveled to New Orleans for a couple weeks to train...before facing off against Cincy. The was before there was even a league, by the way — teams just challenged each other and collected points (by winning a 3-game series) to take the pennant.

In 1928, Harold Johnson of the *Chicago American* interviewed Coach Jimmy Burke about Spring Training in the 'old days.' Burke started with Peoria in

1895 and hit the bigs in 1898. "Spring Training then was limited to three weeks," Jimmy told the scribe. "Each player was required to lug his own wardrobe, which meant we handled three pieces of baggage consisting of a uniform roll, a bat bag with two clubs and a suitcase. No taxicabs awaited us at the depots, either. Instead we rode to the hotel in a streetcar."

A lot of players kept coming to Hot Springs through the years, on their own, before regular Spring Training began. In 1919, when the Cubs held training camp out West (in Pasadena), the *Chicago Tribune* reported: "Big Jim Vaughn...intends to leave tomorrow for Hot Springs...to begin getting in shape to pitch the opening game."

Given Jim Vaughn's nicknames — "Big Jim" & "Hippo" — he apparently needed some pre-season boiling.

Here's the semi-official listing of Cub camps, once Spring Training became somewhat 'formalized' (rather than just a bunch of fat guys lounging around in bubbling water and occasionally emerging to toss the leather). Notice that it was still pretty seat-of-the-pants, given the multiple-location thing for several of the seasons:

Year	Spring Training Site
1900	Selma, Alabama
1901-1902	Champaign, Illinois (Brr!)
1903-1904	Los Angeles
1905	Santa Monica, California
1906	Champaign & West Baden, Indiana
1907	New Orleans & West Baden
1908	Vicksburg, Mississippi, & West Baden
1909	Hot Springs, Arkansas, & Shreveport, Louisiana
1910	Hot Springs & West Baden
1911	West Baden & New Orleans
1912	New Orleans
1913-1916	Tampa
1917-1920	Pasadena — with a quick trip to Catalina in 1920

Springtime tales

In 1919, the Great War was still on everyone's mind. From the *Chicago Tribune*:

Sergt. Bill Killefer will act as scout for Chicago Cubs to clean out any possible machine gun nests between the city and Pasadena in advance of the Spring Training trips...Killefer does not need any extra conditioning to put him in shape for the pennant race, because he has had plenty of physical training while in uniform at Camp Custer...

The Pasadena weather (and groundskeepers) did their part to help nudge the Cubs across the Channel: the next week, the *Tribune* dutifully reported, "After falling down on the job for three days, California's well-known sun returned this morning...In spite of the mud and chills, the boys were able to stage quite a session of batting practice in regulation style, except that the batting cage had to be placed on one side of the grass to escape the mud at the plate."

Anybody remember Les Mann (no jokes about *his* name, please — he smacked 2 doubles in the 1918 World Series for the Cubs)? He helped create some dissatisfaction in Pasadena, too: "Les Mann objected to the bare floor in the clubhouse," according to the *Tribune*, "so William Wrigley ordered his secretary to have carpet put in before tomorrow."

A ballplayer by the name of Ted Turner (what's with the names in this chapter?) came out to Pasadena the next season — and apparently the Ted didn't enjoy train rides all that much. "The only candidate for Trainer King Brady's satchel of pills was Pitcher Turner, who spent all day Sunday in bed from train sickness," came the *Tribune* dispatch from enroute in Albuquerque. "He was first up this morning, though, leading the way to the dining car — saying he felt bully."

The next day, "Tony Schultz almost lost the train at Barstow, Cal., during a brief stop there...but managed to catch the last car by some hard sprinting...Coach Dolan is thinking of offering a watch as a bribe."

Later on, Abe Bailey paid a visit to the trainer, too — because he "acquired an ailment which Doc was unable to diagnose without the aid of a licensed veterinary, to whom Bailey was sent late today... Alexander and Killefer express the opinion that the rash may be due to cooties, but cannot explain where Abe acquired them."

And then...more troubles for the Pasadena complex appeared in the paper:

The local Association of Commerce is now worrying about where to find housing for the Cubs next spring, as the highly congested conditions of this winter have made the local hotel folks regret the contract they made with the Chicago club a year ago.

If there is no other way, William Wrigley Jr. threatens to build training quarters for the Cubs on the Catalina islands, one of which possesses a level area 400 feet square, the only flat of that size in the new Wrigley domain.

In order to acquaint the Cubs with their possible training camp for next year, the Squire of Avalon plans to escort the Cub party to the islands next Sunday and let them take a day off to look things over as his guests. Some of the rookies were touted by the veteran Cubs to hunt up remedies for seasickness and life preservers in anticipation of a rough passage across the channel.

The site was next to the golf course, which had been there since 1892 (3 holes, expanded to 9 in 1894).

The trip went well. "Landing at Avalon shortly before noon...inspection included an expert survey by Manager Mitchell as to the qualifications of the island for training in case the Spring of 1921 finds California so congested with tourists that the Cubs cannot find sleeping quarters on the mainland. In that case Mr.

There is no record of Wm. Wrigley launching a hot-air balloon to provide Manager Mitchell with this view in 1920, but ya never know. The level site for the future ballfield is the lightly-treed area in the lower left part of this image.

Wrigley can have quarters erected on the island before next year to house his athletes."

Apparently, the little old ladies in Pasadena didn't build enough new hotels to meet Mr. Wrigley's standards for his lads — and the rest became history. The next Spring, Catalina was the place to be...

* Do you suppose his associates called him Daniel, Mr. Daniel, Dan, Danny, Danny-boy, Dan Dan, Double-Dan, or perhaps D.D.? And what do you think the 'M.' stands for, in the midst of all this confusion — I mean, why not just make it Daniel Daniel Daniel?

The Cubbies just came over for a quick looksie in 1920, yet they got a rousing welcome from the good people of Avalon.

1921~1951

A 30-Year Relationship -- Sort Of

"We kind of fell in love with the beauty of it. I spent 11 birthdays on the island, and I really enjoyed it out there. Even Hornsby loved it, even though there weren't any race tracks."

Woody English, in the 1997 issue of *Spring Training* magazine.

Baseball Grounds, Country Club and Golf Links,
Avalon, Catalina Island, California.

"In All The World No Trip Like This"

There seem to be 2 kinds of baseball books.

Some are written like dreary, century-olde volumes...while others come across more like fun-to-read magazines, filled with features. Tome-like baseball books are mostly text, and contain a few grainy pictures — one on about every 20th page or so. The other kind uses graphics and pictures on just about every page. Not only that, they're filled with quotes and trivia and funny tales, rather than a listing of facts in dry order.

Since this is about the history of a particular team during a particular 30-year period, it would've been quite easy to default into the history-book mode. Which would mean it'd sound something like this:

On Thursday, February thirtieth, Nineteen-hundred and eleventeen, twenty-two Chicago Cubs arrived in Avalon at eleven-fifty-seven in the morning, Greenwich Meridian Time minus fourteen. For a complete roster, see table 6.1. For a complete list of each player's height and weight, see table 6.11. For a complete list of each player's career statistics, see table 6.12. For a comprehensive list of each player's hometown, favorite foods, and the color of his toothbrush that season, see table 6.13.

While this book was a labor of love, I certainly hope more than 8 or 9 people actually *buy* it. So, I resisted the urge to simply pound out the facts. Don't get me wrong — facts are good. But it just seemed like it'd be a bit more fun if we tried to avoid the feel of a college biology textbook.

The reason I am explaining all this is because this chapter, entitled "1921-1951," could still easily fall into this mode. Fear not. While there has to be *some* chronology here, the sequence covering these 30 years includes some interesting sidelights about the big picture, too — what actually happened out there in the middle of the Ocean.

So please bear with us as we mention a few dates.

In 1920, the Cubs trained in Pasadena. Mr. Wrigley, who'd just bought Catalina the year before, was a little miffed with the lack of quality at the team's facilities. So, he took the team over to visit Catalina, just for a looksie, one weekend.

In 1921, pitchers and catchers came over to the Isle for pre-camp camp, before heading back to join the rest of the squad in Pasadena. From 1922 onward, the entire team practiced there.

The team came every season through 1942. Wartime travel and safety restrictions meant Spring Training had to take place closer to home — in French Lick, Indiana — from 1943-1945.

From 1946 through 1951, Spring Training returned to Catalina. Sort of. In 1948 and 1949, much of the squad spent more time in Los Angeles than on the Island.

And in 1952, Spring Training became a permanent Arizona event for the Cubs. So, that means the Cubs actually trained on Catalina 26-28 years, depending on whether or not you count 1948 and/or 1949. Some amazing talent showed up: In all, just about half of the Cubs who are in the Hall of Fame (16 ballplayers) practiced on Catalina.

Over these 3 decades, an entire life-cycle took place. At first, there was nervous anticipation and excitement. In the '20s and into the '30s, the heyday — bands and movie stars and laughter everywhere. By the late '30s, a few rainy Springs dampened the enthusiasm, and of course World War II put everything on hold.

After the War, the return was tentative. That, coupled with the general malaise created by losing seasons...and money issues...led to a lot of people being pretty worn out about Catalina by 1951. Over the years, there was a passing parade of managers, with vastly varying practice schedules. The steamships were being replaced by airplanes near the end. And the young reporters, who loved the junket at first, grew old and grumpy about it — turning the good PR from the old days into bad news back in Chicago.

So let's embark on a whirlwind look at these 30 remarkable seasons — with some interesting sidelights sprinkled in.

Movie Stars

Catalina has always been a playground for movie stars. Dozens of movies were filmed on the island, and frequent visitors in the Cub days included Charlie Chaplin, Laurel & Hardy, Cecil B. DeMille, Johnny Weismuller, Betty Grable, Errol Flynn, John Wayne, and plenty of others.

And the Big Bands came out, too: Benny Goodman, Rudy Vallee, Jimmy Dorsey, Woody Herman, Count Basie, and many more.

Local celebs included General George S. Patton (who spent much of his childhood on the Island)...movie cowboy Tom Mix lived on Catalina...and so did novelists Zane Grey and Gene Stratton Porter. Theodore Roosevelt, Herbert Hoover, Winston Churchill and King Olaf V of Norway were members of the Avalon Tuna Club. Coolidge and Hoover came out to visit the Wrigleys; Mr. Coolidge even watched the team practice for a while, at his wife's behest and against his will.

CBS Radio broadcast live Big Band shows from the Casino in those days, like Rudy Vallee's performance with the Hal Grayson Band in 1941.

Fans

Over the years, the Chicago papers frequently mentioned leading bankers, retailers, and other noble citizenry making the wintertime trek with the team — visiting the Cubs on Catalina was apparently a pretty nifty bragging right around the Chicago cocktail circuit in the '30s.

Newsreels & such

Every season, managers muttered under their breaths as the newsreel cameras interrupted workouts. Players mugged it up for the MovieTone teams and the wire service photographers..while no baseball got accomplished.

When the Cubs came, the newsreel cameras appeared too. This was the scene in '38.

In 1930, the *Chicago American*'s 'Jimmy the Cork' Corcoran reported that a particular photographer made a few too many pose requests of crusty manager Joe McCarthy. "We believe that the photographer...is still engaged in the 1930 edition of the Wrigley Channel swim to main land," Jimmy wrote. "Joe wrapped his tongue around a few choice words and phrases and the photog wrapped up his shooting menagerie and went away with his coat tails sticking straight out behind him."

"Upon landing at Avalon," Ed Burns wrote in the *Chicago Tribune* in 1937, "the Cubs rushed to their hotel and without pausing for luncheon, donned their monkey suits and again boarded the steamer. Then, for the accommodation of the movie and other photographers, they clamored down the gangplank, making off like they are so close to their work that they travel in their playing uniforms."

The facilities

At first, the team dressed at the bath house, which hovered over the bay. By 1928, the Country Club was ready — right across Avalon Canyon Road from the field. The course dates back to 1892; the Bobby Jones Golf Tournament was held there from 1931-1955, except during the War.

In this 1936 pub shot, Bill Lee supervises as rookie Ken Weafer rows (while Gene Lillard & Johnny Hutchings look on) -- with the younger trio wondering if ballplayers always fish in their uniforms.

There never seemed to be an official name for the ballpark/field diamond. Most people called it Wrigley Field, but it's also been referred to as Las Casitas ballfield, Cubs' Field, the Recreation Grounds, the Field of Dreams (more recently), or simply the ballpark — you name it.

Nothing but the finest in oceanic 1938 locker rooms: Tex Carleton & Gabby Hartnett don the gear.

The weather

Over the years, rain and wind and sun seemed to get a lot of ink from fickle reporters. Good weather? Happy reports. Clouds? Sad faces. In 1930, Bob Ray wrote this snippet for the *Training Camp Gossip* column of the *Los Angeles Times*:

Training for the Cubs today was confined to such thrilling practices as bridge, pinochle, plain fibbing and a bit of throwing, from which all except the battery men were excluded. This uneventful program was made necessary by a rainy, raw atmosphere

---

"If no mountains fall down tomorrow and the rain stays a while in the heavens, the first intraclub game of the year will be played."

Ed Burns, for the *Chicago Tribune*, 1937

"I remember that time when there was some hail, and maybe some snow — it was very cold," Johnny Klippstein says. "But I've been in Florida when the weather was terrible. It'd rain, then 45 minutes later the sun would be shining."

"The weather didn't matter," Cal McLish said. "If you had to run, you had to run...whether the sun was shining or if it was snowing."

Popular myth suggests the bad weather in 1951 was the reason behind the move to Arizona. The real reason was economics, but the weather *was* lousy that year. From Al Wolf of the *Los Angeles Times*: "When the...Chicago Cubs began their conditioning at Catalina a week ago, they were deluged with rain, pelted with hail and frozen by wintry blasts."

Life goes on

The real world went on while the boys were in paradise. Presidents were inaugurated — starting with Warren Harding in 1921. The great Depression hit. World War II and Korea. "Talkies" replaced silent movies. TV began to replace radio. The world changed while the Cubs played on their Island.

There was a maritime strike in 1937 — which threatened to leave the team stranded offshore. And in the years that followed, the threat of a very real war colored the trip. In 1942, just 3 months after Pearl Harbor, Al Wolf wrote in the *Los Angeles Times*: "The Cubs have just returned to this country from Catalina Island, where they spent the better part of three weeks chasing mountain goats, line drives and submarine rumors."

Family life went on, too. Players got married, babies were born, everyday stuff happened. In 1931, the *Los Angeles Times* reported that Jackie May got hit in the head with a baseball — and everyone was afraid his skull was fractured. Fortunately, the X-ray machine at the tiny Avalon Hospital revealed he'd just have a bad headache for a while.

Infielder Lloyd Lowe, recalling 1948:

"I was a new father, and I didn't have much money to spend. We had our meals, we'd walk down to the ocean — you'd write letters home, you didn't do much on the side. When I was out there, my wife had our first child. My brother-in-law sent a telegram. Charlie Grimm gave it to me after we're done, and he pulls me aside and tells me, go back to the hotel, call your wife, and put it on my bill. In those days, they kept you in the hospital 8-10 days. But I didn't do it — I felt like if I couldn't afford it, I wouldn't ask him to pay for it."

"I went out to Catalina with Cy 2 times, in 1946 and 1947," Harriet Block says. "The 1st time, we stayed at the hotel. The 2nd time, we stayed at the bungalows — I was pregnant. We could have our meals in out hotel, if we wanted. It was a lovely bungalow. We usually ate over at the hotel."

Hopes & dreams

Rookie sensations came. Most went, but some stuck — like Phil Cavaretta. One year, Burns wrote in the *Tribune*: "It is sad to relate that this year's alleged rookie sensation, Ed Baecht, wasn't altogether sensational in his chore of the day, being spanked for ten hits and seven runs during his 5-inning tenancy."

1940 rookie hopeful Clare Bertram. Take one look at his motion, & it becomes quite clear why Clarence never actually appeared in a major league game.

"We didn't have television, we barely had radio — we weren't bothered by anybody," Claude Passeau's wife, BUM*, recalls. "We stayed in the little casitas, and we could walk right down to the beach. And of course, they were right next to the field. Every morning, they'd bring in fresh sweetpeas; it was wonderful. One time when we went to Catalina, I had one child; another time, I had 2. I'd cook the quail; one time, I cooked a boar. We'd walk on the beach."

Opponents

Teams were lining up to play the Cubs on Catalina. The very first season, Mayor Pete Reyes declared a school holiday, gave all employees the day off, and challenged the Cubs to a game against the local All-Stars. "The island boys played as if their lives depended on it," the *Los Angeles Times* reported. UCLA, USC, and Occidental College were among many mainland schools seeking a meeting, too.

* Yep, she really spells her name with all caps...

Giant times: Some of the greatest players of all time visited the Cubs on Catalina in 1932 & 1933.

CARL HUBBELL

"MEL" OTT

BILL TERRY — Lou Gehrig says...

In 1932 and 1933, the New York Giants floated over to play a series of exhibition games. Stars like Carl Hubbell, Bill Terry, Mel Ott and John McGraw (voted "Greatest Manager Ever") applied their skills on the Avalon diamond. Boatloads of mainland tourists came over and crowded the local hotels, and the papers reported 2,500 fans watched — more a testament to the Wrigley PR machine than anything else, because the crackerbox grandstand might've held 300, at the most. The White Sox, training in Pasadena, came over to watch the spectacle.

" 'Tell me about the great John J. McGraw.' He said *Jota* for J."

Manolin, talkin' baseball with Santiago in Ernest Hemingway's *The Old Man and the Sea*

"Word got out that the Giants were coming to town," recalls Avalon native Bob Hoyt, who was in kindergarten in 1932. "I wanted to go down there and see how big those guys were! So I got to the field just as they were walking up, and I remember saying to myself, 'They don't look *that* big!' "

The guys had some fun with their intrasquad games. Just about every year, the half-squads got new names. Some matchups over the years:

> Regulars vs. Sand Dabs
> Regulars vs. Goofs
> Doublemints vs. Spearmints
> Catalinas vs. Avalons (Burns covered these in the *Tribune* as Joseph V. McCarthy's Avalons vs. J. Vincent McCarthy's Catalinas)
> Claghorns vs. Wildcats
> Regulars vs. Rebels
> > Regulars vs. Daisies
> > Regulars vs. Yannigans
> > McCullough's Night Owls vs. Scheffing's Grumpies
> > Whites vs. Grays
> > Roy Johnsons vs. Spud Davises

Bill Terry's Giants returned to Catalina in 1933 for another round against Charlie Grimm's N.L. champ Cubs — Islandball at its finest.

The view from the dugout

So what'd the ballplayers think about Island training?

"All I remember is those shrimp cocktails," Wayne Terwilliger says. "They were really good! I don't think anyplace else I ever trained could compare to Catalina. It was beautiful, it seemed the weather was perfect. We'd take walks in the hills. One season, we got there early and just hiked. Somebody had the idea that'd help us push a few more runs across the plate. But then we'd come down and have a shrimp cocktail — that was hog heaven. They had that big pavilion, the Casino — I don't know if it was operating full-blast."

Twig, contemplating his next shrimp cocktail.

The Cubbies could dress right over the ocean in the '20s.

"It was exciting," Randy Jackson says, "but there wasn't a whole lot to do. We'd get a few dollars in meal money. It was off-season, so there were very few tourists that time of year. There wasn't a theater, I don't think. They had that big Casino, but I'm not sure what they used it for."

"It was the same old baloney," according to Harvey Storey.

"I was just a kid then, the youngest guy in camp," Paul Schramka says. It was a super-nice field. We had a great time, but we only spent about 8 or 9 days there, training, before we went on the road and started playing exhibition games — I don't think we played any exhibition games there."

"I don't know why they didn't keep going out there," Lee Anthony muses. "Wrigley owned the island, and it was a nice set-up."

"It wasn't all that convenient," Cal McLish explains.

At first, the Cubs had to dress in the bath house that was right on the Bay — about a mile's walk to the diamond. But by the late '20s, the Country Club was fully operational (right across Avalon Canyon Road from the field), making things a bit easier. The bath house was removed in the '50s after a big blow, yet the Clubhouse remains intact. In fact, if you choose to duff while on Catalina, you can dress in the old Cubs' locker room — beneath pictures of the ballplayers. And after you've birdied your last putt, you can dine in the restaurant upstairs...with more Cub photos gracing the walls.

The Country Club, where the Cubs could both shower & eat, serves as a nifty working 'museum' in these modern times.

Get a room

One of the few major difference between Avalon then...and Avalon now...is the fact that the Hotel St. Catherine is missing.

Once a grand resort, the hotel was taken over by the Army during the War — and never quite got back up to the old standards. The property fell into disrepair and was finally demolished in 1966. Now, there's a small beach and park there, in Descanso Cove — a short walk past the Casino. Standing on the spot, it is difficult to imagine such a magnificent hotel could fit into that little canyon.

The Cubs usually stayed at the St. Catherine, although families, married players, and some others generally stayed at the bungalows right next to the field — Las Casitas. Some years, an overflow of players would stay at the Atwater Hotel, right in the center of Avalon's tiny downtown. The Atwater is still in business, yet lost in time; there are no telephones in the rooms.

"The St. Catherine Hotel was nice and clean, and they had good food. Once in a while, you'd see a movie star," Phil Cavarretta says.

"I remember going into the hotel dining room all by myself, and gettin' a shoe shine," says Buddy Hartnett, Gabby's son. "My shoes must've been 3 inches long!"

The St. Catherine became one of Charlie Grimm's favorite stages. He'd perform his famed pre-Chevy-Chasian pratfalls (the elevator would arrive in the lobby, for instance, and Cholly would collapse face-first onto the floor). Della Root Arnold (Charlie Root's daughter) recalls one time when Grimm grabbed an armload of silverware and went down the halls, randomly tossing spoons through above-door transoms into the rooms of unsuspecting guests.

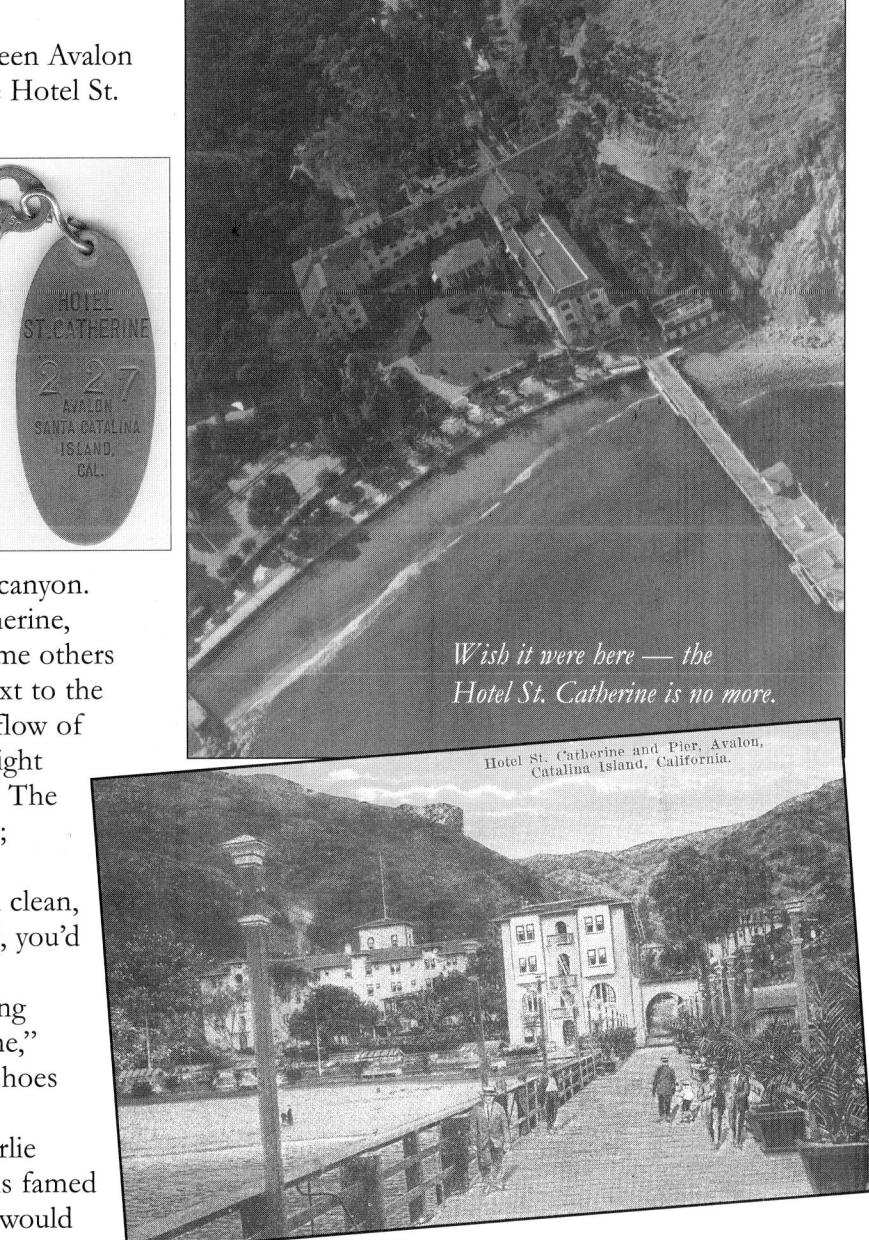

Wish it were here — the Hotel St. Catherine is no more.

Good thing Larry French brought his glove -- he can play catch in the hallways at the Hotel St. Catherine. Bill Lee chose to pack extra shirts instead.

Filling in the blanks

Okay, okay — you do need a few more details about the 30-year thing. How it started so good, and ended up so bad. Like the fortunes of the team itself, the Catalina adventure began as a great William Wrigley idea...which got diluted because PK wasn't all that interested in maintaining anything beyond the gum biz...and everyone's morale eventually deteriorated. When the whole thing started, Bill Wrigley knew the glowing newspaper reports would encourage tourism to the Island; by the end, PK's scaled-down Avalon (less music and dance, for instance) bored the grumpy old reporters to tears, so the company was actually spending all that money to drag all those journalists over there...only to have them bash Catalina daily for Chicago readers!

There were some quizzical glances at first. In 1921, Harry Williams of the *Los Angeles Times* called William Wrigley "the Robinson Crusoe of the modern business world." But enthusiasm soon took over. The *Times* reported manager Johnny Evers "declares Catalina is the best training spot he has found in 20 years of baseball, and hopes to see a permanent camp established there. He regards the island climate as the nearest thing to perfection he has found."

"The boys should be 'fixed comfortably, so that they will want to return again next year.'"

A wireless telegram from Mr. Wrigley, sent in 1921, as reported in the *Catalina Islander*.

The next year, new skipper Bill Killefer beamed to the *Chicago Tribune*, "This is what I would call the last word in ballparks."

Still, some needed a while to be convinced that the experiment would fly. "Several recruits from the Middle West...feared that in case of a downpour the island might become waterlogged and sink, and therefore insisted on sleeping in life preservers," the *Los Angeles Times* suggested in 1926.

"In All the World, No Trip Like This."

The slogan used to promote Catalina vacations in the '20s

But most reporters soon warmed up to Mr. Wrigley's annual junkets — and happily acted as his personal PR team for the folks back home. Harry Hochstadter wrote this glowing view for the *Chicago Evening Post* in 1923:

Pity the poor baseball fan. The man who pays the freight must stay here and endure the wintry blasts while the ball player is forced to board a California-bound rattler and get into playing condition by basking in the glare of California sunshine.

Some one suggested as the Santa Fe pulled out that there should be a training trip for baseball fans to get them ready for the terrible strain of concentrated rooting which starts on April 17.

It's a cruel world but Bill Killefer was not kicking a bit as he assembled his noble athletes for the getaway.

Two days later, as the Cub Special blew through Winslow, Arizona, Harry continued his puff journalism: "It might be worth mentioning," he wrote, "that you don't need any heavy furs or earmuffs in this territory." And the next week, Harry boldly predicted: "It will only be a few years before Catalina will be the Spring camp of more than one big league club."

In 1935, Jim Gallagher — still writing for the *Chicago American*, and not yet the Cubs' GM — reported on some heavy rains, and revealed the first chinks in the armor.

In order to get the field into any kind of shape, they had to burn fifty gallons of gasoline in sawdust over the infield.

Grimm is in a state of mind now to suggest to President Wrigley that the Cubs transfer their Spring activities to Florida.

A few days of sunshine, however, would make everyone cheer up and decide that Catalina is the only place to train after all. For everyone connected with the Cub official family loves this picturesque island.

"Alexander said last week that he was in better shape right then than he was when the season started last year. Why? Catalina!"

Chicago Herald & Examiner, 1921

But the winds of change were already blowing. "As early as last August, when the Cubs first booked games with the Giants around Pensacola," Burns wrote in the *Tribune* in 1936, "it was reported that this trip to California may be the last for the Cubs. St. Petersburg has extended an especially cordial invitation for the Cubs to establish their Spring base in that lively Florida west coast city."

False advertising in 1937? The sun shines brightly in this poster, but unfortunately...it didn't smile on the Cubs in Catalina that Spring.

THE CUBS ARE HERE!
Why don't you come too?

CHICAGO CUBS SPRING TRAINING TRIP - FEB. 21 - MAR. 12
SANTA CATALINA ISLAND

Something must've been in the water at the *Tribune*. The next year, another *Trib* writer referred to the Cubs as "half trained" after they broke camp. Burns sent repeated dispatches about the demise of Catalina, including one headlined "Avalon Still is Beautiful, But Natives Don't Seem to Love Our Cubs Now." In that story, Honest Ed typed, "it is reported that certain former red hot Cub boosters in Avalon sit at their receiving sets and root for the Cubs to get whipped." He went on, "The island never was the perfect training site" and "The glamour has gone for the Cubs." He concluded with, "The future is not desperate, however, for Mr. Wrigley has a swell boarding house in Phoenix, called the Phoenix Biltmore. Don't be surprised if you get your Spring Training news of the Cubs from Arizona, beginning next year."

"The Cubs have no thought of giving up Catalina Island," Edward Cochrane countered in the *American* the following week, "and when you hear reports to the contrary just discount them. They are sent out by irresponsible people."

"Catalina Island will be the training site of the Cubs next season — and probably for many seasons thereafter — unless it ups and falls into the ocean. (Florida papers, please copy.)," Jimmy the Cork had written for the *American* the year before. "Furthermore, neither Lon Warneke nor Gabby Hartnett, two of the team's expert marksmen, see any fun in shooting crocodiles."

Yet Burns seemed bent on bashing Catalina for years to come. After the War, when some players flew to the mainland for exhibitions while others remained on the Island for intra-squad work. Ed wrote, "18 will remain incarcerated on Avalon."

"Mesa made the Cubs an offer that we couldn't refuse."

Philip K. Wrigley, quoted in the *Catalina Islander*, 1951.

Yet Ed was a naif compared to Warren Brown, by then with the *Chicago Herald-American*. Every day in that final, fateful Spring of 1951, Brown devoted an entire column to venting his anti-Avalon wrath — he gave more column inches each day to badmouthing Catalina than he did to actually covering baseball. Consider these gems:

Feb. 25: "A couple of sentimental guys such as R.C. (Lewis) and I might have shed a nostalgic tear over the Catalina contemplated now and the one we first glimpsed in the early '20s..."

March 4: "Since the boat from the mainland does not reach Avalon until 12:10, it is unlikely that the game will get started before one o'clock. By that time, casual tourists will have had a chance to get to the park, after exhausting the possibilities of post card and souvenir shops, one-arm eating joints and other attractions of Avalon's water front."

March 8: "In all the years I've been coming to Catalina Island, the place never has been quite as dreary as during this spell...It seemed to his old friend, after an absence of several days while studying form at Santa Anita, that Frisch rapidly is approaching the talking to himself stage...If Wid (Matthews) intends to return, he didn't say so."

March 9: "Maybe you'd like to have another fill in on the life and times of Avalon, from which 20 Cubs are being paroled today...'I'm glad I had two week-end breaks,' he (Ed Burns) said, 'getting over to the mainland. You know what Lewis wanted? He wanted to know if I was going to the meeting tonight. I asked him what meeting. He said that out his open window, he heard two ladies asking each other if they were going to the meeting. So he said, even if he didn't know what meeting or where, at least there WAS a meeting somewhere, and he thought I ought to know, since it was one lead on some place to go.' In all the world, no place like this."

The truth is, there just wasn't enough action around Avalon for the grizzled sports reporting crew from Chicago — who liked the night life and race tracks. Mr. Wrigley's junkets, while inspired at first, were beginning to backfire — to the point where Brown was even reduced to mocking the old Wrigley slogan from the roaring '20s.

And the Cubs office staff got grumpier, too — less involved, less engaged. By the late '40s, it seems no one was sure about the Cubs' training schedule. "For the first time within memory," Edgar 'the Mouse' Munzel wrote for the *Chicago Sun* in 1948, "the Cubs will not depart in an organized troop."

"You folks on Catalina have been wonderful and most assuredly we leave with fond memories and wish for you all every success."

A telegram from Wid Matthews to the Catalina Chamber of Commerce in 1951.

Yet in 1952, no one was certain that Arizona was going to be permanent, either. Irving Vaughn referred to Mesa in the *Tribune* as "the new Spring camp that, at least temporarily, has displaced the long established training grounds at Santa Catalina Island."

Long after the glory years of Catalina were over — in 1966, when the Cubs moved their Spring Training from Arizona to Long Beach for one season (to accommodate new manager Leo Durocher) — there were still a few lingering remnants of the past. Ancient Munzel, now merged into the *Chicago Sun-Times,* wrote:

Charlie Grimm, one of the Cub Vice Presidents, donned a uniform and helped out with a fungo stick...It's his 50th consecutive Spring Training camp.

One remarkable little island. One legendary ballclub. Three decades of memories. In all the world, no story like this...

Left: Epperly, Kimball, Harrell, Lillard, Higbe, & Carnett leaping, 1939;

Right: Tommy, Jimmy, Robbie, Ernie, & Neil leaping in Cub hand-me-downs, 1947.

Getting There

Trains, Planes, Buses, Steamerships, Streetcars, Cabs, & the Occasional Thumb

"It was a lovely trip, if ya didn't get sick."

Al Epperly

CUBS CATALINA BOUND IN PENNANT QUEST

Good-By Chicago! We'll Be Back in April — **HERALD and EXAMINER SPORTS** — CHICAGO — FRIDAY, FEBRUARY 25, 1927. — *Hello Catalina! Your Sunny Clime Calls Us*

Cubs on train: Guy Bush, Luther Roy, Howard Freigau, Hank Grampp, Earl Adams, Riggs Stephenson, Cliff Heathcote, Hack Wilson, Abe Felson, Johnnie Brillheart, Art Queisser, R. Hanson, N. Lolos, Charlie Hartnett, Webb and Yaiser

Nowadays, you can get from Chicago to Los Angeles in about 3 hours.

Back then, it took about 3 days.

Train to the Coast. Streetcar-like-thing or bus to the pier. Boat to the island. Bus or truck to the hotel. Walk to the clubhouse.

Six weeks later, reverse, repeat.

After the War, the team experimented with flying some of the boys out, too.

All in all, keeping a few dozen young men cooped up together for a couple of months was fertile ground for adventure, mischief, and the occasional mayhem. Fortunately, there were never any disasters — train wrecks or anything like that — but there were some interesting close calls.

In 1938, Kirby Higbe disappeared on the train ride out. They thought he'd boarded in Chicago — but the next morning, no Kirby. "So far," Warren Brown dispatched from Kansas for the *Chicago Herald & Examiner*, "no reward has been offered for the missing pitcher."

Brown explained the mystery years later, in his 1946 history of the Cubs: "He finally reported that he had forgotten a toothbrush or something, and had gone back to Columbia, South Carolina, or thereabouts, to get it." Brown editorialized: "He showed possibilities as a pitcher, but he also showed possibilities as an eccentric." He was traded away soon thereafter.

Even if Kirby Higbe would have thought to pack his toothbrush...he apparently also forgot his shirt, as well. Tsk, tsk.

On the 1934 trip, everybody was accounted for — in fact, an extra character caused the complications. "Manager Charlie Grimm and many of his players narrowly escaped serious injury yesterday," Herb Simons wrote in the *Chicago Times*, "when the bus that was taking them from the train to the boat in Los Angeles crashed into a cow that was nonchalantly crossing the road. The bus swerved off the road, stopping within only a few inches of a telegraph pole. The cow continued crossing the road."*

And in 1937, "Round Robert C. Lewis, traveling secretary of the Cubs, had by far the roughest journey from Los Angeles to the island," the *Chicago Daily News* reported. "First of all, Robert's bus driver lost their way enroute to the dock on the mainland. Then, as R.C. cooled off from that struggle, a sea gull scored the only counter of the voyage on Robert's newly cleaned hat."

Less eventful seasons

Generally, though, the trip was a pretty boring non-event for most of the veterans...and a potentially stressful one for the wanna-bes. A 1937 caption-writer at the *Chicago Tribune* explained that Ken O'Dea got a trim as soon as he boarded the train. "He should have waited," the paper said. "Now he won't have anything to do tomorrow."

As for the rookies, "What journey is so fraught with great possibilities as a baseball training trip?" a pre-Cub-GM Jim Gallagher wondered rhetorically for *Chicago American* readers in 1935.

Let's take a vehicle-by-vehicle look at this well-fraught journey:

Fast as a speeding locomotive

The Cubs would leave from either the Dearborn Street Station or the Polk Street Station on a major rail carrier, like the Santa Fe. Zillions of screaming fans would see their boys off — which was no small sacrifice, given the weather you'd generally get in Chicago in mid-February. Keep in mind, the pitchers and catchers would usually head out a week or so ahead of the rest of the squad...so those loyal Cubbie rooters would actually go out to the station *twice* each pre-Spring. Things usually started smoothly, but there was the occasional incident:

"Gabby Hartnett, star catcher, who apparently has just recovered from trouble with his throwing arm, had trouble with his legs," 'Jimmy the Cork' Corcoran wrote for the *American* in 1930. "Just after the train started, it was discovered that Hartnett was missing. It was brought to a halt and the puffing Hartnett clambered aboard."

Manager Grimm helps the band give the team their send-off in 1938. Hmmm... does it really say 'Oscar Mayer' on his cap?

* The editors feel obliged to point out that this was indeed a long time ago — when was the last time anyone saw a cow in downtown Los Angeles (except, perhaps, atop a bun at a McDonald's) . . . or a telegraph pole, for that matter?

Rookie Al Epperly didn't quite clamber as quickly as Gabby. While Pard would do fine on the 1937 boat-ride leg, his success along the tracks left something to be desired. "That was my first trip on a big boat," he explains. "Everything was new to me. I didn't get sick, but some of the guys did." Well, Al didn't get sick, but he did get lost. The account from the *International New Service* wire, which mistakenly used his middle name:

EPPERLY LOST; FOUND AGAIN

LYNNDYL, Utah — The Chicago Cubs lost pitcher Paul Epperly for a brief period today on an unintentional "release" at Ogden.

When the train carrying the squad to their Catalina Island training camp pulled into Ogden, young Epperly alighted for a stroll. The train was running late and it left without him.

Fortunately, Epperly had only 10 minutes to wait for another train, which reached Salt Lake City while the Cub train was still waiting there

They'd head West on a semi-northern route, which seemed to be the most direct. Then, after breaking camp, they'd take a more leisurely Southern run, where they'd stop off in spots like Phoenix, Bisbee, San Antonio, and Little Rock to play exhibition games.

They spent enough time aboard the trains that the reporters often filed stories while rattling along; in the Spring of '37, *Des Moines Dispatch* columnist Dutch Reagan sent one article home from the rail line:

"CAR 29, BETWEEN LOS ANGELES AND SAN FRANCISCO," he datelined, "It's bound for 'San Antone,' but if the engineer can't keep his mind on his work he'll drive that thing right into the Kankakee opera house and bowling emporium."

Al Epperly desperately attempts to hail a train.

"The train ride out, that was a thrill in itself," says Lennie Merullo. "We all met in Chicago; that was quite a trip out there. I went all by myself. Then I joined up with the team, and I think it took 3 days. It's always a lot of fun. I enjoyed the sightseeing — I'd never been to Chicago, or west of Chicago, before. Most of the guys played cards (especially the veterans), but I wasn't much of a card player. The game they played mostly was Hearts."

"Gabby Hartnett has already established himself the champion rhummy player of the expedition," the *Herald & Examiner* reported in 1937. "On the first day out he relieved Billy Herman, Rip Collins, Johnny Corriden and two newspapermen of what tip money, if any, they had rattling around in their jeans."

"Man alive, we all went barnstorming across the country, to Florida."

Ox Miller

"When I was with the Browns, we used to take the same train out as the Cubs," Ox Miller recalls. "The Browns trained in Anaheim. We left on a special train together. The Cubs had one car, and there was the dining car between us, and we had our own car."

"It was really first-class," Lloyd Lowe says. "We were treated well. I wasn't used to that in the D leagues."

Feel free to use crayons to color the map.
Use brown for the Rockies, & blue for the water.
Other color selections are totally up to your discretion.

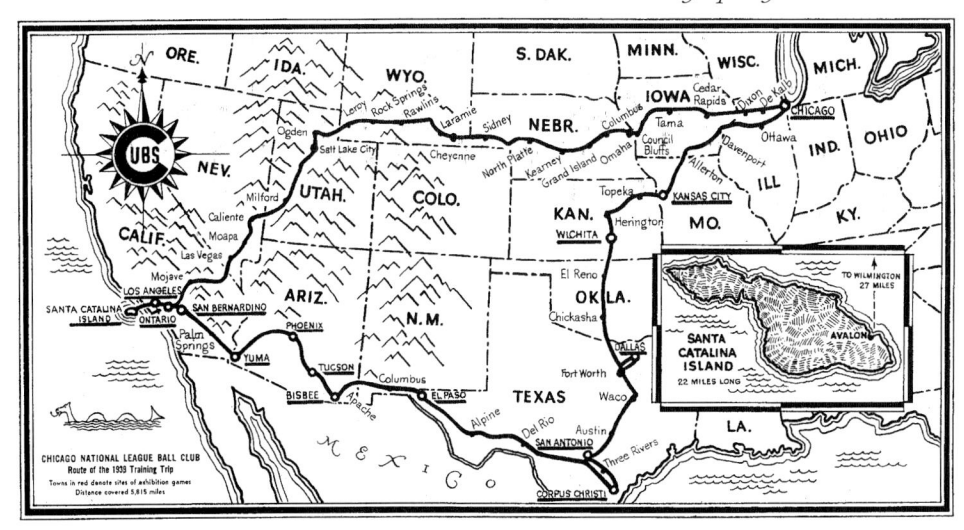

Howard Auman echoed the same sentiments in a letter he wrote home from the Fairmont Hotel on San Francisco's Nob Hill in 1948:

Dear Home Folks,

This is another large city and a nice hotel we are staying in. Left L.A. last night at 7:55 and arrived this morning about 8:30 AM. Play five games while we are here and return to L.A. Tuesday night.

The weather is cool and we have a night game in Oakland tonight. Oakland is across the Bay from here.

We travel in 'class;' all we have to do is be there on time, we pack our bags but they take care of them, see that they get to the train from the hotel. Our baseball things are put in a trunk and we don't see them until we are ready to dress at the park.

It was the invisible-but-always-working support crew, Andy Lotshaw and Yosh Kawano, who made all those trunks suddenly appear at the right place at the right time. While the players got to snooze and play poker on the train, the others were still hard at work.

"What'd I do on the train? I slept!" grins Yoshi, who still takes care of equipment for the Cubs. "That's what everybody always said: 'Yosh is sleeping.' But they had those switches on the tracks, and one of my jobs was to go out, in the middle of the night, and switch the tracks. The railroad guy would say, 'Don't worry — I'll check it. You sleep.' But I thought, I'm not gonna depend on somebody else; what if the train goes to Detroit instead of L.A.? So I went out and did the switching."

Meanwhile, "Trainer Andy Lotshaw has reported all travelers probably will land in good shape except for having to have their clothes pressed," Ed Burns wrote in a 1929 *Tribune* article.

"The trip from Chicago has been devoted largely to proving some of Hoyle's theories..."

'Jimmy the Cork' Corcoran,
in the *Chicago American*, 1938

The dining car was a popular spot, right from year one. "All indications were the dining car would have a good play," the *Tribune* reported in 1921. But there were restrictions, too: "The celebrated Cubs are jogging across the wilds of the Southwestern desert, fuming amongst the cacti...cooped up in Pullmans with common citizens and without a chance to cuss or spit on the floor," the *American* dispatched a few days later.

A luggage tag from the '30s.

"There hasn't been a cross word in the whole party," the Cork wrote for the *American* in 1936. "Most of the fighting so far has been done to reach the chow car. It is very important that you get to the chow car early when you are traveling with ball players because the lads are likely to put a tremendous hole in the 'vittles' long before the average customer can get his dogs planted beneath the board."

"We were rookies — there weren't many tall tales to tell yet!"

Carmen Mauro

"Some anxiety is being felt by the athletes because the train is running an hour late and they have visions of missing breakfast tomorrow," the *Tribune* pointed out in 1929.

The next year, the *American* explained: "Despite the rigors of the cross-country marathon, the traveling secretary has been keeping the boys in good humor by supplying them with plenty of gum...You see, the Cubs are high-priced athletes and must be accorded some of the luxuries of life. We are offering two ducats to the bird who can guess the brand of gum that is being distributed."

Some of the baseball card companies merged ballplayers with the King O'Hearts. Imagine playing 5-card draw on a lengthy train ride, & coming up with a pair of your own face — like Guy Bush might've in 1927, if he'd been using this deck!

Charlie Grimm always brought his banjo along. When Sheriff Blake got married just before the trip and brought his new bride for a Catalina honeymoon, Jolly Cholly struck off a few bars of Mendelssohn's Wedding March. A few harmonicas usually made their way into camel's hair coat pockets, make-shift drumsticks were easy to find, and ukuleles were in vogue back then — so before anybody knew what hit 'em, a band had usually been struck up. Hack Wilson and others were often in fine singing form, so small towns throughout the Midwest often must've wondered who these wandering minstrels might be.

> "The Cubs will spend tomorrow on the great American desert but won't mind. The club car has a really excellent radio."
>
> Ed Burns, in the *Chicago Tribune*, 1937

When neither crooning nor serenading, the boys often told tall tales. "You might say the 1929 N. L. pennant race will be well underway today," Burns told *Tribune* readers, "for manager Joe McCarthy and the members of his first squad of Cub travelers...indicated they are in superb voice. They should have their first 20 games won before their Santa Catalina Special reaches Englewood shortly before 2 o'clock this afternoon. And if the oral pitching holds out, the rest of the league ought to be in a panic by the time the gang gets to Needles Saturday night."

Corcoran reported that the players weren't the only ones gabbing away. "The author's young offspring is affected with talkitis," he wrote for the *American* in 1930, "but so far no one has threatened to toss him off the train. The betting now is that he will not last out the trip."

Another Cub kid almost didn't last out the trip — the very first year the team chugged to Catalina. In 1921, the *Tribune* reported:

PILOT EVERS' SON PULLS A STUNT TO EXCITE CUBS

Williams, Ariz. — Jack Evers, the 11-year old son of Manager Evers...furnished the first excitement on the Cub trip when the train paused at Las Vegas, N.M. for a few minutes.

Jack got off to buy a box of candy. When the train prepared to start he couldn't be found, but soon showed up, much to his parents' relief. He had boarded the train up ahead, being afraid he might miss if he tried for a car further back.

Besides the candy shoppes, there were other interesting stops along the way, "At Joliet the Cubs were greeted by a large group of fans," Jimmy the Cork wrote in 1930. " 'I want to visit the penitentiary here when the club returns,' manager Joe McCarthy told the mayor as the train left the city."

Passing through Tucson in 1934, pranksters Woody English and Billy Jurges loaded some of the highly-touted local garlic crop aboard...and smeared the stuff all over Gabby Hartnett's berth. "The entire caravan suddenly became garlic conscious," Herbert Simons wrote in the *Times*. "Discovering that a little bit of garlic goes a long way, thus having a lot left over, Woody immediately made the rounds of all the berths. A smell time was had by all."

English "exhibited a genius for pranks," Charlie Grimm wrote in his autobiography. "Along came Bill Jurges and Augie (Goo-Goo) Galan to form a conspiratorial threesome. They never struck alone and became known as the Katzenjammer Kids."

Goo-Goo Galan appears to be studying baseball strategies, but in actuality is plotting his next gag with English & Jurges.

"On a trip back to Chicago," Grimm continued, "the Katzenjammer Kids went into action. We were sidetracked one night because of power failure, so we took advantage of the delay to leave our two cars and stretch our legs. It was pitch dark, but our three friends stumbled onto a freight car wheel. I don't know how they did the job without a derrick, but they managed to lug it aboard, gently dropping it into Lon Warneke's lower berth before he returned. He didn't sleep all night."

A brilliantly-executed prank apparently made Lonnie's hair stand straight on end.

"Roy Henshaw was one of the few ballplayers who had graduated from college," says Della Root Arnold, Charlie's daughter. "He was a nice little fella, and he got a tryout. On the train, they were getting ready to go into their berths, and Gabby says, 'Oh, you're in the wrong berth — that's Charlie Root's berth. You're a left-hander.' So he called the porter and he tore up the bed and put it the other way."

The end is in sight

After 3 days aboard a loud, rattling, rolling, often smoke-drafted train, most of the Cubbies were more than ready to disembark. "The boys will be sniffing the salt air of the Pacific in another 24 hours or so, something much desired by some and dreaded by others," the *Chicago Daily News* noted in 1926.

"The day was so bright and clear the Cubs stood on the dock at noon time and saw plainly the snow capped peak of Mount Baldy, 100 miles away behind San Bernardino," the *Herald & Examiner* reported the next season.

"The Bruins, who had been glimpsing snow-clad country all the way to California, welcomed the sunshine here," *American* readers read in 1928.

Transfers

Once the lads made it to Los Angeles, things were supposed to be relatively simple: Take the electric rail to the port, where they'd get on the steamer.

But occasionally, someone couldn't make it to L.A. on the team train — so the kid in question would often be on his own. And since a lot of these young ballplayers had never been to the big city before (let alone off the farm), things could get pretty interesting.

"I didn't know my butt from a teakettle!" Bob Kelly admits. "I arrived in L.A. all by myself — I imagine I didn't have the sense to look into traveling with the team. When I got to L.A., the boat wasn't leaving for the next morning... so I had to find a hotel all on my own. I had to share a room with someone. It was a nightmare. I didn't have enough sense to turn in my expenses! I thought it was better to be seen and not heard."

Fresh from the cross-country train ride, the '36 squad prepares to embark on the cross-L.A. trolley ride to the steamer port.

Harvey Storey was a bit more seasoned, having played in the Pacific Coast League for a while. "I lived in Portland, so I drove down," Harvey says calmly. "The boat ride was not a new experience for me — I'd been to Victoria, on ferries."

"I didn't know my butt from a teakettle!"

Bob Kelly

Ken Raffensberger did a little driving one year, too — nearly 3,000 miles' worth. "Larry French asked if I'd go to Detroit and pick up a car for him," Ken says. "So I drove to Chicago, took the train to Detroit, and drove it to L.A. It took me 2 days."

"I came in late," Paul Schramka says. "I was going to school, and just finished the spring semester. I took a plane to Los Angeles, then flew over to the Island from L.A. on a little plane. It was a real thrill. Somebody met me at the airfield, and got me checked into the hotel."

"I took the train from Arkansas to Los Angeles and caught a cab to catch the boat," Randy Jackson says. "The train was late, and as soon as the cab pulled up, I saw the boat taking off. I asked someone what I could do. They told me that about 20 miles away there was a seaplane I could catch. So I grabbed up my bags and got another cab to catch the plane. I actually got there before the boat did! I gave the traveling secretary, Bob Lewis, my bill for the cab — and he really blew up! His arms were flying all around and everything. I didn't know how a major league team worked. But I explained to him what had happened, and he finally agreed to pay it."

Of course, a player's unique circumstances were occasionally a lot *easier* — like Charlie Root's. "We lived a couple blocks from the old Washington Park in Los Angeles," daughter Della says. "He walked to work. In Chicago, the first couple of years, we were not too far from the park."

As far as our research indicates, none of the Cub rookies ever fell overboard. Of course, none of them ever found the belowdeck bowling alleys, either...

A 3-hour tour...a 3-hour tour...

The players would set out to the Magic Isle from a little seaport town in Southern Cal called Wilmington. Wilmington no longer exists — long since swallowed up by behemoth L.A. — but the exit is still alive on the 405 freeway as you approach Long Beach.

T'was generally a pleasant trip, but there were hazards...like the occasional gust of wind. "I bought a new hat — a cowboy hat," Don Dunker recalls. "When we were coming back, there was a storm. I was up on the 2nd level of the boat, and when I came down the stairs from the top level to the bottom, a big wave came over and the wind blew my hat right off. The last time I saw it, it was going out to sea."

Too bad Don Dunker hadn't yet learned the technique veterans Hartnett, French, & Lee mastered in 1940 — hold on to your hats, boys!

Most years, the Cubs went out on one of 2 grand steamships: the *S.S. Catalina*, or the *S.S. Avalon*. Both, sadly, are long gone.

Mr. Wrigley's company launched the *Catalina* in 1923, and she finally retired from passenger service in 1975. The ship was 301 feet long and could carry about 2,200 people. During the Big Band days, revelers would dance 'til the wee hours of the night.

In World War II, this great white ship was borrowed as an Army Transport and painted dull grey. Afterwards, she returned to the pleasure biz.

Today, she rests in Ensenada Harbor, half-sunk in Mexico. A non-profit group, the *S.S. Catalina* Preservation Association, is trying to raise funds to have her towed back to the U.S. — so she can be restored into a floating museum, shops, restaurants, and such (à la the *Queen Mary*, now permanently anchored at Long Beach Harbor). The group's website is *www.sscatalina.org*.

The S.S. Catalina then . . . and now.

There's a bit less hope for the *S.S. Avalon* — which took the Cubs out their first and final sailing seasons, 1921 and 1950 (the team flew in '51). She was retired in 1951, suffered a series of fires, and found her top sheared off...to be converted to a barge! The barge sank in a storm off Palos Verdes in the early '60s, and for the past 40 years this once-grand steamer has served as a wreck for Scuba divers. The hull sits on a seabottom that's roughly 70 feet deep, and fishies now swim where Cubs and movie stars once danced.

The S.S. Avalon *then . . . and now.*

And in 1942, due to war worries, the team endured the ride over in smaller, scarier water taxis. Even with the big ships, though, rough seas could stir up enough whitecaps to weaken the toughest character's knees. "Some of the boys will get a bit dizzy or lightheaded when they get off the boat," Charlie Grimm told reporters in 1936. "If they went right out and faced Warneke, Lee, French, Henshaw, Carleton, and Shoun, all of whom were throwing curves today, they might get their respective ears torn off or their backs broken going after those hooks."

"All those who aren't seasick on the way can get some prelim exercise by tossing oyster crackers at the seagulls," Jimmy the Cork suggested.

Oyster crackers weren't the only things that got tossed.

"I should remember the boat," Preston Ward admits, "because I got seasick."

"Roy Smalley and I were both going to school at Pepperdine, so we both showed up at Spring Training together," Don Carlsen says. "The boat ride out wasn't bad for me, because I'd been in the Navy, but Smalley got sick."

"On the boat, a couple of the guys weren't feeling too good," Johnny Klippstein remembers. "I've had some trouble on boats, but I did okay out there."

"I got seasick one time," Bobby Mattick admits.

Pitchers Julio Bonetti, Jake Mooty, & Ken Raffensberger pitch crackers to the gulls, 1940.

In 1928, the *American* told the tale after a particularly unsettling crossing: "The betting was 100 to 1 that Hartnett, a poor sailor, would be the sickest fellow in California, when the ship *Catalina* docked here, for a strong wind was blowing all day — but Gabby stood the gaff in surprising fashion and no stretcher-bearers were needed to convey him from the boat."

Some of the ballplayers took their kids, too — since kids love boat rides, right?

"The most significant memory I have is going over on the boat," says Boots Merullo, Lennie's son. "There was a trainer named Joe Dollar, and he was carrying me. I was probably 2 or 3 years old or something — he was holding me up so I could see over the bow, over the railing, and I was terrified! I was scared of falling into the water, I guess. My dad has all these movies of him, rowing madly on this dinghy they'd tied to the back of the ship."

"We took the boat over in 1927. My brother got sick, and I thought that was swell."

Della Root Arnold, told with a sisterly grin

"I was so small, all I can remember is getting sick on the boat," says Larry Burgess, Smoky's son.

"The 2nd year, I had my family with me," Bob Kelly says. "We took the boat all the time. Coming back, it was quite raunchy. Kevin (Chuck Connors) was holding our baby, because I was hanging onto the rail. I can get pretty seasick."

"When one manages a ball club that trains on Catalina Island," states McCarthy, "one has to have sailors as well as ball players. Of course, it is well to have a few who can stand the bumps of the ocean. I have made the rounds of the club and Schulte seems to be the only man with sea-going experience. If the rest get kind of squeamish during the crossing Saturday morning, we at least have one man on the field — so that the Angels can't claim the game via forfeit."

Warren Brown once recounted a tale of a choppy day, long after the Cubs discovered Schulte was better suited for Navy duty than baseball: "Charlie Grimm, aboard the good ship 'Avalon,' offered $500 to anyone who would get him a horse and buggy for the rest of the trip."

Brown also mentioned a later manager, Frankie Frisch, missing the last boat in 1951: "After sundown the only means of getting across the Catalina channel is swimming. The Old Flash doesn't swim that well."

With all that seasickness, good thing prank-loving Doc Lotshaw was around. From the *Tribune* in 1937:

Trainer Andy Lotshaw spent the last day on the train reparing the new Cubs for a serious day of seasickness on the way from Wilmington Harbor to the Island. Their pockets were filled with various things to take as a remedy, including strips of bacon, fried crisp.

Earlier on, Joe McCarthy relied on some other channel-crossing insurance — as reported in Corcoran's *Cork Tips* column in a 1930 edition of the *American*:

There is nothing like having an old sailor on a ball club, especially when it rains on an island where one has to go to and fro via ocean-going boats. The old sailor in question is Johnny Schulte, catcher.

Joe McCarthy keeps Schulte on his payroll for a number of reasons. But one of them is because Johnny doesn't get seasick when he crosses from Catalina to the mainland. This assures Joe that he will have at least one man who will be able to play a ball game in the event that a game is scheduled on the same day that the channel has to be bridged.

The ballplayers who didn't get seasick on the S.S. Avalon in 1934 decided to make the trip seem quicker by taking over the bandstand.

The Welcoming committee

"Hey, seeing those flying fish for the first time, you never forget!" Lennie Merullo says. "I was wide-eyed all the way. And who's greeting you when you get there, but this Mexican band!"

While not out at sea, Johnny Schulte provided solid backup for Gabby Hartnett.

Troubadours, rather than mariachis, greeted the Cubs. Had they learned this distinction, they might have made the World Series a little more often.

Mr. PK Wrigley, with daughters DeeDee & Blanny, welcomed the Cubs on horseback some seasons.

Ah, the Mexican band. Colorful costumes and lively music...and a parade. The locals truly pulled out all the stops, and the Wrigleys themselves often mounted horseback and joined in the festivities. "With the tuneful tinkling of music of Mexican harmonizers and a hearty heigh-ho of the Islanders," Jimmy the Cork painted for *American* readers in 1936, "the Cubs arrived here this afternoon.

"We'd have a parade, a band when they came to town, open buses, old horse-drawn carriages," recalls Avalon Mayor Bud Smith.

Harvey Cowell, a previous Mayor of Avalon, also helped put on the shows. "And of course, the parade," his Honor says. "Mr. Wrigley got out the old stagecoach — he and his children would parade with him and the Cubs."

"We'd ride horses with Dad in some of those parades," says Blanny Wrigley Schreiner, one of PK's daughters. "I have a picture of my dad and my sister and I. I think it was 1937 or 1938. It was a lot of fun, because we just loved to ride horses."

"There was great weather, and the local people were all so nice, always glad to see us," Phil Cavarretta says. "They'd always greet us with a band."

Rogers Hornsby added to the PR imagery in 1929, doing Mr. Wrigley a favor. "As a boon to the photographers' cult," Burns wrote in the *Tribune*, "Hornsby drove a team of ancient plugs, which dragged the newcomers to the hotel a half mile from the pier. The picturesque ride ended the monkey business, for all employees were ordered to be on the practice field in uniform just as soon as they had finished lunch."

Thank you, Orville & Wilbur Wright

While the Cubs kept coming over by steamship during their '30s heyday, they were pioneers in dabbling with aviation. "Cub players are so enthusiastic over the plane trips between here and Wilmington that Hornsby will probably have to make the athletes draw straws to see which lucky ones get to make the trip by air," Bob Ray wrote for the *Los Angeles Times* in 1932. "If the National League ever decides on transporting its players by air, the Cubs will be the first to make the change, for they are an air-minded bunch."

Billy Jurges loved the change. He hurried over by plane in 1936 after showing up late — so he could avoid missing a day's workout.

The Cubs took flight long before most big-league teams. By 1933, they were already frequent flyers.

Ironically, Warren Brown was still grumbling about the new-fangled process, nearly 20 years later. In 1951, his column in the *Herald-American* said: "Against all the advice of old settlers, Wid (Matthews) and the Old Flash have insisted on ferrying the Cub squad to the mainland late Friday afternoon by plane... Obviously, no self-respecting pilot would attempt the table-top landing at Catalina." He quoted traveling secretary Bob Lewis: "What was good enough for Robert Fulton is good enough for Robert Lewis."

Dizzy Dean reaps the benefits of missing the team boat.

In between, in 1946, a Cub troupe headed to the mainland for a charity All-Star game found their flight grounded by 45-mile-an-hour gale winds. "We already had taxied to the end of the runway when they called off our flight back over the channel," Stan Hack said. A few weeks later, a planned series against the Pittsburgh Pirates — on the Island — was called off, because the Pirates didn't want to fly over.

Don Dunker says he couldn't blame the Bucs one bit. "We went over on a plane and came back on a ship," Don remembers. "Of course, the airfield was on top of a mountain! We didn't know anything about it 'til we got there; after we got off, we looked over the edge of the cliff — it was pretty scary! They had a lot of cowboys that came up when we landed. It took us about 2 hours to get down, on the bus."

"Flying off the Catalina airport was scary," Randy Jackson agrees. "The runway was really short — about the length of this desk. The DC-3 would start to take off, and then kinda drop off the end! And landing there, that was something else. It was on the end of this cliff."

"The plane wouldn't haul a ballclub," Johnny Klippstein says. "The airport was on the top of a hill — it was scary, coming down that winding road. One manager said we'd fly other teams over and let them stay on the Island, but nobody would do it."

"We took the boat," Ben Wade recollects. "It was about a 3-4 hour trip in those days — one of the few ways you could get there! Everybody enjoyed it. The majority of the ballplayers were afraid to fly, because the runway was so short."

Of course, a choppy boat ride...or a bumpy flight... would be better than not getting a chance at all. "I never made it to Spring Training," Ed Jabb laments. "They cut me off — I was on the list, and they shipped me to the farm club. I got a fall tryout at Wrigley; I'd just finished high school in Chicago."

Today, the luxury trains are forgotten relics of the past — although if you happen to take in an Atlanta Braves game, there's a nifty Pullman car on display at the ballpark museum. You can still fly to Catalina, but the major airlines are long gone. There is helicopter service now — which lands on the site of the old Catalina Tile & Pottery works. And the boats are faster and smoother...making the former 3-hour journey in about 50 minutes from Long Beach.

With less seasickness, it seems.

Yet the approach by sea is the same: The mainland slowly disappears, and off in the distance is this vague landform, and then the harbor comes into view. "The approach to Avalon is always breathtaking, no matter how many times you've taken it in," writer Jim Allyn smiles. And while there are a few changes, it's similar to the view first seen by Grover Cleveland Alexander and his mates...when the Cubs took their first few tentative steps toward Catalina in 1920...

The trip took 4 years this time, but the Cubs finally made it back over in war-free, French-Lickless 1946.

Hack Miller, Hack Wilson, Stan Hack, & Warren Hacker

An Assortment of Colorful Cubs Just Kept Hacking Away...

"Once, he amazed William Wrigley by pounding a 10-penny nail through a 2-by-4 with his bare hand."

Charlie Grimm, on Hack Miller

Pitchers and catchers and shortstops, oh my.

Within the uniquely amazing backdrop of Catalina Island, a collection of quirky ballplayers visited Cub camps over the years. There were Hall-of-Fame heroes and steady journeymen and a lot of wanna-be hopefuls — several hundred in all.

And their tales are often too outrageous to even be fictional. Let's meet a few...

Hack Miller

Never heard of Hack Miller? Allow Oscar Reichow's 1922 dispatch for the *Chicago News* to introduce you:

AVALON, Catalina Island, Cal. — He bends spikes with his hands, breaks a bat over his knee, drives his fist through a 2-inch plank, holds 6 men at one time, lifts a 200-pound weight over his head with one hand and pulls a 4,500-pound automobile with his teeth.

That is Lawrence "Hack" Miller, the Cubs' new outfielder and only strong-man ballplayer in captivity...If he does not succeed in elevating himself to an exalted position as one of Bill Killefer's regular outfielders, the club can carry him around through the season as a side attraction.

Hack Miller, demonstrating his 'driving-in-a-nail-without-benefit-of-a-hammer' technique, 1922.

The 1st Hack: Good thing Mr. Miller didn't stick around too long, or there wouldn't be any trees left on Catalina today.

Oscar neglected to mention that Hack also uprooted trees to amuse the Islanders, drove nails into boards with his fist, and hoisted the piano at the Hotel, too.

"He wields a bat as I do a toothpick," Harry Hochstadter wrote for the *Chicago Tribune* in 1923.

And Hack could swat that ol' horsehide. He still holds the Cub rookie batting record — .352 that season! He smacked 20 home runs the next year, hitting .301. His lifetime major league average: .322.

"Miller accidentally planted himself in front of Flack to watch infield practice," Reichow wrote later that Spring. "The manager suddenly missed Flack and shouted out, 'Where's Max?' Flack, hearing his name called, stepped out from behind Miller to show that he was ready for service. Miller took the joke good-naturedly, but kept moving around to keep the boys from thinking he was trying to shield the diminutive outfielders, who did not overlook the chance to plant themselves behind the broad-backed player for a few minutes' rest."

But...his massive frame slowed him down, so he couldn't move in the outfield. Alas; all-hit, no-field just didn't work six decades before the DH rule. After a few seasons, the Cubs gave up on his fielding follies and sent him back down to the Pacific Coast League. His minor-league numbers were even more awesome (.328, with power) but defense did him in. He retired to work the docks of San Francisco, undoubtedly hoisting steamships out of the Bay when they needed barnacles removed.

Hack Wilson

At 5'6", Hall-of-Famer Hack Wilson was larger than life. "Hack Wilson not only holds the record for runs batted in...and the National League record for home runs," Bill Veeck said in a Cubs video history, "He also holds the record for most saloons in and out of. And he was also the most colorful ballplayer I think ever to perform in Wrigley Field, and maybe ever to perform in baseball."

"Hackus-Smackus Wilson," Jimmy the Cork Corcoran wrote for his *Cork Tips* column in the *Chicago American* in 1930, "has established himself as a national sporting character.

He was actually nicknamed after Hack Miller, since they cast similar shadows.

Mr. Wilson hit 56 homers for the Cubbies in 1930 (while batting .356), and knocked in 191 runs — still a big-league record, despite today's juiced balls, juiced bats, juiced ballparks with juiced air, juiced batters, and minor-league over-expansion pitching. His lifetime batting average was .307 (.319 in the World Series), and he led the league in dingers 4 times. Hack spent 6 springs on Catalina.

"Maybe you better go in now, Hack — or you'll be too tired to go riding again tonight."

Manager Joe McCarthy to Wilson, after hungover Hack clubbed his 3rd homer in a Spring exhibition game but was barely able to slog around the bases

Hack Wilson hit 56 homers in a season once -- when it actually meant something. And he did it without corked bats, although he did pop a few corks in his time...

"Hack Wilson came down the gangplank today and all the bells in Avalon began to ring, the whistles blew and Jimmy, the barber, had his fife and drum corps at the dock to drum Hack from the pier to his hotel," the *Chicago Times* said in 1931. "Of course, Hack was accompanied by a dozen other Cubs..."

"Bring on this 1931 season," Hack's ghostwriter typed for his column in the *Chicago Times*. "I'm all ready. Or rather, I'm sure I will be after the 7 weeks' training course mapped out for us on the Island."

The locals remember Hack fondly. He was nice to the kids, according to current barber Lolo Saldaña, who got to wear Hack's hand-me-down jersey when he played for the Avalon High team. "Oh, how I wish I'd kept it," Lolo says.

After losing a flyball in the sun during the 1929 World Series, Hack good-naturedly joined the razzing in Catalina. "In the hotel dining room," biographer Clifton Blue Parker wrote, "Wilson pulled the window shade and asked the maître d' to dim the light so he wouldn't misjudge his soup."

By 1933, Hack had already drank himself off the Cub roster.

While at practice, Hack put on a show. "Hack Wilson, who weighed in for the game at 205 ringside," Ed Burns wrote for the *Chicago Tribune* in 1929, "gained two homers and lost six pounds."

"Hack Wilson got ahold of one and drove it farther, according to the boys, than any ball was ever hit on Catalina Island," the *Chicago Times* reported in 1931.

Another day, "Hack...had to be satisfied with 2 puny singles," the *Los Angeles Times* said, covering a Spring game in 1931. "That's like putting an elephant on a slice of melba toast."

"I see 3 balls coming at me and always swing at the one in the middle. It's usually the real one."

Hack Wilson

But, according to Parker, Hack played off-the-field on the Island, too. "Hornsby told reporters: 'Wilson started out breaking training rules at Catalina last spring.'"

"The older ballplayers, they were a different breed," Lennie Merullo says. "Not too many of 'em were educated, they were rough-and-ready guys, from tough towns, they played hard and lived hard."

"Hack Wilson loved to fight — he was in trouble all the time," recalls Della Root Arnold, Charlie's daughter. "As a kid, I used to love it! Hack was always nice to me. His son Bobby was an absolute terror. The box seats had metal pipe railings, and Bobby would hang from his knees and smack people as they went by!"

According to Parker, Hack liked to smack people, too: "One day, a frustrated Hack leapt from the dugout and challenged the entire Cincinnati Reds team to a fight. (He never did like the Reds.)"

Bobby Wilson, getting pointers from Pops on how to smack things.

Stan Hack

Wouldn't ya think a guy who hit .301 over 16 seasons...led the league in hits and steals twice...batted .400 in 3 All-Star games...and walloped out a .384 clip over 4 World Series...oughta be in the Hall of Fame?

We present Stan Hack, and ask: "Why not?"

Smilin' Stan was a slick-fielding 3rd-baseman, too — he led the league in defensive categories 9 times. Islander Sylvester Ryan recalls: "Stan Hack was wonderful to watch. One time, somebody hit a line drive that hit once on the ground in front of him. He was playing deep, behind third base, and went to the right and caught it with his bare hand and threw it to first. I can see that like it was yesterday."

"I had Stan Hack's uniform," says Marcelino Saucedo, who wore it while playing for the Avalon High team. "His name was sewn in there. Stan Hack would tell stories, like how they'd put a hole in the glove, in the old days, so it would close around the ball. There wasn't much leather there in the first place."

Stan made the most of his 13 seasons on Catalina. He danced the night away with movie stars like Joan Crawford at the Casino (he won the open waltz trophy in 1947)...he golfed and took hunting trips with the boys...and later on, he brought his family out. Before baseball, he was a banker in Sacramento — "and not a good one at that," he told Jimmy the Cork in 1936.

"A year ago Hack was a bank teller. Except for baseball, he might still be in a bank teller's cage, with absent-minded customers poking peanuts at him by mistake."

Harry Williams in the *Los Angeles Times*, 1932

He almost didn't get a chance, thanks to a typical rookie-like remark he once made. Charlie Root told a *Chicago Daily News* reporter this story in 1939: "Stanley Hack, as a rookie in 1932, made the funniest crack — without meaning it — I've ever heard in a Spring camp. We had played an exhibition game. Rogers Hornsby, who was managing the Cubs then, was 'on' Hack for grinning all the time during the game. He told him, finally, that he had looked terrible. 'Well,' said Hack to his first major-league manager, 'you didn't look so hot yourself today.' " (But he must've looked good enough that Hornsby forgave the fumble...)

He was a hit with the local kids. "I always admired Stan Hack," says Avalon barber Lolo Saldaña. "One year, before the World Series, the radio announcer said, 'You can't beat those guys.' And Stan Hack told him, 'We're gonna beat 'em just because you said we can't!' "

"I was walkin' off the field, and all the kids were waitin' for Stan Hack," pitcher Ken Weafer says. "I looked a little like him in those days, and he was a big star. And all the kids were lookin' at me, sayin', 'Mr. Hack, sign this!' So I looked over at him, and he shook his head, he nodded, so I signed a few 'Stan Hack.' "

"We were always there, as a gang, we got foul balls — we'd shag 'em," says Hon. Edgar Taylor, now a Superior Court Judge. "Stan Hack would toss 'em to us over the fence."

A lot of Catalina Cubs played for Stan in the minors — he managed at Springfield, Des Moines, and Los Angeles, while also managing the Cubs themselves from 1954-1956. "He was always easy to get along with," recalls Fuzzy Richards.

"Stan Hack was a great guy," says Paul Schramka. "He was my manager in the Western League. We had lots of fun. I was playing for Lincoln one night, and hit a single to centerfield. The lights weren't very good, and the centerfielder reached down and faked the throw to 2nd. Well, I came around 1st, and I faked, and I'd retreat, and he'd fake, and I'd fake, and the crowd was yelling, and all of a sudden the right fielder throws it back to 1st — it had rolled right through the centerfielder's legs! I just made it back to 1st base. The next guy up got a base hit, and Stan Hack is coaching at 3rd when I get there. And he says, 'Way to go, Paul — way to stretch a triple into a single!' "

"Stan Hack was a great gentleman," Ed Chandler says. When the Angels would play up north, "he'd have us over to his home in Sacramento for dinner."

Stan Hack has Hall-of-Fame numbers...but no Hall-of-Fame plaque.

Warren Hacker, looking dapper on Catalina. That's the Pleasure Pier behind him; roommate Corky Van Dyke was behind the camera.

Warren Hacker

Warren Hacker pitched in the big leagues for 12 years — 9 with the Cubs. In 1952, he went 15-9 (with a sparkling 2.58 ERA) for Chicago. But hey, these were the Cubs; the next year, he led the N.L. in losses, with 19. After retiring, Warren was a pitching coach in the A's and Padres' organizations for nearly 20 years. He was a Marine and pitched a no-hitter for the L.A. Angels in 1951, after the Cubbies kept him in California for more seasoning. "He was a three-quarter sidearm pitcher," recalls rookie pitcher Eddie Kowalski. "Nobody wanted to face Warren."

"Our Spring Trainings were too long," Hacker told John Skipper in *Take Me Out to the Cubs Game*. "We were pretty well beat by the time August rolled around."

Warren Hacker was one of the Cub aces in the early '50s — which unfortunately gave him a good shot at losing 20 games each season.

"Warren Hacker and I were pretty close," Bob Rush says. "We talked the game after the game, and stuff like that. Each pitcher had his own way of doing things — trying to do something the way another pitcher did it didn't necessarily mean the other one could do it."

He helped extend one ballplayer's ties with the game. "I roomed with Warren Hacker. He's a good guy," says Corky Van Dyke, who also pitched with Warren in the Pacific Coast League. "We called him 'Happy Hack.' I stayed in baseball a while, but I decided to give it up — I'd lived out of a suitcase for a long enough time. Hacker called me and says, scout for Kansas City. I did it for a while."

"I never went to Catalina with him," Olinda Hacker says, "because most of the time, the wives had to pay their own way...and we had a little girl."

"Me!" says daughter Pam.

"Yeah, you."

Corky Van Dyke

Gordon Van Dyke went to Catalina with the Cubs during 2 Springs. "I was just a punk kid then, straight off the farm," Corky says. "I used to throw the 'hope' ball: you'd try and get it by 'em, and hope you could!"

"Gordon Van Dyke was a hard-throwing pitcher, a power pitcher," Carmen Mauro says. "They were consistently very high on him. He threw like Robin Roberts, but he didn't have that pinpoint control. Ball 3, ball 4, and you have to groove one. I think they want you to have a couple of good games in Spring Training, and he never got there."

The Cubs sent him to the Los Angeles Angels in the old Pacific Coast League, and from there he pitched for the Portland Beavers.

"I was back from the service," Corky says. "It was a pretty good jump from the Central Association to AAA, to Los Angeles. I took a chance — I could have gotten more money from Detroit, Cincinnati, or St. Louis. My dad wanted me to sign with the Cubs. He'd played in Louisville. I've got the credentials. I played with Luke Easter, Minnie Minoso, some pretty good ballplayers in the Coast League. I played against Hank Aaron. I was in Sioux Falls when he was with Eau Claire. I pitched against him. I didn't have any trouble — I used to puff him out once in a while. I threw pretty hard — I could blow pretty good. He did get me one time."

"I used to puff him out once in a while."

Corky Van Dyke, on facing Hank Aaron in the minors

"It was a lot of work, hard work," he recalls. "There were some bad days. You had to keep it going, or they'd give you the slip. I was in Portland, and got called to Chicago, but I got hit in the head with a line drive. I was in the hospital for quite a while. Then they asked what I wanted to do, and they ended up sending me to Des Moines."

He roomed with Cal McLish in L.A. "Cal was quite a character," he says.

"Gordon Van Dyke was a nice guy," McLish recalls. "We pitched together out there and for L.A. He had a good arm."

Corky's other claim to fame: He's a distant cousin of Dick Van Dyke. "I've been a police officer, I've worked in a funeral home, I've done a lot of things," Corky says. "I lost my wife last year. I have a calico cat who keeps me company, now that I'm all alone."

Andy Pafko

"We called Pafko 'Sprushi' because he was a Polak," Corky says.

"A lot of people think I'm Polish," Andy says, "but I'm not Polish. I'm Slovak. "Nobody called me Andy." (We won't tell Corky the nickname was really 'Pruschka,' either.)

They did call him a heckuva ballplayer. During his 17-year career, Andy hit .300 four times, had back-to-back 30-homer seasons (1950 & 1951), and he was a 5-time All-Star. He also played for the Dodgers and the Braves. In all, Andy appeared in 4 World Series, for all 3 teams — including the Cubs' final time, 1945.

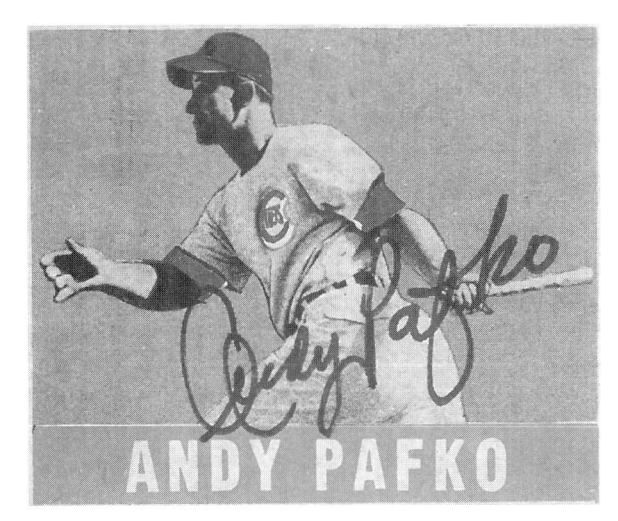

Whatever his nickname was, Andy proved to be a sweet-swinging batsman for the Cubs — as evidenced by his 1948 Leaf card.

"Catalina was a beautiful place to train," Andy says. "Then we'd play exhibition games on the mainland. In the later afternoon, about 2 or 3 o'clock, the breeze came off the ocean. I enjoyed training on Catalina — Mr. Wrigley took good care of us. We used to have a lot of fun in the old days. I played in a good era."

"Andy Pafko was a good guy," Cal McLish says, "and a good ballplayer."

"What a nice guy," Bob Kelly agrees. Bob roomed with Andy on Catalina when Mrs. Pafko wasn't around.

"I was married in 1947, and my wife would come out," Andy says. "We lived just beyond the centerfield wall — it was like a 2nd honeymoon. We stayed at the cottages. There was not much to do. We would go to the dock and watch the tourists come over — that was the routine. I never was much of a fisher or a hunter. Yeah, some of the guys wanted to get me out riding horses. I was a farm boy, raised on a dairy farm. We didn't have riding horses; we had working horses."

*Andy's 1952 Topps card puts him in an elite club with guys like Mickey Mantle & Honus Wagner — 'cuz some Einstein-like person once bought one at auction for $83,870! (As though there might be a reasonable explanation...it's card #1 in the set, & lots of kids rubber-banded their cards together, thus defiling Andy's image. So, it's hard to find one in nice shape. Oh, okay, **that** explains it...)*

One thing Andy wouldn't do on Catalina was hit the links. "To the old-time managers," he says, "golf was taboo in our day! You hit a ball that was standing still, but here in baseball, it's a moving object! I didn't play until I retired."

He did manage to get himself into a little trouble, though. "Outfielder Andy Pafko and Catcher Carl Sawatski got their hands full of poison oak while clambering around the Island during the two-week conditioning vacation offered club members," Al Wolf wrote for the *Los Angeles Times* in 1950. "They'll have to sit out the first few days of official toil." But, Wolf added, "the poison oak didn't hamper their reclining ability."

A few weeks later, according to the *Chicago Tribune*, "Pafko did a series of somersaults on a single, thus providing the runner with an extra base." Manager Frisch, the paper noted, was not amused.

Compared to the Pafko card, Bob Kelly's '52 Topps is a bargain -- easily obtainable for somewhat less than $83,870.

Bob Kelly

Former Pafko roomie Bob Kelly pitched 4 seasons for the Cubs, Redlegs, and Indians. In just 15 starts for the Cubs in 1952, he twirled 2 shutouts.

"The only one who ever really taught me anything about pitching was Bob Kelly," Turk Lown says. "Bob showed me how to throw the slider — I had a real good fastball. I was fortunate; it moved. A lot of guys can throw hard, but you need some movement on the ball."

"I was throwing a curve," Bob says. "I had a real good curve then. They had everybody watch." It was a nerve-wracking time for a rookie. "That 1st year, I can hardly remember," he says.

But he remembered right about his breakin' pitch: "He had a heck of a curveball," Paul Schramka says. Schramka roomed with Kelly later, and so did Randy Jackson.

"We were taking batting practice one day, and Bob was pitching," Randy says about one particularly memorable Spring afternoon. "Bob didn't wear a cup, and he chewed this huge wad of tobacco. Somebody hit a sharp one-hopper back to the mound, and it hit him right where the cup is supposed to be. He fell down and swallowed his tobacco, and he's lying there as green as could be, begging someone to kill him."

Paul Schramka, hustling out on Catalina.

Paul Schramka

Besides rooming with Kelly, Paul Schramka can boast of several Cub claims-to-fame:

1. "Schramka is the only ballplayer around who swings like Ted Williams," Cubbie Director of Player Personnel Wid Matthews swooned once.

2. Unlike Teddy — or Babe Ruth or Joe DiMaggio — Paul can truthfully say that he never struck out in a major-league game during his entire career.

3. His uniform number, 14, was retired by the Cubs.

Okay, so Wid was wrong...Paul didn't get a single at-bat during the 2 games he played...and Ernie Banks wore #14 after he did. But why all this quibbling?

"Paul Schramka was a good left-handed hitter," Cal McLish says.

"I remember the way he'd run and hustle," says Johnny Klippstein. "He loved the game."

"I left all the base-hits in the jersey for you."

#14 Paul Schramka's telegram to #14 Ernie Banks, when the Cubs retired the number in 1982

Paul played both basketball and baseball at the University of San Francisco. "I'd just come back from the service," he says, "and I was the #7 man in the outfield — I knew my place. I was a streak hitter. My biggest weakness was the pitched ball."

"I was just a kid then, the youngest guy in camp," Schramka says. They roomed him with veteran Johnny Vander Meer to keep him out of trouble. "You didn't get too familiar; you were just there a short time. I was just moseying around, and knew I wasn't going to be there."

But he kept right on being there. "I got to replace Sauer when he broke his finger," Paul recalls. "That's how I got my little window opening. I was fortunate; I had a good spring. I got 2 pinch-hit home runs, one against the Giants and one against the Red Sox in the "B" squad games. At the end of the month, I came in, and I was kinda hangin' around the hotel, and you expect to get called in — and they'd tell you where you were gonna be assigned, which minor league team. But every day, I'm in the starting line-up again, and I'm hitting about .320 in Spring Training."

Paul took good care of jersey #14 for Ernie Banks, making sure to not soil it too much during games.

But then...Schramka became perhaps the only ballplayer whose major-league career was called on account of rain. "The opening series, the City Series, got rained out," he says. "Then, we went to Cincinnati, and it rained...and when it finally stopped raining, Hank was able to play again."

So he tried to have fun in the minors: "I was playing in Omaha, and Earl Weaver was playing 2nd. I was out in right field. Those were the days when the ballplayers would leave their gloves on the field, on the grass. I don't know why, but I had a plastic snake in my pocket. So I put that friggin' snake in Weaver's glove. He kicked it all the way around the outfield."

After he retired, Schramka joined the family funeral-home business — but he still kept playing semi-pro ball. "I played until I was 40," he says. "We had the global world baseball tournament in Milwaukee — teams from 4 continents."

"I'm gonna see Paul Schramka in a few weeks for an Old-Timers meeting," Klippstein says. "I'm the president of the Chicago Old-Timers' Association, and he heads the one in Wisconsin. He's a heck of a guy — he has a great sense of humor."

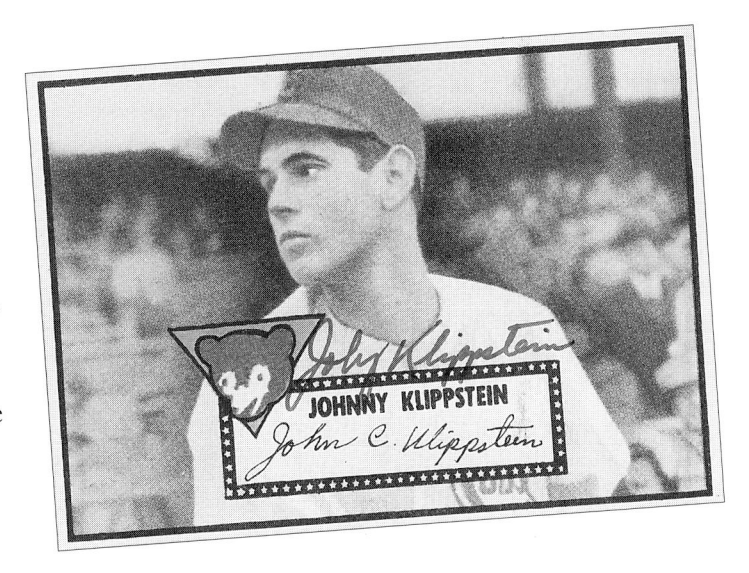

Johnny started his career as a Catalina Cub, as evidenced by this 1952 Topps card — also not as valuable as Pafko's.

Johnny Klippstein

Johnny Klippstein overcame control problems — he was nicknamed 'the wild man of Borneo' early on — and enjoyed a slightly longer career than Schramka. In fact, Johnny was one of the last 2 remaining Catalina Cubs in the big leagues in 1967 (along with Smoky Burgess). During his 18-year career, Johnny won 101 ballgames, led the league in saves in 1960, and appeared in 2 World Series (1959 for the Dodgers, 1965 for the Twins)...where he pitched 4 2/3 scoreless innings. "You have to be in the right place at the right time," he says.

He was a student of pitching. As a rookie on Catalina, he sought out veteran Vander Meer: "We'd have some great chats," John says. "It was toward the end of his career. We'd talk mostly about how to handle it, how to approach the game, rather than specific pitches. Of course, he was a left-handed pitcher, and I was right-handed, so we'd have to pitched to hitters differently, anyway. He talked about his experiences in baseball; he said it was important to choose the right kind of people to hang out with when you're young."

Of course, there weren't many bad boys to run with on Catalina. "It was very quiet — the quietest place to train I ever went," he says. "There was hardly anybody on the island. If you went for a walk in town, it seemed like there were only about 10 people you'd walk by."

When he wasn't closing down the town at, say, 8:30 or 9, Johnny spent time gleaning from Dutch Leonard. "Dutch and I, we talked pitching all the time," he says. He later married Dutch's niece — and the Klippsteins just celebrated their 50th anniversary.

Many Springs later, Johnny was still at it — although by 1965, he'd apparently lost his cap. No matter; he made it to the World Series that Fall, a concern he never had with Chicago.

"I was probably a fastball pitcher the first 5 or 6 years of my major league career, and all through the minors, of course," Klippstein says. "I threw some curves, but my fastball was my best pitch. We didn't have radar guns in those days, but I'm guessing I threw 93, 94 miles an hour. I could get some in there — I developed better control. Later, I started throwing more sliders, more breaking balls; I'd change speeds. And I became a relief pitcher in 1959."

"It was good to have him on the team — he was a high-class individual," Bob Rush says. "He had a great attitude."

But that wild streak was always lurking in the background. "He hit me in the head once," Wayne Terwilliger says. "I had a helmet on; it cracked the helmet. It felt like I wasn't wearing a helmet, like it cracked my head. I just lost the ball."

Wayne Terwilliger

But Twig survived the beaning, about 50 years ago, and he's still a professional baseball coach.

Yep. Now in his 7th decade of pro ball...we present Wayne Terwilliger, manager of the Fort Worth Cats.

It would be impossible to sum up a career that started in the 1940s...that's still going...but let us try to list a few of the highlights here:

* He collected 8 straight hits while playing for the Cubs once — in 1949

* He also got a base-hit against Satchell Paige, and a homer off Whitey Ford

* He was in the Brooklyn dugout when Bobby Thomson's homer beat the Dodgers to end the 1951 season — an infielder who turned double-plays with Jackie Robinson

* He was playing big-league ball before Mantle or Mays started

* As a Marine, he participated in the initial assault on Iwo Jima

Twig played in the majors for 9 seasons — 666 games in all, perhaps making him the Anti-Ballplayer. After retiring, he won 2 World Series rings (1987 & 1991, with the Twins) and was an A.L. All-Star Game coach twice. He's writing a book about his never-ending career.

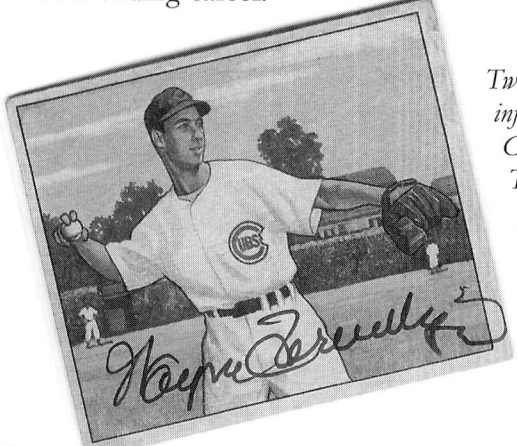

Wanna know how long Twig's been around? He appeared in the very 1st Topps baseball set, way back in 1951.

Twig works some infield in a 1950 California Spring Training session... for his Bowman card portrait. That's the Los Angeles version of Wrigley Field behind him.

Of course, like many others...his major-league debut was a rather inauspicious one. "The Cubs called me up from L.A. to finish the season," he says. "I was excited, but I'd kinda thought maybe they would, 'cuz I'd had a good year and the Cubs were struggling. My first at-bat, Johnny Antonelli struck me out on 3 fastballs."

But he did well enough to earn another trip to the Island in the Spring of 1950.

"We went out on the boat," Twig says. "It was a great trip — really exciting. I don't think anyplace else I ever trained could compare to Catalina. It was beautiful, it seemed the weather was perfect. We'd take walks in the hills. Hard Rock Johnson hit fungoes to me. Goin' out and eating, that was about all we did. I used to hang out with Chuck Connors. He was a real character; we really hit it off."

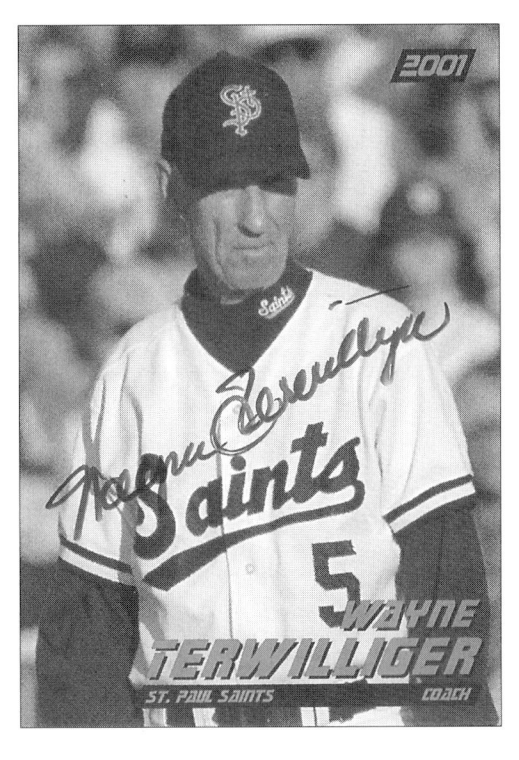

Exactly 50 seasons after his Topps Red-Back debut, Wayne is still appearing on new baseball cards each spring.

Twig, who seems to remember everything, will occasionally shout, "Time out!" in mid-story, when another one comes back to him.

"Time out!" he calls. (See? We told ya.) "In the showers one day, somebody asked Johnny Vander Meer if he was a Dutchman, so everybody started talking about nationalities. Somebody asked me what I was, and I said, 'I dunno, a mixture — German, Dutch, English...' And Vander Meer exploded on me — I mean, he just blew up. 'Don't you know what "Terwilliger" is? There's a whole truck-ful of 'em in New York — that's Dutch!' "

Our minds reeled with plenty of caption ideas to go here, below Dutch Leonard's 1941 Play Ball card, but we decided to let you come up with your own.

Dutch Leonard

We suppose Dutch Leonard (no relation to Dutch Reagan) was aware of his lineage. Between Twig and Dutch, you almost have an uninterrupted line back to Alexander Doubleday's fabled invention of baseball in 1839. Leonard finished his 20-year career with the Cubbies in 1953 — at the age of 44 — when he appeared in 45 games. (He broke in with the Brooklyn Dodgers in 1933.) He won 190 games and sported a nifty 3.25 career ERA — thanks to his pioneering use of the knuckleball.

"Baseball has given me enough reward — a lovely family, a home, some security" he told the *Los Angeles Times* in 1951. "And it took me out of the coal mines."

In 1949 — his 1st Spring with the Cubs — the paper reported that his presence was stirring up the Cubbie camp. "Up came an assortment of the dipsy-do knuckleballs for which he is feared and famous. The hitters couldn't hit him — which Grimm chose to attribute to Leonard's magic rather than mass blindness on the part of the batters — and Scheffing couldn't catch him, except with his chin, shins, and elbows. 'What a summer this is going to be,' moaned brother Scheffing.

" 'Yea, bo!' yelled the delighted Mr. Grimm. 'Why, Dutch was never better. We'll crank him up and really go places this season. Hot dog!' "

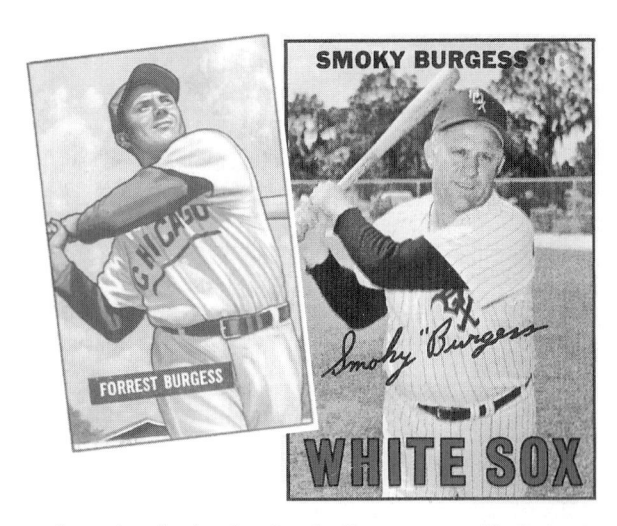

Spanning the decades: Smoky Burgess was still playing in 1967, 16 seasons after the Cubs last scuttled to Catalina.

Smoky Burgess

While the oldest Cub in the 1949 camp was Dutch, the youngest was Smoky Burgess — who happened to be one of the beleaguered catchers assigned to hunt down Leonard's flutterers.

Of course, Smoky stuck around for a while himself...and, along with teammate Johnny Klippstein, was one of only 2 Catalina Cubs still playing in 1967. During Smoky's 18-year career, he hit .295 and collected 145 pinch-hits — the major-league record until Matty Alou eclipsed it to 150. Smoky hit .333 in the 1960 World Series for Pittsburgh. He was a 7-time All-Star, and was the catcher for Harvey Haddix's 12-inning perfect game.

His son Larry remembers going to Catalina with daddy when he was just 3 years old. And Smoky's widow, Margaret, recalls visiting the bird park and the beach. "At the barbecues, it would be a player affair, a family-oriented thing," she says.

Smoky was a laid-back country boy. When asked how he felt, he'd say, "Felt pretty good when I got up this morning. But I got over it."

Howard Auman

Howard Auman, another southern boy, took the train from Greensboro with Smoky to meet the Cubs in 1948. He'd earned his tryout after winning 20 for Macon. Howard made the Texas League All-Star team in 1949, and was also an All-Star in the SALLY League and Tobacco State League (when he won 22 for Sanford in 1946). A tough, gritty old-fashioned pitcher, he was known for pitching both ends of double-headers — and completing both games. Howard played briefly for the Los Angeles Angels in the Pacific Coast League in 1948, but never made it to the show.

"Fifty-four years ago, I was in Spring Training with the Chicago Cubs on Catalina Island," he says. "Seems like a dream today. I just looked around, and enjoyed the scenery. I used to do a lot of walking, when I was in the cities, and I'd just walk the streets around Catalina.

Part of a letter Howard wrote from the Fairmont Hotel, Nob Hill, San Francisco, March 19, 1948:

Got a haircut today and they charged $1.25. Things are certainly higher here than they are back East.

Heard from Maxine today, and also a letter from Bobby. Maxine certainly did enjoy her stay with you all. Maybe it won't be long before we can be together.

Don't know when they begin cutting our squad down. Saw in the paper yesterday that they would have some players with L.A. when we leave next Sunday. I'm in hopes if I don't get to Chicago I'll be placed with Nashville or someplace back that way. I don't care to play out here on the West Coast. If I should happen to be placed in Nashville, I plan to go by there and get Maxine before I report. Still I haven't any idea where I'll be.

Haven't pitched any more since I pitched against Los Angeles. Don't know when I will, but expect to while we are here. There's not much news. Hope you are all fine.

Love, Howard

An epilogue: Wish we could report that Howard no-hit the Oaks...but according to the Bay Area papers, he didn't get to pitch for the Cubs against Oakland that weekend after all.

The Cubs sent Howard Auman across the channel to L.A. for more seasoning. Unfortunately for Howard, they never asked for him back.

"I thought I'd be back — I never thought it would be my only time with the Cubs. Those are the breaks of the game. They optioned my contact to Los Angeles, the Angels. I started the 2nd ballgame of the season for Los Angeles, vs. San Diego in the Pacific Coast League. I got into 2 more games, then I was optioned to Shreveport in the Texas League. I won 14 for Shreveport that summer. I just knew I was going back to Chicago — but they had another pitcher, Warren Hacker. So I played with Shreveport 2 more seasons, and made the All-Star team again...but then, I began having some arm trouble, so they sold my contract to Texarkana in the Texas State League, further on down in the minors, and I knew when I was going down I'd never go back up."

During his baseball odyssey, Howard started his family. "I got married in 1947. She came out when the season opened in Los Angeles. We were leaving for Oakland for a week, and she arrived just as I'd gotten on the train. But I got to talk with her on the telephone." He'd served in the Air Force during World War II. "They sent me overseas, to the Pacific," he said. "We were onboard the ship 57 days, from Seattle to Okinawa. We docked at 2 places for 2 or 3 weeks, and by the time we finally got there the war was just about over."

Back home, he managed a semi-pro team in the '50s...ran a grocery store...worked for a big furniture manufacturer...then retired. But, "after I retired, people started asking me to refinish their furniture for them, and I've been busy ever since. We have 2 daughters and 3 granddaughters. I've had a pretty good life."

Randy Jackson

Handsome Ransom Jackson was part of the same rookie class as Howard Auman. He played 3rd base for 10 seasons — with the Indians and Dodgers, too. A 2-time All-Star, he played in the 1956 World Series for Brooklyn, moved with the team to Los Angeles, and ended up with 103 home runs...including 21 in 1955. A multi-sport star, he played in the 1945 and 1946 Cotton Bowls for Texas, with QB Bobby Layne.

"I was shaving one day, and the telephone rang," Randy says. "My dad was calling to tell me I was the answer to a trivia question on *Good Morning America!* They said I was the last player to hit a home run for the Brooklyn Dodgers. I hadn't known that!"

Long before Randy became the answer to a trivia question on ABC-TV, the folks at Bowman decided to see how he'd look on the tube in 1955.

"He was a good ballplayer," says Lennie Merullo, "real handsome, what you'd expect a Texan to look like. When I started scouting, I always arranged for ballplayers to get a locker next to him — because he'd talk to them, get them feeling good about the organization. He was always a good influence."

He was 'a snappy fielder,' according to his 1953 Bowman bubblegum card — but things weren't always that way. "In college, people behind 1st base said they needed gloves," Randy says, " 'cuz I threw the ball over to them sometimes instead of to the 1st baseman!"

His football career took a few interesting turns, too. "I was 6'1" and about 140 pounds then. Coach asked, 'What position do you play?' I told him I didn't know. He put me on the line. So I went out, and the biggest guy was about 225 pounds, and I was beating against them and I looked up and saw the backfield guys tossing the ball around and laughing. So after that 1st practice, I went back to the coach and said, 'I play backfield!' " But he didn't need much motivation to hit the books. "If you flunked," Randy points out, "they'd send you to where you'd have to fight."

"We'd wander around town.
That took about 15 minutes."

Randy Jackson

The Cubs offered him a tryout while he was still in college — which went well. "I hit a bunch of balls into the bleachers," he says. He signed a 2-year deal for the minimum, $6,000, and "they sent me a letter assigning me to come to Catalina and be part of the 40-man roster. I took the train from Arkansas to Los Angeles." Once on the Island, "It was exciting, but there wasn't a whole lot to do. We'd get a few dollars in meal money. It was off-season, so there were very few tourists that time of year."

He played a lot of golf — after icing his ankles. "Some idiot at the front office had us come out there a week early and walk the paths in the mountains that the goats made," he said. "We'd start in the morning, and hike all day. Everybody had shinsplints — dumb! I don't think there was a lot of wisdom running around."

"We had a 154-game schedule and after the first ballgame he'd say, '153 to go!' "

Eddie Miksis, on Randy Jackson
in *Banks to Sandberg to Grace*

As the assigned 3rd-sacker, he'd play Hank Sauer deep — to avoid losing his scalp. "I used to do that with Ralph Kiner, too — Ernie Banks and I would both back up to the outfield grass. We all teased each other — you had to. I don't think I ever met anybody I played with that I didn't like; you had to have some fun. Sometimes you'd have a phantom infield, without balls, you'd play pepper games, do crazy things."

Fans keep the pleasant memories alive, too. "About a month ago, I got a letter from a guy in Florida," Randy says. "The guy's probably 60 now. He said after a game in Chicago, he and his little brother were trying to get autographs, but all the guys were in a hurry. 'But you stood there and answered all our questions and signed autographs — I'll never forget that.' "

Lennie Merullo

Lennie Merullo played for the Cubs from 1941 to 1947, before a bad back ended his career. The slick shortstop played in the 1945 World Series, and after retiring he scouted for the Cubs for 25 years. His grandson, Matt, caught for the Indians & White Sox.

On the day when his son was born in 1942, Lennie set a major-league record by making 4 errors in a single inning. They named the baby 'Boots.'

"Merullo was a good friend," Phil Cavarretta says. "He was my roommate. Actually, I was the one who brought up that name, 'Boots,' to him. He was kinda searchin' around for a name. I told him he had a good game. He said, 'Screw you.' I said it again — yeah, a pretty good game. He said, 'Screw you.' I told him, 'Boots,' that'd be a good name. And he laughed."

"Merullo was a funny guy," Red Adams says. "He had a dry sense of humor; he saw the humor in everything."

He'd been playing baseball at Villanova in 1939, but the Cubs sent him a small check — so he got kicked off the baseball team. No problem; Catalina awaited. "I was wide-eyed all the way," he says.

"There was always something to do — just being there was great. We used to dress at the golf course, at the Country Club. Just walkin' in there with your pals was terrific. I had 2 pals from my area here — Eddie Waitkus and Barney Olsen. Barney had such talent, more than the other 2 of us combined, but things didn't work out."

Lennie Merullo on Catalina, full of energy by only having a 50-foot commute from the Casitas beyond the fence.

Lennie & Boots pose for the lensman, as Lennie concentrates hard on not dropping the oncoming ball.

He went boar hunting with Cavy and took in some fishing. In 1946, he had an incident with a horse — he was suffering from "soreness in the leg that resulted from ramming into a tree while horseback riding," the *Chicago Sun* reported. "It wasn't serious."

And while not partaking in the equestrian events, he soaked up all the baseball knowledge he could. "Just listening to these fellas, especially prior to going down to the field, sittin' around with the club, was fun." And the Great One, Dizzy Dean — he had a special impact on young Merullo. "I always felt I played better, just when he was in the game," Lennie says. "Diz used to kid me, called me Poosh 'Em Up, like Lazzeri, 'cuz I was Italian. I was erratic — I had a good arm, and I could run like a son of a buck, and I always did better when he was pitching. He used to kid me — but everybody had fun with ol' Diz."

Life, like baseball, went on. "I married the girl next door in 1941," Lennie says. "We grew up together. The 1st few years, she didn't come out. You never made the money, so you always tried to save; you'd always say, 'Maybe next year.' After the 1st couple of years, she got to come over — and my oldest came. Out there, maybe we'd do nothing. We'd just go down and listen to the music — it was beautiful."

Boots remembered the boat ride...and getting to run around the field. "As a kid," Boots says, "being around those guys, it was wonderful. I thought I'd died and gone to Heaven. I'd run on the field while they were hitting." Boots got to play in the Cape Cod League, like his dad did in the '30s. "The living conditions weren't the best — you'd stay in some old lady's loft. The ballplayers would stick an extra ball in their back pocket. When the fog came in, they'd call the game when somebody hit a fly to left field, and a ball would come in from right." Boots signed with the Pirates in 1961 — but he hurt his leg and had to get a day job.

Lennie's career ended with an injury, too. "I did try to play, but that back wouldn't hold up. I figured, I had a college education, so I could find something." The Cubs called after a while. "I scouted for less money than I was making at the Prince Macaroni Company!" A highlight: He was on hand when Ernie Banks signed up.

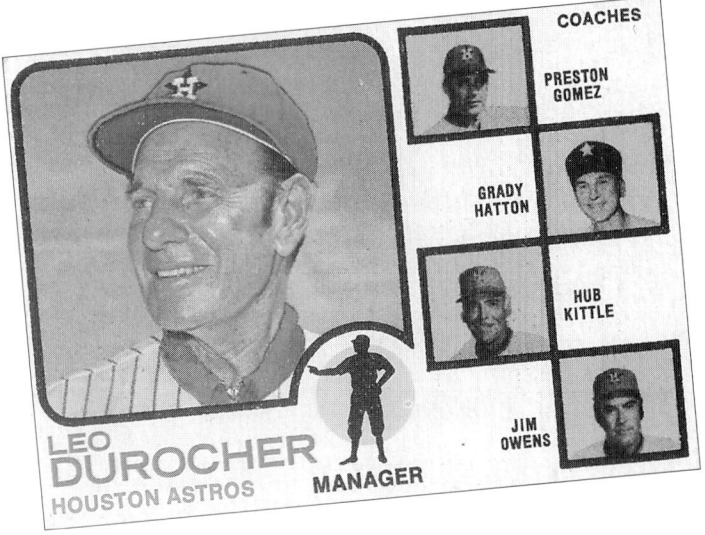

By the time he'd been in baseball for 5 decades, Hub Kittle finally appeared on a Topps card. Sort of.

Hub Kittle

Another long-time scout who played on Catalina was Hub Kittle. Hub won a World Series ring as a Cardinals coach in 1982, and still scouts for the Seattle Mariners — in his *8th* decade of professional baseball.

No, that is not a typo. Hub first pitched batting practice for the Cubs on Catalina in 1936. He spent 20 seasons playing in the minors (winning 144 games)...coached for the Cards, Astros, and numerous minor-league teams...managed (winning 1,371 games & 4 league championships)...ran ballclubs as a GM (the Sporting News named him Minor League Executive of the Year in 1960)...scouted...and then *played* some more.

Nope, no typo there, either. Know who's the oldest man to ever play in a professional baseball game? Not Satchel Paige — Hub Kittle. In 1980, at the tender age of 63, Hub pitched an inning for Springfield. A *shutout* inning: "I got out there," Hub says, "and that first sucker bunted on me! So on the next pitch, I knocked him on his rear-end. I got a standing ovation. I retired the side."

By his 6th decade in pro ball, Hub earned himself a World Series ring — as Whitey Herzog's pitching coach.

(By the way, Hub had previously set the Southern League age record, 11 years earlier, when he pitched 1 2/3 innings for the Savannah Senators in 1969... when he was a mere 52.)

"Hub Kittle was way past 60, with a face as worn as an old Rawlings mitt, by the time he came to the Cardinals as my pitching coach," Whitey Herzog wrote in his autobiography. "He'd spent 4 decades hitting fungoes, steering buses, sleeping in back seats, telling stories of the old days, and sharing the secrets of making a hitter look foolish with a thousand beanpole kids you and I never heard of. Name the place, Hub had been there. God bless guys like him. They *are* the game."

"He was just a fun-loving guy," Bobby Mattick says. "He got to be a great coach, 'cuz he was so good with the kids."

"I'd see him take an 18-year-old pitcher who couldn't throw 83 miles an hour off to the side, and 10 minutes later, the guy's out on a rubber humming it 88, 89. I can't even tell you how he did it except to use those 5 magic words: 'He was a baseball man.'"

Whitey Herzog, on Hub Kittle

While on Catalina, Hub danced at the Casino — and won a prize with Hard Rock Johnson's daughter. He sang on the '30s equivalent of 'open-mike' night — with some of the world's biggest Big Bands. He tossed easy ones to Dutch Reagan, dated a few movie stars, and twirled a couple of no-hitters for the semi-pro Catalina team.

"Hub Kittle was a champion dancer," says Mattick. "he won all kinds of trophies."

"Hub Kittle, that son-of-a-gun — he was a ladies' man," Lefty Carnett recalls. "Boy, what a good dancer — he could flat *dance*. He was at Spring Training with us in 1939. He was a competitor — he had a good curveball. Hub was the kind of guy you like to have on your team. He was always laughin' — always in the middle. Whatever it was goin' on, he was in the thick of it."

A decade after winning the World Series, Hub was still showing young pitchers how to twirl the forkball.

The Wrigleys funded a semi-pro squad — which played in the summer, after the Chicago Cubs were long gone — to provide a fresh supply of potential material for the Los Angeles Angels (and, eventually, the parent team). Sometimes called the Catalina Angels, sometimes called the Catalina Cubs, they imported teams from the mainland...and occasionally played in L.A. themselves. Hub was a mainstay.

"That's how he knew all the gals," Lefty says, " 'cuz he lived out there."

Although the Mariners' scout is 247 years old now (& likely planning his next pitching appearance), he was a youngster himself once — singin', dancin', & tossin' forkballs past befuddled batters.

"The Cubs hired me for 50 bucks a month in 1936," Hub recalls. "My 1st contract was with the Angels. I pitched for the Rookie League team on Catalina. I had a heck of a year — I was 15-3." Future Red Sox catcher Roy Partee was one of his backstops, and future Cub Lou Stringer was a mainland-based opponent.

"Hub Kittle, he's full of baseball stories," says Cal McLish, who's also still scouting with the Mariners. And there are stories aplenty about him, too; for instance, Cards pitcher Dave LaPoint likes to tell about finding always-coaching Kittle in a hotel lobby at 3 a.m. — trying to teach a bellhop how to throw a forkball.

"I played semi-pro ball in L.A.," Stringer recalls, "and almost signed with the Catalina Cubs. I played against Hub — he's a real goer."

"Baseball was #1 to me," Hub says. "Nothing else mattered."

Well, maybe the dancing? "Hub Kittle was a great dancer," says Yosh Kawano, still with the Cubs as an equipment manager...and also in his 8th decade of pro baseball. "He and I are good friends. I saw him this spring in Arizona — he was down there with the Mariners. Hub was just a kid then — he threw batting practice for Doc Brooks."

Hub had 7 kids, but "none of 'em played ball," he says. So, he figured, he may as well keep right on playing himself.

Steve Mesner

Steve Mesner once got hit by a Hub Kittle pitch on Catalina. Hub got sent to the showers, cussed out by Grimm; Mesner went on to other near-misses and disasters...

* One Spring, he swallowed his chaw...and earned himself a free trip to the emergency room to experience the joys of stomach-pumping.

* Another Spring, he caught a Cavarretta pop-up and got a big hand from the crowd...but "Steve was so busy accepting the congratulations," Irving Vaughn wrote for the *Tribune* in 1937, "that he forgot there was a runner on base. By the time he awakened, Billy Herman had scooted from first to second."

* And he led National League 3rd-basemen in errors twice.

I don't know about you, but I sure wouldn't send Steve Mesner out to buy the crystal or the china.

Steve joined the Los Angeles Angels in 1934, at the age of 16. The next season, while just 17, he hit .331. He played in the majors for 6 seasons — 1938 & 1939 with the Cubs, then with St. Louis and Cincy. A big star in the Pacific Coast League, he played 21 years in pro ball...with a lifetime .305 average in the minors. After that, he ran a batting cage in San Diego.

KiKi Cuyler

KiKi Cuyler, on the other hand, was a big star in the *major* leagues. During his 18 seasons at the show, this Hall-of-Fame outfielder hit .321...and at various times led the league in doubles, triples, runs scored, and steals. He appeared in 3 World Series (1929 & 1932 for the Cubs), and also played for the Pirates, Reds, & Dodgers from 1921-1938. After he retired, KiKi managed in the minors (cultivating future Catalina Cubs like Ox Miller) & coached for the Cubs & Red Sox.

He got his nickname (pronounced KI-KI, like HI-HI, rather than KEE-KEE, as in HEE-HEE) in the minors, when infielders would yell out, "Cuy, Cuy" when a pop-up was his. He desperately needed a nickname; for some reason, his folks saddled him with being Hazen Shirley Cuyler.

"What a ballplayer!"

KiKi's 1933 Goudey bubblegum card

On Catalina, his speed and fancy footwork translated into dancing prowess: During his 8 Springs on the Island, he won the dancing contests that Andy Lotshaw or Hub Kittle didn't take. (KiKi was particularly known for his waltzing skills.)

"He was the closest approach baseball ever had to a matinee idol," Charlie Grimm wrote in his autobiography. "He wore his uniform like a tuxedo. KiKi's teammates often accused Andy Lotshaw of brushing off Cuyler's uniforms between innings!"

Ox Miller

Ox Miller was no relation to Hack Miller — but *boy*, do those Miller guys get some nifty nicknames! Actually, he was a distant relative of Ty Cobb's.

Ox was a pitcher, but his career batting numbers were actually more impressive — very Cobb-like. He went 3-for-7 in his one season with the Cubs (1947), hitting .429 (hey, Ted Williams only got to .343 that year) — and one of those hits was a grand slam!

He does look like he's strong as an ox, doesn't he?

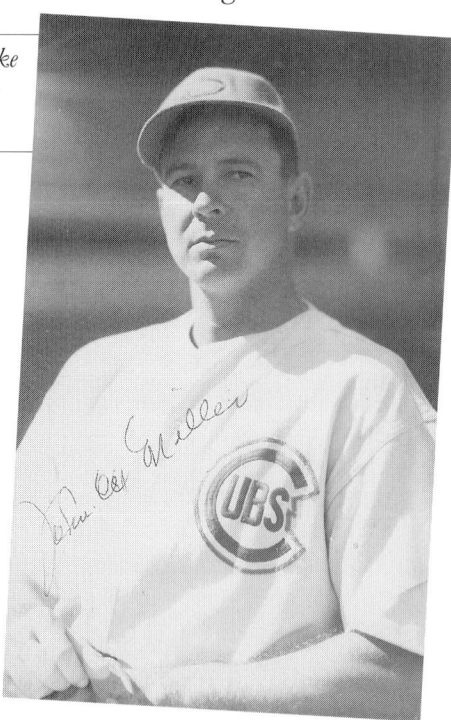

Ah, but the pitching... In 4 tries with the St. Louis Browns, Washington Senators, and the Cubbies — cellar-dwellers all — Ox went 4-6 lifetime, with an ERA of 6.38. (Actually, that ERA would probably contend him for Cy Young honors these days!) For the Cubs, he was 1-2, with a less-than-impressive 10.13 ERA. He fanned 27 during his career, walking just 33, in 91 2/3 innings.

He got his nickname early on: "That happened in the minor leagues," he says. "I pitched both games of a double-header in Lincoln, Nebraska, out in the Western League. The morning paper came out and said, 'That young John Miller is strong as an ox.' The papers were competing, and the evening paper came out and said, 'He's as dumb as an ox — he's gonna hurt his arm!'"

After baseball, he was a mailman in rural Texas... and coached little league teams. "I'm retired now," Ox says, "and Shorty and I pretty much stay here in Live Oak County, Texas — we don't get out much."

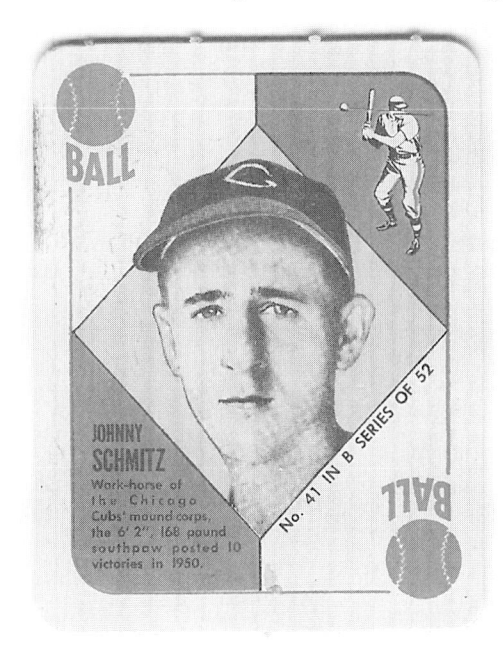

While this 1951 Topps Blue-Back card of Johnny Schmitz is interesting enough in itself, one must wonder what's going on with that cartoon in the upper right-hand corner...

Johnny Schmitz

So if Ox wasn't the ace of the '47 Cub staff, who was? Why, Johnny Schmitz, of course. Bear Tracks went 13-18 that year (leading the N.L. in losses — hey, this was the Cubs!), one of several seasons where he didn't exactly get a lot of offensive support.

Johnny pitched for 13 seasons (1941-1951 for the Cubs, interrupted by the War). He led the N.L. in strikeouts in 1946, and came close to winning 100 games lifetime — which would've been miraculous, considering he also played for the Senators, Red Sox, Reds and Orioles (with momentary stints for Brooklyn and the Yankees). He was a 2-time All-Star. And while he was no Ox Miller at the plate, he did hit 2 home runs over the years.

His finest achievement, however, was appearing in the Norman Rockwell Cub painting that graced the cover of the *Saturday Evening Post* in 1948.

"The most enjoyable thing about Catalina was playing golf after workouts," he says. "They had a nice 9-hole course." Johnny's too modest — he tore it up on the Avalon links, carding the best score just about every season he was there. His tallies were often under par.

After he quit pitching, he got back to his other love — working as a golf course greenskeeper for more than 30 years.

Paul Erickson

Paul Erickson would often play Schmitz stroke-for-stroke on Catalina's little course. Li'l Abner pitched for the Cubs from 1941-1948, and got into 4 games of the 1945 World Series in relief. As a rookie, Paul pitched a 1-hitter against the Pirates in 1941.

In 1946, when outfielder Swish Nicholson was holding out, Paul spent some time shagging flies in the Island sunshine. The *Tribune* reported: "Paul Erickson, after pulling down his 3rd flyball in right field, yelled: 'I guess Bill Nicholson will sign up in a hurry when he reads about this!'"

"Paul Erickson, that big son of a gun," Red Adams smiles. "They called him Abner. He was a character. He could throw hard — I liked to watch him pitch."

Besides throwing hard, he also threw with, uhm, purpose. Kirby Higbe, pitching for Brooklyn against his old Cub mates, once decked a few batters in a 1942 contest. When he came up to bat in the next inning — against Erickson — Higbe later said "the first 2 pitches were between my head and my cap."

He was known for being zany. "Paul Erickson has been described as a new Dizzy Dean," Warren Brown commented in his *So They Tell Me* column for the *Sun* in 1946. "Does there HAVE to be another Dizzy Dean? Erickson has been given ample opportunity to be a pitcher first and an eccentric afterwards."

*Do **YOU** think Paul Erickson looks like Li'l Abner?*

Hank Sauer

When Schmitz and Erickson made it a threesome on the Avalon links, Hank Sauer was their 3rd. "Sauer was outa my class," duffer Ed Chandler says. "He'd hit that ball 800 miles."

"Years later," Frank Saldaña says, "we were still talking about where it went."

"Oh, my, he could drive that ball," Carmen Mauro recalls. "He was a terrific athlete."

Before posing for his 1953 Bowman card, Hank must've misplaced his 75-pound warclub — so he had to carry 2 woosy-bats instead.

Golf balls, baseballs — Hank swatted 'em all with authority. "Randy Jackson used to make fun of Bill Serena because of the way he'd play Sauer," Islander Marcelino Saucedo says. "The players would call him names, even the fans in the crowd would razz him, because he wouldn't play at 3rd base, he'd play in the outfield! And the shortstop would play him deep, too. Years later, I ran into him when he was scouting...and he said he was glad he never had to play against Sauer, because he didn't think he'd be able to play him at the position he was supposed to!"

Sauer Slams 487-footer

AVALON, Cal. (AP) — Hank Sauer hammered a 487-foot homer to give the Whites a 3-2 win over the Grays in the Cubs' first intrasquad game today.

Hank Sauer might've broken all kinds of records...if he'd have just gotten off the fence. (By the way, that's PK Wrigley, bringing up the rear, riding his Arabian du jour.)

"Yeah, we played deep for Hank Sauer," Wayne Terwilliger acknowledges. But, "he couldn't run, so it didn't matter if you were back — he couldn't beat it out."

That 1st Spring in Mesa did Hank some good: The first Hammerin' Hank led the league in homers and RBIs, winning the 1952 N.L. MVP title. He hit 288 home runs in his 15 seasons, and he got to play against his brother Ed a few times — Ed was briefly a Wartime Cub. Ironically, Ed got to play in the 1945 World Series for Chicago, but Hank never made the Fall Classic. Off the field, Hank appeared in *The Winning Team* with Dutch Reagan in 1952.

"It was beautiful there," Hank told Cub newsletter *Vine Lines* in 1998, "but I don't believe it was a great place for Spring Training." He said PK Wrigley once stopped the guys from hiking to the top of a ridge, because "he was afraid the pigs or boars would attack us."

Back on the diamond, Ed Burns told *Tribune* readers that Sauer's bats were the biggest in the majors. "We were in awe of Hank Sauer's bats," Marse Saucedo says. "On the field, we'd pick it up. They weighed something like 52 ounces! The ones we used were about 34 ounces. The left field fence was about 370 feet; he used to hit it half way up the hill to the Country Club!"

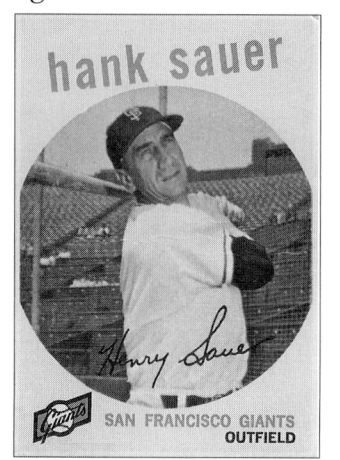

A decade after pounding 'em across Catalina, Hank Sauer was still drilling home runs out in California.

Ed Chandler

"We were so busy climbin' mountains," Ed Chandler says, "there wasn't time for much golf. There were no carts. Frisch wouldn't let us golf much, anyway."

Ed went to Catalina in 1950 and 1951. He pitched for the Los Angeles Angels and San Francisco Seals in the Pacific Coast League for several years until 1957. He'd broken in with Brooklyn in 1947 after going 22-6 in Ft. Worth. His lifetime major league record wasn't quite as good: 0-1.

"They had the ballroom open," he says, "but I didn't go down to see it — the manager might be there. I'm not a fisherman. I was raised in Alabama, working the sawmills. I was married then, but I didn't take my wife — we had to pay our own expenses for that!"

He played island ball with the Dodgers, too — Spring Training in the Dominican Republic one year, and an exhibition game in Cuba. "When I finished baseball in 1956," Ed says, "I pitched batting practice for the Dodgers for several years. I worked with Ben Wade. Alston was a good friend of mine. I couldn't throw, but I could still pitch batting practice."

After Ed Chandler took the boat back to L.A., he stayed on for a while — pitching in the P.C.L. & then chucking batting practice for the Dodgers.

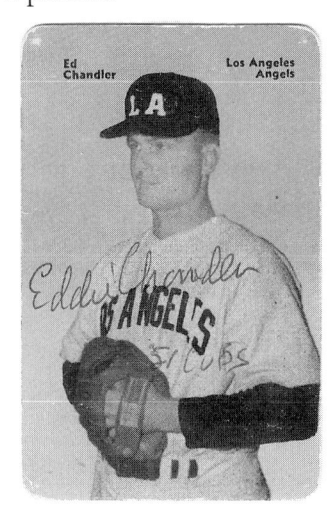

Ben Wade

Ben Wade pitched for Cubs in 1948. He also played for the Cards, Pirates, and Dodgers during his 5-year career — which included a World Series appearance for Brooklyn in 1953. He once hit 2 homers in a single game, while pitching (and batting!) against Warren Spahn. His older brother, Jake, also pitched in the majors.

Later, Ben became the first West Coast scout for the New York Mets. After that, he scouted for the Dodgers from 1963-1973. He became Scouting Director in 1973, and stayed on for 18 seasons until 1991. In all, Ben spent *7 decades* in professional baseball...after debuting in 1939.

Ben Wade got to the World Series after the Cubs traded him away. He was so grateful to the Dodgers . . . he was still working for 'em 5 decades later.

"Nicknamed 'Virg' because of his penchant for calling everyone 'Virgil.'"

Ben Wade's 1961 Union Oil San Diego Padres card

"We took the boat," Ben says. "It was about a 3-4 hour trip in those days — one of the few ways you could get there. The ballclub was pretty much secluded — we played a lot of cards."

Bill Voiselle

Around the time Ben Wade was coming up, another big Carolina boy was wrapping up his pitching career on Catalina. Bill Voiselle was from a little town called Ninety-Six, South Carolina — a number he proudly displayed on his uniform, wherever he could.

"Matthews got one look at the number '96' on the back of the shirt assigned to Connors," Warren Brown wrote for the *Herald-American* in 1951, "and ordered trainer Andy Lotshaw to issue a new one to Connors today. Needless to say, that '96' reminded Wid of Bill Voiselle, the man who introduced it, and nothing else, in his brief stay with the club."

"Bill Voiselle was at the tail end of his career, trying to get back," Corky Van Dyke says. "We'd put on a rubber suit, and we'd go in the mountains. Bill would sweat, that poor old soul — I always felt bad for him. He suffered so bad. He had to weigh in every day, and they'd put the whip on him on the scales."

"Voiselle reported to host Frisch on the Avalon dock that he had left his Carolina home a sleek 230," Burns told *Tribune* readers, "but that he had encountered cold weather enroute and had to eat especially large portions of victuals to keep warm."

"We all had shinsplints so bad we couldn't move," Bob Kelly says. "Bill Voiselle just sat down — he couldn't take another step. He was such a nice guy — I felt bad for him."

"I could still throw hard," Bill says. "But I didn't get along with Frisch; I don't think he liked me when I was pitching for the Giants. The sportswriters were getting on me too."

65

NEW STAR to join ranks of the Cubs is Bill Voiselle, star performer on the mound for the Giants and Braves before coming to the Cubs last winter. Bill is counted on to help the Cubs come up in the N. L. flag race.

Voiselle had been one of the premier pitchers in the game several years earlier. In 1944, he won 21 for the Giants — leading the league in strikeouts. During his 9-year career, he also led the N.L. in complete games (twice) and innings pitched...and he played in the 1948 World Series for the Braves. But by the time he reached Catalina, it was gone. He went 0-4 for the Cubbies in 1950 with a 5.79 ERA, and retired.

The kids really liked him. "Ol' 96, Bill Voiselle, he was real nice," says Foxie Saucedo, who was playing for the Avalon High team that year. "He'd show me some pitching tips."

"I had to get permission from the commissioner to wear that number," Bill says about one of his claims to fame. Ironically, he didn't get to wear it in 1944 during his other moment in the spotlight — the year he was the best pitcher in the National League.*

Swish Nicholson

Meanwhile, in Chicago...Bill Nicholson was having as good a 1944 at the plate as Ol' 96 was having on the mound. He led the N.L. in homers and RBIs — for the 2nd straight year — and he also led the league in runs scored. Bill broke in with Connie Mack's A's in 1936. During his 16-year career, he walloped 235 homers...and knocked in 8 runs during the 1945 World Series, a record at that time.

In fact, Bill finished 2nd in MVP voting in both 1943 & 1944. He was so feared that he was once walked with the bases loaded.

"Those years, when you managed, you coached 3rd base, too," Red Adams says. "One time, Grimm was coaching at 3rd. Bill Nicholson was coming around — he ran like a fullback. He's coming around, and he's gonna score, and all of a sudden Grimm holds him up. It was a little late for him to make that call, and Grimm was right in his path. Well, Bill ran right over him — he really ran him down — and I think Nicholson did score. Charlie could've been hurt — he was flat on his back."

Nicholson hunted wild boar on Catalina with Ken Raffensberger. And "Cavarretta, Peanuts Lowrey, Bill Nicholson — we played cards on the train, we'd shoot craps," Gene Mauch says.

Andy Pafko says Swish helped him when he first came to the Cubs. "I had my locker next to Cavarretta, between him and Nicholson — 2 of the greatest Cubs who ever lived," Andy says. "Nicholson was great, to help me from centerfield; I didn't know the hitters, so he moved me around. Big Nick would say, 'He's a pull hitter,' or 'Play this guy straight away.' "

"Swish was an old country boy," Lennie Merullo says. "I'd always try to visit with him — he was one of those guys who loved to hunt and fish, and I could sit for hours and listen to them talk."

*Swish! Bill Nicholson hit more homers than the rest of the Cubs **combined** in 1943.*

---

* Bill wore #17 that season.

Galan appears confused. Besides the fact that he wore tennis shoes to work, he's swinging away from the pitcher's rubber in the bullpen, rather than home plate.

Augie Galan

Augie Galan finished his playing career where Swish started — at Connie Mack's place. Augie then began his coaching career for the A's. Augie played for 16 years in the majors...in Chicago from 1934 through 1941. He hit .300 half a dozen times, led the league in runs scored during his 2nd season, led the league in steals (twice), and exhibited his patience by topping the circuit in walks twice. Augie played in the 1935 & 1938 World Series for the Cubs...and also in the 1941 Classic for the Dodgers.

"Augie Galan, he was quite a ballplayer," says Lonny Frey.

You think Mickey Mantle was the first guy to homer from both sides of the plate...in a single game? Augie did it in 1937 — when the Mick was 5 years old. The year before, he became the 1st Cub to homer in an All-Star game. And he hustled: "Little Augie Galan...never feared a concrete fence or a wall when he was going after the ball," the 1949 Eureka Sportstamps Album claimed. Multi-nicknamed, he was called Frenchy and Gu-Gu (or Goo-Goo) at various times.

In 1932, when Augie was playing for the San Francisco Seals of the Pacific Coast League, he was invited to join a group of big-leaguers who were headed to Hawaii to play some exhibition games. Augie got the okay to go...if he could find a replacement. Teammate Vince DiMaggio mentioned that he had a kid brother at home — a 17-year-old named Joe.

"August Galan, he was a great guy — kind of a ladies' man," recalls Yosh Kawano. And a funny man, too...according to Charlie Root's daughter:

"When it would rain," Della Root Arnold says, "the boys would gather in somebody's room at the St. Catherine. This one time, they were in Dad's — Mother and Charlie and I were out. They were playing cards, and Augie Galan didn't like to play cards. Dad and Larry French were playing 3-handed pinochle — that was their game. The beds had these big metal frames, and Augie took out a nail file and scratched 'Charlie Root' into it. When we checked out, there was an item on the bill: 'Using bedstand as autograph album, $25.' Augie paid it for him, and they all thought that was pretty funny."

Lonny Frey

Linus Frey played shortstop for 14 years, from 1933 through 1948. He was only on Catalina once — in 1937 — although he was traded back to Chicago right after the 1947 season started. Lonny also played for the Dodgers, Reds, Yankees, and Giants. He led N.L. in steals in 1940, topped his loop in fielding categories half a dozen times, and played in 3 World Series. As a Brooklyn rookie in 1933, he hit .319 in a partial season. He was a 3-time All-Star.

"I didn't fit in with that bunch," Lonny says. "I didn't enjoy that bunch. It was cliquey, hard for a newcomer to break in, so I was glad when they traded me to Cincinnati."

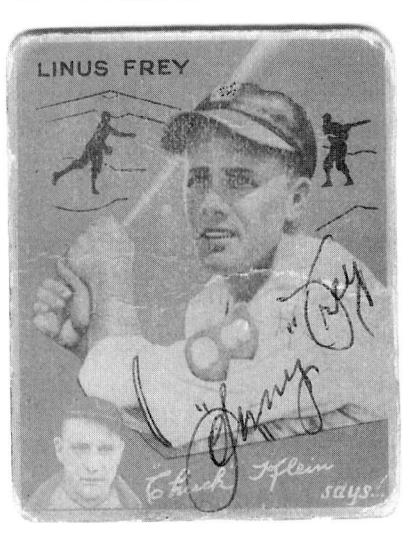

Lonny Frey's rookie card, from the 1934 Goudey set.

They must've gotten it fixed. "A big happy gang is a good one," new manager Gabby Hartnett told reporters in the Spring of 1939, "but rarely represents the truth. I have seen many cliques on the Cubs, but this year there are apparently...no insurgencies. I have no fears of the old clique menace."

Leaping Linus, 1937.

"We should have won the pennant that year," Lonny says. "I was really upset we didn't win — we had a 6-game lead going into September, and everybody was spending their World Series money before they had it! All the wives were out shopping already."

Fortunately for Lonny's wife, he got to other World Series in other cities — the last in 1947, with the Yankees, despite communication difficulties. "I could never understand what Stengel was saying," Linus says.

And like a later Yankee, Roger Maris, Lonny hit 61 homers. It simply took him 14 seasons . . .

Woody English

The Cubs traded an aging Woody English for Frey after the 1936 season. In the early '30s, Woody was among the premier shortstops in the game. He hit .335 in 1930 and .319 the next year. With teammate and roommate Rogers Hornsby, he was part of the best double-play combo in the N.L. He played in the 1929 & 1932 World Series for the Cubs, and hit .286 during his 12-year career. He made the 1st-ever N.L. All-Star team in 1933, and after he retired...he stayed on with Mr. Wrigley, managing the Grand Rapids entry in the All-American Girls Professional Baseball League.

Since his eyes are closed, we must wonder if Elwood English is daydreaming about torching newspapers, managing ballplayers who wear skirts, or necktie destruction.

He was memorable off the field, too. "Woody English would get down on his hands and knees and crawl up toward someone who was reading the paper," recalls Della Root Arnold, "and he'd light the bottom of the paper on fire."

"His escape is made during the smoldering stage," *Des Moines Dispatch* columnist Dutch Reagan reported from California in 1937, "and he is innocently dozing when the reader finds himself possessed of a flaming torch. He batted about .999 this trip and would have made a perfect average, but he tried it on Charlie Root one night. When Charles discovered his handful of unnecessarily hot news he carried the torch across the lobby and dropped it right in Woody's lap."

Woody's sense of humor was right up manager Grimm's alley. When the Cubs won the pennant in 1935, "Woody English brought his scissors along and snipped off every tie in sight, including Phil Wrigley's," Grimm wrote later.

Billy Jurges' irrational fear was falling into the ocean. His rational fear was being plugged by a deranged fan.

Billy Jurges

Billy Jurges pretty much took over English's shortstop job as Woody was eased over to 3rd...then over to Brooklyn. Billy played 17 years — starting (1931) and ending (1947) with the Cubs, interrupted by 7 seasons with the New York Giants. He was a so-so hitter but a great fielder. He played in 3 World Series and took 2 bullets from an unhappy girlfriend. Yep, Billy was the 1st Cub to audition for the role of Roy Hobbs, getting shot in a Chicago hotel room.

He started out with a bang. "I want to play alongside of Jurges in some of the games and give him a chance with the Regulars in battles," manager Hornsby told reporters in the Spring of 1931. "His work in the practice games at Catalina Island was great. Never saw a better-looking rookie."

A few seasons later, though, he was still trying to get oriented around Avalon. "Bill Jurges has 'Island Fever,'" wrote Jimmy Corcoran for his *Cork Tips* column in the *American*, 1936. "He states that it wouldn't be so bad if he thought he could walk someplace without falling into the drink."

Lloyd Lowe

As Jurges was wrapping up his second Cub gestation, another shortstop was gunning for his job: Lloyd Lowe. Lloyd played in the Cubs' and Cardinals' organizations from 1943-1950.

"We went to Catalina Island in 1948," Lloyd says. "I went to Los Angeles, and Bob Lewis was the traveling secretary — he handled all that, and sent out a train ticket. When we came back, we started playing exhibition games and would work our way back East. It was an exciting time, a new experience. It's a nice place to have Spring Training. It's a little foggy, so the grass is wet 'til about 10 o'clock."

And it was a long way from home. "I was a new father," he says, "and I didn't have much money to spend. We had our meals, we'd walk down to the ocean — you'd write letters home, you didn't do much on the side. We weren't in the habit of picking up the telephone and calling home. I was just a rookie, and I'd make $5,000 a year once the season started."

The pressure was on for rookies, Lloyd says. "I was new to the organization. It was tough to break in — they had so many good ballplayers." But the incentives were obvious: "The bad thing about the lower leagues, especially the Texas League, was when you'd go on the road...the trains were air conditioned, but the hotels were not. In San Antonio, in the summertime, after the game, the dressing rooms were hot and sweaty...instead of a locker, they'd have a hook for you to hang your clothes on — it was not as delightful as you might think. That bat was pretty light at the beginning of the season, but every month...the bat got a little heavier."

But at least he was climbing. "Hark Rock Johnson was managing when I was in class D, in Jamestown," Lloyd recalls. "I was making a whopping $90 a month. I met him up there. I was just 18, and the season had started when I graduated from high school. I had to write home to my mother for trainfare after the season."

But with the Cubs, "it was really 1st-class, we were treated well — I wasn't used to that in the D leagues. At Jamestown, they'd give you a dollar and a quarter a day to live on. You'd eat corn flakes for breakfast, a hot dog for lunch, and scrambled eggs for dinner — and that was it!"

> "I had to write home to my mother for trainfare."
>
> Lloyd Lowe

Lloyd was closing in on the big time, though. "I went out to the P.C.L.," he says, "after having a good Spring Training on Catalina. Most of the Angels were ex-major league players. The weather was good. Bill Kelly was the manager. On opening day, he said every job was wide open — but they already had their regular team picked out. It took us a week or 10 days to have a chance to have batting practice. After the regulars would go in, the rookies would throw batting practice to themselves. Finally, we had the opportunity to get in there with the regulars. Red Barrett was pitching. He was really heavy, but he didn't throw very hard. The very first pitch he threw to me, I hit outa the ballpark, see, and ya got everybody standing around watching you. Rube Novotney was catching, and he gives the sign, and the next pitch came right at my head. So I go falling down, and as I get up I'm brushing off the dirt, and I said to Rube, 'Does he think he's pitching the World Series?'

"And Rube says, 'I think you hurt his feelings.'

"So I said, 'But he doesn't throw hard enough to hurt anybody.'

"And Rube says, 'Don't tell him that!'"

But the Cubs didn't call, and part-way through that year...the Angels sent him down to Springfield. "I had a problem with my financial situation. At the end of the season, you've gotta get a job. By that time, I had a wife and 2 kids — I wish I could have continued, but it was a matter of economics. I didn't want to quit; it gets in your blood, like an addiction."

Fuzzy was a Cub on Catalina for a while, but not long enough — they shipped him to the L.A. club.

Fuzzy Richards

Another Cub hopeful who spent more time in Los Angeles (rather than Chicago) than he'd have preferred...was Fuzzy Richards. Fred, a 1st-sacker, hit a respectable .296 for the 1951 Cubs in 10 games. He played several years in the Pacific Coast League — a starter for the Angels in 1953 and 1954.

"For me, it was very unique," Fuzz says. "I'd never been to California. I took the train from Ohio to Chicago, met the team, and we took the Chief across the country. We took the boat over from Los Angeles. I was only 21 or 22, so it was quite an experience."

He'd started in 1946 and was with Des Moines. "I played well, so I got the opportunity with the Cubs." But he suffered a broken leg, so when he went to Catalina in 1951, "I spent most of the time in the whirlpool, exercising, stretching, walking, running. Lotshaw was elderly by then, but he was a lot of fun. A real nice guy."

The Cubs/Angels sold him to the Giants in 1955, where his Minneapolis Millers won the American Association Little World Series. "In 1956, they wanted to send me to Dallas, and I had to make a decision. I decided to come back and see what was going on here. Within a few months, I was a firefighter."

Dee Fondy

The 1st-base sack was crowded in those days — besides Richards, and Chuck Connors, Dee Fondy was also looking for a job. Dee played 8 years in the majors — batting .300 three times. In 1953, he secured the Cub position by clubbing 18 homers and hitting .309.

In 1951, "Chuck Connors had an outstanding Spring and Dee Fondy did not," Roy Smalley says. "So, Chuck made the Cubs, and Dee went to L.A."

Fondy was leading the Coast League at a torrid .376 clip, while Connors was limping along at .239 in Chicago. "Dee tore up the Coast League, and Chuck did not do well, so they switched," Roy explains. "That's how Chuck got back to Los Angeles, and he let that show-biz personality develop."

"Dee Fondy was a good ballplayer, and he had a terrific glove," Andy Pafko says. "He was a good spray hitter, and he could hit some home runs."

Dee Fondy did a lot of bending & stretching exercises so he could beat Chuck Connors out for the 1st-baseman's job — but he could've taken it easy if he'd known that Chuck would soon switch careers.

Eddie Miksis might beg to differ on Andy's fielding report for Fondy — Eddie thought he got credited with a few too many throwing errors, thanks to Dee's, uhm, proficiency. "You might as well have had a statue out there," Miksis told Carrie Muskat in *Banks to Sandberg to Grace*. "He was a butcher."

Cy Block

Cy Block was another infielder who could *hit*. In fact, his lifetime big-league average is .302! He only played a total of 17 games over 3 seasons — but he did get to pinch-run in the 1945 World Series.

Unfortunately for Cy, he played 3rd base...when should-be-Hall-of-Famer Stan Hack was around. His first Catalina camp was in 1942. "Cy came up under Jimmie Wilson, and Jimmie Wilson loved him," Harriet Block says. She and Cy were married the next year, and the War interrupted his career after he'd hit .364 in 33 rookie at-bats.

"Cy Block was a good ballplayer," says Lou Stringer, who played in Los Angeles too. "He had good hands." And a good bat; Cy tore it up in the minors. He was Sally League MVP in 1941 (his .357 average and 109 RBI led the league)...he set a Southern Association record by smacking 50 doubles in 1947 (while batting .363)...and he finished his career with a .325 lifetime average in pro ball.

And he hustled: "Block gained considerable attention in the 1942 Spring camp by his noisy Brooklynese chatter," Edgar 'the Mouse' Munzel wrote in the *Chicago Sun* in 1946, "specializing in such pep phrases as 'that's the old razzmatazz' and 'let's give 'em the hipper-dipper.' "

Cy Block couldn't get Stan Hack's job, although his lifetime batting average was one point higher.

"I went out to Catalina with Cy 2 times, in 1946 and 1947," Harriet says. "The 1st time, we stayed at the hotel. The 2nd time, we stayed at the bungalows — I was pregnant. We went over on a Flying Tiger. We sat on the floor, and landed on a diamond. It was quite bumpy. The next time, we took the boat...and I got seasick. We could have our meals in our hotel, if we wanted. It was a lovely bungalow. We usually ate over at the hotel. We liked to dance at the hotel. There wasn't much entertainment — it was February."

But Charlie Grimm wouldn't play Cy. "They dropped him off in Los Angeles," Mrs. B. recalls, "and from there he was traded to Nashville." He hung up his spikes in 1951. The couple had 3 daughters and 6 grandchildren...and Cy got the best revenge: He made a heck of a lot more money than he would've, even if he'd been given a chance to become a big-league star.

"After he retired, Cy went into life insurance," Harriet says. "He was a legend with Mutual Benefit." Cy hired some former ballplayers he'd met along the way, like Ralph Branca, and kept on breaking records in his new field. "He was the leading agent in the U.S.!" Harriet smiles.

Lou Stringer

Lou Stringer played 3 seasons for the Cubs, then 3 for the Red Sox. Before, in-between, and after...he played in the Pacific Coast League and was actually managing the Hollywood Stars when Boston called him up in 1948. He was a utility infielder with some power — one of only 2 ballplayers to ever hit a home run over the 30-foot-high, 410-foot centerfield fence at Hollywood's Gilmore Field. (Even his Stars roomie, Frankie Kelleher, didn't ever do that.)

He challenged Merullo for infielding prowerss: In Lou's 1st big-league game, he set an N.L. record by chalking up 4 errors. Boots Stringer?

"A very versatile guy, he plays the saxophone."
Lou's 1947 Signal Oil Los Angeles Angels card

On his first trip to Catalina, in 1941, Lou was single — so he took his mother over with him for a vacation. "She cooked for me," Lou says. "We went to that beautiful little church there, St. Michael's Catholic Church. We stayed at our own place, right next to the ballpark — Las Casitas.

Lou Stringer's major-league debut left a little to be desired.

"It's a beautiful island. I played a lot of golf. I'd play with Bobby Sturgeon, Peanuts Lowery, Gene Mauch, Metkovich — we grew up together, there were 8 of us who'd played in high school. Priddy tried to turn pro. Peanuts was the best golfer, and a good poker player."

It was a quiet Spring. "I never met anybody there," Lou says. "I just didn't do too much. I was just thrilled to get to play ball. Most of the other players were just kids themselves." He got married later that year, then went into the Air Corps as a mechanic.

"In 1946, my wife came out," he says. "There wasn't a heck of a lot to do. We went dancing. Cavarretta and those guys, they'd get on a bus or somethin' and hunt the boar. I don't know why I never went with 'em. They were kinda cliquish. I wasn't very close to a lot of 'em — I was a different kind of person."

After baseball, Lou stayed in Southern California. "I've been there once or twice since then," he says. "We took a 10-day boat trip."

Dim-Dom Dallessandro

Another Catalina Cub who also played for the Red Sox was Dim-Dom Dallessandro (not to be confused with Dom DiMaggio) — except Dim-Dom did it the other way around, trying Boston first. The diminutive outfielder (he towered at a Hack-Wilsonian 5'6") played big-league ball for 8 seasons. He was with the Cubs from 1940-1947, and he led the N.L. in pinch-hits in 1942. In 1944, he hit .304. And, like Stringer, he was a long-time Pacific Coast League standout — leading the league with a .368 average for San Diego in 1939.

He almost stayed out of the War — Dom flunked his eye test. But that pesky .304 average in the thick of things caught his draft board's attention, and he was invited to re-apply. He got the job, and although he only had to serve for one season...it happened to be the season that his Cubbies made it to the World Series.

"Can you read the top line on the chart, Mr. Dallessandro? Thank you. Now, can you see the seams on this curveball?"

Practice, Practice, Practice

Goat Trails, Medicine Balls, & A Dash of Pepper

"My biggest weakness was the pitched ball."
Paul Schramka

Charlie Grimm, Ripper Collins, & Gabby Hartnett play a bit of pepper, 1938.

When all the tourists and movie stars and Big Band clarinet players cleared out, the Cubs could get down to business. After all, it *was* called Spring *Training*.

Before there were computerized fitness tables and aqua-robics classes and fat-gram counters, how did the boys manage to get themselves into shape? They must've done something right, winning all those National League pennants. Let's take a look...

Evers was succeeded by 'Reindeer Bill' Killefer the next season. "Killefer instituted the most arduous system of road work ever designed to make a sorely tired ballplayer wish he had taken up some other means of livelihood," Warren Brown wrote in his Cubs' history. "Save for the picturesque bay on which the town of Avalon is situated...Catalina's contours were made by nature for wild goats rather than for ballplayers. There are still men alive who...will swear that once Bill looked them over on the flat, he knew they weren't all major-league ballplayers, and so they might as well try to be mountain goats."

" 'That guy Killefer must think we walk across the plate instead of trying to throw the ball past it,' groaned Jackie May, a lefty pitcher," Charlie Grimm wrote in his autobiography.

Killefer soon changed his tune. After a pair of disastrous exhibition losses against Portland and Vernon of the Pacific Coast League, "Hikes over the mountains have been tabooed," Oscar Reichow wrote for the *Chicago Daily News*. "From now on it will be baseball almost morning, noon and night."

A bright idea, from day one

Catalina's unique geography — as in, plunging cliffs — caught everyone's attention on the 1920 scouting trip. From that moment on, the hills and mountains were an important part of the training regimen.

"We miss the mountains," manager Johnny Evers lamented after heading back to the mainland in 1921. "Those long hikes up steep trails did the pitchers and catchers more good than any form of training I ever saw. I would not trade one week spent at Catalina for a month of ordinary training."

"We did a lot of running," Paul Schramka says. "I was standing next to Frisch because I didn't know better — I was just a dumb kid! I'm on the far right. Klippstein was next to me. Preston Ward is the tall guy, next to Klippstein — he could motor. Bob Ramazzotti was in that group, too."

Take a moment to consider Catalina's hiking cliffs — fun to look at, not so fun to scale.

"Manager Killefer...was an advocate of strength-by-walking," Grimm wrote, "and the setting was perfect. If a player was detected loafing, Reindeer Bill would sentence him to stroll up that sharp hill behind the grandstand. I'll tell you from personal experience, it looked like a mountain when you were climbing it. At the crest was a wooden reservoir. Hack Miller found a way to beat Killefer's evil designs and turn this train of woe to his advantage. He'd send a lad up to the top with some goodies for lunch and then deliberately loaf so that Killefer would sentence him to the long hike."

Years later, the torture-by-trail-hike went merrily on. "We'd be there for a few weeks — you had to get yourself in shape," says Phil Cavarretta. "We'd go after the mountain goats and the wild boar. Frankie Frisch was a tough guy — he was from the old school. He was a great player, a Hall-of-Famer, but he didn't get along with everybody. I wasn't his favorite — maybe he didn't like Italians. He'd take us up some days — Catalina is all mountains — and he'd take all the ballclub up and we'd start walking hills. And after half an hour or so, guys would start falling, even though we were young. With this drill, a lot of us ended up with shinsplints."

"Some idiot at the front office had us come out there a week early and walk the paths in the mountains that the goats made," Randy Jackson shrugs. "You couldn't play catch or hit, because of league rules. We'd start in the morning, and hike all day. Everybody had shinsplints — dumb! I don't think there was a lot of wisdom running around."

"Some of the boys...actually acquired bunions and cactus needles," Ed Burns wrote for the *Chicago Tribune*.

Since Frisch's pre-camp regimen started before teams could officially invoke Spring Training, no baseball was allowed. "It is interpreted that baseballs, bats, gloves, and spiked shoes will cease to become illicit instruments at midnight Tuesday," Burns updated.

"Moving around on the flat was sort of tricky after days of shinnying up and skidding down the hills," Irving Vaughn told *Trib* readers.

"I hope they've got banked turns in the National League infields," Gabby Hartnett said back then, "because one of my legs is shorter than the other from trying to navigate those dad-gummed hills."

"It was a lot of work, hard work. There were some bad days. You had to keep it going, or they'd give you the slip."

Corky Van Dyke

"Frisch had us all go out early," Bob Kelly says, "and he had us climbing the mountains up the rough side...then we'd walk down the path. We all had shinsplints so bad we couldn't move. Bill Voiselle just sat down — he couldn't take another step. He was such a nice guy — I felt bad for him."

"Hank Sauer uses fire extinguisher to cool Clarence Maddern's feet after the two Cub outfielders returned from hike over hills of Catalina Island," this Chicago Tribune *photo revealed in 1950.*

"Somebody had the idea that'd help us push a few more runs across the plate," Wayne Terwilliger suggests.

But they didn't push many runs past the plate that season — the Cubs just got sore muscles.

Earlier, in 1924, the *Chicago American* reported: "The mountain climbing seems to have seized Ace Elliott's angora. 'Gee, I spent the Winter putting on 14 pounds,' lamented the rookie first-sacker, 'and in two days I've lost it all. If I have to hike again I won't be strong enough to hit past the infield.' "

"I must have run a thousand miles that Spring," Kirby Higbe wrote (about 1939) years later.

Doc to the rescue: "Saltwater baths, massages, and applications of magic oil by Trainer Andy Lotshaw and his rubbing assistant soon will have the limping players thoroughly unlimbered," Harold Johnson wrote in a 1938 issue of the *American*.

Off the mountaintop, onto the field

When they finally came in from hiking, the boys got going on the Avalon practice field. Hopefully, after the long winter's layoff...and all that marching...they remembered the fine points of the game.

> " 'Now kiddies,' began Mr. C.J. Grimm, 'this is a baseball. And this is a bat.' "
>
> John C. Hoffman in the *Chicago Daily Times*, 1938

The methods varied from skipper to skipper, as you might imagine. Evers started with a short morning baseball drill, followed by infinite afternoon hikes. Joe McCarthy required a 2-hour morning session and another after lunch — less hillwork. Rogers Hornsby introduced new-fangled regimens, like soccer. Charlie Grimm banned lunch in favor of a single 4-hour session, from 11-3.

"An old-fashioned game of leapfrog first was staged, with all hands hopping merrily from the home plate out to the left field limits and back," the *Tribune* covered in 1928. "Next came the great Cubs' base-circling relay race."

The relay race was a holdover from the previous season, although "Hartnett's side won, mainly because the runners are accustomed to cheating a little rounding second," according to the *Herald & Examiner*.

"We worked out — we went 2 times a day," says Claude Passeau, who worked hard enough to pitch a 1-hitter in the 1945 World Series. "You know how practice is, they throw, they run. We had the late afternoons off."

The 1933 Cubs felt the baseballs would seem lighter if they practiced chucking the massive medicine ball first. It didn't work; they fell from 1st place to 3rd that season.

"We practice 4 hours every day," Fuzzy Richards wrote home in 1950. He neglected to mention the goats, most likely due to space limitations.

Gabby Hartnett just wanted 'em to play baseball: "None of those mountain climbing, medicine ball or soccer notions which from time to time harassed Cub candidates," Burns told *Tribune* fans in 1939.

Whatever the method, the result was generally the same: *Pain*.

"These guys will feel like rolling over and dying tomorrow morning," Frisch observed in 1951, "but a few days of this stuff will put them in shape. Looks like some of these guys did their winter conditioning in a rocking chair."

"Hack Wilson had been perspiring for about 20 minutes in the opening workout when he asked Jimmy Burke how long this had to go on," the *American* reported in 1930. "'Another hour,' responded Jeems. 'I may be here in spirit,' snapped Hack, 'but not in person.'"

"We went someplace and took a steam bath," recalls Bob Scheffing's son Bob, who came out twice in the late '40s when he was a little guy. "In those days, of course, not many of the ballplayers lifted weights during the offseason, and some of 'em got pretty big! So they sent 'em to the steam baths. I remember Swish Nicholson being in the steam room. Swish was a good guy — in my mind, he was Babe Ruth! My dad was big, about 6-foot-2, but Swish — he was huge! I played with him a lot; he was great with the kids."

Howard Roberts of the *Daily News* sent home this piece in 1938:

AVALON, Calif., — *Charlie Grimm today tackled several weighty problems.*

"Look at them," he blubbered, pointing to several members of his squad of Chicago Cubs as they cavorted about the practice field. "They do nothing but exercise with a knife and fork all winter. Then, when they report at training camp, they come to me and say, 'Look, Charlie.'" And Grimm threw out his chest, tucked in his tummy and waved the palm of his hand perpendicularly from chest to waist. "They think maybe they're fooling somebody," Grimm snorted. "No fat...phooie."

> "Skull practice has become a daily part of the training. It was incorrectly reported yesterday that at the skull drill, Hack Wilson had pulled a ligament in his cerebellum."
>
> The Chicago Daily Times, 1931

Springtime weight problems are as old as the game itself. "The most conspicuous rubber shirt fellow was Julian Tubb, rookie pitcher...from Marion, Ala., where folks are supposed to subsist on grits exclusively but obviously do not," Burns wrote in a 1940 edition of the *Tribune*. "The roster gives Julian's weight as 177, but doesn't say what year he weighed."

Julian Tubb, a svelte 177?

If he were managing today, Gabby's Burger Diet would probably be atop the New York Times best-seller list.

And so today the more portly members of the squad were forced to toil extra hard in a long drill that included lots of batting and plenty of running. A session in the steam room followed, to peel off some more of the extra beef.

A rather portly member who is coming in for excess toil is Steve Mesner, who is as stubby and broad of beam as a tugboat. "I'll run some of that heft off in a hurry," declared Grimm, and Steven promptly did a lot of running, even though that is the one thing he doesn't like to do on a ball field.

Apparently, Cholly's programs got results. In 1946, the *Sun* reported:

As for the weight chart, that is a very paradoxical situation. Most of the boys actually are gaining. But Grimm is pleased about it all.

"It just goes to prove we haven't any fat boys this spring," said Grimm. They're working hard and the food is good enough to keep their weight up. Fellows who haven't any blubber on them are inclined to add weight in the Spring because the hard work after a winter of loafing stimulates their appetites and hardens the muscles."

And they kept it off. Consider Warren Brown's column from a 1951 *Herald-American*: "Manager Frank Frisch...and his coaches profess to be pleased with the anti-blubber rules all members of the squad appear to have obeyed during the off season. The anti-blubber rules certainly trimmed catcher Forrest Burgess down to a point where he actually appears tiny."

The Wrigleys had front-row seats for all this reducing. William Wrigley seemed to attend practice every day — even if he was entertaining, say, a U.S. President, like Calvin Coolidge. In fact, "William Wrigley built his house so his bedroom suite would look down on the field," according to the Hon. Edgar Taylor, U.S. Superior Court Judge — who grew up playing ball as an Avalon schoolkid. But after the elder Wrigley passed away in 1932, son Phil was less conspicuous at games — he "came out one day and he sat in the sun for a while, then he left," recalls Don Dunker.

Once they got out of the mountains, off the scales, and finally worked their way onto the practice field...there were good days, and there were bad days. On one of the badder days, Grimm threatened to cancel one of Mr. Wrigley's fabled barbecues. The account in a 1938 *Chicago Daily Times*: " 'We've got to get something done,' said Mr. Grimm with a finality that shook the mountains. 'I like Mr. Wrigley's spirit, but we have a pennant to win and we can't win it by playing around up in the hills with goats.' " Jolly Cholly relented, though — as if anyone didn't think he would — and the boys rode up the mountain for a feast and a rodeo the following afternoon.

> "Look at those guys. I was going to give them a day off next Monday, but it looks like they're taking it today."
>
> John C. Hoffman, quoting manager Charlie Grimm in the *Chicago Daily Times*, 1938

Trainer Andy Lotshaw records rookie Vern Olsen's weight at an even 175. Andy did not, however, record a reason why the rookie (clad otherwise in only his jock strap) chose also to wear his cap at the time.

On the better afternoons, young ballplayers took home memories they'd never forget — when they got to be hero for a day. "Folks about the training camp have been perking up their ears at Johnny Moore. Johnny went into the palm trees behind center field to pull down a drive by Hartnett in the seventh inning," Burns wrote for the *Tribune* in 1929.

You can bank on it: Johnny Moore told his grandkids about his catch. Of course, he ended up with a pretty good career, too — a .307 hitter over 10 seasons, Johnny played in the '32 World Series.

Throughout the process, hope and dreams bloomed...and faded. "A left-hander, a tall, stringy, and very scared one, reported at Catalina one Spring," Warren Brown wrote in the team history. "His first pitch was 5 feet over the head of the catcher. He got better. By the time the Cubs let him go he was missing the catcher by no more than 2 feet at a pitch."

Reality eventually hit: "They were all better than me," pitcher 'Stub' Stabelfeld (who never made a regular-season Cub roster) admits candidly.

There were kids who couldn't miss...who did. "Jim Asbell...has been knocking shingles off the cottages of the natives who live near the ball park with such regularity that the board is bulging with pride and expectation that he is the answer to their prayers," the *Daily News* flashed in 1938. Asbell went on to rack up a lifetime batting average of .182 for the Cubs, without a single homer in a major-league game.

> "When I pitched my 1st intra-squad game, I was scared to death."
>
> Bob Kelly

Another rookie sensation was Dick Bass, Catalina class of '39. Like Roy Hobbs, Bass had toiled in the minors for more than a decade. "That fellow has something," Cub Al Todd observed. Unfortunately for pitcher Bass, it was the wrong thing: His major-league career consisted of one game — which he lost.

The opposite happened, too. Lefty O'Doul had a brief Catalina tryout, but did not impress and was dumped. Within three years, he hit .398 — for another team.

> "The Regulars hit the pitching of Henshaw and Kowalik to all parts of Avalon. Even the goats were running for cover."
>
> The *Chicago Daily Times*, 1936

"For the rookies, it was an entirely different atmosphere," Bob Rush remembers. "They'd call ya 'bush,' and run you outa the batting cage. But once you were accepted, you were made one of the group. They wanted to see what you were made of. A hotfoot, that was one of the things some of the guys would do. One guy would talk to you, and the other would sneak a match in between the sole and the toe of your foot, and light it. No, I never did that! I don't think anybody tried it on me. I just kept quiet, tried to make the ballclub..."

For some, torching rookie toes wasn't enough. "Jack Dittmer and Walker Cooper used to put a lit match between the pants and belt in the back to catch somebody's uniform on fire," Andy Pafko recalls.

Whether hot or cold, dry or wet, the pranksterism rolled on. "One time, I went and opened up my locker, and there was a big stingray in it!" Al Epperly recalls. "It was movin' around — it was still alive. I took it back down and put it back in the ocean. I'd gone fishing a lot, so it didn't bother me."

Bob Rush's rookie card. He is carefully eyeing the dugout for open flames.

"It was the same old baloney," explains Harvey Storey. "Jimmie Wilson was the manager. I guess he was the manager — he never paid any attention to me. After 2 weeks, I finally went up to him and introduced myself. He said, 'I know who you are.'"

Lloyd Lowe wasn't quite as badly neglected by Grimm, but he didn't have an easy time, either. "It was tough to break in — they had so many good ballplayers," Lloyd says. "They were good guys — they liked to hustle."

"At that time, there were not a lot of college kids in sports," Paul Schramka says. "One of the pitchers came up to me and asked, 'Paul, how old are ya, where were you born, where'd you go to high school, oh, you went to a university? What'd you take?' So I told him, and he says, 'Maybe you better think about it, when you're out in the outfield, when you have to call, "I got it, I got it," since you're a college boy, maybe you better yell, "I have it, I have it!"'"

"Basically, you came with what you had...and they'd fine-tune you a little bit," Rush says. "If you were outa synch, if you were overstriding a bit, they'd fix you back up."

"I guess the coaches did some," Preston Ward says. "Of course, spring training, you know, you go through all the rigoramorool, all the stretching, the exercises."

"We didn't get a lot of coaching, not in those days — not really," Andy Pafko says. "You relied on your God-given talent. Roy Johnson was a hard worker — a real nice fella. He was one of the best coaches ever. If you had a problem, you could come to see him. If you wanted to take some extra batting practice, he'd be there. That's why they called him 'Hard Rock' — because he was such a hard worker, always working with the kids."

Lennie Merullo, who liked to hustle.

The rookies sorta kinda expected a little coaching help...but it wasn't always readily available. "Rogers Hornsby was supposed to be the batting coach one year," Randy Jackson says. "He'd stand behind the batting cage and watch us, then run off to the race track. He never said anything to anybody, never offered any advice."

"We didn't have special coaches like they do now," says Wayne Terwilliger, still managing/coaching in Fort Worth, more than 50 years later. "Rogers Hornsby was there one spring. Here was this Hall-of-Famer who took batting practice and made it look easy, but he couldn't teach anybody to do it like he did."

Some of the older players gave tips to the rookies. "Charlie Root helped me," Al Epperly recalls from 1937. "He got me to throw a sinker, and a slider. He worked with all the young pitchers. Red Corriden was a coach. Did he help us rookies? I don't think so. He was workin' with some of the money pitchers."

"Charlie Root took me aside and gave me some tips," says Bob Kelly, who came along after Root had retired to become a coach. "I didn't learn to pitch until after I was out of baseball!"

"There was no coaching in those days — no instruction," says Gene Mauch, who went on to manage for 26 seasons. "I mean, *zero.*"

Carl Reynolds, 1938.

Hub Kittle recalls how the process eventually helped him:

"Grimm took me out one time — I was a wild son of a gun, and I hit Steve Mesner on the knee. Grimm said, "Get that blankety-blank so-and-so Indian outa there — he's gonna kill all my players!"*

"The next day, he told George Uhle to help me. My delivery was all over the place — I had this fancy twisted-up wind-up. He straightened my delivery out, cleaned up my mechanics. I'll never forget what he taught me that day. He said, 'Stick that stinky stuff — hold the ball in front of you, turn it like this, anticipate the ball into the catcher's glove.' And all of a sudden, I threw strikes!"

When the batters weren't getting plunked, the sluggers had some interesting targets to aim for. "We were in awe of Hank Sauer's bats," says Islander Marcelino Saucedo. "On the field, we'd pick it up. They weighed 52 ounces! The ones we used were about 34 ounces. The left field fence was about 370 feet; he used to hit it half way up the hill to the Country Club! Randy Jackson and Bill Serena used to kid each other about playing Sauer so deep."

"The field was big," says Marse's brother, Foxie Saucedo. "Left field must've been 425, 430 feet. Left center, right center, that was close to 500 — that's where they had the sliding pits for the players. I never saw anybody hit one out, but the older kids said Novikoff hit one out."

"We all played at Wrigley's field," Frank Saldaña agrees. "The dimensions were long, like the field in Chicago — 331 feet to right, 444 to left, and way out in center, it was almost 500 feet!"

While the *exact* dimensions are a matter of memory, the fact is that things looked pretty tempting beyond the first-base line. "Bill Nicholson has found the range of the right-field fence for several 'homers'," Edgar 'the Mouse' Munzel wrote for the *Sun* in 1947, "but it's only 315 feet from the plate. 'Unfortunately, we can't take that fence with us to Wrigley Field,' observed (GM Jim) Gallagher."

Not only short porches, but also a shortage of batting-practice pitchers, may have given some of the Spring Cubs illusions of grandeur. In 1949, the coaches lined up 5 last-minute batting-practice hurlers from the Los Angeles area. "If we have to use them in those games," Grimm observed, "the scores may sound like a basketball contest."

"In general, it was a loose atmosphere," Red Adams recalls "It wasn't under a magnifying glass, the way it is today."

Whatever the dimensions, this is where the Cubs practiced.

SPRING TRAINING GROUNDS OF THE NATIONAL LEAGUE CHICAGO CUBS

Catalina's baseball park is distinguished by its scenic setting at the foot of towering mountains and by the absence of billboards and high fences.

F4472

* *Jolly Cholly was referring to the fact that he was aware Hub had been pitching in Ponca City, Oklahoma — which is pretty much surrounded by the 'Kaw Nation' Native American reservation.*

"Catalina was a great place for practicing," Phil Cavarretta says. The park itself was great, always in good shape — there were no potholes."

Despite the well-kept field...players did get hurt from time to time, unfortunately. In 1938, All-Star Billy Herman got plugged by a stray pitch and "dropped as if shot," Braven Dyer wrote for the *Los Angeles Times*. "The groan he let out must have been heard on the mainland. The ball hit him on the point of the left elbow but traveled so swiftly that most of us on the sidelines did not know immediately what part of Billy's anatomy had been dented." After the ding proved to be less-than-life-threatening, "Charlie Grimm's leathery countenance — which had resembled the sea-green tinge of a sick spinster crossing the channel — took on its natural hue again and everybody breathed a sign of relief."

That same Spring, the *American* said that "Tony Kaufmann has acquired a sore neck. 'I must have a strained ligament trying to think,' declared the home-bred while undergoing treatment for the affliction."

In 1929, Hartnett got sore feet from golfing in his dancing pumps, while Hack Wilson's drinking buddy, Pat Malone, claimed his upset stomach was due to overexertion on the previous day's goat hunt. The next year, a flying bat clunked pitcher Lon Warneke in the nose — resulting in 3 stitches.

In 1946, the *Sun* reported that "There was one casualty due to injury. Johnny McPartland, rookie southpaw, was blinking through a 'shiner.' He kept his eye too much on the ball yesterday when it came bouncing off the scoreboard."

Billy Herman — feeling much better now, thank you.

After all that soccer, volleyball, leap-frog, medicine-ball tossing, & a variety of other assorted sports tore up the turf, Charlie Grimm & Gabby Hartnett took it upon themselves to make sure there were no potholes in the Spring of 1935.

As a sidelight, Dyer pointed out that "Occasion of the near-catastrophe was the first Spring game between the regulars and rookies, won by the veterans in a photo finish, 20-6." Not a bad 21st-century score for a game in 1938.

"Bouncing bats off athletes' heads has been stopped. (McCarthy) believes the bats are too valuable."

Jimmy Corcoran, writing in his *Cork Tips* column for the *Chicago American*, 1930

Doc Lotshaw to the rookie's rescue...

Johnny Schmitz's size-14 cleats provided more space for blisters. Johnny suffered a bad case in 1950, but must've recovered quickly — later that afternoon, he went out and shot a 72 on the Catalina golf course. "Catalina is a wonderful place to train," he says. Apparently, for him, it was...

Johnny Schmitz, pitching in the shadow of Catalina's fabled hiking peaks.

Of course, everybody wanted a piece of the exhibition action. The very first year, a team of local 'All-Stars' took on the Cubs — and got creamed. Colleges came over to play. Comedian and baseball nut Joe E. Brown would assemble celebrity teams to scrimmage the Cubs. And in 1928, a Navy team from the U.S.S. Tennessee took the plunge. Two Springs later, a squad from the U.S. Revenue Cutter *Algonquin* (this was during Prohibition, remember, and rum-runners liked to hide out behind the islands) took on the Cubbies. "Something resembling a ball game was played," Jimmy the Cork wrote for the *American*, "but the only reason that it could be called such was that there were 9 men on a side and a lot of cussing was done. At the finish 3 mountain goats were brought down from the mountains to play outfield for the rubberlegs."

Pacific Coast League teams (particularly the Wrigley-owned Los Angeles Angels) often came to scrimmage, and in 1932 and 1933, the New York Giants stopped by for several games. "The Angels are now gloating," the American said in 1930, "because they are the champs of Catalina Island. This makes the Cubs mad because this happens to be their Island."

GM Wid Matthews tried to introduce a pre-little-league-style batting tee in 1950. Players teed off too easily, though, and the item was relegated to the junk trunk.

On one particularly rainy day in 1927, the *Los Angeles Times* reported that the team moved their practice inside, to the dancing pavilion: "The indoor drill in the afternoon was marked by more frivolity and horse-play than usually is permitted by Mr. McCarthy. The chief form of exercise was a basketball game in which a tin pail and a wooden box served as baskets."

The famous mudslide of '37, which blocked the path to the diamond, "restricted their exercise to running up and down hotel corridors, interspersed with lobby pacing," Burns wrote for the *Chicago Tribune*.

While torrential rains did happen a few times, the weather was generally less of a factor. "The only thing some of the ballplayers had against it was the prevailing wind that came across right field," Lee Anthony says. "It bothered a few of them a little. It was a cool breeze. The pitchers didn't like it, and the right fielders didn't like it. Other than that, I don't know why they didn't keep going out there — Wrigley owned the island, and it was a nice set-up."

Lee Anthony escaped the Catalina winds and went on to play for Mr. Wrigley's other team — which let him wear his initials on his cap.

"The weather didn't matter," Cal McLish says. "If you had to run, you had to run...whether the sun was shining or if it was snowing."

"I remember that time when there was some hail, and maybe some snow — it was very cold," says Johnny Klippstein. "But I've been in Florida when the weather was terrible, too.

"It was cold over there," Ed Chandler recalls. "When Frisch got through running us around the outfield, we'd walk back to the hotel as fast as we could. The wind was blowin', it was raining — to pitch, it'd take 20 minutes to warm up. Frisch got the better pitchers in shape — if I wasn't gonna pitch, I wasn't gonna do any good. It was frustrating."

Islander Jack Cowell was familiar with the local atmospheric nuances. "One thing that was funny was, they'd take that fungo bat, and Gabby would hit that ball so high up, outa sight, and that breeze came down the canyon and blew it all around — the players had to run around in circles trying to catch it," Jack says. "They used to laugh about that."

Players also got the giggles when one teammate's wife would work out alongside the guys. "She wasn't really fat," a former Cub who requested anonymity says, "but she had this huge chest. She'd come out when we were having calisthenics, and she'd wear this tight t-shirt, and she'd be standing off to the side, but she'd be doing calisthenics right along with us. And man, all the guys were looking over there..."

> During practice a big Scotch collie, entitled 'Rags,' insisted upon browsing amongst the athletes, shagging balls and generally manifesting keen interest in the game.
>
> The *Chicago American*, 1924

"Gabby Hartnett and his 17 battery men, without the accompaniment of radio stars, newsreel grinders and miscellaneous photographers, today got down to concentrated conditioning processes in their training camp at Catalina Island," reported Burns in the *Tribune*, 1939.

> "It seemed like mass hysteria sometimes, but we managed to get some baseball in."
>
> Carmen Mauro

As early as 1923, non-Cubs were suiting up. "Edward Sargent, owner of the Kalamazoo club, joined the players at the St. Catherine and takes baseball practice at the Cub training camp each day." Big Band members often talked their way onto the

Manager Hartnett, at the left, begs the Movietone folks to go back to Hollywood so his boys can get to work in the Spring of 1939.

Distractions of all kinds

Managers have always had a tough time keeping players focused. But Catalina seemed to bring an entirely new level of distraction possibilities — besides the mountain goats. There was a golf course within view of the field, and chances to dance, and an ocean, and movie stars, and...well, you get the idea.

field. John Payne (as opposed to Wayne), who played the good lawyer** in *Miracle on 34th Street*, also practiced a bit. And of course, Cub radio announcer Dutch Reagan took a few swings in 1936 and 1937.

Speaking of lawyers, a 1929 report in the *Catalina Islander* instructed fans that they must now park in the road (rather than the outfield), because several windshields were broken during the previous Spring.

In 1926, new manager Joe McCarthy issued a few edicts, according to the *Chicago Daily News*. "There will be no more poker and pinochle games while playing. This means of diversion, Joe has found, only makes the boys nervous and fidgety." But Marse Joe's rules were kiddie's play compared to the edicts enacted by his successor, Rogers Hornsby. No reading or going to the movies, for instance — although a rolled-up copy of the daily racing forum (and its 6-point type) was clearly visible sticking up from his hip pocket at all times.

> "My brother was 5 years younger. He'd embarrass us! Every year, we were on Catalina during his birthday, so he'd always make the rounds to tell all the ballplayers, and they'd give him money! Mother wanted to throttle him..."
>
> Della Root Arnold, Charlie Root's daughter

"They only had one high school," Phil Cavarretta says, "and they'd bring in those kids 2 or 3 times — around 9:30 or 10 o'clock in the morning, before our workout. We'd take a little batting practice with 'em, and the pitchers would go down to the bullpen and work with the pitching instructor. We'd try and teach them something."

Photo opp! A particularly clever journalist suggested Gabby could go 'fishing' for a pair of ballplayers named Sturgeon (Bobby) & Bass (Richard) — get it?

And some 'fans' could get on ballplayer nerves. One afternoon at the team hotel, Charlie Root found catcher John Schulte bellowing out the window at a roofing crew. "Hit those rivets harder! You, with the bandana on your head — move a little faster!" Schulte howled, with a few obscenities thrown in for good measure. "Pick up the pace, or you'll never get through!" Charlie asked him why he was shouting at those hapless souls. "Because," Schulte replied, "they're the guys who yell at me when *I'm* working!"

Beyond grown-up distractions, kids were a factor too. Besides the occasional player's kid, Avalon was loaded with youngsters who spent every waking second at the ballpark.

After the Cubs would head East

Mid-March was a bittersweet time for Islanders... as they said goodbye to their Cubbies for another year.

But Mr. Wrigley did not leave his Island baseball-less. He sponsored a semi-pro team, the Catalina Cubs, throughout most of the Chicago Cubs training years. They acted as somewhat of a combination practice squad and farm team for the Los Angeles Angels, and for a time went by the name 'Angels,' too.

** Yes, we recognize that the term "good lawyer" is a *non-sequitor*. But recall that the character in question was in a *movie*, not real life — so please engage your 'willing suspension of disbelief' in this situation, that we may get back to the Cubs . . .

The Catalina Cubs, when they were the Catalina Angels, sporting hand-me-down L.A. Angels uniforms.

The Catalina Cubs occasionally went to the mainland to play, but usually floated opponents to Avalon. Over time, they played just about anybody — but generally, their regular opponents included:

* The Paramount Cubs
* Shell Oil
* Pepley's All-Stars
* The Croatians
* Fox Studios
* Standard Oil
* Procter & Gamble
* Richfield Oil

Hub Kittle was a regular. In 1936, "I was 15-3 on Catalina," Hub says. "Playing over there, the team belonged to the Santa Catalina Island Company — we were the Catalina Island Angels. Doc Brooks was the manager. Old Hoss Lelivelt and Truck Hannah, they coached us. They sent 'em over on a boat to play us — I had a heck of a year. I pitched 2 no-hitters. Roy Partee was on that team; he went up to the Coast League, then to Boston."

"We were working for the Santa Catalina Island Company," Hub says. "They hired us to play ball, but since we worked for Mr. Wrigley's company...we did other things, too. They had us pick up the garbage, empty the cans by the ballpark — it was part of our work."

The competition was sometimes stiff, sometimes not — but always interesting. The Paramount and Fox Studios teams, unfortunately, included "no stars, just a bunch of stage-hands," although stars (like Bing Crosby) sometimes suited up for photo-op games.

Since Mr. Wrigley was behind the Catalina Cubs, they had sponsors & programs & everything — this scorecard was from a game in late September, 1930.

"I played for the Richfield Oilers," recalls Chuck Stevens, who played for the St. Louis Browns in the '40s and then several more years for the Hollywood Stars. "My uncles worked at Richfield and ran the club. I started out when I was a sophomore in high school. They'd 'freeload' ya transport to and from the Island, and they'd put you up in these semi-tents near the ballpark over Saturday and Sunday, before putting you back on the old Catalina steamer Sunday night. We'd go to the Casino sometimes, and we'd get out and push the ladies around the dance floor a little."

The 1932 Catalina Cubs semi-pro squad championship ball.

86

Another of the semi-pro Catalina Cubs was Clarence Kumalae — the Hawaiian pitcher who also tossed batting practice for Chicago. Occasionally, a Catalina Cub or two would get a tryout with the Chicago version; in 1928, Catalina outfielder Frank Califano and pitcher Clarence Steube (a pitcher who chucked a no-hitter that Spring) got a look from Los Angeles Angels manager Marty Krug. Neither one made it.

And Islander Spud Ryan also caught — and scouted — for the Island team. Charlie Grimm would occasionally use Spud in right field for practice games...teasing reporters at first by calling him 'John Doe.'

But the War got in the way, and the Catalina Cubs never re-emerged — so when their Chicago 'parent' pulled up stakes in 1951, both professional and semi pro ball on the Island came to an end.

Hub Kittle wore this 'away' jersey & cap (on the right) while pitching for the Catalina Cubs in the late '30s. The Cubbie blue is in place, but the bright red was replaced with yellow. The home jerseys used the same colors, but a less-fancy font.

Catalina cop Spud Ryan was also a Catalina Cub catcher.

How does a ballplayer get to the Hall of Fame? Practice, practice, practice . . .

After Practice

Snipe Hunts, a Friendly Game of Cards, & Putt Perfection: What's a Boy (On an Island) to Do?

"Snipe Hansen was just a kid. Grimm, Gabby, and some of the guys that liked to stir something up took him on a back road behind the St. Catherine — there weren't many roads out there then. He listened, and said, 'Yessir, I'm gonna catch them snipes!' And back at the hotel, they all laughed and laughed..."

Della Root Arnold, Charlie Root's daughter

You're on an island in the Pacific Ocean. You only have to work 4 hours a day. What're you gonna do in your spare time?

While the Cubbies were on Catalina, they found plenty to do. Most of the time, it was good clean fun. But boys will be boys — so there was a bit of mischief from time to time...

They'd fish. They'd hunt. They'd golf, play tennis, or go to the local arcade for billiards or bowling. There was dancing. And Mr. Wrigley would have a barbecue and rodeo at his ranch.

"People ask me what I do in winter when there's no baseball. I'll tell you what I do. I stare out the window and wait for spring."

Rogers Hornsby

ROY HANSEN
Pitcher. "Snipe" throws left handed, bats either. He is 25 years of age, weighs 195 lbs., and is 6 ft. 3 in. tall. He came up first time to the "Phillies" in 1930; was sent back for more seasoning and came up in 1932 to stay. He signed his first major contract at 17. "Snipe" is also a basket-ball star. His home is in Chicago.

ROY HANSEN
Philadelphia "Phillies"

And then there were rookies.

Rookies require pranksterism, and one of the all-time great stunts took place on Catalina in the Spring of 1927. The mark was a rookie batting-practice pitcher by the name of Roy Emil Frederick Hansen — but the joke was so profound, it even changed the kid's name.

Kid, indeed. Roy was in his last few days of being a teenager, scheduled to turn 20 the next week. And, thanks to the benevolence of his elders, he was about to learn the fine art of snipe hunting. Snipe, of course, seem to exist only in the imaginations of jokesters — who are more than willing to help youngsters try to bag a few. Woody English, Billy Herman, Gabby Hartnett, and Charlie Grimm emerged as the prime perpetrators this particular day.

Too bad Snipe didn't have any of these matches with him whilst on his snipe hunt — he might've lit a fire to keep warm after the sun began to set.

88

In snipe hunting, the rookie is given a burlap sack and placed in the center of a canyon. The seasoned snipers will separate and each climb an opposite canyon wall, where they will locate said snipe and chase them downhill. The rookie will be perfectly positioned to bag the beasts, so that a fine snipe roast will ensue. A key: the rookie must be patient, and stay in place for a long time...because snipe are known to be wily critters. Meanwhile, "All the rest of us...went down to the hotel, had dinner, and sat around the lobby," Grimm recalled later, "waiting for our victim to show up."

Most rookies, of course, don't follow instructions well — so even if they agree to hunt snipe, they'll give up their vigil within a half an hour or so, at the most.

But not Roy Emil Frederick Hansen.

For on this February afternoon in 1927, Roy was determined to be the best dad-gummed sniper on the Island. So he stood. And he waited. And waited. And waited...until the afternoon ceased to be afternoon, and became dusk, and became evening, while those stubborn snipe refused to be rooted.

It was dark. Some of the ballplayers began to worry about young Roy — shouldn't we send out a search party? But some of the jokesters suggested he'd have the last laugh...and actually come in with a sackful of snipe.

Clearly, Snipe never recovered; years later, he was once discovered in the St. Louis bullpen... imitating a flamingo.

The rookie finally trudged back to the Hotel St. Catherine — at around *9:30* p.m., with steam fuming from his reddened ears — to a chorus of laughter they must've heard all the way over on the mainland.*

"We chased hundreds of snipe in your direction," Woody scolded the lad, "and you didn't even catch one!"

Roy hadn't bagged any snipe, but he did earn a new nickname. Ladies & gents, Snipe Hansen — a name so solidly engrained in baseball consciousness that he's listed that way (rather than 'Roy') in the *Baseball Encyclopedia*.

So young Snipe took out his aggressions on the field. "Yesterday 'Snipe,' casting the last 3 sessions, granted no base hits," the *Chicago American* reported the next Spring. Sweet revenge: "He got off to a flying start by fanning Hartnett." In all, he pitched in the big leagues for 6 seasons.

"Nights here present a riot of 'dissipation,' . . . the movies and then back to the hotel for cards, pool, the horse-race game, and quiet reading. The lobby is usually empty by 11."

Jimmy 'the Cork' Corcoran, in his *Cork Tips* column for the *Chicago American*, 1936

Other pranks of note

Snipe was not the only victim. Pranks and jokes were never in short supply on the Island — and the victims often set themselves up.

A 1921 rookie commented on the quality of the salted mackerel. "Salted mackerel nothing," Grover Alexander corrected, "that's a tuna."

"Don't spoof me," the rookie shot back. "I've seen tuna in Des Moines. It always comes in cans."

That same season, according to the *Los Angeles Times*, the team took a glass-bottom boat tour of Avalon Bay: "One young and handsome rookie gazing through the bottom of the boat saw a shovel-nosed shark looking back at him, and he thought it was his own reflection. When he found out that the vessel doesn't carry a mirror on its keel he regained a good opinion of himself."

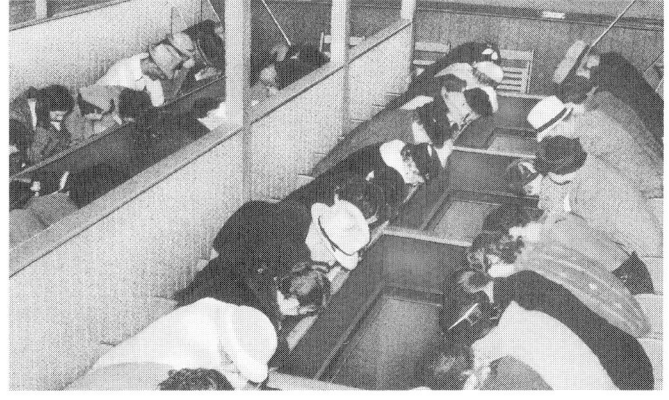

During the glass-bottom boat tour, Catalina visitors pray that the Cubs will win the pennant in 1939.

---

* *Variations of the yarn exist, even amongst eye-witnesses; Della Root Arnold, who was also there, swears Snipe snuck in the back door to the hotel before the perpetrators...and thus earned the laugh on them!*

Ah, the ol' exploding golf ball routine.

Prey of the day: Clay Bryant.

"The new Bruins are also looking forward with keen anticipation to the pleasure of snipe hunting, dog and badger fights, and bucket fishing," Gentleman Jim Gallagher wrote for the *American* in 1937.

The guys didn't wait to get all the way to Catalina to send the rookies off on a wild goose chase (or snipe chase, as the case may be). A 1926 caption in the *Los Angeles Times* said, "On the left is Percy Lee Jones, a southpaw hurler who is still wondering where the bowling alleys are on the boats going to Avalon."

The bowling-alley-on-the-boat routine was a common one. In Charlie Grimm's book, he writes of the rookie-victim-du-jour on a particularly choppy crossing:

He bounced around the deck and finally poked his head into the stateroom of Bob Lewis, who was so sick he was hoping the boat would sink. "Where IS everybody?" asked this indomitable youngster.

"They're all downstairs bowling," answered Bob. "Just turn to your left and go down the steps."

The youngster...thanked Bob and went off to find the bowling lanes. When we finally arrived safe and sound at Avalon, this youngster went up to Lewis and asked, "Where do we go now?"

"St. Catherine Hotel. Check in, and you'll be assigned a roommate," said Bob. "And, by the way — did you ever locate the bowling alley?"

"No, I looked all over the boat and finally wound up in the engine room," said the lad. "By the time I tried a few other places the whistle blew and I figured I'd go upstairs to see what it was all about. And, when you're figuring out roommates like you just told me, please don't put me in with you!"

"Extra-curricular activity hasn't been clamped down on by Hartnett, with the natural exception of such sports as walking the streets after midnight, shuffling the pasteboards for excessive sums or indulging in distillates."

Herbert Simons, for the *Chicago Daily Times*, 1940

The set-up was always a good routine. In 1922, the manager of the Atwater Hotel showed pitcher Virgil Cheeves a trick, but said he couldn't make it work. He pressed a dime against his forehead and said the objective was to make it fall...without hitting your nose. Of course, the dime hit his nose...and of course, Cheeves wanted a try. The hotelman obliged, pressing the dime onto the ballplayer's noggin...but sneaking it away. "The impression was so hard," Oscar Reichow wrote in the *Chicago Daily News*, "that Cheeves thought it was still there, and corrugated his brow for nearly 5 minutes trying to make the dime (that was not there) fall — while the gathered athletes laughed heartily."

By the time this portrait was made, Virgil Cheeves had removed all loose change from his face.

In 1924, trainer Andy Lotshaw did a bit of double-reverse-prankstering. He stuck a buttonfish into one of Hack Miller's flannel pantlegs before a workout. Lotshaw then watched Miller jump and dance and sputter and cuss, and calmly informed him that he'd seen Gabby Hartnett fooling around his locker. Miller threatened to throw Gabby off the pier, but Hartnett swore he was innocent. The next morning, dressing for practice, Gabby found a harmless-yet-alarming garter snake in his hip pocket. Once again, Andy was on the scene...reminding him of the previous day's confrontation with Miller. After a day or so of uneasy calm, Andy confided in both men that he really thought rookie Ace Elliott was the culprit. So, Hack and Gabby teamed up to stuff lima beans into Ace's spiffy new two-tone shoes...and simply add water. The expanding beans busted the seams. (Only later was the true villain unmasked.)

Three stars: Chuck Klein, Babe Herman, & an ample starfish.

"The fishy odor of the camp itself," the *Chicago Times* reported in 1934, "was something else. It must be charged up to the playboy infielders, Billy Jurges and Woody English, who went out last night and caught themselves some assorted finny specimens — which in a moment of playfulness they threw over the transom into the bedroom of Charles Dunkley, the well-known Press Service sports editor. Before Mr. Dunkley awoke this morning, the entire corridor of the hotel had been perfumed with the odor of neglected fish."

But not everybody was up for fun and games. "In Catalina, I'll tell ya what I did," Harvey Storey says. "After those 2 workouts, on the way back to the hotel, I'd get 5 pounds of Epsom salts and then lay in the bathtub the rest of the day to try and get better."

"The lawn of the Cubs' Spanish clubhouse today became a nudist camp," Ed Burns wrote for the *Chicago Tribune* in 1941, "as the thermometer moved toward 80 degrees. The athletes, naked as Mexican hairless canines, frisked and gambooled in the glorious sun. It was quite a sight, everything considered."

Other times, fashion statements were more civilized. "Last year," the *Chicago Daily News* reported in 1926, "Alexander was the only one who wore knickers, but now all the boys have them — including the rookies."

Did Woody English really catch this 270-pound porpoise? Was he wearing his uniform at the time? Doesn't he believe in dolphin-safe tuna? And why is superfan Danny Cahill wearing Woody's cap — backwards?

"I crocheted a rug for the house while I was out there in '48. Some of the guys didn't let me forget that when they heard about it."

Lee Anthony

Babe Phelps, Bud Tinning, & Dutch Seebold . . . with the whoppers-in-the-making of 1934.

Fishing tales

When you're surrounded completely by water, fishing comes to mind. Some of the ballplayers fished from the piers, and others took to the deep blue sea. The results were often entertaining.

"Trainer Andy Lotshaw had the thrill of his young lifetime," the *American* reported in 1924, "when he hooked a giant devilfish. Andy yanked it almost to his level, only to let loose when the fish emitted streams of terrifying fluid."

Meanwhile, said the paper, "Coach Oscar Dugey hooked a giant eel from the spring board fronting the Cubs' dressing quarters and had the time of his life yanking the wriggling denizen of the deep to the dock, where a battle royal ensued before it was taught to say, 'Uncle.'"

Pitcher Ray 'Cowboy' Harrell displays his haul — not quite over the 1939 season limit.

Des Moines Dispatch columnist Dutch Reagan recorded a particularly creative Catalina fish prank in 1937. "Gabby Hartnett is both persecution and victim," Dutch wrote, "and is the loudest guy on the coast in both. He was taking a salt bath one day when the boys found an undersized octopus (sailors call 'em squid). That combination could have but one result, and did Leo talk when his unexpected tub mate (in the usual defensive gesture of his kind) surrounded himself and Gabby with a cloud of ink! What the best catcher in the business said then would stunt your growth."

Dutch also described a prank often plied on rookie fishermen: tying a kettle or bucket to the greenhorn's line, as the unsuspecting angler tries to land a big one from the back of the boat. "It may sound silly," Dutch observed, "but his efforts — combined with a little sly boat maneuvering — can give all the effect of an irate fish. Charlie Grimm had a visitor in camp work one hour and 30 minutes landing a tin lid one day. The poor guy was punch drunk for a week."

There were other perils, too. "Killefer allowed the hired hands half a day off Sunday," said the *Tribune* in 1923, "and most of the athletes boarded *The Quest* for a trip around the island. The Pacific was not so pacific, and neither were the ballplayers when they returned."

Others enjoyed a bit more success. "Charlie Root has established himself as the champion fisherman," the *Daily News* said in 1926, "by catching a yellow tail."

Decades later, Cal McLish mastered the sport, too: "When I played in the Coast League," Cal says, "we'd take one of those charter boats and go fishing for calico bass and striped bass out there. It was kinda fun to see those fish grab ahold of your bait — the water was so clear, you could see down 20 or 30 feet!"

"Fishing, I know — the one that got away!"

Olinda Hacker, Warren's wife

Bob Kelly found himself exposed to species he'd never encountered in fresh water back home. "I threw in a line, and went fishing off the rocks," says Bob. "I caught all kinds of things — fish with bumps all over 'em."

"The Cubs were taken on the glass-bottom boat trip today," *Chicago Sun* readers found out in 1946, thanks to Edgar 'the Mouse' Munzel, "with Bob Lewis volunteering to handle the announcing megaphone so the boys won't get sand dabs and swordfish confused."

Getting somebody's goat

"Tomorrow," Burns wrote for the *Tribune* in 1935, "the first formal goat hunt of the training season will be staged. A new lodge has been built in the midst of the thickest goat habitat and the nimrods on the team will hunt in style and elegance."

"During their spare moments," the *Los Angeles Times* told in 1932, "the boys are training a wild Catalina goat which later will be designated as the St. Louis Cardinal goat."

Cholly Grimm tries to determine if his catch is as large as the other one that's on display at the pier.

Mr. PK Wrigley asks manager Charles Grimm why he is riding a goat, rather than riding the ballplayers or hunting the goat.

Charlie is contemplating a snappy reply.

Boaring tales

When they weren't fishin', the boys might be found huntin'. Catalina's hills and gullys offered a wide variety of game — besides snipe and jackalope (a creature that looks like a rabbit but has antlers), there were also wild boar (technically feral pigs, for the statisticians in the crowd), Spanish range goats, and even bison (which tend to imitate buffaloes).

"Another mountain goat hunting expedition was to be staged today," Ed Smith of the *American* reported in 1928, "with Blake, Bush, Root, Grimm, and Jones manning the firearms. The first named trio of moundsmen were gunning in the wild woods, 16 miles from Avalon, yesterday — and when they appeared declared they had brought down 19 goats at distances ranging from 300-500 yards. Their yarn is being investigated. Last Spring, Roy Fred Hansen, the angular southpaw rookie, starred as the hero in a snipe hunting party, but no such low comedy has been attempted this season."

Somehow, we don't quite picture Spring Training as looking exactly like this any longer...

Local pranksters led Rip Russell to believe that this little BB gun would fell a wild beast.

"Charlie Root is lazy and says he is full of cactus," the paper reported the next week. "Isn't that the stuff they make tequila out of down across the line? Says he got it on a goat hunt. I was up there one time and didn't get back for 2 days. Never saw either goats or cactus." Two days later, Guy Bush was in on the act. "Now that I have picked all those cactus barbs out of my left leg, collected while mountain climbing, I am ready to do a lot of pitching. Those stickers knocked me out of at least 4 goat hunts."

Pat Malone & Lon Warneke hope they have a better day than the goat did.

"Perhaps," Billy Herman surmised in 1938, "I could shag more flies if mounted upon a swift steed."

Happy trails

Yet there were hazards beyond weaponry. "Tony Kaufmann and Howard Freigau have taken to horseback riding," the *Daily News* reported in 1926, "but not for long. They're so stiff now that they can't climb into the saddle without aid."

"I went with Sauer and Pafko," Carmen Mauro says. "But boy, those horses were educated; you had to push 'em up, but once they got to the pinnacle... they took you down those narrow trails, in a *hurry*."

Des Moines Dispatch columnist Dutch Reagan attested to the hazards of the goat hunt in 1937.

"These ponies...I suspect are in league with the goats," he wrote. "You do a shuffle foot, one foot, two foot for the nearest bump on a horizon as full of bumps as an unmade bed. On the level, though, it's not bad going except that you don't stay on the level. Skipping over a strained interlude of hillside touched here and there with cactus, we'll put you on a ridge. This is where you stop breathing and resolve to die with a devil-may-care smile 'neath your sunburned nose."

Nothing a little Worcestershire Sauce wouldn't fix up...

"Dizzy Dean withdrew from the party," Burns wrote for the *Tribune* in 1939. "His withdrawal came not through fear of shooting himself or being shot instead of a goat, but because of fear that the recoil from the heavy rifles used in goat slaying might injure his mending right shoulder."

Hy Vandenburg & Hard Rock Johnson spent a little too much time on horseback in the Spring of 1946.

This little piggie got blown away

According to the *Sun*'s Munzel, in 1947 there were about 4,000 wild boar on the Island. He said 30 had been imported in the early '20s to help eliminate the rattlesnake population, and after 25 years, "rattlers are few and far between."

"I've even done some boar hunting!" laughs Lennie Merullo. "Imagine that, a kid from the city, going boar hunting."

Phil Cavarretta adds, "The instructor told Merullo and me, 'Be careful when you shoot; you have to kill it, because if not, it'll hide in a corner and charge you.'

"Well, sure enough, this dumb Dago hit one. And Merullo says, 'No, don't go after it — you'll get hurt.' But I go towards it anyway — and sure enough, it comes charging up. But we were young, so we had good reflexes, and it goes to the right, and I managed to get it. Boy, we were stupid."

The Curse of Snipe must've lingered: "Bob Chipman went out hunting boar one time when it was getting dark," Bob Kelly says. "It got really late that night, and he didn't come back. He finally showed up — I remember being pretty scared for him."

Others got a little better at it. "The hunting party of Stan Hack, Bill Nicholson, Phil Cavarretta, Henry Wyse, Mickey Livingstone, and Bill Fleming bagged 10 wild boar," according to the *Chicago Sun*, 1946.

Other assorted fauna

"They had quail by the hundreds," Cavarretta says. "The instructor told us what to do; when they hear you, they bunch up, and they won't come up until you practically step on 'em."

And in 1937, John C. Hoffman of the *Times* sent home an unusual report: "Wrestling with an 18-month-old leopard the other day, Larry French had his short torn off...Larry at first swore the only thing that would satisfy him would be a leopard skin to replace the shirt...but discreetly let the matter drop."

"Hobby is catching and training mountain lions."

From the back of Red Adams' 1949 Bowman P.C.L. card

"Oh, by the way," Catalina hole-in-oner Lefty Carnett points out: "The #1 tee of the golf course is about halfway up the hill behind me. We used it a lot."

Tall tales from the links

The Catalina course is actually the oldest on the West Coast — the fairways heard their first swear words in 1892, assuming there were swear words then. But not everybody had their lovely walk spoiled there:

"A hole-in-one on the 105-yard 2nd hole of the golf course here was the top development of the camp," the *Daily News* reported in 1939. "The ace was scored by Edwin Carnett, a young left-handed pitcher who will probably end up in Los Angeles for the season, despite his excellent tee shots."

"After practice, we played golf," Carnett smiles fondly. "Several of the guys played: Gene Lillard, Al Epperly, Woody English."

Alas, Lefty got shipped out to the Coast League — so he had to practice his putts in Seattle. That left room for others to make their move. "Top golfer is Charlie Root," the *Daily Times* reported in 1940, "with a 76 after taking an 8 on the first hole."

See? Lefty really did it!

Finding that baseballs were not small enough, a few of the '28 Cubs decided to swing at tinier round objects. Some of the boys didn't take things too seriously . . .

Fanatics? Obsessives? Nah. "Paul Erickson and Hank Sauer won top honors for stamina," Munzel informed *Chicago Sun* readers in 1946. "They played 54 holes of golf...Johnny Schmitz made it for 45."

A week or so later, Schmitz drove the 1st green — a 320-yard shot which had last been accomplished by Sam Snead, several years earlier. "The most enjoyable thing about Catalina was playing golf after workouts," Schmitz recalls. "They had a nice 9-hole course." Yeah, but would Johnny have enjoyed it as much...if they'd made him play all 54 holes, rather than just 45?

> "I don't want to play golf. When I hit a ball, I want someone else to go chase it."
>
> Rogers Hornsby

Dizzy Dean told *Daily News* reporter James Kearns about one teammate's golfing temperament in 1939: "That Ferrell — he doesn't only throw his clubs and break 'em on a bad shot...he slammed himself down on the ground. Honest, now, it's hard to believe, but he started buttin' his head against the tee marker. Pretty soon he stopped for a minute...Then he butted his head a few more times before he cooled off."

Others appreciated the talent they saw, rather than the tantrums. "Sauer was outa my class," Ed Chandler says. "He'd hit that ball 800 miles."

Del Walker, the Avalon High baseball coach, was also the golf pro for a while. "It was a very narrow course," Del says, "and the ballplayers were strong, heavy hitters — not necessarily accurate. I sold more golf balls than any other time. I remember very vividly running out of new balls; I'd send the kids into the hills to look for 'em."

Bill Voiselle was smart enough to enjoy the course...without tempting himself to frustration. "Most of 'em played golf," Ol' 96 says. "I didn't play golf then, so I caddied for 'em — Mickey Owen, Bob Rush, and the country club manager.

It's hard to tell from this great a distance, but bad words were being spoken at the time this shot was being snapped.

Games of skill & chance

Cards? Bowling? (There really were lanes on the Island!) Ping-pong? Horseshoes? You name it, a ballplayer could do it on Catalina...

Just shut up & shuffle the deck

"The pinochle tournament has reached the fifth pukka," reported the *Los Angeles Times* in 1928, "with Charlie Grimm showing unusual form and enjoying a slight favortism in the betting."

"There was always some card-playin' going on," Cal McLish says. "No poker, because they usually had a rule against that — we just played for nickels and dimes."

"In the '30s," Grimm recounted later, "we had some loud games of chance. Crummy rummy was my favorite for many years. We played it for one cent a spot and double if a player went out at once. I was better at hearts, especially when Andy Lotshaw was one of the other contestants. Lotshaw knew that I would be very unhappy if I would collect that awful card and often, when he could make me take it, he'd back away. That's what I call loyalty."

"Peeking wasn't considered cheating," Grimm wrote. "and Hartnett was the champion. Once we persuaded Phil Wrigley to join our jolly group, and what I and Gabby and Burns did to him was a shame. He stayed clear of us after that."

Peeking may've been kosher, but betting certainly was not. "Gambling amongst us will not be tolerated," Commissioner Happy Chandler edicted while the Cubs were back on Catalina in 1946. "It is put to us to shun all appearance of evil. We must keep baseball on a high plane."

Before the Commissh's rule, the boys weren't into shunning evil (nor the appearance thereof), apparently: "Old Jack Doyle took a lot of money away from some brash youngsters in a poker game which had 8 players, 7 kibitzers, and 3 assistant kibitzers," Gentleman Jim Gallagher wrote for the *American* in 1935.

But the next year, it came around for the ol' scout. "Jack Doyle," Jimmy the Cork wrote for the *American* in 1936, "was no little irked today because the 'young punks' showed him how to play poker last night."

Jack Doyle scouted for the Cubs from about 1776-1951. During that time, he won a lot of chips . . . until Cavarretta came along.

The 'young punks' happened to be teenager Phil Cavarretta. Here's Phillibuck's rendition of things which transpired the night before:

Jack Doyle was our #1 scout. He'd come to Spring Training and watch the players and grade 'em. He was a great scout and a great guy. In those days, we were allowed to play poker — we'd play a quarter and a half. My first year, one night, I was just 18 — but I got together enough money to get into a game with Doyle, Gabby, Augie Galan, and Charlie Root. We had to stop at 12 o'clock — we had a midnight curfew. It was getting late, so it was time for the last pot.

I'm doin' pretty good — I got lotsa quarters. Jack Doyle was on my left, and Gabby was next to him, then Galan. We're playing five-card stud, and I opened for a half. Jack Doyle looked at me with those hard Irish eyes and said, "Well, I'll call." Same with Gabby, and Augie, and Charlie — they all call. So he asks, "How many cards you want?"

And I said, "I don't want any — I'll stand pat."

And Doyle cusses me out and says, "You little Dago, what're you doin'?" And I said, "I don't want any cards, Mr. Doyle" — very polite. So Gabby wants 2 — I figure he's got three of a kind — and Galan asks for 3, so he's got a pair. Okay, so now comes the betting. Now, I'm standing pat, okay? So I bet a half. And he looked at me again, and cusses me out. So everybody's in, they all call, so it's back to me, and I raise it to a dollar. He calls me names again, and everybody calls, and it comes back to me again.

And I say, "I'll raise you."

And Doyle says, "You little Dago so-and-so." We're allowed 3 raises, and the others drop out, and it's just me and Doyle, and I raise it another half. He calls me a dirty name and says, "I'm out," and throws his cards down. So I rake it in — I've got 2 pocketfuls of money, this little Italian boy from Chicago, with lotsa money. So I pick up the cards to start to shuffle, and Doyle says wait — I wanna see your hand. But I didn't have a thing — just and ace and a jack — and he had 3 kings! He said, "Listen, Dago — if you become half as good a ballplayer as you are a card player, you'll have a good career!" And every time we played cards after that, he'd tell that story.

Years earlier — when Cavy was still in diapers, or at least knickers — there were already hustlers on the club. "The only pastime they have engaged in," said the *Tribune* in 1922, "is in pitching coins in front of the clubhouse. Virgil Cheeves won most of the money with his control."

Pony rides

Some of the boys — and all of the press crew — would occasionally head to the mainland to catch a horse race or two. Or three. Or... The hot tracks in those days were Agua Caliente, across the border in Mexico (where there were greyhound races, too); Del Mar, near San Diego; Hollywood Park; Santa Anita; and Los Alamitos. In the '30s, there were several gambling barges that operated out of Los Angeles — but California Attorney General Earl Warren shut 'em down by 1939.

"Agua Caliente," Corcoran wrote in his *Cork Tips* column for the *American* in 1930, "is a place that was built so Americans could realize how it feels to be broke on foreign soil. Few Americans who visit Agua Caliente, we hear, fail to send greetings back home. They usually read, 'Please wire me one hundred.' The Mexican jail at Tijuana is said to be very accommodating. The gendarmes wouldn't think of annoying your kin by telling them where you are incarcerated."

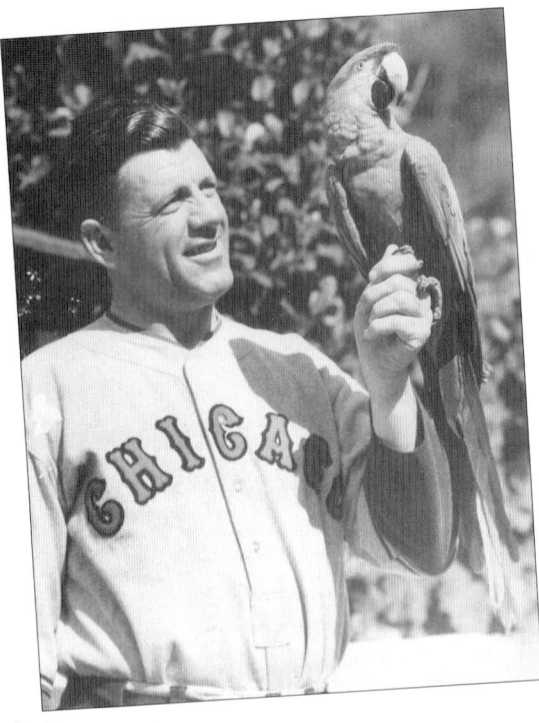

Charlie Grimm makes acquaintance with Rags, the world-famous talking macaw who lived at the Catalina Bird Park in 1934.

Kiki Cuyler thinks this is an ostrich, so don't tell him it's really a cassowary.

Miscellaneous sporting events

"Mr. and Mrs. Gene Lillard have flipped for the game of badminton," Jimmy the Cork wrote for the *American* in 1936. "Jack Doyle will tell you there weren't any badminton or other sissy games with McGraw and the old Orioles."

"Larry French is the badminton master," Howard Roberts told *Daily News* readers in 1938, "as Clay Bryant is willing to admit after chasing miles after the little white bird." The *Herald & Examiner* said French was trying to convert everyone to the badminton courts — but with little success.

Mr. Lillard, while Mrs. Lillard went to the powder room to change into her badminton outfit.

"It may be badminton when you play it," Doyle said, "but it'll be worse minton when I get out there."

Pool brought on unique challenges, too. "The finest bit of shooting was turned in by little Steve Mesner," the *Daily News* tattled in 1938, "who tried 3 times to 'break the rack' without even so much as touching a ball. His first shot jumped clear over the bunch and off the table, barely missing scoring a bulls-eye on Logan's head. The second shot went careening into a corner pocket. On the third attempt Steve drew back the cue so far he jabbed it into the end of the table. The odds at once rose to 5-2-0, and even that he'd miss the rack on the 4th try. But Steve fooled everyone — he not only hit the rack, but he kelleyed!"

After the Lillards were gone, Larry French took up the indoor badminton torch. He's playing at the community center, which is now a Von's Express grocery store; if you go inside to buy a Milky Way Midnight, you can see the same ceiling rafters.

There were unusual athletic feats to watch, too. In 1924, as the Cubs boated back to the mainland, a daredevil flyer buzzed their steamer as his partner did headstands on the wings. In 1927, a famous lady swimmer was training to swim the San Pedro Channel...by dancing with the Cubs. And the team often boated over to L.A. to take in boxing matches, as guests of Mr. Wrigley.

Stan Hack, Turk Stainback, & Joe Marty kibbitz while Gabby aligns, 1937.

Charlie Root had some fun with the rookies. Everybody knew he pitched righthanded, but few realized he was ambidextrous...and did just about everything else as a lefty. He'd challenge the youngsters to a game of pool, and when they'd hesitate, he'd generously offer: "I'll tell you what I'll do; I'll play you left-handed!" He'd then proceed to clear the table.

An instant celeb after winning the World's Featherweight Championship in 1933, pugilist Freddie Miller went a few rounds with Babe Herman — who might just have had a slight reach advantage.

The Cubs bowled at the same place where the archers arched — the Pavilion. (We can only hope none of the veteran pranksters painted targets on the seats of rookie pants!)

Indoor archery, at the fabled Pavilion: Rookies Ray Campbell, Al Epperly, Julian Tubb, & Clare Bertram hope they have a shot at making the 1940 roster.

And they finally found the bowling alleys. "Ken Raffensberger, the promising rookie southpaw, established himself as the bowling king with a 233 game," the *Daily Times* reported in 1940. (The paper failed to mention Raffensberger's best score on the below-deck bowling alley aboard ship.)

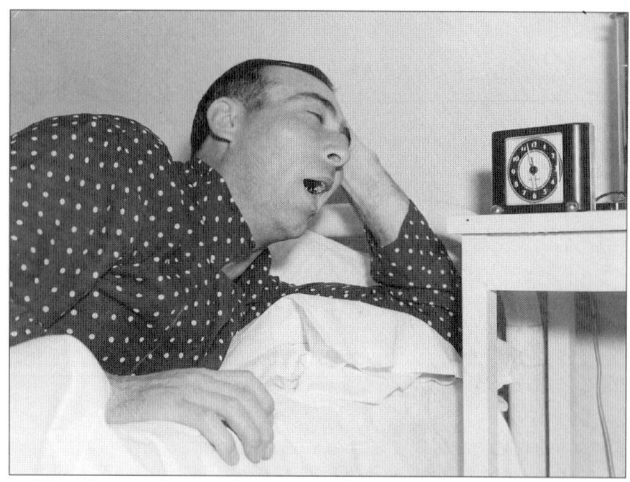

Tony Lazzeri pays the price for last night's curfew violation.

Curfews & such

"One night," Johnny Klippstein recalls, "I came in about 3 minutes before the midnight curfew. Frisch was there with 2 or 3 of the coaches, and he made this comment about 'These young kids, comin' in late,' and one of the coaches said something similar.

"But I said to him, 'I'm in before the curfew, so I'm within my rights. I'll respect the fact that 12 o'clock is 12 o'clock, and I'm on time.' And Frisch never got on me after that."

The big building on the right is the fabled Sportland Pavilion/arcade, where Cubs improved their eye-hand coordination in stirring contests with the locals.

"Dewey Williams was a catcher," Islander Foxie Saucedo remembers. "There used to be a place, Sportland — it was an arcade, where the Pavilion Lodge is, and all the ballplayers used to go there to shoot pool or bowl, things like that. Well, ol' Dewey was walking in one night with a couple of the ballplayers, and they were wearing sportcoats, and a couple of the ballplayers behind him kept yelling, 'Hey, Dewey! Hey, Dewey!' He finally turned around. He had a bottle of whiskey in his back pocket, and it was sticking out over the tail of his jacket! So when they told him, he covered it up."

"The night before we left," Kirby Higbe recalled from 1937 when he wrote his autobiography, "they threw a dandy party for us with beer and whiskey flowing. We played bingo for cash prizes. When the big game for $500 started, it was hard to see the cards. Whoever won it had to be the last one that could see the cards."

Still, Bill Voiselle says, "There wasn't too much drinking. I played for years, never drank. I tried to live right."

"The players were pretty good," agrees Harriet Block, Cy's wife. "They drank beer. The old-timers were more involved with alcohol — maybe it was too expensive for the younger players."

"Us rookies, we weren't out with the big shots," Al Epperly says. "I used to go out and run around with Dizzy. We'd go to shows. He didn't like to go with the stars. We'd play pool, go swimming, go fishing. I didn't even own a camera then — I was only getting $500 a month!"

"They wouldn't let you do anything."
Preston Ward

Money — or the lack of it — was a recurring theme for rookies. "I didn't take any pictures," Ed Chandler says. "I didn't have the money to buy film!"

"It was a great set-up," Cavy says. "Catalina was one of the best places to have Spring Training. I likedit better than Mesa, in a way. As a manager, for a few weeks, all they had was a small movie house, a Catholic church, and a hotel — there was no place to get a beer or get in trouble."

Ben Wade agrees on that count — no way to get into trouble. "There was *ab-so-lute-ly* nothing to do!" he says. "There was no traffic, no automobiles, there was one bowling alley, and you could walk to the Casino — where there was no gambling."

Dewey Williams, practicing up the hill but thinking of Sportland — say, what's what sticking out of his back pocket?

"Dean Grimm," Burns wrote for the *Tribune* in 1938, "confirmed rumors that there is to be an 11:30 o'clock curfew each night. This is not so startling or arduous as the 7:30 a.m. business."

But that didn't bother Billy Rogell. "I don't dance, I don't drink — never did," he says. "I'm one of them home boys. I was a stupid ol' jackass — I never was a night guy."

"I didn't fit in with that bunch, I didn't enjoy that bunch," Lonny Frey says. "It was cliquey, hard for a newcomer to break in, so I was glad when they traded me to Cincinnati. They liked to carouse around, and I didn't go with anybody."

At least they changed their spikes: Al Epperly, Hal Sueme, & Tex Carleton see who'll be the 1st hoopster to commit a slam-dunk on the Island in 1937.

Let's go to the Wrigleys' place

William Wrigley built his mansion high on a hill overlooking Avalon, the Bay, and the playing field. He used a telescope to watch...from his bedroom...on the rare occasions he wasn't down on the field. He'd take the players for tours of the Island, and his son PK would host enormous barbecues on their back-island place, *El Rancho Escondido* — where there would be an informal mini-rodeo. If a player was loafing, he'd 'invite' him to run up the steep hill to the mansion... to say 'hello' after practice.

Yikes! Better not loaf at practice, 'cuz that's a pretty lofty penalty box...

When the New York Giants returned to Avalon in 1933, the chef announced that he wouldn't serve cabrito — also known as baby goat — at that year's barbecue, due to popular un-demand. "Anybody who ever tried to bite a chunk out of a mountain goat can realize how tough we are going to make it on the invaders," Ed Burns had written for the *Chicago Tribune* the year before.

"The year we were there," Paul Schramka says, "it really impressed me how Wrigley treated us. He took us for a tour of the island. We went to this big ranch, and there were all these cowhands, and they gave us a tour of the house and put on a rodeo for us. Jeffcoat even got to perform for us. They paraded these Arabian stallions, and there was one kingpin who wouldn't perform with the other horses, only all by himself."

"Hal Jeffcoat...won the grand prize for roping," the Catalina Islander reported in 1951, "and Carmen Mauro...won first prize in the 'goat scramble' event."

Roping...the 'goat scramble' event...and, get this, even auto mechanics: "Things you'd have to see to believe," previewed Munzel in the *Sun*, 1946: "P.K. Wrigley, multimillionaire gum tycoon, tinkering with a balky motor-scooter, belonging to Otis Shepard, right on a downtown street of Avalon...and making it work." Only on Catalina...

From Warren Hacker's scrapbook, 1950:

Roomies Corky Van Dyke & Warren Hacker wonder if any corn is stuck in their teeth.

Don Carlsen, Don Watkins, & Bob Borkowski get settled in at the barbecue.

Randy Jackson occupies Row 1, while Hacker, Carmen Mauro, & Bob Kelly man Row 2.

Warren probably took this photo because he was wondering why all the trees on Catalina leaned to the left.

Mr. Wrigley imported large quantities of picnic tables from the mainland for his parties.

Since the smiles are subdued, we assume Carlsen & Hacker realized they did indeed have corn stuck in their teeth.

I can hear music

They were the rock stars of their era — except they wore bowties and rubbed Vaseline into their hair. Catalina was a top destination for Big Band concerts in the '30s, and CBS Radio even broadcast live shows from the Casino ballroom. Ballplayers were more than happy to listen...and dance the night away.

"The Big Bands played there," Cavarretta remembers with a smile. "Wayne King, the Waltz King, and Tommy Dorsey...There were a lot of stars on Catalina. Stan Hack, Ol' Diz, Turk Stainback, the reserve outfielder — they'd go with the stars. They'd go to the Casino and dance." Hack was seen dancing with Joan Crawford from time to time on the enormous circular dance floor...which could hold as many as a thousand couples.

The Casino played host to dances, concerts, movies, & even a live CBS Radio program in the '30s.

Time to change the cleats & slip into the dancin' shoes...

"Jan Garber, the orchestra leader, used to play at the Casino," Hub Kittle says. "I used to sing — I sang 'Old Man River' at the Casino. Hard Rock's daughter Joanne and me, we won the dancing contest at the St. Catherine Ballroom."

"Hub Kittle was a great dancer," Yosh Kawano confirms. "He was just a kid then."

"I never could dance too much. I had 2 left feet, I think. I could only do okay if we went real slow, and the dance floor was crowded."

Bob Rush, glad that he was on Catalina with his wife, rather than trying to impress a date!

There were plenty of great rug-cutters in the Cub crowd. "In the annual Avalon-Chicago Cubs' dance contest," AP reported in 1947, "Stan Hack took first prize in the modern waltz contest last night. Veteran Trainer Andy Lotshaw got a prize for his interpretation of the old-fashioned waltz." Dim-Dom Dallessandro took 2nd, behind Hack, the team newsletter noted. Way to go, Dim-Dom!

Years before — in 1926 — "Young John Welch is one of the beau brummels of the team," the *Daily News* said (whatever that means!**). "He can do the Charleston, which makes him a favorite with the young women."

But not everybody joined the party. "Here's an item of news," flashed the *American* in 1930: "Rogers Hornsby established a precedent when he dropped in at the village dance last night. But he didn't dance. The latter isn't news."

Yet most of the boys gave it a whirl. "I never was much of a dancer," Andy Pafko admits. "My wife was a wonderful dancer, though, so I'd come along and watch her! When I first got married, I had to go to Fred Astaire lessons..."

Moving pictures, too

When the Casino was completed in 1929, it was the largest theater ever built for motion pictures — not to mention the tallest building in Los Angeles County. The theater was one floor below the dance hall. Trouble was, the film quality and selections were not as impressive as the musical offings.

** Beau Brummel was the dashing title character in a 1924 John Barrymore flick, re-made in 1954 — should anyone care but not be interested enough to surf Google to find out.

"We would walk every night to the Casino and see the same doggone picture," Della Root Arnold says.

"Every night," Bob Lewis told Warren Brown of the *Herald & Examiner* in 1936, "I decided that I've just seen the worst picture ever made. So I have to go back the next night to make sure the record hasn't been broken."

But it wasn't always so bad. "The Cubs were given special permission to stay out late tonight," the *Herald & Examiner* revealed in 1927, "to attend the first showing of the new picture, 'Slide, Kelly, Slide.' " (Since talkies were not introduced until 1929, we must wonder how Kelly knew he was supposed to slide in the plot climax. Apparently, signals had been introduced by then...)

"The village cinema draws its best Cub patronage on nights when Western thrillers, referred to as 'Shoot 'em Downs,' are playing," the *Daily News* mentioned in 1939.

That's Jolly Cholly Grimm, playing some early Bob Dylan licks on the banjo. He's accompanied by Cliff Heathcote.

"Occupying leisure time is no problem for Turk Lown, playing piano, musically inclined member of the Cub squad," the Chicago Tribune *transmitted from Catalina in 1951. Wayne Terwilliger, disembodied by an overzealous touch-up artist, stands behind.*

Strike up the ballplayers

Not always content to wait for Benny Goodman to show up, the Cubbies would often get the gang and do a show on their own.

"The musical bug has bitten the Cubs — they've got a band!" Wayne 'T-Bone' Otto of the *Chicago Herald & Examiner* wrote in 1924. "Vogel sawed on the violin; Raymond Pierce played the bass horn (borrowed from the police chief); Hack Miller strummed the guitar; Friberg massaged the banjo, and Killefer did the directing. Thursday Sparkie Adams, a good trombone player, joined the outfit."

"I was a banjo man from the start," Jolly Cholly wrote. "Every Saturday night we got together for a schlag-fest with all the trimmings, which, naturally, included a keg to wet down the vocal chords." According to Grimm, Miller's guitar was held together with bicycle tape and Cliff Heathcote came along later with his ukulele.

"If anything, I remember he was a banjo player and a singer," Don Dunker recalls. "He'd get us gathered around in a big room and sing — usually country songs. He was a country singer."

But baseball practice could get in the way. "Charlie Grimm is too tired these days even to strum his guitar," said the *Daily News* in 1926. "He passes his evenings sprawled in a soft chair."

And all good things ground to an end. The music died with the War, and the old life didn't return quickly. By their last few Catalina trips, things were pretty quiet out there. "It was off-season, so there were very few tourists that time of year," Randy Jackson says. "There wasn't a theater, I don't think. They had that big Casino, but I'm not sure what they used it for..."

Good grub

The question must inevitably arise: After one bags a wild boar, what does one do with it?

"They'd barbecue 'em at the hotel," Al Epperly says.

Ken Raffensberger took the entire nasty business a step further. "I sent it back to the family," he says. "I shipped it airmail, frozen. Nobody cared for it — but the chef out there, at the hotel, he made it for us, for the team, and we had it for dinner one night."

"We had this big barbecue," Don Dunker remembers, "but they didn't taste too good! It was very tough, not like the pork you buy from the butcher."

Ah, well. So what else is on the menu?

Don Carlsen snapped this shot with his Brownie in 1949, while enjoying Mr. Wrigley's annual Catalina team picnic at El Rancho Escondido. Little did he know he was photographing his dinner . . .

"Some of those nuts would take fried chicken up to their rooms, and they'd eat it all night," Corky Van Dyke says. "You could get as much food as you wanted on the island — you just signed the check."

"They gave us a meal ticket, meal money," Cal McLish says. "There were 5 or 6 places to eat on the island. Italian, Chinese, they had a few places. You'd just sign the check."

T'was too much of a temptation for some of the lads, who'd never had carte blanche before: "There are three hospital candidates now, reported the *Daily News* in 1926. "Touchstone has a festered shin, while Cooper and Kelly ate too much."

The next season, another Cubbie caught the same disease. The *Herald-Examiner* explained, "Art Quiesser, young Chicago catcher, was taken down with sandabitis. He ate 5 sandabs for breakfast yesterday."

Kids were not immune. "Jane Killefer, the manager's only daughter, 2 years old, is a good 2-fisted eater," the *Tribune* reported in 1922. "In the dining room she was discovered demolishing a dish of ice cream with 2 spoons. Coach Dugey observed her and said she came by this naturally, as her dad has always been a ravenous packer away of food."

Reindeer Bill Killefer & his bouncing baby Jane enjoy the fragrances emanating from the hotel kitchen in 1922.

"There was one weepy member of the Cub party in camp Thursday," the *American* regretfully reported in 1930. "Charlie Root Jr. had a birthday party, and by the time he had passed out slices of his cake to the athletes...he didn't have a cut left for himself."

But it wasn't always so tragic for the Root family. "The last year in Catalina was the only year we stayed in the bungalows," remembers Charlie's big sister, Della Root Arnold. "You had to cook your own meals there, so we liked to stay at the hotel instead. They didn't really have waitresses assigned, but they kind of adopted you. Edna would say, 'And Mr. Root, are you going to have the sand dabs this morning?'"

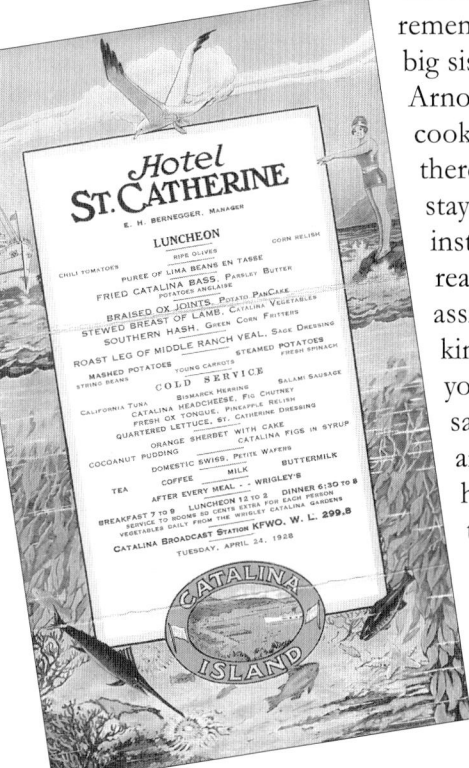

A 1928 lunch menu from the Hotel St. Catherine.

105

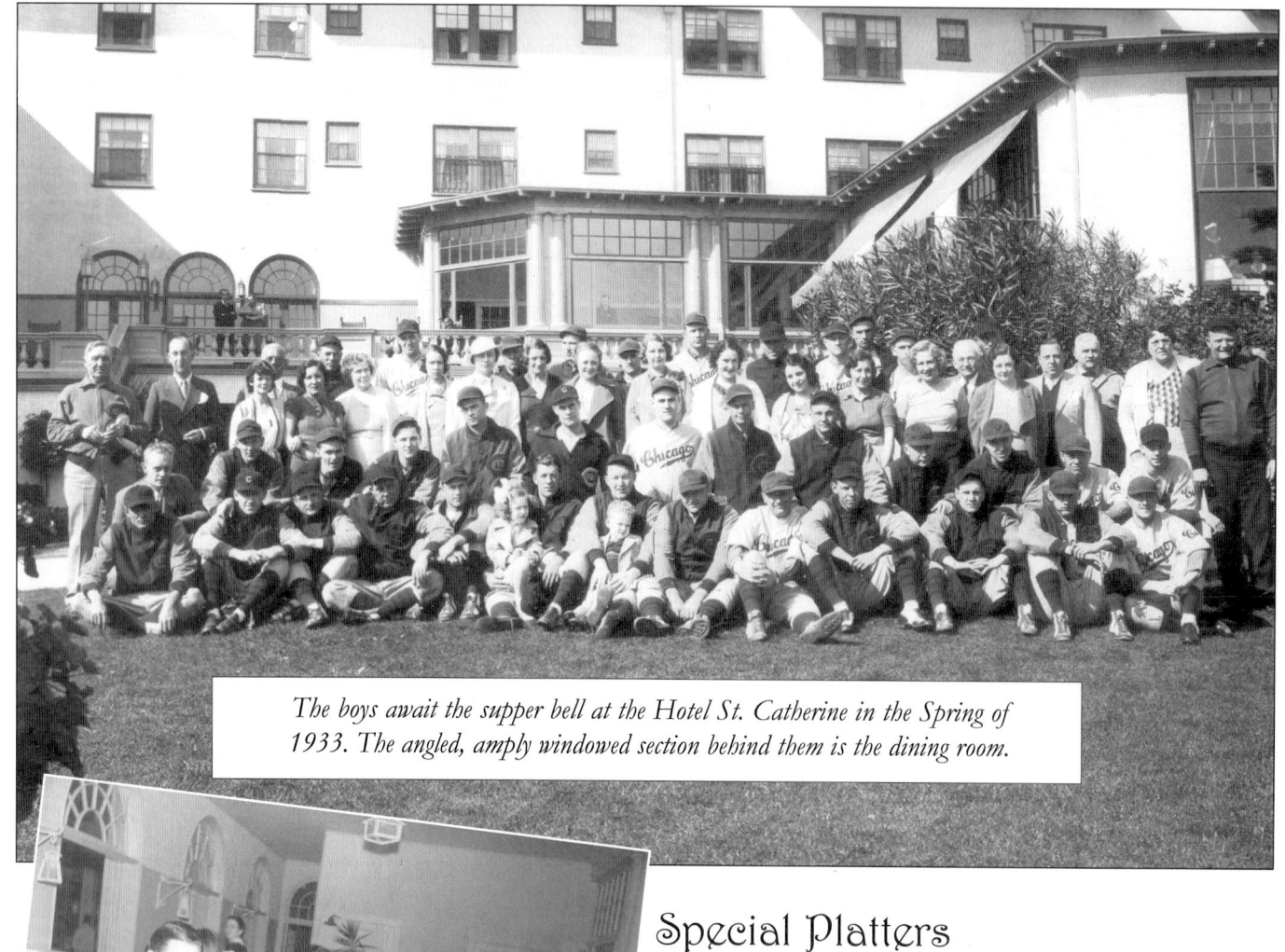

The boys await the supper bell at the Hotel St. Catherine in the Spring of 1933. The angled, amply windowed section behind them is the dining room.

Special Platters

Catalina was home to a world-famous Tile & Pottery works back then. The factory made for some pretty fun photo opportunities, and the boys were happy to oblige. The plant is long gone, though — replaced by a helicopter landing & alighting site — while the artifacts fetch big bucks on ebay.

Larry & Thelma French sample the St. Catherine cuisine with Jim Gleeson & galpal Dorothy Harris.

Pop Joiner, Bill Lee, & Ole Ward carefully approach a kiln.

When they didn't stay at the Hotel St. Catherine, some of the Cubbies ate fried chicken in their rooms at the Hotel Atwater — which, unlike the St. Catherine, is still standing & taking guests.

Pat Malone, Charlie Root, & Gabby Hartnett shop for mugs to give their wives.

Johnny Schmitz had to deal with the same financial restraints. "I got married in 1949," he says, but "I didn't bring my wife to Spring Training — I didn't make that kind of money like they do now."

"My wife came out in 1951," says Roy Smalley, Jr. "She liked Ellen Pafko a great deal — and Rube Walker's wife. They went down in Avalon and hit all the shops, go to the beach, sometimes watch the workouts. They went to the bird park, which was a nice nature study in those days. I think the pottery was still operating."

"I was married in 1947," Andy Pafko says, "and we lived just beyond the centerfield wall — it was like a 2nd honeymoon. The Smalleys, they were a real nice couple. Roy is a high-class person. We all hung out together. Our wives went shopping."

Fabulous families

Yes, some of the ballplayers brought their families along to Catalina. In fact, Billy Rogell's wife was responsible for him coming over. Detroit had traded him to Chicago, and "I was ready to quit in 1939," Billy says, "but my wife wanted to go to Catalina!" Even when camp ended and Billy hit the road, his family decided to stay behind. "After I left, Mum — I called her Mum — she spent a month there. We took our 2 boys out."

Claude Passeau says he'd go fishing or hunt some quail for dinner. "I'd cook the quail; one time, I cooked a boar," his wife, BUM, says. "We didn't have television, we barely had radio — we weren't bothered by anybody. We stayed in the little casitas, and we could walk right down to the beach. And of course, they were right next to the field. Every morning, they'd bring in fresh sweetpeas; it was wonderful."

Harriet Block, Cy's wife, also has fond memories of Catalina. "We were friends with the Merullos," she says. "We were entertained by Mrs. Wrigley at her home. We watched practice, then went to the club for lunch. We toured the island, we socialized. We liked to dance at the hotel."

"I married the girl next door in 1941," says Lennie Merullo. "We grew up together. The first few years, she didn't come out. You never made the money, so you always tried to save; you'd say, 'Maybe next year.' After the first couple of years, she got to come over."

Larry French shows Larry French the view from Catalina, 1940.

Bob Rush was a newlywed on Catalina, too. "We'd gotten married in November of the year before, so it was kind of like a honeymoon — it worked both ways! We stayed in a small place right next to the park. It was real nice, especially being so young. Basically, we'd walk around, go to a movie, take in the island — for us, it felt like a vacation. It was very relaxing. A couple of times, we took the glass-bottomed boat. Bert Wilson, who was the Cubs' announcer at that time, brought his wife. Our wives got to be good friends, and we went around together."

Bob Scheffing & Charlie Gilbert explain the ground rules to Bobby Jr. & Barbara Ann in 1947.

"My parents first stayed at the Casitas on their honeymoon in 1940," says Bob Scheffing, Jr. "They drove from Missouri, and zig-zagged all over. At their bungalow, my mother couldn't get the stove lit. She didn't realize you had to put 50 cents into it to get the gas started. She thought, oh, no, my husband's gonna think I don't know how to cook! So we laughed about that for years..."

Margaret Burgess, Smokey's widow, says, "We spent some time with the Jeffcoats and Chuck Connors. We'd go out to dinner sometimes, but mostly we'd do our own cooking — there weren't many places to go, and we didn't make that much money then. There was a zoo above the playing field, where they had all kinds of exotic birds. Or we'd go down to the beach. At the barbecues, it would be a player affair, a family-oriented thing. I made scrapbooks."

Bob Kelly had daddy duty. "The 2nd year, I had my family with me," he says. "I took the baby in a buggy, and we walked along the level part near the harbor, then up a craggly hill. With a baby, we were pretty busy. We did have some time to ourselves because my sister-in-law, Barbara, came along. We went on a boat ride, and she dove off. There were a lot of seals swimming in the water, and she tried to get back in the boat — but she had a difficult time doing it. I had to keep looking the other way, because her swimsuit almost kept coming off..."

Some of the players' kids got to come, too. Della Root Arnold says dad Charlie brought her out to Catalina for 14 seasons — and she remembers plenty of 'Penny Lane' images. "We stayed at the Hotel St. Catherine," says Della. "It was beautiful. They had a great big lobby with oriental rugs and big, soft furniture. They had a jewelry store and a little curio shop. The dining room was all glass, overlooking the ocean. Off to the left, they had this little room where the guests could play pool.

"We went to the bird farm with my brother Charles and Patsy Malone. When Charles was 6, and Patsy was 5 or 6, they went downtown by themselves, and when they came back they both had handfuls of these polished shells. Mother asked where they got them, and they told her they'd gathered them on the beach. But she knew — she'd seen the baskets in front of the stores — so she marched them back, but the store owner said they could keep them. They didn't take any more shells after that!

A few ballplayers posed with the Missus on Catalina in 1947. Red Adams' 3-year-old daughter, Lila, is sitting on Bettie's lap — with proud Daddy standing behind. The couples, left to right: Mr. & Mrs. Russ Bauers, Bob Chipman, Cy Block, Red Adams, Charlie Grimm, Lennie Merullo, & Ray Prim.

"In the morning, after breakfast, we'd go to the ballgames, and we we'd be out there until maybe one o'clock. They had mynah birds that would talk — this one bird named Jimmy would say, 'Wooshy, wooshy, anybody's laundry.' We'd go to the shops, and we were well-behaved — Dad would look at us with those beady blue eyes and say, 'I've spoken once, don't make me speak again.'"

Billy Herman got Billy Jr. to shag flies for him in 1938.

If only the *ballplayers* were as well-behaved as the kids while guests on Catalina; case in point, Woody English. "You can spot Woody," *Des Moines Dispatch* columnist Dutch Reagan wrote in 1937, "as the guy who slips up to the house dick, who doesn't know him, and mutters, 'What do you hear from the mob?'"

Odd couples

Like other ballclubs, the Cubs would usually try to pair a rookie with a veteran when it came time to assign roommates. The logic was, the old guy could teach the young kid something...and keep an eye on him, to keep him outa trouble...and the young guy's mere presence would keep the older guy in line, since he'd feel like he had to set an example. At least a little bit of an example.

"I roomed with Diz until his wife came out," Lefty Carnett remembers from 1939. "He kind of adopted me — we were both from Oklahoma — he'd go around after the rookies. He was one heck of a guy. After his arm was hurt, he pitched on his nerves, his guts. He was just an ol' country boy. I learned what a great competitor was — don't ever give up, period. All the guys always took time for the kids."

Apparently, not all roommates were as memorable as the great Dean. "I roomed with another rookie — I think he was from L.A.," says Al Epperly. The name? Lost for the ages...

The name combinations were sometimes amusing. Fuzzy Richards roomed with Monk Dubiel, for instance. As in, 'this is Fuzzy & Monk's room.'

If this ain't the cutest baseball picture of all time, we'll take nominations. Gabby Hartnett & Buddy.

There were occasional compatibility issues, as you might expect. "I was roomin' with Johnny Schmitz," Corky Van Dyke says, "but he smoked so much and spit a lot on the floor, so I asked to be removed from him. He was a nervous guy. Then I roomed with Warren Hacker. He's a good guy. I used to room with McLish. Cal was quite a character. He could throw left-handed and right handed, either way."

> "Lee Anthony was my roommate for half a year. He took a little suitcase on the road, and seemed to have a different outfit every day. Everybody wondered how he did it. His suits must've been reversible."
>
> Cal McLish

Lee Anthony is wearing one of his reversible Cub uniforms, which he crocheted himself.

The conversation could be lively. "Bobby Sturgeon was my roommate," Harvey Storey says. "Back in the room, we'd second-guess the starters, the way they acted."

And some roomies got to be lifelong friends — like Phil Cavarretta and Lennie Merullo. "We roomed together for 8 years," Lennie says. "We got along great. He had this way about him, he was hard to get to know, it took a little time. Grimm used to call us 'the Grand Opera Kids,' because we were both Italians, and both kinda small."

The Grand Opera Kids — roomies Merullo & Cavarretta.

"Merullo's a good friend," Cavy says — and Lennie had interesting shoes to fill, since one of Phil's previous roomies — Clay Bryant — dated movie star Grace Bradley. "They'd go to the Casino and dance."

In fact, Roy Smalley, Jr. met his wife because of his assigned roomate. "Jolene and I were married in 1950 — she's Gene Mauch's sister. Gene came to the Cubs in 1948 from Brooklyn. We were roommates and became friends, and that's how I met her."

> "My roommate? Carl Sawatski. He liked to eat. He'd eat most everything. You couldn't get anything past him."
>
> Lefty Sloat

"My very first roommate was a guy by the name of Andy Pafko," Bob Kelly says. "He'd been around — what a nice guy. He'd talk to his wife on the phone, and he'd call *her* 'Pruschka'!"

Mr. Pruschka lasted a while, so he ended up with additional roomies over time. And a coincidental selection: "My roommates were Johnny Schmitz, Rube Walker, and Bob Rush — the guys from the Norman Rockwell painting!" Andy says.

Lou Stringer was another roommate swapper — but in a slightly less conventional mode. "In 1941," Lou says, "I was young and single — my mother stayed with me. Mother and I were very close — she cooked for me. We went to that beautiful little church there, St. Michael's Catholic Church. We stayed at our own place, right next to the ballpark — Las Casitas. In 1946, my wife came out. We went dancing."

Corky Van Dyke studies up on batters' weaknesses in the Hotel Atwater during the Spring of 1950 — photography courtesy roommate Warren Hacker, who did not spit on the floor (which was a step up for Corky).

The ultimate Catalina odd couple award goes to Don Carlsen and Smalley. They both came out early to train, so they spent more time together in one of the cottages by the ballpark. "We were roommates at Las Casitas," Don says. "Smalley would cook — he was good at that, he kinda liked it. He'd cook, and I'd do the housekeeping."

"When we were out on Catalina rooming together," Roy says, "you know how with roommates there's always nonsense going on. We were sharing a casita. I started kidding him about brushing your teeth — when you first get up, or after breakfast. I said it doesn't make sense to do it before you eat, and he disagreed, and this banter went back and forth — and he said, 'You know, I've had this experience before with a friend in Denver, and it got stupid, and one day I knocked him on his rear end.' So I decided to end the tooth-brushing debate right there!"

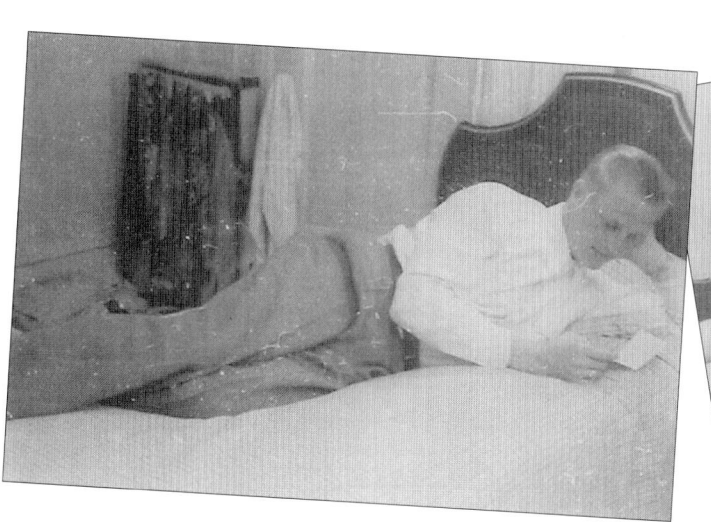

Warren Hacker models the accommodations, as photographed by shutterbug roomie Corky Van Dyke.

This is the Carlsen-Smalley house, still standing next to the field on Catalina — site of great debates regarding appropriate oral hygiene for athletes.

The Natives are Female!
Dames, Skirts, & Even an Occasional Broad

"Feminine companionship was nice to have, after being in the mountains with pigs and goats and buffaloes!"

Roy Smalley, Jr.

Ah, Springtime...when a young man's thoughts turn toward...

Since baseball is a game of statistics, we can imagine how many times a scene like this was repeated: Suppose it's a late February evening in 1935 at the Hotel St. Catherine. Two rookies have just checked into their room, and chat as they get settled in.

One mentions that he's heard there are about 3,000 residents of Avalon. He picks up the room's fountain pen and begins to scribble on a sheet of the hotel's letterhead. That would mean there are about 1,500 women...and say, they're aged from 0-90, that means...carry the 3...there are 16 women of each age — 16 18-year-olds, 16 19-year-olds, and so on. (Ballplayers were not allowed to use hand-held calculators in those days, don't forget — but it's okay, because they learned long division in school from scowling nuns who would hit their knuckles with a ruler if they did not turn in their assignments promptly.)

So if we take women between the ages of, um, 18 and, heck, let's go up to 30...that's 12 years times 16 women per year...that's 192 women in the eligible age range. Let's say 2/3 of 'em are married, and that leaves...64 single gals.

Now, there are 40 of us ballplayers, and 9 of the guys are married — leaving 31 single guys. But Hack tells all the dames he's not hitched, so let's say 32 guys will be chasing the 64 skirts.

The rookie who got a "B+" in elementary school math suddenly looks up with fire in his eyes: *That's two dolls for each of us, Lefty!*

Okay, okay — this is a non-fiction book, so enough of the surmising. But c'mon...don't tell me you doubt this conversation happened every year out on Catalina. Repeatedly.

Now, keep in mind, the '2-girls-for-every-boy' theory doesn't even count the band singers, the movie starlets, and the other tourist ladies from the mainland. But we'll get to that later. For now, we're gonna focus on Island girls...

A brochure from the roaring '20s.

Indeed, there were females on the Isle; here, Cubs Billy Herman, Jimmie Wilson, Dizzy Dean, & Larry French practice good public relations skills to benefit the Wm. Wrigley Company in 1941 . . . with Island belles Joan Johnson (Hard Rock's daughter), Peggy McKenzie, & Nancy Harris.

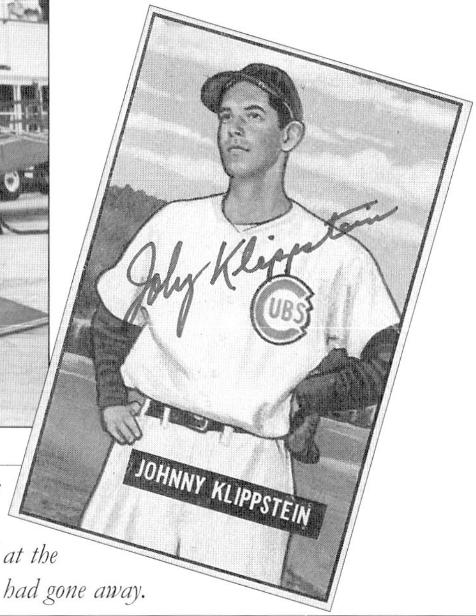

Johnny expresses frustration at learning the girl at the Port of Avalon had gone away.

"You couldn't get into trouble out there," Johnny Klippstein says. "I was single, and I dated one of the girls who worked at the recreation center there. We talked, we walked around the island — that was about it. We played some table tennis."

But even on a little island, things can change. "She wasn't there that 2nd year! I don't know what happened to her. So I had to be a loner! There was nobody on the island." Such a sad story — there must be a silver lining: "So, you could spend more time working on the fundamentals, more time training." Short-term pain for long-term gain: All that extra work paid off, since Johnny ended up as one of the last 2 Catalina Cubs still playing in the big leagues, nearly 2 decades later, in 1967.

Roy Smalley spent a winter on the island, doing ranch work in the hills — nearly qualifying as a local himself. Pitcher Don Carlsen came out before the rest of the team, and the 2 bachelors shared a cottage at Las Casitas — right next to the ballfield.

"We met a couple of local girls," Roy says. "There wasn't a heck of a lot to do. Feminine companionship was nice to have after being in the mountains with pigs and goats and buffaloes!

"It was strictly a local romance. They'd entertained us in their apartment one evening — one worked for the Island Company. They cooked dinner for us. It was a nice casual relationship, certainly a relief for me. The Casino wasn't open then — just a couple of the local bars. We could do some dancing in the apartment, but it was small."

"We followed Roy Smalley around," says Islander Frank Saldaña, who was just a kid at the time, "and there were these famous pro golfers out on the course. We could see Roy out there, having fun with the girls, talking to 'em, flirting, trying to go out with 'em."

Whilst checking in at the Hotel St. Catherine, Gabby Hartnett wonders if local gal Allison Gildner generally dresses like that for the local guys, too.

But after Roy's 1st year or so on Catalina, the action would be limited to the field. "Don knew Gene Mauch — Gene had played for Don's dad on a kids' team. The first time I heard my wife's name, Don and I were both at Pepperdine. He'd known Joelene — she's Gene Mauch's sister — and asked her for a date. That's how I got to know her. She and I were married in 1950."

Okay, so Mauch and Carlsen conspired to take one of their mates out of circulation. That's okay — there were still plenty of other Cubs out at sea.

"I dated one of the 3 or 4 girls on the island."

Johnny Klippstein

"I'm not going to say I was a saint," Randy Jackson confessed in *Banks to Sandberg to Grace*, "but at least I went home at a reasonable hour. I was prone to stay out all night when things weren't going too good. I think there was one time when the season started and I was hitting every ball on the nose and wasn't getting any hits. I stayed out all night long and I started getting some hits after that.

"It was the old-timers playing back in the '40s who did a lot of staying out late. Most of the younger guys were pretty conscientious. It's nice to go out occasionally; you can't go from a game to home. It was a different story if you had a family."

But Al Epperly bit the dust, too. "I went out with a gal who lived on the island," Pard says. "We went swimming, and fishing, and we'd go to the shows. I only went out with her the one year, because I got married the next year."

Imagine if he'd been wearing a uniform! Coach Grover Alexander shows off his penmanship skills for the local ladies.

Ripper Collins provides complimentary batting instructions to Catalina resident Kay Todd — a public service, on behalf of major league baseball.

"I was single then," Don Dunker says, "But there weren't too many girls out there. Once you get into the pro leagues, you have to keep good care of yourself! Most of the guys out there were pretty straight-laced, getting ready to play."

Most, not all.

"One of the local guy's nieces dated Hack Wilson," says the Barber of Avalon, Lolo Saldaña, "but she didn't tell anybody. When I heard about it, I asked her what he was like. She said, 'He was the worst date and the biggest drunk I ever met in my life!'"

> Chuck Connors related his conversation with Mr. Rickey: "Chuck, do you run around with fast women?"
>
> "No, sir."
>
> "Do you drink hard liquor?"
>
> Chuck swears he answered, "Mr. Rickey, if I have to drink to play for you, I want to be traded." Later he was traded to the Cubs.
>
> Carl Erskine, in *Tales from the Dodger Dugout*

"They had their fun," agrees brother and fellow barber Frank. "They like to have a few bottles, but they were in Spring Training. They'd look for girls, but they had their curfews."

Curfews, eh? Weren't curfews, like other training rules, meant to be broken?

"I was waiting for the June League to start," says Hub Kittle — who pitched batting practice for the Chicago Cubs on Catalina in the spring, then stayed on with the semi-pro Catalina Cubs. "We stayed at the cabañas by the ballpark. Doc Brooks used to check us in every night by flashlight, at 11 p.m. We'd be down at the Casino, and we'd dance until a quarter 'til — then we'd race to see who could get back 1st so we'd make our bed check. All the ballplayers would meet the gals by the 18th tee — we'd sneak back out."

Hub Kittle (next to Hank Majeski & Lefty Logan's right arm in 1938) is supposed to be listening to the coach, but he's thinking about the dame he met at the Casino the night before.

"Out there, we had a curfew and they did a bed check," recalls Corky Van Dyke. "I never did get caught, although I did go with some of them dollies. Some of the girls from L.A. would come over."

After the Cubs sent Corky over to play for the Los Angeles Angels, he maintained his interest in local talent — and of course, there were a few more girls across the channel. "A lot of big stars would come to the park in L.A. and in Hollywood. Bing Crosby, Lauren Bacall, Humphrey Bogart. I was just a punk kid then, straight off the farm. We had a lotta fun — it was a good life. I made about $15,000 a year in those days. I met some of the extras, the girls who worked in the movies, and some of us dated a few of them."

Charlie Grimm gets acquainted with Mary Gibson, Joan Johnson (yep, Hard Rock's daughter again), & Maxine Weisel.

"They'd take pictures of girls in bathing suits with the ballplayers," Ken Weafer recalls. "We were the single guys, so they brought us out there. I made a date with one of 'em, but I broke it to go out with another one of those starlets that came over. But she got a note to go back to the studio, so I called the 1st one. She said, 'As long as you're on this Island, you'll never have another date with me!'"

Of course, some of the local Avalon gals made it big. Norma Jean Dougherty was a teen bride living on Catalina during the war (when the Cubs were training in the Midwest) but the Catalina Cub team still worked out occasionally. "I got pictures of Marilyn Monroe — out on Catalina. She was a good ball fan, she came to the park," Kittle says. Unfortunately for all the boys, Norma Jean was hitched during her Catalina stay; her husband was actually stationed on the Island.

Norma Jean Dougherty, when she was a local Avalon girl — before she picked up her alliterative nickname and married a ballplayer who was with the New York Yankees.

Since the boys didn't have cable in those days, they didn't necessarily recognize stars — so they couldn't always tell 'em apart from locals. Clay Bryant dated an actress and Phil Cavarretta played ping-pong with another, among the more notable path-crossings. But you'll have to wait 'til chapter 14 for all the juicy details.

"There was this Greek guy on the island who had a restaurant," Yosh Kawano recalls. "He asked me, 'How do I get more business?' I told him he needed to have girls in there. He got this waitress, but she wasn't very nice to me. She just ignored me!"

Yosh says most of the players weren't there long enough to meet girls, but there were a few exceptions. "August Galan, he was a great guy — kind of a ladies' man."

Bud Smith, who grew up to become Mayor of Avalon says, "A lot of them were single, and of course good-looking — some of them dated my wife. Louie Stringer, Paul Erickson."

"We'd just hang around, go to Sportland — it was good clean fun," says Marie Smith, defending herself.

"I was going with one of the ballplayers, Dan Haley," recalls Florence Johnson Hamlin, who graduated from Avalon High in 1931. "He was a rookie. My sister went with another of them. We'd go out together. We'd go to the Casino, and they had a Pavilion where they had those games — you'd put a quarter in — and a bowling alley. We went down and watched them play. After they left, we wrote letters."

One of Florence's friends also dated a Cub. "We'd go down after school to watch them practice," Helen Ross recalls. "All the high school girls, we liked to see the rookies...becuase they were more our age. We got to talking with them — they were very nice, very friendly."

Helen worked at the Casino when it opened, and also got to go out with a young pitcher there: "Right before the team would leave, they'd have a beautiful, beautiful dance at the Casino," she recalls. "It was very formal. One of the rookies, Malcolm Moss, invited me in 1930. We won a prize, doing the 2-step — but I didn't even know what the 2-step was! We won a picture of the Island, which I still have."

Mal Moss was still so fired up about dating an Avalon gal that he went out and threw a no-hitter in the Pacific Coast League the next season.

"My sister Tina used to date Cal McLish," says local Foxie Saucedo. "They'd go to the movies."

"She was about 21, 22," recalls other brother, Marcelino. "My sister was pretty square. They went bowling, they went to the show. There were a lot of girls who dated the ballplayers — a lot of groupies would come over from the mainland, and hang out at the ballpark. Catalina is the island of romance."

"I was single when I came out in 1946, but I didn't date any of the local girls. I'm kinda the bashful type."

Andy Pafko, who was anything *but* bashful with N.L. pitching

The front grounds at the team hotel were well-known for providing pleasant views of indigenous species . . .

. . . but watch out, ladies! Jolly Cholly Grimm decided to give the local bathing beauties a run for their money out on Descanso Beach in '47 — striking quite a pose himself.

Dutch

How a Plucky Young Radio Man Parlayed His Catalina Trip into a Career in Hollywood... & Another in Washington

"Jimmy Cork...took a swing at the man from Des Moines, who ducked. The Cork's punch landed in the expansive midriff of Ed Burns. The target he missed was the kid from Iowa...Ronald Reagan."

Charlie Grimm, describing a typically relaxing Springtime evening on quiet Catalina Island

Back in 1936 and 1937, it wasn't too unusual for young journalists to accompany the Cubs to Catalina.

What might be considered a wee bit out of the ordinary, though, was that one of 'em would eventually become the President of the United States.

Dutch Reagan was a radio announcer for WHO in Des Moines back then. (He also wrote a column in the defunct *Des Moines Dispatch*, called *Around the World of Sports with Dutch Reagan*). And he was ambitious enough to talk his way out of a Midwestern winter...and onto the Cubs train to Catalina.

While there, he interviewed the players... sweet-talked Charlie Grimm into letting him suit up and practice with the team a few times...and snuck back to the mainland for a screen test with Warner Bros.

And oh yeah, he got himself into a barroom brawl, too.

But first, the baseball.

Dutch Reagan, a great communicator in the early '30s.

"Dutch would put on a uniform and work out from time to time," recalls Della Root Arnold, Charlie Root's daughter. Her dad got to toss Reagan a few slowballs.

"He thought he could hit!" Phil Cavarretta laughs. "Two or three times, he came and suited up and worked out with us. How good was he? Well, ya know — like we say in Italian, '*Mangia-mangia*.'* His performance wasn't very good. He fractured a bat. The batting-practice pitcher didn't put too much on the ball — Grimm told him, 'Don't hurt the guy!' Charlie Grimm was a happy guy, and he liked Reagan. So he made an agreement with him: If you get hurt, you're on your own — you can't sue the club!

"He had what I call a 'slow bat.' We kinda teased him on that. That was what I liked about him: He was the kind of person you could joke with, and he'd take it in a proper manner."

---

* Phil is being figurative. The term means, "Eat, feast, enjoy," — but here, it's more like, "Go for it, dude...keep tryin', fatten up so you'll be big and strong."

To Join Cubs

RONALD "DUTCH" REAGAN

Announcer for radio station WHO, Des Moines, who will leave that city Saturday morning for Catalina Island. He has been assigned by the station management to spend the next six weeks at the training camps of the Chicago Cubs and White Sox baseball teams, according to word received by his parents, Mr. and Mrs. J. E. Reagan this morning. He will be with the two Chicago teams during their spring training season and then accompany one of the teams on the return trip to Chicago, gathering material for his regular summer broadcast of the major league games.

"We used to tease him a lot," Yosh Kawano says, "just kidding around."

"He was just the greatest guy," Della recalls. "All the Cub players really liked him, and certainly no one thought when we were joking around that our young friend would become President."

Cavarretta adds, "He said to me, 'Phil, why don't you come out a little early in the morning and help me out? Please, Phil, show me some tips!'"

"I was ball-shy at batting," Dutch recalled years later. "When I stood at the plate, the ball appeared out of nowhere about two feet in front of me. I was always the last chosen for a side in any game."

"He was blind as a bat," says Norman Wymbs, Chairman, Ronald Reagan Boyhood Home Restoration Foundation. "He had very poor eyesight. He couldn't see very well — that's why he took up swimming, because you didn't have to see. You could just go back and forth, back and forth in the pool. He really wanted to play baseball, but there was no place they could put him!"

"Yeah, I remember Reagan being out there," growls Hub Kittle, one of the batting practice pitchers that Grimm had told to toss gently. Al Epperly received the same chucking orders.

"I remember Dutch Reagan, because he was from my home town," says Al. "He was broadcasting the games in Iowa. We talked a lot about 'back home.' I threw to him, but not hard. He was a nice guy. Us rookies, we weren't out with the big shots. We'd play pool, go swimming, go fishing."

Dutch came out with the team for the first time in 1936. "I was the only radio man there," he recalled later — as you can see in this photo, where he's reaching down to adjust his equipment behind the microphone tripod (while the more dominant newsreels whir away). Stan Hack, interviewed for the fans back home later that day, takes a healthy cut in the foreground.

"The Iowa winters...were beginning to give me a yen for warmth and sunshine and make me a collector of travel folders. I did some sharp figuring and talked the station into the idea that if they would put up the money, I would put up the time — and my vacation could be spent accompanying the Chicago Cubs on their training trip to Catalina Island. I made quite a pitch about what this would do for me in filling me with color and atmosphere for the coming baseball season. It worked."

Ronald Reagan, *My Early Life*, 1965

Reagan did take advantage of the Island's many recreational benefits. "I was really having a vacation, riding horses, boating, and seeing the Catalina scenery," he wrote in his 1965 autobiography. Yet it wasn't always easy to manage a steed on those narrow mountain trails — which he mentioned in one of his 1937 newspaper columns. "Of course," young Dutch wrote, "there is the small matter of getting off one mountain and onto the next."

In fact, his first attempt at vacationing on Catalina didn't quite go right. "The day I arrived was really unusual weather," he recalled. "It was a record-breaking 82 degrees in February. I, of course, assumed it was just standard. I wasn't in the hotel in Catalina 10 minutes before, clad in trunks, I was running out to the end of the pier. I dived into the coldest water that was still liquid that I've ever known.

"Awe-struck natives watched me as if I were from outer space, and I rewarded them. I swear I didn't swim — I walked ashore on top of the waves."

And he teased the girls. "At that time, polo coats were the rage," smiles Della, then a teenager. "They were big wrap-around coats — it was the new big thing. Mother dressed us to kill. I had two — a camel's hair one, and a white one. Dutch was teasing me about it — he asked, 'Where'd you get that coat?'

"He took us all to the ship when we left and waved goodbye. The 2nd year, his mother Nelle came out. I sat next to her on the ship on the way to the island. She was a very nice lady, very tiny. We talked about Illinois, about the Midwest; Mother had grown up on a farm, so we had a lot in common. She had a little hat on that was all flowers."

Actually, Dutch almost never made it over in 1937. He arrived in Los Angeles during a stormy few days, and chose to miss the boat. The seaplane ride over the whitecaps alarmed him enough that he refused to fly again for years afterward.

"I have very fond memories of Catalina Island..."

Dutch Reagan

Once he made it over, he got to work. "Ronald Reagan did the broadcasting back then, and once in a while, he'd do interviews before the ballgame," Phil Cavarretta says. "One day out on Catalina, he came up to me, and I didn't know who he was, and somebody told me what he was doing. He was a real nice guy, very polished in his mannerisms. I thought, 'My gosh, this guy's good-looking.' And I liked the fact he wasn't looking for dirt, like a lot of these guys were. So he interviewed me a couple times."

"The Cubs were at the top of the heap in those days," President Reagan told *Inside Sports* magazine in 1981. "Two or three times while I was broadcasting, they won the pennant."

Reagan had graduated from Eureka College in Illinois in 1932, seven years after the Cubs began broadcasting their games. In December, he landed a job at WOC in Davenport, Iowa. The next April, WOC merged with WHO of Des Moines. He moved there to be WHO's chief sports announcer. One of his responsibilities was to re-create Chicago Cub games, using information from telegraph reports and sound effects. Occasionally, a little extra creativity was needed, too: In 1934, the wire went dead in the middle of a Cubs-Cardinals contest...with Augie Galan at the plate.

"I had a ball on the way to the plate and there was no way to call it back," Dutch recalled years later. "So, I had Augie foul this pitch down the left field line. He fouled for 6 minutes and 45 seconds. My voice was riding in pitch and threatening to crack — and then, bless him, Curly started typing. I clutched at the slip. It said: 'Galan popped out on the 1st ball pitched.'"

See the happy smile? Augie's wrists were well-rested by the time he posed for this Topps card, some 20 years after fouling off pitches for 6-7 minutes in Dutch's vivid imagination.

Things tended to go a little more smoothly on Catalina, where Dutch spoke into a massive microphone and recorded the action onto phonograph records. In Edmund Morris' biography, *Dutch*, there's a transcript of a Reagan interview with trainer Andy Lotshaw: "Excuse me, Andy, I want to see Charlie Root over here. Say, Charlie, I noticed today you kept refusing Stephenson's signs. Did that mean he was calling them wrong?"

Although Reagan was also a print journalist, the crusty old newspapermen didn't exactly welcome the kid with open arms.

"Like any rookie, I was due for some hazing," he wrote rather diplomatically in *My Early Life*. "Some of it was good-natured, some of it was unkind. I was the only radio man there and the newspapermen had an understandable amount of resentment. The ball players, the fellows I really wanted to know, took no part in this hazing and, as a matter of fact, included me in their activities — I think mainly because they are wary of sports writers as actors are wary of critics. It was a case of any victim of the writers being automatically a friend."

Charlie Grimm was a bit more candid in his own autobiography.

The most spectacular incident in the White Cap occurred when the Cubs were getting ready for the 1937 season...A handsome young man bearing the credentials of WHO...joined our jolly press group that Spring. The press table, down at the field, wasn't more than 12 feet long, but this fellow, arriving early, grabbed at least half of the space...The Chicago writers took a dim view. What was this guy doing there, crowding them out? In those days, the newspaper reporters looked on all radio announcers, even if they were nice people, as interlopers. Who did they think they were, barging in like this? I had seen this show of hostility many years before in Chicago...They told the people, with their typewriters, the game's story. Now, this strange breed had invaded the scene, and they resented it.

The reporters were indignant. Warren Brown and Ed Burns gave him a baleful glance. And so did Jimmy Corcoran, a little red-thatched Irishman who was everybody's friend.

That night, in a gathering of the clan in the White Cap, this man from WHO showed up. There were words, and Jimmy Cork, who would have to eat a stalk of bananas to make the lightweight limit, went into action. He took a swing at the man from Des Moines, who ducked. The Cork's punch landed in the expansive midriff of Ed Burns. The target he missed was the kid from Iowa...Ronald Reagan.

"Those are some great human beings," Phil Cavarratta says, dripping with sincerity. "Ed Burns, he was a great writer. Warren Brown, he was good too. The articles they wrote — they were tough! They all thought we should play like Ruth and Gehrig. They'd bury you if they didn't like you. I don't know what the press would do — I didn't stay up that late. A lot of 'em were freeloaders. You'd buy 'em a drink, and they'd write good things about you."

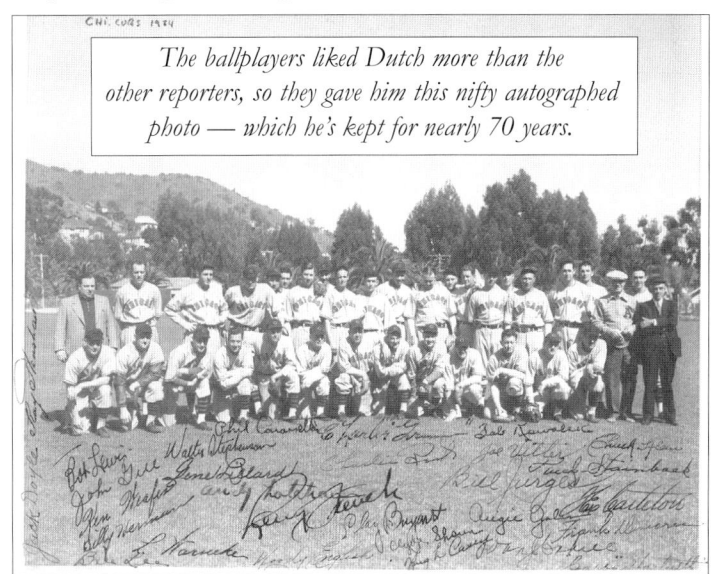

The ballplayers liked Dutch more than the other reporters, so they gave him this nifty autographed photo — which he's kept for nearly 70 years.

The way the reporters felt about Dutch was apparent in their 1936-1938 dispatches from the Catalina trips. Since there really was no news to report for 2 solid months each season, they got to write puff pieces about anything and everything — from Grimm's banjo playing to who won that night's card game to every hangnail suffered on the field. And they showered each other with ink, too — so it's rather telling that there is no mention of Reagan by name — even in 1938, where it seemed their joking might naturally include wondering who'd be the next movie star to emerge from the group. The closest anybody came to actually acknowledging their 2-month traveling companion:

"(En route to California with the Cubs, March 9) — Nineteen Cubs and their accompanying galaxy of scribes, radio announcers, club officials and addicts pushed through the desert, Catalina-bound, today — under the protective wing of Herr Charlie Grimm." (John Hoffman, in the *Chicago Times*):

"Newspaper and radio men and Dan Cahill (Chicago's No. 1 Cubs and fire fan) and wives accompanied the party." (Corcoran, in the *American*).

Even more telling: In 1938, Ed Cochrane of the *American* mentioned that "radio announcer Pat Flanagan" was en route.

But he didn't have time to worry about popularity contests at the Chicago Press Club — Dutch Reagan was a young man in a hurry. From Catalina, he called Joy Hodges — a singer-actress from Des Moines, who he'd interviewed on WHO — and he asked her for some help in breaking into the movies.

Back in 1936 & 1937, when Dutch was out on Catalina, you could get a mini-pennant like this with a piece of candy.

"One day on Catalina, Charlie Grimm, the Cubs' manager, bawled me out for not even showing up at the practice field," Reagan wrote. "How could I tell him that somewhere within myself was the knowledge I would no longer be a sports announcer?"

Joy introduced him to her agent, George Ward of the Meiklejohn Agency — who also represented stars like Betty Grable and Jane Wyman. George scheduled 2 screen tests. The first, at Paramount, never happened; the studio kept him waiting, but he had to broadcast a Cubs exhibition game. He got up and walked out. The 2nd was with Warner Bros. It went well, but Dutch left on the train the next day.

"I had come to like Reagan," Jolly Cholly wrote. "A few days after the White Cap caper, Ron came around to say goodbye. He was leaving the Magic Isle to take a movie test. At first, I didn't think he was serious, but Bob Lewis took him over to the boat dock after practice. And that's the last I saw of Ronald Reagan."

Back home, Dutch got a telegram from his agent:

> **WARNER'S OFFER CONTRACT 7 YEARS, 1 YEAR'S OPTION, STARTING AT $200 A WEEK. WHAT SHALL I DO?**
>
> **BILL MEIKLEJOHN**

"I tore the envelope open, read the first line, and threw all the rest of my mail away," he told the *Dixon Evening Telegraph*. "Reagan also leaped about three feet in the air and let out an Indian war-whoop, those who were standing nearby said. 'I admit that it's got my head spinning like a top,' he said."

Years later, in his own account, Reagan explained: "I wrote back, SIGN BEFORE THEY CHANGE THEIR MINDS — and then I yelled."

His first role at Warners, appropriately enough, was as a brash radio announcer...in *Love is in the Air*."

After he left, though, the Cubbies did manage to fill the radio booth again. Jack Brickhouse joined the team in 1941 — and stayed on for more than 40 seasons. Bert Wilson, legendary WIND announcer in the '40s and '50s, once said, "I don't care who wins, as long as it's the Cubs." And of course, in later years, there was Harry Caray. Today, Joe Carter and Chip Caray (grandson of Harry) call the games for WGN-TV, while Ron Santo and Pat Hughes handle the mike for Cubs radio.

JACK BRICKHOUSE
WGN-TV

BERT WILSON
WIND

Dutch, now Ronald (Ronnie to his friends), portraying Grover Cleveland Alexander at Wrigley Field/L.A. in 1952.

Let's go to the movies

And so a star was born — although his name was generally on the marquee of 'B' movies rather than the major releases. Still...he was a genuine-article Hollywood star. And he maintained his ties to the game. In 1946, for instance, he was the emcee at the annual Association of Professional Baseball Players banquet, at the Biltmore Bowl — where Joy Hodges had been performing in 1937. He shared the stage with Abbott & Costello, Roy Rogers, Jimmy Durante, and other Hollywood 1st-stringers.

"I knew Ronald Reagan had a close association with the Cubs," says Red Adams, "because after we went back to L.A., we'd have a big dinner at the Biltmore Hotel, a special occasion. And I can remember Ronald Reagan being there. Somebody, one of the old-timers, spoke — Charlie Grimm was a great storyteller. Bob Lewis, the traveling secretary, talked about Reagan, introduced him — he talked about how they used to call him Dutch. I always liked him, he seemed like a nice guy."

He was a family friend of the Wrigleys. "I met Ronald Reagan at the Biltmore in Arizona, when he was on his honeymoon," says Blanny Wrigley Schreiner, PK's daughter. "I'd gone to the Latin school in Chicago with Nancy Davis. Dad let Ronnie and Nancy use one of the cabañas — they were staying at the one next to ours. Years later, we'd all go to the campfires together at the Biltmore. Patty was about the same age as my daughter Blanny; Ron was a baby then. All the kids would have skits, and sing, and we'd have a hayride. I think that was the last time I saw him, during one of those campfires."

"I got to meet Ronald Reagan," Don Carlsen recalls. "I had a whirlpool with him. I was pitching for L.A., and he was in Hollywood, and we had the same doctor. I'd hurt my arm, and he hurt his ankle, and we were in the office at the same time one day. So we were in the whirlpool, and we got to talk."

When he wasn't acting or taking a dip in the hot tub, Dutch — now Ronald — was already dabbling with his next career choice, politics.

"I first met Ronnie Reagan when I was doing a picture off the coast of California, on Catalina Island," Gene Autry later told the Screen Actors Guild. "He came out because he was announcing ball games for the Chicago Cubs and they held their spring training on the Island. So he spent the day out there with me and my band. He said, 'Gene, this actor's union intrigues me. How do you go about getting in it?' He became head of the Screen Actors Guild and held that position for a long time."

The real Mrs. Grover Alexander (middle) makes sure the artificial Mrs. Alexander (Doris Day) smiles properly when accompanied by the artificial Mr. Alexander (Dutch).

"I got to know Ronald Reagan and Bill Frawley** out at the banquets in L.A.," says Lefty Chambers. "I talked to Reagan several times, just small talk. All the stars came to those: Bob Hope, Esther Williams, Danny Kaye. Frawley was a big baseball fan. One time we were talking — he always talked out of the side of his mouth, like he did on *I Love Lucy* — and he told me Reagan was the most respected man in Hollywood. I asked why. He said because he was the president of the Screen Actors' Guild, and that was the toughest job in the world — because actors are the screwiest people in the world. That's why he was so highly respected, as an administrator. That was really the start of his being an administrator, when he ran the actors' union."

** William Frawley was a co-owner of the Pacific Coast League's Hollywood Stars, cross-town rivals of Wrigley's L.A. Angels. Later, when the major leagues came to town, Frawley became a director of the American League version of the L.A. Angels.

But professional politics was still a ways off — this acting thing was a little too fun. In fact, he got to play a Catalina Cub in the 1952 flick, *The Winning Team* — the story of pitcher Grover Cleveland Alexander. His co-star was Doris Day, who later starred in *The Glass-Bottom Boat*...which was set on Catalina.

The movie was filmed at Wrigley Field in L.A., of all places, and included several big-league ballplayers: Bob Lemon, Jerry Priddy, George Metkovich, Irv Noren, Al Zarilla, and 3 Catalina Cubs (Hank Sauer, Gene Mauch, and Peanuts Lowery).

Dutch, as Alex, arrayed in Cub garb.

Lowery was the player that plunked Reagan with a ball between the eyes as he ran for 2nd in one scene. "We used a cotton ball...when I hit him, I shouted, 'Look out!'" P-nuts said in *The New Era Cubs*. "But the director said, 'Cut!' He figured I'd get an extra $350 for having a speaking role so we reshot the scene; after I hit Reagan, I had to look sad and keep my face down as Reagan was sprawled on the ground. I looked plenty sad, thinking of the lost $350."

Lemon, a Hall-of-Fame pitcher and later a manager for teams like the Yankees, Kansas City Royals, and the Pacific Coast League Sacramento Solons, helped Reagan with some baseball moves. "He was very graceful and east to teach," Lemon recalled. "I had this little quirk in my own motion where I did a little hop after I released the ball so I would be in position to field a ball hit back at me. By the time they started shooting the movie, Reagan was doing exactly the same thing."

Besides Alexander, other old Catalina Cubs were portrayed in the film — including Bill and Margaret Killefer...and Rogers Hornsby.

Reagan's final acting connection to Catalina, it seems, took place in 1961 — when he appeared in an episode of *Zane Grey Theater* — advancing the reputation of the long-time Catalina resident novelist.

More career changes

In 1965, he decided to give writing another try, apparently — publishing his autobiography. The next year, he decided to become Governor of Catalina Island and the Rest of California. Unlike the reprised writing career, which only lasted one year, he stayed on in Sacramento for 8 seasons. While there, he occasionally took side trips to San Francisco, Oakland, and Los Angeles to throw out first pitches or simply attend ballgames.

Unfortunately, he was too busy to make regular pilgrimages back to Catalina. "No, he never took us out there," says eldest son Michael Reagan, now a radio talk-show host himself. "We never went. Yeah, you'd think we might have gone over."

Former radioman/slow-batted ballplayer/actor/author Ronald Reagan, Governor of Catalina Island & the Rest of California, discusses career options with Joe DiMaggio, former fisherman/ballplayer who was then a Coach for the Oakland A's, 1968.

He liked to kid about his baseball past — but not everybody always got the joke. Tip O'Neill told this story, but seemed to miss the light-heartedness: "He's sitting over there (by his desk in the Oval Office) and says, 'Hey, Grover Cleveland. I played him in the movies.' I said no, you played Grover Cleveland Alexander, the baseball player. And then I knew the nation was in tough shape from that moment on."***

"He was a great fan of Dad's," Della says. "When Dad died, he sent a nice letter to us, saying Dad was his favorite player. And when the Hall of Fame players came to the White House when he was President, he asked, 'Anybody got a Charlie Root card?'"

"Nostalgia bubbles within me and I might have to be dragged away," Reagan said that day. And at a 1983 Old-Timers Game, he said, "This is really more fun than being President. I really do love baseball and I wish we could do this on the lawn every day."

"I think the President enjoyed this visit even more that we did," said Joltin' Joe DiMaggio, who saw then-Governor Reagan occasionally while DiMag was coaching for the Oakland A's in the late '60s.

"I wouldn't even complain if a stray ball came through the Oval Office window now and then," the Prez commented once.

Trouble was, Gorbachov was always calling or something, so the President only made it to 4 games while in the White House: 3 Orioles contests, including the 1983 World Series, and one magical afternoon at Wrigley Field in Chicago...

After all those career changes and name changes, Dutch/Ronnie/Mr. President/whoever re-lives fond Catalina memories with a snowball in 1986 — exactly 50 years after his first trip to the Island.

"Ronald Reagan and I became good buddies through the years," Della Root Arnold says. "I was active in politics in California when he was Governor. When we lived in Lancaster, he was going to be the speaker at our Chamber of Commerce dinner. When I was introduced to him, I reminded him that I was Charlie Root's daughter. He pulled me off to the side as everyone came by to be introduced, and talked to me between all the introductions!"

Dutch finally retired in 1974, replaced by Jerry 'Moonbeam' Brown — unusual that 2 back-to-back governors would *both* have cool nicknames. But Dutch/Ronald got restless again, and in 1980 he applied to become leader of the free world. His application was accepted.

Dutch finally achieved every ballplayer's dream in 2002:

He appeared on a Topps card (outfitted in Cub regalia, no less). Unfortunately, due to budget cuts announced during his 2nd administration, he had to share his rookie card with a piece of an old wooden chair.

*** Reagan, later: "There are some things that are current today and sweeping the country...that I haven't had time to get familiar with. Pac-Man, for example. I asked about it, and somebody told me it was a round thing that gobbled up money. I thought that was Tip O'Neill!"

After a 52-year absence, Dutch made it back to the booth to call a Cubs game... with none other than Harry Caray.

Just 4 months before Reagan left office (on Sept. 30, 1980), the Cubs lost to the Pirates, 10-9. Nothing new there. But the headlines that day were the fact that the President of the United States threw out the 1st pitch (or a pair of 1st pitches, actually)...and the fact that the old Cubs broadcaster climbed back into the booth to broadcast an inning and a half. (The year before, he had phoned in and chatted with Harry Caray, on-air, during a game.)

"You know," he said over the airwaves from the Wrigley Field press box, "in a few months I'm going to be out of work and I thought I might as well audition."

"You could tell he was an old radio guy," Harry mused. "He never once looked at the TV monitor."

Other Presidents on Catalina

Dutch Reagan was neither the first — nor the last — American president to land on Catalina soil. There were several others, in fact.

The Cub/Chief Executive connection goes way back. William Wrigley and his initial partners bought the Cubs in 1916 from William Howard Taft's brother, Charles. Herbert Hoover attended the 1929 World Series, and Franklin Roosevelt came by the old ballyard in 1932.

Warren Harding was actually on his way down to visit the Wrigleys on Catalina in 1923, but he got sick in San Francisco and died first.

Hoover visited the Island both before...and after... his highly-successful 1-term presidency.

And Calvin Coolidge came over in 1930 — actually sitting in on a practice session, against his will.

Warren Harding planned on being the first U.S. president to visit Catalina Island, but he died first and got to appear on a postage stamp instead.

Jimmy the Cork, who later took a barroom swing at a man who would eventually replace Cal, described the Cubs' arrival in the *American*:

"C'mon down and see the Cubs come in," said Bill to the ex-President.

"New additions to your zoo?" mused Coolidge.

"No, the Cubs are my favorite sporting enterprise," corrected Bill.

"But I am not interested in football," said Coolidge, without batting an eye.

Mrs. Coolidge, however, accompanied Mr. & Mrs. Wrigley to the docks to see the athletes. Mrs. Coolidge waved her hand at the boys.

Meanwhile, the ex-President remained in the study of the Wrigley shanty at the top of the mountain. Nearby goats nibbled at the shrubbery, but Coolidge showed little or no interest.

The former President is not a baseball fan. You can bet your spats on that. However, we're not picking on Coolidge. Any man who was forced to do the catching for some of the senatorial washouts for seven years should be overstuffed on all manner of sport and those connected with it.

Mrs. Coolidge was actually a big baseball fan — a lifetime Red Sox supporter in her native New England.

President Coolidge preferred to discuss the relative merits of chewing gum with his host, rather than whether or not a curve ball actually curves or not.

Two-score and one years later, after the Cubs had ceased to visit Avalon, Dick Nixon stopped by. RM came by with daughter Tricia and non-mobster pal Bebe Rebozo of Miami for a quick peek at the shoppes along Crescent Street. Mayor Harvey Cowell greeted the small party and their larger United States Marine Corps entourage.

A final few presidential notes:

* "I met Richard Nixon when I was with the Senators," Wayne Terwilliger recalls. "Ted Williams was a good friend of his, and he came to a couple of games. Eisenhower threw out the first pitch."

While Mr. Harding avoided impeachment by passing away, Mr. Nixon merely had to resign — although it meant he had to wait to appear on a postage stamp. He did not have to wait for the next available ferryboat to Catalina, though, because as President he was entitled to ride a helicopter over — pretty tricky. Here, Dick and daughter Tricia meet Avalon mayor Harvey Cowell in 1971, while Bebe Rebozo, not of the mafia, prefers the comfort of Secret Service protection.

* The *Chicago Cubs News* told fans in 1948: "Cliff Chambers, another of the youngsters determined to make the Cubs the League's best, for years to come, is a distant relative of William Howard Taft."

* A year later, the same team newsletter also reported: "Cal McLish was named after the 29th president of the United States, but doesn't know why…'All my family are Democrats!' he says."

* Pitcher Gordon Van Dyke says, "We were from Cooksville, Illinois. It's about 15 minutes from Eureka College, where they have all sorts of things set up about Ronald Reagan."

* And rumor has it that Grover Cleveland Alexander might've been named after a U.S. president.

Lefty Carnett, Lefty Chambers, Lefty Minner, Lefty O'Doul, & Lefty Sloat

Where's a Good Southpaw When You Need One?

"The oddest situation in the camp to date is the presence of more left-handed pitchers than the team can use. There are 5 of the portside critters...Lefty French... Roy Henshaw...Lefty Charley Flowers...Lefty Shoun... and Lefty Clauson Vines, winningest pitcher on the roster."

Ed Burns, in the Chicago Tribune, 1936

And let's not forget Lefty Logan, Lefty Pierce, Lefty Milstead, Lefty Westnedge, Lefty Weinert, or Lefty Reinhart and Lefty Tyler — the first 2 on Catalina.

(Don'tcha wonder why you never see a guy nicknamed 'Righty'? Think about that one for a moment.)

Nonetheless. Let's meet a few *more* interesting Catalina Cubs who populated the Isle in those days...

Manager Charlie Grimm wonders why, as a left-handed pitcher, Bob 'Lefty' Logan raises his right foot in the air before releasing the ball.

Lefty Carnett

Eddie Carnett lost his nickname along the way.

He came up to the Cubs in 1939 as a southpaw pitcher, but changed his mind after that and became an outfielder. And an infielder too, sometimes. Once he left the mound, nobody would call him 'Lefty' anymore, although he still chose to wear a glove on his right hand.

"As I progressed further up the ladder," Whatever-you-wanna-call-him says, "I hurt my arm and went to outfield and 1st base. The media dropped the 'Lefty' and started calling me 'Eddie.'"

Lefty Carnett, before he lost his nickname.

Lefty, aka Edwin, dba Eddie, was certainly among the most versatile athletes ever to don a Cub flannel on Catalina. Besides his multi-purpose baseball play, he owns a unique Island claim to fame: Of all the Cubbies to whack at a golf ball while in Avalon over a 30-year span, Lefty Carnett is the only one to ever card a hole-in-one. Spring o'39, 2nd hole, ker-plunk.

"I sure as heck did!" he remembers. "There's a camelback green, a humpback, and it went over there…but I didn't think anything of it when I hit it."

Lefty's big-league career was interesting: Pitcher for the Boston Braves, 1941. Starting outfielder for the White Sox, 1944 — batting a respectable .276. And a few games at each spot for the Indians in 1945. During his 20 seasons in pro ball, he's one of the few members of the 100/100 club (129 wins, 114 homers) in the minors…where his lifetime average was .314. He had a few seasons to write home about:

* In 1937, for Tulsa, he won 15 games while hitting .304 as a 1st-baseman

* In 1943, for Seattle, he hit .300 as an outfielder…and still pitched in 11 games

* In 1948, he hit .409 with 33 home runs for Borger in the West Texas/New Mexico League ("That was a renegade league!" Lefty says. "We had some good ballplayers out there.")

* And in 1950, still with Borger (now as a pitcher-outfielder-manager), Lefty led the league with a 3.14 ERA…and hit .361 with 24 homers

"I'd hurt my arm, and it never quite came back," Lefty says. "I was a pretty good hitter, I could throw hard, I had good control, I wasn't afraid to push you back."

Then, like now, timing was everything. "You gotta get the breaks," he says. "There were a lot of really good ballplayers who never made the majors. I was traded to the Yankee organization and sent to Milwaukee. We didn't make any money, but we had a great time — meeting the guys, traveling. We did make good money out there in the Coast League, when I was with Seattle."

He spent a lot of time on the West Coast. Besides Seattle and the Catalina stop, Lefty pitched for the Los Angeles Angels in the late '30s, too. "It was great, off the coast," he says. "Mr. Wrigley owned the island. That Catalina is something else, another world. After practice, we played golf. Some went fishing. We had a horseshoe tournament, we went bowling, and out at the Casino ballroom, we had all the great guys, the big bands."

As 1939 camp wound down, Charles Drake — the Cubs' PR man — hosted a going-away shin-dig for the boys. "Mr. Drake took us up to the Wrigley mansion the last night we were on the Island," Lefty says. "There was a lotta food, a lotta everything. What a hot time we had that night — Hub Kittle and Goo-Goo Galan and Billy Herman, a lot of the guys — Gabby turned us loose, and we made a lot of noise. We even rolled a few 55-gallon drums down the hill. We came down around 3 in the morning, and the police stopped us and told us to go back to the hotel."

He roomed with another wallflower, Dizzy Dean, for a while — and got to know Diz's brother Daffy while managing in Texas. In the Navy, he played against greats like Bob Feller. And as a kid, he got to meet one of the New York Giants who pitched a few exhibition games on Catalina: "Carl Hubbell was my idol," says Lefty, not needing to mention that King Carl was a southpaw. "I saw the 1933 World Series. All of us kids, we were there behind the fence, screaming for autographs. Hubbell took my scorecard, and he came back with a bunch of autographs on it."

While still playing, he began to manage in the minors for the Cubs. After 10 seasons, it was time to move on: "The Cubs told me I was a lousy manager," he says, "so I went to work at the Burlington Country Club in Iowa." Retired now, "I play golf, go fishing. I shot my age the other day — 42, 43! We have 3 kids. Oh, well, that was a long time ago and many memories for an 85 year-old."

Lefty Chambers

Cliff Chambers pitched in the majors for 6 seasons. He came up with the Cubs in 1948 after dominating the Pacific Coast League with Los Angeles for 2 seasons (he went 24-9 the previous year). Over the Winter, Chicago traded Lefty to Pittsburgh for Cal McLish. A few years later, the Pirates dealt him to St. Louis for Joe Garagiola. During his stop in Pittsburgh, Left went and winged himself a no-hitter against the Braves.

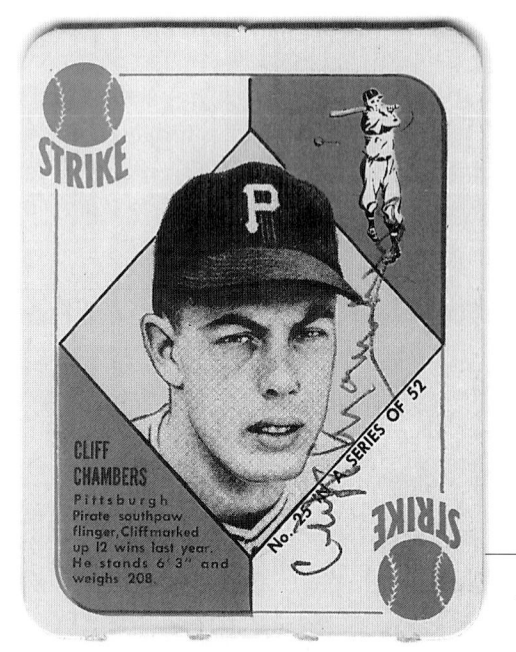

"I was out on Catalina with the Cubs 2 years," Lefty recalls, "1947 and 1948. "In '47, I started out East with the team, but when we got to Arizona they sent Red Adams and me back to L.A. — they had too much talent, too many pitchers. My 1st year with the Cubs, they paid me $8,500 — the minimum was $6,500, and they screamed like a wounded Turk to pay me that!"

After practice, he'd head off to visit PK Wrigley's stables. "I used to ride his Arabians," Lefty says. "About half the guys would go hunting, the other half would fish, or they'd play golf. We'd go pig hunting. Wrigley brought the boars out to kill all the rattlesnakes. We were only there 2 to 3 weeks, then we'd live at the Biltmore in Los Angeles and play at Wrigley Field."

It was a quiet environment. "Avalon was a very seasonal community — hardly anybody lived there. The tourists just came and left. It was a great field — but I had shinsplints pretty bad. I don't know if it was because of the field, but they sure caused me a lot of problems. It was beautiful, but we couldn't play any games because nobody wanted to take the boat ride over, so it wasn't that good a deal. We stayed in a 2-story hotel, with a telephone hanging on the wall. My wife came over on the boat a couple of times. The wives would come over in the morning, and spend the day. We'd just 'hang out,' like the young people say."

He says he didn't get a lot of actual training there, though. "The coaches just ran us through our drills," Lefty recalls. "Everything I learned was from other pitchers. From Bill Posedel — he was in Seattle when I was in L.A. — I learned the change. From Hugh Casey, in Brooklyn, I learned how to get the ball over the plate. I got a college degree — Danny Litwhiler and I were about the only big league ballplayers in those days who had college degrees, and here's some guy who barely finished high school, he's supposed to be your coach!" Yet it eventually added up: "I was pitching against Willie Mays in 1951, he wasn't hittin' Molly Potts," says Lefty, "but Durocher stuck with him. A lot of guys were like that — they'd tear it up in the minors, but the big league pitchers saw their weaknesses and capitalized on 'em. That's what happened to Steve Bilko."

Lefty's retired to Idaho now. "We live on a ranch," he says. "We go horseback riding, do some hunting — we have 160 acres and an airstrip, next to the national park. Bill Buckner lives nearby."

Lefty Chambers in 1951 — the year he no-hit Boston.

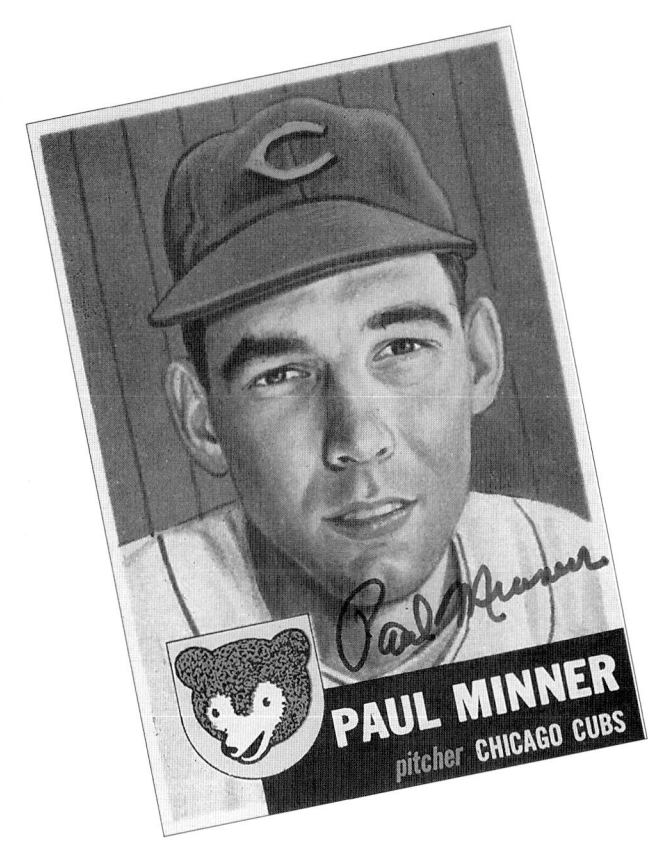

Did Lefty Minner really look like Ben Affleck when he was young?

Lefty Minner

Paul Minner pitched for the Cubs from 1950-1956, after 3 seasons in Brooklyn. He appeared in a World Series game for the Dodgers 1949. As one of Chicago's starting aces in the '50s, that meant he got to have a turn at leading the N.L. in losses — going 6-17 in 1951, despite a respectable ERA.

"The pitchers and catchers came out early — about ten days," says Lefty. "We took the boat over to Catalina. We did nothing — we didn't leave the Island until we went East. It was a wonderful place, great for a vacation, with a small town."

He still visits Spring Training (and joins in at Fantasy Baseball Camps), but now in Arizona. Lefty island-hopped in his day: "With the Dodgers," he says, "we trained in Havana in 1947 and Santo Domingo in 1948. Then we went into Vero Beach, where the team bought the old air base. I was one of the original tenants."

"Spring training changed from Catalina to Mesa," according to Lefty. In Arizona, "We had teams to play — none ever came over to Catalina. It was better to play different clubs." Yet Catalina had its charms: "There was golf out there, and Mr. Wrigley had a ranch. We went over there for picnics."

Lefty became a southpaw insurance man in Florida, then moved back to his native Pennsylvania... enjoying retirement and, still, the annual pilgrimage southward to baseball camp every February.

Lefty Sloat

Dwain Sloat also did Dodger-Cub duty — tossing a few games for Brooklyn in 1948 before coming to Chicago the following year. He pitched 3 more seasons in the minors before hanging it up.

"Seems like you couldn't do much of anything," he says. "We'd set around, and shoot the bull with the guys. There were always some stories going. The Cubs had kind of an older team then." Most of the team practiced in Los Angeles that Spring, and Lefty spent most of his time at Wrigely Field in L.A.

He didn't get any decisions in his 5 games with the '49 Cubs...after going 0-1 for the '48 Bums. So Lefty ended his big-league career at a very Cub-like 0-1 lifetime mark. And he got to do the multiple-island thing: Training on Catalina, Cuba, and Hispaniola before playing on Long Island and Manhattan.

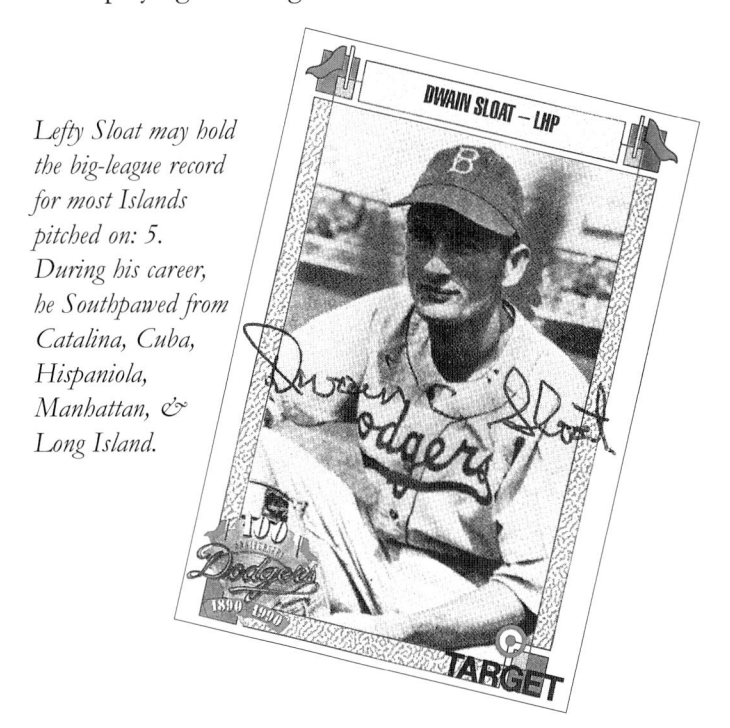

Lefty Sloat may hold the big-league record for most Islands pitched on: 5. During his career, he Southpawed from Catalina, Cuba, Hispaniola, Manhattan, & Long Island.

Lefty O'Doul

Francis Joseph O'Doul is the stuff legends are made of — his career spanned decades and continents, and he's famous for different reasons in different circles. Yet hardly anyone thinks of Lefty as having anything to do with the Chicago Cubs.

He pitched for the Yankees and Red Sox from 1919-1923 — a teammate of Babe Ruth. He pulled a Lefty Carnett and switched to the outfield...but did even better at it: He hit .300 for 5 straight years, leading the league twice (at a blistering *.398* once, with 32 homers for the 1929 Phillies). His lifetime average: .349. (Lefty also went 1-for-1 in the 1933 World Series for the Giants.)

The multi-generational, multi-continental, multi-environmental (but never a Cub) Lefty O'Doul.

Then, he went to work. Lefty is a Pacific Coast League legend, winning more than 2,000 games as a manager from 1935-1957. He spent most of those seasons heading the San Francisco Seals, where he cultivated talent like Joe DiMaggio. (In fact, Lefty and Mrs. O'D. were the only guests when Joe married that actress who used to live on Catalina, Norma Jeane Dougherty.) There's even a bridge in San Francisco named after him — not far from the Giants' ballpark. He's credited with pioneering baseball in Japan — taking teams on barnstorming tours before World War II and afterward, serving as a goodwill ambassador. Lefty even climbed off the bench to pinch-hit in a Coast League game in 1956 — when he was 59 years old — and when the outfielders crept in, he lined a triple over their heads!

But 1926 was the year that will live in infamy for Cub fans. William Wrigley bought Lefty's minor-league contract, but skipper Joe McCarthy cut him. "Marse Joe, sad to relate, made a monumental mistake that Spring," Charlie Grimm wrote in his autobiography. O'Doul went across the channel to Hollywood and hit .338. The next year, back home in San Francisco, he hit .378 and won the league MVP award. The New York Giants called, and he hit .319 as a semi-rookie in 1928.

"Later on," Warren Brown wrote in his history of the Cubs, "when O'Doul broke back into the National League and either led it in hitting or caused damage to some Cub pitching hopes, Wrigley would sigh: 'Oh, that O'Doul...my O'Doul!'"

Dizzy Dean

The press liked to call him 'The Great One' — and Hall-of-Famer Dizzy Dean was as great a showman off the field as he was on the mound.

Great, indeed: in a 5-year span, Diz led the N.L. in *20* pitching categories. He went 30-7 in 1934, and won 28 the next year — leading the league in strikeouts 4 straight seasons. One year, he won 24...and led the league in saves, too! And his 2-win performance in the 1934 World Series for the Gas House Gang Cardinals is legend — brother Daffy won the other 2.

Then he hurt his arm.

But no matter — the Cubs picked him up in 1938, and he responded with a 7-1 mark and a 1.81 ERA, including some heroic World Series play.

"Bear in mind that Dean's arm was gone," Bill Veeck said in the Cubs' video history, "and he pitched one of the more remarkable games in the World Series history. He couldn't throw hard enough to break a light bulb! And he finessed 'em. You see, the opposition still believed that he could throw. And so he would go into that great wind-up, and then nothing would happen...and the ball would eventually arrive at the plate. He was a tough competitor, with nothing. He was brave to get out there — I thought he might get killed!"

"To watch him pitch, you talk about courage," Phil Cavarretta agrees. "In 1938, he could hit you right between the eyes and not hurt you. But he was smart, and he had outstanding control. Before that, you talk about 95, 100 miles an hour — this guy could bring it up there, maybe quicker than that. The secret to a good fastball is control."

Dizzy even tricked the bubblegum card company into using his incorrect name.

Most folks remember Dizzy as a Card, not a Cub — but he performed some heroics for the Wrigleys, too.

"He was anything but a shrinking violet, to be sure," Warren Brown wrote in the Cubs' history, "but when his fast ball was at his beck and call, he could make any batsman roll over and play dead — and frequently did."

"Dizzy Dean stepped on a vagrant baseball...as he walked toward the clubhouse," Burns wrote in the Spring of 1941. "Diz was assisted to the first aid bay, screaming with agony, but after many poultices had been applied, said he didn't believe the injury was serious." The next day, when it was time for an exhibition all-star game on the mainland, "Dizzy...experienced a miraculous recovery."

"Dizzy Dean asked for — and got — permission to go over to the mainland Friday to fill a radio engagement," Brown wrote for the *Chicago Herald & Examiner* in 1939. "Then somebody suggested that maybe Old Diz, instead of returning with the 2nd squad on Saturday morning, might miss the boat and get out to Santa Anita for the $100,000 handicap. Old Diz thought that was a pretty good idea...'But I can't go missing me no boat,' decided Old Diz. 'If I do, it'll cost me the 4-500 I can pick up doing my radio stuff. Ain't that right, Gabby.'"

No matter where he went — when he was on top, and after he blew his arm out— Diz was the center of attention. "Dizzy Dean was the best," Harvey Storey says. "He conducted the Dizzy Dean Show every noon at the clubhouse at Catalina — telling stories. He kept everyone laughing."

"Whenever he pitched, the ballpark was full," says Cavarretta.

"The consensus is that the great man will not be very late in arriving at the Cubs' training grounds," Ed Burns reported in the *Chicago Tribune* in 1940. "Next Friday is camera and newsreel day at Avalon and it is felt Diz surely will not miss that."

"Dizzy Dean remains exuberant," Burns told *Tribune* readers in 1939, "even though...he is not permitted to play golf and he can't win at rummy. He has told so many folks out here that he's going to win upwards of 20 games that he's beginning to believe it himself."

"They were a bunch of cut-ups," Islander Doug Bombard recalls. "I met Dizzy Dean when he joined the Cubs, when he was trying to make a comeback."

He toyed with reporters about his name (telling some it was Jay, others that he was Jerome)...and his age. Listing player ages in the *Tribune* in 1939, Burns entered: "Dizzy Dean, 28, he says." (He was in fact 29.)

AVALON, Cal. — The baseball season was officially opened at 8:30 this morning, when Dizzy Dean threw out the first autograph.

Warren Brown, the *Chicago Herald & Examiner*, 1939

"Dizzy was a case," says Della Root Arnold, Charlie's daughter. "Other than my Dad, he was my favorite ballplayer — he as such a neat guy. He and Pat spent a lot of time at our apartment — she'd been Miss San Antonio. She allowed him $20 per day, because he'd buy every kid he saw a hot dog, every freeloader a Coke or ice cream. The Cards bought his enlistment up, out of the army, and they sent him to Tulsa. Ty Cobb was managing Tulsa. Dizzy got to the ballpark, but nobody would talk to him. He got dressed and went and sat on the bench — 'and here come that mean Mr. Cobb.'

"Cobb asked him, 'Are you that hot new rookie I heard about from Arkansas?'

" 'Yes, sir, Mr. Cobb.'

"And Cobb said, 'Do you know what we do with hot new rookies from Arkansas?'

"And Dizzy said, 'Do you know what we do with cobs in Arkansas?' And Ty Cobb didn't have a comeback for that."

"Dizzy never went to school," Yosh Kawano says, "but he was a bright guy."

"He couldn't read or write at first," Della says. But "Pat worked with him, and he learned to read."

Lennie Merullo played with Diz in the Texas League, where Dean was on a rehab assignment. "They sent Dizzy down there because of the hot weather, to help loosen his arm up," Lennie says. "That was the best thing that ever happened, because he really filled up the ballparks — everybody wanted to see him. The fans brought out baskets of food for us, watermelon — we ate well. He lived in Garland, between Dallas and Ft. Worth. We'd be sittin' in front of the old Jefferson Hotel, and he'd come driving by in his big old station wagon and say, 'Ya want a ride?' We went out to his farmhouse, and it was empty — there was no furniture in it — except in one room, there were more press clippings than I ever saw."

"To be honest, he was a big star then," says Phil Cavarretta, just a youngster at the time, "so we didn't go with him. There were a lot of stars on Catalina. Stan Hack, Ol' Diz, Turk Stainback, the reserve outfielder — they'd go with the stars."

He was an inspiration to the rookies, because of his work ethic between the lines. "Dean is one of the hardest workers in camp," Burns told *Tribune* readers in 1939. "He snags flies, makes a great deal of noise, autographs while catching his breath, but is fast-losing his West Coast reputation as a pop-off guy."

Goo-Goo Galan (on the right) does his best to keep Diz from lifting 2 checkers at a time.

And he'd challenge hitters, too. "Now, these guys dig in," says Bobby Mattick, who was a teammate of Dizzy's on Catalina. "That's all Dizzy'd have to see, and down you'd go."

But with a sore arm, the team was nervous about his aggressive attitude on the field. "Dizzy Dean has acquired an official guardian, and there was considerable curiosity afoot in the training camp of the Cubs today as to how far the crusade to save Dizzy from himself might be carried," James Kearns wrote in the *Daily News* in 1939. "Yesterday the great man chose to turn loose a few throws over a 75-foot distance along 1st base...and Charles Drake, assistant to Owner P.K. Wrigley, promptly scurried out from the sidelines to tell Jay Hanna that such doings couldn't go on." So Diz was relegated to R&R. "Diz spent the afternoon playing checkers with Clay Bryant despite the fact that Mr. Drake had not applied scales or calipers to the checkers to test them for size and weight. Some observers felt that reaching for the king row would constitute a strain on Dizzy's arm. The Dean evening program featured a cumulative rhummy game with a foursome including Hartnett and Drake. Dizzy held a few cards bigger than sixes, causing a few onlookers to wonder whether it had been officially decided that picture cards were too heavy for Jay Hanna to be lifting. All in all the Dizzy One is being thoroughly chaperoned."

"Dizzy Dean was a good boy today," Burns told *Tribune* readers a day later. "He pitched about a half dozen to Hartnett, then was halted. He did no sneak pitching to Bob Garbark."

Hard-working as he was, it generally took Diz a while to get to camp — part of his center-of-attention strategy. He held out just about every year:

1936 (AP): "Holdout Jerome 'Dizzy' Dean made peace with the St. Louis Cardinals today, signed a pledge of loyalty...and agreed to talk salary figures tomorrow."

1937 (INS): "The Dizzy Dean, the loquacious one who said he was going to quit major league baseball, arrived here this afternoon and is expected to sign a contract..."

1937 (*Los Angeles Times* headline): "Dean Retires — Yes, Again."

1938 (AP): "Dizzy Dean ended his annual salary squabble...today..."

1940 (*Los Angeles Times*): "Diz, if he shows up, will not be permitted to mount the gangplank unless he signs."

1940 (Burns, in the *Tribune*): "Come sailing time, no Diz and that was that. There was no talk of delaying the steamer's churn out into the Pacific Ocean, however."

(3 weeks later): "Dizzy Dean appears to have been sunk without trace, but this isn't so serious, except to cameramen and radio agents."

1940 (Herbert Simons, in the *Chicago Times*): "A little soft music, please, professor; the curtain is up again on another revival of that tear-jerking opus, 'The Holdout.' Dean is getting little but mock sympathy from what is left of his public. After all, a fellow who won but 6 games last year and 7 the year before hasn't much of a leg to stand on, yet alone much of an arm to pitch with. The Diz's threats to sit in Dallas and 'starve' rather than occasionally exert his carcass for a mere 5 C's a week aren't disturbing the tranquillity of this Pacific isle.

Once he'd eventually make it there, Dizzy had a good time on Catalina. Here, the Great One discusses seams with actress Jane Frazee (who made 50 movies during her career).

"The absence of the salary-sulking Dizzy Dean, whose presence used to arouse more or less natural resentment through his wittingly and unwittingly hogging the spotlight while contributing little, is causing no perturbance here. In fact, his name is infrequently mentioned. When it is, it's usually in a gag, such as one wag's suggesting that Dizzy should be paid what he's holding out for — if he promises to continue to stay away!"

It grew old in the front office. "Dizzy got to going back and forth with Mr. Wrigley about his contract," Lefty Carnett says. "Finally, Mr. Wrigley just send Diz a blank one, and said, 'You fill in what you think is fair.' Well, Dizzy didn't like that — he thought it put him on the spot."

As Dizzy's ERA rose, his stock sank. "We expect him to be a pitcher from now on and not a side-show attraction," PK Wrigley said before the 1940 season.

A year later, it was over. In the Cubs' history, Brown wrote: "The eager critics, much as they approved of Dean as an aid to spirited copy, any time, anywhere, anyhow, soon began to refer to Dizzy's 'nothing' ball...which came toward the plate with all the fury of something blown out of a bubble pipe."

Diz embarked on his broadcasting career — which got him into hot water with English teachers. In 1947, appalled with the St. Louis Browns' atrocious pitching he was forced to watch day after day, the former Great One took to the mound one last time. He threw 4 shutout innings, and — always the showman — managed a base hit in his only plate appearance. Yessah, Dizzy went out batting a thousand.

Billy Rogell

Billy Rogell enjoyed a solid 14-year career in the big leagues, yet he's best known for a single play involving Dizzy Dean.

Billy broke in with the Red Sox in 1925 — his 1st hit was a double, off Walter Johnson. He came to Detroit in 1930, and was their starting shortstop for a decade. He finished his career with the Cubs in 1940 — Billy was ready to retire, but his wife wanted to see Catalina, so he made the trip.

And he started in the 1934 World Series for the Tigers, where he achieved his Dizzy claim to fame.

"I was the guy who hit him on the head in the World Series," Billy says at the tender age of 98. "I never did see the man when I threw the ball to first! What were they doin' anyway, usin' a star pitcher for a pinch runner?"

When Billy Rogell wasn't rendering opponents unconscious, he was a slick-fielding infielder throughout the '30s.

Game 4, Dizzy is pinch-running for Spud Davis — for some reason. Rogell steps on the bag as Dizzy barrels into 2nd, trying to bust up a double play. Billy fires to 1st, but the ball pops Diz in the noggin instead...bouncing 30 feet into the sky. Dean was out cold.

Dizzy later said, "The x-rays of my head revealed nothing." (Popular myth suggests that was the headline in a St. Louis paper; it wasn't.) When Dizzy was revived, the 1st thing he said was, "Did I break up the double play?" He was scheduled to pitch the next day, and didn't doubt for a moment that he would: "You can't hurt no Dean by hittin' him on the head."

Sportswriter Bob Broeg says, "Somebody asked Paul Dean what Dizzy was saying, and Paul said, 'He wasn't sayin' nothin'.'"

Billy didn't just knock Dizzy in the head that day; he knocked in 4 runs, leading the Tigers to victory. Diz pitched 8 innings the next afternoon but lost 3-1. (He won his other 2 starts in the Series.)

"Everybody expects me to remember who bunted 70 years ago!"

Billy Rogell, in his 99th season

Things weren't the same with the Cubs. "We didn't have a good club," he admits. But Spring Training made it worthwhile: "Catalina Island is a beautiful island, believe me," he says. "It must be the prettiest island there is. We had an apartment there. The boys were too kid-young to work out with the team — Billy, he was only 6."

"Baseball is a great sport. I tell ya, I don't care what they say: Baseball is the toughest sport to play. I did the best I could."

After baseball, Billy entered politics: He served as an alderman on Detroit's city council for 40 years, from 1942-1981. He was so instrumental in developing Detroit's airport...that Metro Airport's entrance road is named after him: Rogell Drive.

"Here I am," he says, "almost 100 years old, and I'm up every morning at 5, and have breakfast at 6. I'm not on my butt, like people say today — I go walkin' around."

Billy Herman

Billy Rogell's double-play partner for the Cubs was Hall-of-Fame 2nd-sacker Billy Herman. Billy played with Chicago from 1931-1941, then put in a few more seasons with Brooklyn and the Boston Braves...before player-managing the Pirates in 1947. His lifetime average was .304 — a point higher than Pete Rose — and he led the N.L. in hits, doubles, and triples at one time or another (not to mention numerous fielding categories). A 10-time All-Star, Billy played in 3 World Series for the Cubs, and one more for the Dodgers. He coached for years, then managed the cellar-dwelling Red Sox from 1964-1966.

He hustled — appearing at camp in shape, a sharp contrast to a lot of post-winter bulging ballplayers in the '30s. "His arms and legs are in excellent condition," Herbert Simons wrote for the *Times* in 1934, "as a result of several weeks solo training on his 1,000-acre ranch in Texas. His only trouble at the moment is a shortage of wind, perhaps as a result of running out all those hits yesterday."

Before Lennie Merullo came along, Herman roomed with rookie Phil Cavarretta. "Billy Herman helped me become a better ballplayer," Cavy says. "He gave me run-downs on the pitchers, and he helped me understand how to play the infield."

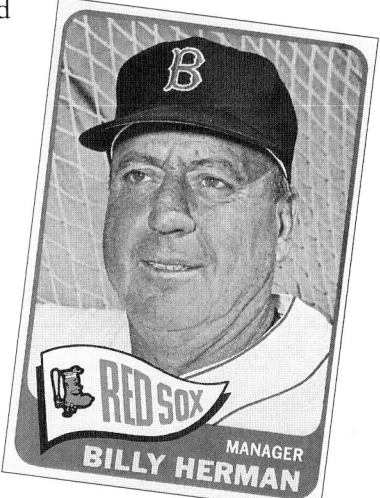

Long after Catalina, Billy Herman managed another fine ballclub.

Billy was not only a student of the game, but a keen observer of human nature — which helped him as a coach and manager. And it gave him an edge early on, too: When Herman was a rookie playing for Rogers Hornsby, "He ignored me completely, and I figured it was because I was a rookie," Billy said. "But then I saw he ignored everybody."

Herman determined to not repeat those mistakes. When Bob Borkowski was in the service, Herman helped him get a shot at pro ball. "I was stationed in Hawaii, with the Navy," Bob says, "and I took care of the infield. Billy Herman was the manager. I asked him if I could pitch batting practice, and he asked if I could get it over the plate." He did, and got a contract — always grateful that Herman gave him a chance.

In 1953, with his Cub years behind him, Bob Borkowski got to play for the hometown team.

Bob Borkowski

Bob Borkowski did break in as a pitcher, but he hit close to .400 in the minors — twice — so he morphed into an outfielder. Bush was with the Cubs from 1950-1951, the Reds from 1952-1955, and he finished as a Brooklyn Dodger. He hit .251 lifetime.

"When I was little, I had this long hair," he says, explaining the nickname, "and they couldn't pronounce my father's name, Borkowski. I hope it wasn't because anybody thought I was a bush-leaguer!"

He loved his 2 Springs on Catalina. "It was lots of fun," Bob remembers. "We used to dress in the Country Club, and walk up there. After practice, we used to take off our shoes and play golf. It was quite a nice place to have it. A lot of them used to go fish. We used to go away on weekends, back to California. It was great — the best place I ever trained. I stayed in the little cottages, where a lot of the ballplayers stayed with their wives. In town, we'd eat out a lot. We were a bunch of young guys, just trying to build the team up. Most of 'em were down to earth — there weren't really any clowns in the bunch."

Once he finished at the Show, "I played in the Coast League after I was with the Dodgers, up in Portland. I played in Nashville, too. I came back to Ohio, worked for a printing outfit." Now retired, "I play a lot of golf. Wally Post lives up the road; I've played in his golf tourney."

Hal Jeffcoat

Another Catalina Cub who switched positions was Hal Jeffcoat — except Hal did it the other way around. He was a Cub outfielder starting in 1948... before taking to the mound in 1954. He pitched almost exclusively for the Reds and Cards from 1956-1959. His older brother, George, pitched for the Dodgers and Braves from 1936-1943.

"When we were out on Catalina," Carmen Mauro says, "Wrigley had a rodeo on his ranch. They selected Hal Jeffcoat and me to chase some pigs inside a ring there — I guess they wanted people who could run and dive. They let 'em loose in this area, all covered with oil and grease and the dirt flying — but we did it! We tackled 'em. Those were the ones that were gonna be roasted."

Oh, they played some baseball on the Island, too. "I enjoyed it very much," Hal says. "Back then, playing ball was all I cared about. We took the boat — we took the plane once. You land, you see the ocean coming, it was an experience. They were a nice group, all the old veterans. We played golf, we ran, we hiked through the mountains. My wife and I had just gotten married."

"We had 3 children, 1-2-3, right together," Valma Jeffcoat adds, "so I didn't go out. We got to talk by phone, and he wrote letters. I still have them somewhere. He took some 8-millimeter movies. We had a camera, but it broke. They're all in a closet somewhere. When Jeff was playing — I called him Jeff — I kept them for our children."

Valma may've called him 'Jeff' — but Charlie Grimm called him Hotfoot Hal. Yet when he wasn't jokestering, Hal liked to hustle. In 1950, the *Tribune* reported that "Jeffcoat, having learned that Frisch likes the boys to run wild, immediately stole home, and the maneuver so surprised McCall he heaved the ball to the backscreen."

In Avalon, Hal played in the outfield. Notice the Catalina hiking course behind him on his 1951 Bowman card.

After playing outfield for 6 seasons, Hal changed his mind — & pitched for 6 more.

Carmen Mauro

When he wasn't chasing pigs with Jeffcoat, Carmen Mauro played a little ball, too. Carmen shagged flies for Chicago from 1948-1951, then completed a trifecta in 1953 — playing for the Dodgers, Washington Nationals, and A's in a single season.

Carmen's debut was about as good as you can get: He smacked an inside-the-park home run past Stan Musial!

"Murray Dickson...threw me something that was supposed to be a knuckleball, but it didn't knuck," Carmen smiles. "He really put it in my wheelhouse, and I lined it to centerfield. I came around 1st and picked up Charlie Grimm at 3rd. He was jumping up and down frantically. We were in 6th or 7th place at the time, and I'm just a rookie, and he's screaming, 'I want you to score!' — I could hear him! So I turned the volume on and rounded 3rd. Del Rice was the catcher, and I slid under the ball. So my very 1st hit in the big leagues was an inside-the-park home run! My family was in Chicago, listening to the game on the radio, and they were jumping up and down. It was the last game, so I went home to a great party at our house. That one, I couldn't surpass."

He'd spent the Spring on Catalina with the Cubs. "I was in Chicago, so I came out with the team. We took the train out," he says. "We played a lot of cards. Then, they put us on a boat — we came out from San Pedro. That was very interesting. I'd never been to Catalina. The main street is not too long — it extended from the pier to the Casino. But the ballroom was closed for the winter that year. We stayed at a small hotel, the Atwater. I wrote some letters. I tried to play golf. I went with Hank Sauer. Oh, my, he could drive that ball; he was a terrific athlete."

Carmen imported his own fan club. "I had some people from Morton High School (in Cicero, Illinois) come out," he says. "Some people came and watched us practice. I remember a lot of kids, and the sportswriters — it seemed like mass hysteria sometimes, but we managed to get some baseball in. People wanted to see the players."

In a way, the pressure was off, though. "I was a rookie," he says, "and I didn't think I was gonna break into that outfield — Pafko, Hank Sauer, and Peanuts Lowrey. I was some young kid who could run and hit. In the minors, they wanted to switch me to a home-run hitter, change my stance. They felt Wrigley was a hitter's park, with that wind and that fence."

He got a better shot with the Dodgers, because Montreal manager Walter Alston cultivated his strengths — telling him, "With your running and bunting ability, you could beat out 30 bunts a year." As a lead-off hitter, Carmen hit .327 ahead of Don Hoak and Junior Gilliam...with Tommy Lasorda on the mound. ("He was a curveball pitcher, a gutty little pitcher," Carmen says. "He'd string you out with a fastball, and wasn't afraid to drill you.") So Brooklyn called. "But who's my competition: Duke Snider in center, and Carl Furillo, in the prime of their careers!"

Mauro was managing from the bench himself, even as a rookie in Catalina. "We'd sit and chew the fat, and say we have a good club... we could win the pennant," he says. "It boils down to pitching and tight defense. And clutch hitting. We had lots of sessions in the hotel lobby — Chuck Connors and the other jokers, it was a lot of fun, just horsing around. But Frank Frisch was a taskmaster; he wanted us to look the part, to not come down from the room without a coat and tie. 'You need to look like Chicago Cubs,' he'd say. We'd go to Los Angeles, then Phoenix — where we'd stay at the Biltmore, which Wrigley also owned. That's where Frisch was really rough on us. I had a lotta hair, and he wanted us to keep our hair neat. Ballplayers would come down with their shirts open, no necktie, and he'd say, you can't go to the dining room that way. So we had to bring sportscoats or suits, and look professional."

Seems everybody else was bossing Carmen around, too. Once, he went flying off a horse at the Isthmus side of Catalina — right into some scrub brush. Mr. Wrigley's ranch hand "threw me right back on the horse," Carmen says, "and told me it was because he didn't want the horse picking up any bad habits!"

After his 4 seasons in the majors, Carmen starred for several years in the Pacific Coast League. A bad back forced him to retire in 1959, and he turned to coaching — heading several college baseball teams on the West Coast.

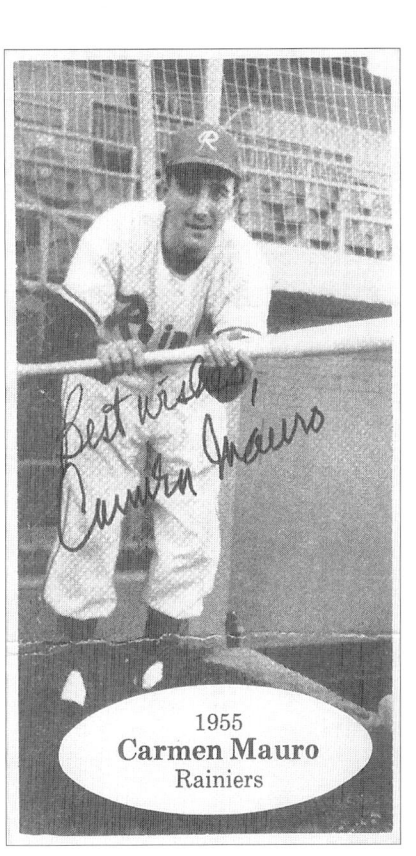

Peanuts Lowrey

Carmen Mauro wasn't the only guy who had a tough time trying to take All-Star Peanuts Lowrey's job away from him. P-nuts enjoyed a solid 14-year career, starting with the Cubs (from 1942-1949), and finishing with the Phillies in 1955 (after stops at Cincinnati and St. Louis). He hit .310 for the Cubs in the 1945 World Series and led the N.L. in pinch-hits twice.

Movie star, golf shark, diminutive ballplayer — Peanuts Lowrey.

He got his nickname early on, and he only made it to 5'8". As a kid, he acted in some silent movies...and appeared with Dutch Reagan in *The Winning Team* in 1952 (he's the one that plunked Reagan, as Grover Alexander, in the head with a ball). He also landed bit parts in *Pride of the Yankees* and *The Stratton Story*. When practice was over on Catalina, he was easy to find — just head for the golf course.

Peanuts was a man of principle, and a smart businessman. "If there is going to be something different in baseball," Warren Brown wrote in the Spring of 1946 for his *So They Tell Me* column in the *Sun*, "you can trust the Cubs to come up with it. Their latest 'holdout' problem, that of Left Fielder Harry Lowrey, is a new touch. James T. Gallagher very properly awarded Lowrey a bonus for his splendid work in 1945, but Lowrey didn't want it to reach him until 1946, because of the matter of the annual income tax. Gallagher, being a firm believer in getting 1945's business completed in 1945, didn't wait, and now Lowrey is a holdout — the first on record who ever became miffed when a club gave him more than his contract called for."

After retiring, he coached for Phil Cavarretta in Buffalo. From 1960 through 1981, he coached for 5 major league teams — including the Cubs, under Leo Durocher.

Wimpy Quinn

Another food-related nickname: Wimpy Quinn, whose penchant for the burger got him the same moniker as Popeye's cartoon friend. Actually, he had a pretty cool real name: Wellington Hunt Quinn. Unfortunately, he didn't have a very cool curve ball; his entire big-league career took place in 1941, where he went winless with a 7.20 ERA. To Wellington's credit, he did go 1-for-2 at the plate, chalking up a lifetime .500 major-league batting average (to accompany his lifetime 1.000 fielding percentage, perfectly handling his lone chance).

Yet the irony of his hitting better than his pitching grows...when you realize he wasn't really a pitcher. The Wimpster was actually a 1st-baseman, and when he was invited to Catalina that Spring...silly him...he thought that's why he was there. (In 1940, he'd hit .342 with 27 homers in the minors.) "Wimpy Quinn was a good little 1st-baseman in L.A.," says Bobby Mattick. But manager Jimmie Wilson, faced with a shortage of moundsmen, was impressed with Quinn's strong arm. He had Quinn throw a bit, and made an executive decision — which may've cost Wimpy a serious shot at a big-league career. He languished in the minors for 2 seasons, pitching badly (but still hitting well) before going off to War.

Was Wimpy Quinn a pitcher, an infielder, or a power forward? Perhaps only Andy Lotshaw knew for sure...

When Quinn returned home, Wilson was gone, fortunately — so he could get back to the plate. But unfortunately, his pop was gone by then, too. Wimpy hit well in the low minors, but it was too late — he'd missed his window. He finished in 1951, as a player-manager for Bakersfield in the California League.

By the way, there's another unique side twist to Wimpy's career: Not only was he a multi-position guy, he was a multi-sport athlete. Before the War, he'd played both baseball and basketball at the University of Oregon. (In fact, he was a member of the 1st-ever NCAA-Championship basketball team in 1939.) When he got back from World War II, he played 1st base for Los Angeles in the Pacific Coast League. Then, he tried to revive his *basketball* career — and did well enough that he was the 1st Duck basketball player to be selected in a pro draft.

Thing is, he was picked by the Toronto Huskies in 1947, after their 1st season in the new BAA (Basketball Association of America)...but Toronto folded before playing a 2nd season! (The BAA merged with the NBL — National Basketball League — to form the NBA in 1949, by the way.) So, Wimpy's hoop dreams were about as problematic as his baseball fantasies. He went back from the hardwoods to the diamond. Ya just gotta wonder how far Wimpy Quinn might've gone...if he'd been able to stay as focused on his athletic career as his dining desires.

Pea Ridge Day

The Cubs' all-culinary nickname squad continues to grow. Consider Pea Ridge Day, whose momma named him Clyde when she birthed him in 1899...in Pea Ridge, Arkansas. Mr. Day (or Mr. Ridge, or perhaps the guys just called him 'Pea' for short?) pitched for St. Louis, Cincinnati, and Brooklyn from 1924-1931. (His lifetime mark: 5-7, with an ERA not worth mentioning.) He never quite made the Cub roster — probably because he couldn't quite find his way to Catalina. Irving Vaughn wrote this final dispatch from Chicago for the *Tribune* in 1929:

One little item of no particular importance remains to be settled before the advance squad of the Cubs can pull out of here Thursday in the direction of Catalina Island and spring labors.

The item that prevents completing all necessary preliminaries is Clyde Day, a young man who pitched for Omaha last season and resides in a town the post office guide mentions as Pea Ridge, Ark

The Cubs purchased this lad from Omaha thinking he would welcome a big league opportunity, which his 1928 record of 17 wins and 18 losses hardly warranted, but instead of expressing his thanks the fellow has sent back his contract with no signature attached.

President Veeck admitted yesterday that he had written the youngster several letters without success, so it is probable that unless Day alters his attitude and reaches here in time to climb aboard with the others on Thursday, his big league career will be as short as his name and he will shortly find himself headed back to Omaha, or Pea Ridge, or both.

From the smirk on Pea Ridge Day's face, we can surmise he knew exactly what he was doing in ignoring Cub pleas to come to Catalina...

While enroute 4 days later, Burns followed up: "While Mr. Burke joined at Kansas City with great difficulty, the same cannot be said of Pitcher Clyde Day, pride of Pea Ridge, Ark., nor was word received regarding his intentions. Manager McCarthy ventured the opinion that Clyde may have conceived the idea of traveling from Pea Ridge to California in a covered wagon. If Clyde has done this he will be tendered his contract and permitted to proceed just as if he hadn't vexed the management all this anxiety."

On Catalina, 2 days later, Burns sent the final Pea Ridge update: "The Cubs have but one hold-out, and they aren't worrying about him because it's 'Pea Ridge' Day, the clown chucker who made Marty Krug lose his temper several times when he was dropping ball games for the Angels a couple of seasons ago."

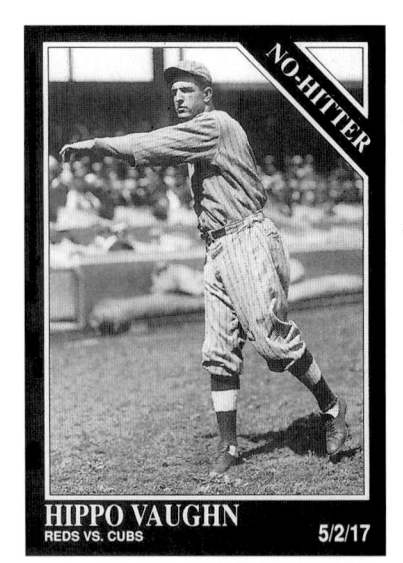

From this vantage point, one might scratch his or her head wondering how James earned a nickname like 'Hippo.'

Hippo Vaughn

We suppose there must be some form of animal that eats hippos, so Hippo Vaughn's nickname also qualifies as an edible one. Hippo was the star pitcher of the 1918 season — leading the N.L. in wins, ERA, strikeouts, and shutouts, then pitching splendidly in the World Series. He'd pitched in the A.L. from 1908-1912, before he came to Chicago...where he became a dominating pitcher. Over the next 9 seasons, Jimbo won 20 games 5 times...and ended up with a lifetime ERA of just 2.49.

Hippo was winding up his career in 1921 when the Cubs first trained in Catalina — part of that great staff that also included Grover Cleveland Alexander. He was the losing pitcher in the only double no-hitter ever pitched, in 1917, when Hippo and Cincy's Fred Toney both no-noed through 9; Jim Thorpe knocked in a run against Vaughn in the 10th.

Jigger Statz

Fans who like to quench their thirsts after a game may think Jigger Statz was named after a beverage-related utensil, but Arnold actually earned his nickname through his golfing prowess: a jigger is also an iron used to approach greens. The Jigmeister was a good major-league hitter (he hit .319 in 1923), but he was one of the all-time great minor-league batsmen.

In the majors, he played 8 years (Cubs, Dodgers, Giants, and Red Sox)...with a solid .285 average. He also played 18 seasons with the Los Angeles Angels in the Pacific Coast League — a single-club record for the minors. There, he collected 3,356 hits (which, combined with his 737 in the bigs, totals 4,093 — not many guys in the 4,000-hit club, at any level)...and a lifetime .315 average. Fast of foot, he led the league in steals 3 times, and once stole 6 in a single game.

Later on, Jigger was a Cub scout — in Southern California, of course. While there, he helped coach actor Ronald Reagan on how to look like a ballplayer when *The Winning Team* was being filmed. "Your coaching made this 'so, so' baseball player into a believeable big leaguer," Reagan wrote to Statz from the White House in 1983, "and that was quite a chore!"

He won his job on the Cubs by hustling. "Statz," Oscar Reichow of the *News* wrote in 1922, "appears to be as trim as a race horse...He reported to the club in tip-top shape. That is how ambitious he is of making good in the big show."

And could he golf! "Arnold Statz, Cub outfielder, expects to inject a lot of golf in his training program on Catalina Island," the *Tribune* reported in 1923 — accompanied by a photo of Jigger swinging a jigger. "He is recognized as the best golfer in baseball. Statz is one of the longest drivers in the game and rates among the nation's leading amateurs."

Had Jigger Statz known where he was supposed to wear his glove, he might have enjoyed a longer and more illustrious major-league career.

Coaker Triplett

You might think Coaker Triplett had a pretty great nickname, too — but actually, he had a pretty great *middle* name. We are pleased to introduce Herman Coaker Triplett, a Catalina Cub outfielder.

Coaker broke in with the Cubs in 1938, batting .250 in a dozen games — a 27-year-old rookie who'd toiled in the minors after scoring a lot of touchdowns at Appalachian State in his native North Carolina. The Cubs dealt him away, and he played 5 more years for St. Louis and Philly...before extending his career in the minors again, leading the International League in hitting in 1948.

Herman Coaker Triplett: A man who needs no introduction.

Like a lot of guys in the pre-DH days, Coaker had the bat to make the big time...but left his glove at home in the Appalachian foothills: "Dean Grimm has become convinced that H. Coaker Triplett, who led the Southern Association in hitting last year with .356, has a chance to stick in the outfield if he can learn to pick up more fly balls," Burns wrote for the *Tribune* in 1938.

Chick "Slug" Tolson

Perhaps the most nicknamedly-challenged Catalina Cub was Chick "Slug" Tolson, who wore a nickname atop his nickname. Charles Julius Tolson broke in with Cleveland in 1925, then spent 4 unusual seasons with the Cubs. As a rookie in 1926, he hit .313 — leading the N.L. in pinch-hits and pinch-hit-at-bats. He had a similar season in 1927, didn't play the next year, came back in 1929 but didn't do as well (going 0-for-1 in the World Series), and finished up in 1930 at an even .300.

'Slug'? Here's a clue: He made it to the basepaths exactly 100 times during his career — and swiped a single bag.

His career pinch-hitting mark was .311 — all as a Cub. But he was a 1st-baseman by trade, unfortunately at a time when Charlie Grimm owned that spot — at least most of the time. "There is some possibility," the *Los Angeles Times* reported from Avalon in 1926, "that Tolson may start at first in place of Grimm as that young man's hand is somewhat mauled as a result of his nose dive into a gulley while chasing a foul on Tuesday."

You can call me Chick, or you can call me Slug...

Turk Lown

What survey of Cub nicknames would be complete without a look at Omar 'Turk' Lown?

Turk pitched for the Northsiders from 1951-1958, before a brief pit-stop in Cincinnati and then a 1958-1962 career on the Southside. The trade did him good — he got a visit to the World Series with the White Sox in 1959, pitching 3 1/3 innings of shutout ball in 3 games. Turk led his league in saves, relief wins, relief losses (hey, '50s Cubs), and games at one time or another.

"Boy, it sure was great out on Catalina," Turk says. "We really enjoyed it. There was a lot of solitude; we didn't have to worry about anything. I went hiking a little bit out there. I wasn't into golf then. I really enjoyed reading mysteries — still do. I read on the boat going over."

What a name, what a wind-up — it could only be Omar Lown.

It was a long way from Turk's native Brooklyn — but fortunately, a Cub teammate was from the same borough. "You remember Chuck Connors," Turk says. "We played together in Montreal and Newport News, too. I finally got him horseback riding in the mountains — a guy from Brooklyn on horseback."

Turk played on another island (winter ball in Cuba), and before his Cub tryout, he went *really* far away: to Venezuela with Durocher's Dodgers. In L.A., he roomed with another future Cub. "Steve Bilko, he could really hit the long ball. Poor Steve — I had to ask for another roommate — he snored so loud!"

Early in his career, he moved to Pueblo, Colorado (where he'd pitched for the Dodgers in 1947). "My folks said, 'They still have the stage coach out there?' He coached his own kids in American Legion ball, and he's in the Pueblo Sports Hall of Fame. "My sons played in college, and then my grandson. My wife, Violet, was at the ballpark for 50 years. She'd tell my grandson what he was doing wrong when he was in a slump. She knows baseball."

Tuck Stainback

Before Turk Lown, there was Tuck Stainback — also known as the more Egyptian-oriented 'Tut' Stainback. (We feel the problem was a lack of Internet access in those days; everyone simply repeated what they heard...and on noisy trains, steamships, or ballfields surrounded by the roar of a crowd, it's hard to tell the variations apart.) Actually, his middle name was 'Tucker,' so 'Tuck' surely came first...

George was a pretty good ballplayer. His 13-year career started with the Cubs (1934-1937), followed by stops with half a dozen other teams (including the Yankees, who let him play in the 1942 & 1943 World Series). Afterwards, he was instrumental in organizing the first pension system for old ballplayers.

He started strong, batting .306 as a rookie outfielder in 1934...but peaked too early, since that was his best season. How could he not come out with a bang, given the rave reviews he drew from eternal superscout Jack Doyle: "He's the greatest ball player I ever saw go up from the minors," Doyle drooled to Bill Veeck in the Spring of 1933. "He's ready for the big leagues right now. Of course, he'll improve with experience, but he's got everything right now that any ball player needs. He can run like a deer, with great long strides. He has a marvelous throwing arm. He can hit anything."

Tut-tut. His lifetime average was .259, with 17 homers, 27 steals, and a meager .965 outfielding average. His rookie average of .306 dipped to .255 for his 2nd year...and .173 the next. Perhaps his problem was he was really, really good at one other thing:

"All that I am today," Tuck told the press in the Spring of 1935, "I owe to home cooking."

Please tell the press that Mr. Stainback's name is 'Tuck,' rather than 'Tut.'

Do you suppose Greek George is awaiting a baseball...or some ice cream...to come falling from the sky?

Greek George

After Tut but before Turk, Greek George played for the Cubs. Charlie's career was interesting: over a 10-year period, he played parts of 5 seasons for 4 different teams. His batting averages during those glory years:

.000
.195
.200
.156
.174

This amounts to a career clip of .177, with no home runs and no steals — which we can overlook, since Greek was a catcher when catchers were supposed to be especially slow-of-foot.

Greek was Gabby Hartnett's heir-apparent — or at least had a chance to be — putting in his Cub year in 1941. While he wasn't around long, he at least endeared himself to a few folks in the Cub camp: "The Greek was one of my all-time favorites," Bill Veeck wrote in his autobiography. "I knew that any time I wandered around with him, something was going to happen."

The Greek shares a good laugh with the photographer over his most recent batting average.

Veeck describes an afternoon when Greek bombed bald-headed targets with Eskimo Pies from a moving Ferris wheel — and the two had to run for their lives when they got off "through a bitter and ugly crowd, a crowd reeking of vengeance and ice cream."

Good thing the Eureka SportStamp company hadn't decided to use players' full names in 1949, or they'd have had a problem with Cal McLish's stamp.

Calvin Coolidge Julius Caesar Tuskahoma McLish

The Catalina Cub with the most names is undoubtedly Calvin Coolidge Julius Caesar Tuskahoma McLish. Strange as it seems, Cal also has a nickname — 'Buster'.

HUMBLE REPORTER: Cal, how come a guy with 6 names needs a nickname?

C. C. J. C. T. 'B.' McL.: I weighed 12 pounds when I was born! I had more nicknames than I could tell you. In high school, they called me Archie because I shot basketballs up into the rafters, like the comic book Archie. And of course, anything that had to do with being Indian — a lot of people called me Chief. I'm not even half Indian — maybe one-sixteenth!

Cal pitched for Cubs in 1949 and 1951. He also pitched for Brooklyn, Pittsburgh, Cleveland, Cincinnati, the White Sox, and Phillies in a career that lasted from 1944-1964. He had some good seasons: 16-8 in 1958 (with a 2.99 ERA), 19-8 in 1959. He earned the save in the 2nd 1959 All-Star Game. Cal also pitched 6 years in the Pacific Coast League with Los Angeles and San Diego — winning 20 for the Angels in 1950.

And today, nearly 60 years after breaking in with the Dodgers as a teenager, Cal is still a roving scout for the Mariners, specializing in pitchers — along with Hub Kittle and Chris Bosio.

"I went to Catalina in 1949 and 1951," Buster says. "We took the boat over — it was a nice little ride. All you could do over there was run and throw. It was nice, something different...beautiful scenery. There was a little golf course — 9 holes, I think. We played a couple times. I never went hunting, but Phil Wrigley had a big cookout at his place. He had a kind of rodeo. They'd run down a rope and pull a ribbon off a calf's head. It wasn't a real rodeo."

"Cal McLish was a character," Randy Jackson remembers. "He never won a lot of games, but with the Cubs in those days, winning 6 or 7 was fantastic!"

Cal finished his playing long after Catalina, from whence he began coaching for former Cubmate Gene Mauch.

So Archie became a student of pitching, to soak as many wins out of those Cub teams as anybody could. "When I'm around pitchers, I'm baseball-oriented," the Chief says. "I don't tell a lot of stories — I mostly like to talk about pitching. I watched all the pitchers. At Wrigley, they had those slots — 345 to left-center, to right-center, so you'd better learn to keep the ball down. I learned to be a sinker-ball pitcher."

As a green Dodger rookie, he got some tips from a fellow Oklahoman who was wrapping up his career. "In 1944, in Cuba, we worked out of the old West Point Field House," J. C. says. "Paul Waner told me I only had a fastball — no change-up or slider — and I needed to work on that. I'd started out trying to throw fastballs — I tried to cross-seam everything, to be like Feller. I finally realized I needed to be the kind of pitcher I should have been."

Actually, his whole career was a comeback — he'd hurt his arm pitching for the Army in Europe. "In fact, the Dodgers started making an infielder out of me," Big Mac recalls. "In Havana, I played 16 games as an infielder on Pepper Martin's team until the 1947 season started."

But his arm got better, and he got back to the mound in time to go to Catalina. He got married between Catalina trips, but his wife couldn't come out in 1951. "She'd just had our 1st baby," Pops says. "She was pregnant the next year, too — we had kids every 3 months!" (Editor's note: Good thing there were lots of family names to dole out.)

His retirement blended into this coaching career: Cal's manager at Philadelphia, former Cub Gene Mauch, sent him to the minors and the Puerto Rican winter league to see if his arm would come back... while he coached and scouted a little. He followed Skip to Montreal in 1969, and eventually made his way to the World Series with Milwaukee in 1982.

Gene Mauch

Skip skippered for 26 years in the big leagues — starting with the Phillies (1960) and finishing with the Angels (1987). In between, he managed Montreal and Minnesota. Gene's Angel teams made it to the League Championship Series twice, and he was N.L. Manager of the Year 3 times. He's on a few all-time lists: Games (5th), wins (9th), and losses (3rd).

Before that, he played infield for half a dozen teams from 1944-1957. From 1948 to 1949, he trained with the Cubs in Southern California. A perennial All-Star in the Pacific Coast League — for the Los Angeles Angels, where he'd later manage — Mauch broke into big leagues as a 17 year-old.

"Gene Mauch was one of those feisty players," Bob Rush says. "He wasn't afraid to get his uniform dirty. He had the desire — he was into the game all the way, doing anything he could."

Before he Skipped, he played — Gene Mauch in 1957.

While most players practice to play in ballgames, it seems Mauch played in ballgames to practice managing — right from day one. "Gene Mauch, he was what we called a bench jockey," Jim Kirby says. "If you didn't do something right, he'd jump all over you — and he was just a utility infielder! One time, they put me in to pinch run, and I think it was Harry Walker got a soft hit to right, and I went all the way from 1st to 3rd — and Mauch just about went bezerk! Now, that was the way I always played ball, but he didn't like it — he thought I put myself in a position to get thrown out, and he didn't have any trouble telling me so!"

"Gene Mauch was a tough kid, and later on it was nice to play for him," says Johnny Klippstein, who was a Phillie in 1963 & 1964. "He was always in the game, he always talked the game — all the time."

Skip even analyzed the managers he was playing for. "Durocher was the highest-profile," he says, and "Billy Southworth was great with the 1948 Braves. Southworth told me one time, 'Skipper, you'll be a manager one day. Here's one piece of advice: Don't fall in love with your ballplayers.' The saddest thing is, that's exactly what he did, and it hurt him; he brought over some guys he'd had in St. Louis, and they just couldn't perform any more."

Mauch spent 5 decades in baseball, with tales spanning from the Brooklyn Dodgers of the early '40s through today's vastly-different game. He recalls the old days vividly: "Cavarretta, Peanuts Lowrey, Bill Nicholson — we played cards on the train, we'd shoot craps," he remembers, often amazing himself with how clearly the Spring of 1948 comes back ("Where'd *that* come from?" he says frequently, when recalling a player or a play from a ballpark that's long gone).

Bob Scheffing

During Gene Mauch's 1st season with Chicago, 1948, Bob Scheffing was the starting Cub catcher — batting .300. Scheffing also went on to manage in the majors (Cubs, 1957-1959, and Tigers, 1961-1963). He played for the Cubbies from 1941-1950, then finished briefly with the Reds and Cards. He led the N.L. in pinch-hits in 1946.

"The best I ever played for," Mauch says, "was Bob Scheffing, in Los Angeles. I was good at that level, and he made me feel like I was super. He knew how to handle me. He'd say things quietly, like I wasn't supposed to hear. He'd stand by the batting cage and kinda whisper loudly, 'That Mauch sure is a great hitter' to somebody. He'd say, 'Aw, I don't think he can hear me.' He was a very shrewd man."

Bob Scheffing, the master motivator — from behind the plate & inside the dugout.

"Casey Stengel would do that too," Bobby Mattick says.

Scheff actually started managing while still playing in the minors, in 1939 — at age 26 — before hitting the big leagues. "Bob Scheffing was a good catcher," Howard Auman recalls. "He was very good. You know, he motivated you. When he'd come to the mound, sometimes the catcher would say something to get your mind off what's happening, maybe tell a joke. Whenever it wasn't going good, we wished we had a chute we could walk into to get to the dugout!"

Scheffing's Tigers won 101 games in 1961, and he was named A.L. Manager of the Year, but...Roger Maris and Mickey Mantle played for the Yankees that season, so Detroit finished 2nd. As General Manager of the Mets, he won a pennant in 1973.

Bob & Bob Jr. on Catalina, 1947.

Bobby Mattick

Another Cub-turned-manager was Bobby Mattick. Mattick played for the Cubs from 1938-1940, then went to Cincinnati for 2 seasons. He managed the Toronto Blue Jays from 1980-81. His dad, Chick, played for the White Sox and Cards from 1912-1918. Like Hub Kittle, Bobby's been in pro ball for 8 decades — he's still Vice President of Baseball Operations for the Jays.

Bobby's 1938 Cub debut was impressive. He batted 1.000 for the season, knocking in a run with his first major-league at-bat.

He'd already spent 4 years in the minors, signing after his sophomore year in high school. "They had a semi-pro team on Catalina," Bobby says, "that and Ponca City, where guys like Hub Kittle were playing. Lelivelt liked me, and I only weighed about 150 pounds then, and he didn't think I'd do too good in that hot weather, so he kept me in L.A." He made several trips to the Island. "Avalon, that wouldn't be a bad place to live. We stayed at the St. Catherine. We'd eat there — it was a real nice place. It was a good outfit then."

He says "the older players, like Larry French, went fishing or boar hunting" — but he kept his nose to the grindstone, like Mauch, the other manager-in-training. "Heck no, I was all baseball — I put it in front of everything else."

Bobby Mattick was the oldest rookie manager in history when he suited up for the brand-new Blue Jays in 1980 — 42 Springs after Catalina.

Larry French

Besides chasing wild boar on Catalina, Larry French was also a starting pitcher for the Cubs from 1935-1941. In all, he pitched 14 years — starting with Pittsburgh in 1929 and finishing with Brooklyn in 1942. He won 197 games and led the N.L. is shutouts 2 straight years for the Cubs. He pitched in the 1935 and 1938 World Series for Chicago, and another for the Dodgers. He never quite won 20, but came close plenty of times — including 1936, when he went 18-9. His best pitches were screwballs and knuckleballs.

He was a badminton champion on Catalina, too — and quite a practical joker.

"Larry and Dad were roommates," says Della Root Arnold, Charlie's daughter, "and they were devils! One time, they were at their table, eating soup, and Dad never looks up and says, 'I'll bet you can't hit that bald guy on the head with a cracker.' And Larry does it! So the fella looks up and seems to recognize them, but doesn't get up, doesn't do anything, doesn't say anything — he just finishes eating and pays his bill. But then he went over to their table, picked up the ketchup, sprinkled both of them on the head, and left."

He was a devoted family guy — bringing his son to Catalina every Spring. Yet once he put on that uniform, Larry was a fierce competitor. He "was one of the few rookies I ever saw talk back," Dick Bartell wrote in his autobiography. "He'd be pitching batting practice and really pouring it on. The hitters complained, told him to take it easy. 'Nothing doing,' he said. 'I'm not out here to make you guys look good. I'm here trying to earn a job.'"

French enlisted in the Navy during World War II and retired 27 years later, in 1969.

The Larry Frenches, 1940.

Judging by his expression, you'd think Larry French was remembering those great times he spent with Charlie Root — lobbing crackers at unsuspecting diners.

Dick Bartell

Rowdy Richard Bartell was a good ballplayer — he hit .300 half a dozen times during his 18-year career — but his nickname explains why such a good ballplayer bounced around to 5 teams during his career. He only lasted 1 year with the Cubs, a disastrous 1939 season where the press and the fans pretty much rode him out of town.

Dick was a 2-time All-Star who ended up with 2,165 hits. He played in 3 World Series, and managed the Sacramento Solons in the Pacific Coast League before coaching briefly for the Tigers and Reds. Fired, fired, fired.

The Cubs traded him for Billy Rogell in the Winter of 1939 — which a reporter described as "one worn-out shortstop for another." But Bartell anchored the infield for the 1940 Tigers, helping lead 'em to the World Series — and getting the last laugh.

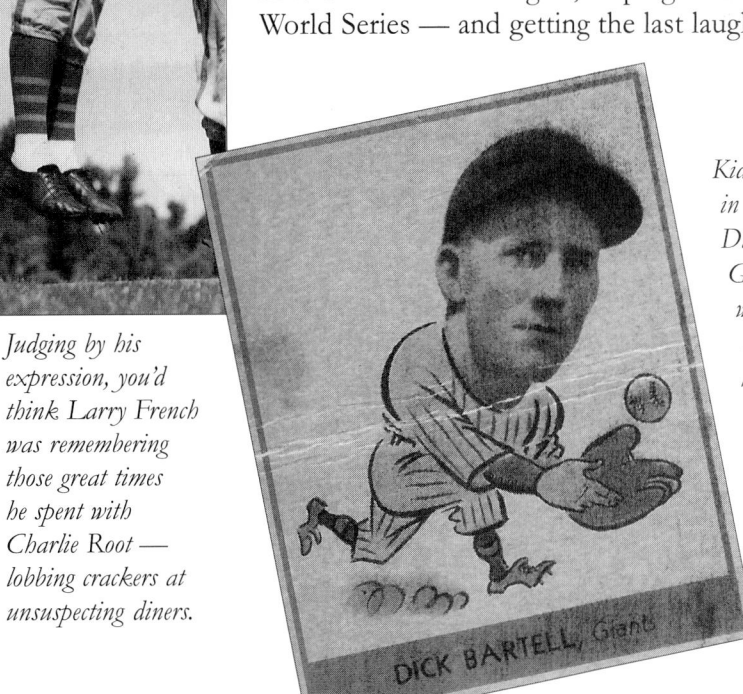

Kids, find the answer in the picture on Dick Bartell's 1938 Goudey card: Why was Rowdy Richard always getting himself into trouble?

Roy Smalley, Jr.

Roy Smalley manned the Cub shortstop post a little while longer than Bartell — 6 seasons, to be precise, from 1948-1953. In 1950, he suddenly must've realized he was playing in Wrigley Field — and he smacked 21 home runs. (Actually, the team had put him on a weight-gaining milkshake diet. But maybe he slurped one too many: He also led the league in strikeouts.) Roy played 5 more years, for the Braves and Phillies. His son, Roy III, played 13 seasons in the '70s and '80s...at the same position.

He went out to Catalina early and worked the back country (chasing goats and buffalo and such), then roomed with Don Carlsen, who was a schoolmate at Pepperdine. Bob Rush and Wayne Terwilliger also spent some time rooming with Smalley.

"What a great guy!" Twig says. "Very easy-goin', laid back, but some fire inside."

The fire came out at the plate. "Roy Smalley hit 12 home runs that spring," Gene Mauch says. "He and I had a deal — we'd put up a buck for each homer. I'd only hit one all spring. I had to buy him 2 pair of Argyle socks. They cost about $12. I told him, "That's $6 a foot!""

And then there was the infield.

"He had a super-terrific arm," Paul Schramka says.

"They liked Roy Smalley for his strong arm and his range," Carmen Mauro says.

"The fans in Chicago made it tough on Smalley — just 'cuz he threw it over the 1st-baseman's head," Phil Cavarretta says.

But Bob Rush clarifies: "He'd get the ball most people wouldn't get, then they'd get on him for the throw he made. He got some bad publicity, which was unfortunate. Roy Smalley was a top-notch guy."

So a Chicago racetrack announcer penned a poem entitled, "Terwilliger to Smalley to the Dugout," which he renamed "Miksis to Smalley to Addison Street" the next year.

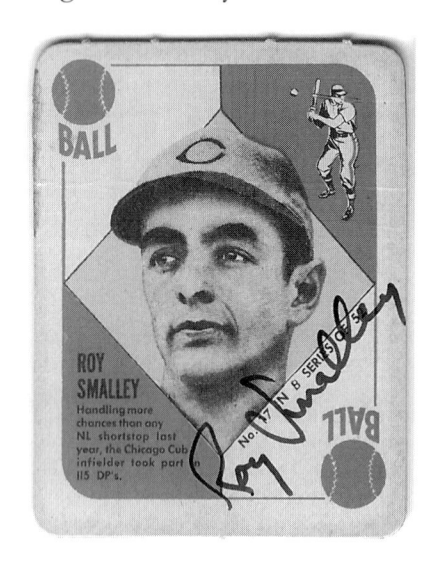

Roy Smalley herded buffalo & mass-consumed milkshakes on Catalina to aid in his career.

"He had a tremendous arm, one of the best arms in baseball," Eddie Miksis told Carrie Muskat in *Banks to Sandberg to Grace*.

Roy could joke about it. "One year," he says in *Essential Cubs*, "I led the National League in errors. They named a vitamin after me — One-a-Day." The forgotten asterisk: He also led the N.L. in putouts, assists, and double plays that season.

And he was a favorite with the local kids every Spring — always taking time to give 'em some tips. He served in the Navy during World War II, and in 1975 he got to watch his son play in his 1st major-league baseball game.

Bob Rush

Bob Rush survived pitching for the Cubs for 10 seasons, from 1948-1957, before being traded to Milwaukee. He was rewarded for his patience by getting to play in the 1958 World Series. He played another year and a half for the Braves, before finishing up with the White Sox in 1960. He managed to average 11 wins a year with the Cubs — no small feat in those days — and got to take his turn leading the N.L. in losses in 1950, with 20. Bob won the 1952 All-Star game, and he was a good enough pitcher that if he'd been with the Yankees all those years...he might be in the Hall of Fame. "Charlie Grimm was fine to play for," Bob says. "Of course, the ballclubs he had weren't exceptionally good." Bob's claim to fame is that he's the guy on the left in the Norman Rockwell painting that appeared on the cover of the *Saturday Evening Post* in 1948.

"I don't know if anybody besides Feller threw 100 miles an hour in those days," Islander Foxie Saudcedo says, "but he sure threw hard."

"We winced," says Foxie's brother Marse.

When he wasn't scaring the local kids behind the batting cage to death, Bob also golfed on Catalina — carding the best net 2-round score in the pre-training tournament with a 118. But, according to the *Cubs News*, the competition wasn't all that stiff — he had a 21 handicap.

Rush worked hard — coming out early to get in shape with Smalley and Don Carlsen. "I went a couple of weeks before the team came over," he remembers. "I went out with my wife. I just wanted to get out early, because at the time I lived in South Bend, Indiana, and it was still winter! So I just wanted to get a jump on getting in shape. We threw, and did some running around the field. Some light tossing, just to get the arm ready. We ran up the goat paths when Frisch got there!"

It was an adventure, he says. "Most of the time, we took the boat out. Once or twice, we flew to Los Angeles for some reason, maybe to play an exhibition game. When we came up on Catalina Island and looked down on the Island, it didn't even look as big as an aircraft carrier — I thought, 'We'd better have a good pilot!' And when we'd take off, it was like we ran off a cliff."

After he retired, Bob worked at Motorola...then a swimming pool company. He had 2 daughters, and 2 sons who played baseball in high school.

Hank Borowy

Hank Borowy was finishing up his Cub pitching career when Rush came along, in 1948. Hank pitched for 10 seasons, from 1942-1951. The Yankees sold him to Chicago in the midst of the 1945 pennant race, and Borowy responded — going 11-2 for the Cubbies (21-7 for the year), and winning 2 games in the World Series. In fact, he started 3 games and appeared in 4 of the 7 — working 3 in a row. He won 108 games in all, and also appeared in 2 Fall Classics for the Yankees.

In order to throw the ball 100 miles an hour, Bob had to get some momentum going during his wind-up.

Hank Borowy showed William Bendix how to throw for The Babe Ruth Story *at the White Sox Spring Training camp in Pasadena. (Manager Charlie Grimm, looking on, contemplates whether or not to mention that the Babe was a Southpaw.)*

Hard work, but good times. "Of course, I was young. I enjoyed it. I was lucky — I got off to a good start. The attitude, the atmosphere is different for each era — it changes. After the War, the only people left on the teams were the guys who got rejected, or the guys who were older — that's how I got my break. The main person who helped me was my dad. He had a cup of coffee with the Browns, but he found he could make more money playing in the industrial leagues!"

Borowy was known as a gritty ballplayer who didn't need much managing. "Look at that Borowy over there," Charlie Grimm told reporters in 1946. "He must've gained all of 5 ounces over the Winter. I'll order him to take 2 steam baths a day. Then he won't have to open the door to come out — he can just fall through one of the cracks."

Hank casually suggests that Bill Bendix change from his White Sox uniform to Yankee pinstripes.

Claude Passeau

The Cubs' other pitching star/workhorse in the 1945 World Series was Claude Passeau. Long before Yogi leaped into Don Larsen's arms, Claude pitched a World Series 1-hitter against the Tigers. During his 13 seasons with the Pirates, Phillies, and Cubs...he won 162 games. He came to Chicago in 1939 and finished his career there in 1947. His best year was 1940, when he won 20 — 1 season after leading the league in strikeouts.

"Spring training there was interesting," Claude says. "It was a vacation, and it was also getting in shape. A few times, my wife came out on the island for 3-4 weeks. Then, of course, we went to L.A., and played against the White Sox and whoever else would come out there to play against us. My son and my daughter came out — they were just 3 or 4 years old at the time. We all had a good time."

His wife, BUM ("I had one older brother," she says, "and one younger, and they couldn't say Bernyce, so they started calling me BUM. You spell that with all capital letters.") would take care of the kids and the cooking. "It was wonderful," she says.

Since Claude Passeau threw a pitch other than a fastball, he did not have to kick as high as Bob Rush did.

Claude brought a laid-back country attitude to the mound. He was a few weeks late for Spring Training in 1942, and flew out West to join the rest of the squad: "Let's let it go that I had some 'unfinished business,' " he told Herbert Simons of the *Chicago Times*. " 'Confidentially, though,' he drawled, 'I just wasn't in any hurry to get here. I didn't need the work.' "

But when he was good and ready, Claude was focused — earning a reputation for brushing hitters back. Once, after Hank Sauer hit a home run, Passeau decked him on his next at-bat. "Try hittin' it that way," Claude shouted when Hank was still in the dirt.

"I didn't have a curve ball, just a fastball, and one that moved a little — they call it a slider now," he says. "Some people said I threw a spitball, but I couldn't throw a spitball if I had to. Clyde McCullough was at a banquet, and one of the guests asked if I threw a spitter. They asked what he thought of Bill Lee, of Charlie Root, and so on. He said, 'Well, I know one thing. One of 'em threw a fastball, one of 'em threw the curve, and Passeau was a pretty good pitcher.' "

"What a specimen," Red Adams says. "He was a big guy, with a big frame; he didn't have an ounce of fat on him in his prime — raw bone. He had some ability. He was 37, and he could still throw hard — there was no finesse. He had a hard slider, and he came in on the hands of those left-handed hitters. He was nice to us kids."

Claude went back to the farm in Mississippi after baseball, growing tung nuts and running a John Deere dealership. "My son runs it now — he has for the last 19 or 20 years," Claude says. "He signed with Cincinnati — but he didn't like it, so he quit. He had good stuff, as good or better than I did."

Yet he was a well-respected field general — 'managing' the starting half of the team during some Avalon intrasquad games. He went on to coach for several big-league teams, and he managed in the minors, too.

"Clyde McCullough was one of a kind," Gene Mauch says. "Baseball was all he knew, all he cared about. He had a great arm, and he was so proud of it. He threw the ball with such perfect backspin, you could catch it bare-handed — hard, but it felt like a feather cuz of the backspin. I caught it one time bare-handed when he threw down to 2nd, and he wanted to kill me. I told him it was a compliment to his throwing — I wasn't trying to show him up."

Bill Lee

When Clyde wasn't catching Claude's, uhm, non-spitters, he was calling Bill Lee's fastballs. Not to be confused with 'Spaceman' Bill Lee (who pitched for the Red Sox more recently), Big Bill Lee was one of the premier hurlers of the late '30s. In 1938, he led the Cubs to the World Series with his league-topping 22 wins, 2.66 ERA, and 9 shutouts. In fact, 4 of 'em were in a row — tying a big-league record. A 2-time All-Star, his 14-year career started and ended in Chicago (1934-1947), with brief interludes in Boston and Philadelphia. He won 169 games, led the N.L. in 9 categories, and pitched in the 1935 World Series too.

Clyde McCullough, the catcher's catcher. Who needs a mask?

Clyde McCullough

Clyde McCullough caught for 15 seasons, and there's no telling how many times he got his fingers wet during that period. He started with the Cubs in 1940 and finished with the Cubs in 1956, with a 4-year side-trip to Pittsburgh in the middle. A 1948 All-Star, he hit .252 lifetime and got to play in the 1945 World Series (despite not playing during the regular season), thanks to special Wartime rules. He was a tough, gritty, old-fashioned ballplayer — one of the last catchers to play without a chest protector — and in 1955 he called the 1st no-hitter in Wrigley Field in 38 years.

Clyde was truly a stereotypical catcher — Yogi-Berraesque as they come. His teammates brought him a birthday cake on Catalina in 1947, and sang, "Happy Birthday, Dear Meathead..."

Big Bill Lee, 1939.

Bill stopped by the Catalina Pottery to make a teacup for the missus, or something.

"Bill Lee, he was their ace pitcher," Islander Roger Upton remembers. "I got to do a little batting practice with him. He threw me an easy one, and I hit it right back to him."

General Lee was a big country boy who worked hard in the warm Southern Winters. On the 1st day of '38 Spring practice, Andy Lotshaw told reporters: "I was helping to fit Bill's uniform in the clubhouse before we came out to work. I noticed calluses on the 1st 2 fingers of his throwing hand. That told the story. He's been throwing quite a bit in Louisiana and he's already in shape to pitch batting practice."

But with success comes the other stuff. A few years later, in 1941, Bill was late for camp. In the *Tribune*, Ed Burns wrote: "If Lee stays out too much longer we aren't going to pick the Cubs to win the pennant and that will be an upset, our civic pride being what it is." In a special for the *Los Angeles Times*, Burns said Lee was "suffering from shock he underwent when he took a 1st look at this year's salary offer. Bill...is said to have passed into a coma."

Yet a few more seasons brought things back full circle. "Bill Lee, trying a comeback with the Cubs, reported to Catalina in such good shape that he starting pitching batting practice an hour after getting off the boat from the mainland," the *Cubs News* informed fans in 1947.

Ken Raffensberger

Ken Raffensberger came to Catalina in 1940 and 1941, when the Cubs weren't sure if Lee could still carry the load. Ken ended up pitching for 15 seasons — mostly with the Reds and Phillies. He won 113 games, primarily on cellar-dwelling teams — forced to lead the league in losses twice, while also leading the N.L. in shutouts twice and saves once. He won the 1944 All-Star game.

"That was a nice place to train," Ken says. "We'd get a day off now and then; we'd go up in the mountains and hunt wild boar. Bill Nicholson came along. We had a guide who took us up in the mountains, on a Jeep. We bagged one. We went fishing, too. They had a big dock at the end of the Hotel St. Catherine, where we stayed. We caught a lot of fish, we caught anything — nothing big — with some guys from Catalina. We'd troll, catch some small tuna." When the Cubs sent him to Los Angeles, he kept right on fishing. "Every Monday was a day off," he says, "so we'd go deep sea fishing off Santa Monica." While in L.A., Ken rented Cub/Angel teammate Lou Novikoff's house in South Gate... when Lou was up with the Cubs.

He returned to the minors after the Reds let him go in 1954. "I played in Cuba, and in the Piedmont League, with Baltimore," he says. Then, "I managed for the Cubs in 1955-1957, at Lafayette, Louisiana, in the Evangeline League, then at Burlington in the III league. I came back to York and worked in sales, before retiring and taking life easy."

Ken Raffensberger, a Catalina rookie in 1940.

There weren't many baseball cards made during the War — paper rationing, you see. But the MP Novelty Company (a carnival supply firm) issued this appropriately-designed card of Lou Novikoff in 1943.

Lou Novikoff

Lou Novikoff had a certain advantage over most other ballplayers: He was nuts. Looney. Certifiable. Absolutely over-the-top crazy.

The Mad Russian once stole 3rd with the bases loaded, saying he couldn't resist getting such a good jump on the pitcher. He sometimes sang to the fans. He'd have his wife sit behind the plate while he was playing, and berate him — loudly. He'd pub-crawl his way from the hotel to the ballpark. And he was so terrified of the ivy at Wrigley Field that he'd let balls drop rather than getting close to the wall.

"That's why I played centerfield," Ed Jabb recalls. "I had to back him up!"

"Novikoff was there," Harvey Storey says. "After he'd fill up with beer, he'd grab the microphone and put on a show at any cabaret in town. He'd stay up all night, then come to practice the next day."

But when he was on, he was on. As a starting outfielder for the Cubs in 1942, he hit exactly .300. He played parts of 5 seasons in all, led the league in pinch-hits in 1945, and batted .304 in his final part-season. In the minors, he won 4 straight batting championships...with a lifetime average of .338. He dominated the Pacific Coast League in 1940 for the Los Angeles Angels, batting .363 with 41 homers.

And he was the 1st player to have an agent.

"Neither Novikoff nor his agent, Joe Rodgers, communicated with the Cubs today," the *Los Angeles Times* reported in 1941, with Cub GM Jim Gallagher saying Lou's alternative was to "make a living in some other line of endeavor." The report went on to explain that Cub brass "would rather know how he can do in National League parks than how his magnificently muscular body shows up in rotogravure."

A few days later, Ed Burns wrote: "AVALON — Lou Novikoff, slugger, tenor, harmonicist, and muscular marvel, accepted Cub terms here this afternoon. The 25-year-old ex-Angel was accompanied by Joe Rodgers, who has been described as his discoverer, friend, agent, and adviser."

"Novikoff's 4-day holdout ended yesterday," Herbert Simons wrote in the *Chicago Times*, "when, in company with 'his pal' and personal adviser, Joe Rodgers, he coyly came over from the mainland with the other Sunday sightseers 'to see the bird farm.' Accidentally on purpose, he bumped into General Manager Jim Gallagher, who accidentally on purpose happened to be in the way of said bumping."

The Man Russian wows the crowd in the Spring of '41.

"In his 1st Spring Training session," Warren Brown wrote in the Cubs' history, "(Manager Jimmie) Wilson might have gained 1st place in the Attention Derby, all by himself, if it were not for the advent of the one, the only, the original Lou Novikoff."

"As a character," Simons wrote a few days later, "Novikoff's naiveté has lived up to all the advance press-agentry...He'll sit in the hotel lobby with you and go heavily on a Russian accent to all passers-by and then turn to you with a Russian shrug and 'Vell, vot can I do? They vant me to make bub-licity.'"

But "Inside baseball and signal systems were things with which he couldn't be annoyed at all," Brown wrote.

Lou's inability to handle big-league ivy kept him relegated to the minors for most of his career — appearing on obscure card sets issued with anything but gum. His 1947 Centennial Pancake & Waffle Flour card is another good example. (Is that woman behind Lou screaming at him?)

Grimm tried everything he could to get past the fielding issues. "I thought at first he was susceptible to hay fever," Cholly told Brown, "so I got me some samples of golden rod and proved to Lou that the vines weren't that. He seemed relieved, but next time a guy hit a ball over his head he stayed farther away from the vines than ever. Bob Lewis...said maybe Novikoff thought the stuff was poison ivy. So I took him out again, and...when I was sure Mr. Wrigley wasn't looking, I pulled a bunch of vines off the wall and rubbed them all over my face and hands. I even chewed a couple of the leaves to prove they couldn't harm anyone. All Novikoff had to say was he wondered what kind of smoke they would make. But he wouldn't go near 'em to find out."

Back in the Coast League in 1948, Seattle manager JoJo White sent Lou in to pinch-hit — but Lou wasn't in the building. The Rainiers sent him packing. After retiring, he played semi-pro softball for years...and was the 1st member ever elected to the International Softball Congress Hall of Fame.

Gene Lillard

Another Coast League superstar who didn't fare as well at the Show was Gene Lillard. Unlike Novikoff, though, Gene's cap was screwed on snugly.

Gene smacked 56 homers and hit .361 for the L.A. Angels in 1935. So obviously, the Cubs called him up. And just as obviously...

...they tried to make him a pitcher.

Lillard, bored on the Cub bench, had offered to toss batting practice. His arm impressed the Cub braintrust...and since All-Everything Stan Hack was in front of Gene at 3rd...it seemed to make sense. But in the long run, it jettisoned his career.

Gene and his wife had fun on Catalina, though — he golfed, and together they made a mean badminton tandem.

His major league totals: .182 with no homers in 44 at-bats for the Cubs in 1936 and 1939...and pitching, 3-5 for the Cubs in 1939, 0-1 for the Cards in 1940.

His minor league totals: 345 home runs and a .303 average over 22 seasons. He hit 43 homers as a teenager in L.A., and at age 35 batted .364 for Phoenix to lead the league. Gene then hit .300 in the minors 4 more times after that — including his last season, at age 40. Another Cub experiment, gone horribly wrong...

In 1947, when Gene Lillard wasn't with the Cubs, his manager in Oakland (Casey Stengel) said he didn't have to pitch any more.

Once everybody figured out what his name was, Ken O'Dea enjoyed a 12-year career in the major leagues.

Ken O'Dea

Ken O'Dea was a back-up backstop catching some of Lillard's tosses. Ken went by his middle name, which confused reporters early on — they wanted to call him 'Jim.' He played 12 seasons, breaking in with the Cubs (1935-1938), then to the Giants, then the Cards, and finishing with the Braves in 1946. He hit .300 twice for Chicago, subbing for Gabby Hartnett, and tore it up in 5 World Series — hitting .462. He batted 1.000 for the Cubs in the 1935 Series, and smacked a homer against the Yanks 3 years later.

"Ken O'Dea, rookie catcher, was paired with Stainback for superlatives," the *Los Angeles Times* reported in 1935. "It was O'Dea's hitting which brought Grimm's superlatives...Grimm expressed hope that the long quest for a catcher capable of giving Hartnett a lift in double-headers and on hot days may have ended."

"O'Dea, whose hitting is getting long and often, is a capable reserve and should give Hartnett that needed day off (which he'll spend fishing)," agreed *Des Moines Dispatch* columnist Dutch Reagan in 1937.

Mickey Owen

Mickey Owen caught for the Cubs too, but he's more famous for 2 non-Cub reasons: a goof in the 1941 World Series, and a long-time baseball camp after he retired.

Mickey's career started as a Cardinal in 1937, then Brooklyn. He jumped to the renegade Mexican League with a few others in 1946, was banned from U.S. baseball, and returned to the Cubs in 1949. After 3 years in Chicago, he finished up with the Red Sox in 1954. A great fielder, he set catching records for Brooklyn in 1941...but dropped a slippery spitter of a 3rd strike (which was supposed to be the final out of the Series), and the Yankees came back to win.

"I remember them telling us it was beautiful out there," Charlie Owen says about his parents' time on Catalina. "Mr. Wrigley owned it, and he took good care of it — it was a heavenly place. Dad was working, and mom enjoyed looking around. She described some of the most beautiful horses she'd ever seen, and she had some knowledge of horses — since dad tried to raise some. Mother always had a twinkle in her eye when she talked about that place."

Like Bill Buckner, Mickey Owen is remembered for a single World Series play...rather than a pretty impressive major league career.

Harry Chiti

A hopeful successor to Mickey Owen behind the Cub plate was Harry Chiti. Harry caught for the Cubs from 1950-1956, then bounced around with a few teams until 1962. That year, he was traded for himself: The Indians dealt him to the Mets for a player to be named later. After Harry hit .195 in 15 games, the Mets realized they didn't need him, so they named him as the player to be named later and shipped him back. Harry's lifetime average was .238.

He displayed the potential for power early on — smacking a 425-foot triple in a Catalina intrasquad game once — but he needed work. "Harry Chiti was this big, 18 year-old kid," says Islander Marcelino Saucedo, "but he couldn't throw the ball back to the pitcher. I guess he learned how!"

"The master minds are high on 18-year-old Harry Chiti, a 215-pound catcher," Frank Finch wrote in the *Los Angeles Times*. "The Detroit youngster looks eligible for the Chicago Bears."

Can't run, can't throw, can't even be traded away — but boy, can the youngster hit!

"They were grooming Harry Chiti," says Carmen Mauro. "He had a good arm, and he was big and strong, but not much power. They'd jam him, and get that little dribbler."

Big, strong, slow — definitely a catcher. "In the old days," Mike Royko reminisced for *Tribune* readers in 1985, "you could watch Harry Chiti run to 1st base in 35 seconds flat."

Lee Anthony

Lee Anthony was one of the rookie pitchers tossing to the rookie catchers on Catalina. His career in pro baseball spanned 6 decades as a player, manager, coach, and scout. Lee never made it to the Show with the Cubs, but he won more than a hundred games in the minors...and was a top-notch pitcher in the tough Pacific Coast League for several years, playing for the Hollywood Stars and Los Angeles Angels. He won 16 for the Angels in 1948, after the Cubs went back to Chicago. Besides his time on Catalina, the New York Giants also gave him a shot at their Spring site in Phoenix in 1956.

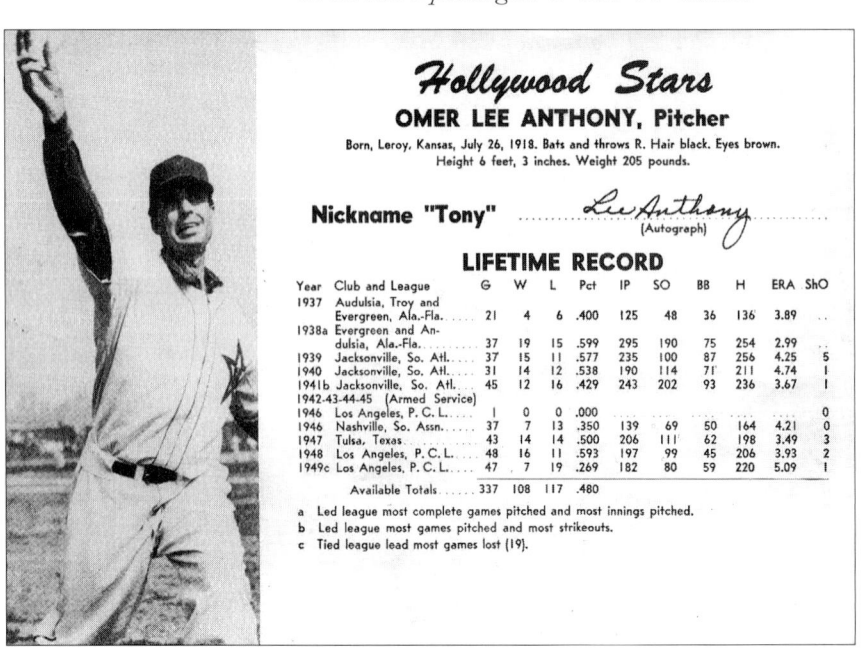

Lee pitched in the minors for nearly 20 years, from 1937-1956, then managed in the A's organization before moving into their scouting office. He later scouted for the Senators and stayed with the team when they became the Texas Rangers — finally retiring in 1986.

"I don't know why they didn't keep going out there," Lee says about Catalina. "Wrigley owned the island, and it was a nice set-up."

When practice was done, they made the most of the locale, Anthony recalls. "They had a lot of rattlesnakes out there, and they brought in some wild hogs to clean 'em up. We had one day off where some of the ballplayers went fishing out at sea, and some of the others went hunting after the hogs." But still, he stayed pretty focused. "I was pretty interested in baseball, that's all," he says. "I'd go from the hotel to the restaurant to the ballpark and back. I got married in 1947. My wife had a couple of brothers in Los Angeles, and she stayed with them, and she came over a couple of times on a boat from Long Beach and spent the night at the hotel."

Lee's career highlight was also a lowlight. In 1938, while still a teenager, he pitched a no-hitter in the Alabama-Florida League. But thanks to poor fielding behind him...he lost the game!

During his 6 decades in professional baseball, Lee Anthony once played for a fabled team called the Hollywood Stars — pitching his home games at Gilmore Field, which has since been bulldozed & turned into a parking lot at CBS TV studios.

Hollywood Stars
OMER LEE ANTHONY, Pitcher

Born, Leroy, Kansas, July 26, 1918. Bats and throws R. Hair black. Eyes brown.
Height 6 feet, 3 inches. Weight 205 pounds.

Nickname "Tony"

LIFETIME RECORD

Year	Club and League	G	W	L	Pct	IP	SO	BB	H	ERA	ShO
1937	Audulsia, Troy and Evergreen, Ala.-Fla.	21	4	6	.400	125	48	36	136	3.89	
1938a	Evergreen and Andulsia, Ala.-Fla.	37	19	15	.599	295	190	75	254	2.99	
1939	Jacksonville, So. Atl.	37	15	11	.577	235	100	87	256	4.25	5
1940	Jacksonville, So. Atl.	31	14	12	.538	190	114	71	211	4.74	1
1941b	Jacksonville, So. Atl.	45	12	16	.429	243	202	93	236	3.67	1
1942-43-44-45	(Armed Service)										
1946	Los Angeles, P.C.L.	1	0	0	.000						0
1946	Nashville, So. Assn.	37	7	13	.350	139	69	50	164	4.21	0
1947	Tulsa, Texas	43	14	14	.500	206	111	62	198	3.49	3
1948	Los Angeles, P.C.L.	48	16	11	.593	197	99	45	206	3.93	2
1949c	Los Angeles, P.C.L.	47	7	19	.269	182	80	59	220	5.09	1
	Available Totals	337	108	117	.480						

a Led league most complete games pitched and most innings pitched.
b Led league most games pitched and most strikeouts.
c Tied league lead most games lost (19).

Red Adams actually had a couple of different baseball careers in Southern California over the years...

LOS ANGELES ANGELS

CHARLES DWIGHT ADAMS, Pitcher

Born, Parlier, Calif., October 7, 1921. Bats and throws R. Hair red. Eyes green.
Height 6 feet, 2 inches. Weight 192 pounds.

Nickname "Red"

LIFETIME RECORD

Year	Club and League	G	W	L	Pct.	IP	SO	BB	H	ERA	ShO
1939	Bisbee, Ariz.-Tex...	27	16	8	.667	216	116	62	244	4.36	0
1940	Bisbee, Ariz.-Tex...	31	13	12	.520	240	191	68	188	5.29	..
1941	Vancouver, W. Intl..	32	6	15	.286	171	95	67	207	4.95	0
1942	Los Angeles, P.C...	11	6	4	.600	67	21	31	69	4.10	..
1942	Tulsa, Texas......	18	4	8	.333	90	44	37	93	4.40	..
1943	(Inactive)										
1944*	Los Angeles, P.C...	44	10	7	.588	186	87	56	176	3.58	3
1945	Los Angeles, P.C...	41	21	15	.583	298	160	90	269	2.72	2
1946	Chicago, N.L......	8	0	1	.000	12	8	7	18	8.25	0
1946	Los Angeles, P.C...	17	9	4	.692	104	61	25	96	2.68	..
1947*	Los Angeles, P.C...	34	14	12	.538	236	134	57	230	3.51	0
	Totals....	263	99	86	.535	1620	917	500	1590		5

*—Pennant-winning clubs.

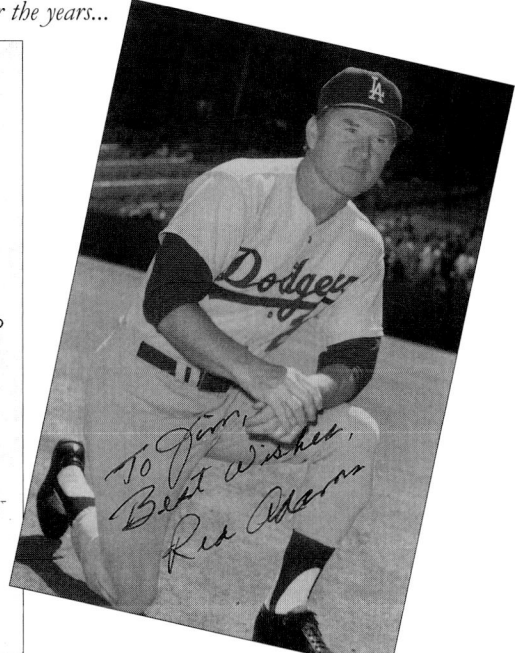

Red Adams

Like Lee Anthony, Red Adams spent a few years alternating between the Cubs and their top farm team in L.A. And, also like teammate Lee, his playing career was a prelude to another, lengthier career in baseball.

Red won 21 for the Angels in 1945, earning a trip to Catalina in 1946. He went 0-1 in Chicago, and got a train ticket back West. He was invited back to the Island in 1947, but never made it to the majors again — at least as a player. But as a coach, he spent more than a decade shaping some of the most successful young pitching careers in the league.

As the Dodgers' pitching coach from 1969-1980, Red cultivated guys like Claude Osteen, Tommy John, Fernando Valenzuela, and Don Sutton. Talk about high praise: when inducted into the Hall of Fame, Sutton said, "Red Adams is a standard by which every pitching coach should be measured. No person ever meant more to my career than Red Adams, and without him I wouldn't be standing in Cooperstown today."

"Red Adams," Edgar 'the Mouse' Munzel wrote for the *Sun* in 1946, "radiates more cold determination than any recruit the Cubs have had in camp in several years. He is so much a carbon copy of Charlie Root...both in courage and his side-arm delivery, that Grimm calls him 'Root Junior.'"

"My stuff was pretty mediocre," Red says, "nothing exceptional. Oh, my fastball might've been a little busy. I was pretty much a run-of-the-mill journeyman pitcher. Had it not been for the War, I'd have probably been released."

"That kid has a real pitching heart," coach Dutch Ruether said that Spring. "However, he will be duck soup for left-handed hitters unless he learns to keep that ball low and outside."

Rookie rough-housing may have cost Red a major league career. In 1939, 17-year-old Adams was wrestling with some of his teammates in Bisbee, Arizona — when he dove through a glass door that he didn't know was shut. "After I hurt my arm," Red says, "I'd throw from all different angles. Underneath, that caused less pain."

Yet 7 seasons later, he earned himself a ticket to Avalon. "I have nothing but good thoughts about Catalina," he recalls. "We went over on the boat from San Pedro, and my wife went with me. We had one little girl; she was about 2 years old. We were only actually over there 2-3 weeks. Then we'd come to L.A. and play some exhibition games. It's a real tiny town — you're a stone's throw from anything. I was over there 2 different years — in 1947, I stayed in the hotel with the team. There were some wild boar, but I didn't do any of that. I'd fish. They had that beautiful ballroom. One time, I remember having a dance — some big orchestra came in. Those were the days of the Big Bands."

Red stuck around in the P. C. L. for several more years: besides L.A., he also pitched for San Diego, Portland, and Sacramento. Then, his winter carpentry job became full-time. "I wish I'd have had enough brains to go to college," he says. But he did okay — getting into the movies as a set-builder and working with some big stars, including former Catalina Cub Chuck Connors. Then, back to the game.

"When I think back on my baseball life," Red says, "I was fortunate. The thing that pops out the most are the people I've met. There were a lot of great guys."

Before he was a Society, Emil Verban was an Antelope — as the back of his 1949 Bowman card informs collectors.

Emil Verban

Emil Verban, who also got a cup o'coffee with the Cubs in the late '40s, achieved some post-playing notoriety, as well.

Emil played 2nd base from 1944-1950 for several teams...and was a 3-time All-Star. As a rookie, he hit .412 in the 1944 World Series for the Cards (driving in the Series-winning run), and got to have 2 nicknames: 'Dutch' and 'The Antelope.' His greatest achievement as a Cub was that he only struck out *twice* in 1949 — in 351 at-bats! (To put this into perspective: All-time major-league-leading whiff king Reggie Jackson, the most over-rated player in the history of the game, averaged **92** strikeouts per 351 at-bats.)*

Emil has a most unique fan club these days. It's called the Emil Verban Memorial Society, and its 700 members — including a lot of former Cubs — simply celebrate Cubdom. "I got together with Swish sometimes at the Emil Verban Memorial Society," Lennie Merullo says. "Every year, they have a 2-3 day event with a dinner."

Emil was selected as the marquee name (edging out Roy Smalley at the last minute) because he represents the typical old-time Cub player: Hard-working, a solid ballplayer, but obscure. He bristled at first, but realized it wasn't ridicule when Dutch Reagan — a member — invited him to the White House.

Eddie Waitkus

Eddie Waitkus was also a Cub infielder in the late '40s — until he got shot by a deranged fan. Like Emil, Eddie has become larger than life after his career...thanks to being a prototype for Roy Hobbs in *The Natural*.

Eddie played 1st base for the Cubs from 1941-1948, then played 7 more seasons — mostly for the Phillies. He hit .304 as a rookie, and was an All-Star for the Cubs in 1948 — so naturally, they traded him away. Eddie was batting .306 for the Phillies in 1949 when he got plugged in a hotel room — ironically, in Chicago. After 4 surgeries, he was okay. The next season, he helped lead the Whiz Kids to the World Series.

Preston Ward

Preston Ward hoped to replace Waitkus as the Cubs' 1st-sacker. He played for about a team a year during his 9 seasons — breaking in with Brooklyn (1948) and hanging up his spikes with the A's in 1959. He hit .253 during his career, with a little power.

He wishes he could've spent more time on Catalina. "We were only there 2 weeks," he says. "I liked it, I enjoyed it, I think Frisch liked me. They wouldn't let you do anything." Then, he missed a couple of Springs because he was drafted.

Preston's career took another bump, too. "Of course, I got hurt early," he says. "I was stealing 2nd, and I tried to switch the direction I was sliding, but it was too late. I hurt my ankle, and I was out most of the summer. That really hurt — there's nothing worse that getting a good start, and getting injured." After that, no more Catalina: "I hated for the trade to go to Pittsburgh. He was gettin' rid of everybody, started a new team, almost."

When he retired, Preston had a Hallmark shop in Beverly Hills. "We had 2 girls, and a grandchild," he says. "I'd like more!"

Preston Ward contemplates whether or not his 1950 Bowman card shows a series of UFOs lining up in landing formation behind him.

---

* Since we're at it, let the record show that Emil's lifetime average was 10 points higher than Reggie's... and his World Series batting average was 55 points higher than "Mr. October" got.

160

Don Carlsen spent a few years pitching in Southern California, even when he wasn't out on Catalina Island.

Don Carlsen

Don Carlsen was on Catalina at the same time as Ward. He'd gotten into 1 game for the Cubs in 1948 — pitching an inning — then played for the Pirates in 1951 and 1952.

He started as a shortstop, hitting .299 at age 17 before the Navy called. Converted to a pitcher in Los Angeles (while he was also going to Pepperdine), Don got an invitation to Catalina. He roomed with Roy Smalley at a bungalow next to the ballpark.

"Catalina was my 1st spring training," Don says. "There wasn't a lot to do — not a lot of activity. Avalon was a quiet little town. There was golf available. There was sightseeing, and there was one little theater. I think Smalley and I went to a show or two. Playing cards, we'd do that a lot. I had a pretty good moving fastball. A couple years later, I ran into arm trouble."

"Don Carlsen was a good guy," Bob Rush says. "In baseball, like anything else, you have to be at the right place, at the right time."

Don Dunker

Don Dunker was invited to Catalina in 1946, but he really wasn't in the right place at the right time, either — he pitched in the minors from 1945-1953, but never made a big-league roster.

Pitching for Indiana University, Don was MVP in the Big 10 — in 1941. He went into the service. "I was selected to the All-Service All-Star team that played the American League All-Stars in Cleveland," he says. "I was the only college boy on the baseball team, so I was invited to pitch batting practice in Chicago, at Wrigley Field. I was in the service from 4 months after Pearl Harbor to 1945. When the war wound down, I went to spring training."

"His one handicap was imposed by the War," Munzel wrote in the *Sun* in 1946. "He was in the Navy for the last few years and now already is 27 without any experience in organized baseball."

Once he made it to Catalina, "The basic training out there wasn't much different," he says, but "the environment was different. As far as the training went, we had all the same kinds of facilities they had on the mainland. There wasn't too much happening; we were only there 2 or 3 weeks."

What about spare time? "They had wild hogs on the mountains," Don laughs. "Some of the guys went after 'em — they bagged 'em. I chummed around with Johnny Schmitz some, and Russ Meers. You could go bowling, or swimming — they had recreation facilities. It's kind of a tourist place. A lot of those guys would go fishing. They had a pier right there. One time, there was a school of barracuda following the ship, because of the food they toss over. They were big! A lot of 'em would go golfing. Me, personally, I went fishing, and bowling, I went to the movies several times — they had shows. Of course, you didn't always feel like doing anything — it was a long practice!"

Hoosier pitcher today? Don Dunker shut down Big 10 batters for Indiana U, but Catalina was as close as he ever got to the Show.

But for Don, the timing just wasn't quite right. "I had an injury — I didn't have the fastball I had before," he says. "I wasn't gonna stay with 'em — they wanted to send me to the Coast League, but I decided against it. So I went and played for a few other teams, Evansville and Memphis and Ft. Lauderdale." After he'd had enough of the minors, Don became a scout for 20 years — with the Reds, Royals, Dodgers, and Mets — and won numerous championships, coaching high school baseball for 40 years and kids' leagues in the summer. He was inducted into the Indiana Baseball Hall of Fame in 1984.

Al Epperly's unusual career included a 12-year gap, a perfect 2-0 lifetime record, & an early-in-the-career injury that inspires the question, "What if...?"

Al Epperly

Al Epperly's pitching career was even more unusual than Dunker's. Pard pitched for the Cubs in 1938 — going 2-0 — and he vanished into the minors and the service and the minors again and didn't re-emerge until 1950, when he tossed 5 decision-less games for the Dodgers. Thus, a sparkling career mark of 2-0 — with a 12-year gap between big-league appearances.

In between, he won 170 games...pitching for the Los Angeles Angels, San Francisco Seals, and numerous other teams (including a few in Cuba) over a 17-year minor-league career.

"Grimm is sweet on Albert Paul Epperly," Braven Dyer wrote for the *Los Angeles Times* in 1938, "a 19-year-old farm boy from Iowa who has plenty of stuff on the ball. In batting practice even the regulars have experienced considerable trouble hitting his fast-breaking curve."

Gabby Hartnett called Epperly the best-looking rookie he'd seen in years...and manager Charlie Grimm beamed, "I think the kid is going places."

"I started 2 games for Chicago," Al says, "and I hurt my arm."

But in the Spring, before he got hurt, all was magical. "The St. Catherine was a beautiful hotel," he says. "They'd let us go hunting once in a while. We'd catch some wild boar, and they'd barbecue 'em at the hotel. We'd go to the shows downtown. I didn't even own a camera then — I was only getting $500 a month! The older players, they stayed among themselves. They had some great pitchers then; of course, they had great teams in those days. Charlie Root, Larry French, Tex Carleton, Clay Bryant. I was just a young guy — I looked up to 'em."

Yet young guys in camp were prime targets for a prank or 2. "One time," he says, "I went and opened up my locker, and there was a big stingray in it! It was movin' around — it was still alive. I took it back down and put it back in the ocean. I'd gone fishing a lot, so it didn't bother me."

Back in Iowa, he farmed in the off-season, then spent 30 years at the local sheriff's department. "I have 2 grandchildren, and 2 great-great grandchildren," Pard smiles.

Tarzan Parmelee

As Epperly was coming up, Tarzan Parmelee was finishing his career with the Cubs. Roy pitched 10 seasons in the bigs — mostly with the Giants — from 1929 through 1939. While with New York, he pitched several exhibition games on Catalina. Another time, Cub ace Lon Warneke walked the bases loaded to face Parmelee — and Tarzan smashed a game-winning grand-slam.

The original Wild Thing, Roy Parmelee, ignores a few tips from Gabby Hatrnett.

He got his nickname because he truly was wild — leading the league in walks once and hit-batsmen 4 times. Tarzan came to his 1st Cub camp in 1937, and made a prediction: "Tarzan Parmelee, the new Cub pitcher, didn't want to go out on a limb," Jimmy the Cork wrote for the *American*, "but thought he'd win 15 games."

He went 7-8 with a sorry ERA, and came back to Catalina camp in 1938 — but had to "come up with a more definite idea about the dimensions of the home plate," Ed Burns wrote for the *Los Angeles Times*.

"Gabby spent an hour with LeRoy Parmelee, the wild man, trying to get the ex-Giant and ex-Cardinal into the habit of following through in his delivery," Irving Vaughn wrote for the *Times* 2 weeks later. "The theory is that this will eliminate Tarzan's habit of throwing the ball every place except over the plate."

Grimm and Hartnett finally thought they fixed his control problem by removing a jerk from his delivery. "Wouldn't it be funny if I never threw another bad pitch?" Tarzan asked. But said jerk returned...and Parmelee never pitched for the Cubs again.

(By the way, Tarzan Parmelee was not related to Tarzan Wallis — ironically, another Cub — who got his moniker by jumping from cliffs near the team's Spring Training site in Arizona.)

Lon Warneke

Lonnie Warneke did not suffer from control problems. He won 193 games in 15 seasons, starting with the Cubs in 1930 and winning 20 games there 3 times in 7 years. He dominated N.L. hitting in '32 — leading the league in wins, ERA, and shutouts. He went 2-1 in the 1932 and 1935 World Series for Chicago, pitched a no-hitter in 1941, and finished with the Cubs during the War (after a hiatus to St. Louis). A perennial All-Star, he pitched in the 1st-ever All-Star contest. He could often be found strumming a ukulele by his locker at the Catalina Country Club.

He apparently had control during the after-practice rodeo sports, too — dubbed "the big Arkansas goat-roper" by *Des Moines Dispatch* columnist Dutch Reagan in 1936. "Lon is the mayhem-minded type of guy Grimm yearns for," Dutch wrote from Catalina, "and that is the entire secret behind his being branded as a tough cookie in the pinches."

After retiring, Warneke was an N.L. umpire for 10 seasons, then served as a county judge in Texas.

Guy Bush

Guy Bush was an ace in the same starting rotation as Warneke. Guy pitched for the Cubs from 1923 through 1934, then pitched for 4 other teams over 5 seasons. He won 176 games during his 17-season career — yet led the league in saves a couple times, too — and went 1-1 in 2 World Series for the Cubs.

He's also infamously known for giving up Babe Ruth's last 2 homers.

The Mississippi Mudcat was definitely a country boy, with country ways. "Guy Bush takes cod-liver oil during the Winter," Herbert Simons told *Chicago Times* readers in 1934, "And usually he switches to yeast during the Summer. This Spring, however, his stamina-building diet is malted milks... thrice daily."

Guy quickly got a reputation as a greenhorn, but pretty quickly eliminated any doubt about his smarts. He said he was scared of gangster-infested Chicago, so he traveled there under an assumed name for for his rookie trip. And he missed his sleeper train because he didn't know what a Pullman was — so he sat in the station all night, waiting for a 'normal' one.

When he finally made it to Catalina, he broke a batter's wrist. Some of the veterans told him he'd be fined; when Bush said he didn't have any money, the guys told him he'd have to go to jail. But the rookie got his revenge on the train ride back to the big city; the boys graciously invited him to join their pokerfest, and Guy obliged by cleaning their clocks to the tune of several hundred dollars.

In 1932, nobody could hit Lonnie Warneke.

Guy Bush let his teammates think he was a busher — just long enough to remove all their money from them at the poker table on the train.

But he was still susceptible to the occasional prank. "One time, in the '30s, Mother bought this kaleidoscope," recalls Della Root Arnold. "She put black powder around the end, where your eye goes. And she goes up to Guy Bush and says, 'Wait'll you see what I got for the kids!' And she had him put it up to his left eye, and take a look. And then she tells him to look through the other eye, and of course the powder made big black circles around his eyes. Guy went to eat at the drugstore. He sat down at the counter, and they had this big mirror there. He took one look at himself and thought he was sick enough that he was about to die!"

Riggs Stephenson

Riggs Stephenson provided the offense to accompany Guy Bush's defense during those Cub glory years. After he spent 5 seasons with Cleveland, Old Hoss was a constant in the Cub outfield from 1926-1934. He hit anywhere from .319 to .367 for 8 straight years, with some punch — leading the N.L. with 46 doubles in 1927. He hit .378 in the 1929 and 1932 World Series, and finished his 14 seasons at .336. A bum arm kept his fielding at bay, which probably kept him out of the Hall of Fame.

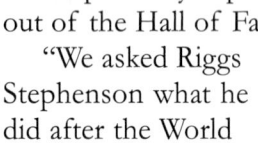

Riggs Stephenson hit .324 in 1932, then batted .444 in the World Series.

"We asked Riggs Stephenson what he did after the World Series," Jimmy Corcoran mentioned in his *Cork Tips* column in the *American* in 1930. " 'O,' he drawled, 'I just spent the Winter.' Riggs is the minute man of the team. He opens his mouth once per minute."

Joe Munson

Joe Munson patrolled the same outfield as Stephenson — just not as long. His big-league career consisted of 1925 and 1926. As a rookie, he hit .371 in 9 games...and his average fell to a more earthbound .257 the next year.

But Joe's major-league stopover was merely a brief interruption to a brilliant minor-league career, which spanned from 1918 through 1934. He batted an impressive .335 with 208 home runs, collecting more than 2,000 hits. He led his league in hitting categories a dozen times, including homers (twice), triples (twice), steals, and average (3 times).

Joe Munson let go of his camera long enough to let someone else snap this picture of him in the Spring of 1926.

He hit .400 at Harrisburg in 1925 — leading the league in homers, runs, hits, triples, and RBI — which earned him a ticket to the Show.

Reporters took note. "Joe Munson, left-handed outfielder who opened the eyes of Cub fans last fall...has been slamming the horsehide with great glee," the *Chicago Daily News* reported from Catalina in 1926. "But, as has been said, it's too early to mention anything about the end of the pastime."

"Munson may have thick legs," the paper said the next week, "but he certainly can travel around the outfield. There aren't many faster than he."

Yet Joe knew how to have fun, too. "Joe Munson has been walking around the Island with a camera in his hand, taking snapshots of every gable and window," the paper said one more week into camp. "He even speculated on the advisability of snapping the lights in the middle of the main street."

Joe Marty

A decade after shutterbug Munson manned the outfield on the Island, another youngster came along whose major-league career seemed only a sidelight to his minor-league superstardom. Joe Marty spent 6 seasons at the Show — the 1st 3 with Chicago, starting in 1937 — but his true calling was the Pacific Coast League.

Marty came up as a teammate of Joe DiMaggio with the San Francisco Seals (hitting .359 in 1936)...and after his major league career, he hit .309 during 7 seasons with the Sacramento Solons (where he also managed). In fact, his old pub there is still in business...next door to the site of the old ballpark (which is now a Target store).

He made a splash on Catalina as a rookie: "Joe Marty will play in the Cubs' outfield this year," John Hoffman wrote in the *Daily Times*. "Manager Grimm was sure of it, the Islanders were sure of it, and even the seals barked in approval. Marty is no second Ty Cobb, but then who is? 'This boy looks mighty good to me,' Grimm said later. 'He handles a bat like a toothpick and doesn't move it much before he swings. He'll do.' "

Joe Marty on his 1949 Bowman PCL card — happily back home in Sacramento.

Harvey Storey

Up the Coast a ways, Harvey Storey was also enjoying star-status in the minors. He anchored 3rd for the Portland Beavers for years, and also played for San Diego and San Francisco. He won the Coast League batting title in 1946 (.326) and led the circuit in doubles the next year — he popped 51. The man was a metronome of consistency — once hitting .305 for 2 straight years.

The Cubs offered him a tryout in 1941, but — like so many others — his assignment was to wrest Stan Hack's job away from him. *Next!*

"I was in San Francisco," Harvey says, "and was sold to Chicago. I lived in Portland, so I drove down." But manager Jimmie Wilson ignored him for 2 weeks, so Storey finally introduced himself. "The big boys never spoke to me. Some of 'em hunted wild boar — Bill Nicholson. Root was friendly. There wasn't any television then, of course, so we'd listen to the races from Santa Anita. There were not any girls there."

He had other obstacles to overcome. "I'd broken my leg, so I wasn't ready to play yet," he says. "They didn't set my leg right, then they said I was too old. Andy Lotshaw tried to do a lot for my bad leg, but there's nothing much he could do. He got up early one morning and took me down for X-rays. They told me what a lousy job the doctor in San Francisco had done. In Los Angeles, I could only go a week at a time. I stayed in L.A. when they went on to Chicago. It still hurts, even right now."

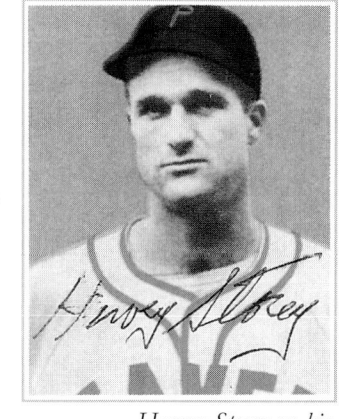

Harvey Storey on his 1949 Bowman PCL card — happily back home in Portland.

After retiring, he stayed in Portland and spent more than 30 years working for a couple of oil companies. "I still live in the same house I've owned for 52 years," he says. And the good old days are still with him: "All we wanted to do was play ball," he says.

Ken Weafer

Pitcher Ken Weafer also got a 1-season shot with the Cubs, in 1936. He made the club, but before playing in any games was dealt to the Braves. His major-league record consists of 1 game for Boston, with no decision. He's listed in the *Baseball Encyclopedia* as Hal Weafer — nicknamed 'Al' — but he says his brother went by Hal and he goes by Ken.

"On Catalina, they really worked ya," Ken says. "We went over on the ship from LA, and no sooner were we there than they ran ya up to the plateau where the field was from that big swimming bathhouse that was on the water. They really ran ya. Charlie Grimm was a great fella."

He made some good contacts in a hurry: As one of the single rookies, photographers picked him to pose in publicity shots with some of the local ladies. And, "at the Casino, I got to know the daughter of the architect," Ken says. "They had a yacht out there, and they'd have us out."

The War interrupted his career; he went into the Navy, and then pitched in the minors for several seasons before going into sales in his native New England.

Ken Weafer is supposed to be looking at the camera, but his gaze has wistfully meandered toward the beach.

Chuck Klein's 1934 Goudey card included the "Lou Gehrig says..." bio on the back — but Chuck was so good in 1933, other cards in the set started with "Chuck Klein says..."

Chuck Klein

Hall-of-Fame outfielder Chuck Klein was also on Catalina that Spring — his last trip to the Island. He only played 3 seasons with the Cubs during his stellar 17-year career. He led the N.L. in offensive categories 19 times (including homers 4 times), won an MVP award and a triple crown, and retired with a .320 average (and exactly 300 dingers) after 1944.

Klein hit .368 the year before coming to the Cubs — and while he hit .304 for his 1st Chicago season, it's hard to live up to such lofty expectations. "Chuck Klein, the dormant genius, this morning knocked 6 full-bloom homers on 6 pitched balls, and enthusiasm is rampant on Catalina Island," Ed Burns wrote for the *Los Angeles Times* in 1935.

Tony Lazzeri

Tony Lazzeri didn't put up his best numbers for the Cubbies, either. But his case was a little easier to understand — after all, Tony was near the end of his career, and he'd put away a few drinks by then. He earned his Hall-of-Fame status with the Yankees, manning 2nd and appearing in 6 World Series from 1926-1937. His lone season with Chicago came next, before he split time between Brooklyn and the Giants in 1939. He returned to his native Bay Area for 1 final season with the San Francisco Seals in 1941.

Know who's the 1st player to ever hit 60 home runs in professional baseball? Not the Babe. Tony smacked 60 for Salt Lake City in the Pacific Coast League in 1925, earning his trip to the Show.

"The vet from San Francisco is not a chatterbox," Burns wrote for the *Los Angeles Times* in 1938, "and will have no part in heckling classes. He may teach a few gutteral insults later on but will not be asked to give any lectures on atta boy hollering or repartee for distance."

"Lazzeri is a man of few words," John Hoffman agreed in the next day's *Chicago Times*. "Even when asked how long he was with the Yankees, the lithe Italian replied '12' and not '12 years.'"

You'd expect to see Tony Lazzeri in Yankee pinstripes, but he did spend one Spring on Catalina with the Cubs. That's Avalon policeman Spud Ryan behind the plate.

Alex was so great, Hollywood made a movie about his life. Dutch Reagan played the lead role — pictured on this card in a minor-league uniform. Long-time Cub trainer Andy Lotshaw was Grover's catcher on that Galesburg team.

Grover Cleveland Alexander

Grover Cleveland Alexander whiffed rookie Lazzeri with the bags full in the 1926 World Series — a climactic scene in a movie we'll mention in a moment. How good was Ol' Pete? He won 28 as a rookie in 1911. He won *30* games — not a mere 20 — 3 straight years. His ERA was below 2.00 for 6 consecutive seasons. And he once pitched 16 shutouts in a single year.

His career? 373 wins, a 2.56 ERA, 90 shutouts. He led the league in some pitching category or another *45* times. And all this, after inhaling mustard gas in World War I, suffering from epilepsy, and having a battle with strong drink. No wonder they made a film about his life — *The Winning Team*, starring Dutch Reagan, in 1952.

Grover Cleveland Alexander spent quite a few seasons limbering up under Catalina's comforting sunshine.

He retired in 1930, after 20 gutsy seasons. Grover pitched for the Cubs from 1918-1926, so he was part of the first contingent that practiced on Catalina. A couple of seasons after he retired, when he was 45, he talked his way into a job pitching batting practice on Catalina for $100 plus room and board at the Hotel St. Catherine — he needed the money, and he still dreamed of making yet another comeback.

According to legend, his control was so great that he once put on a Springtime demonstration for reporters. Catcher Bill Killefer held a gallon-sized can with the ends cut out, and Alex threw several dozen pitches through — without missing a single one.

He did have fun on Catalina. "Grover Alexander, who has been getting his arm 'golf broke' during his two weeks at the Island, was led into temptation," the *Los Angeles Times* wrote that first Spring, 1921. "Chasing a foul, he was caught trying to roll the horse-hide into a hole on a nearby green."

"There was a double-header birthday in the Alexander household, with the pitcher and Mrs. Alexander both celebrating," the *American* told readers in 1924. "The famous right-hander is 37, but he feels only 21, he says. He observed the occasion by working overtime during the practice session."

Mr. & Mrs. Alex, the birthday kids. Do you think they look like Ronald Reagan & Doris Day?

He was always helping the younger pitchers. In 1922, Manager Killefer "put Grover Alexander to work in instructing George Stueland in the art of letting the curve slip off his fingertips," Oscar Reichow wrote for the *Chicago News*. "The recruit took Alexander's advice."

In 1934, when he was 47, Ol' Pete was still hurling batting practice — & teaching the Cub kids — on Catalina. Here, he takes a break with Charlie Grimm & Gabby Hartnett.

In 1924, "Alexander the Great intends to take the youngster (Fred Blake) in hand and teach him an efficient overhand delivery," the *Tribune* reported.

The following week, the *American* said "Northside fans would enjoy watching Alex in action with the rookie boxmen. There isn't a trick about pitching known to the grizzled Nebraskan that he has not cheerfully taught to the recruits."

And the rest

Hundreds of Cubs and Cub hopefuls took to the Isle over the years. Here are a few of the others...who are at least footnote-worthy:

* **Hi Bithorn**, who grew up hurling on another island (Puerto Rico), pitched for the Cubs from 1942-1946. He won 18 in 1943. The year before, he threw at a Brooklyn Dodger, as pitchers occasionally will do — but the Dodger was *manager* Leo Durocher, who was in the *dugout*. And, in the *Chicago Sun* in 1946, Warren Brown wrote: "What is going to happen now that Hi Bithorn is in camp is something I do not care to contemplate. If he goes through the same slow-motion conditioning this time, he will be of as much help to the Cubs as Bob Lewis, whom he resembled greatly in general contours, late in 1945." The stadium in San Juan (where the Cubs played some games against the Expos years later) was named after him.

* **Footsie Blair** is included because, well, how can you not include a guy named 'Footsie'? He hit .319 as a rookie in '29, and played in the World Series that Fall.

* **Sheriff Blake** spent 1924-1931 with the Cubs, averaging just over 10 wins a year. In 1928, he won 17 and tied for the league lead with 4 shutouts.

* **Tex Carleton's** career was shortened by arm trouble. But he accomplished a lot in 8 years — 100 wins, and 3 World Series appearances. Tex spent 4 seasons in Chicago (1935-1938). In one of his last starts (for the Dodgers, in 1940) he threw a no-hitter. With the Cubs, he led the N.L. in shutouts in 1936.

Tex, 1937

Rip Collins, 1939

* **Ripper Collins**, known as 'Jim' to his mother, led the N.L. in homers in 1934, while batting .333. He hit .300 or better 4 times in his brief 9-year career, which included 3 World Series seasons.

* **Jackie Cusick's** 1st homer at Wrigley Field was a grand-slam. An inside-the-park grand-slam. He hit one more for the 1951 Cubs, and none for the 1952 Braves. His lifetime average was .174. He also got a pro basketball trial — and while on Catalina, he amazed the locals with his hoopster skills.

* **Frank Demaree** spent the first 6 seasons of his 13-year career with the Cubs — hitting .300 on 3 occasions, including .350 in 1936. He hit a homer in the 1932 World Series and played in a pair of All-Star games.

* **Paul Derringer** won 223 games (4 times, he won 20+) in 15 seasons, finishing with the Cubs (1943-1945) and playing in his 4th World Series to end his career. Once, Charlie Grimm invited the team to a compulsory picnic. "When the final call was made," Cholly wrote, "Derringer was missing. We finally located him in a rose bush."

* **Vallie Eaves** "had methods of his own for breaking every rule of training and development ever devised by a baseball club," Warren Brown wrote in the Cubs' history. "Eaves...should have been a great pitcher, but just didn't get around to it." His 5-year career ended with 2 seasons for the Cubs, from 1941-1942. His lifetime pitching record was 4-8.

* **Jim Gleeson** hit .313 as a starting Cubbie outfielder in 1940, so he was promptly traded to the Reds for a backup infielder who'd hit .202. Gee Gee got over it, though, and went on to a successful career coaching, managing, and scouting in the Yankee system.

Gee Gee selects some lumber, then dances the night away with pal Dorothy Harris.

* **Monk Dubiel** pitched for the Cubs from 1948-1952 after 3 seasons with the Yanks and Phils. He was a favorite with the local kids. "Walt Dubiel, he was a character, a jokester, he was always telling jokes," Islander Frank Saldaña recalls.

When Monk Dubiel wasn't cracking one-liners, he might be found roping... or trying to run away from PK Wrigley (wearing the shades, at the left).

* ***Mike Gonzalez*** was the 1st Cuban-born manager in the majors. Before that, he caught for 17 seasons — backing up Gabby Hartnett from 1925-1929, and playing in the World Series his final year as a Cub. A true island-baseball booster, he was a national hero in Cuba — where he owned a minor-league team.

* ***Burleigh Grimes*** threw spitters for 19 seasons and resides now in the Hall of Fame. A Cub on Catalina for 2 seasons, he got shelled in the 1932 World Series. In his autobiography, Frankie Frisch called Grimes "the master of the knockdown pitch."

* ***Babe Herman*** (as opposed to Billy Herman) only played 2 seasons for the Cubs — 1933 & 1934 — hitting .289 and .304. His 13-year average (.324) should've put him in the Hall of Fame.

* ***Kirby Higbe*** didn't do much as a Cub, but went on to win 22 for the 1941 Dodgers (before getting shelled in the World Series). Higbe led the league in walks 4 times during his 12-year career, which was laced with eccentricity. He was traded repeatedly.

* ***Johnny Hutchings***, the 1936 rookie who thought he'd landed in Mexico, pitched 6 seasons in the majors — including the 1940 World Series (for Cincinnati). He gave up Mel Ott's 500th homer in 1945. Johnny's career mark was 12-18, and he never played for the Cubs during the regular season — despite high hopes: "He has plenty and he's gonna be heard from," Coach Red Corriden said in 1936.

* ***Ed Jabb*** was a centerfielder who had a Cub tryout in 1937, then played several years in the minors. "I got a fall tryout at Wrigley," he says. Like Phil Cavarretta, "I'd just gotten out of high school in Chicago. I didn't care about the individual statistics and all that — I was a team player. I slid into 2nd one time and broke my leg. I started in 1934, and I never got a pink slip from any of 'em, not even in the minors."

* ***Don Johnson*** played 2nd for the Cubs during the mid-1940s, hitting .302 in 1945 and starting in the World Series. For fun, Don and Peanuts Lowrey would pretend to be vegetable dealers in hotel lobbies and argue about the price of carrots — just to see how people would react.

* ***Tony Kaufmann*** pitched for the Cubs from 1921-1927 — a pupil of Grover Alexander. "Tony Kaufmann has acquired a sore neck," the *Chicago American* reported from Avalon in 1924. " 'I must have a strained ligament trying to think,' declared the home-bred while undergoing treatment for the affliction."

* ***Jim Kirby*** played centerfield in the minors from 1941 through the early 1950s. He got a tryout with the Cubs in 1949. "I just didn't fit in with the big leagues. The rent was so high, having my wife and children back home, I don't know how we could have afforded 2 places. You won't believe this, son, but I didn't even have a sportscoat — just a jacket. We were poor."

* ***Fabian Kowalik*** went to Catalina with the Cubs in 1935 and 1936...and he got to go to the World Series with 'em too, pitching well in 4 1/3 relief innings. Fabian was traded to the Phillies with future Hall-of-Famer Chuck Klein after the 1936 season. He slow-pitched to Dutch Reagan in batting practice, and had no need of a nickname himself.

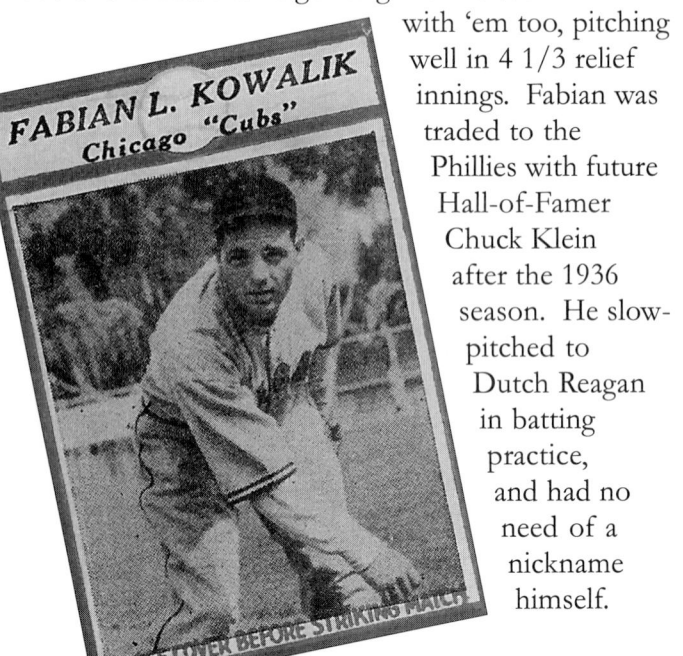

* **Clarence Kumalae** "pitched batting practice for the Cubs for a long time, a long, long time," according to Hub Kittle. "He was a left-hander, and he could throw strikes like nobody. He'd hit a cup if you put it up there, knock it right off. He went to Fairfax High in L.A. The Cubs saw him pitching, he got acquainted with some of the players and got invited to try out for the Angels as their batting practice pitcher, then he went to the Cubs." When Islander Jack Cowell returned from Chicago to California after the 1938 season, Clarence was kind enough to give him a cross-country lift.

Hawaiian fans idolize Prince Oana, who hit the bigs in 1934 — but less-well-known is Hawaii native Clare Kumalae, who pitched for L.A. in 1933 & then tossed BP in Chicago for years.

* **Emil Kush** went 21-12 for the Cubs — from 1941-1948. He got thrown out of Wrigley Field when he first attempted to try out, but snuck back in, trotted to the mound, grabbed a ball, and started to throw.

* **Doyle Lade** pitched for the Cubs from 1946-1950. He won 25, but lost 29. His nickname was Porky, which most of us would find quite disconcerting. "Lade needs constant attention," Warren Brown wrote in the *Herald-American* in 1951, "first to get him in shape, and next to keep him there."

* **Hank Leiber** was late coming to Avalon in 1941. "Wilson said he hadn't heard from Leiber, who is resting in Tucson, apparently during the duration of the Cubs' stay on Catalina Island," the *Tribune* reported. "Last spring Hank rested during the Catalina traveling span in his native Phoenix. The Cub management hasn't been able to find whether the resting is better in Phoenix than in Tucson or vice versa." Not surprisingly, Hank never pitched for the Cubs. He spent his entire big-league career with the Giants in 1942, pitching a single game and losing. Thus, 0-1 lifetime.

* **Fat Freddie Lindstrom** had even more to complain about from a nickname standpoint. Yet Hall-of-Fame 3rd-sacker Fred enjoyed a fab 13-season career, mostly with the Giants — his lifetime average was .311. He came to Catalina to start 1935, played in the World Series to finish it, and moved on to Brooklyn before retiring the next year. Before that, he played a few exhibition games on the Isle in '32, while still a Giant.

* **Pat Malone** was Hack Wilson's drinking/brawling buddy. He had Hall-of Fame talent, but blew it. Pat averaged 20 wins in his 1st 3 Cub seasons (starting in 1928), but was through within 10 years and dead at 40.

* **Dutch McCall** set a Cub record in 1948: 13 straight losses. Bob ended the year 4-13.

* **Babe Phelps** hit .364, .367, .313, and .308 as Brooklyn's starting catcher in the late '30s — after the Cubs waived him away due to his neuroses. Babe tended to stay up all night, fearful that he'd pass away if his heart skipped 4 beats; he was also afraid to fly, and retired rather than take the team plane. His chow-related nickname, "Blimp," was thus amended to "The Grounded Blimp."

Carl Reynolds, 1938

* **Carl Sawatski** played 3 seasons with the Cubs starting in 1948, and 8 more years on several teams. A backup catcher, Swats made it into the 1957 World Series for Milwaukee. He led his league in homers 3 times in the minors. "Carl Sawatski was my roommate," Paul Schramka says. "He'd take a case of beer after a game! I woke up one time at 5 o'clock in the morning, and Sawatski's comin' in! So that day, I'm sitting on the bench, and Sawatski's in catching — but instead of a catcher's mitt, he looked like he had on a boxing glove, punching the balls."

* **Johnny Schulte** caught for 5 teams in 10 years, starting in 1923. He backed up Gabby Hartnett in '29. The next Spring, Jimmy the Cork Corcoran of the *American* gave a rundown of Cubs in camp...describing Schulte as "Fat and not fancy, but valuable."

* **Carl Reynolds** is truly one of the forgotten stars of the '30s. Over 13 seasons, he hit .302. A pillar of consistency, that's also what he hit as a starting outfielder for the Cubs in 1938...before playing in the World Series that year.

* **Marv Rickert** played for the Cubs from 1942-1947, then got traded around a bit. He hit .247 lifetime, and hit a homer in the 1948 World Series for the Braves. He once caught the largest steelhead trout ever (29 pounds, 9 ounces) — but didn't get credited for the world record because he didn't report it soon enough. He earned a starting job in 1946 by hitting .556 on Avalon, but fell to .263 in continental ballparks.

* **Bob Schultz** sometimes went by 'Bill,' although his middle name was Duffy. Go figure. He pitched for the Cubs from 1951-1953, going 9-11 on the mound.

* **Rip Russell** had a great rookie year with the Cubs in 1939, but after a series of injuries he was gone by 1942. Redeemed by the Red Sox, he batted 1.000 in the 1946 World Series — a perfect 2-for-2 pinch-hitting.

Rip Russell, 1942

* **Bill Schuster** engaged in Lou-Novikoffian antics with the same teams — the Cubs and L.A. Angels — except he was good-naturedly funny. He hit .234 in the majors (Broadway Billy was with the Cubs during the War, and got to play in the 1945 World Series). He'd climb backstops, dive into the stands, and run to the pitcher's mound on easy ground-outs, among numerous other crowd-pleasing antics.

* **Bill Serena** played 3rd for Chicago from 1949-1954. He loved to golf on Catalina, and was "a 2-fingered piano player," Wayne Terwilliger says. "They had an old piano in the hotel lobby, and he'd do pretty good; he'd make music!" He later scouted with Avalon native Marcelino Saucedo in Northern California.

* **Hal Sueme** was an All-Star catcher in the Pacific Coast League, but never made the Show. He went to a few Cub camps on Catalina. "Sueme might be ready for major league society right now," Edward Cochrane wrote for the *American* in 1937, "but he is hard of hearing, which is a sad handicap for a ball player and especially a catcher. Birmingham is happy to have him back."

* **Zack Taylor** caught for 16 seasons — backing up Gabby Hartnett for the Cubs from 1929-1933. Later on, while managing the St. Louis Browns for Bill Veeck, Zack was the manager who pinch-hit midget Eddie Gaedel in 1951.

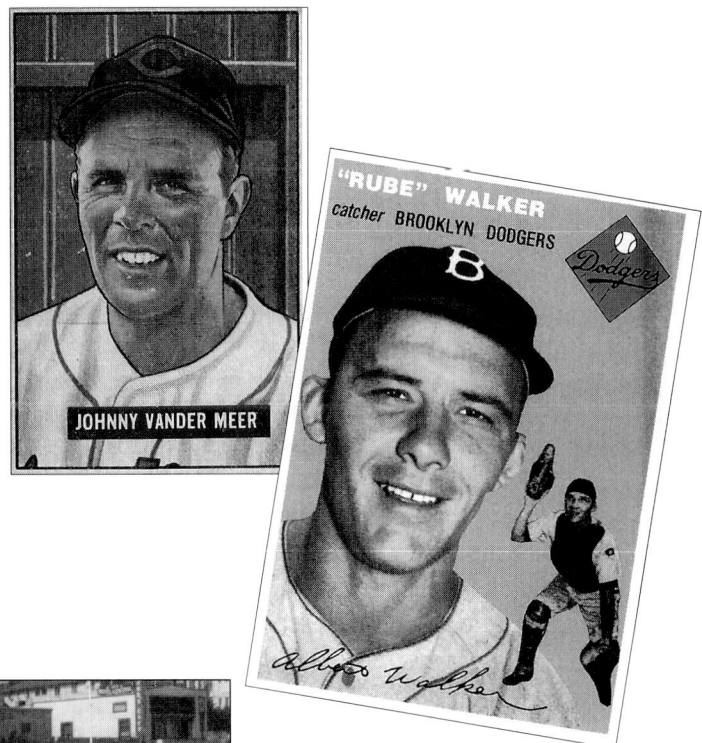

Babe 'Blimp' Phelps, Bud Tinning, & Dutch Seebold try to avoid sinking the boat.

* **Bud Tinning** went 13-6 for the Cubs in 1933, after pitching a couple scoreless innings in the 1932 World Series — as a rookie. On the mound, he showed good control; unfortunately, he didn't carry that habit to the training table. "He reported 20 pounds overweight," the *American* reported in 1933, "and because of his inability to deny his appetite, has made little progress toward cutting off the surplus avoirdupois. This, naturally, has affected his pitching, and in his one appearance in a practice contest, he was pounded all over the lot." The Cubs canned him the next year.

* **Johnny Vander Meer** is the only man to ever pitch back-to-back no-hitters — he did it in 1938. He came to Catalina in 1950, trying to squeeze another year out of his career. Johnny always took time for the younger pitchers...and the local kids.

* **Rube Walker** caught for the Cubs from 1948-1951, then for the Dodgers from mid-1951 through 1958. He played in the 1956 World Series for Brooklyn. Al was part of a few famous moments: He's in the Normal Rockwell Cubs painting...he was catching when Bobby Thomson's 1951 homer allowed the Giants to win the pennant...and he was the pitching coach for Seaver, Koosman, and Nolan Ryan when the Amazin' Mets won the 1969 World Series.

* **Hank Wyse** won 22 for the 1945 Cubs with his great sinker, helping lead the team to the World Series. Hooks started strong in 1942, but injuries shortened his career to 8 seasons. Looking for work during the Depression, he approached a manufacturer for a job. The company had a sandlot team, and the deal was simple: Win, and you're hired...lose, and forget it. Hank pitched a no-hitter. After baseball, he worked as an electrician for 40 years — where he made a lot more money.

Norma Jeane

The Stars Really Came Out...
While the Cubs Played on Catalina

"I would've liked to have known you, but I was just a kid..."

Writer Bernie Taupin, in his 1973 ode to Marilyn Monroe

Mrs. Norma Jeane Dougherty, a teenage bride, moved to Catalina in 1943.

Welcome, Norma Jeane.

She was a newlywed, all of 16 — goin' on 17. Her husband, Jim, was a Chief Petty Officer...recently assigned to Avalon for training and such. They stayed there about a year and a half.

(Since Catalina was right between Pearl Harbor and the West Coast, U.S. military bigwigs thought it'd be a good idea to station a few troops there during the War...and the Doughertys were part of that effort.)

After the War, Norma Jeane modified her name (a habit of many good ballplayers, it should be noted, who went from being something like 'Clarence' to a more original ID, like, say, 'Lefty' or 'Hack.'). Armed with her new moniker, Marilyn Monroe, Norma Jeane pursued a career in acting. She later married a baseball player, as a matter of fact — a former Pacific Coast League star by the name of Joseph P. DiMaggio, who played outfield for one of the East Coast teams.*

Quite the baseball aficionado, that Norma Jeane.

Unfortunately for the Chicago Cubs, they had to train in icy, flooded, frosty French Lick, Indiana while she was around the Magic Isle. (Like they needed another reason to hate French Lick?) But the semi-pro guys were still hangin' around:

"I got pictures of Marilyn Monroe — out on Catalina. She was a good ball fan, she came to the park," says Hub Kittle, the Cub batting-practice hurler who stayed on to pitch for the semi-pro Catalina Cubs.

While husband Jim was off-duty, the couple would go swimming. She'd walk their dog Muggsie. And she probably spent hours thinking about the old days, when she was a standout player on her Hollygrove Orphanage softball team, across the channel.

When Jim was away at work, shelling whales or a similar shore-defending assignment, Norma Jeane had her days to herself. Rolling out the red carpet of Island hospitality, a few of the Islanders later claimed they spent some time with her.

---

* As a writer, I feel compelled to point out that after she was married to DiMaggio, Marilyn married a writer. Hmph.

Marilyn's rookie card, from the 2002 Topps American Pie set.

"A couple of the local guys say they used to take her out," Islander Marcelino Saucedo says. Some of Marilyn's biographies say her husband was suspicious and jealous, even then — but did he have any reason? After all, wasn't she just a shy kid who didn't really know anybody? "Avalon is so small, everybody gets to know everyone else pretty quickly," Marse explains. A few Marilyn historians suggest she was a big hit at a Stan Kenton Big Band performance at the Casino. "She was young and kinda flighty — they said they'd just take her around town, or go for a walk in the hills on the golf course, under the moonlight," according to Marse.

Another Islander, Scooter Hansen, maintains more innocent memories of his former neighbor. "Marilyn Monroe babysat for me once or twice!" says Scooter, who was 10 at the time. "Her name was Norma Jeane then. She lived a few doors down from us, on Descanso Avenue — in the middle of the block, between Beacon Street and Third Street, on the East side there. My dad knew her because he

Newlywed Norma Jeane, feeling maternal on Catalina — holding another Islander's future Cub star pitcher. They're standing on Sumner Avenue, about 3 blocks from the ballpark.

went around and read all the meters. She was married to a merchant marine. When Dad had to go Overtown, he asked her to come over. She made sure I was all right — she was very nice to me. Of course, she had brown hair then — dishwater blonde, maybe. Later on, I knew it was her."

When hubby shipped out, Norma Jeane moved back to L.A. from Catalina in short order — so poor Scooter had to host other babysitters from then on.

The Dougherty family in Avalon, between Crescent Street & the beach, with the Pleasure Pier behind them.

The post-Dougherty Marilyn appeared on other Southern California baseball diamonds from time to time in the '50s — throwing out the first pitch at Hollywood Stars and Los Angeles Angels games occasionally. And of course, she sang the title cut from that fine and memorable film, *Diamonds are a Girl's Best Friend*. Hey, as long as *we* know she was really thinking about *baseball* diamonds...

Marilyn spends some quality time with Hank Majeski, Gus Zernial, & Joe Dobson.

Gus Zernial, who smacked 40 homers for Hollywood in 1948 (on his way to being the Pacific Coast League MVP), got to do a Pasadena photo shoot with Marilyn during Spring Training, 1951. "The people in the movie industry, they brought her out for some publicity with different ballplayers," Gus recalls. "But later on, she sure didn't need any publicity from ballplayers. I never saw her after that." Legend has it that Joltin' Joe DiMaggio asked to meet Marilyn after seeing those very shots.

Gus says she chatted with the boys about the game. "I always remembered her as one of the nicest young ladies I've ever met — very intelligent, not the way she was portrayed," he says. "We talked about her career, what she wanted to pursue — she was making a film at the time. We talked a little about baseball — how the game was played, just chit-chatting back and forth about hitting and fielding, the normal chit-chat you'd have with a person. She didn't flirt or try to show off — she was very much a lady."

Of course, Catalina was a star-studded location — Lady Norma Jeane wasn't the only star (or star-in-the-making) who came in contact with the Cubs there. "There were a good many movie stars there, making publicity pictures and one thing and another," Kirby Higbe wrote in his autobiography. "Betty Grable, Loretta Young, Anita Louise and loads of starlets. Ronald Reagan and John Payne were there. All those movie people were great, and we had lots of fun."

Let's roll the credits:

Betty Grable, the Catalina ping-pong MVP

Phil Cavarretta, the National League MVP of 1945, was a teenage Catalina rookie in 1935. He was just minding his own business one evening, when another future star leaped into his path.

"The St. Catherine Hotel was nice and clean, and they had good food. Once in a while, you'd see a movie star," Phillibuck says. "I met Betty Grable there when she first came up — my wife doesn't like to hear this story! She had this group, I think they called themselves the *Whoopee Girls*** — there were five of 'em, and they sang at the Casino.

Believe it or not, Betty Grable appeared on a Topps card before Phil Cavarretta did! In 1948, Topps issued a set of tiny 'magic' cards that needed water (or kid spit — let's get real here!) to develop the image. Here's Betty's well-spat card...

"Betty Grable was one of them, and they stayed at the hotel we were at," Cavy continues — much to his wife's chagrin. "After dinner one night, some of the guys were downstairs playing ping-pong — and

** *Betty Grable's first movie role — an uncredited one, at that — was in the 1930 Eddie Cantor flick,* Makin' Whoopee, *which popularized the song of the same name. Betty and the gang were singing on the Island; early in her career, she was known more as a singer than an actress (or a pin-up queen).*

she was over on the side, watching us play. She comes over, all full of life, and looks right at me, and she says, 'I wanna play you.' And I looked back at her, and she says, 'I can beat you!' So I say okay, and I gave her a paddle."

Um...we know whatcha mean, Phil, but...you wanna maybe rephrase that one?

Of course, it was in front of all the guys — so young Cavarretta's honor was at stake, playing against a *girl*. "And you know what," Cavy says, "she was pretty good! I had to really concentrate to beat her, so all the guys wouldn't get on me. But I was tricky when I played — I'd put a little slice on the ball, give it some 'English' — it was the only way I could stay close to her! But that was the last time I saw her."

"I wanna play you. I can beat you."

Betty Grable, challenging Phil Cavarretta to a ping-pong match on Catalina, 1935

Years later, on another Spring Training trip, Wayne Terwilliger had an interesting encounter with Betty, too. After the Cubs broke camp on Catalina, they were playing some exhibition ball in Arizona.

"I met Betty Grable," Twig says. "She was out in Phoenix with the Harry James Orchestra during Spring Training with the Giants one year. Harry asked me for a cap. I don't think I could find one, so I think I gave him mine. I told her I'd gotten her autograph as a kid. She'd sent me a snapshot — it was really beautiful — she was with a dog, leanin' out the window of a car. She got a kick out of that!"

The basement of the Hotel St. Catherine, where Cavy's Grable incident took place. Unfortunately, due to bulldozers, this room is now underneath a park.

"Betty Grable was married to Harry James, the bandleader," long-time Cubs equipment manager and jack-of-all-emergencies Yosh Kawano explains. "He was good friends with my brother Nobe. Nobe worked for the Hollywood Stars, and Salt Lake City, then the Dodgers."

Olivia de Havilland, gone with the publicist

When she was very young and just starting out, Olivia de Havilland had an interesting brush with the Cubs on Catalina...also at the Hotel St. Catherine.

"The starlets would come over," recalls Della Root Arnold, Charlie's daughter. "When I was 17, some of the agents had them rope off tables in the dining rooms, where only the stars could eat — there was hardly any room left for all the rest of us! Anita Louise was there, and Olivia de Havilland, when she was about my age. This was before she was a big star, before *Gone With the Wind*.

"I was in the lobby, and Olivia de Havilland came over and was so apologetic. 'I've never been so embarrassed in my whole life,' she said. They were just young girls my age, and we got to talking, and they said they always wanted to see a game. We invited them to come to the ballpark the next morning, but they had to go back."

Back in the '30s, ballplayers weren't the only ones who got to see their faces on cards — there were movie star cards for little sisters, too. Here's Olivia de Havilland's rookie card.

Anita Louise was a well-known starlet in the '30s and '40s, too — she appeared in Blondie's Big Moment *&* The Phantom Submarine.

177

The next spring, Olivia was back out on the Island — celebrating St. Patrick's Day at the Casino. (She'd been busy in between, making no less than half a dozen films in 1936 and 1937.) While there, she chatted for a moment with a "charming young man," she recalled to PBS in 1989. This particular fellow, "full of good nature and affability and grace," turned out to be a radio announcer from Iowa...by the name of Dutch Reagan.

Hopalong now, Miss Bradley

In fact, some of the Catalina Cubs even dated a movie star or 2 on the Island. Stan Hack, who won a few dance contests at the Casino, was rumored to have gone out with his occasional dance-card partner, Joan Crawford. And pitcher Clay Bryant went out with Grace Bradley, who instead married actor William Boyd the next season — thereby becoming Mrs. Hopalong Cassidy, or actually 'Mrs. Hoppy' to legions of fans. "Clay Bryant was a big, good-lookin' fella," Al Epperly points out. "He was a real ladies' man."

"Clay Bryant was a nice-looking guy," recalls Della Root Arnold.

"There were a lot of stars on Catalina. Stan Hack, Ol' Diz, Turk Stainback, the reserve outfielder...they'd go with the stars," Cavarretta remembers. "Another of my ex-roommates, Clay Bryant — he almost married one. Grace Bradley was one of those *Whoopee Girls*. She was in a few pictures. They'd go to the Casino and dance. But that was only open once a week, on Saturday nights, that time of year. The Big Bands played there: Wayne King, the Waltz King, and Tommy Dorsey..."

Grace, now 89 and still teaching fitness classes in Los Angeles, smiles coyly. "I dated any number of them. Clay Bryant, I remember him — I *might* have dated him. You'd go dancing, you might go out on one of the boats and go fishing — there were so many lovely places to go."

She was born in Brooklyn in 1913 and appeared in 3 dozen pictures from 1932-1949 — including 2 flicks with Betty Grable in 1935 and 1936. She was actually on Catalina to rest up from overworking herself into exhaustion.

"I'd been working 20 hours a day," she recalls. "I was under contract with Paramount. If another studio wanted you, they'd pay — and Paramount would loan you out. Harold Lloyd wanted me for *Cat's Paw* — it was his last picture. I was getting $250 a week, which was great for the Depression. I was working on a picture at Paramount, *Come on Marines*, with Richard Arlen. Doing one of those dances would have been censored! Harold paid $2,500 a week for me. He started early; we had to be at his set at 8, and we'd work until 6. Then I'd go back to Paramount, and work until 6 a.m.

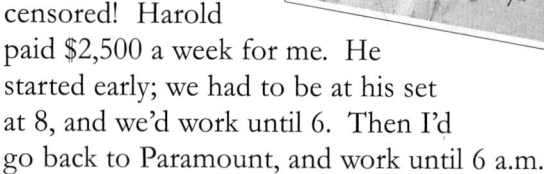

"I did that for 6 or 7 days, and about half way through...I was hallucinating! I didn't go to bed; all I'd do was shower, re-apply my makeup, and go back to work. Finally, when I got to go to bed, I just collapsed. My mother took me to the doctor. He said, 'Grace, you've got to stop something.' He put me on brandy — a tablespoon every 4 hours. I put it in a laxative bottle. My mother made a reservation for us to go to Catalina.

"Catalina was a great place — very alive, things going on, people had their boats," she says. "There were beautiful little places there; it was a great little getaway. We flew those seaplanes over, with the enormous pontoons, and you'd also take the boat."

Once she got a few good days' sleep, she was ready for some fun. "I don't think I was performing on Catalina, but I was there — I might've gotten up to sing once or twice," Grace recollects. "I did some singing, but didn't consider myself a singer. Catalina had all the Big Bands coming in. I remember Ben Birney. They were in a movie with George Raft. Ben's singer was Frank Prince, and I dated him a few times. I knew the Wrigleys had Arabians — they were *beautiful*." And, like Betty Grable: "Oh, I played ping-pong. It was very popular then..."

Grace Bradley with the fella who managed to lasso her heart, Hopalong Cassidy.

When Clay wasn't chasing skirts, he was busy running after some of God's other lovely creatures. Warren Brown wrote this piece for the *Chicago Herald & Examiner* in 1939:

BUTTERFLY INJURES CLAY

Bryant himself admitted to a little soreness after the strenuous workouts that have been going on since Friday. Clay also has a sore index finger, having jammed it against a wire fence while trying to capture one of the butterflies that John "Red" Corriden is training for early Fall delivery to a few preferred clients.

His career started with some stellar expectations. "He's the fastest thing I've seen since Walter Johnson," legendary scout Jack Doyle gushed in 1936.

The journalists echoed those sentiments. "Bryant continues to look like a rising sensation," Dutch Reagan cabled home to *Des Moines Dispatch* readers the next Spring. Everything seemed to be on track: Clay won 19 in the 1938 World Series season...but also led the league in both strikeouts *and* walks. In other words, he threw too many pitches. His arm was gone 2 years later.

Terwilliger, who knew Bryant years later (in 1952), says ol' Clay still knew how to put it on. "Clay Bryant was my manager at St. Paul. He was always impeccably dressed — never any wrinkles. Even in his baseball uniform!"

Larger than life, Clay was one of the few ballplayers deemed worth of his own caricature. This flattering image — must be his best side — graced the pages of the Chicago Daily News *in 1939.*

Clay coached and managed for more than 30 years. His teams won 3 pennants in the Dodger farm system, before he jumped to big-league coaching with the Dodgers and the Cleveland Indians. And, in a sideways sort of way, he influenced Hall-of-Fame Dodger skipper Tommy Lasorda — who usually didn't have much bad to say about anybody. "I remember thinking," Tommy wrote in his autobiography, "as I watched him strut around the Greenville clubhouse one day, that if I did manage a club, I would do everything precisely the opposite of the way he did things.

"Bryant might not be the worst person I ever met in baseball," Tommy explained, "but he is definitely a finalist. My father tried to teach me to look inside a person for his goodness. I am convinced a fully equipped search party working for six months couldn't have found any goodness inside Bryant. He never tried to teach us anything, or encourage us, or boost our confidence; he just ruled by fear."

Golly-whillikers, Tommy, whadd'ya really think?

"He was the kind of man you always wanted to be managing the other team."

(In Clay's defense... he probably was just still a little sore about the whole Hopalong thing.)

Even Clay Bryant got to appear on a Topps card eventually — with his head strangely disembodied, to Mr. Lasorda's delight.

John Payne: Miracle on Avalon Canyon Road

John Payne (this is not a typo for John *Wayne*) made dozens of pictures. He's best known for portraying the lawyer who proved Santa Claus was indeed Santa Claus in *Miracle on 34th Street.* He's least known for *almost* being the first James Bond; John optioned the rights to *Moonraker* in 1955, but never developed the project. *Bond. Payne Bond...*

"Movie stars flocked to the retreat, mostly fans," Charlie Grimm wrote in his autobiography, "including John Payne, who worked out with the Cubs."

"John Payne was a handsome leading man — I did know him," Mrs. Hoppy says. "He was quite athletic, so I wouldn't be the least bit surprised if he'd played baseball."

Unlike some Norma Jeane tales, the John Payne sightings could be verified. "I remember John Payne coming over," Marse Saucedo says. "I saw him on the pier. He was athletic." And Islander Jack Cowell was later assigned to the same flight program with Payne in the Air Force.

John Wayne (not to be confused with John Payne), with Catalina's #1 diver, Duke Fishman (what kind of nickname is that — 'Duke'?)...who did not ever need Mr. Wayne to rescue him.

"John Payne, he was there all the time at batting practice," recalls Hub Kittle, who lobbed a few fat ones over the plate for celebs. "He wouldn't come out in the field — he'd just play catch. They wanted to hit. We gave 'em easy stuff, and they had fun."

While nobody claims to have seen John *Wayne* bat on the Cub diamond, Duke was a Catalina regular — and a big sports guy, who'd played college football at USC. "Harry the Monk was a local diver," Marse recalls. "One time, he didn't come up. John Wayne was at the Isthmus — he went in after him, and pulled him up. He was an incredible athlete, very strong."

Not just any dummy

Edgar Bergen and Charlie McCarthy came out in 1939. For the younger set, Edgar Bergen was dad to Candice Bergen (Murphy Brown), and Charlie was his wooden dummy. Edgar was a ventriloquist who performed on the radio.

Think about that for a moment; it ought to make your head hurt.

"The McCarthy stunt," Ed Burns wrote in the *Chicago Tribune*, "was perhaps the most interesting of the perennial photog and newsreel stunts, the annual act usually consisting of something like jumping through a paper hoop made up to represent a huge baseball."

Try reading this caption without moving your lips, and you may end up with a successful radio ventriloquism career — as Edgar Bergen & Charlie McCarthy had by 1939, where they were invited to Catalina. Fortunately, none of the Cubs mistook Charlie for a bat.

("Movie men have to be humored," the *Trib* had reported in 1919 from the Cubs' Pasadena camp.)

"McCarthy's weight," Warren Brown wrote for the *Herald & Examiner*, "was given at 31 pounds — unlike the ball players, most of the weight being in his head."

Gabby doubles his pleasure

The Doublemint Twins are a longtime Wrigley advertising icon. Catcher Gabby Hartnett seems to thus be the ultimate company man, if we're to believe this 1931 publicity photo from the Catalina ballfield.

"I SAW HIM FIRST," this 1931 photo headlines. "Gabby Hartnett of the Chicago Cubs has promised a ball to the girl who reaches it first. Rochelle Hudson and Arline Judge, Radio Pictures featured players, reach for the baseball instead of the sweet."

Rochelle and Arline made half a dozen pictures together, including *The Public Defender* (the same year this clearly-spontaneous photo was snapped) — which featured a young Boris Karloff in a bit part.

Now, for our younger readers who might not recall these particular starlets: They were big names in Hollywood at the time. Consider these credentials:

Rochelle Hudson made more than 130 pictures. She played Claudette Colbert's daughter in *Imitation of Life* (1934), and Natalie Wood's mother in *Rebel Without a Cause* (1955). She had her own 2-season sitcom from 1954-1955, called *That's My Boy*, and she guest-starred on 3 episodes of Catalina Cub Chuck Connors' show, *Branded*, in 1965. And she sure liked Gabby, didn't she?

Rochelle Hudson's rookie card.

Arline Judge — would you guess she won the contest, based on her pose? — made 53 films. She was married almost that many times, too. (Well, okay — 8. *Eight*?! Refer back to the pose...) Her 1st hubby, Wesley Ruggles (who appeared as an actor in 9 Charlie Chaplin films), discovered her on a train (refer back to...oh, never mind). After they split, Wesley went on to direct a picture entitled *Too Many Husbands* in 1940, while she was working on her 3rd. (Husband, not picture.) For younger TV fans, Arline appeared in a Perry Mason episode in 1957. We feel she liked Gabby, too.

We are pleased to present Arline Judge's rookie card, imported from merry olde England. The card clearly underwent a lot of trading over the years.

A parade of stars

Other Catalina brushes with fame:

* "Charlie Chaplin was a regular in our store," former Avalon Mayor Harvey Cowell says. "I had an incident with him one time. He and his wife at that time, Paulette Goddard, were in there, and I went up to him and said, 'Mr. Chaplin, I had so much fun watching your movies as a kid...I really enjoyed them.' But he turned his face away from me and didn't say a word!"

* "I was driving a bus at the time," Harvey also recalls, "giving the motor tours of the island, and I saw Jean Harlow walking from the Yacht Club to the Tuna Club — and she had a real bad sunburn. Later on, I heard they had to have her hospitalized, it was so bad." (Tuna Club members included Theodore Roosevelt, Herbert Hoover, Winston Churchill, Norway's King Olaf V, Chaplin, and Cecil B. DeMille.)

* "When they filmed *Mutiny on the Bounty* there," says Harvey's brother Jack, "they had a school picnic, and I played ping-pong with Clark Gable and Charles Laughton. I had some pictures of them." (Anybody else noticing a pattern of some sort — what's with movie stars and ping-pong out there?)

* Rookie pitcher Ken Weafer recalls from 1936: "The starlet with all the freckles, Joan Crawford — they were all interested in Big Bill Lee, but he was faithful to his wife. They had their eye on him, but he turned 'em down."

* Cowboy movie star Tom Mix actually lived on Catalina back then, and speaking of Cowboys...Gene Autry (who later owned the California Angels of the American League) met Dutch Reagan on Catalina in 1937, when Gene's band was performing there.

* Radio stars Fibber McGee & Molly stopped by for a visit once, and joshed with the boys.

* Red Adams worked as a carpenter on several films after his stint as a Catalina Cub. His credits include gigs at the Goldwyn studios on movies like *Porgy and Bess*, *The Big Country*, *The Loretta Young Show*, and *The Apartment*...with Charleton Heston, Gregory Peck, Jack Lemmon, Sammy Davis Jr., Pearl Bailey, Burl Ives, Fred MacMurray, Ray Walston, Sidney Poitier...and former Catalina Cub Chuck Connors.

They sure look better in person than they do on the radio! Fibber McGee & Molly, sporting NBC logos, say hello to Gabby at the Cubs' Catalina camp.

* Former Avalon High baseball coach Del Walker, who ran the pro shop for a while, says former Tarzan star Johnny Weismuller golfed on the Island frequently — "He was a good golfer" — and "A fella by the name of Harry Cohn, who ran one of the studios, he'd come over with Rita Hayworth. She went out and played. She wore high heels, so we had to get some tennis shoes for her. I don't think she played much!"

* Comedian Joe E. Brown brought teams of movie stars to play the Cubs on Catalina for several years.

* "All the big bands used to come out and have hitting practice with us," Hub Kittle recalls. Benny Goodman, Rudy Vallee, Jimmy Dorsey, Stan Kenton, Woody Herman, Count Basie, Buddy Rogers, Ben Bernie, Jan Garber, and Kay Kyser all played at the Casino or the St. Catherine. Islander Jack Cowell traveled with the Kay Kyser band for a time. Perry Como started out on Catalina with Ted Weems' orchestra — after working on the Island as a barber.

* Charlie Grimm, Hank Borowy, and Cavarretta gave baseball tips when *The Babe Ruth Story* was being filmed. Of course, Hank Sauer, Gene Mauch, and Peanuts Lowrey appeared with Dutch Reagan in *The Winning Team*. (Jigger Statz, by then a Cub scout in L.A., offered some baseball tips to Dutch.) Lou Stringer played a ballplayer, of all things, in *The Jackie Robinson Story*. And the oft-interviewed Grimm was invited onto Bing Crosby's radio show in 1937.

Grimm shoots the breeze with William Bendix, on location filming The Babe Ruth Story, *before an exhibition game at the White Sox Spring Training park in Pasadena.*

* Another local celebrity was Zane Grey, who wrote 89 novels — most of which were best-sellers. Zane might've occasioned the ballpark from time to time, since he'd played minor-league baseball in the 1890s. "Zane Grey wasn't there much," Jack Cowell says. "He was always traveling around the world."

In 1921, one of Zane's fishing buddies threw a big party for the Cubs to welcome them on their 1st trip out to the Island. But the famous author didn't always make much of an impression: "He refused to speak to anyone," Della Root Arnold says, so her dad Charlie "never read another Zane Grey book!"

Zane Grey's lifetime minor league batting average was .323!

* The semi-pro Catalina Cubs often hosted teams from Paramount Studios and 20th Century Fox.

* Cub pitcher Corky Van Dyke is a distant relative of Dick and Jerry Van Dyke.

* Sometimes they took a break from practice...to watch. "The ten members of the second squad arrived a bit after noon today," the *Los Angeles Times* reported in 1933, "the boat being somewhat late because it paused to participate in a movie shot at the Catalina Isthmus, 12 miles northwest of Avalon." And in 1936, the Cubs took a special side trip to the Isthmus: "A company is on location there and the Grimm party will remain overnight to make a study of how cinema stars spend their leisure," the *Chicago Tribune* explained.

Star-search, '30s style...

Lights...camera...baseball!

Every Spring, the newsreel crews would set up on Catalina to take moving pictures of the Cubs...to send to theaters all across the country. It started early on; the *Los Angeles Times* reported in 1921 that "the Cubs had their tryout of movie work, posing in uniform and registering action before the movie cameras, with Avalon in the background."

In 1926, the paper said the Cubs were accompanied from port by so much moviemaking equipment that the trip required "a fleet consisting of a schooner, a tug, a barge, a speed boat, and a seaplane. The only means of aquatic transportation they forgot were a submarine and a pair of water wings."

> "Which one of these guys is Dizzy Dean?"
>
> Warren Brown of the *Chicago Herald & Examiner*, quoting 'the full squad of photographers' in 1939

"You should see today's workout at your favorite cinema on next week's bill," the *Tribune*'s Burns promised readers in 1936.

Advances, like talkies, made the whole thing even more thrilling. "Within the next few days," Burns told *Trib* readers in 1942, "you will be able to go see the Cubs on the silver screen and listen to them, too, for the sound equipment is to be brought over with the cameras."

And of course, the old story in Hollywood has always been, 'it's who ya know.' In 1947, cute little Timmy Gallagher, age 5 and all decked out in full Chicago regalia, was the star of a newsreel segment — a great coincidence that Timmy was son to Cub General Manager Jim Gallagher.

A picture worth at least a thousand words

When researching a book about the Cubs, most tasks are obvious: Interview Cavarretta, find out Paul Schramka's fielding average, that sort of thing. But in the process, a few new questions materialize. Hidden within the microfilm of old newspapers, a photo emerged of a Cub, a leopard, and a lady on Catalina in 1937. It raised more questions than the caption answered:

Larry French, Chicago Cub mound ace, met a real cub yesterday when Mrs. Linton Wells, prominent writer, brought her pet leopard cub to visit the Catalina training camp.

On the surface, it was just a cute publicity shot — leopard Cub, Chicago Cub, get it? But then, ya gotta wonder...Who is she? Why does she have a leopard? And, more subtly...when all the other women on the Island were wearing frilly dresses, silk stockings with seams, flowery hats, and probably even gloves in 1937...who is this spunky gal, wearing slacks and a leather jacket?

Turns out Mrs. Linton Wells was none other than Fay Gillis Wells, a bit of a celeb in those days. She was one of the 1st female pilots on earth — a true pioneer whose flying buddies were Amelia Earhart and Charles Lindbergh. Born in 1908, she got her pilot's license in the 1920s...helped Wiley Post try to fly around the world in 1933 from her posts in Moscow and Siberia...and decades later covered the Nixon trip to China as a broadcast journalist. Along the way, she was the first woman aviator to parachute from a disabled plane...and, along with her husband, founded the Overseas Press Club in New York in 1939. They were the 1st married couple to have side-by-side front-page bylines as foreign correspondents.

But...what's with the leopard?

"It came about from our trip to Ethiopia," Fay says at the age of 94. "My husband and I covered the Ethiopian war." (Mussolini had invaded in 1935, during the early pre-U.S. stages of World War II. While there, the adventurous couple survived firefights.) "For amusement, the natives brought us a baby leopard that was wandering around — and also a cheetah. We kept both in the hotel room. Fortunately, they had 2 big balconies. We kept one on one balcony, and another on the other side.

"I called her the Queen of Sheba, because she was from Ethiopia — Snooks for short."

Soon after that, "we came back to America, and Snooks returned with us. We stayed at a hacienda in Puerto Rico. We were down there 6 months while my husband wrote his autobiography. Then we went to California, where we visited his parents. I covered Hollywood for the *New York Herald-Tribune*, and took her to all the studios. Everyone went bananas, and they all wanted pictures with her."

And Avalon? "Santa Catalina Island was one of our pleasure trips. The bellboys took care of her, and sat her on the front desk; when all the guests would come in, they'd see her there! She was about 6 feet long, to the end of her tail, and she weighed about 100 pounds...but when I first got her, I could hold her in my hands. We had to take her one time a month to the zoo, to have the curve of her claws clipped."

In 1938, David Sarnoff (who invented NBC, network radio, and network TV) asked the couple to start radio in South America. "He sent us on a 5-month tour of Latin America," Fay says, "but we couldn't take Snooks. I took her to the Broadmoor Hotel in Colorado Springs — but when we came back, she was dead. They'd bred her."

Fay, 1929.

Whew. All that adventure, from one funny little publicity photo. So next time somebody repeats the oft-repeated phrase, "A picture is worth a thousand words," you'll know what they mean.

And let's not forget Norman Rockwell

Magazines were big in those days, too — like *The Saturday Evening Post*. On September 4, 1948, the lovable-loser Cubs appeared on the cover...in mid-defeat. The Norman Rockwell painting was entitled simply, "The Dugout,' and it featured 4 Catalina Cubs: Bob Rush, Johnny Schmitz, Rube Walker, and manager Charlie Grimm. Also included was the Boston Braves' batboy (albeit disguised in Cub garb), which was semi-appropriate because the scene had been set up there...rather than in Chicago.

We're supposed to think they're sad because they're losing, but the fact is Norman Rockwell just informed them that they're not being paid to pose.

"We were playing in Boston," Bob Rush recalls, "and Norman Rockwell came down on the field before the game. He took photographs of us in the dugout. He took each one individually — not all together, like you see on the poster he painted. He did the poster from the individual photographs."

"Tell you the truth," Johnny Schmitz admits, "I don't even know doing that. It's been a long time to remember that but it sure was fun doing it. People ask me about that and I tell them the picture shows what it's like having a bad day or year."

"When I saw it, I couldn't believe it!" Rush laughs. "I always got *the Saturday Evening Post* because of the covers — so I was pretty honored, and surprised. While he was doing it, they told us it was gonna be on a poster or something — we didn't know for sure it was gonna be a *Saturday Evening Post* cover until it came out."

Rush says "Nobody teased us or gave us a hard time about it; most everybody thought it was kinda neat. Attitudes were different in those days!"

"No, they like the picture," Schmitz agrees.

Ironically, "We didn't get paid for it," Rush shrugs. "Today, each guy would've probably gotten $300,000 for it! Things were different then..."

Dutch & Norma Jeane debate whether Kiki Cuyler or Phil Cavarretta was the better clutch hitter.

The Great Quake of '33

California Rolled Out More Than Just The Red Carpet One March Afternoon

"Oh, boy, it was a hum-dinger!"

Della Root Arnold, Charlie's daughter -- who was 13 when the big one hit

---

The Cubs battled more than on-the-field opponents during Spring Training — they also faced disasters (natural and un-natural) of all kinds.

Like landslides, bank closings, wars and rumors of wars, and the Quake of '33.

While some earthquakes are more famous — like the great San Francisco Quake of 1906 and the Loma Prieta Quake of '89, which was broadcast live by Al Michaels during the A's-Giants "Between the Bay" World Series — others seem forgotten to the history books.

CHICAGO AMERICAN — COMPLETE MARKETS
VOL. XXXIII, NO. 211 P.M. — CHICAGO, SATURDAY, MARCH 11, 1933 — PRICE FIVE CENTS

DEATH TOLL 141 IN QUAKE

26th Temblor Spreads Long Beach Ruin

ECONOMY BILL PASSED BY HOUSE

Foes in Senate Delay Vote on Measure Until Next Week.

WASHINGTON, March 11. — (AP) — The House rallied behind President Roosevelt this afternoon to pass his drastic economy bill.

WASHINGTON, March 11. — (AP) — The Roosevelt economy program collided with vigorous opposition in Congress today that made delay certain and defeat a distinct possibility.

Beaten on their own caucus Democratic leaders sought to rush it through the House and appeared to have fair chance for success, in view of Republican support.

PAYROLL CASH RELEASED BY BANKS HERE

Firms Get 5 to 25 Pct. of Money, Business Monday, View.

A number of Chicago banks today released from 5 to 25 per cent of their usual Saturday payroll cash for regular customers.

STRICKEN TOWN DIGS OUT FROM UNDER

2,000 SERIOUSLY INJURED AS RESCUERS COMB DEBRIS; LOSS NEAR $35,000,000

LATE BULLETIN

26TH TEMBLOR ROCKS LONG BEACH.
LONG BEACH, Cal., March 11. — (By International News Service.) — Following another earthquake shock, the twenty-sixth, at 11:55 a.m. (1:55 p.m., Chicago time), which shook downtown buildings, all structures in that district were ordered evacuated by military authorities.

(Other Bulletins on Page 2.)

BY TED SMITS.
International News Service Staff Correspondent.

LOS ANGELES, March 11. — Southern California's death toll from a series of earthquakes that rocked a 200-mile long coast strip for more than fifteen hours mounted to 141 today.

Thousands were injured, available hospital and relief station reports placing the more seriously hurt at upward of 2,500, with more than

Nobody seems to know about the Long Beach Earthquake of Friday, March 10, 1933, although it was a major one:

* More than 120 people died, and some 600 others were injured

* Property damage was about $50 million (in 1933 dollars), which is closer to a billion of today's bucks

* The entire city of Compton was leveled

* It registered 6.4 on Mr. Richter's scale, epicentered 3 miles south of Huntington Beach (less than 10 miles from John Wayne/Orange County Airport)...dozens of schools collapsed, and thousands of children were spared because it happened at 5:54 in the afternoon

And it shook up a whole lot of Chicago Cubs.

"The Biltmore Hotel swayed 7 feet!" says Della Root Arnold (Charlie's daughter), then 13.

"Riggs Stephenson, the left-fielder, was rooming with a young rookie, who was from the same area," Della says. "The Cubs tried to put older members with a younger guy. They were in their room at the Biltmore, and the young guy said, 'You know, Riggs, I just got a bottle of White Lightning from my uncle — should we have a sip?'

"And they took a sip just as the quake hit — and Riggs said, 'Boy that's powerful corn!' "

If you'd listened to your mother re: the evils of strong drink, Riggs, you might just not tip over like that...

"When the Quake hit," Jolly Cholly Grimm wrote in his autobiography — although not so jolly at just that moment — "it sounded like someone had thrown a bowling ball against a wall. I was in my room and must have set a speed record coming down the stairway. I didn't wait for an elevator."

The Cubs had just boated over from Catalina to complete their exhibition series against the New York Giants. They'd played a few games out on the Island, and the next contest was scheduled for the day after the Quake.

"Few of the players on either team got much sleep during the long night following the severe earthquake yesterday afternoon," Gentleman Jim Gallagher nervously typed for the *Chicago American*, years before he became the team's GM. "Even the few hardy souls who dared to go to their rooms couldn't sleep because of the slight tremors which recurred constantly through the night." The headline on the story was, "QUAKE LEAVES CUBS SHAKEN."

There were dozens of aftershocks over the next few weeks. "William Veeck tried to calm us after this scary experience while we sat in the lobby talking to each other, as tight as a drum," Grimm recounted. "We were waiting for the next shock, knowing that's the way quakes travel.

" 'Well, boys,' he said along about 9 pm, 'I think the worst is over. I'm going up to bed and I think you all should retire too, because we're playing the Giants tomorrow.'

"As this fine gentleman, the very picture of relaxation, was strolling toward the elevators, another tremor hit. He turned right around and came back."

Actually, most of the Cubs left the hotel altogether.

"My dad called down to the Biltmore Hotel and said, if any of you boys want to come here, the house is safe — we didn't have any damage," Della recalls. "18 of 'em came!" Charlie had played for the Los Angeles Angels in the Pacific Coast League before coming to the Cubs, and still had his house in L.A. — so that's where he stayed with his family during part of the Spring drills. "Woody English and a couple of the other infielders came, and they never left! They stayed about 10 days, until the team left town.

Charlie Root had L.A. roots, so some of the Cubs moved in with him after the Quake hit.

"I was in our house on Maryland Drive," Della remembers. "We didn't have TV then, but we had radio — and I was listening to Chandu the Magician. When it hit, I ran through the front door...but my mother, my dad, and my brother ran to the back. When Mother realized I wasn't with them, she said, 'Get Della!' So Dad came running by the shaking house. The road looked like waves!"

"At this precise time," Grimm wrote, "Buck Newsome, then a Cub rookie pitcher, had a full face of lather down at the barber shop. When someone hollered, 'Earthquake!' Buck bolted out of his chair and rushed upstairs into the lobby and through the revolving doors. Buck dashed across the street into Pershing Square, a grassy knoll that attracted the hippies of the era, a considerably older bunch than the present breed."

By 1953, Buck Newsome had gotten that shave finished... but he'd been so unnerved by the whole episode that he'd changed his name (so no more quakes could find him, apparently) and his hair had turned grey.

The Hartnetts dashed out to the park, too.

"My parents were getting ready to go out," Sheila Hartnett Hornof says. She wasn't born yet, but her parents had told the tale. "Dad was shaving and had a high-ball on the counter. Everything started shaking."

"I was in a bathtub — I don't know why this stands out," remembers older brother Buddy Hartnett, who was just 3 at the time. "The door was open, and my dad had a drink that was sitting on a bureau — and I noticed that the drink was movin' across that thing, and it fell off. They yanked me outa the tub and we ran out. You couldn't use the elevator, so we were all comin' down the stairs. I remember there was a lady wearin' a fur coat. We went across the street to the park."

"Martha Hartnett, she never participated, really, but she came that time," Della says. "She was bathing their little boy in the hotel. She grabbed him out of the tub, and put on her dress backwards! And she never changed it. She didn't come out too often, and after that she never came again."

Other ballplayers endured embarrassing moments, too — like some of the White Sox, training in Pasadena. "Perhaps the funniest incident centered around Charlie Berry," the *Chicago American* reported. "He was getting a rubdown, but when the first rumblings came the masseur shouted: 'Earthquake! Every man for himself!' He made a hurried exit to the street, but poor Charlie's sense of modesty won out over his desire to flee."

Al Simmons was getting a shave but only suffered a nick, the paper said. And "Mule Haas was shaving in his room when the Quake was felt, but checked himself in the hallway when he recalled he had nothing on from the waist up." Some of the fully-clothed players ventured out for a look, according to the paper: "Manager Lew Fonseca and several other members of the club motored in the direction of Long Beach to view the raging fire on Signal Hill, where there is a veritable forest of oil wells."

The Hartnetts, back on solid ground, seeing Gabby off (unaccompanied) to Catalina in 1936 — 3 years after the Quake. Fortunately, Mrs. Hartnett had time to adjust her outfit before the photographer arrived.

189

"Dad got through to the police," Della says, and he was able to get to Compton, which was completely demolished."

The visiting Giants were staying at the Biltmore alongside the Cubs. Bill Terry was rooming with traveling secretary Jim Tierney, and they darted down the stairwell. "Tierney, in the lead, was praying and crossing himself," Grimm wrote. "Terry, a 32nd-degree mason, put his hand on Jim's shoulder and said: 'I don't understand everything you're doing, but whatever it is, I'm with you!'"

Stephenson and his rookie roommate, fresh from the White Lightning storm, were also bidding a hasty retreat. "They ran to the door, and the room was still shaking," Della says. "And a man was running down the hall with a twin bed mattress on his head! And Riggs said, 'Don't worry — we'll be all right!' But the man shouted at him and cussed him out.

"That night, we had Zack Taylor, who was a catcher for Dad, over for dinner," Della continues. "He was from Florida. He was the nicest guy! By golly, I tell you — running through those halls, seeing the dining room table — mother had already set it. She had pineapple and cottage cheese salad out, and it went up, and landed right on the chairs!

"Zack and Gabby and about everybody — they weren't from California, so they didn't know about earthquakes. Zack, that night, he had a hat and gloves on, even though it was pretty warm, and he went out and walked up and down the street, he was so upset."

"Lonnie, you probably know, is a man of iron nerves. Earthquakes mean little or nothing to him. But then on the other hand a couple of earthquakes known as Ruth and Gehrig are something else again."

The Cubs' previous season had ended at the hands of the Babe & his trusty sidekick, Lou — the ill-fated 1932 World Series was a much greater disaster to Cub fans than any geologic incident.

Corcoran spent his nervous energy lampooning everything in sight. "Now they've found the cause of the earthquake," he typed. "The Giants beat the Cubs Friday afternoon. When the Giants win a ball game, even on a training trip, it is likely to start most anything. So perhaps it's just as well that they finish on the short end from now on.

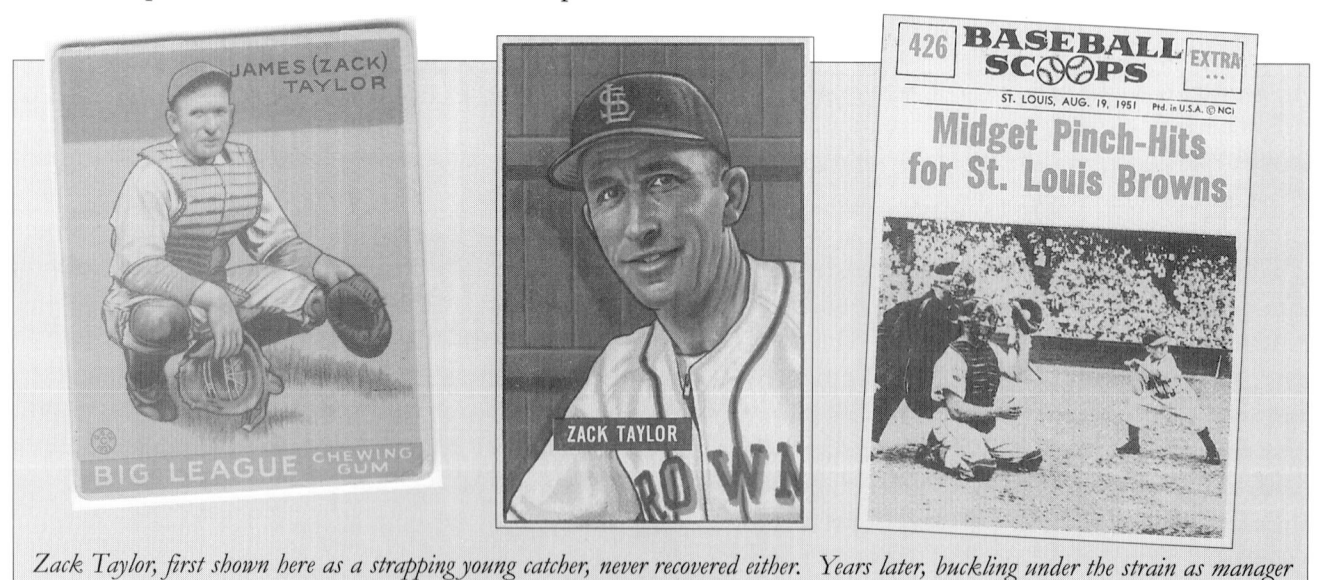

Zack Taylor, first shown here as a strapping young catcher, never recovered either. Years later, buckling under the strain as manager of the St. Louis Brown, he collaborated with Bill Veeck's son, Bill, to insert a midget as a pinch-hitter in a major league game.

In his *Cork Tips* column for the *American*, Jimmy Corcoran wrote: "When Lonnie Warneke woke up Saturday morning after sleeping for 12 hours, he said: 'Someone was trying to wake me up all night. This is a deuce of a place to try for a little sleep.'

"One of the real benefits of the quake," the Cork (clearly a Chicago architectural snob) rambled on, "is that it should promote some fresh new buildings along the coast. Providing, of course, that anyone has money." FDR had closed the banks that week, so financial earthquakes were also shaking things up.

Aftershocks kept rolling the landscape. "When Warneke woke Bush, his roommate, during yesterday's morning tremblor, the worst since Friday," Gallagher reported the next week, "Guy just rolled over and said: 'What is it? Another of those dang things?'"

There were aftershocks of another sort — on the field, too. On Sunday, "Buck Newsome, still suffering from earthquake shakes, was wild in the fifth," Gallagher wrote. On Tuesday, he sent back word that Grimm was "still refusing to go to bed" and that several veterans "and most of the younger players have done very little sleeping since the big jolt.

"The earthquake just about put a final kibosh on any hopes of the Giants' training here next season," Gallagher reported. "Big Jim Tierney, secretary of the club, dashed from the hotel just after the first shock, declaring himself all for New York's blizzards in preference to climate."

"After this nerve-shaking experience," Grimm penned, "Terry pulled the Giants out of California for Spring Training. I've always thought it was ironic that, 25 years later, the Giants left New York to set up shop in San Francisco, whose 1906 earthquake made this little eruption to the south seem like kid's stuff."

"This may go down in history as the year an earthquake decided a National League pennant race," Gallagher wrote a few days later. His words proved prophetic: The Cubs, defending champs, lost out to none other than the Giants! "The great Quake of March 10 and the series of after-shocks which have continued ever since have completely shattered the nerves of the Chicago Cubs. It's a question even now whether some members of the troupe will be able to recover their morale before the season opens. And if these earth tremors continue, it's a cinch they won't.

"Young Bill Herman, who should be the best 2nd baseman in the big leagues this season, is a nervous wreck. He hasn't slept and has hardly eaten since Friday night, and yesterday, while the Cubs were losing to Los Angeles, 10-8, he was out of the lineup for the first time since joining the Cubs in the Fall of 1931.

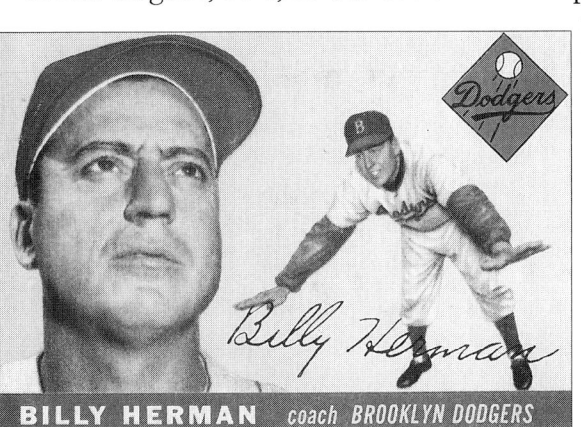

Billy Herman, feeling a bit more safe! with the Dodgers.

"Herman's wife, a very nervous young woman, left for home yesterday, and manager Charlie Grimm hopes his young second sacker will get back his grip on himself now that he need no longer worry about his helpmate.

"Burleigh Grimes, veteran spitball pitcher, is another whose nerves are wrecked. A sick man last season, he reported fit as a fiddle, and was expecting to stage a fine comeback. He has visibly aged since the shock Friday night and can't do much concentrating on his work."

But they did go on — and kept coming back to Catalina. The following season, Herbert Simons wrote in the *Chicago Daily Times*: "Five Cub wives, survivors of the 1933 earthquake, were game enough to return to California this year...the Mmes. Grimm, Malone, Tinning, Cuyler and Lotshaw."

"This is the 9th anniversary of the Southern California earthquake," Ed Burns opened one piece from Avalon for the *Chicago Tribune* in 1942. "This shake, it was recalled today, so upset the Cubs in 1933 that they couldn't defend their National League championship won in 1932, but so frightened the New York Giants, who trained in Los Angeles that year, that they didn't stop running until they had won the 1933 World Championship."

Burns reported that only a few remained from 1932, but "most missed in this reunion of survivors was Bill Herman, who has passed on to the Dodgers since the eighth anniversary observed here last year. Bill had a nervous reaction to the Quake that sent him to bed for several days."

Ed noted that "residents of Avalon refused to participate in recollections of the Quake. 'It was nothing to the shake this Island got shortly after Dec. 7, and has been getting ever since,' is the way one resident businessman explained apathy toward the anniversary." The resident was right; while the quake couldn't keep the Cubs away, Pearl Harbor did.

As late as 1950, the old-timers on Catalina still recalled the '33 shake. From the *Tribune*:

> *While the Cubs were sailing across the channel from Catalina, their heel and toe paradise, to the mainland of the United States, none aboard except Trainer Andy Lotshaw and Traveling Secretary Bob Lewis were able to recall that 17 years ago, Cubs of another era bravely were defying an earthquake to shake their noble courage. Lotshaw slept at second base at Wrigley Field and Lewis sat up all night in Pershing Square, a park across the street from the Cubs hotel.*

Actually, the Cubs felt another earthquake during their Catalina jaunts — ironically, it came in 1946, their first year back after the war. The Walker Pass Quake took place on March 15, miles away in the California high desert. There were a few dozen aftershocks. It was about as severe as the Long Beach Quake (6.3 on the Richter Scale), but far less damaging because it was so remote.

"Watching the chandeliers swing during yesterday morning's li'l earthquake apparently left the Chicago Cubs a bit cockeyed," wrote seasoned earthquake veteran Al Wolf of the *Los Angeles Times*, "for they were able to collect only six hits while dropping an afternoon exhibition game against the St. Louis Browns, 7-2, before 1500 Wrigley Field kibbitzers.

"Of course...the chucking for the American Leaguers may have had something to do with it, but the tremblors certainly provided a swell alibi."

Poor lads. Seems a large quake knocked the entire team off their feet at once.

Other plagues & such

In his autobio, Grimm referred to additional obstacles faced by ballplayers. "Hughie Critz, the great little second baseman of the Giants, who had a cotton plantation in his native Mississippi, sighed, 'Earthquakes in the Spring and boll weevils in the Summer.'"

Not to mention the Great Depression, which did hurt attendance in the early '30s — even at exhibition games. And of course, World War II.

In March of 1933 — ironically, the same week as the Quake — FDR closed the banks. Most of the Chicago sportswriters expressed concern that fans would be able to find the spare change around the house to attend Spring exhibition games.

And then there was the weather. The Cubs also had to avoid massive walls of mud on occasion. "Our hotel was up quite a ways from downtown — it was a pretty good walk," Ken Raffensberger says. "If you had a storm, the mudslides would block the road."

Knowing that there were fewer landslides in Florida, where the Redlegs trained, Ken breathed a sigh of relief when dealt there.

"The sea is belching waves at a furious clip. The rain fell so hard and steady that even the most loyal Californians would be forced to admit that it was more than a 'mist.'"

'Jimmy the Cork' Corcoran,
in the *Chicago American*, 1930

The biggest landslide of all took place in 1937, after an unseasonable amount of rainfall.

"CHICAGO CUBS MAROONED BY LANDSLIDE," was the headline in the *Chicago Tribune* sports section. Burns wrote, "A huge landslide over the road which leads from the Cubs' hotel to the village of Avalon, the Cub clubhouse and the practice field, today marooned the athletes who came here to bask in the sunshine while conditioning themselves for the National League pennant race.

"Confined to a canyon which was under a constant downpour all day, the Cubs, perforce, restricted their exercise to running up and down hotel corridors, interspersed with lobby pacing."

Bud Smith, later a Mayor of Avalon, recalls, "One year, there was a lot of rain, and they were staying at the Hotel St. Catherine — about a mile outside of town. There was so much rain they had a big dirt slide — it completely blocked the walk. The only way to the hotel was by boat, so Mr. Wrigley took a big glass-bottom boat to the Pleasure Pier, and they'd go do their training, then back downtown, and back on their boat to the hotel. That went on for a couple of weeks. It was rainy a little bit, and they'd hang around Sportland, bowling, playing pool, badminton, and the kids would hang out."

"Manager Charlie Grimm called off the practice session for the day. Just in time, too, for another 'high fog' almost drowned him on the way back to the hotel."

Gentleman Jim Gallagher,
in the *Chicago American*, 1935

The next day, Burns waxed poetically:

AVALON — Mountains falling down, rain pouring out of black skies, seals, millions of seals, barking saucy reprimands at angry Neptune as he kicks the Pacific to the very bedsteads of winter-soft athletes. Thus the Cubs' $35,000 trainingless training season goes on apace. And mud, very sticky mud, is everywhere.

This morning Manager Grimm said, with wild enthusiasm, "The weatherman is in error. It ain't goin' to rain no more."

But the weatherman wasn't in error. For no sooner had the Cubs donned their monkey suits and hied to the gummy practice field that rain started coming down in a very spirited way. In booming disgust Mr. Grimm called off everything and the boys returned to their clubhouse.

Meanwhile, Gentleman Jim was clarifying errors for readers of the *American*, who apparently may've heard some radio reports that the bell tower had been washed into the ocean: "The report is about as authentic as the one sent out at the time of the Long Beach earthquake that Catalina Island had disappeared, when it hardly felt the shock at all," James explained.

Apparently the engineers needed more than one year to shore things up. The following season, the *American*'s sports editor, Ed Cochrane, reported: "That annual Spring extravaganza known as 'The Landslides of Catalina' opened a 1938 engagement today when a large portion of the mountain that skirts the highway leading from the hotel where the Cubs are quartered to the village at the beach and the ball park, came tumbling into the road and marooned the athletes in the fodder shop.

"It is hardly fair to say that athletes object to being marooned in the fodder shop. Their chief reason for reporting at the Spring camp on Phil Wrigley's playground out here in the Pacific is to start eating large meals at the expense of the boss."

The Cubs repaid PK for all those large meals by winning the N.L. pennant that fall.

Still, somebody was always trying to outsmart the elements. In his *Cork Tips* column in the 1930 *American*, Corcoran wrote about a Charlie Grimm scheme, from his pre-managerial playing days:

Cholly Grimm came into camp yesterday with the latest device and it happens to be a weather indicator. "It's this way. Every time it is going to rain, I know in advance. When it is going to be cold, I know it." And then he held out his left mitt that was damaged late last season.

Jolly Cholly checks tomorrow's forecast.

"Still a little sensitive," he said, "when the weather is going to change — but outside of that it doesn't bother me in the least. Guess I ought to be the most valuable man on the team when I can tell Joe McCarthy 24 hours in advance whether it is going to be rainy or fair. Of course, I haven't gone into the situation thoroughly with Joe, but if he ever needs any advice on the weather, I'll just say, 'C'mon, paw; do your stuff. This ought to supply Joe with that sixth sense of vision and probably it will win a lot of ball games for us."

*Body snatchers, too?
Gabby seems to have vanished, 1939.*

Jolly Cholly, Gabby, Old Flash, Cavy, & Other Managerial Types

A Collection of Colorful Coaches & Skippers Came Over to Keep the Boys in Line

"That music in the background is by Cholly Grimm, the only man in captivity who can play a left-handed banjo and cuss at Gabby Hartnett at the same time."

'Jimmy the Cork' Corcoran, in the *Chicago American*, 1930

Half a dozen Hall-of-Famers managed the Cubs on Catalina. If you think some of the ballplayers were characters...imagine these guys, with another few decades (and several thousand more ballgames) under their belts.

There are a few general truisms we can draw:

1. Pretty much everybody loved Charlie Grimm.

2. Pretty much everybody hated Frankie Frisch.

3. There was no correlation between winning and a manager's style: Stern skippers won big and lost hard, while fun-loving field bosses took home pennants and also scrubbed the cellars.

So let's visit the helm, and meet these grizzled ol' baseball lifers...

Before Catalina

When William Wrigley was but a wee lad, and the Cubs had no Catalina connection, the team employed some large-name managers. Albert Spalding, Cap Anson, and all 3 members of the legendary Tinker-to-Evers-to-Chance double-play combo ran the team for a time.

In 1920, when Mr. W. brought the team over from Pasadena for a look-over, Fred Mitchell was in his 4th (and final) year as Chicago's manager. He'd led the Cubs to their 1918 World Series appearance against the Red Sox (starring pitcher George Ruth). But the team slid to 3rd place, then 6th...and Fred was off to lead the Boston Braves.

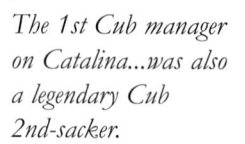

The 1st Cub manager on Catalina...was also a legendary Cub 2nd-sacker.

Tinker to this guy to Chance

Hall-of-Famer Johnny Evers player-managed the Cubs to a respectable 3rd-place finish in 1913, but didn't manage again until 1921. Lucky John: That means he was the 1st-ever Catalina Cub manager. But his team's challenge for last place didn't endear him with Mr. Wrigley, so he was replaced before the season was over.

Dealing with ballplayers was difficult, he conceded. "Temperamentally," Johnny told the *Los Angeles Times* upon his Island arrival, "the director of a bunch of grand opera stars has nothing on me."

Johnny Evers

* Nickname: Crab
* N.L. MVP in 1914 — although he only hit 1 homer!
* Played 18 years, stole 324 bases

A Reindeer for Catalina's hills

Reindeer Bill Killefer managed the Cubs from 1921 through 1925. His teams never finished better than 4th. He was Grover Cleveland Alexander's catcher with the Phillies, and helped squeeze several more good seasons out of Ol' Pete. He also managed the St. Louis Browns in the '30s, and several minor-league teams — including a stint back in California, with the Pacific Coast League Sacramento Solons.

Not known for his batting prowess, he knew how to handle pitchers. "A juggler in a vaudeville act as nothing on Killefer," the *Times* said in 1921. "The very tips of Killefer's fingers must be magneted — the ball just sticks to them."

Bill Killefer

* Bill & his wife were important characters in the 1952 Ronald Reagan movie, "The Winning Team" — the story of Grover Alexander

* His career spanned 6 decades (1909-1958) as a player, manager, coach, & scout

Reindeer Bill Killefer (playing catch on the beach at Avalon Bay in 1922) hoped the actor who portrayed him in that Reagan movie was as handsome a chap as he was in real life.

Do these 2 guys count?

The Cubs suffered a bit of disarray in 1925 — in pre-Steinbrenneresque fashion, they employed 3 managers. Yet only Killefer managed on Catalina, so the other 2 will get a quick asterisk here.

Rabbit Maranville played 23 years and is in the Hall of Fame — but don't ask why. His lifetime average was a piddling .258 (when guys hit .400 all over the place). He never hit .300 in a full season. He only hit 28 home runs — in 23 seasons! And the only time he ever led the league in a batting category...was when he paced the N.L. with 672 *at-bats* in 1922.

Dazzling.

Could it be his managerial prowess? Debatable. Lifetime mark: 23-30 (.434, last place) for the mid-1925 Cubs.

Nonetheless. Our task here is neither to trash nor besmirch the reputation of a fine human being. Rather, we only wish to note that he managed the Cubs once. And that he was quite the colorful character — truly an early-on players' manager, and a teammate/playmate of Charlie Grimm: He dropped water balloons from hotel windows (onto Cub front-office execs), got into a brawl with a cabbie (which got Rabbit thrown into the slammer), and doused train passengers from a spittoon.

While he was the Cubs' <u>manager</u>!

On Catalina one Spring, Bill Veeck says a photographer asked the Rabbit to stage a golf pose with Grimm: Charlie lying on his back with a tee in his teeth, Maranville with club. "Rabbit took a vicious swing and knocked the ball out of Charlie's teeth," Veeck wrote in his autobiography. "Charlie arose, white as a sheet because...Rabbit had only played a few rounds of golf in his life."

Next! George Gibson finished the season by leading the Cubs to a 12-14 mark. He also managed the Pirates for 6 seasons and had been a big-league catcher for 14 years. He was not nearly as colorful as Maranville...which suited Mr. Wrigley just fine.

The greatest manager of all time?

Quick trivia: Name the manager with the best career win-loss percentage...the best career World Series win-loss percentage...and the most World Championships.

Hint: Same guy who was the 1st to win a World Series for both leagues...and the 1st to win 4 straight World Championships...during his 24 seasons at a helm.

You're right: Hall-of-Famer Joe McCarthy, who rookie-managed the Cubs on Catalina from 1926-1930...including a league championship in 1929. (We regret to report that Marse Joe's next team, the Yankees of New York, beat the Cubbies in the 1932 and 1938 World Series.) All this, from a chap who never played in a major league game!

Hornsby should've stuck with pointing to where he'd hit the ball.

The Yankees made McCarthy a genius long before they did it for Stengel. Earlier, in 1928 (when he was merely excellent), he rated the rookies with coach Jimmy Burke.

"The two great requisites for a baseball manager," the *Chicago Herald & Examiner* editorialized in 1927, "are baseball knowledge and control of players. McCarthy has those assets."

But William Wrigley's hopes were a bit too high. After finishing 2nd in 1930, the under-appreciated McCarthy jumped to Yankee Stadium...and all the Cubs could do after that was eat his dust.

Joe McCarthy

* Finished 1st 9 times, 2nd 8 times
* Never finished worse than 4th
* Joe DiMaggio said, "Never a day went by when you didn't learn something from McCarthy."

He couldn't manage, but he sure could hit!

The Cubs' next Hall-of-Fame manager got there with his bat, rather than his neat penmanship on line-up cards. Rogers Hornsby hit .400 — *3 times* — and his .358 lifetime average is second only to Ty Cobb. Rajah led the league in hitting 6 straight years, and he even hit more home runs than Babe Ruth twice. He managed the Cubs for only one full season, taking over the last week of 1930 and getting the boot part-way through 1932. After managing the Cubs, he piloted the Browns and Reds for 8 seasons — and always finished in 6th, 7th, or last place. In between, the Cubs brought him back to teach some kids how to hit...but he didn't.

"He didn't know how to handle men," Charlie Grimm observed. He refused to let players drink soda pop in the clubhouse, watch movies or read the papers — but you could see the *Racing Forum* sticking out of his back pocket."

"You can picture Rogers roosting in a corner of a divan in the lobby of the St. Catherine Hotel," wrote Jimmy Corcoran in his *Cork Tips* column for the *Chicago American* during the Spring of 1930. "He is sitting alone. Very much alone. He is not reading. He is thinking. But just what he's thinking about is none of our business."

He wrote the book on irascible: He led the Cards to the 1926 World Championship as player-manager, but was traded after the season! And in 1932, he managed the first 99 Cubs games before being fired (the team was in 2nd place at the time) — but after Grimm took over and led the team to the World Series, the players voted *against* giving Hornsby a share.

"Rogers Hornsby was supposed to be the batting coach," Randy Jackson says. "He'd stand behind the batting cage and watch us, then run off to the race track. He never said anything to anybody, never offered any advice."

William Wrigley threatens to punch Rajah in the mouth; Pat Malone officiates, making sure they don't fall overboard.

"Here was this Hall-of-Famer," Wayne Terwilliger says, "and he took batting practice and made it look easy. But he couldn't teach anybody to do it like he did."

"What makes you think you're smarter than your daddy was?"
Bill Veeck's mother, when he hired Hornsby to manage the Browns in 1952

"What did I tell you?"
Mom, 2 months later, when Bill fired him

He had a good eye, though — conducting a baseball camp for kids, and he was one of the Cubs' 1st TV announcers in 1949. "He kinda took a liking to me," Phil Cavarretta says. "I guess he liked the way I hustled, the way I played hard. When I became manager, and we'd take batting practice, he'd come behind the batting cage and he'd talk to me about the games, trying to give me good advice about what a player was doing."

Rogers Hornsby

* *In his 1st season playing for the Cubs (1929), Hornsby was named league MVP — hitting .380 with 39 homers*
* *Led the league in hitting categories more than 40 times during his 23 seasons*
* *Like Killefer, Hornsby was portrayed in the Dutch Reagan flick, "The Winning Team"*

Jolly good times

Charlie Grimm loved baseball — *really* loved baseball — but more than that, he loved his ballplayers.

He told stories and played practical jokes and strummed his banjo and ran and jumped and tumbled (even as manager), always quick with a smile or a word of encouragement...when he wasn't mugging it up for a camera lens or posing for a Norman Rockwell painting or taking a few minutes to chat with a star-struck kid in Avalon.

Jolly Cholly Grimm, surveying the Catalina diamond from atop the press box wall — while cooking up his next 1-liner.

Jolly Cholly served 3 separate tenures as Cub manager, in the '30s...'40s...and finally in 1960. Before that, he was one of the best 1st-basemen in the National League. He hit .300 half a dozen times during his 20-year career (*.345* in 1923), and led the league in fielding 9 straight years. He managed for 19 campaigns in all.

His 1st managerial assignment with the Cubs was unusual; he took over in mid-season 1932, and led the team to a pennant. And he left in mid-season 1938 — when the team also won the pennant. Right smack in the middle, he got 'em to the 1935 World Series (all by himself). Cholly also skippered the 1945 N.L. champ team during his 2nd gestation (1944-1949), but was too old in 1960 and started 6-11 before being traded to Cleveland for broadcaster Lou

---

"The best banjo player in baseball."

Columnist Dutch Reagan, describing Charlie Grimm in a Spring report from Catalina for the *Des Moines Dispatch*, 1936

Boudreau — a fittingly unusual end to a most unusual career. (In between, he was a radio announcer himself...and from 1952-1956, he managed the Braves.) "My heart belongs to Chicago and the Cubs," he wrote — and his wife asked if she could scatter his ashes over Wrigley Field.

"Charlie," Cub superscout Salty Saltwell eulogized in 1983, "always saw something good in everything."

"I always thought a pat on the back, an encouraging word, or a wisecrack paid off a lot more than a brilliantly executed piece of strategy," he wrote in his autobiography. "In my 3 pennant years, I had the horses, and it was more or less a matter of giving them the ball and letting them take over."

"He seemed to draw the best out in them," Saltwell said.

He often did it quietly, behind the scenes — like one particular Catalina episode. "I was a new father," Lloyd Lowe says, "and I didn't have much money to spend. When I was out there, my wife had out 1st child. My brother-in-law sent a telegram. Charlie Grimm gave it to me after we're done, and he pulls me aside and tells me, go back to the hotel, call your wife, and put it on my bill."

Grimm truly inspired loyalty. "I came up when I was 18," Phil Cavarretta says, "and I can thank Charlie Grimm for that. A lot of people in the organization said, he's only 18, with just a little Class A experience... send him to Double-A. But he disagreed: "I don't care how old he is — 18, or 25 — as long as he shows me he can play. He's hitting .350, .360, he's a great fielder — and the best thing I like is, he gives 100%. What more do you want?' "

He let visitors suit up an work out with the team: movie stars, big banders, and of course the radio broadcaster, Dutch Reagan. And he gave locals on Catalina a chance, too — like Conrad Lopez, who got a contract, and barber-to-be Lolo Saldaña. He'd let the kids (like Foxie Saucedo) caddy for him while he was golfing, and he was always generous. "I got the first glove I ever got from Charlie Grimm," says

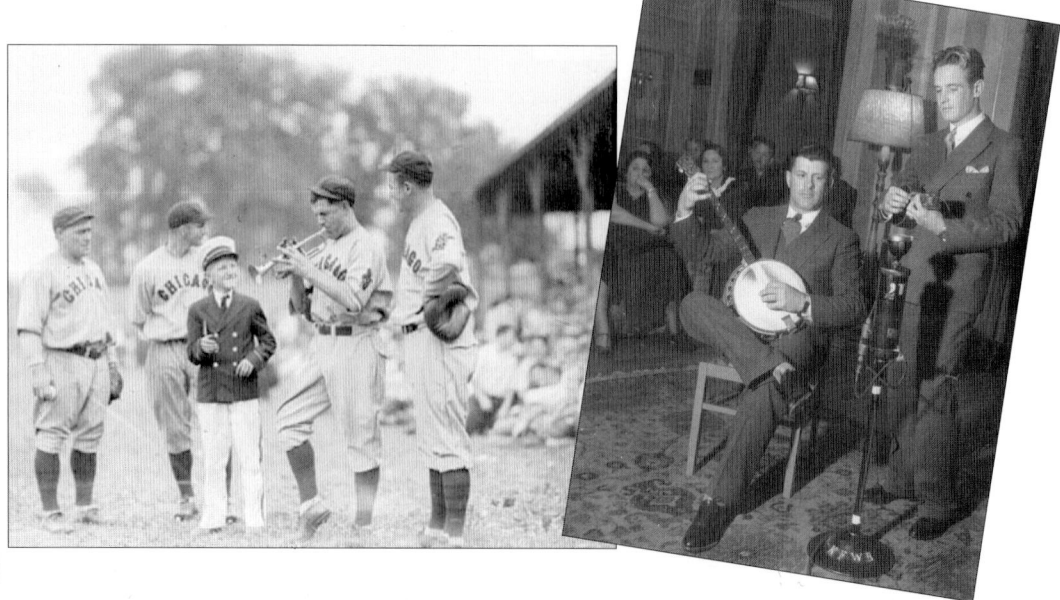

Charles was a serious student of music. While performing with the stringed instruments, he was accompanied here by Mr. Tuck Stainback

Islander Roger Upton. "I was 8, hanging over the fence, he handed it to me. One of those old-time gloves, with the short fingers — I kept it for years. I might still have it."

But most of the time, he was just having fun.

"One of the problems to be answered," the *Los Angeles Times* wondered in 1929, "is the one about who is to play first base if Charlie Grimm cuts his hand on a banjo string or something."

Although he sometimes came across as a softie while managing, Charlie was a rough-and-tough ballplayer in his heyday.

"The camp social season is on in full swing," Herbert Simons wrote in the *Chicago Daily Times*, 1934. "Saturday night was marked by Manager Grimm's 'sausage dinner' to club officials and newspapermen in which 'Der Kaptink' served sausage made on his own farm, with homemade sauerkraut from Treasurer Boots Weber's place as a side dish."

"Jolly Cholly was the funniest man in baseball," Lefty Chambers says. "He should've been on the stage. I never laughed so much, but we finished last! In those days, you couldn't argue with the umpire — you'd get thrown out of the game. So when there was a close play, he'd come out and stand next to Bob Scheffing, the catcher, and he'd yell and kick dirt but not look toward the umpire. The ump would ask Grimm what he wanted, and he'd tell the ump, 'I'm not talking to you!' So he wouldn't get thrown out.

"We had our own night club on Catalina, a spot called the White Cap," he wrote later. "The natives...seldom came into the place. They were probably scared away by the noise."

His antics were legendary. "One time," Doyle Lade told John Skipper in *Take Me Out to the Cubs Game*, "we were getting the daylights beat out of us and Charlie dug a hole in front of the dugout and buried the lineup card in the hole."

"When he'd be coaching 3rd base, if a line drive would come flying by, he'd collapse — he'd keep you loose," Lowe says.

> "Ol' Charlie Grimm, he was crazier'n a bed bug."
>
> Corky Van Dyke

Over time, his reputation preceded him. "One morning, just after daybreak," he wrote, describing an encounter with William Wrigley, "Andy Lotshaw and I were strolling toward the ballpark when W.W. came along on his beautiful black horse. As he reined, he gave us a cheery greeting and then said, 'Why don't you lads go back to the hotel and get some sleep so that you'll be able to work out?' By his tone, both Andy and I knew he thought we were just getting in after a night in Avalon. The only reason we had made such an early start was because I was going to help Andy hang up some sweatshirts!"

"In those days, managers would coach 3rd base," Andy Pafko says. "He went through so many gyrations. Charlie was a fan favorite; he'd give so many signs, and half of 'em didn't mean anything."

"I was trying to get Charlie Grimm to buy me from Boston," Bill Voiselle says. "I always liked the way he managed."

"He was loose, very low-key," Paul Schramka recalls, "the type of manager you wanted to like, to play good for him."

"One time, we lost both ends of a double-header at Wrigley Field — the 2nd game in 10 innings," Lefty Chambers says. "Everybody came into the clubhouse, all upset, wondering what Grimm was gonna say. He says, 'I'm gonna go to my farm in Missouri and let the birds crap all over me.' Well, everybody laughed — that really broke the tension and lightened things up."

"I loved Charlie Grimm," Roy Smalley says. "Charlie was a guy who just let you play; he'd give you a bat and a ball and a glove, and you could go."

Of course, he did have to get tough sometimes. "I've been a good fellow in the past," he told reporters in 1935, "but from now on I'll make Simon Legree look like Pollyanna."

Sure, Cholly.

"We were kinda slow, a little sore," Phil Cavarretta says. "Charlie Grimm knew this, because he'd played — he was one of the best-fielding 1st-basemen I've ever seen, and he could hit, too, over .300. He was a good manager. Some people didn't take him seriously; people say, 'Jolly Cholly.' Hey, the guy won."

And play he had. "When Charlie Grimm busted a screaming liner over Cliff Heathcote's noble dome in the 9th inning of today's game, he not only got himself a homer...but prevented the Goofs from winning the 4th of 5 games from the Regulars," Bill Henry wrote in the *Los Angeles Times* in 1926. "Not only did Grimm bring the game to an end with his last-minute blow, but he featured the earlier proceeding with a sensational swan dive into the wash back of the grandstand while making a desperate attempt to retrieve a towering foul. Beyond getting his pants filled with Mr. Wrigley's expensive gravel, Charlie's effort was fruitless."

He saw, she saw: Charlie ponders how the cassowary might taste grilled; Marion wonders instead how the feathers/plumes might appear in a new hat.

He paid the price for his Chevy-Chasian physical play: "The triumph gave Chicago 2 straight against the Giants," Bob Ray wrote for the *Los Angeles Times* in 1933, "and it also practically cleared up Manager Charlie Grimm's attack of lumbago. In fact, Charlie felt so fine this evening that he was patting himself on the back without suffering any pain at all." But when small crowds turned out after the earthquake, Charlie opted against playing: "It would be an insult to my lumbago to exhibit it to such a slender turnout," he told Ray.

"Grimm tried for a high foul yesterday," the *Chicago Daily News* reported in 1926, "and just as he reached out for the ball he disappeared from sight. He reappeared a second later with dirt and burrs all over his shirt. He had taken a head-on dive into the mountain."

When he wasn't leaping into gulleys, he was known for giving nicknames to everybody. Cholly was responsible for Cavarretta becoming 'Phillibuck.' Cavy and roommate Lennie Merullo were 'the Grand Opera Kids.' Hank Wyse was 'Hankus Pankus.' And then there was Andy Pafko.

"I don't really know why Grimm started calling me Pruschka," Pruschka says. "You'd have to ask him. He never told me why — I'm not really sure. He had nicknames for everybody. I'm Slovak. In Slovak, Hruschka means pear. I guess I was built like a pear, kinda round. I mean, I was in shape, but...I never asked. And all the guys on the other teams got wind of it, and they'd be yelling, 'Hey, Pruschka...' Nobody called me Andy."

He was multi-monikered himself. "Charlie Grimm was doubled in a 3 no-trump bid in bridge last night and lost," according to a 1926 issue of the *Daily News*. "Since then he has been nicknamed 'No Trump Charlie.'" A week later, the paper provided an update: "Since 'No Trump' Charlie had that terrible setback, the boys have taken to bridge."

But even with all the fun — and the pennants — there were still detractors.

"There's only been one like him," Gene Mauch says. "He'd take us out onto the field and say, 'Here's a bat, here's a ball — let's play!' He gave us signs in Spring Training: 'If I hold up 1 finger, that means you take the pitch. If I put my hand behind my back, you bunt.' That's pretty simple, I thought. But he didn't say anything else. So I asked him, Charlie, how about a squeeze play? What's the signal for that? He said, 'We don't have a squeeze play.'"

"Ah, he wasn't much of a manager," Lefty Sloat says. "He was no Durocher. He was always puttin' on an act or something, he liked to fool around. It seemed like Leo always knew what was going on 5 innings from now."*

Older yet wiser when Topps took this picture — Charlie was still too youthfully optimistic in 1960, when he agreed to manage the Cubs one more time.

Before Mr. Wrigley let Hartnett manage his baseball team, he wanted to see how well Gabby could do managing the glass-bottom boat ride division.

"In 1942, Cy was a rookie," Harriet Block says. "He led the league in batting in 1947 — he hit .364! But there was no free agency then, and they wouldn't trade him. Charlie Grimm wouldn't play him. Grimm wasn't a nice man, in spite of all the 'Jolly Cholly' you hear."

"I can't say a good word about him — I can't say anything at all," Ed Jabb says. "He wouldn't let me hit! I grabbed a bat, and he said, 'Sit down over there!' So I sat down on the bench. Charlie Grimm ran that ballclub, he ruled that bench. I don't know what he was thinking."

(Ah, yes — the view from the bench is always quite clear!)

"He should be in the Hall of Fame," Cavy says — with the last word on Jolly Cholly Grimm.

Charlie Grimm

* Won 100 games in a 154-game season, 1935
* Broke in for Connie Mack's A's as a 17-year-old
* Hit .389 in the 1929 World Series for the Cubs, .333 in the '32 Fall Classic as player-manager — .364 lifetime

---

* For the record, Grimm's lifetime win-loss percentage was .547; Durocher's, .540. Both men won 3 pennants — Grimm in 19 seasons, Leo with 24 chances.

Gabbin' away

"I liked Gabby, because he was always with the kids," Avalon barber Lolo Saldaña says. "He loved the kids."

Charles Leo Hartnett was a big kid himself — not to mention one of the greatest catchers to ever put on a mask. During his 20-year Hall-of-Fame career, he was the 1935 N.L. MVP...a 6-time All-Star...and he led the league in fielding, assists, double-plays half a dozen times apiece. He also hit .300 that many times, and appeared in 4 World Series. From 1938-1940, he was player-manager. Gabby took over from Charlie Grimm in mid-1938 (at Charlie's suggestion), and skippered the team to a league title. After that, he managed in the minors and coached for the Kansas City A's in the '60s.

Most people who knew his chattery ways thought his nickname was obvious — but actually, it came about because the shy rookie was so *quiet* on the 1922 train ride toward Catalina. According to the *New York Times*, "An exasperated newspaperman, failing to get any quotes from the rookie, turned to a player and said, 'There's the gabbiest guy that ever went to spring training.'"

> "The perfect catcher."
> Manager Joe McCarthy

That changed in a hurry. "Hartnett did a lot of yelling," the *Los Angeles Times* reported in 1927, "and sweated off about 5 pounds by that form of exercise." Years later, he was still at it: "His line of chatter would make 8 mummies rip off their wrappings," the paper said in 1936.

"He says 'hello' from here to the next county," Dutch Reagan wrote in his *Des Moines Dispatch* column during the 1937 Springtime trip to Catalina. And, Dutch added, Gabby "has a heart as big as Wrigley Field."

Like Grimm, he displayed a wickedly wonderful sense of humor. "One of the innovations planned... by Manager Hartnett perished today," Ed Burns wrote for the *Chicago Tribune* in 1939. "Gabby thought it would be nice to assign each of the sluggers to room numbers corresponding to their batting averages...but the plan had to be abandoned because of congestion in room 202."

"Most catchers are so ugly," modest Gab once mentioned, "they don't have to wear a mask — but I have to wear one because I'm so good-looking."

Mrs. Hartnett was kind enough to snap this shot of her handsome hunk while Islanding with him in the early 1930s.

He was truly a celebrity on Catalina, always in-demand with the photographers and newsreel teams...not to mention the local little guys. "Gabby Hartnett and I played catch," Jack Cowell remembers. "He threw that ball so hard, it'd sting like crazy — but I wouldn't let him know." Gabby even gave Jack an old glove. And years later, when Jack hitchhiked to Chicago, Gabby helped him get settled in — and wrote him a nice letter of recommendation.

"In batting practice, he'd be catching," Lolo says, "and he could throw the runner out at 2nd without coming out of his crouch — his arm was that good."

"He was a good inspiration," Lonny Frey recalls. "He was in the game all the time."

"Gabby knew what to call — he was one of the great ones," says Al Epperly. Of course, when I was a rookie, all he could call was a fastball or a curve!"

Another rookie pitcher, Kirby Higbe, learned the hard way. In 1937, Higbe was protecting a 5-0 lead...and made the mistake of shaking Gabby off 3 times, when the veteran backstop kept calling for a curve against feared slugger Johnny Mize. Gabby called time and went to the mound. "Okay, busher — I'm going to let you throw the fast ball," Gabby told Higbe, "but when you do, the score will be 5-2." In his autobiography, Higbe tells what happened next:

Big Jawn sure did hit my Sunday fast ball. The last I saw, it was headed over some apartment buildings, and it may still be going. After the game, which I won, Gabby called me over to his locker and said, "Hig, with that good arm of yours, you can be a major-league pitcher, but let me think for you for a while."

Of course, there was more to life than baseball. "Gabby is more worried about his bad luck at keeno than anything else," Braven Dyer wrote for *The Sports Parade* column in the *Chicago Times* in 1938. "Until last night he had played 2 solid weeks without winning a game. But finally the worm turned and last night he bagged 2 juicy pots. 'That's all I needed,' said Gabby as they shoved the money over to him. 'We're off now and nobody will stop us, even the Giants.'"

And then he became the manager. Although he's credited as leading the charge to the pennant that first year...Gabby was generally considered a great player who didn't exactly light up the dugout. "To put it plainly," Dick Bartell wrote in his autobiography, "he couldn't manage my Aunt Kate."

Always the consummate ballplayer, Gabby raises his hand to ask Manager McCarthy if he may leave the field to visit the boys' room.

But not everyone shared that view. "He was a wonderful guy," Ken Raffensberger says, "a great manager, a great catcher. He helped a lot with the pitchers. He told me one time I wouldn't be a winning pitcher until I learned to change up."

Lefty Carnett said manager Gabby was fair and honest with him, too: "Gabby was great. I never got to pitch to him. I thought I had the club made, but Gabby said, 'We've got too many good pitchers — you'd sit on the bench.' So he sent me to Milwaukee, where I could pitch. But somebody got hurt, and I could hit pretty good, so I went to 1st base."

"Baseball's a funny thing, a funny game," says Billy Rogell. "I remember a lot of really good guys. There's some guys ya like, who you got along with, and others you didn't. *I don't remember Gabby Hartnett.*"

A family guy

Gabby was the quintessential family man — bringing his clan to Catalina whenever he could. "Mr. and Mrs. Hartnett are making the trip their honeymoon," Bob Ray wrote in the *Los Angeles Times* in 1929, "and the Cub players and the steamship Catalina orchestra gave the newlyweds a reception as they got on the boat yesterday. Guy Bush, Cub pitcher, showed that he has plenty of control by knocking Gabby's hat off with a paper sack full of rice while the orchestra played *Here Comes the Bride*."

But behind the scenes, the boys were a little more mischievous. "Martha came on their honeymoon," recalls Della Root Arnold, Charlie's daughter. "But she thought the players were so raunchy, she swore she'd never come again. They sewed dead fish into their pillows, and they'd change the beds every half hour. As soon as they'd leave the room, the ballplayers would sneak in and change the beds; they switched to 2 twin beds! Gabby and Martha would come back, and make the hotel switch 'em back — but as soon as they'd leave again, the guys would come back in — out went the double bed. She didn't think that was too humorous. She was a nice lady. A *lady*. The others were more raucous, so she had a bad trip."

"My mother was working at Montgomery Ward's when she met my dad," Buddy Hartnett says. "She thought he was a laborer because he had all these calluses on his hands from the bats!" Buddy spent several Springs on Catalina: "I remember sliding down the hill with my mother. The glass-bottom boat, where you could see the bottom of the ocean, I remember doing that with my mother."

Of course, the grass can tend to be greener — wherever you are. "Goin' to the ballgames," Buddy says, "I had to get all dressed up. My mother and I were treated great. I was dressed up like Little Lord Fauntleroy. I was sitting in the stands, and I noticed a bunch of other kids, sneaking into the park — I remember thinking, I wish I was one of them."

Buddy was suffering another little-lad indignity, a bath, when the Quake of '33 hit. But the pleasant memories far outweigh the 'Aw, Mom!' ones. "I remember them taking this picture of Ann Sheridan and Toby Wing, pulling dad from these actresses, when Dutch Reagan was around," he says.

Buddy's little sister, Sheila, came along 6 years later — so she doesn't have any Catalina memories. But she visited the Island years later, and ran into Frank Saldaña...who promptly directed her to the barber shop, where the brothers regaled her with tales. "Lolo and Frank, they're great," she says. "I was shocked — in the barber shop, it's still all the old Cubs! It brought back a lot of memories, of what my parents had told me."

You'd think Martha would look a bit happier on her Catalina honeymoon — unless, of course, she knew what the boys were doing to her room just then.

Gabby's fun-loving ways rubbed off. Buddy helped with Gabby's post-baseball bowling alley outside Chicago, but he's retired these days. "Nowdays," Buddy Hartnett says, "I take it easy, go fishin', which I'm gonna do now."

Gabby Hartnett

* Still holds the N.L. career record for double-plays by a catcher — 163
* Held the major-league home run record for catchers (236), until Yogi Berra (and then Johnny Bench) topped it
* Hit .300 at the age of 40, finishing his career in 1941 with the New York Giants — who held Spring Training in Miami that year (his only non-Catalina season)

Gabby tries to pass a few tips onto Buddy Hartnett.

The wartime skipper

Jimmie Wilson managed the Phillies and Cubs for 9 seasons. He finished last 3 times, 2nd-to-last thrice, 6th twice, and in his banner season he took 5th. His stellar Cub career spanned World War II, 1941-1944. He traded Hall-of-Famer Billy Herman (a lifetime .324 hitter) for a .242 hitter and a .229 hitter — because he saw Herman as a candidate to succeed him. And Stan Hack retired on Wilson's watch, because they didn't get along — but the next season, after Wilson was gone, Charlie Grimm talked Stan into coming back for 4 productive seasons

He'd been a pretty good ballplayer, though — catching for 18 seasons, hitting .300 several times and even batting .353 in the 1940 World Series, at the age of 40.

Harvey Storey says Wilson didn't talk to him at all for 2 solid weeks. Frustrated, Harv finally went up to Wilson and introduced himself. Wilson told Storey, 'I know who you are,' but soon shipped him to Los Angeles.

Harvey Storey, trying to catch Jimmie Wilson's attention in 1941.

"Jimmie Wilson lied to me," Raffensberger says. "We had 26 players, and he told me, 'You're worried about staying — don't worry, you're on my team.' But he let me go to St. Paul."

"Heck," Roy Hughes told Kit Crissey in *Teenagers, Graybeards and 4-F's*, "you could've handed him a bunch of home-run champions at each position and he wouldn't have known what to do with them."

He was kind of a poor man's Rogers Hornsby: A good ballplayer (but not as good), yet a lousy manager (but not as bad), because of a void of people skills. Like Rajah before him, he loved rules for the players: The *Chicago Tribune* listed some of Wilson's Catalina commandments for 1942:

Bowling is no good for ballplayers.

No poker and no horse betting. Players shall not even mention the names of horses while conducting conversations in the clubhouse or on the field.

No sitting around the ball field. Sitting...permissible upon retreat to the clubhouse.

No fooling or wrestling in the clubhouse.

No throwing ice water on nude ballplayers either in the showers or elsewhere.

...And like Hornsby, he seemed to like to excuse himself from his hard-line regulations: "Jim Wilson ordered today's Cub intra-club game started at 11 o'clock instead of the usual 1 o'clock because he wanted to go fishing," Burns wrote for the *Trib* a few days later.

Frankie is smiling here because he knows he is about to be ejected from the game, so he can get home to his petunias.

The Flash grew dim

Hall-of-Famer Frankie Frisch, 'The Fordham Flash,' was one of the slickest 2nd-baseman in history during the '20s and '30s. But by the time he was managing the Cubs (from 1949-1951) he was even calling himself the 'Old Flash,' and he'd lost his spark.

As a player, he hit .300 or better 13 seasons (.316 lifetime)...and starred in 8 World Series for John McGraw's New York Giants and the St. Louis Cardinals. As a manager, he led the Gas House Gang Cards to a World Title in 1934 (while hitting .305 himself). He skippered a total of 16 seasons, managing in Pittsburgh too. (With the Pirates, he once mocked umps by opening an umbrella on the field — becoming the subject of a Norman Rockwell painting.)

He'd been coaching with the Giants in mid-1949 when he got the call to replace Charlie Grimm in Chicago. So Frankie Frisch was the last Cub manager to take the team to Catalina.

Jimmie Wilson's wartime rules allowed fishing but disallowed bowling, poker, naked ice showers...& winning ballgames.

"No! Absolutely not!"

Frank Frisch's wife Ada, reacting to the Cubs' offer to manage in 1949

Jimmie Wilson

* *Caught in the 1st All-Star Game, 1933*
* *Played in 4 World Series*
* *Managed the Cubs on Catalina twice...& in French Lick twice*

By the end, he was either quite sarcastic...or quite delusionsal. In Avalon, between last-place and 2nd-to-last-place finishes, he said: "I've never been in a training camp before where the players have shown such spirit...and if this spirit keeps up, the Cubs are going to be the surprise of the 1950 season."

"Frankie Frisch was a wonderful ballplayer," Gene Mauch says. "And I guess he did a wonderful job managing St. Louis and Pittsburgh in the '30s and '40s. But by the time he got to Chicago, he didn't want to manage any more — he didn't seem to care. I played with a lot of managers, and there was only one I didn't get along with — Frankie Frisch."

"Frisch was a *%*$!," says Ed Chandler. "I was with the club until July, and he didn't talk to me the whole time. I'd be out in the bullpen and start to warm up — he'd tell the coach to have me sit down."

"Frisch, that *$%@#*^!," says Corky Van Dyke. "He was a character. One time, he asked me, 'Aren't you gonna play ball any more?' He liked to cuss and spit. Another time, Sauer missed the ball and Frisch yelled out, 'You couldn't catch it in a bushel basket!' He was a hard-nosed guy — he'd stick ya. He liked to drink a little booze."

The Old Flash's greatest achievement on Catalina was the fact that he was personally responsible for dozens of new adjectives being introduced into the Island dialect.

"Nope, him and I didn't get along," Bob Borkowski says. "He was no good. I was down there playing, and my brother came back from Korea. He was injured. He came on the field, and we were talking, and Frisch comes over and says, 'I don't care who you are, you get off this field!' We got into a big argument, and he wouldn't play me after that."

C'mon, guys, don't mince words. Whaddya really think?

"Frisch was a jerk," Lefty Chambers recalls.

"I didn't get along with Frisch," Bill Voiselle says. "I don't think he liked me."

"Everybody hated Frisch," says catcher Bob Scheffing's son, Bob. "He broke his leg, going into those sliding pits, and a lot of the ballplayers just laughed about it."

Rookie pitcher Eddie Kowalski remains missing from *The Baseball Encyclopedia* due to Frisch's motivational expertise. Kowalski got called to the Show for the last 6 weeks of the 1949 season — "but I didn't get to play in a game," he says. "I suited up at Wrigley, and went on road trips to Pittsburgh and St. Louis. Frisch was the manager. He wasn't the best. The Cubs were out of it by then, but he told me, 'We're facing teams in a pennant race — I can't use a rookie.' So what could I say?"

Ah — Smalley to the rescue! "I liked Frisch, although I know a lot of the guys didn't like him," Roy says. "I liked Frankie, and he liked me — it's hard to dislike somebody who plays you!"

Frisch, avoiding Grimm-like motivational tactics in Avalon.

Islander Marcelino Saucedo says the players would even complain to the kids about the burned-out Flash. "Frisch was really bad," Marse says. "He didn't like anybody complaining. One game, I was listening on the radio, and Dubiel walked 5 or 6 in a row during an exhibition game in L.A. Later, when they were back on the Island, I asked him why that happened. He told me Frisch wouldn't take him out. He came to the mound and Dubiel told him he didn't have his stuff, he needed to come out — but Frisch said, 'I'm gonna leave you in, I'm gonna let you suffer.' So he walked a few more guys, and Frisch finally came out and pulled him. Later in the dugout, Dubiel told him he'd better not say a word, or he'd beat the daylights out of him."

"I'm gonna leave you in, I'm gonna let you suffer."

Frankie Frisch, using positive reinforcement on pitcher Monk Dubiel

"He had his guys he picked on, if he knew they wouldn't fight back, if they had that kind of temperament," Johnny Klippstein says. "He was on Carmen Mauro all spring — he embarrassed that kid to death."

Still, some managed to find the humor in Frisch's antics. "He was a card himself," Fuzzy Richards remembers. "He was a little banty rooster — he was a little rough."

Klippstein says, "There were times during ballgames that he'd get so upset, he'd say, 'Somebody bring me a bucket — I've gotta throw up. Major-league baseball, my butt!' He even left one time. He was a dandy."

"He was from New York," Turk Lown says. "Every time he'd go there, he'd get thrown out of a game and go home."

"Whenever we played in New York, especially Brooklyn," Bob Rush recalls, "everybody would kid him about his going home early to do some gardening. One day game, out at home plate when they were having the usual meeting between the managers and the umpires, I actually heard one of the umpires tell Frisch: 'I don't care what you do today, you're not gettin' thrown outa this game so you can go home and tend your petunias!'"

"Frisch didn't really care," Randy Jackson says. "He didn't come to the field until it was time for the game to start."

"He'd had a lot of great ballclubs with St. Louis, perennial winners," Paul Schramka says, "and I guess he'd started his big slide, his downward spiral with all those losing teams in Chicago. One time, he was sitting in the dugout, and it must've been in a prolonged losing streak. It was about the 2nd or 3rd inning, and we're losing 8-to-nothing, or something like that, and he throws his hands in the air and says, 'I can't stand this any longer — I'm goin' home.' And he got up, and I guess he did!"

Schramka came up as a rookie under Jolly Cholly Grimm — so the contrast was dramatic. "There was a big difference with Frisch — he ranted like a little Napoleon. He used to get these fellas before the workout and say, today we're gonna do this and we're gonna do that. And Roy Johnson would always say, 'Right, Frank.' This went on every day for 2 or 3 days. One day, he's sittin' there, and he starts going through it. And he says to Roy, we're gonna do this and that. And for some reason, that day Roy says, 'Well, Frank, don't you think...' And Frisch cuts him off and says, we're gonna do this and that. And Roy says, 'Yeah, but...' And Frisch says, we're gonna do this and that. And Roy starts to ask something again, but Frisch starts yellin' and cussin' and says blankety-blank it, Roy, we're gonna do this and that! So Roy just said, 'Right, Frank.'"

"Take a deep cleansing breath," Frankie is likely advising his squad. "Think happy thoughts..."

"Frankie Frisch was a tough guy," Phil Cavarretta says. "He was from the old school. He was a great player, a Hall-of-Famer, but he didn't get along with everybody. I wasn't his favorite — maybe he didn't like Italians."

"I believe what finally got Frisch fired," Cavy says, "was he was reading a novel in the dugout, during a game. We would run in and out, playing the game, and all Frisch was doing was turning pages — reading his book. Well, Bill Serena strikes out, and Frisch starts cussin' and says, 'What a buncha lousy ballplayers,' and he throws the book right onto the field — he almost hits the 3rd base coach with it! And Wid Matthews, who was sittin' in the dugout, he gets up right then and leaves. And after the game, Frisch gets fired."

Frank Frisch

* 1931 N.L. MVP
* Hit .300 for 11 straight seasons
* Managed the Cubs after being elected to the Hall of Fame in 1947 (Oops! No more mountains left to climb...)
* Led N.L. Managers in 'Thumbs' by being ejected 6 times in 1950

In the Spring of 1954, as usual, Cavy was gonna call 'em as he saw 'em. Unfortunately, Mr. PK Wrigley didn't see things the same way.

Cavy

When Frisch got canned halfway through the 1951 season, Phil Cavarretta became the player-manager. That means Cavy was actually the Cubs' 1st Mesa manager — he never headed the team during a Catalina Spring.

"Phil Cavarretta, about to conduct his first training season as skipper," Arch Ward wrote for the *Chicago Tribune* in the Spring o'1952, "has been...assuring listeners that the 'Cubs will be a hustling ball club.'

It has been suggested that somebody freshen up Phillibuck's script...Zeal is important, but it is something managers promise when they have little else to offer, a trite bit of sop..."

His 1951-1953 tenure ended unceremoniously in the Spring of 1954, when he basically said the team sucked. PK Wrigley fired Cavy for a 'defeatist attitude' — an odd observation, considering Cavarretta was always known for hustling, always working hard.

"I liked Cavarretta a lot," says Roy Smalley. "Phil was as generous as can be. He expected you to give 120%, as he did — and sorry if you don't like that."

He was a favorite with the locals. "Cavarretta was a chatterbox, always talkin'," Catalina barber Lolo Saldaña says. "He was a real ballplayer — I always liked to be around him."

Like all good executives, Cavy mastered the art of blasting his way out of a sand trap.

"Cavarretta, he was tough," Paul Schramka says, "a good baseball man. He played with the Cubs in their golden era. He hated to lose — a great competitor. After the game, the players would get changed, and he'd complain, 'You can't wait to get outa here!' So they'd wait until he started dressing."

Cavy at work. Or play. Or both.

His playing career started with a bang: Cavy hit a game-winning homer — at the age of *17* — in his 1st big-league appearance, the last week of 1934. "Cavarretta, who won't be 18 until July," Jim Gallagher wrote in the *Chicago American* the next Spring, "handled himself around the bag like a veteran." Gentleman Jim called the rookie's performance on Catalina an "impressive showing."

"You should be in high school," Babe Ruth told him before a game. Or maybe he should've been in the World Series — where he hit .317 in the Cubs' final 3 Series appearances.

Charlie Grimm said Cavy "must have been the inspiration for whoever coined the phrase, 'He came to play.'" Well, most of the time, anyway, when he wasn't being a bit too youthful: "Grimm says he is getting in shape so he can play first base if Phil Cavarretta gets stomach miseries like he did several days last season after eating too many raviolis," Burns wrote for the *Tribune* in 1936.

"Cavarretta was a serious manager," Johnny Klippstein says. "If you played for Phil, you had to give 100% every day. He was great to play for because he was always in the game."

Bob Kelly credits Cavy as giving him a career boost. "Phil Cavarretta game me my best shot," he says. "He took me out of the bullpen and gave me a chance to start."

"Cavarretta was a great student of the game," Lefty Minner agrees.

And he liked to teach. "I was the batting instructor for William Bendix in *The Babe Ruth Story*," Cavy says. "The White Sox were training in Pasadena, by the Rose Bowl — it's a very beautiful place. We'd play 'em in a few games. William Bendix was there one day, and they're makin' the movie, but I thought it was just some publicity stunt for the White Sox. We were gettin' ready, taking batting practice, watchin' what they were doing, and this guy comes runnin' up, he's the director or something, and he asks me if I could help Mr. Bendix — at least show him how to stand at home plate. So I went up and introduced myself, and said maybe I could give him some pointers. He said, 'Boy, do I need 'em!' I shows him how to bend his knees, how to lean, how to plant his feet, and he says, 'That sounds pretty good. It feels pretty comfortable; it feels like I'm sittin' on the commode!'"

"So then I tell him, don't be too stiff, your body action is important, here's how to stride — keeping your body in balance is important. And the 1st swing, he fell right on his fanny. But we went through this whole procedure in 15 or 20 minutes, and he got the knack. So they tried him in live-action, and he did real good. After they filmed him, he came over and put his arm around me and thanked me, said he really appreciated it. Heck, today I'd get $10,000 for that!"

Cavy helped William Bendix swing like a real ballplayer in The Babe Ruth Story — *he just couldn't teach him to actually* look *like the Babe. This photo was taken immediately before Cavy's lesson on not standing pigeon-toed at the plate.*

After retiring, Cavy managed in the minors... coached and scouted for Detroit...and was the Mets' batting instructor in the '70s.

Phil Cavarretta

* The 1945 N.L. MVP, led the league with a .355 average
* Led the N.L. in pinch-hits in 1951 — while he was manager
* 1st big-league manager to ever get fired during Spring Training
* When PK Wrigley fired him after 20 years as a Cub, Phil played for the White Sox in 1954 & 1955

And after that...

A few other Catalina Cubbies managed to manage:

* Stan Hack succeeded Cavarretta, but with little more success. Smilin' Stan was fired after the 1956 season, when he finished dead last with a stirring .390 win-loss percentage.

Stan Hack replaced Cavy, but the Cubs needed more than mere managerial help by 1955.

* Catalina Cub Bob Scheffing replaced Hack. In 3 seasons (1957-1959), his squads were unable to break .500. Things had gotten so bad that PK Wrigley resurrected 953-year-old Charlie Grimm from the grave to manage in 1960. (After a 6-11 start, PK traded Jolly Cholly for a radio broadcaster.)

* Clay Bryant managed in the minors for years, winning 3 pennants, and also coached in the bigs for Cleveland.

* Catalina alum Bobby Mattick managed the expansion Toronto Blue Jays in 1980 and 1981. His record came in at .388 — last-place, both times — a very Cub-like showing.

* Billy Jurges coached for the Cubbies in 1948, before managing the Boston Red Sox into the cellar from 1959-1960.

Billy Jurges the player, long before he evolved into a manager.

* Billy Herman took a crack at the Red Sox a few years later (from 1964-1966)...but didn't fare much better.

* And of course, there's Gene Mauch...who managed for 26 seasons in the big leagues from 1960-1987. Skip's lifetime tally is .483, with a pair of post-season appearances to his credit.

Skip was the last Catalina-era Cub still wearing a big-league uniform — managing for the Angels until 1987.

Lippy put an end to this 'College of Coaches' silliness, once and for all — ushering the Cubs into their next dynasty.

(Or not...)

And finally, let's not forget that PK Wrigley instituted the manager-less rotating 'College of Coaches' system from 1961-1962, which was replaced by the 'Head Coach' plus 'Athletic Director' system (1963-64), which finally died with only one 'Head Coach' in 1965. (Leo Durocher came on as a genuine baseball manager in 1966.) During PK's 5-year experiment, the Cubbies finished 7th, 9th (with 100 losses, a Cub first), 7th, 8th, and 8th. Rah, team...

Catalina Cub Coaches

Speaking of coaches, quite a cast populated Santa Catalina Island during the great days. Among the most notable was a man who lived in Avalon during the off-season...and stepped in as interim manager in 1944, until Grimm's train could get to the station.

Hard Rock, Catalina Island

Roy Johnson's lifetime managerial record, 0-1, ain't exactly Hall-of-Fame stats. But Hard Rock was one of the Cubbies' most beloved coaches during his 18-year tenure. From 1935 through 1953, Hard Rock gave his all for better baseball. He roved, too... managing minor-league teams in the Cub system whenever (and wherever) he was needed. Garden spots like Bisbee, Ponca City, Tulsa, and Lockport. They sent him down low 'cuz they knew he could develop talent to send up the line. After coaching and managing, he became the Cubs' head scout in the '50s.

He pitched briefly for Mr. Mack's Philadelphia A's in 1918, but arm trouble ended his career too early. Lest we create any confusion, there was another Roy Johnson (also from Oklahoma) in the big leagues way-back-when, but *that* Roy Johnson was an outfielder (whose brother Bob was also an outfielder). Neither one was Roy Johnson, the outfielder who played for the Expos in the 1980s. Got it?

> "He was on the job for but one playing day and then turned the team over to Grimm without even asking for a receipt."
>
> Warren Brown, in his Cubs history, discussing Hard Rock's lengthy major-league managerial career

So the question naturally arises: How does one come to earn the nickname, 'Hard Rock'? Press clips over the years tell the story:

The only casualty is Coach Roy Johnson, who stopped a ball with his left ear.
— *American*, 1936

Coach Roy Johnson, hit in the eye with a badminton arrow, is going to be all right, unless he gets kicked by a parrot. — *Tribune*, 1938

Coach Roy Johnson still has the endurance to wear out a man 20 years younger. He even keeps right on pitching batting practice although his jaw was broken last summer while engaged in the same pursuit.
— *Cubs News*, 1947

Roy Johnson...was hit in the right eye by a ball from the bat of...Hal Jeffcoat. Johnson was taken to Avalon Hospital, where several stitches were required to close the wound. — *Tribune*, 1951

Hard Rock, indeed.

"Hey, Pardner!" — Hard Rock Johnson.

"One time he got into an argument on the bench with a coach from Philadelphia, Benny Culp," Yosh Kawano says, "and Culp went right to the bench and said, 'If you weren't so old, I'd go in there and get ya!'

"But Hard Rock said, 'Don't let age make a coward out of you!'"

That 'getting-hit-in-the-head' thing must've run in the family: "Hard Rock had his nephew or his grandson out there," recalls Bob Scheffing Jr., who came to Catalina twice in the late '40s when he was little. "I broke his nose! I was pushin' a tricycle, real fast, and at the end we went down these steps. The week before that, we'd gone sand-dab fishing, and I found a little bat, and I was swinging it. On the backswing, I'd hit that same kid — he went down, out cold, and I thought I'd killed him! He was an accident waiting to happen."

Hard Rock takes a break from being beaned to enjoy the Avalon sunshine — his home town! In this 1941 photo, he's relaxing on the links with Rip Russell & skipper Jimmie Wilson.

"Hard Rock hit fungoes to me," Wayne Terwilliger says. "That was a good name for him — he looked like a Hard Rock. He had a craggly face, a rough old guy."

"The players loved and respected him," Cholly Grimm wrote. "Roy could handle a fungo stick like a monkey with a coconut. He was tireless on the field and pitched in batting practice sessions after he reached his 60s."

"Roy Johnson was my favorite of all my favorites," Lennie Merullo says. "He was just one of these men who was a worker. He threw batting practice for us, and he got hit by more line drives! He couldn't throw hard — he couldn't hurt you if he hit you — but he'd challenge you."

"Roy Johnson helped me the most during my career," Bob Rush agrees. "Being a rookie, if I needed someone to talk to, he was there — he basically made me feel like I belonged."

"He was one of the best coaches ever," Andy Pafko says. "If you had a problem, you could come to see him. If you wanted to take some extra batting practice, he'd be there."

"Johnson was a story-teller," Cal McLish says, "an old-time baseball guy."

"He was always poppin' off," recalls Al Epperly. "He'd read somethin' in particular in the paper, and he'd be talkin' about it all day."

And he always had time for the kids — his neighbors — on Avalon. "Emil Verban broke his bat...it was a hairline crack," says Islander Foxie Saucedo. "Roy Johnson was looking at the bat — he used to call everybody, 'Pardner,' and he says to me, 'Hey, Pardner, you want this?' So I got a bunch of nails and tape and wrapped it all up. That thing was heavy! The following week, we were playing against a high school from San Diego, and I got 4 hits. We went into extra innings, and in the bottom of the 12th I hit a long fly ball over the leftfielder, a homer, and knocked in the game-winning run. I came back to the plate, but the bat was broken — so I threw it away."

"Hard Rock ran the local team before Doc Brooks," says Yosh Kawano, referring to the semi-pro Catalina Cubs — where Hub Kittle pitched for years.

"Hard Rock's daughter Joanne and me, we won the dancing contest at the St. Catherine Ballroom," Hub says.

"Roy Johnson's daughter, Joan — we went to school together," says Islander Jack Cowell. "He lived across the street — so two weeks before the team came, he'd ask me to play catch with him. So I'd go down to the field and shag balls. Every year, he'd ask me to warm him up, so he'd be broken in."

Hard Rock passed away in 1986, at the tender age of 90. He's one of those guys whose career seems sadly misrepresented by the major-league record books — where he only played in 10 games and managed 1, coming out as little more than an asterisk. He'll never make the Hall of Fame, but he helped shape a lot of careers during his 6 decades in the game.

Hard Rock joins Tony Lazzeri, Carl Reynolds, Clyde Shoun, & Cholly Grimm for a 1938 skull session on the mound — but it was all for naught, since Shoun was traded for Dizzy Dean a few weeks later.

Charlie Root — famous for the wrong thing

Charlie Root is best-known for something that didn't really happen. Ah, yes — Babe Ruth's so-called shot in the 1932 World Series.

"He was a real tiger — hitters didn't get away with anything," Johnny Klippstein says. "Knowing Charlie, I never believed that Babe Ruth 'called shot' story," "Charlie would've decked him."

"You better believe it, he was *real* old school," Bob Rush says. "Even if you dug in on him, he'd put you on your back."

"Charlie Root, he should be in the Hall of Fame," Phil Cavarretta says. "And he was tough! If you'd get a base hit off him, especially 2 — that 3rd time, you'd be on your back. He was a great competitor. He was my pitching coach."

Charlie's daughter was there. "In the 1932 World Series, I was sitting in Box 58, Tier 12, right at the edge of the screen," Della Root Arnold recalls. "After the 1st strike, he raised his hand with 1 finger up — that's 1 strike. After the 2nd, he raised 2 fingers. He was hollering at Guy Bush in the dugout: 'I'm gonna have you out there tomorrow.' I heard him. The yelling was so bad, on both teams, Landis called 'em in. Mrs. Ruth gave this big interview about the fans throwing lemons — but who had the money to buy lemons in 1932? Babe was on Hal Totten's show, and he said, 'I'd have been a fool to point at a pitcher like Charlie Root.' The story just got big later on. We went to Australia right after the Series, and didn't know anything about it."

Bill Veeck believes Ruth was pointing at Lotshaw, since the 2 old buddies had been calling each other names. And Charlie Grimm, in the dugout at the time, confirms Della's account — saying Ruth was yelling at Bush. "I hate to ruin a good story," Jolly Cholly wrote, "but the Babe actually was pointing to the mound. As he pointed, I heard Ruth growl: 'You'll be out here tomorrow — so we'll see what you can do with me, you so-and-so tightwad.'"

"Would those eyes let a fat guy hit a home run?" Della Root Arnold asks.

"At Des Moines, Charlie Root was my manager," Corky Van Dyke says. "He'd beat ya up — if a fan would get on him, he'd go to the railing and say, 'Meet me after the game, outside the park.' And he was up in years then! He'd take your head off in a minute — not like these candies today. It was a hard-rock game then. If you didn't produce, you were gone."

"Charlie Root, he had all kinds of great stories," Randy Jackson remembers. "He said Ruth didn't call his shot — he'd have knocked him down if he had. It never happened — 'I was too much of a mean son-of-a-gun.'"

And by the way, none of the news accounts that day made any mention of Ruth pointing to the bleachers.

Jackson says Root liked to tell another less-famous Ruth story. "But he said he did see this: a pitcher was throwing to Ruth, and he finished his delivery and was in his stance to field, and Ruth hit a line drive right between his legs that just missed him. The centerfielder caught it on the fly, threw the ball to the infield, and back to the pitcher. The pitcher got to thinking about it, and then they tossed the ball to him he fainted — when he thought about what *could* have happened!"

When he wasn't bearing down, he liked to laugh — and to pull a good practical joke. "Dad was quiet, but he loved tricks and pranks," says daughter Della. "Dad would bring home tricks from the trick shops in New York. One time he brought this long rubber tube that had bladders on both ends. He said, 'We're gonna put this under the tablecloth, and put one end under her plate.' He kept the other end in his hand, and every time she'd try to take a bite, Mother's plate would jump! "She said, 'Charlie Root, I know you're doing something, and I want you to quit it!' Another time, he told the housekeeper to slip this white pill into Mother's coffee. It fizzed and boiled!"

Between his pranks, his Cub pitching career, and coaching, Charlie took his family to Catalina for years — daughter Della got to go for 14 seasons, and enjoyed the ride. "The teachers would say to Mother, 'You can't take these kids out of school!'

"But Mother said, 'Would you rather go to school, or go to Catalina?' I did have a tutor, because we were out of school so much. Mrs. Briggs complained to Mother, and Mother told her, 'Mrs. Briggs, Della is going to live with people, not in school.'"

Della Root's 13 in this 1932 photo . . . Charlie Jr. is 8 . . . Charlie Sr. is 32 . . . & Dorothy ain't tellin'.

In fact, Charlie Root Jr. got a tryout on Catalina in 1947, but Manager Grimm shipped him over to the mainland for more seasoning at the Class-C Visalia camp.

Della says an old friend from Catalina, Dutch Reagan, "was a great fan of Dad's — when Dad died, he sent a nice letter to us, saying Dad was his favorite player. And when the Hall of Fame players came to the White House when he was President, he asked, 'Anybody got a Charlie Root card?'"

Dutch Reagan would've been delighted to pull this card from a gumwrapperful of heroes in 1933.

"Anybody got a Charlie Root card?"

Dutch Reagan, when a group of ballplayers visited his White House

Oh, yeah — by the way. Charlie coached for the Cubs from 1951-1953 and again in 1960...and he liked to give the younger guys tips while he was still playing. "Charlie Root helped me," Al Epperly says. "He got me to throw a sinker, and a slider. He worked with all the young pitchers." Between playing and coaching, Charlie pitched and managed with the Hollywood Stars in the Pacific Coast League (winning 15 in 1943 as a 44-year-old player-manager).

One Spring afternoon in 1960, Charlie was pitching batting practice for the Cubs — at the tender age of 60. A brash rookie stepped in and pointed toward the outfield. Charlie decked him on 3 straight pitches that barely missed the rook's chin. The kid, still sitting in the dust, yelled to the mound: "He didn't point, Charlie! I know he didn't point!"

Charlie pitched in the bigs for 17 seasons — and 4 World Series. He won 201 games. He led the N.L. with 26 wins in 1927, went 19-6 in 1929 to lead the league with a .760 winning clip, and paced the senior circuit with 4 shutouts in 1930. "Just let me get 9 more pitchers like Charlie Root," Manager McCarthy told reporters in 1928. Which begs the question: Why ain't Charlie Root in the Hall of Fame?

Other assorted coaches

Hall-of-Famers Jimmy Foxx and Kiki Cuyler coached for the Cubs too — as well as a gnarly assortment of old-timers who sometimes taught, and sometimes didn't.

"There was no coaching in those days," Gene Mauch says. "No instruction. I mean, *zero*."

"Back in my day," recalls Claude Passeau, "we didn't have pitching coaches — we learned the hard way."

"We didn't have pitching coaches or batting coaches or any of that crap," says Mattick.

"I guess the coaches did some," says Preston Ward. "Of course, Spring Training, you know, you go through all the rigoramorool, all the stretching, the exercises."

"We didn't get a lot of coaching, not in those days — not really," Andy Pafko says. "You relied on your God-given talent."

"The coaches didn't help you much in those days," says Bob Kelly. "I didn't learn to pitch until after I was out of baseball!"

"All the time I was in the big leagues, I never was with a team that had a pitching coach!" Ben Wade says. "The guy who helped me the most was an infielder, Gene Handley, in Hollywood."

"They expected if you reach that level, you know how to play," Lennie Merullo says. "I found mostly, the coaches in those days, if you were a hitter, they spent time with you. Coaching today, sometimes it's overcoaching."

"Unlike today, where there seems to be about 1 coach per player, there were not a lot of coaches," Don Carlsen says.

"We didn't have special coaches like they do now," says Wayne Terwilliger, still coaching and managing in Fort Worth. "Somebody from the front office came down and tried to help me with my hitting."

So...what did those guys who collected a check for coaching actually do? "The coaches were there to be disciplinarians in those days," Carmen Mauro says. "They wanted us to stay out of trouble, to stay in the hotel." Some of the more noted Catalina Cub coaches who tried to keep the boys in line:

Red Smith (1945-1948). "When the photographers came to Grimm in the clubhouse asking where they could find Smith," Edgar 'the Mouse' Munzel wrote for the *Chicago Sun* in 1946, Charlie said: 'You won't have any trouble knowing him; just look for the guy who doesn't look any more like an athlete than this ash tray.'"

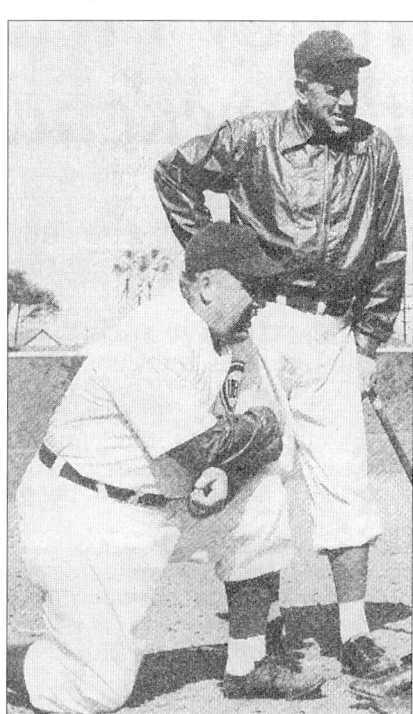

Red Smith begs Manager Grimm to grab him a hot dog & a Coke from the concession stand between innings.

In his defense, Red — whose nickname became 'Smorgasbord' after his playing weight of 185 rose to a coaching weight of 220 — was quite an athlete in his day. He played college football for Knute Rockne at Notre Dame, and pro ball for the Green Bay Packers and football's New York Yankees. "Coach Red Smith, who doubles as a line mentor for the New York Giants grid team, didn't have to wait long to get ribbed about their defeat in the title game," Munzel reported the next year. "Grimm had hung a big sign over Red's locker reading, 'Bears 47, Giants 14.' What happened? The inaccuracy of the score, which was 23-14, just added to Red's fury."

Oh, baseball. In 1927, multi-sport non-athlete Red (one of 4 Red Smiths in the *Baseball Encyclopedia*, by the way, in case the whole Roy Johnson affair didn't confuse you enough) enjoyed a stellar major-league baseball career. Red caught an inning for the Giants and chalked himself up a put-out (with no errors) for a major-league record career fielding average of 1.000 (take that, Hartnett!). Alas, Smorgy didn't get to the plate that afternoon...

Red Corriden (1932-1940). "Red Corriden was a great one," says Lonny Frey. "He knew his way around the ballfield. You could always talk to him. He was always keeping 'em in the game." A career .205 hitter in 5 seasons, he played for the Cubs from 1913-1915. His son, John Jr., appeared in a game for the Dodgers in 1946, and Red managed the White Sox in 1950. In 1937, Ed Burns recorded a Corriden primer on coaching for *Tribune* readers:

If a coach plucks at his ear or rubs his chin, he's giving a 'touching skin' sign, and if he pulls down the visor of his cap or dusts off his bloomers, he is giving a 'touching cloth' sign, usually an entirely different message. The coach must be careful, of course, not to touch skin and cloth at the same time, for all pandemonium is apt to bust loose, as you readily can understand.

Spud Davis hit .308 lifetime — no small potatoes.

Spud Davis (1950-1953). "Big Spud — he was a jovial type, a good guy," says Terwilliger. A multiple-pre-Cub connection: Future Cub Dizzy Dean was pinch-running for future Cub coach Davis in the 1934 World Series (at the behest of future Cub manager Frankie Frisch)...when future Cub Billy Rogell knocked Diz out cold while trying to throw to 1st. Future Cub Tex Carleton watched from the bird bullpen, while future Cub Ripper Collins and future Cub manager Leo Durocher watched from the St. Louis dugout. In 16 big-league seasons, Spud hit .308 — including a perfect 2-for-2 in that fabled '34 Series.

Milt Stock (1944-1948) played in the bigs for 14 seasons and hit .300 5 times. **Merv Shea** (1949) hit .220 over 11 years at the show, but he was a big star with the Sacramento Solons in the Pacific Coast League. He scouted the West Coast for the Cubs for a long time, with **Jigger Statz** — another P.C.L. star. And "**Max Carey**, who stole over 700 bases in his major league career, was brought in to provide base running instructions," the *Cubs News* told fans in 1949.

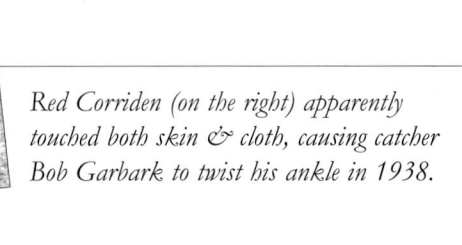

Red Corriden (on the right) apparently touched both skin & cloth, causing catcher Bob Garbark to twist his ankle in 1938.

Bill Baker (1950). Bill had come to Catalina as a seasoned 28-year-old pre-rookie catcher in 1939. "I just turned 91 years old!" Bill says. "I don't know if I can remember much. I came along as a catcher. I coached for Frankie Frisch after I quit playing. I was in the bullpen." He must've picked up a lot of tips, going to Spring Training with some of the game's all-time greats: "I spent a few years in the minors, I sure did — the Yankees sent me to Newark. I was with the Oakland Oaks in 1937, went to Spring Training with the Yankees. I knew Babe Ruth and Lou Gehrig well — I was in Spring Training with them for 2 years. I knew DiMaggio and played on the Cardinals with Stan Musial."

Even now, at 134 years of age, Jack Doyle could whip you & me both.

Once tough, always tough: "Here, at the tender age of 66, grizzled and gray and as gnarled as the old oak — but as sturdy — he's batting out fungoes to the lads who weren't even around when he was in his prime," Jimmy the Cork wrote for the *American* in 1936. "An all-night rain has made the field soft and soggy so the hired hands were instructed to take it easy. But Jack Doyle didn't know about that. He slithered and skidded in the mud...After 20 minutes of 'fungoing,' Jack tossed the bat aside and the players, with their tongues wagging on their chins, breathed a sigh of relief."

"At 11 o'clock o'an evening at Avalon," Warren Brown wrote in his *So They Tell Me* column for the *Chicago Herald & Examiner* in 1936, "John 'Red' Corriden, Charlie Grimm and Jack Doyle begin to debate the issue whether Dan Howley was a better ball player than Jimmy Burke...At midnight, Grimm went to bed...At 2 a.m., Doyle was still holding forth on the subject, and hadn't noticed that Corriden was asleep in his chair."

As a Cub catcher, Bill Baker honed his future coaching skills. Here, he observes that the pitch is just a <u>shade</u> outside.

Jack Doyle was a long-time Cub scout. But 'Dirty Jack' was no cub scout on the field; while with Chicago, he once climbed into the stands of the Polo Grounds to slug a fan...and the year before, he got into a brawl with an umpire. The Irish-born, uh, slugger played for 9 major league teams from 1889-1905 (wonder why he kept getting traded?), including one season with the Cubs (1901). His lifetime average was .299 — that's rough — and he managed the New York Giants and Washington Senators for partial seasons.

"See this?" Doyle is instructing Ole Ward in 1934. "Throw it at somebody's head."

Doc

They Don't Make 'em Like Andy Lotshaw ... Or Yosh Kawano ... Any More

"Andy Lotshaw's Cub training room was like a vaudeville stage most of the time."

Charlie Grimm

Andy Lotshaw was the perfect combination of Yogi Berra and Fred Flintstone.

He was a big ol' lovable lug who massacred the English language...and kept the Cubs' muscles in fine working form for more than 30 years. Andy was the Cubs' trainer, and he made every Cub trip to Catalina but one.

He was a master of psychology before anybody studied such a thing — knowing just which buttons to push for motivating terrified rookies as well as burned-out old veterans. One of the great Andy Lotshaw legends goes like this: He's giving a rubdown to a rookie. At the very end, he splashes on a palmful of Coca-Cola and hands the kid the bottle...so the ballplayer thinks Coke was the trainer's secret formula.

"I could tell ya stories about Andy Lotshaw for an hour," Gene Mauch says. "You know those knee injuries kids get — they call 'em ACL now? He'd pour Coke on it and say, 'Come back and see me tomorrow.' I got hurt, and he'd spit on my knee! We didn't have MRIs — I played 30 years and didn't know what a hamstring was. He'd rub toothpaste on it. He was a good old guy."

Sheriff Blake, Guy Bush, Cliff Heathcote, & Bob Lewis help stuff Andy Lotshaw neatly into a trunk for the 1930 sojourn Westward.

Andy was a man of many talents. He'd been quite a baseball player in his own right, before getting hurt. He was also the Chicago Bears' trainer — helping win some pre-Super-Bowl World Championships with guys like George Halas, Red Grange ('The Galloping Ghost'), and Bronco Nagurski. And, seemingly a bit outa character in this day and age, he was a perennial dancing contest champion out on Catalina, partnering with his wife Laura.

And he was a man of many nicknames: They called him Dr. Lotshaw, or Doc Lotshaw, or just plain Doc — although he didn't even has a high-school diploma. Sometimes he was 'Iodine.' A Chicago paper called him "the student of Shakespeare" once. And the press often used 'Andrew Hemingway Lotshaw' as his full name, although it wasn't.

> Andrew Lotshaw's murdering of the king's English has begun early. He told the players: "Now, when you get to Avalon, don't run off right away. Congratulate on the pier so they can get a picture."
>
> Edgar Munzel, in the *Chicago Sun*, 1946

Most of all, those who knew him best agreed: Andy Lotshaw had a heart of gold.

Of all his claims to fame, he was *most* famous for 2 things: his verbal malapropisms, and his own brand of body rub, which trainers at all levels swore by for decades.

"Andy Lotshaw was the dandiest guy," laughs Della Root Arnold, Charlie's daughter — "but he could mess up the English language! One time, Dad and Andy went to see Red Barber at station WOLF in New York. They arrived at the studio, and at the reception desk Andy said, 'We'd like to see Mr. Wolf.'

"They finally got to the program, and Red asked Dad the usual stuff. And of course, Andy was also the trainer for the Chicago Bears. So Red asked him the difference between baseball players and football players. Andy said, 'Them baseball players, they're like tissue paper. They slide into 2nd, and they're out for a week. Football players, they get knocked down in the 1st quarter, I tape 'em up, and they're back in. And they get knocked down in the 2nd quarter, I tape 'em up, and they're back in. And they get knocked down in the 3rd quarter, I tape 'em up, and they're back in. And they get knocked down in the 4th quarter, I tape 'em up, and they're back in, fight-fight-fight for the old alma-gater.'"

"Lotshaw was a character," Lou Stringer agrees. "People didn't think he was too smart, but he was smart enough to know his bread and butter. I wouldn't get too close to the trainer's table — he'd spit tobacco juice on you."

"Lotshaw, he was no dummy — although he liked to act like he was," Bobby Mattick says.

Della says the Lotshaws and the Roots got to be good friends. "Andy and Laura would come to the apartment. They didn't have any kids. He finished the 2nd grade, I think, and she finished the 3rd — it was like a TV show, the banter back and forth.

> "Ballplayers are different — there's no comparent."
>
> A typical Andy-Lotshawism, quoted by Della Root Arnold, Charlie's daughter

In fact, a lot of people (who were actually around at the time) think Andy Lotshaw was at the heart of Babe Ruth's fabled 'Called Shot' home run...off Charlie Root. It took place at Wrigley Field in 1932; legend holds that Ruth pointed to the bleachers before teeing off, but all the ballplayers who knew Charlie agree that Root would've leveled the Bambino if he'd been showing off like that. So what's the Lotshaw connection?

"Ruth was pointing at Andy Lotshaw," Bill Veeck said in a later interview. "Right from the start, players from both benches were insulting each other. The loudest Cubs were pitchers Pat Malone, Burleigh Grimes and trainer Andy Lotshaw, who shouted at Ruth, 'If I had you, I'd hitch you to a wagon, you potbelly.'

" 'I don't mind no ballplayers yellin' at me,' Ruth said. "But the trainer cuttin' in...that made me sore.' "

Andy takes a break from malaproping on Catalina to pose with Danny Cahill, Chicago superfan

Ruth and Lotshaw had been great buddies for years — and they loved to ride each other. In Phil Cavarretta's rookie season — when he was still a wide-eyed teenager — he recalls his first trip to Boston, to play the Braves, during Ruth's swan song for that team. "All of a sudden," Cavy said, "I hear a voice that sounds like a big ole bear. The voice says, 'Where is Andy Lotshaw? I want to kill that big old so-and-so Dutchman.' I look around and who do I see, the big guy, Babe Ruth...The Babe and the late Andy Lotshaw, our trainer, were very, very good friends, and they were always kidding, happy, and having a lot of fun."

"What do you guys think you're doin' out there? You're bringin' us to the brink of an abscess!"

Andy's attempt to rouse the team (after 4 straight losses), late in the 1929 pennant race

---

Lotshaw "was a fabulous minor league slugger," Charlie Grimm wrote in his autobiography. "He always contended that except for a chivalrous action he might have been enrolled up there with Babe Ruth. The way he told it, the Cleveland Indians had just bought him when he heard a fellow insult a young lady in a hotel lobby. Andy said his target ducked and that he busted his hand on a pillar and never got another chance in the big time."

Grimm wasn't exaggerating. Lotshaw set a Kitty League record for triples — *24* — in his rookie year, 1906. That record still stands, nearly 100 seasons later. And he possessed some other impressive stats, too; in fact, Andy carried aging news clips in his wallet...in case any younger player doubted his heroics. Yosh Kawano says, "He told Swish Nicholson one time, 'Lookit here' — and he pulled out the old batting averages from the Three-I League.

"Nicholson said, 'But look, you only had 300 at-bats.'

"Andy said, 'Yeah, but wouldn't you have played me, hittin' like that?'"

In 1931, the *Chicago Daily Times* ran an on-going column that was supposedly written by Hack Wilson. (Yeah, and Wrigley Field is on an island in the Pacific Ocean. What's that? It is? Oops, bad analogy. Anyhow, you know what we mean...) In this column, Hack's ghostwriter typed: "Andy says he likes to take care of home run hitters. Perhaps it's because he was one himself not so long ago. He was one of the original home run kings of baseball and can show you newspaper clippings to prove it."

"Age seems to be no handicap to the 67-year-old Lotshaw," Edgar 'the Mouse' Munzel wrote in the *Chicago Sun* in 1946. "He still has the last word in every clubhouse argument...As an added 'stopper' for the popoffs this spring he has a police badge from the local constabulatory and he has also armed himself

Andy Lotshaw was a bit of a celebrity himself — appearing on the front page of The Sporting News *in 1937.*

with a faded old clipping dated July 11, 1914, which shows that Lotshaw, then playing for Champaign of the Illinois-Missouri League was leading the circuit in hitting with an average of .387."

In fact, Andy was Grover Cleveland Alexander's batterymate in Galesburg, Illinois, in 1909. His connection with Ol' Pete led to his becoming the Cubs' trainer. In 1921, he did an emergency repair job on Alexander's arm during the City Series against the White Sox. "I must have done Alex some good, because he came back to beat the Sox in a 19-inning game," Andy said later.

The train was resting on a siding near Albuquerque, waiting for the Sante Fe's new streamliner to whiz past. As it zipped past the Cub Pullmans, Andy puffed out his chest. "Reminds me of Lotshaw on the base paths," he cracked.

Howard Roberts, in the
Chicago Daily News, 1938

"I didn't know much about taping athletes when I began training the Bears," he explained, "but it didn't take me long to learn. I bought a few rolls and practiced taping my wife...until I learned the correct way."

"Andy...practiced bandaging his wife Laura until sometimes she looked like an Egyptian mummy," Bill Veeck said.

"That's easy. Call a doctor."

What Andy said when asked
what he'd do if a player broke a
leg, in *Quotations on the Chicago Cubs*

"Andy was an excellent baseball player, but he knew nothing about medicine!" Yoshi says. "He *was* a bright guy. His line was always, 'I never helped anybody — but I never hurt anybody, either.'"

But he did help. Enormously.

"Ol' Diz — when we got him, he had a bad arm," Cavarretta says. "But to watch him pitch, you talk about courage! Every day, before he'd start, he'd go in the training room, and old Andy Lotshaw would rub him with this capsicum he'd invented himself. I don't know what this sucker put in there — it was so strong, his pitching arm looked like a lobster. But he'd go out and throw three or four innings, a little here, a little there, and every once in a while...he'd buzz one in there pretty good."

Chuck Klein became afflicted with muscular knots known as a 'charley horse.' It was so resistant to all the ministrations of trainer Doc Lotshaw that he finally confided to Manager Grimm he was afraid Chuck's ailment was 'chronicle.' No charley horse in all baseball history could compare with the knots Doc Lotshaw could tie in the English language.

Warren Brown, in *The Chicago Cubs*

"Andy had his Andy Lotshaw Body Rub," Andy Pafko says, "and he told me he used to rub Dizzy Dean with it. And Diz would say, 'Oh, does that feel good. I want a bottle of that.' And Andy handed him a bottle of Coke."

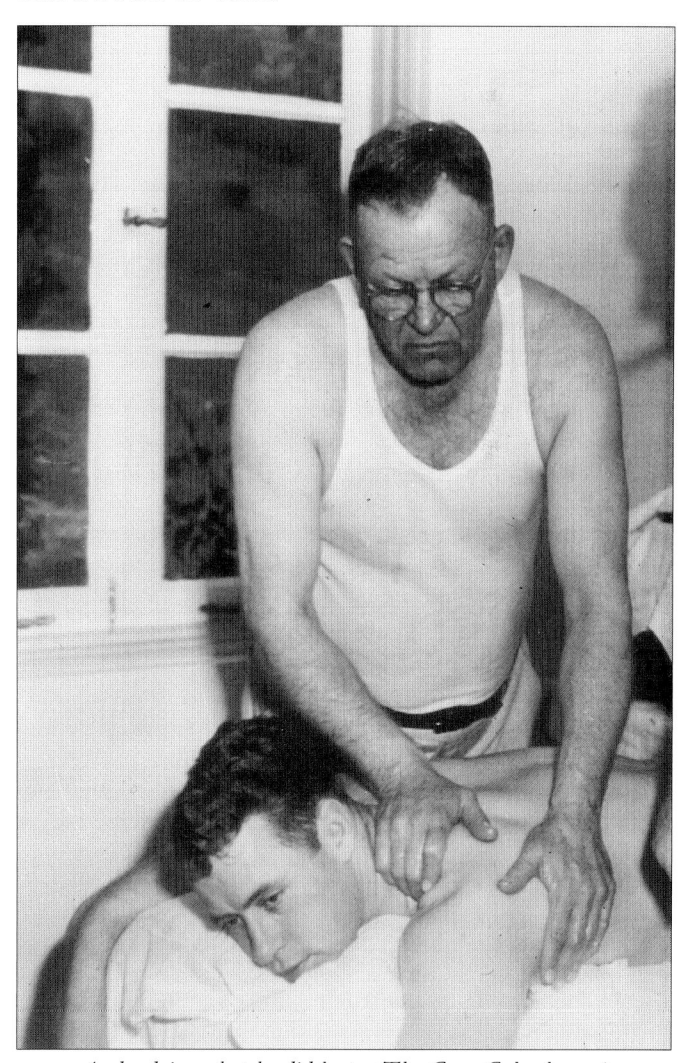

Andy, doing what he did best. (The Coca-Cola chaser is soon to follow.) The patient, this particular Catalina afternoon in 1946: Rookie pitcher Johnny McPartland.

Andy Lotshaw's World-Famous Body Rub

Andy's rub was a big seller for years — advertised in sports publications and elsewhere. People swore by the strong-smelling stuff.

Della Root Arnold recalls, "Dad was being interviewed on the radio by Hal Totten, and the program was sponsored by Andy's Rub. Hal asked Dad what he though of it. Dad said, 'It's good stuff — in fact, here comes the good Doctor now!'

"So Andy came on, and said, 'It's good for sore muscles, women's chests, and skin abortions.'"

If you bought a set of Cub team photos in the '30s or '40s, you'd find this coupon inside.

"My mother was a maid cleaning Las Casitas," Islander Marcelino Saucedo says. "Andy Lotshaw gave her some of that lotion, and we used it. The label said he was the famous trainer for the Chicago Cubs and the Chicago Bears, so as kids we wanted some of that — we thought, if the pro ballplayers use it before the games, so should we!"

> "Turpentine, lemon oil, olive oil, and some other things I ain't tellin'."
>
> Andy Lotshaw, enumerating the ingredients of his product

Grimm provided some enlightenment to the manufacturing and shipping process in his book: "Lotshaw, just to add a little class to his tape and arnica department, persuaded the club to buy him a $30 copy of *Materia Medica*. The investment wasn't a total waste. He used the pages to wrap up bottles of his famous Lotshaw's Body Rub."

Of course, Doc was far from a one-trick trainer; his bag of tricks was stuffed to the edges.

"Andy had Hack (Wilson) in one of those big, high old tubs, sobering him up," Veeck wrote in his autobiography, *Veeck as in Wreck*. "In the tub with Hack was a 50-pound cake of ice....Everytime Hack's head would bob up, Andy would shove it back down...It was a fascinating sight, watching them bob in perfect rhythm, first Hack's head, then the ice, then Hack's head, then the ice."

Despite this cruel and unusual training, Hack idolized Andy. In his, um, column in the *Times*, Hack, um, wrote these words: "I have often been asked what person I thought helped me most along my baseball route. The man to whom I believe I owe the most is a man behind the scenes — Andy Lotshaw, the trainer of the Cubs. I weigh 210 pounds. Yet I have about the smallest feet in baseball. I wear size 5 ½ shoes. He uses more than a mile of tape on me every season, he says." For each game, Lotshaw would use about 10 yards of adhesive tape on Wilson's weak ankles.

The *Chicago American* reported in 1937 that "Andy Lotshaw, who rubs away aches and pains of ailing members of the North Side club, has his lotions, pills, saws, etc. packed and is ready for any emergency, which we hope won't arise."

> The Cubs have begun a blind bogey golf tourney. "They ought to do pretty good at that," said Lotshaw, "because some of 'em look blind when they're hitting at a baseball."
>
> Edgar Munzel, in *The Chicago Sun*, 1947

"Lotshaw was a character," Al Epperly says. "He was supposed to be a trainer, but he didn't know anything! He didn't rub me with Coca-Cola, but I saw him do it."

"Lotshaw claims a rubber suit will remove Hartnett's double chin," the *Chicago Herald & Examiner* told in 1927, "even if the rubber does not touch his chin."

"Joe Westnedge...tried to climb a mountain too fast and half way up he caved in," according to a 1925 issue of the *Tribune*. "When he reached the hotel he was having chills. He was over them by morning, however, for a couple of Lotshaw's pink pellets fixed him up."

LEAVE IT TO ANDY

Hack Wilson owes much of his success to Andy Lotshaw, Cub trainer. There's lots of heft on Hack's slim ankles and if it weren't for the way Andy binds 'em up, Hack probably wouldn't do so well. Andy's right on the job in the above picture.

Andy keeps Hack Wilson taped to the table, so Hack can't go drinking with Pat Malone.

"Dr. Lotshaw arises early so that he may make the rounds of his patients and discover if any of the rookies had colic during the night," Warren Brown detailed in his *So They Tell Me* column, for the *Herald & Examiner* in 1938, "or if the rheumatism of the veterans will permit them to get out of bed when the 'Good morning! It's 7:30!' phone rings. And as long as he has to get up, no matter when he gets in, Dr. Lotshaw has it all figured out that he might as well stay up."

Of course, some of the ballplayers wanted to keep Andy *less* busy — because after all, a trip to the training room often meant you had a problem. Lonny Frey was one: "I wanted to stay outa there!" he says.

"Dr. Andy Lotshaw's supply of ointments, balms and astringents, alongside a whistling steam bath, electric cabinets, needle and whirlpool devices seemed ominous to the lads who believed the hosts' assurance that the gathering here was to be 'a 10-day get-acquainted holiday,' " Ed Burns wrote in the *Trib*, 24 Springs later — when a lot of that rookie crop hadn't even been born when Doc first ventured to the Island.

"Andy was blustery, of the old school," Carmen Mauro says. "If you had an ache or pain, just rub some dirt on it and play. Rubdowns were meant for starting pitchers."

"I couldn't get in the trainer's room if I wanted to," Ed Chandler says. "I didn't throw enough for the Cubs to get in there."

But Johnny Klippstein thinks a lot of the rookies were mistakenly intimidated — Andy's bark was worse than his bite. "He was one of the hardest-working guys I ever saw," Johnny says. "He never refused a ballplayer who needed a rubdown or something, and he was always jovial."

Hard-working, indeed. "Andy Lotshaw — the iron man," wrote Gentleman Jim Gallagher for the *Chicago American* in 1933. "After unloading all the trunks at the clubhouse, he came out and batted all afternoon. Then, back to rub down 21 aching athletes. Warneke was the most active man on the lot, fielding bunts, bunting...and shagging flies for Andy Lotshaw...and did Lotshaw chase him!"

> "I couldn't forget Andy Lotshaw — he was an old fart, a gruff old guy. He didn't fool around with the rookies much — he didn't have any sympathy for rookies who got banged up. He'd say, 'I don't wannna see any blinkety-blank rookies in here!' "
>
> Wayne Terwilliger

Others didn't mind a little attention — even if it was unnecessary. In his autobiography, eccentric pitcher Kirby Higbe recounted a Lotshaw episode from his rookie year, 1937: "You were supposed to get your arm loosened up by the trainer every day before throwing batting practice. The first time I went in, Andy Lotshaw started rubbing my left arm, and he rubbed it all Spring. About two days before we left the Island, Gabby Hartnett came in and said, 'Andy, Hig is a right-handed pitcher.'

"Andy covered for both of us with a joke. 'I know, Gabby, but he thinks he's left-handed, and his left arm gets sore, too.' After Gabby left, Andy gave me down the country for letting him rub my left arm all Spring.

" 'My arm never bothers me, so it didn't need any rubbing anyway,' I told him. 'I figured you might as well work on my left arm because I didn't want to deprive you of a job.' "

Sure cleans up nice, don't he? Doc wins another waltz trophy, this time with local gal Hulda Eichelberger as his dance-card partner.

"Well," said Andy, "I only missed one and you missed three. That don't make you look so good, does it?"

— Bill Henry, in the *Los Angeles Times*

Sparky, lookin' good.

The merry prankster

Yet despite all the hard work, Andy found time for a little fun and games. No, make that a *lot* of fun and games. Sometimes, he was the jokester. Other times, he let himself be the butt of the joke. Here's a partial highlight reel, over the years:

1924: Fish tales
Trainer Andy Lotshaw indulged in a bit of horseplay at the expense of Manager Killefer today. Prior to the start for the practice field, the muscle manipulator bought a rubber fish 3 feet long and filled it with water, attaching it and a weight to Killefer's fishing line.

Yep, Bill fell for it. — *Chicago American*

1926: Yer out!
Mr. Andy Lotshaw, the combination umpire and trainer, scored a verbal knockout over Sparky Adams when he called the young man out on strikes during a desperate rally by the regulars. "You sure missed that one," said Sparky reproachfully as he started for the bench.

Dr. Andrew Hemingway Lotshaw reached midseason form shortly after the bus left the Sante Fe station en route to Wilmington. The doctor, complimenting Tex Carleton on his snappy regalia, said: "If you didn't have that hat on, I'd take you for one of those college sophomores."

Chicago Herald & Examiner, 1937

1927: Rookies, beware
Trainer Lotshaw has been the life of the party so far. He had a group of youngsters 'listening' in on the Taylor-Shea fight reports on a phony radio rigged up in the club car last night and has the same bunch all set for a bowling tournament on the boat between San Pedro and Catalina.

— *Chicago Herald & Examiner*

1929: Rookies, keep on being ware

The rookies are going to hear some hair-raising stories that they've never heard before and never will hear again unless Andy is able to improve on his original versions.

— Irving Vaughn, in the *Tribune*

1929: For the birds

When we say the Cubs are happy we don't include the trainer, Dr. Iodine Lotshaw, who is busier than the proverbial bee. Doc thinks Avalon is the grandest place on earth were it not for the sea gulls and the California laws protecting them. He brought a shoe box full of food and a bottle of milk from the hotel down to the beach today, anticipating a quiet retreat on the sand. When his attention was diverted, a sea gull made off with the box lunch. He turned to find another trying to figure how he'd hoist the milk bottle.

— Ed Burns, condensing his *Chicago Tribune* story for the *Los Angeles Times*

Whadd'ya suppose he really kept in that big black bag of his?

1937: The name game

Four Los Angeles pitchers, whose names Dr. Lotshaw will never know, are here to pitch batting practice.

Pat Malone, teasing Lotshaw, asked who was the Los Angeles manager. Andy's comeback: "I don't know, but you better find out. That's where you'll be playing ball in a couple of weeks."

The umpires were to be the Messrs. Bob Lewis and Doctor Andrew (Humming Bird) Lotshaw. Dr. Lotshaw worked far into the night memorizing the names of the batteries so he wouldn't announce Cherry as Strawberry and Majeski as Majestic.

— John C. Hoffman, for the *Chicago Daily Times*

"He called me Huey because he couldn't say Dewey."

Dewey Williams, in *Wrigleyville*

1937: A hearty congrats

Last night a good time was had by all at the hotel, where a benefit dance was staged, with prizes and everything. There was some muttering today because in the draw for prizes only one of the Cub party won anything.

By a strange coincidence it was Dr. Lotshaw who won a prize. The coincidence consisted in the fact that he won while drawing the numbers himself.

His prize was a roll of tape.

— *Chicago Herald & Examiner*

1938: Seeing Red

Trainer Andy Lotshaw is captain of the bowlers, but is greatly upset because the eligibility of Red Sedgewich has been questioned. Red, one of the coast pitchers borrowed for batting practice, is the best bowler of the bunch, but being only a batting practice hurler, is he eligible to compete as a Cub? It is an earth-shaking problem to the good Dr. Lotshaw.

— Howard Roberts, in the *Chicago Daily News*

1938: More congratulations are in order

The annual Cub dance was staged last night and trainer Andy Lotshaw, many years an island waltzing champion, was nosed out by Stainback. Andy was more or less perturbed about the loss of the title until the prize was awarded. It was a caged red rooster, the tail of which was improved by the presence of an ostrich feather.

— Irving Vaughn, condensing his *Chicago Tribune* story for the *Los Angeles Times*

Stainback now regrets beating Lotshaw in the 1938 Island-wide waltz-off.

1939: Keep your head down

Andy, tired of hearing (Hank) Leiber and his teammates talk of Hank's ability to hit a golf ball out of sight, challenged him to a driving contest. One of Andy's bosom buddies on the Island was Roy Phillips, the golf pro. He was to referee and furnish the balls.

Lotshaw insisted on shooting first. When he sliced the ball no more than 150 yards...Leiber stepped up confidently. Hank connected solidly on a teriffic swing — but the ball exploded, the fragments flying in all directions. — *Jolly Cholly's Story*

Andy tangles the king's English occasionally but he doesn't let it slow him down. The other day he remarked that someone was "dressed in the nude."

Edgar Munzel, in the *Chicago Sun*, 1946

1946: Keep your head up

The eucalyptus trees on the third base side are being trimmed because they were casting too much shadow. Doc Lotshaw had to run for his life when he decided to haul up his socks just when a sawed-off branch was tumbling down.

— Edgar Munzel, in the *Chicago Sun*

An overall great guy

For all his practical jokes and rough edges, Andy simply cared about people. In an era when a lot of ballplayers advocated racism, Andy stood up for fairness. "When the first black ballplayers came up," Yosh Kawano says, "and some guys started complaining about it, Andy said, 'You wouldn't worry about 'em if you were better — if you're better, they won't take your job.'"

And while some ballplayers were too busy to pay much attention to kids and other locals in Avalon, Andy always had the time. "I talked to Andy Lotshaw," Foxie Saucedo says. "He was truly a real nice guy. He asked how I was doing in baseball."

In fact, when Islander Jack Cowell showed up at the ballpark (in *Chicago!*) one day looking for work, Andy helped out...and then, "Andy Lotshaw wrote a real nice letter of reference for me, and he had Gabby sign it, too."

He even shared his expertise with the people on Catalina: "Trainer Andy Lotshaw has been inviting the townsmen to come out and let him display his ability as an osteopath and a masseur," the *Chicago Daily News* reported in 1926. "He says he doesn't get enough practice from the players."

The waitstaff inside the Hotel St. Catherine keep a careful eye on Andy & Laura Lotshaw in 1933, eagerly anticipating what they might do next...

> He was asked one day by a curious interviewer who wanted to know if Doc believed in God. "In course," said Lotshaw. "What do you think I am — an amethyst?"
>
> Warren Brown, in *The Chicago Cubs*

"Nobody was more loyal or true," Gent Jim Gallagher eulogized in 1953. "I never heard of Andy hurting anyone all the years I knew him. No one will ever know how much money he spent helping other people."

Truly an American original, it's too bad Doc was around before there were sound bytes — he'd surely be in our minds with a whole bunch of classics. Andy truly was one of the all-time great Catalina Cubs.

Doc was the team doc for the World Champion Chicago Bears, too.

Also in this 1932 team photo: George Halas, Red Grange ('The Galloping Ghost'), & Bronco Nagurski.

Top Row—Dr. J. F. Davis, C. Tackwell, John Sisk, John Doehring, Bill Buckler, Paul Franklin, Tiny Engebretsen, A. Lotshaw, Ralph Jones. Middle Row—Charles Bidwill, George Trafton, Don Murry, L. Burdick, Gil Bergerson, Bronko Nagurski, Luke Johnsos, Bert Pearson, George Halas. Front Row—Dick Nesbitt, Bill Hewitt, Carl Brumbaugh, Keith Molesworth, Red Grange, George Corbett, Ookie Miller, Jules Carlsen, Joe Kopcha.

Yosh Kawano at 16 — already a veteran in 1938.

Yosh Kawano: The All-Century Cub

To put Yosh Kawano's major-league career into perspective:

Yosh knew Babe Ruth — on a professional level — and Yosh is *still* working for the Cubs.

He's been in baseball for 70 years now — spanning *eight* decades — yet most fans don't know the name. And that's okay with him — because Yosh is one of those guys who loves to work hard, behind the scenes, and not get any credit. Old school. *Very* old school.

Yosh started out as a batboy for a variety of teams in the early 1930s. He worked with the White Sox and Cubs during their Southern California Spring Training camps; during the regular season, he worked for the San Diego Padres and the Los Angeles Angels. He knew Ted Williams in the minors, and they became good fishing buddies. All the stars of the past 8 decades — Ruth, Gehrig, DiMaggio, Williams, Musial, Mantle, Mays, Aaron — these guys know and respect Yosh Kawano.

"I've known Yosh for more than 60 years!" says Gene Mauch, who's been in professional baseball for more than half a century himself. "He's a very astute baseball personality. He knows the players, he knows their weaknesses. He won't say 9 words, but what you could get out of him, if ya could, it was remarkable what he knew. We'd sit and talk; he didn't profess to be a scout or anything like that, but when you could get him to put an opinion out, it was remarkable how often he was right about a particular ballplayer or something about the game. I guess maybe I felt that way because he agreed with me so much!

"He won't say how old he is, but I knew him in 1941, at Reese High School, in L.A."

"Yosh has to be the guy who's been with a club the longest in the history of baseball," Andy Pafko says. "He looks the same as he did 30-40 years ago. I'd ask him, 'How old are you, Yosh?' And he'd say, 'I dunno.' He's always working, never stops."

Yosh Kawano, then or now or somewhere in between... currently in his 8th decade of major-league baseball.

"He was the quietest man I ever knew," Johnny Klippstein says. "He was the kind of person who was seen, and not heard. And usually not even seen. I always thought he'd be with the Cubs for the rest of his life."

"Yosh says he doesn't own anything with the Cubs' logo on it," Carrie Muskat wrote in *Banks to Sandberg to Grace*. "He prefers to be anonymous."

Anonymity has its benefits — like staying under the radar. "Later on," Bobby Mattick says, "he got to where he was probably runnin' the club!"

Always working, quietly. "Yosh was my roommate in Chicago for a while when I was single," Randy Jackson says. "Sometimes I'd be kind of waking up in the morning and see him pulling the blanket over me, like a momma might do. He'd do anything for you, whatever needed to be done."

"You know, a ballplayer can't do anything for himself," Yosh told Muskat. "Once he puts on that uniform, somebody's got to do things for him."

Always paying attention. "I was watching TV," Paul Schramka says, "and it was a rainout, so they got to talking about who wore number 14 before Ernie Banks. Well, Yosh came up from the clubhouse and said it was Paul Schramka. And Jack Brickhouse said, 'Who the heck is that?'"

Always trying to keep the new manager happy. When Leo Durocher took over in 1966 — and the Cubs moved Spring Training back to Southern California for one brief shining season, to Long Beach — Yosh dodged a Durocher bullet. "Clubhouse custodian Yosh Kawano took Durocher's order of no water in the dugout so seriously that he didn't have any in the clubhouse either, but that was changed just in time to save his scalp," the also-eternal Mouse Munzel wrote for the *Chicago Sun-Times*.

Always cookin': in the 1994 book, *The Cubs R Cookin' by Cub Wives for Family Rescue*, a featured recipe was Yosh Kawano's Chopped Chicken Livers. Mmm...

Always thinking ahead. "We called him Yoshi," Phil Cavarretta says. "He's a good friend of mine. When we were training in Mesa, he'd take me out to the middle of the desert after the workout and ask, 'What do you see here, Phillibuck?'

"I'd say, 'All I see are rattlesnakes!'

"He said, 'Buy yourself 2-300 acres — it's only $10 an acre.'

"I told him, 'You're crazy!' But he bought a lot of land, and...do you have any idea what it's worth today?"

Yosh spent quite a few years on Catalina, too.

"They used to play golf a lot," Yoshi says. "The funniest thing I can remember was when Frankie Frisch heard they played golf up there. He borrowed Mr. Wrigley's clubs, and off he went to the 1st tee, at the top of the hills. Well, his 1st ball he hit went way out to the right...and the next one went way out left.

Yosh has appeared on more than a dozen Topps cards, when the sets included team photos. Here, on his 1956 rookie card, he's even identified for posterity.

He had a couple of coaches shaggin' balls, and me caddying. By the time he got to the 3rd hole, he had lots of people following him, watching — a big crowd. And he turned to me and said, 'If I lose another ball, I'm gonna get a new boy on the next boat over!' So he hit a slice, right through the trees, and everybody was laughing and running, headed for the bushes. I didn't know what to do — there wasn't another ball, but by gosh, it was in the fairway! I said to him, 'There's your ball!' The other guys had already looked there. He said, 'You're the greatest — I don't know how it got there.' Frisch gave me 20 bucks.

"Jim Gallagher, and all of Mr. Wrigley's friends said, 'I can't believe you did something like that!' For years, everybody said, 'Yosh dropped the ball there.' But it was a mystery to me — he must've hit a tree or a rock or something. Who'd have believed it — the ball made a turn!"

Yosh was born in Seattle in 1921 — but don't tell anybody. His parents, searching for work, moved to Southern California when he was little. "I came out of the Depression. It was a hard time. These guys have no idea."

Because of his Japanese ancestry — even though he was a U.S. citizen — Yosh was sent to a 'relocation camp' along with the rest of his family. "I was in an internment camp, in Arizona," he says, "but they could draft you out of that! One minute, you're a risk to national security... the next minute, you can serve your country."

So Yosh went off to serve in the Pacific. The only silver lining was...he didn't have to endure French Lick.

"My brother Nobe was in the camp, too. He worked for the Hollywood Stars, and Salt Lake City, then the Dodgers. He lives in Los Angeles and Hawaii now." Nobe drew a little media attention a few years back in his quest to help Dodger skipper Tommy Lasorda slim down. He had one of Lasorda's jersey's made up with LASAGNE across the back, above Lasorda's number 2...and he made Tommy a t-shirt that said "Do not feed the manager" in 5 languages.

Yosh, the quieter one, went back to the Cubs. "After I got out of the Service, the General Manager wouldn't let me work — he said, 'You should go to school with the GI Bill.' But I didn't want to. So he said, 'Yosh, you'll always have a job here if you want to work.' "

And so he does — taking care of the visitors' clubhouse at Wrigley Field. (The home clubhouse is named after him, by the way.) "I don't know any other life," he said in *Banks to Sandberg to Grace*. "I'll tell you what. I never thought I'd be here this long."

Looks like Andy got the last laugh on Blake, Bush, Heathcote, & Lewis — say, anybody seen those 4 fellas lately?

Chuck Connors, The Branded Rifleman

After Dutch, Another Strapping Visitor From the East Hopped Over to Hollywood From the Catalina Diamond

"Chuck Connors almost ran over my wife and me, coming down one of those steep hills on a bike one day!"

Roy Smalley, Jr.

If you grew up watching TV in the '50s, you remember Chuck Connors as Lucas McCain on *The Rifleman*.

If you grew up watching TV in the '60s, you remember Chuck Connors as Jason McCord on *Branded*.

If you grew up in the '70s, you remember him from flicks like *Soylent Green* and for his Emmy-nominated role as evil slavemerchant Tom Moore in the *Roots* miniseries.

But if you grew up on Catalina Island...you remember Chuck Connors as one of the Chicago Cubs.

Before he appeared in more than a hundred movies and television shows, Chuck was a larger-than-life, outrageous, funny, cantankerous, boisterous, loud, never-dull member of the 1951 Cubs. Before that, he played for his hometown Brooklyn Dodgers. (Chuck was originally drafted by the New York Yankees before being dealt away.) His career average is .238, with 2 homers in 202 at-bats.

Not only that, he was one of the rare multi-pro-sport stars of his times... playing in the pre-NBA for the Boston Celtics while working his way through the minor leagues.

Chuck Connors, as most people remember him.

Chuck Connors, as the 1951 Chicago Cubs remember him.

At 6'5", he loomed large. Yet his showmanship and magnetic ultra-personality were early clues that this guy was going someplace.

He really was a big star, which us older folks remember; if you're among the young (and thus say things like, "You mean Paul McCartney was in another band before *Wings*?"), consider this: his co-stars included John Wayne, Charleton Heston, Gregory Peck, Katherine Hepburn, and Spencer Tracy. He has his own star on the Hollywood Walk of Fame.

And he wasn't a bad ballplayer, either:

* Chuck led the Piedmont league in home runs in 1946
* He hit .300 in the minors 3 times
* He hit 3 homers in a game once for Los Angeles
* And in 1951, he smacked 22 homers in just 98 games (while batting .321) for L.A., before Mr. Wrigley summoned him to Chicago

He was always doing something outrageous. Considering the fact that he really only spent a few weeks with the Cubs, it's impressive that just about every teammate had Chuck Connors tales to tell.

"They paid me $500 for my week's work in that movie. I figured they'd made some mistake on the adding machine. 'Baseball,' I told myself, 'just lost a first baseman.'"

Chuck Connors, explaining why he switched careers after appearing in *Pat & Mike*, his first film, in 1952 (from *Chuck Connors: The Man Behind the Rifle*)

(Lest we confuse you, his name was Kevin Joseph Aloysius Connors. When he was playing ball, some people called him 'Kevin.')

Let the stories begin...

"We did a bus tour of the island," Bob Borkowski says. "We were going to Mr. Wrigley's ranch, in the center of the island. He'd have a barbecue, and contests like greased pigs — you'd get a gift, get a watch. Chuck stood up, right in the front of the bus, he took the mike — it was a tour bus — and he recited 'Casey at the Bat.' He was the most interesting character we had. He was always piddling around, doing something different."

"Chuck would do anything for a laugh. But on the diamond he was as intense as I was, which was probably the reason we became close friends."

Tommy Lasorda, in his autobiography

"He'd give you a hot foot," Phil Cavarretta says. "I'd be sittin' in the dugout, trying to concentrate on the game, trying to see what kinda stuff the pitcher had, and all of a sudden — your shoe's on fire!

"He liked to be in front of people. He'd sing, he'd play the harmonica, he'd entertain us — in my thinking, this guy's good! On the team bus, he'd sit in the back and he'd whip out that harmonica. The

1st thing he'd play was always *Take Me Out to the Ball Game*. The guy was good. He tried baseball, he gave his best — but I think he made the right choice."

"Connors was crazy," Randy Jackson smiles. "He'd do anything. He'd lie down in front of moving cars, right on the street. I mean, they went slow out there, but still...

"One time we were sitting in a restaurant — there were 4 of us in a booth, and they had maybe 15 tourists in there. And Chuck says, 'I'm gonna do something. No matter what you do, don't look up.' So he stands up, right in the middle of this crowded restaurant, and he puts his hands around his mouth, real theatrical, and as loud as he could, he yells this really nasty obscenity. Well, we were all too embarrassed to look up — he didn't need to tell us — but nobody else looked up, either! I guess they were all too embarrassed, too. So I guess he found his niche in acting!"

Randy Jackson chose to move to Brooklyn rather than having to dine with Chuck again.

"Chuck Connors was a different kinda guy," Johnny Klippstein grins. "One time, we were walking down the street and he had one of his sons on his shoulders — he was probably about 2 or 3. And Chuck was reciting poetry: 'Today, I killed a man, and I'm not sorry at all...' And he was doing it real loudly, and people were stopping and turning to look. It was pretty embarrassing! I started walking 2 or 3 steps behind him. He was a real character — but down deep, Chuck was a really nice guy."

"I knew Chuck Connors well, when he was with Montreal," Lloyd Lowe says. "Chuck takes us to this place, it's like in the movies — jam-packed with people, filled with smoke, and the bartender had a revolver — not in a holster, but right in his pants! I asked Chuck if he comes in here very often. And I could just picture, if they raided this place, and put my picture in the paper, and everybody back home saw it, what would I say?"

"Chuck Connors, he was a wonder."

Gene Mauch

"My mother told this story about Chuck Connors," Boots Merullo says. "He had this whole box of cheap engagement rings, and he'd pass 'em out every 5 minutes."

"He kept things going a bit," adds Fuzzy Richards.

"Connors was a character," Paul Schramka says. "He was a real cut-up. One time it started raining, and what happened was the ballpark, Wrigley Field, the one in L.A., was filled, and the management didn't wanna call the game — all those people! Connors grabs a couple of bats, and went and sat on the pitchers' mound, and he pretended the bats were oars, and he started rowing! Well, they finally started the game up, and as soon as they threw the 1st ball, the ump called the game — cuz the umpire had control of the game once it started!"

He also raised a few eyebrows at L.A.'s Wrigley Field by cartwheeling around the bases after hitting a homer one time.

Connors liked to tell about the day he was called into Dodger legend Branch Rickey's office. Rickey asked a series of questions, like whether Connors drank. Chuck claims he answered, 'Mr. Rickey, if I have to drink to play for you, I want to be traded.'"

"We took the boat all the time," Bob Kelly says. "Coming back, it was quite raunchy. Kevin was holding our baby, because I was hanging onto the rail. I can get pretty seasick."

"I finally got him horseback riding in the mountains — a guy from Brooklyn on horseback," Turk Lown says. "Chuck, he'd never gotten on a horse! He just wasn't interested. So I always thought it was pretty funny, him ending up on a western, where he rode a horse all the time!"

"We went up into the mountains, horseback riding," Wayne Terwilliger says. "I'd never been riding before. We stopped on this ridge, and I guess I let my reins down, since the bit went crooked in the horse's mouth — and he took off running! I grabbed his neck, 'cuz that's all I could do. I was scared spitless, scared to death that we were goin' over the edge of a cliff. But he finally got settled down and started walkin'. And Chuck was just laughin' his head off."

"We'd go to the movies and he always had a water gun on him," Eddie Miksis told Carrie Muskat in *Banks to Sandberg to Grace*. "When he was sitting up in the upper deck, he'd find some bald-headed guy."

In the '50s, you could get a baseball card of your favorite Pacific Coast League ballplayer — like this strapping fella — with a purchase of Mother's Cookies.

Connors and Dee Fondy were battling it out for the 1st-baseman's job on Catalina in 1951. At the end of Spring Training, Frankie Frisch brought Fondy back to Chicago...and sent Chuck to the Los Angeles Angels. "I met Chuck Connors once," Joe Fondy says. "He said my dad helped him get into TV! My dad said he'd told him the same thing, too."

"When I was with the Los Angeles Angels," Carmen Mauro says, "he was already in the movies. He'd come to watch the games. He knew me, and although he was no longer in baseball, he'd come down on the field during batting practice and he'd say, 'You can't hit — gimme that bat!' And he'd take it! And he'd hit pretty good. Of course, we were buddies, so it was fun."

"About the time I was getting done," Lefty Chambers recollects, "Chuck Connors came through. He was a pretty fair hitter, but he just couldn't hit the long ball. In those days, 1st-basemen had to hit for some power. Dee Fondy took his job away from him."

"Chuck Connors was my favorite 1st-baseman," Cavarretta says. "Here was another guy who had some talent, but probably not enough for the big leagues. He was a little slow with the bat. In the Coast League, he did okay, but when he came to the Cubs...he'd break more bats than Louisville Slugger could put out."

"The chance for Kevin Connors to prove himself in actual ball games was lost when he came up with a sore arm. He will remain on the Island...while the bulk of the squad is in the North."

Warren Brown, writing in the *Chicago Herald & Examiner*, 1951

Red Adams worked with Chuck again, after their playing days were over. "I got to know Chuck a little," Red says. "I worked in the studio a bit — I was one of the grips. I got in good with the Goldwyn studios. I went on location, working on *The Big Country*. Chuck Connors was in that, before he made it real big."

"Chuck Connors was an interesting guy, a good friend — of course, he was from Brooklyn, too," Harriet Block (Cy's wife) recalls. "We saw them a lot. We went out to California in the '60s. We sent him a telegram, and we went out to the studio. He got us in, and we enjoyed seeing him."

Round, round, get around, Chuck got around

It is interesting to note that Chuck Connors, who only spent about 6 weeks with the Cubs on Catalina...and a couple of months with the team in Chicago...must've roomed with everybody at one time or another. This is a mystery that cannot be solved in a single volume of this length.

Turk Lown: *"I may've roomed with Chuck on Catalina."*

Fuzzy Richards: *"I roomed with Chuck Connors."*

Larry Burgess (Smoky's son): *"They were roommates."*

Paul Minner: *"I roomed with Chuck Connors."*

Valma Jeffcoat: *"Chuck was Hal's roommate."*

"Chuck Connors owes me money!" Islander Marcelino Saucedo says. "We were all having a refreshment at the soda fountain at the Island Pharmacy. He walked in, ordered something, then as he's leaving, he says, 'Charge it to Marse,' then walked out! I was only 17, and my sister was working at the fountain. It was only 50 cents, but I kept kidding him about it.

"He was real friendly, real outgoing, a jokester, he liked to play tricks, fast ones — a real character. Connors and some of the other guys on the Cubs would come watch our games. They'd say, 'I'll give you a quarter for every hit you get.' So we'd get 3 hits, and go to 'em and say, 'You owe me 75 cents.' But they'd say, 'Oh, no, not bloopers; those don't count. The real ones: line drives.' They still owe us money."

Chuck passed away in 1992 — way too many Marlboros. His love for the Cubs will always be apparent to anyone who visits his gravesite...because the Cubs logo appears on Chuck's tombstone.

Other multi-sport Cubs

There were other multi-taskers on the Island:

* Ace Parker played for Brooklyn in the NFL, and got a Cubs tryout in 1947 — at age 34
* Frank Baumholtz played pro basketball for the Cleveland Rebels
* Preston Ward played pro basketball for the St. Louis Bombers
* Wimpy Quinn played college hoops at Oregon and was drafted by the Toronto Huskies, but never got to play pro basketball
* Paul Erickson and Eddie Waitkus played high school hockey — Erickson as a goalie
* Ray Mack turned down an offer from the Chicago Bears in 1938 to play baseball
* Trainer Andy Lotshaw also rubbed away the aches for the Chicago Bears — where he received a caseful of pre-Super Bowl rings over the decades

"Some of the guys were really good basketball players," Marse Saucedo recalls. "Jackie Cusick played for a short time in the NBA, too. He gave this demonstration one time. They were there at the end of our high school basketball season, and during the halftime of one game, Jackie gave this demonstration of his 2-hand set shot. There were about 400 people there, and we were all amazed. The referee would give him the ball, and he'd move around the circle, and he couldn't miss — swish, swish, swish. And he did it in his street clothes!"

Crazy Legs?

Crazy Legs Hirsch (Elroy to his draft board) is in the NFL Hall of Fame. He played for the defunct Chicago Rockets and then the Los Angeles Rams in the '50s, catching passes from Norm Van Brocklin.

Few fans know he got a Catalina tryout in 1946.

"He had a wonderful time," Ruth Hirsch recalls. They were married 3 months later, in June — but she hadn't gotten to go with him.

"In college he pitched and played in the outfield," Edgar 'the Mouse' Munzel reported in the *Chicago Sun*. "He has quite a reputation as a hitter." The next day, Munzel wrote: "After working out with the Cubs he sighed, 'This still is the best game of all.' He'll make up his mind between football and baseball when and if he gets his discharge."

Elroy choose football, so alas — Cub fans never got to see those crazy legs in action, hawking flyballs on the grass at Wrigley Field...

Topps, 1957.

HIRSCH BIDS 'HIGH' FOR CUB JOB
Lt. Elroy "Crazy Legs" Hirsch, former Wisconsin football star, goes up for a high one for the edification of Manager Charlie Grimm while working out with the Cubs at their Catalina spring camp. Hirsch, a pitcher, has ambitions of becoming an outfielder after he leaves the service. He was granted a three-day leave to try out with the Cubs.

"I'm crazy about that leaping ability," Charlie Grimm must've been thinking as he watched Elroy Hirsch give baseball a go on Catalina in 1946.

Onto the Summer & Into the Fall: Back to the Friendly Confines

Once the Boys Broke Camp, They Spent a Little Time at Wrigley Field, Too

"Cubs fans were the best fans I ever saw."

Randy Jackson

This should be a very short section.

That's because there are 94,353 book about the Chicago Cubs...and all 94,353 are devoted to stuff that happened at Wrigley Field, in Chicago, 'tween April and October.

As in, the ivy on the walls and the lack of lights and Harry Caray and Ernie's 500th home run and the great late-season wilt of 1969 and Gabby's homer in the gloamin' and Babe Ruth's alleged called shot in the 1932 World Series and...well, you get the idea.

In other words, there wouldn't be much new here. No need for this chapter at all — except how could you have a book about the Chicago Cubs that didn't at least tip the cap to the Windy City and the park over on the Northside?

So here is our whirlwind tour of baseball season in Northern Illinois — a few fun little tales emerged during the Catalina research, and bear repeating.

From an interview with Randy Jackson in *Banks to Sandberg to Grace*, Carrie Muskat's delightful remembrance: "I remember — and this is probably true for anyone who has ever played for the Cubs — they love the hours. It's a daytime job. You go to work at 9:30 and get off at 4:30. It was a great place to play because of that.

"Chicago fans were probably the best fans I was ever around. Back then, we drew only 6,000 or 7,000 a game — we were habitually a 7th or 8th-place team...The fans, you love the fans. I really enjoyed being around them. Of course, there were some...but the majority came out to see baseball and loved the Cubs, win or lose."

The hallowed grounds, the Friendly Confines, the stadium formerly known as Weegham Park.

Bob Rush, on the crowd: "The fans in Chicago seemed to get on 2 guys, Roy Smalley and Bill Voiselle. The fans get on you, and the press gets on you, and it kinda builds..."

> "The fans in Chicago made it tough on Smalley — just 'cuz he threw it over the 1st-baseman's head."
>
> Phil Cavarretta

In *Wrigleyville*, Peter Golenbock recounts a Bill Veeck yarn about one of his more successful Ladies' Day promotions:

"One Friday, shortly after the gates were opened, and there were 45,000 spectators inside and thousands outside, an usher came upon a little old woman who was crying. He assured her that he would find her a seat somewhere.

"'I don't want a seat,' she sobbed. 'I want to get out. I came to visit my daughter, who lives near here. Before I knew it I was caught in this terrible mob and swept inside.'"

If ebay had been around in 1940, can you imagine how much this little item might have fetched?

One fan in particular, Chicago fireman Dan Cahill, made pilgrimage with the team to Catalina nearly every Spring — and got plenty of press coverage from his Chicago sportswriting buddies. For instance, this tidbit from the 1927 *Herald & Examiner*: "Danny Cahill was turned down on his application to join the Avalon fire department because he was a complete flop during the Chicago fire of 1871. He will pilot the island sprinkling cart when it stops raining." Another day, the paper said, "Dan hated to miss the Cicero blaze that started just before the rattler left Polk & Dearborn Sts. But he was satisfied when he saw a fire at Streator on the way through."

Cub superfan Danny Cahill asks Lonnie Warneke if he knows about any blazes on the Island, 1933.

"One night," says Charlie Root's daughter, Della Root Arnold, "at the St. Catherine dining room — it was a big solarium where the players ate, and Danny was eating with the press. There was a little foyer that went through, and they had a string quartet playing — it was quite elegant. The waitress brought this huge tray — it had a big turkey cover over it, and they presented it to Danny. When he took off the lid, there were all these live lobsters! And they went off onto the floor, and of course everybody was afraid to pick 'em up! I think the newspapermen and Gabby were behind it — Danny Cahill was real close to Gabby."

That was hardly the only hazing the SuperDan endured. "They were forever hauling him off to the clubhouse for an alcohol rub from Andy Lotshaw," says Della. "He'd pour alcohol all over him, and they'd all laugh and laugh.

"He loved those Cubs, and they loved him — he was the nicest man! Wonderfully funny," Della says. "And when he died, he was buried in a Cubs jacket, holding an autographed Cubs baseball in his hand."

Stan Hack, Danny Cahill, Gabby Hartnett, & Bob Garbark, 1938.

out the other. You could see the talent he had — what a waste of talent.

"I'll tell ya why he couldn't hit in the big leagues," continues Phillibuck. "Players would get called up late in the season, and there was a hotel, a Sheraton, 3 or 4 blocks from Wrigley Field. There must've been 10 or 15 bars between the hotel and the ballpark, and he'd stop at every one and have 2 or 3 beers, and laugh with the people there. That's why he couldn't hit. He'd play his harmonica — he thought he was pretty good — and he'd be buying 'em beers, and by the time he'd come to the clubhouse...all he had was bloodshot eyes."

Fanatics, indeed: In 1928, 2 local Chicago kids (Jack Calvey and Dan Haley) paid their own way all to Catalina in hopes of a tryout. Neither ever made it to the show, but Calvey enjoyed a lengthy minor-league career...and was the starting shortstop for the Sacramento Solons in the '40s.

"They booed me plenty. But I never got mad because I knew they were right."

Dick Bartell, in his autobiography

Not accustomed to the big city, son?

Lou Novikoff was afraid to touch the ivy-covered outfield walls at Wrigley — or even get within a few feet of them. Many errors resulted; the only year he started, 1942, the Mad Russian was charged with more errors than the other 2 starting outfielders *combined*.

"Lou Novikoff, the happy Mad Russian," Phil Cavarretta grins. "All kiddin' aside, he was a great hitter — in the Coast League. But we'd bring him up, and he couldn't hit me. He was always *too* happy — every day was steak day. You'd try and give him some instructions, and it was in one ear...and

While 2,000 miles or so from the ivy-adorned walls at Wrigley, Novikoff had no trouble performing acrobatics in the field.

237

This-n-that...

* President Herbert Hoover attended the 1929 World Series at Wrigley Field. President Franklin Roosevelt attended the 1932 World Series there, too.*

* "It was cold back in Chicago," Carmen Mauro says. "They'd liquefy some of that capsicum and slap it on you, they'd throw it on you to warm you up, and that's it!"

* "In Chicago, we all stayed in a little hotel near Wrigley Field," Ox Miller says. "There wasn't much to do. In the evenings, we'd go to a picture show, or a football game at Soldier Field."

* "I was in Portland, and got called to Chicago," Corky Van Dyke says, "but I got hit in the head with a line drive."

"In Chicago, there was a place near the ballpark, Karo's," Corky adds. "It was a good eating place, and some of the ballplayers used to go in the back and play dice."

* "One time, I went to a game in Chicago — and when I went to the ladies' room," BUM Passeau recalls, "Claude hit a home run, and I missed it!"

"I played in 3 no-hitters, and I was on the bench during Larsen's perfect game," Randy Jackson says. "The greatest thing I saw was Sad Sam Jones throw a no-hitter at Wrigley. He walked about 7 people. In the 9th, he walked the first 3. Scheffing was the manager then — what are you gonna do? But he struck out the next 3."

Andy Pafko was in awe when he first arrived. "I had my locker next to Cavarretta, between him and Nicholson — 2 of the greatest Cubs who ever lived," Andy says. "When I first came up as a rookie in 1943, up from Los Angeles, where we'd won the pennant — the Cubs had 13 games left at the end of the season. I took a 3-day train ride from California. I showed up at Wrigley Field, and the 1st big-league player I met was Stan Hack. Nicholson was great, to help me from centerfield; I didn't know the hitters, so he moved me around. Big Nick would say, 'He's a pull hitter,' or 'Play this guy straight away.'"

Of course, after the career Andy had...fans were in awe of him, too. Randy Jackson tells of a doctor near his home in Athens, Georgia: "A few years ago, he asked me about Andy Pafko — he'd grown up in Chicago, and he and his brother loved the Cubs. He said Andy was their idol. So I wrote to Andy, and he sent this autographed picture, personalized, and it said 'Thanks for remembering me.' I brought it to his office, and I thought he was gonna cry. He loves it; he's still got it up in his office, and a while back he told me, 'My brother hates me for it!'"

Some Cubs (like Woody English) were so dedicated, they started working out in mid-winter, 1934 — using snowballs for chucking practice. Trainer Andy Lotshaw monitors the workout.

Cubs kids

"In Chicago, I can remember us staying at the Knickerbocker Hotel," says Larry Burgess (Smoky's son). "I remember that because I liked the name!"

Lennie Merullo's son Boots recalls Wrigley Field from a child's perspective:

"As a kid, being around those guys, it was wonderful. I thought I'd died and gone to Heaven. They only played during the day, so my father would take me to Wrigley Field. I'd run on the field while they were hitting. Peanuts Lowrey sawed off the end of a bat, so it was light enough for me to swing, and he'd pitch to me. When it got serious, time for them to do

---

* *FDR never claimed to see Babe Ruth point at anything.*

infield, I went into the stands with a sandwich, and I'd watch the game with my mother. There was a big Coke cooler in the clubhouse, and the players put a check-mark next to their name when they took one. I thought that was so great, when I wanted to get a Coke, to put a mark by somebody's name!"

Tiny Beck's dad, Clyde, expresses shock at the kind of things that are going on back in the big city.

Charlie Owen (Mickey's son) also enjoys fond childhood remembrances of Wrigley:

"As a child, I was able to go in the dugout. I could dress out. I got on the hot dog circuit. I was a little guy, real young, kinda cute — all the grown-up women loved me — and I loved hot dogs — so they all gave me hot dogs and peanuts. I got fat! I got in there as a little kid...and came back as a butterball!"

Charlie Root's daughter, Della Root Arnold, also had some frightening ganster-era memories to accompany the pleasant ones:

"In Chicago, we lived in the Swanville Apartments. One day, I noticed a car following us. I was so frightened, I still remember the license number: 319 405.** I was taking care of my brother and Tiny Beck, who was 9 months old. This man stepped out and said, 'Okay, kid, in the car!' I grabbed Tiny; my brother and got to the stairs, and I'd gotten out one scream. They rented the basement to a tailor, and he ran out — the man in the car took off. Dad asked the police to keep it out of the papers, and they did.

"One day, a man came up to Dad at the ballpark and said, 'I understand you had some trouble with your little girl. It's been taken care of.' That really scared him. And the guy said, 'If you ever have any trouble with any of these umpires, let us know.' And that *really* scared him. The car had been a rental, so we never did find out what happened. I went to stay with my grandmother in Ohio for the rest of the school year."

Gabby Hartnett, chatting with a fan at Wrigley Field. The fan turned out to be Al 'Scarface' Capone; the picture appeared in all the papers; the Commissioner was less than enthused.

Of course, Boots Murillo got his name because of nervous dad Lennie's performance at Wrigley — but Randy Jackson's 1st child narrowly escaped a similar moniker. "My first child was born at about 3 or 4 in the morning," Randy says, "so I didn't get any sleep. The game that afternoon was close; there was a runner on 2nd and 2 outs. The batter hit a grounder to me. I went over and stepped on the bag, then threw the ball to the pitcher's mound! I was half asleep. Everybody was running around and hollering; it was very embarrassing."

*** Della was 83 years old when recounting this story from 70 years earlier. This is particularly impressive to me, given the fact that I don't even know my own license plate number!*

What I Did During My Winter Non-Vacation

In Those Days, Most Ballplayers Slogged Through Blue-Collar Wintertime Jobs ... Once They'd Made It Back Home at Season's End

"I went into the funeral business with my dad, with my 2 brothers. My dad said, 'Business is bad — nobody's even sick.'"

Paul Schramka

Is Paul Schramka holding a bat, or is that the end of a shovel?

Hard to believe, but true: We're just a single generation removed from ballplayers actually having to hold down an off-season job — and we're not talking about being a sports shoe spokesmodel, ya know.

Most of the Catalina Cubs trudged their way through post-season work. And 'work' is the operative word here; sure, some of 'em had office jobs, but most of these guys plowed the back 9 somewhere, or fitted machine parts, or drove a truck. They worked farms and factories and thought nothing of it — that's what gritty, hard-working family men did after they came back from the war. They had to; baseball just didn't pay enough in those days. "My first year with the Cubs, they paid me $8,500," Lefty Chambers says. "The minimum was $6,500, and they screamed like a wounded Turk to pay me that!"

"If I had my way, I'd have stayed in the minors — so I could work another job," Jim Kirby says. "I just didn't fit in with the big leagues. The rent was so high, having my wife and children back home, I don't know how we could have afforded 2 places. The Cubs drafted me, and signed me for $800 a month. But I was making $600 at Shreveport, and that was my main reason for not caring if I went up or not — I could pick up jobs in the minors, which I couldn't do at the higher levels. After I come down from

I magine, for a moment, Barry Bonds carrying a big metal lunch bucket...wearing a hard-hat...clocking in at a factory on a cold winter's day in the Rustbelt.

Not. Poor fella might damage his manicure or get his earring caught in the machinery.

Chicago, I had the opportunity to go to Sacramento or Augusta, class A. I went there instead of AAA, for $1500, because I could work the 2nd job and end up making more money."

Lloyd Lowe felt the same pressures. "I wish I could have continued," he said, "but it was a matter of economics. Hark Rock Johnson was managing when I was in class D, in Jamestown, making a whopping $90 a month. I met him up there. I was just 18, and the season had started when I graduated from high school. I had to write home to my mother for trainfare after the season.

"In 1951, they started with the bonus ballplayers. I had a problem with my financial situation. At the end of the season, you've gotta get a job. By that time, I had a wife and 2 kids — it was a matter of economics.

"I did some welding in the offseason. After that, I was a truck driver. Our family kept getting bigger. We had 6 children — a houseful."

"Percy Jones spent the winter doing heavy work around an oil lease in Texas, so the Spring Training appeals to him like a picnic."

The Chicago Tribune, 1921

"Percy Jones, the left-hand T. & . P. Freight brakeman... after a winter of juggling box cars...will need only a little work to get himself in readiness for his summer's toil."

The Los Angeles Times, 1928

Earl Webb — who set a single-season major league record by smacking 67 doubles in 1931, after leaving Catalina for the Red Sox — was featured in the *Chicago Tribune* in 1928 for his off-season accomplishments:

Webb is a product of the coal mines. At the age of 12, he was a trapper in the anthracite mines of Tennessee, his native state. In those days he toiled 10 hours at a stretch, earning the magnificent sum of 40 cents.

Later, accepting a job as a mule driver, Earl was paid $1.50 a day at the mines. Frequently he labored 6 days...and on the Sabbath trudged 7 miles over rocky mountain trails to pitch a double-header, getting no compensation for his diamond efforts.

He still loves the vast open spaces, for we saw the big Southerner at 7 o'clock the other morning returning from a hossback ride through the canyons which abound hereabouts. He had been up and about since sunrise.

So here's a listing of the off-season jobs your Catalina Cubs plied...as well as their post-baseball careers:

Chuck Connors played basketball for the Boston Celtics. After baseball, he went to Hollywood, where he memorized scripts for a living.

Dutch Reagan, a Cubs radio man in the '30s, actually enjoyed several post-Catalina careers. He also memorized scripts for pay, then became president of the Screen Actors' Guild. After that, he became president of a global superpower. In between, he was the Governor of Catalina Island (and, as noted earlier, the rest of California, too).

Incidentally, Mr. Reagan appeared as former Catalina Cub Grover Alexander in a film entitled *The Winning Team*. This 1952 extravaganza also provided post-season employment for a handful of other ballplayers, including Cubs **Peanuts Lowery**, **Hank Sauer**, **Gene Mauch**. Lowery was a grip on several other films between baseball seasons.

The newsreel crews loved to cover the Cubs on Catalina. Sometimes, they'd let the boys help out: In 1936, Johnny Hutchings, Hal Sueme, & Lonnie Warneke got the gig.

Bill Voiselle worked for Liberty Life Insurance, and at Parke-Davis at a capsicum plant. Being mere baseball fans, we are yet to discover what 'capsicum' is.

"I had me a car lot. I sold new and used cars. The Chevrolet people put me in as a manager in Salisbury, North Carolina."

Bill Baker

Claude Passeau was a John Deere dealer. "My son runs it now," Claude says. "He has for the last 19 or 20 years." Claude also grew corn and had a grove of tung nuts in Mississippi. According to Ox Miller, who apparently discussed farming with Claude, tung nuts are used in paint, rather than cooking.

"Roy Parmelee revealed he had loafed all winter at his home in Lambertville, Michigan. He admitted he came close to getting a job as a salesman, but refused it on the grounds that it was cheaper to loaf than work for the salary offered."

Chicago Daily Times, 1938

Cy Block went into life insurance. "He was a legend with Mutual Benefit," Harriet Block beams. "He was the leading agent in the U.S.!"

Need any insurance? Before he retired, Cy Block would've fixed ya up.

Bob Garbark worked in a zipper factory in Meadville, Pennsylvania — and was pleased to learn the new Cub uniforms would be equipped with zippers, rather than the more traditional button-down front, for 1938. "If any of the boys...have any difficulty getting in or out of the zipper-equipped suits," Warren Brown wrote for the *Chicago Herald and Examiner*, "it is a consoling thought to know that there is a zipper expert no farther away than the bullpen."

Bob Garbark in 1938. Note the fashionable new style in flannels, with the zippered front replacing the archaic button-up technology.

Dewey Williams, who lived in Georgia in 1946 (the year a convoluted gubernatorial election left 3 men claiming the job), told sportswriters how he spent the winter: "I was busy reading the papers every day to find out who was governor."

Carmen Mauro: "In the off-season, I went back to Chicago," Carmen says. "My family had a little snack shop — a small restaurant in Cicero. We served spaghetti and had a fountain in a Polish and Czechoslovakian neighborhood." After that, he was a college baseball coach/athletic director — having discovered that he should have either A) moved the shop to Little Italy, or B) sold kielbasa sausage instead.

Ed Jabb went on to battle blazes for the Chicago Fire Department — for more than 25 years.

Paul Erickson worked — really worked — in a steel plant in Fon du Lac, Wisconsin. "No tummy on me this spring," he told the papers in 1947...before going 7-12.

Billy Rogell is probably the only Catalina Cub who has a street named after him. He was a city councilman in Detroit for *40* years, from 1942 through 1981. Among his achievements: Billy was instrumental in making the Detroit airport a world-class facility, so the entrance road is called "Rogell Drive."

Dad! There was apparently a Cub population explosion in 1951. Johnny Schmitz, Bob Rush, Bob Ramazotti, Frank Hiller, and Ron Northey all paced the waiting room while their respective wives gave birth that winter. (Photo-showing was definitely big on Catalina that Spring!)

Coaker Triplett owned his own gas station in Boone, North Carolina.

Guy Bush, pumpin' gas — a competitor of Coaker Triplett's?

Lefty Chambers ran a community recreation program in Spokane, before becoming a Certified Financial planner.

Gabby Hartnett apparently *ate* during the offseason: "The mere suggestion of a hill climb," the *Chicago Evening American* reported in 1924, "brought tears to the eyes of 'Gabby' Hartnett, who is 20 pounds overweight."

Lon Warneke gobbled, too. In 1935, manager Charlie Grimm said: "I'm especially ticked over Warneke. He has gained twelve pounds this winter. I asked him how he did it and he told me he had been on a 'quail diet.' He hunted for sixty consecutive days and shot 261 birds.'"

"After I finished playing ball, I came back and took an examination and got a mail carrier's job. I got an appointment from President Harry Truman to carry the mail, and I did that for 30 years. I'm retired now, and Shorty and I pretty much stay here in Live Oak County, Texas — we don't get out much."

Ox Miller

Grover Cleveland Alexander apparently tried a similar diet. The *Chicago Tribune* reported in 1923 that "Alex...spent the winter in St. Paul, Nebraska, in the open air, playing golf and hunting birds and rabbits."

Bob Scheffing, like ***Matthew*** (of New Testament fame) was a tax collector.

Matthew, not Scheffing.

Otto Vogel coached high school basketball in Elgin, Illinois in the '20s...and **Kiki Cuyler** played basketball... while **Al Todd**, **Clyde McCullough**, and **Ted Pawelek** refereed basketball games in the '40s.

Line Drive Nelson — a very, *very* bad name for a pitcher* — was a pugilist. He "thought he might make his living via the jolt and the jab," wrote 'Jimmy the Cork' (a much better nickname) Corcoran for the *Chicago American* in 1930. "He looks the part of your rough and ready athlete."

See? We're really not making this stuff up!

Paul Schramka, while not embalming: "I still played semi-pro ball until I was 40. We had the global world baseball tournament in Milwaukee — teams from 4 continents."

Johnny Klippstein: "I'm gonna see Paul Schramka in a few weeks for an Old-Timers meeting. I'm the president of the Chicago Old-Timers' Association, and he heads the one in Wisconsin. He's a heck of a guy — he has a great sense of humor. He gave me a card from his funeral home, and on the back it says, 'Thank you for smoking.'"

"Did you hear what the funeral director said? 'Drop over sometime.'"

Paul Schramka

Several more stayed in baseball. **Mickey Owen** ran a world-famous baseball school, for instance. Here's how some of the others kept close to the game . . .

Corky Van Dyke: "Warren Hacker called me and says, scout for Kansas City. I did it for a while, but I'd lived out of a suitcase for a long enough time. I've been a police officer, I've worked in a funeral home, I've done a lot of things."

Lee Anthony spent more than 50 years in baseball. After playing, he managed the Seminole, Oklahoma team for the Kansas City A's...then scouted for the A's from 1958-1963. "Twinkletoes Selkirk wanted me to go to Washington D.C. with the Senators." When the franchise went to Texas as the Rangers, he continued to scout for them. He finally retired from the scouting bureau in 1986 — after spending 6 decades in professional baseball.

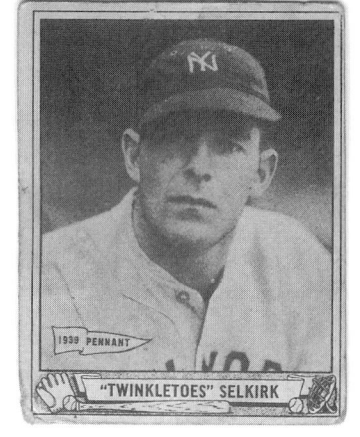

Nope — definitely can't make this stuff up!

Hub Kittle is now in his 8th decade of pro ball. Hub coached on the World Champ St. Louis Cardinals in 1982...2 years after he finally retired from active play at the age of 63. (He's the oldest man to ever play in a professional game, pitching a shutout inning for Springfield in 1980...at the age of 63.) He's still active as a scout for the Seattle Mariners, well into his 80s.

As a youngster trying to make his mark on Catalina, Hub went fishin'. "One of my great friends, Gene Feeling, an outfielder — we had a rowboat, and we'd go where they took the glass-bottom boat," Hub says. "I talked him into rowing so he could strengthen his arms, since I'd been fishing and in the boats ever since I was a kid. There was a Greek restaurant, the Acme Cafe, on the corner there near where the boats launched. We made him a deal: I'd furnish all the fish, and he'd give me a $5 meal ticket, all punched with holes. We'd fill the boat all the way up with sheephead and fish like that. We ate well!"

Bobby Mattick is in his 8th decade of pro ball, too. He's still VP of Baseball Operations for the Toronto Blue Jays...after years of scouting, front-office work,

---

* *Line Drive Nelson's lifetime ERA was 5.25; his won-loss record, 33-42. 'Line Drive,' indeed!*

coaching, and managing (he was the Jays' 1st-ever skipper, in 1980). But before that, he needed an off-season job in the late '30s. "I went up to PK Wrigley," Bobby recalls, "and I said, 'Mr. Wrigley, I want to get started working in the off-season.'

"And he said, 'I'll put you to work in St. Louis.' That's where I was living. So I went with this guy, and we're goin' to all the grocery stores, puttin' up displays with gum in 'em. I went home that night, and told my folks I wasn't gonna do this — I guess I thought I was gonna be president or somethin'! So I quit after one day."

Cal McLish is still scouting, too. He started with the Phillies in 1964, then followed Gene Mauch to the Expos. "After that, I coached in Milwaukee for 7 years and was there for the World Series in 1982. I went to the front office after that, then was out of baseball for a while, before joining Seattle part-time for Spring Training in 1992."

Ben Wade was the first West Coast scout for the New York Mets in the early '60s. Then, he was a scout for the Dodgers for 10 years, starting in 1963. From 1973 to 1991, Ben was Scouting Director for the Dodgers. He started in pro ball in 1939 — which means Ben spent 7 decades in professional baseball.

Wayne Terwilliger is still managing in pro baseball — working for the Fort Worth Cats. Twig coached for the Minnesota Twins from 1986-1993 — where he won 2 World Series rings and was an A.L. All-Star Game coach twice. He was named the top 1st base coach in the A.L. by *USA Today* in 1991. But he still has grandiose career schemes: "I went back in the off-season and got my degree from Western Michigan — I wanted to do some writing. I'm writing a book now."

Turk Lown, recently inducted into the Pueblo Sports Hall of Fame in Colorado: "I coached American Legion ball, and of course my kids played for years."

Don Dunker is another Hall-of-Famer — he's a plaque-toting member of the Indiana Sports Hall of Fame. Don was also was a pro scout for 20 years...for the Reds, Royals, Dodgers, and Mets.

Lennie Merullo scouted for the Cubs for 25 years. (His grandson, Matt — who caught for the Indians and White Sox — is now a scout for the Arizona Diamondbacks.) "I was in the office when they signed Ernie Banks," Lennie says. "When I took the scouting job, it was for less money than I was making at the Prince Macaroni Company!"

Della Root Arnold, Charlie Root's daughter:

"In 1937, I went to Boots Weber and said, 'I'd like a summer job.' He told me I could do Ladies' Night tickets, 'but don't tell anybody who you are — because you don't need a job, and they do.'

"So I was in the sorting room, and Dad comes through and says, 'Hello, Della!'

"And Stan Hack comes through and says, 'Hello, Della!'

"And Dizzy comes through and says, 'Hello, Della!' So everybody wonders, who's this 18-year-old blonde who seems to know all the ballplayers?! I got quite a reputation. And I got $5."

Gene Mauch spent a lot of years in dugouts, punctuated by the occasional jaunt to the field to have a friendly chat with an umpire.

Gene Mauch's post-playing '2nd' baseball career was probably the most famous of all the Catalina Cubs: Skip was a major-league manager for 26 years, from 1960-87.

Philadelphia Phillies	1960-1968
Montreal Expos (their 1st manager)	1969-1975
Minnesota Twins	1976-1980
California Angels	1981-1987

His teams made it to the League Championship Series with the Angels in 1982 and 1986. And he's on 3 all-time lists for managers:

Games managed	5th, 3942 games
Wins	9th, 1902 victories
Losses	3rd, 2037 defeats

Some players had *dual* post-playing careers: they stayed in baseball, and they also did something else. A few notable examples:

Ed Chandler pitched batting practice for the Dodgers after retiring. Then, "I went into the stock brokerage business in Los Angeles, and did that for more than 20 years. I was a member of the Wilshire Country Club in Los Angeles for 35 years. That was major league living — in baseball, I only made $5,000 a year for a couple years!"

Lefty Carnett managed in the minors, but "The Cubs told me I was a lousy manager, so I went to work at the Burlington Country Club in Iowa. I stayed 5 years, then went into the chemical business for 20 years."

Howard Auman: "After I retired from playing in 1951, Milltown had a semi-pro baseball team...and they wanted me to manage. So they gave me a job. I thought I could still play, but I couldn't. After that, I bought a grocery store in Fayetteville...then, I sold that and moved to Sanford in 1958 and went to work for a furniture manufacturer. I spent 25 years at the plant. It was sold to Singer, and I worked for Singer for 14 years as a supervisor. I retired 19 years ago. After I retired, people started asking me to refinish their furniture for them, and I've been busy ever since."

Red Adams was the Los Angeles Dodgers pitching coach from 1969-1980. He was a pretty good one, too, if you believe what Don Sutton had to say:

"Red Adams is a standard by which every pitching coach should be measured. No person ever meant more to me in my career than Red Adams, and without him I wouldn't be standing in Cooperstown today."

Don Sutton, while being inducted into the Major League Baseball Hall of Fame in 1998

Red took an interesting detour between his playing days...and his coaching career:

"I wish I'd have had enough brains to go to college. I grew up doing farm work. Years later, I got into carpentry. I was a carpenter in the off-season, and I knew a guy who was working for the studios, so I went over there...and they offered me a job.

"I worked in the studio a bit — I was one of the grips. I was lucky enough to get in on some shows. It was grunt work; you'd do the rigging off some scaffolding, setting up, tearing sets down. You had to get some miles on you to do a TV show — that was a gravy job. I worked for a few different studios. You'd go down to the union hall, and go 2 or 3 places over the course of a few weeks.

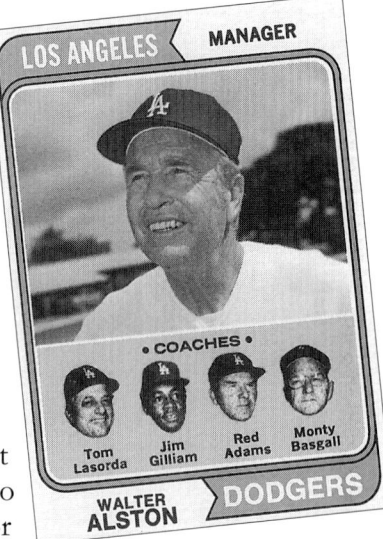

"I got in good with the Goldwyn studios. I worked on *Porgy and Bess*, and went on location to Red Rock Canyon, working on *The Big Country*. Chuck Connors was in that, before he made it real big. So was Burl Ives, and Charleton Heston, and Gregory Peck. It was a big Western extravaganza; we worked out there for several weeks.

"In the studio itself, I worked on *The Loretta Young Show*. And *The Apartment* — Billy Wilder directed that. He was a funny guy. Jack Lemmon and Shirley MacLaine were in that."

Red Adams in 1947, warming up for a series of careers.

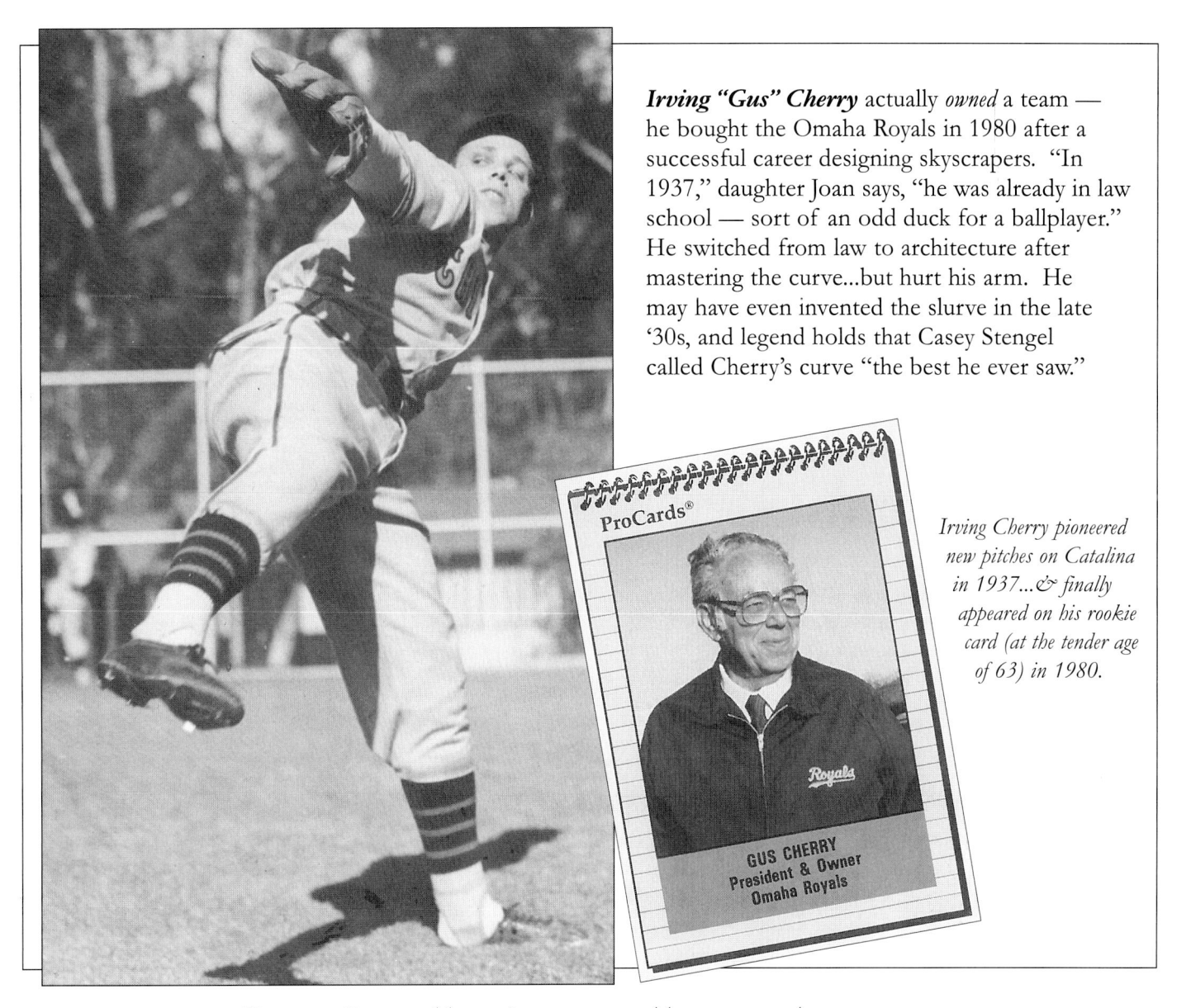

Irving "Gus" Cherry actually *owned* a team — he bought the Omaha Royals in 1980 after a successful career designing skyscrapers. "In 1937," daughter Joan says, "he was already in law school — sort of an odd duck for a ballplayer." He switched from law to architecture after mastering the curve...but hurt his arm. He may have even invented the slurve in the late '30s, and legend holds that Casey Stengel called Cherry's curve "the best he ever saw."

Irving Cherry pioneered new pitches on Catalina in 1937...& finally appeared on his rookie card (at the tender age of 63) in 1980.

GUS CHERRY
President & Owner
Omaha Royals

Roy Smalley's excellent adventure

Roy Smalley, Jr. must claim the prize for the most unusual off-season career. The Cubs News reported it innocuously enough in 1949:

Roy Smalley, whose home is in Los Angeles, spent most of the winter on Catalina Island working as a laborer to toughen up and put on weight.

While that may sound pretty much like the unglamorous stuff which occupied the other guys, consider that Roy did things like herding buffalo.** Perhaps we should just let Roy tell the tales:

"I had a more-than-unusual experience on Catalina. I was there for a couple of months one winter. My 1st off-season, I spent a winter there in the high country.

"I spent the winter of 1948-1949 there. After the last game, I got all packed up and was going to my car — PK and some of the staff were still there working around, looking for ways to improve the park. He was a very nice man, and he stopped me to say goodbye. I went home and after 2 or 3 weeks, I got a letter from him saying, 'You looked tired and worn out. Charlie Grimm's a great outdoorsman, like you — do you want to go to Catalina and work outside, and have some fun working there?'

"I wasn't married at the time, so that sounded like a pretty good idea. I worked for an old cowboy who was Wrigley's 1st horse-wrangler — Jack White, the old cowboy who was a fixture there for many years. He was a jack-of-all-trades, ran the livestock and was a deputy sheriff — he was born on a ranch in New Mexico, that's where he and his wife Elma were from — he was the real article.

** The 'buffalo' on Catalina are technically bison. I include this footnote to avoid getting letters from half a dozen irate purists.

"We'd hunt wild boar and shoot quail, and arrange the hunting parties for guests — they'd hunt deer. We went into wild areas, and dug out springs.

"Don (Carlsen) and I shared a unit — his cleaning was probably better than my cooking! We met a couple of local girls; there wasn't a heck of a lot to do. Feminine companionship was nice to have after being in the mountains with pigs and goats and buffaloes!

With the buffalo droppings washed off, Smalley is now able to swing away once again.

"I was only involved twice with the buffaloes. A writer and photographer from the *Los Angeles Times* came over — our job was to find them, so they could observe them. That was kinda fun. Those buffalo are big, strong, independent creatures — Jack said you can only 'loosely' herd them, just sort of encourage them to move in a particular direction.

"The other time with the buffalo was, somebody called the ranch one day and said one was hurt. They had gone through an area called Middle Canyon, and had seen a buffalo struggling on a high hill, as though caught in some barbed wire. Jack and I jumped in a jeep and went to that area, and saw this pretty big lump on top of a pretty steep hill. This buffalo cow had caught one of her hind legs on an ancient barbed-wire fence, and had fallen head-down. Thing is, buffalo don't have an esophagus, so with the head below — there's no way it could survive very long, and it had choked. She was dead, and stiff as can be — so we had to cut her loose and try to push her down the hill. Well, we had to work at it for quite a while, and we pushed and pushed, and finally there she went — rear-end over teakettle, tumbling down the hillside. Then she came to a stop, lodged against some rocks. By the time we caught up with her, she was loose as a rag doll. We started to skin her out. She was older, so she was real tough, and we were cutting away and wondering how we were gonna haul all this off when this truckload of Hispanic workers came by. Jack was real fluent in Spanish, so he starts talking to these guys, and they worked out a deal: We'll skin her out and make the hide, and you can have the meat. They were all over that — they really liked that, so it worked out okay.

"One day — it was a cold, rainy day — I got together with Hard Rock Johnson and Jack White and Larry French. We went out on horseback to hunt quail. Now, California quail are runners; they don't hold still, so the way you hunt 'em is to ride across the foothills, stop and listen at the canyons. If you hear them, you get off your horse and go on foot. It's fairly rigorous hunting, but fun. This day, we rode and rode and came to a split; to the left there was a canyon, and another smaller canyon to the right.

No, you're not looking at the back of a nickel; these are direct descendants of the buffs that Roy Smalley worked with.

Roy said, "You ride up this one, and we'll go the other way." I went up, and pretty soon I heard some quail. So I got off my horse, and started climbing — I felt like an Indian. I heard the singing, and I brought up my shotgun and peered over the edge of a creekbed. There was this giant dead tree, about 50 feet long, I

feeding. We drove around the herd to cut them off, but they got scared and ran — the wanted to get back to the rocky coastal part where they like to stay. But we ran them toward the dry wash, and they started going up the top, where it was too steep. It was like a shooting gallery — we burned a lot of powder. We ended up with 22 goats, and some were big, with spreading horns. We stacked 'em in the back of the truck and filled that up. Then we started tying their legs together and laying them over the front of the fork part in front of the jeep. We got them back, and it was my job to skin them out — all 22! I smelled like a goat for 3 weeks...

"I never liked to eat goat meat, but some of the locals liked the young goats."

Jack White takes a break from managing the ranch in '33...to show Lon Warneke a few of the ropin' tricks he performs when the Cubs are back East.

guess, lying on its side, with all the branches making a lot of brush. The quail had gathered there, and there were dozens of 'em — they looked like ants! But I was dumb — instead of getting the other guys, I figured I can get 25 of 'em! But they all flew off, and it sounded like thunder — and when I got over there, I'd only gotten one! They never let me hear the end of that goof! I really took a beating from those guys — I shouldn't have told them!

"Before Spring Training began, we were taking care of the bird park. One of the things Jack White did was keep meat for the meat-eating birds. They had eagles, hawks, and vultures — they don't mess around with mice or anything little like that — yeah, they eat meat! Somebody came by and let him know the meat was getting low. So we picked up another cowboy, a guy named John, and we went past the Isthmus toward the West End of the island. John had his pickup truck, and Jack had his jeep with the bulldozer attachment at the front, something like a forklift. I had a 30-30 carbine, and they had their guns too. It was a balmy day, and we were out there early. We saw a herd of goats on the flatlands,

The back of Roy's 1954 Bowman card tells us:

"Frankie Frisch, who used to manage the Cubs, always said that Roy looked like a movie star..."

Yessir, the Catalina Cubs — like other ballplayers of their time — were tough characters. And while there are certainly some strong-willed competitors on today's teams...

...somehow, I can't quite picture Barry Bonds skinning a buffalo...

The Other Channel Islands...
& Isles Further Out To Sea

There Were a Few Other Ports Around the Deep Blue Oceans...

"I didn't like it. You're tied up, you can't do anything. I just wouldn't like to ever live on an island. I went to Hawaii — and I couldn't wait to get home. Did I ever go back to Catalina? Are you kidding? I'm a city boy."

Lonny Frey

You say potato, Lonny Frey says patata.

I say tomato, Lonny says tamata.

Golly, I'd walk on hot coals sprinkled with broken glass to get to an island; Mr. Linus Frey prefers the security blanket of a big city. All kinds, it takes.

Islands. Baseball islands. As we mentioned at the outset, it's not a combo you usually think of. But it brings to mind some interesting trivia:

Name the **4** major league teams who've played their home games on an island.

First: The New York Giants, whose Polo Grounds occupied a chunk of northern Manhattan. So yes, "The Giants win the pennant, the Giants win the pennant..." was uttered on an isle. Willie Mays played his rookie season on an isle. The last man to hit .400 in the *National* League (Bill

Whatever you do, don't tell Lonny Frey that he spent the 1st 4 years of his major-league career (1933-36, Brooklyn/Long Island) & the last season (1948, New York Giants/Manhattan Island) playing his home games out at sea. (Notice his desperation to keep both feet off island soil.)

250

Terry, 1930, .401)...did it playing his home games on an island.

Ironically, Yankee Stadium — in view, across the Harlem River in the Bronx borough — is *not* on an island, but mainland New York state. Go figure.

So natch, the Brooklyn Dodgers also played on an island — Long Island, to be precise. Yes, after all these years, we must shift our brains to realize that Ebbets Field sat on the surface of an isle.

The 3rd island-based big-league squad? A hint, if you still require one: They're still doing it! Yes, Virginia, there is a major league team that still plays their home games on an island, out to sea. It's the Mets, o'course — but they aren't on Manhattan. Like the Dodgers, years before, they, too, go to work on Long Island...at Shea Stadium.

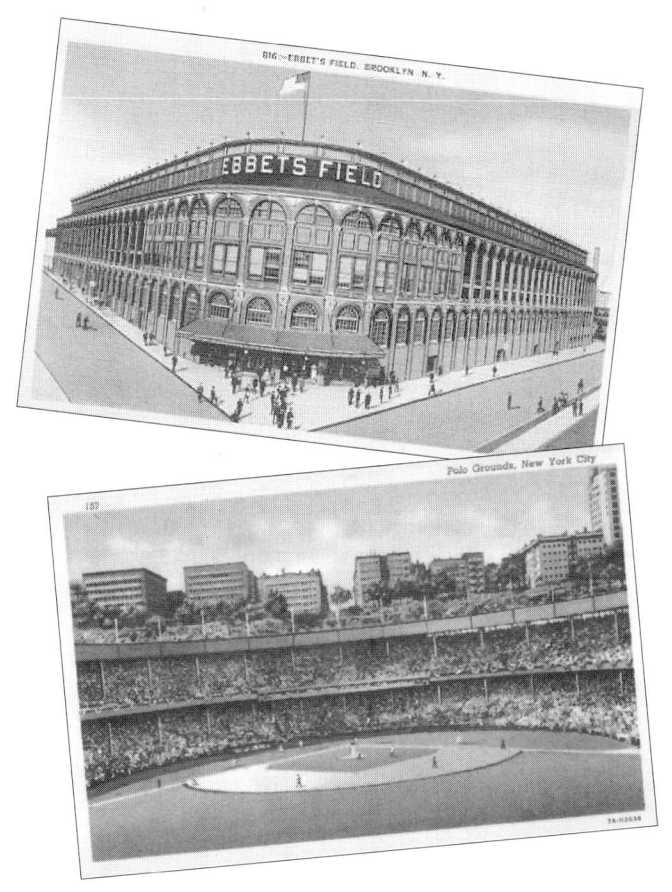

Youse tellin' me these ballparks was on islands? Fu-getta-bout-it!

Not to disparage New York, but it just ain't da same. I mean, when I think of islands, I think sunshine and swaying palms and all that — not skyrise tenements and snow on the sidewalks and the fragrance of diesel smoke in the air, with a thousand yellow taxicabs soaring by as the drivers cuss me out with a thick Bronxian dialect. I *do* ♥ New York, Rudy, but — it just don't feel like no island, yuh know what I mean?

Oh, by the way, as though it matters to anyone — the 4th is the Montréal Expos. Both their original ballyard (Jarry Park) and newer rendition (Olympic Stadium) occupy the Île-de-Montréal, which is surrounded by a pair of rivers. In 2003, the lightly-attended Expos decided to play 22 of their home games on yet another isle, Puerto Rico. (Hope it helps.) Ironically, the home field in San Juan is Hiram Bithorn Stadium — named after the one-time Cub pitcher!

Which brings us back to Catalina. And more island trivia.

A lot of people don't know there even *is* a Catalina Island, and even fewer know there's a whole chain of islands off the Southern California coast. They're called the Channel Islands, which seems to make some sense since they're across the Channel from the mainland. There are 8 of them (not counting semi-artificial Balboa Island at Newport Beach... totally-artificial and industrially-zoned Terminal Island...those funky little oil-riggy semi-islands in Long Beach Harbor...or assorted and sundry harbor rocks):

* Santa Cruz, the largest

* Santa Barbara, the smallest

* Anacapa, the closest to the mainland — 11 miles away

* San Miguel, the most remote

* Santa Rosa, between San Miguel and Santa Cruz

* San Nicolas, used by the U.S. Navy for target practice and thus off-limits to most humans

* San Clemente, also a bomb-lobbing ground, also forbidden

* And Santa Catalina (the official name), usually shortened to 'Catalina,' and formerly used for baseball

Several years ago, in fact, there was a nifty novel called *A Little Piece of Paradise* — which was set on the islands. A lovely book, that. Unfortunately, I think it's out of print now. Nonetheless, there is a copy in the one-room Avalon library, and they'd be happy to lend it to you for a look.

Bill Voiselle recalls, "We'd set around the lobby, went fishin' — the mayor took a bunch of us out to Seal Island." (Seal Island is an uninhabitable rocky outcropping, covered with bird poop.)

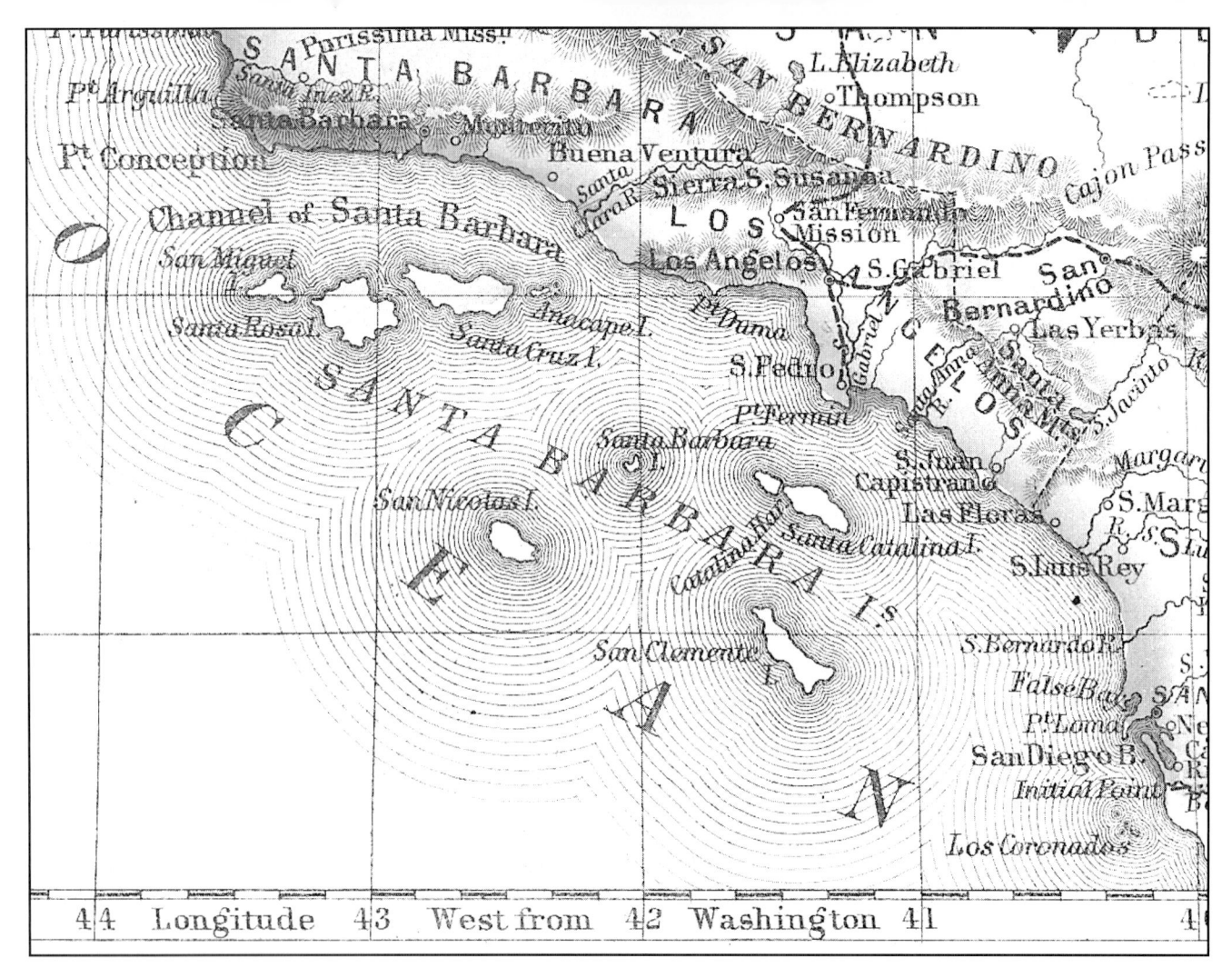

"When I played in the Coast League," Cal McLish says, "we'd take a charter boats and go fishing for calico bass and striped bass out there. It was kinda fun to see those fish grab ahold of your bait — the water was so clear, you could see down 20 or 30 feet!"

There's no record of baseball on the other Channel Islands, although we suspect that some takes place on San Nicolas and San Clemente — since servicemen are stationed there, and where servicemen are stationed a baseball match is often known to break out.

Except for those 2 (and Catalina), the rest make up the Channel Islands National Park. That means you can camp there, with permits and all that, if you like to hike and cook things over the Sterno.

Other offshore Spring Training sites

The trivia mounts: Did ya know other big league teams took Spring drills on other islands? True, true. The publishers provide this handy chart as a public service:

Team	Island in Question	Years in Particular
Yankees, New York	Bermuda	1913
Giants, New York	Cuba	1937
Dodgers, Brooklyn	Cuba	1941-1942 & 1947*
Dodgers, Brooklyn	Hispaniola**	1948
Pirates, Pittsburgh	Cuba	1953

*Should the words, "1947" & "Brooklyn Dodgers" also bring the phrase, "Jackie Robinson" to mind, take yourself an extra plantain for heads-up play. It is sadly fascinating to note that in Spring Training of his breakthrough year, Jackie was not allowed to stay at the team hotel in Havana, the fabled Hotel Nacionál (where Desi Arnaz performed before he became Ricky Ricardo). Jackie had to bunk in a military dorm.

**The Dodgers actually trained in the Domincan Republic, which shares the island of Hispaniola with Haiti. Or is that getting to be more information than you, or Sammy Sosa of said D.R., would care to know?

The White Sox gave Mexico City a try in 1907. While Mexico City is not on an island, it is technically overseas, which doesn't quite make sense but we'll go with it anyway.

Because of the frequent trades between the Bums and the Cubbies, a lot of Catalina Cubs actually went to Spring Training on both Catalina and Cuba — multi-island players, particularly when they played their road games on Manhattan Island against the Giants or Long Island while with the Dodgers.

> "The great DiMaggio is himself again...Do you remember when he used to come to the Terrace? I wanted to take him fishing but I was too timid to ask him."
>
> Santiago (chatting with subtitles to Manolin), in Cojímar, Cuba, as recorded by E. Hemingway in *The Old Man and the Sea*

And plenty of the guys played post-season ball in the Caribbean, too — like Ken Raffensberger and Turk Lown. "I played Winter ball in Cuba, went to Venezuela with the Dodgers, with Durocher," Turk says. "Talk about great baseball fans — they really love the game, know the game down there."

"In Cuba, we worked out of the old West Point Field House," Cal McLish recalls.

John J. McGraw, legendary manager of the New York Giants, got around when he was in Cuba — like the great DiMaggio, he earned himself a mention in *The Old Man and the Sea*:

"Tell me about the great John J. McGraw." He said *Jota* for J.

"He used to come to the terrace sometimes too in the older days. But he was rough and harsh-spoken and difficult when he was drinking. His mind was on horses as well as baseball. At least he carried lists of horses at all times in his pocket and frequently spoke the names of horses on the telephone."

"He was a great manager," the boy said. "My father thinks he was the greatest."

"Because he came here the most times," the old man said. "If Durocher had continued to come here each year then your father would think him the greatest manager."

And then ol' *Jota* came to Catalina, for a series of exhibition games against the Cubs. Harry Williams, writing in the *Los Angeles Times*, 1932:

"Rather a unique event for two major league clubs, representing the two largest cities in American, to clash on an island a short distance off the coast of Southern California."

"But it will offer no new sensation for John J. McGraw. He is the barnstorming buccaneer of baseball, figuratively speaking. Twice he has cruised the Spanish Main and its environs demonstrating inside baseball to those sitting in darkness and playing cricket and ukuleles. He has invaded the Hawaiian Islands, the Philippine Islands, Ceylon, the British Isles and Brooklyn with baseball teams during his travels. After showing the inhabitants of Catalina and the Cubs how the game is played he will tour the Thousand Islands and perhaps retire."

John Jota McGraw, wearing a sweater because he apparently did not yet realize that you could play baseball on islands that were warm & sunny, rather than cold & grey.

> "I was in the Pacific, and we went to all those islands — we didn't know the names of half of 'em!"
>
> Ed Jabb, recalling his ballplaying days with Uncle Sam's squads

Another notable islander: Mike Gonzalez, a Cuba native and national hero there. Mike was a Catalina Cub, before becoming the first Cuban manager in the major leagues (for the Cards). The *Chicago American* reported in 1928,

"Don Miguel Gonzalez has informed Marse Joe (McCarthy) that he is now roaring to go...The Don, who Winters in Cuba, underwent a preliminary conditioning siege at Havana, working out for ten days before embarking for the magic island, and now whips the ball around the diamond in mid-season style."

Mike Gonzalez: multi-lingual, multi-islandic baseball man.

More recently, the Dodgers were fined $75,000 in 1999 by the U.S. Treasury Dept. for holding a tryout camp in currently-embargoed Cuba. Cuba is embargoed, in part, because we don't like the way Fidel Castro, the unanimously-elected *presidente* (or some such), runs it. Of course, Mr. Castro, a big *beisbol* fan and former lousy pitcher, actually got a tryout with the Washington Senators (of all teams!) in the '40s.

Ed Chandler, who was based on Tinian Island in World War II, island-hopped throughout his pre-Catalina career. "I trained with the Dodgers in Santo Domingo, and we flew over from Vero Beach and played a game in Cuba," he says. Lloyd Lowe was stationed on Treasure Island, up the coast in San Francisco Bay. Cy Block served on Ellis Island. And Bob Borkowski also enjoyed isle-based duty — in fact, he was stationed in Hawaii with the Navy when he got a tryout (and a contract) with the Cubs.

And beyond...

For years, Oahu has been the home diamondhead for the Hawaii Islanders of the Pacific Coast League — after the Sacramento Solons jumped pond to bring near-major-league ball to Honolulu in 1961. Quite a few stars have passed through paradise to the bigs — like Tony Gwynn, Barry Bonds, Mets skipper Bobby Valentine, and San Francisco Giants bench coach Ron Wotus (a future major league managers in the wings). And lest we forget, long-time Catalina batting-practice hurler Clarence Kumalae originally hailed from Hawaii.

Between his major league appearances (Cubs, 1938, & Dodgers, 1950), Al Epperly pitched all over the place — including Cienfuegos, Cuba.

In the early '30s, in fact, Babe Ruth smacked a few dingers on Hawaii (or *off* Hawaii, actually)...as he and other Hall-of-Famers (like Lou Gehrig) barnstormed to Japan. Speaking of Japan, there's more islandball. Have you caught any of the recently-televised major league games from thither? And don't forget: Sadaharu Oh of the Tokyo Giants blasted more homers than anybody (even Hammerin' Hank Aaron).

Before there was Ichiro, Sadaharu Oh hit 868 home runs — all on islands in the Pacific.

前人未踏の記録へ挑戦！

So there ya have it. You didn't think they played baseball on islands, did ya? Catalina, Manhattan, Long, Bermuda, Cuba, Hispaniola, Île-de-Montréal, Puerto Rico, Oahu, Japan — the list goes on. Hope I have enough Spray Mount to make scrapbooks for all of those!

Mr. Wrigley, PK, & The Executive Team

Meanwhile, Back at the Tower... They Made A Lot of Chewing Gum, a Few Good Baseball Decisions, & Way Too Many Bad Ones

"I have always wanted a World Championship team."
William Wrigley, 1930

"They still do play a World Series, don't they? It's been so long, I don't remember."
Philip Wrigley, 36 championship-less years later

A brief primer for the casual fan: There were 2 Wrigleys. There was the dad, William Wrigley, Jr., and the son, Philip — known to many as PK.

One built a baseball dynasty; the other dismantled it.

William Wrigley, Jr.

William Wrigley was a giant. A captain of industry. A hero of Horatio-Algeresish and Walt-Disneyesque proportion. He built an empire, turned a fledgling industry into a massive one, and had a positive impact on thousands of families.

He began working in the family soap business (that's right, soap — not gum) as a child, hawking bars of the stuff in Philly (that's right, Philly — not Chicago). Ever the brilliant promoter, he tested different premiums to see which sold the most soap. Sticks of gum won, hands-down. Before long, more people wanted the gum than the soap. Bill got the message.

He invested in the Cubs in 1916 and became owner in 1919. Meanwhile, he had a winter place in Pasadena. From there, the leap to Catalina is easy to see. He bought the Island in 1919, too — quite a year for the accountants!

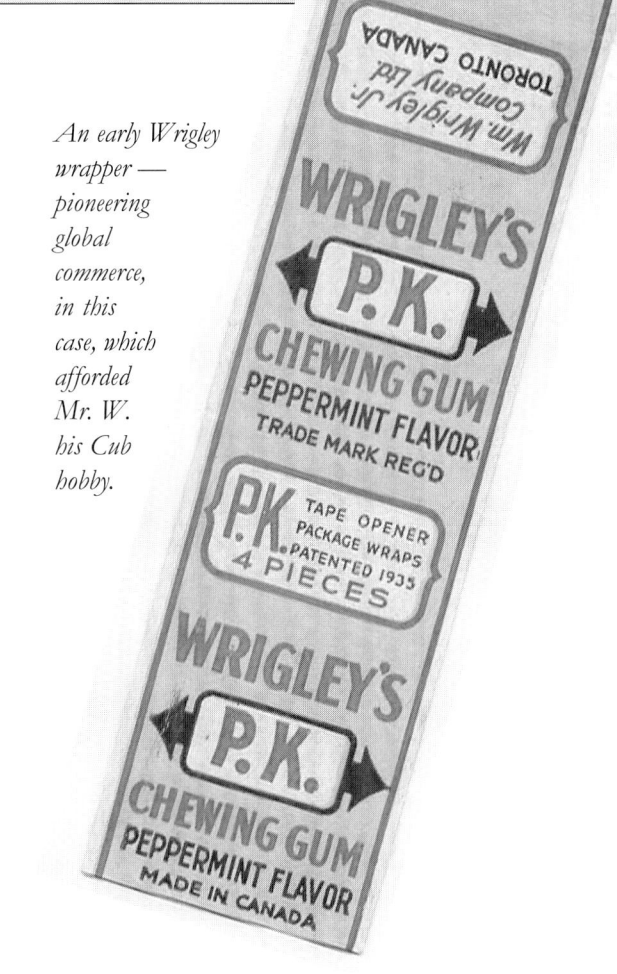

An early Wrigley wrapper — pioneering global commerce, in this case, which afforded Mr. W. his Cub hobby.

Always the dapper dresser, William Wrigley welcomes manager Rogers Hornsby & family to his private isle in 1931.

Mr. Wrigley practically invented Catalina during the '20s, pouring millions into his private island. He paved roads, built homes and hotels, added piers and steamships and installed utilities, put up the Casino and just about everything else that's there now except the mountains themselves. The Avalon you see today, basically, is the same as the one he'd completed before his death in 1932.

He built his mansion on a hilltop overlooking everything — the mainland, the town, the Bay, the back of the Island, and of course the ballpark. It's called Mt. Ada, after his wife. Today, it's a bed-n-breakfast. "William Wrigley built his house so his bedroom suite would look down on the field," says the Hon. Edgar Taylor, who grew up on the Island before becoming a Superior Court Judge in San Jose.

He hosted baseball meetings there, like the 1926 annual convention of the National Association of Professional Baseball Leagues. Judge Kennesaw Mountain Landis gave the opening speech, and plenty of other dignitaries were on hand. He also hosted President Calvin Coolidge and President Herbert Hoover. When President Warren G. Harding died in San Francisco in 1923, he was on his way to visit the Wrigleys on Catalina.

Islanders still worship William Wrigley; he started new companies (like the Catalina Pottery there) during the Depression primarily to create jobs, and was generous with just about everyone.

He loved baseball. "To me," he said in a speech honoring baseball players who'd served in World War I, "the Cubs are my greatest asset." His enthusiasm was easy to see. In the Spring of 1921, when he was 60, *the Los Angeles Times* reported,

"Mr. Wrigley was out on the field to see the boys work out and he stayed throughout the morning. He seemed as full of zip and ginger as any of the youngsters. His spontaneous laugh and appreciative encouragement seemed to put the boys on their mettle and the morning's work was the snappiest since Evers has been trying them out."

For many years, the Cubs issued a team set of baseball cards — available at the park or by mail. This is Mr. Wrigley's 1932 card, honoring him right after he passed away.

The Guiding Genius and Still the Team's Inspiration.

His passion for the game, for his team, and for promotion planted the seeds of a Cub dynasty by the late '20s. The team's foundation was so solid that it stayed strong for years after his death, despite the neglect that soon overtook his work.

William Wrigley also invented the 'all-inclusive' vacation package that's supposed to be a modern innovation: your trip to Catalina included a train ride in L.A., steam passage over, hotel accommodations and meals, tours on the Island, passes to the Bird Park, and of course free seats at the ballpark.

Of course, the gum fueled the engine. Consider this tidbit from the *Chicago Herald and Examiner*, when baseball's commissioner (then called president) Ford Frick visited Catalina:

"President Frick and the Mrs. were duly photographed in the interests of Avalon and baseball publicity. The president was chewing gum at the time and the Mrs. allowed that this was rather undignified, whereupon one of the innocent bystanders suggested that on Santa Catalina Island you chew gum or else..."

His final great baseball legacy was bringing John *Jota* McGraw's New York Giants over for a series of exhibition games. Unfortunately, he set up the contests for 1932 and 1933 — but passed away just a month before the 1st pitch.

Seems there's only one thing William Wrigley, Jr. couldn't do: He couldn't pass his baseball gene onto his son, Philip.

Sorry, Sandals did not invent all-inclusive vacations in Jamaica — it happened on another island, at the brilliance of one Wm. Wrigley.

PK

Everybody called Phil Wrigley 'PK.' We will also do so here in an effort to conserve ink and the precious natural resources used to make ink, which are...say, what *is* ink made of, anyway?

PK took over the Cubs (and, oh yeah, the gum biz) in 1932, when he was 38. Over the next 40 years, he grew the gum thing into a global giant with offices in 54,867,221 cities in 9,308 countries on 14 continents on 3 planets. Or something like that. So clearly, he was a brilliant man and an astounding executive.

His problem was, he just wasn't into baseball.

Oh, he tried. He really did — for a while, anyway, although he said, "I don't want the job." He was admirably loyal to his pop, but with 20/20 hindsight...he shoulda just kept his nose outa the Cubs. Sure, stay in place as the figurehead to honor father's memory, but *let the baseball guys do their thing.*

William Wrigley informs the lads of the many health benefits associated with chewing certain brands of gum, 1928.

Since he didn't, the Cubs crumbled. They became a shadow of their former selves…and for the past 60 seasons or so, they've never been able to recover.

Yet for someone who wasn't interested in baseball, he certainly was interested in meddling. He hired psychologists to try and find out the causes of losing, he hired a guy to try and put a hex on the opposing pitchers, he hired an athletic director, he attempted the no-manager method of rotating head coaches later on — everything but putting a crowbar to his wallet.

In this photo, Bob Kennedy is muttering, "Can you believe that PK Wrigley? Whoever heard of a 'head coach' in baseball? There's no 'head coaching' in baseball!

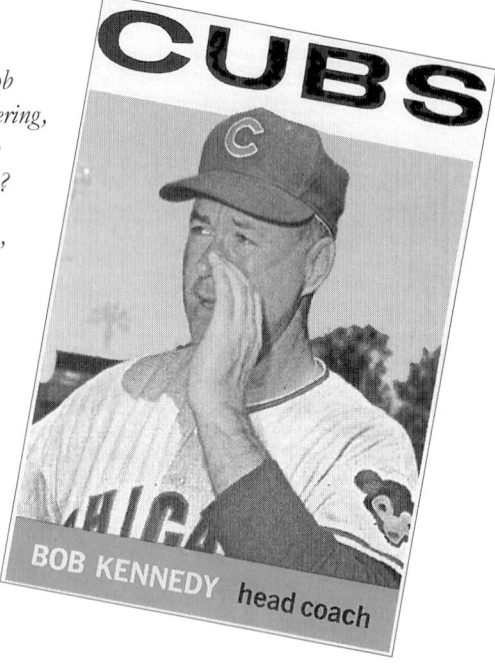

A 1938 experiment was amusing; he sent 2 research scientists to Catalina to try and discover the mental attributes of great players. "Professor Grimm, dean of diamond performance, is perplexed by this whole business," reported Edward Cochrane in the *Chicago American*. He concluded his dispatch by editorializing, "This research business may be all right, but wouldn't it be just as well to spend the same amount of time, energy and money bringing into the fold a pair of sluggers for the outfield and a pair of pitchers who could stave off the Giants, Cardinals and Pirate attacks? Or wouldn't it?"

The next day, Cochrane suggested that "after some extensive scientific research Manager Grimm will be able to state with authority what athletes he has whose skulls are thin enough to be of value."

Always tinkering. Never learning.

"We had a big turnover every year — managers, players," Bob Rush says. "I don't think the organization was baseball-oriented, like the Yankees or the Cardinals. From the top on down to the batboy, they knew what they wanted to do. It wasn't because Wrigley didn't want to spend the money.

The farm system, I don't think it was extremely good. You watch the D-leagues, all the way to the major league level in those organizations, and they played the same kind of baseball — you could see it in the routine plays. When people came up with the Cubs, they didn't seem to have good skills, and they needed to be taught, it seemed like."

PK's dad attended almost every practice session on Catalina, but PK was notable by his absence. "Wrigley came out one day and he sat in the sun for a while," Don Dunker says, "then he left."

His kids would occasionally come out too. "We'd just sit in the grandstand with everybody else," says PK's daughter Blanny Wrigley Schreiner. "But mostly, we were on the back side of the Island — we wanted to be riding our horses."

"He wasn't like his dad; he was more behind-the-scenes," adds Randy Jackson. "Most folks didn't know him from a sack of salt."

"Phil Wrigley has one overriding flaw," Bill Veeck, Jr. wrote in his autobiography. "He knows more about things and less about people than any man I have ever met."

PK died in 1977, and the Cubs eventually became part of the *Tribune* empire. Ah, hope! They could infuse the club with money (as in, salaries), to bring back the winning ways. Hmm, think again; games are sold out already, TV rights are worth a fortune, and there's a sort of sad romantic comedy to the Cubs being lovable losers. In other words, spending a hundred million more won't *possibly* bring in another hundred million more. Thus, with spending decisions now being made at the bean-counting suite of the Trib tower, the Cubs are forever stuck in the cellar.

Thus, PK's legacy. Of course, we can enjoy the perfection of hindsight — clearly, PK's intentions were good. So we will focus on the fact that the ballplayers thought of him as a kind-hearted human being and a devoted family person, along with his wonderful wife Helen.

This is PK Wrigley's 1931 Rookie Card. It is worth slightly less than Ernie Banks' Rookie Card.

"We'd eat at 11 at the country club, outside, with Phil Wrigley and his family — with his little girl Dee Dee," Lefty Chambers says. "He had horses, and I used to ride his Arabians..."

Harvey Cowell, future Mayor of Avalon, says: "One of my most vivid memories was Mr. Wrigley's Island Company would put on a program — a dinner-dance at the Hotel St. Catherine. They'd invite the Cubs and anybody in town who'd want to partake. And of course, the parade — Mr. Wrigley got out the old stagecoach — he and his children would parade with him and the Cubs."

"I think my wife has a bedspread Mrs. Wrigley sent to the wives in the '40s," Ken Raffensberger remembers. "They were real nice people."

"We were entertained by Mrs. Wrigley," Harriet Block (Cy's wife) recalls. "We watched practice, then went to the club for lunch. We toured the island, we socialized. It was a lovely vacation. Mrs. Wrigley had the wives over for lunch at their home, then took us out on their yacht. She was a lovely woman. They had a school room in their home; I suppose after the Lindbergh kidnapping, they were worried about that."

"Mr. and Mrs. Wrigley were very nice to me, always," says Yosh Kawano

"Mr. Wrigley took good care of us," adds Andy Pafko.

"Mrs. Wrigley been berry, berry good to me," Sammy Sosa would've said, if he'd been born 50 years earlier. Here, Mrs. Wm. Wrigley (as opposed to Mrs. PK Wrigley) entertains the President of the United States.

Some of the younger ballplayers were surprised to have any contact at all with the club's owner. "The year we were there, it really impressed me how Wrigley treated us," says Paul Schramka.

"One of the 1st couple of days I was out there, I went walking down this long pier that went way out into the ocean," remembers Wayne Terwilliger. "There was nobody else on the pier — I was all by myself. I went to the end, and looked into the water to see if I could see any fish. Well, here comes this guy in a suit, and I think, 'Is he gonna tell me I'm not supposed to be here?' And it turned out to be Mr. PK Wrigley. He was real nice, and he welcomed me, and told me to let him know if there was anything he could do."

Years earlier, batting-practice pitcher Hub Kittle had a similar encounter. "Ol' man Wrigley, he was a great guy," Hub smiles. "Grimm took me out one time — I was a wild son of a gun, and I hit Steve Mesner on the knee. Grimm said, 'Get that blankety-blank outa there — he's gonna kill all my players! So I was walking up the hill to the locker room, and this guy in a suit has his arm around me and says, 'Don't let it get ya down.' And I looked up, and if it wasn't Mr. PK Wrigley himself!"

Lloyd Lowe tells another similar story:

"One of the biggest thrills I had, I was a green rookie, and a lot of the older ballplayers wouldn't talk to us — Lowrey and Borowy, they wouldn't talk to us. And one day at practice, I saw this big car coming down the hill; it stopped, this big black limousine, and the chauffeur was like in the old movies, wearing a cap with a beak, a black jacket and a black tie, boots from the knee on down — and Mr. Wrigley came out. Charlie Grimm ran over and greeted him, and took him over to the rookies, and Mr. Wrigley put his arm around my shoulder and said, 'Lloyd, you're new to the organization, so I'd like to welcome you. We're trying to turn things around, and get out of being in 6th or 7th place, and have a winning ballclub.' He was really nice — it was very surprising that a man of his caliber would come out and talk to us."

Players who did get to know him recall PK with fondness. Gene Mauch says, "I knew Phil Wrigley quite well. He was a personal friend."

Of course, the shortest distance to a ballplayer's heart is through is taste buds — and PK made sure there were plenty of cook-outs on the Island for the boys and their families. "The old man would have barbecues," Corky Van Dyke says, "then we had to go back to work. Wrigley was always out there. They treated us pretty good."

Olinda Hacker echoes those memories. Although she didn't get to go, Warren told her about his experiences on Catalina. "He said Mr. Wrigley treated them to a big barbecue, and they were treated royally — they had a good time. Warren really enjoyed it there. Mr. Wrigley made them feel like family."

Mr. PK Wrigley enters the rodeo ring on Catalina, as photographed by Warren Hacker.

One year, the team chipped in and bought him a watch to show their appreciation. "He kind of couldn't hardly say anything!" Olinda says. "Mr. Wrigley's wife said, 'PK's really broken up, really touched — most of the time, he's not on the receiving end...he's on the giving end.' Warren said he could have bought dozens of watches like that — but it really touched him for us to have shown our appreciation. No matter how much money is involved, it's people that count."

Preston Ward recalls the event a little differently. "On the backside of the island, they had a barbecue. We all chipped in and bought him a gold watch. In accepting it, he said it wasn't much, but it was the thought that counted!"

Johnny Klippstein adds, "It was the 1st time I'd seen a grown man cry — I think because it was the first time anybody ever gave him anything!"

Of course, PK is the one who moved the Cubs' Spring Training site from Catalina to Arizona in 1951. In a lot of ways, the move made sense by then; but ya never know how things might have been different if his dad's influence had lasted a little longer...

Two years before PK passed away, the Wrigley family donated 86% of the Island to the Santa Catalina Island Conservancy, a non-profit group whose goal is to preserve Catalina's land and wildlife. So while PK's baseball legacy left a bit to be desired, his Catalina legacy is more profound

The ballplayers chipped in and got PK a watch.

We must wonder if the back was engraved, "Time for you to find us new ownership, please!"

An assortment of Wrigley-made gum cards from 1933.

Bubblegum cards?

How ironic. Baseball cards and bubblegum are permanently interwoven in our culture. The Cubs and Wrigley's gum are similarly connected. Ain't it odd that the Wm. Wrigley Company never sold cards with gum?

Sure, bubblegum is different from chewing gum, but — so what? Can't ya package a Snipe Hansen rookie card just as well with a stick of Juicy Fruit...as you can with a pink piece o'Bazooka?

Actually, there was *one* such set during the Catalina days. In 1933, Wrigley subsidiary Orbit Gum issued a 60-card run with their Tattoo gum. (Notice that Orbit has been re-introduced in recent years.) There was also a set of cards that you had to moisten and blot to develop the image...and pins, so you could wear your favorite ballplayers. But for the most part, the Wrigleys left the card biz to the Goudeys and the Bowmans and the Toppses of the world.

The other guys who wore suits to work

Besides the fellas with the Wrigley DNA, there were a few other assorted characters that made life interesting for the Catalina Cubs. Such as...

Veeck, Veeck

As with 2 Wrigleys, there were 2 Veecks — both Bills, to complicate things.

Bill was a sportswriter who regularly ragged on the Cubs. So William Wrigley suggested that if Veeck knew so much about baseball, he should run the club himself. Bill agreed, and was president of the team from 1919 to 1933. He invented brilliant and successful promotions, like Ladies' Day — and radio broadcasts of Cubs game began under his watch. Impatient with managers, he went through 7 during his tenure — but he also produced 2 pennant winners.

Bill the dad.

Bill, on the other hand, is the more famous character. He's the guy who planted the ivy on the outfield walls at Wrigley Field. He's the guy who sent midget Eddie Gaedel in to pinch hit for the St. Louis Browns. He's the guy behind the White Sox infamous Disco Demolition Night promotion, where the game had to be called because fans were flinging Bee-Gees hits all about, and an unruly crowd of thousands stormed the field. His autobiography is entitled, *VEECK — As In Wreck*. He was a fan's owner, beloved throughout Chicago — he was Harry Caray before Harry Caray was.

"My daddy built his pennant winners with the most rollicking, raucous, rowdy and roistering crew in big-league history," Bill wrote about Bill.

Son/grandson Mike is still in baseball — he co-owns the St. Paul Saints with actor Bill Murray and a pig they alternately call Hammy Davis, Jr. or Kevin Bacon. (Catalina Cub Wayne Terwilliger was a Saints coach for several seasons recently.)

Bill the boy.

Gentleman Jim

James Gallagher was a *fabulous* writer for the *Chicago American*. He was a less-than-fabulous General Manager for the Cubs during the 1940s, with "no talent for judging horseflesh," according to author Peter Golenbock. Nevertheless, PK followed in his father's footsteps — sort of — by putting a sportswriter in the GM position.

"He didn't know his backside from a baseball," says Lefty Chambers. "It always amazed me how guys like Wrigley, who were so smart, could hire guys who didn't know anything about baseball. Some guy would work his way up through ticket sales or something, and all of a sudden he's making decisions about ballplayers. Gallagher was a newspaperman, not a baseball man, and that really hurt the team."

Starting with low expectations can help. In *The Game is Never Over*, author Jim Langford wrote that 'Gentleman Jim' took the job "on the premise that he had to do better than his predecessor because he couldn't do any worse."

"Jim Gallagher, I knew him real well," says Bobby Mattick. "They always told the story that a scout woke him up in the middle of the night, 2 or 3 o'clock in the morning, wantin' permission to sign a pitcher. He said the guy's 6-2, 190 pounds, with a good fastball — it moves — and a good curve. But Gallagher said, 'A moving fastball? Forget about him; we've already got enough of those kinda guys.'"

Some players appreciated Gent Jim's talents, but others did not. Lennie Merullo's last experience with the Cubs — in Gallagher's office — was not a pleasant one. "The clubhouse manager says Mr. Gallagher wants to see you. So I go in and he says, 'Sit down, Lennie,' so I sit in the chair — and he seemed to stare at me for 25 minutes, without saying a word. He finally says, instead of saying we're gonna send you to Los Angeles or we're gonna release you, he says, 'Who should we get to room with Cavy?' I couldn't believe it — I wanted to ask him if that was all he had to say, but I just said, 'Anybody you'd like to.'"

Andy Lotshaw leads exercises in the late '20s, while a young Bill Veeck (standing in front) helps out.

Manager Grimm scouts future Cub star Gentleboy Jim Gallagher Jr. (nickname: Timmy/age 4) on Catalina in 1947.

Wid Matthews.

His fellow journalists liked to give him plenty of ink — more than a lot of the players, it seemed sometimes. Warren Brown described him as "a small man with a big voice and positive opinions," and a unique talent: "He can outcuss the most profane ballplayer if occasion arises."

Carmen Mauro liked him, though. "He was very personable," Carmen recalls — pretty high praise for a fellow who wasn't particularly esteemed in many Cub circles.

The replacement

Wid Matthews replaced Gentleman Jim. He'd been Branch Rickey's right hand guy in Brooklyn. "Matthews, it turned out, hadn't learned much from the master," Golenbock wrote. He especially didn't learn much from Rickey about integration; the Cubs were among the last teams to pluck talent from the Negro Leagues, and even when the did...they were slow to import anyone to Chicago. The back of Gene Baker's 1957 Topps card innocuously tells the tale, replete with copy between the lines:

"Gene started in baseball in '50 and was a star on the Pacific Coast for three years before coming to the Cubs."

At least Wid continued to tighten the negotiating screws that PK and Gallagher enjoyed twisting. Randy Jackson tells of contract talks with Wid:

"It was a lot different in those days. Nobody had an agent — we weren't making a lot of money. My 1st 2 years with the Cubs, I made $6,000, then $7,000. I got my contract after the 1951 season, when I'd hit 16 home runs and had 76 RBI, and led the league in putouts and assists — not a bad year — and I got a letter with my contract, saying they'd give me a raise to $8,000. I wrote back and said I'd heard a couple of other teams were interested in me, and I deserve more. I got a letter back from Wid Matthews, who was the general manager at the time, and he said "*Nobody* else wants you — the one team that was interested in you offered us two old balls, a broken bat, and a busted catcher's mask — so you better get your butt to practice." So I took it. Back then, you didn't say 'I'm not gonna come to Spring Practice.' "

Carmen Mauro, who spoke so highly of Jim Gallagher, had a tougher time with Wid:

"He was the one that...well, I don't know if he liked me very much. I was sent a contract, and had a family discussion about it, considering the kind of year I'd had. The session was, well, we don't — we have to save the raises for the big players. I was just asking for $200 more, to cover some expenses. He was not very nice, sitting behind that big desk, and he finally said,

'I'll have to ask for permission.' And I said, well, if it's such a big deal...but he said, 'Well, I'll talk to the powers that be.' So he went to the other room, then finally came back. I got it, but I really took a scraping. It reminded me of Branch Rickey — he'd make players feel unworthy: 'We didn't draw a million people, you were a commodity.' But every day of the year in Chicago, you saw full houses, 45,000 people — if they didn't draw, nobody drew. But Wrigley was gonna give to guys who'd had a good year."

The multi-nicknamed Bob Lewis, umpiring with gusto in 1936. Hartnett appears to approve of the call; English does not.

Big Bob Lewis

Bob Lewis was the traveling secretary for the Cubs since time began. The players seemed to like him a little better than they liked the GM fellas — getting to dole out meal money, rather than having to chop salaries, had its benefits.

"It is a great night for the rookies, at least those who are short on dough," Ed Burns wrote for the *Chicago Tribune* in the Spring of 1929. "Tonight, Traveling Secretary Bob Lewis dealt out subsistence money and joy reigned supreme."

"Bob Lewis was a nice guy," Al Epperly recalls from the '30s.

Charlie Grimm called him "my all-time champion of traveling secretaries."

Yosh Kawano says, "Bob Lewis was a good guy, very funny — he had a good sense of humor."

Hard Rock Johnson once told Bob that he had to pay some local kids $2.50 a day to shag balls hit beyond the fence. "Who didja hire, the town banker?" Lewis quipped back.

In 1936, the Cubs wilted at the end of the season and lost the pennant to the Giants. Charlie Grimm said they ran outa gas because the spring exhibition schedule had been too strenuous. Lewis, who often entertained the troops with Jolly, said, "It was those slot machines in Florida that got the boys down. They developed arm muscles they never knew they had, and couldn't use in baseball. Some of those guys are still trying to hit the jackpot instead of a ball."

Ever devoted, he lived in the 6-room apartment (beyond left field) — right on the grounds at Wrigley in Chicago. And like Gallagher, he could get loud at Spring practice sessions. "R. Clarendon Lewis, who has been indisposed since arrival, made his first appearance at the practice field today," Warren Brown wrote for the *Herald & Examiner* in 1939. "Until then, it was a very quiet Sunday."

He co-umpired games on Catalina with Doc Lotshaw and always had something interesting going. In 1950, Burns ended his day's camp report with this tale:

"Secretary Bob Lewis was made happy today. In front of the hotel are benches for resting in the sun, when the sun shines, and Mr. Lewis complained about a lack of seating space for a guest. So the hotel has set up a sign, saying 'This spot is reserved for R.C. Lewis.' "

Bobby Mattick remembers another incident at the hotel: "We'd always eat our evening meals there, and they'd have a harpist playing. One time, Bob Lewis and Grimm must've had a few drinks before dinner, and Lewis said, 'I could walk through that and get more music out of it than she is!' "

Once, Bob fell asleep while fishing with some of the boys. Charlie Root grabbed a skate fish, sewed a cigar into the fish's mouth, attached it to Lewis' hook, and gathered everyone to watch. Sure enough, the line jerked...the victim awoke...and he reeled in his catch to everyone's laughter.

Round Robert, passing out tickets so the boys can get to Catalina for the final time, 1951.

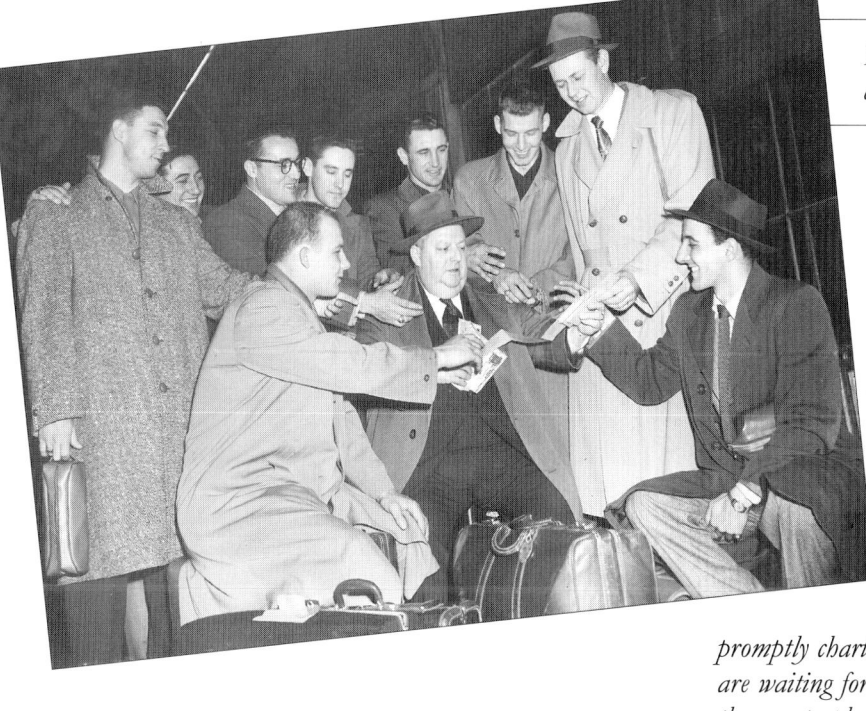

The press loved to tell Bob Lewis tales on their dispatches home from Catalina. He seemed to get more monikers that anybody else. A sampling:

* R.C. (Warren Brown in the *Sun*)
* Round & Ruddy (Edgar Munzel, also in the *Sun*)
* Round Robert (Ed Burns in the *Tribune*)

"Big Bob Lewis, ya couldn't miss him," recalls Wayne 'Twig' Terwilliger from the other end of the height/weight ratio chart.

His girth got him into trouble a couple times. Brown described a round of golf in his *Sun* column, *So They Tell Me*:

The mighty shot R.C. made trickled off the tee, rolled a bit of the way into that rough country and remained there in plain cussing sight.

Now never let anyone tell you that R.C. is not determined. He went right into that rough country without a guide or even a day's rations. He stood over the ball and took another mighty swipe. He wasn't wearing spiked shoes, so his feet slipped out from under him and R.C., instead of the golf ball, started to roll and roll and roll.

Fortunately, he didn't make the canyon. (It is out of bounds, anyhow.) But while he was on the roll, the man at the seismo-graph at CalTech...or maybe it was U.C.L.A.... promptly charted a new earthquake. To this day the scientists are waiting for reports to come in, telling the exact location of the worst upheaval Southern California had experienced since Knute Rockne's Notre Dame team upset the Trojans, 27 to 0.

Ever since then R.C. has remained so far away from golf he couldn't tell Byron Nelson from Ben Hogan, even with a program.

Other assorted characters

Pants Rowland — whose mother actually named him Clarence — was among the best multi-taskers to ever work the Cubs office. He was also a minor league catcher, major league manager (World Champ, with the 1917 White Sox — he left before the scandal), president of the Pacific Coast League, and even an American League umpire.

Pants was a tough negotiator before Gallagher came to town. Ed Burns moonlighted this piece for the *Los Angeles Times* in 1940:

"Front man Rowland said the Cubs had not been in touch with (Hank) Leiber for three weeks. In his last letter Leiber got around to quoting the demand of $17,500. It is said Hank has no more chance to get $17,500 than he has to obtain the Cub franchise."

John Seys, another key Cub exec, was described by the *Chicago Times* in 1931 as "superintendent of peanuts and popcorn at the north side emporium."

FIRST ROW: Littlefield, Wise, Fanning, Batboy Incledon, Elston, Will, Long. SECOND ROW: Lown, Coach Mueller, Trav. Sec'y. Lewis, Mgr. Scheffing, Coach Fitzsimmons, Coach Myatt, Walls, Moryn. THIRD ROW: Tr. Scheuneman, Bolger, Rush, Morgan, Neeman, Brosnan, Banks, Tanner, Eq. Mgr. Kawano. FOURTH ROW: Kindall, Hillman, Littrell, Drott, Drabowsky, Speake, Kaiser, Poholsky.

Bob achieved the highest honor in baseball (besides Cooperstown, o'course): he appeared on a few Topps cards in the '50s.

Only on an island: The artist joins the trainer & the traveling secretary to comprise the umpiring crew. (Otis Shepard, Andy Lotshaw, & Bob Lewis.)

Otis the artist

Otis Shepard was quite the famous artist in his day. Otis designed...

* Many of the classic Wrigley's gum ads that collectors buy and sell on ebay

* Programs for the Cubs and the Los Angeles Angels

* The uniforms for PK Wrigley's All-American Girls Professional Baseball League

* Even Crescent Street and Via Casino Way, the oceanfront avenues in Avalon; these architectural and landscaping gems give tourists their 1st taste of the town

And he had a spot o'fun with the boys, too: "More interesting than the game probably will be the work of the umpires," Munzel wrote in the *Sun* in 1947, "with Trainer Andy Lotshaw behind the plate and Traveling Secretary Bob Lewis and Otis Shepard, Wrigley artist, on the bases."

"On a close play," Charlie Grimm wrote in his autobiography, "he gave the 'out' sign to Phil Cavarretta, who must have been the inspiration for whoever coined the phrase, 'He came to play.' This game didn't mean a thing, but Phil stormed against Shepard with the fervor of a base runner who who had been called out in a World Series battle. Thereafter, Otis left the umpiring to Andy and Bob."

Ah, only in a world created by guys like Disney or Wrigley...can an artist be an umpire on an island...

For years, Wrigley's Chicago ad agency (BBD&O, a significant Otis link) maintained a 1-man Avalon outpost...right next to Lolo's Barbershop.

The handiwork of Mr. Wrigley's versatile designer...

Otis Shepard designed a little bit of everything for the Wrigleys: Ads, posters, & flyers...programs for the Cubs & L.A. Angels...Crescent Street on Catalina (seen here modeled by Corky Van Dyke)...& even uniforms for PK's All-American Girls Professional Baseball League (modeled here by All-Star Pep Peppas of the Kalamazoo Lassies, who probably could've beat PK's National League entry some seasons).

The War, & the Dreary Front At a Place Called French Lick

Spring Training in the Snow, While the Others Had Traded Their Bats For Bayonets

"Oh, those were happy days. That wasn't a place for Spring Training. The weather was terrible. We had to work out inside the hotel, and at the stables. It was so cold, even the horse droppings were frozen!"

Phil Cavarretta

Pearl Harbor changed everything. Catalina went from carefree, youthful paradise...to floating military base. As the only thing standing between the mainland and enemy headquarters, its strategic importance was obvious.

The Merchant Marines took over the ballfield and turned it into a training ground. They took the gilded Hotel St. Catherine and made it into a barracks, using the ballroom as a mess hall. There would be no more dances there — at least not for now. And just offshore, the Navy draped submarine nets throughout the channel.

On the way over, Ed Burns wrote in the *Chicago Tribune* that the team was "en route to Catalina Island, out in the still blue but no longer peaceful Pacific." The next day, Burns grumbled that correspondents faced numerous restrictions: besides travel restraints, they couldn't report on anything military that they saw...or even the weather. "Taking weather news away from a baseball writer on Catalina," he typed, "would be like yanking the ribbon off his typewriter or poking the lead out of his pencil."

Al Wolf of the *Los Angeles Times* battled the tension with humor, too. "For fear that Hirohito may be a White Sox fan," Wolf wrote, "Generalissimo Gallagher refuses to divulge whether the lads will depart the mainland by air or sea or pontoon bridge."

The team ended up taking water taxis over, since the great steamships had been

"Hey, Pardner," sailor Harold Epperly says to his brother Al. Hal stopped by for shore leave when the U.S.S. Colorado anchored off Avalon in March, 1937. A few months later, out in the Pacific, the Colorado led the search for Amelia Earhart.

drafted (and painted dull grey.) Scribe Burns described the taxis as "craft thought too small and fast to be hit by torpedo or bomb, just in case."

It seems odd now that the Cubs trained on Catalina in February of 1942, barely 2 months after we went to War. They would not come back until 1946.

It was eerily quiet. "After returning to their hotel," Burns dispatched, "the Cubs were able to spend a very restful day on account the hotel has no other guests." There was no bus service on the Island, and no press car due to rubber rationing — tires, you know. There were rumors about blackouts, highways being closed on the mainland, and U.S. vessels being shelled or sunk. "I'm not afraid," pitcher Bob Bowman (who'd worked in a coal mine during the off-season) quipped to reporters. "We've got mines in West Virginia, too."

Heinz Becker felt a unique kind of pressure; the Berlin native was the only German-born player during the war. The Cub infielder smartly tried to head off incidents from unruly fans by taking on a new nickname that'd help hide his roots: *Dutch*.

Hank Wyse, recalling the same incident in *Wrigleyville*, said, "We dove in the bushes."

Camp finally came to an end. The papers reported that the departure hour would be kept secret, but it had to be pretty early — so the boats could clear the submarine nets and the immigration barge before nightfall. There was no organized farewell celebration.

"We're still trying to figure out why the Cubs are here this year."

Ed Burns, in the *Chicago Tribune*, 1942

"Today," Wolf wrote in the *Times*, "the Cubs held their last drill...probably their last on the Island for several years at least."

(An interesting asterisk: The St. Louis Browns had decided to move to Los Angeles, starting in 1942. They were planning on making this announcement

At first, this is a beautiful view from the front of the Hotel St. Catherine, where the Cubs stayed on Catalina. But if you scan the horizon, you'll see some ugly grey clouds looming — or at least an ugly grey warship & submarine set — patrolling the channel.

Most of the ballplayers were thinking they'd be drafted — soon. There were censorship and curfews...and fear in the air.

"We'd be out there working out, and those planes — P-38s, I think — would be coming back from patrol duty," recalls Ken Raffensberger. "They'd come down over the park, they swooped down...one time, one of 'em hit the high tension wire."

on...December 8th, 1941. Needless to say, it never happened...and major league baseball stayed East of the Mississippi for another 16 years.)

So without any Cubs news on Catalina for the next 3 years, the only item of interest to report is that Chief Petty Officer Jim Dougherty was stationed on Catalina during 1943 and 1944 with his teenage wife, Norma Jeane.

This photo appeared on the front page of the Chicago Tribune *Sports section on March 21st, 1944. The headline: WHO NAMED IT SPRING TRAINING? The caption: The Cubs do not have to hustle like this — they have the alternative of freezing — as they go from their horse barn training headquarters to the hotel in French Lick, Ind., where they opened practice yesterday. Someone said it was the first day of Spring, but they find little evidence of that fact.*

Indiana Dreamin'

Besides the fact that...

* There was snow on the ground in French Lick during Spring Training

* If there wasn't snow, it's because the thermometer leaped into the low 40s and the snow melted and the local creek flooded its banks onto the ballfield

* There was in fact no ballfield — only a hastily re-shaped diamond on the 14th green of a golf course

* The West Baden Hotel ballroom was too small to practice inside, although a pitchers' mound was actually wheelbarrowed in and 'built' on the floor (*now* do you believe Doc Lotshaw was a handy character to have around?)

* There was nowhere else to practice inside, so the team found a couple of old uninsulated, unheated barns to use

* The journey to French Lick, short as it was, was a nightmare of train rides and bus transfers, often around flooded roads

* When the boys *could* get outside to play, it was seldom 'warmer' than 45 degrees

* The war was dragging on, and none of the potential-draftee ballplayers knew when it would end

* Rationing and other travel restrictions limited the boys from doing just about anything after practice

...besides those minor inconveniences...Spring Training in French Lick was *great* fun.

"There's no place like Arizona, Florida, or California," says Andy Pafko. It's way too cold — you couldn't break a sweat. We practiced with the horses. We'd wake up in the morning and say, 'This isn't spring training!'"

The White Sox tried to practice there, too — misery loving company, we suppose. Yet journalistic integrity obliges reporting that the last season the Cubs made it to the World Series, 1945, was the year of their final French Lick camp...

Burns, bundled in his overcoat, wrote that the Cubs "had learned of several auction barns in the community and they hoped to engage one that could be prepared for use with some energetic use of pitchforks and possibly a rake or two."

"I don't think we worked outdoors more than 3 or 4 times."

Charlie Grimm, recalling the 1945 camp in his biography

New hazards emerged. Irving Vaughn, for the *Chicago Tribune* in 1944: "Paul Derringer, who was hobbling on crutches as the result of an ankle sprain suffered yesterday on the horse track, was graduated to a cane this afternoon."

There were temptations, too. "It was a wide-open gamblin' town," Swish Nicholson told journalist/historian Harrington Crissey later. "I don't know much about gamblin' 'cept every little place you went in had dice games, roulette, and all that. Fellas got to playin' 'em a little bit. We didn't have much money to win or lose."

And the floods hit more than once, apparently to punish them for all that gambling. Edgar 'the Mouse' Munzel, for the *Chicago Sun*, in 1945: "Yep, the Lost River has gone and done it again. The perverse little overgrown 'crick' that meanders through the golf course on which the Cubs have their Spring diamond spilled over its banks yesterday...all roads have been closed until the flood recedes."

"We'll get as near to the hotel as we can and then toss out our lines and do some fishing," Manager Grimm told Munzel. "I need the rest anyhow, after a couple weeks on the banquet circuit."

A week later, Munzel and the rest of the troupe were still scratching their heads. "The Cub practice field, which seems ideally suited for a swimming pool" he wrote, "still was partially under water today... Grimm divided his workout between the hotel auditorium and a little island of dry land discovered on the 9th fairway."

Two weeks after that, Munzel (still in a state of wonder): "Andy Lotshaw, who was become an expert on marine topography, promises all water will be off the field tomorrow and he'll have it in shape for the workout."

"The Cubs practice field has just about come to the surface."

Ed Burns, in the *Chicago Tribune*, 1943

Of course, there's always one guy in the crowd who can spot the pony in there somewhere. In his 1946 history of the Cubs, Warren Brown wrote: "The hotel was a roomy place, the food was excellent, and the surrounding acreage was much greater than had been at the disposal at the Cubs in their many spring sessions at Catalina Island." I suppose no one mentioned to Warren that those massive grounds were either frozen solid or submerged under water; perhaps Warren was at a watering hole himself at the time.

"It wasn't much of a Spring Training," Don Johnson said in *Wrigleyville*. "But we felt it was better to be in French Lick than in Europe."

Lou Stringer, later a manager for the Hollywood Stars, expresses the bottom line well in managerial terms: "French Lick was horrible."

'Pluto Water'?

"The Home of Pluto Water"
French Lick Springs Hotel, French Lick, Ind.

The ballfield lost its charm for a few seasons.

Home at last

The Cubs announced during their 1945 World Series appearance — just a few months after war's end — that they'd happily return to Catalina the next Spring.

"Everything is shipshape for arrival of the Cubs at their Catalina Island spring base Tuesday, right on down to plans for one of those parades with which the townspeople of Avalon used to welcome the Chicago team in the merrier prewar days," Munzel wrote for his *Sun* readers.

The *S.S. Avalon* got a fresh coat of white paint and steamed the team into place. All was well again in paradise.

Charlie Grimm, whose French Lick load was increased by the lack of available talent, could hardly contain himself. "The last few years of wartime baseball," he told the press, "we were hoping every morning that some hitchhikers would show up so that we'd have enough men to round out two teams for a game."

Gunships manned Avalon Bay during the War, and baseball was very far away.

272

What'd you do in the war, pops?

Need a good laugh, after all this serious talk? Okay. Try and picture some of today's baseball super-de-dooper-stars wearing helmets, sleeping in a foxhole, and obeying orders.

"The attitude, the atmosphere is different for each era — it changes," says Bob Rush.

They were a different breed, that rough-and-ready grey flannel crowd. Plenty of Catalina Cubs went into the service — stateside, Europe, the South Pacific. Some were in the thick of battle, while others pretty much played ball on military bases here in the U.S.

Fortunately, no Cubs were seriously wounded overseas. A unique exception was Cal McLish, who suffered a *baseball*-related injury while serving in Europe. "I had a bad arm — I hurt it overseas, in 1946. I was in the Army, in Europe, and after the War was over and they decided they weren't going to send us to Japan, they started us playing division-level baseball. I hadn't thrown for a year or so, and I hurt my arm pitching in the 2nd or 3rd game."

Others faced more hazardous duty. "I was in the Field Artillery division, and went to France 6 days after D-Day," Jim Kirby recalls. "We went to

Veterans like Dale Alderson got to wear the "Ruptured Duck" patch on their left sleeve in 1946 — indicating they'd served & received an honorable discharge.

While it's clear how the War hurt numerous careers, openings were created for some of the younger players. "Had it not been for the war, I'd have probably been released," admits Red Adams. "My stuff was pretty mediocre, nothing exceptional. Oh, my fastball might've been a little busy. I was pretty much a run-of-the-mill journeyman pitcher."

Rush thinks the same thing happened for his career, too. "After the War, the only people left on the teams were the guys who got rejected, or the guys who were older," Bob says. "That's how I got my break." (Bob, always humble, neglects to mention that having a 1.61 ERA in Des Moines may have helped, too!) "I was lucky — I got off to a good start."

Omaha Beach, all up and down the coast, and it was a mess — I think we got lost."

Ed Jabb was half a world away. "In 1941, I went into the Army — on May 5th! How do ya like that. I was in the Pacific, and we went to all those islands — we didn't know the names of half of 'em!"

"I was pitching at Washington State, and several outfits were after me. I was gonna go pro after my junior year, but when Pearl Harbor happened everything got mixed up."

Lefty Chambers

273

Humble heroes, the men of our greatest generation. "I was in the Service 4 years, in Germany," Lefty Sloat says. "I missed the Bulge by a few hours."

"In World War II, I was with the Army Corps of Engineers in France — the 391st," says Ben Wade.

"I was with the Enola Gay group, the 20th Air Group, on Tinian Island. After World War II, I was just glad to get to play ball again!"

Ed Chandler

"I was in the 101st Air Force Infantry, 517th parachute Regiment," says Hal Jeffcoat. "We were stationed in Italy and South France. We landed before D-Day; we jumped about 2 months after the invasion, into South France." A silver lining: Hal met his wife, then a WAC, when they were both stationed in Naples, Italy.

The War interrupted Centerfielder Jimmie "Rabbit" Vitti's collegiate career at the University of Oregon (after he turned down a Yankee contract, before he coached at UCLA); he's seen here stationed in England, just a few weeks before hitting Omaha Beach on D-Day, enroute to the Battle of the Bulge.

Here's a brief partial roster of how some of the other Catalina Cubs served their country during World War II:

Lloyd Lowe: "During the War, I was attached to a sub-chaser repair base in Treasure Island, APO San Francisco. We had boot camp in Farragut, Idaho, during the winter. I learned how to march, and to salute anything with gold stripes. We'd patrol the area around San Francisco Bay, along the West Coast. There was a lot of secrecy. We had a World War I destroyer sunk just outside the Golden Gate Bridge, about 10 miles out. We had German POWs on Treasure Island."

Don Dunker: "I pitched for the U.S. Military Service All-Stars against the A.L. All-Stars in Cleveland during the War. I was stationed at Great Lakes. I was the only college boy on the baseball team, so I was invited to pitch batting practice in Chicago, at Wrigley Field, which I did a few times. I was in the service from 4 months after Pearl Harbor to 1945."

Harriet Block: "Cy was in the Coast Guard, stationed at Ellis Island. They were going to transfer him to the USS Monticello, which was going to the Pacific, but the War ended."

Howard Auman: "I served in the Air Force in Wilmington, North Carolina, at an airfield there until 1944. Then, I was out of Columbia, South Carolina before they sent me overseas, to the Pacific. We were onboard the ship 57 days, from Seattle to Okinawa. We docked at 2 places for 2 or 3 weeks, and by the time we finally got there the war was just about over."

Don Carlsen: "I went into the service for 2 years. I was in the Navy, in the Pacific. We were all over the place — Honolulu, Korea."

Roy Smalley, Jr.: "I was in the Navy in World War II, in San Diego and at Roosevelt Base in San Pedro. The Cubs sent me to L.A. My folks had been hit pretty hard by the Depression and wanted to start over. They were thinking about Washington D.C. or California, and this made it easy. At the end of the 1944 season, I was drafted. I was in the service for 22 months."

Ken Raffensberger: "I was sent to the Bainbridge Naval Training Station in Maryland."

Lou Stringer: "I enlisted in the Air Corps and went to Arizona. I was a mechanic. I was taking an AT-9 engine off the trolley, the hoist, and strained my back — so I was disqualified from going overseas."

Larry French joined the Navy in 1943, retiring in 1969 as a captain.

Lefty Chambers: "I was in the Army Air Corps for 3 years."

Bob Kelly: "I played for the Army team when the Cubs picked me up."

Ox Miller: "I was in the Service shortly, in 1944. But I got banged up, hurt my back, so I went back to the Browns. I was stationed at Camp Walters in Mineral Wells, Texas."

> "I was in the parts department, but I didn't know the difference between an anchor and a propeller."
> Lloyd Lowe

Bob Borkowski: "I played in the service. One umpire's dad was a scout for the Cubs. I was stationed in Hawaii, with the Navy, and I took care of the infield. Billy Herman was the manager. I asked him if I could pitch batting practice, and he asked if I could get it over the plate. I did that for a few days, and they signed me up as a pitcher — no bonus, no nothing."

Yosh Kawano: "I was in the Service, in the Pacific." *

After the war was over, **Johnny Klippstein** and **Corky Van Dyke** also interrupted their careers for a brief hitch. **Paul Schramka** was in the service in between from 1951-1952, stationed in Germany — where he played in the GI World Series. **Preston Ward** served during the Korean conflict.

Bennie Warren, proudly sporting his "Ruptured Duck" emblem in '46.

Lefty Carnett: "I was in the Navy, stationed at Great Lakes, where we had B-17s. Bob Feller had a club up there — Walker Cooper, Pinky Higgins, Denny Galehouse — we had some exciting games."

Bill Baker: "I was in the Navy at Great Lakes, at Iowa Pre-Flight, at Chapel Hill. I looked after the equipment there. They sent me to Dallas and Oklahoma City — I got home the day before Christmas."

> "In the service, I was stationed at Fort Riley, Kansas. I had 3 kids, and another on the way — I don't know how they got me. I was all crippled up, had a bad leg and a bad ankle — I couldn't wear those high-topped boots."
> Lonny Frey, who was 33 when he was drafted at the end of the 1943 season

* *See chapter 17 for a few missing details.*

Better salute, boys: Lotshaw's running rifle-handling drills with bats again.

And the Catalina locals pitched in, too: Future Avalon Mayor Bud Smith flew B-25 for the Army Air Corps here at home, and Harvey Cowell, also a future Mayor, served in the air force. "I ended up in a flight program with John Payne," he said, recalling the *Miracle on 34th Street* actor who used to suit up and shag grounders with the Cubs in Avalon. Harvey's brother Jack did a European hitch with the air force after working at aircraft plants. PK Wrigley's daughter, Blanny, became a WAC. Heck, even Grace Bradley pitched in: "I was working on a picture at Paramount, *Come on Marines*, with Richard Arlen."

> "What would you consider your most interesting or unusual experience while in the military service?"
>
> **GETTING DISCHARGED!!!**
>
> Chuck Connors, on his 1946
> American Baseball Bureau questionnaire

Andy Lotshaw, cleverly camouflaged as an umpire, tries to sneak a closer look at Bennie Warren's "Ruptured Duck" insignia.

The other World War

A previous generation of Cubs also fought in Europe — most notably Grover Cleveland Alexander, whose career (and life) apparently suffered the consequences of mustard gas poisoning there.

Parke Brown, Foreign New Service correspondent, sent this cable to the *Chicago Tribune* in 1919:

KYLLBURG, Germany, March 6 — Within 24 hours, Grover Cleveland Alexander probably will be on his way to rejoin the Cubs…He will be mustered out in New York…"That's the best news I've heard all winter," exclaimed President Mitchell of the Cubs.

Take another look?

Dim Dom Dallesandro didn't have to go into the Army — he flunked his eye test. But later, in 1944, he hit .309. Oops! The Army reconsidered, and invited Dom to join anyhow…

Not your average military career

Hey, these are the Cubs…so you might expect a less-than-ordinary tale. Consider Randy Jackson's Naval career:

"At Texas and TCU, I was in the Navy officer training program. In the Navy, I got my commission in 1946. Two years later, I was playing for Des Moines and I got a letter saying they'd promote me to Lt. Junior Grade if I'd just take a correspondence course. I was on the road, and it seemed pretty easy, so I thought, 'Why not?' So a few years later, I got another letter, saying they'd promote me to Full Lieutenant, same thing — a correspondence course. So I became a Lieutenant in the Navy without ever putting an officer's uniform on.

"In 1948, we all had to register for the draft. I was in Des Moines, and here comes the Korean War. In 1951, I got this letter from my draft board saying I have to come into the Army. But I'm in the Naval Reserve! But they said it doesn't make any difference to us.

"So I called and got an appointment with Mr. Wrigley, and I went down to the top floor of the Wrigley Building. His office was so big, you could get lost in it. I told him my problem, and he said, 'I'll tell you what I'll do. You go with my son-in-law, and drive up to Great Lakes. The Admiral is a friend of mine, and he'll straighten this out.' So we went up, but the Admiral wasn't there. So we saw his chief of staff, a captain, and he called in his flunkie and told him what to do: Tell the Army Ransom Jackson is our property, and if worse comes to worse, we'll call you back in and let you play at Great Lakes. Two weeks later, we were in St. Louis, and I got a letter back from the Army. They said they wouldn't be needing my services, and they wished me the best. As time went by, I found out some of my buddies had been called back in — so it wasn't bad to have Mr. Wrigley on my side."

The Press

Jimmy the Cork, T-Bone Otto, Gentleman Jim, & a Variety of Others With Ink in Their Veins

"Sometimes the typewriter is mightier than the 38-ounce bat."

Charlie Grimm, in Jolly Cholly's Story

Hank Borowy, Heinz Becker, & Charlie Grimm cavort with a pair of photographers in this super image, probably snapped by cub reporter Jimmy Olsen of The Daily Planet.

Some of 'em were caricatures as outrageous as the players they covered — so the press corps following the Cubs on Catalina always stirred something up.

When William Wrigley decided to send his Cubs to his Island, he knew it'd be the ideal time for press junkets. After all, if you send a sports writer (who's fed up with the Chicago winter) on an all-expenses-paid trip to a sunny isle in the Pacific in February and March...you might just end up with some nifty publicity for your tourism business.

The thing was, there really was no news to report — after all, until they were ready for exhibition games (several weeks after camp started), all the ballplayers did was exercise. So the reporters were forced to spin gold from straw, and the stories they sent back allow us some pretty personal glimpses of the players as people...and what it was like to live on Mr. Wrigley's magical Isle in years past.

"Not much to write about in this camp," Harry A. Williams sent back to the *Chicago Times* in 1932, "for not a Cub has got himself banged up since landing. At this time of year a loose toe nail rattling around on the hoof of a $40,000 athlete is good for 100,000 words daily in the various publications."

He echoed a sentiment that began in Year 1: "There is nothing new or startling to report about the Cubs," Harry Neily wrote for the *Chicago American* in 1921.

These aces of the TIMES sports staff will keep TIMES wires crackling with the latest, most complete Spring Training news! They'll give you stories fresh as a $50,000 rookie, written in a style breezy as infield chatter.

A self-promoting ad in *the Daily Times*, 1940

Various publications, indeed. These days, when most big cities have just 1 paper...and even Chicago only offers a few...it's hard to imagine the journalism wars of the '20s, '30s, and '40s. The proliferation of papers was magnificent — something like the number of cable stations today. At any one time, there were more than half a dozen dailies in Chicago...all trying to find an edge against the others. "There were probably as many newspaper reporters as there were Cubs," recalls Harvey Cowell, who went on to become Mayor of Avalon. "They had a big following of old-time reporters." So, the Catalina coverage was a big deal. Some papers would send a pair of reporters, a photographer, and their wives — all at the Cubs' expense, of course.

And the press ate it up. When they'd arrive on Catalina, they'd be treated just as royally as the ballplayers in the big 'welcome' parade: "The gentlemen of the press, a bit nervous withal, rode in an especially high wheeled coach but scarcely added color to the rugged pageant," Ed Burns of the *Chicago Tribune* wrote in 1939.

But the job wasn't always easy — particularly limited by the technology of the times. "Reports of the Cubs' arrival in Pasadena last night were delayed owing to interruptions of wire service by a severe storm in the territory west of Denver," the *Tribune* apologized in 1919.

"War correspondents flashing dispatches from camp back to Chicago are greatly aided by the use of a 27-mile stretch of cable, connecting Avalon and San Pedro," the *Chicago American* revealed to fans back home in 1924.

They unabashedly liked to write about themselves, happily becoming part of the story. Harry Hochstadter wrote this lead for the *Chicago Post* in 1923:

> CATALINA ISLAND, California — Well, the first squad of the 1923 Cub ball club is here, and the veracious newspaper correspondents are ready to inform the eager populace about the cavortings of the athletes.

In 1921, the *Los Angeles Times* reported, "In order to get first-hand dope, Harry Neily and Oscar Reichow of the Chicago press joined the batting aggregation."

The tradition continued. In 1930, *American* readers learned that "After the regular game, the scribes, piloted by Secretary Bob Lewis, scored their second straight victory over the Cub executives, this time by a score of 14-11."

Pretty heady stuff for the grizzled scribes — being included in the parades. Here's the 1947 rendition.

They went overboard — Edward W. Cochrane wrote this piece for the *American* in 1937, reporting on reporters playing golf when the assignment was Cubs' camp: "The first golf victory occurred yesterday when Charles Drake and your correspondent managed to beat Jim Kearns and John Hoffman, 2-up. Manager Grimm has said okay to golf and a tournament is being arranged with the players and newspapermen taking part."

Some could write brilliant prose, and some could be mean-spirited and petty. The ballplayers generally considered sports reporters to be a necessary evil.

"They'd bury you if they didn't like you," Phil Cavarretta says. "The articles they wrote — they were tough! They all thought we should play like Ruth and Gehrig. I don't know what the press would do on Catalina — I didn't stay up that late. A lot of 'em were freeloaders. You'd buy 'em a drink, and they'd write good things about you."

"I could only imagine what they used to do out there," Andy Pafko said. "I never followed them around."

Edward Cochrane, more interested in writers golfing than baseball?

Charlie Grimm once thought a reporter was good-naturedly teasing him as he followed him around, but was actually being quite condescending. "Ralph Cannon, a hard-working and somewhat humorless man was telling the readers of the *Daily News* about us. Every time he saw me in Spring Training...he would call me 'Major,'" Jolly Cholly wrote in his autobiography. "One day curiosity got the better of me. I asked Ralph why he kept calling me 'Major.'

" 'Your boys remind me of those amateurs Major Bowes has on his radio program,' said Ralph. He was slightly off base in his early assessment of my 1935 boys." (Grimm did get the last laugh — the Cubs won the pennant that year!)

Jolly Cholly Grimm seems to be serving up some juicy quotes, but the members of the 4th estate seem to have lost interest in note-taking...

Cavy, seen here contemplating a nice hemlock cocktail for some favorite newspaper buddies.

Grimm also tells how some sportswriters ganged up on shortstop Dick Bartell in 1939:

Ed Burns was a portly gentleman, with an expansive middle that would have been the envy of Santa Claus. Bob Lewis, the demon traveling secretary, also was on the mailing list of the Fat Men's Shoppe. On this beautiful morning on Catalina, Bartell proceeded to utter the six most costly words of his career. "When does the balloon go up?" he shouted.

Unfortunately, Bartell hadn't been introduced to Burns...when those fatal words came tumbling out of his mouth. Bartell didn't know it, but his 12th big-league season was to be a distressing one. Burns, a master needler, never let up on Dick during the season. Errors were magnified into major crimes.

Dick Bartell, neither mouthing off nor committing an error just then — because he looked every bit like he was busy trying to reach a runaway balloon.

"After a mild winter and plenty of well-cooked meals," Warren Brown explained in his book, "both were inclined to be a few pounds, 50 or a hundred at a quick guess, overweight."

"Ed Burns was a big, heavy-set guy," says Bobby Mattick, the shortstop who replaced Bartell. "Everybody always said, don't cross him."

Bartell got to give his side in his own autobiography:

Dizzy Dean, Woody English and I were walking up the path to the park one day. Up ahead of us was a rotund, heavyset guy. He had to turn sideways to get through the gate.

I called out, "Hey, what time does the balloon go up?" It was a common barb we used to throw at overweight ballplayers.

Dean said, "You know who that is?"

I said no.

"That's Ed Burns, the writer for the Chicago Tribune.*"*

Burns turned and pointed a finger at me. "You'll hear from me all summer," he said.

Somebody in Chicago heard about it and when Burns got back to his office he found his desk covered with balloons. Boy, did Burns blow a fuse. Well, the season started and I found that I was being charged with errors on plays where there was no error, like a double play we didn't finish. But Burns was the official scorer. He would give me one, anyhow. And anything that might've been called a hit for me, he'd charge the other team with an error. So the headline in the Tribune *would read, "Cubs win, Bartell makes error No. 14." Stuff like that.*

The Wrigley Field press box had a public address system for the official scorer to announce his decisions so everybody in the area could hear them. They heard, "Error, Bartell," so often, every time I booted a ball...the whole press box sang out, "Error, Bartell."

For the record, Dick's lifetime fielding average was .955. That season, it was .943 — a full 12 points lower than normal.

"The sportswriters were getting on me."

Bill Voiselle, voicing a common ballplayer complaint

Of course, one of the press highlights on Catalina — unreported at the time — was the barroom brawl with WHO radioman Dutch Reagan, where Jimmy 'the Cork' Corcoran took a swing at Dutch, who ducked, and the blow landed right into Burns' ballooned girth.

"*Those* are 2 great human beings," Cavy says, dripping with sarcasm. "Ed Burns, he was a great writer..."

Grimm echoed the faint praise about Burns, for those who can read between the lines: "One of the most delightful men I've met in sports," Cholly wrote.

There was a more famous brawl between Cubbies and pressies, but this one took place in Cincinnati... rather than Catalina. In 1931, the team was about to hop the train back home, when Harold Johnson (of the *American*) and Wayne 'T-Bone' Otto (of the *Herald & Examiner*) taunted pitcher Pat Malone. Pat, who'd had a few two many Coca-Colas (or some such) at the depot bar opted to pummel both men, as Hack Wilson stood nearby and may've muttered, "Oh, please, Pat, stop beating those nice fellas" (or perhaps not). Malone was fined $500 and ordered to pay the doctor bills; Hack was benched for the rest of the season.

Curiously to today's tabloid-fed fans, the papers didn't mention it — until the penalties had been levied, 4 days later. Even then, the coverage of the incident was lopsided at best (saying the reporters were trying to engage the boys in some friendly banter...and that Malone attacked "without warning or justification")...and self-righteous at worst, at least subtly revealing that the press had been antagonizing Malone and Wilson:

"Occasionally there is constructive criticism, but only when it pertains to something that the public should know," Edward Geiger, Sports Editor of the *American* wrote the next week. "If Malone felt he had been unjustly criticized by any member of the press he could appeal to Manager Hornsby, to President Veeck, to the sports editor or the editor-in-chief."

Yeah, right. (And be sure to carefully place those appeals into the *round* file...)

Geiger continued his finger-wagging. "Hornsby comes in for criticism because he permitted this conduct. Apparently he has lost control of the situation."

Hack Wilson & Pat Malone, contemplating their next friendly chat with their favorite reporters. (Notice that Hack has learned his lesson, & is holding Pat back.)

"These guys in the press, the thing I had against some of 'em was, they thought they were gods," Randy Jackson said. "The team had rooms for 'em, and drinks, and really nurtured them, so they'd write good things. If they didn't like you, they'd run you out of town. Some of 'em just go too far. My first year with the Dodgers, a lot of the players told me, there's one reporter from Long Island — do your best to stay away from him. He'd say, 'Are you still beating your wife?' What's your answer — either way, he'll try and make a story of it. He'll flavor it. It was Howard Cosell."

Fortunately, Howard never made the Cub train to Catalina. But there were plenty more where he came from. "There was a reporter at Spring Training in 1950, with the *Sun-Times,* I think," Carmen Mauro says. "I'd had a terrific spring, but he was always trying to write something. If I made an error, or if I got picked off base, he'd say, here's that kid, he made an error, he'd really get on me. My father saved the clips. He'd talk to me on the field, we'd laugh — he liked the fact that I made a joke out of it."

"He'd even watch you on the bus to the next town," Carmen adds. "If your arm fell off the armrest, he'd say you were likely to get picked off. I'd ask my dad, what's that got to do with it? I don't know — it never happened."

Of course, if you hit .300 — with power — you might get an easier time of it. "They were great to me," Pafko remembers. "Ed Burns, the old *Tribune* writer, wrote about me when I missed a fly ball one day — it was pretty windy. He wrote, 'Pafko in centerfield, should have been going north, when he was going south.' He was pretty clever."

Pafko recalls Warren Brown's famous prediction for the 1945 World Series (the Cubs' last) against the Detroit Tigers: "Warren Brown made the remark that nobody's gonna win. My wife was always so afraid of him — he always had a frown on his face. But you could get to know him..."

Warren Brown, who didn't want to be overzealous about the Cubs' chances in the '45 Series.

281

Some guys just liked to dig for dirt. "They were married in May, 1918," Della Root Arnold says about her parents. "I was born in February, 1919. Irving Vaughn once asked Mother, 'How long were you married when Della was born?' Mother told him, 'Long enough!'"

Fortunately for some, you could stay beneath the radar. "The press, they didn't fool around with rookies like me," Red Adams says.

"The newspaper guys, they didn't have anything to do with us," Al Epperly agrees.

"I used to carry papers when I was a kid."

Corky Van Dyke, on his successful career transition from journalism to baseball

---

Yet they could be useful — sportswriters gave Ox Miller his nickname. "That happened in the minor leagues," he recalls. "I pitched both games of a double-header in Lincoln, Nebraska, out in the Western League. The morning paper came out and said, 'That young John Miller is strong as an ox.' The papers were competing, and the evening paper came out and said, 'He's as dumb as an ox — he's gonna hurt his arm!'"

Harry Neily, a long-time sportswriter, helped William Wrigley design and build the ballpark on the Island. And Bill Veeck was president of the team from 1919-1933 — after Wrigley hired him away from the press corps. Wrigley didn't like Veeck's criticisms, so he challenged him: If you can do better, let's see your stuff. Veeck delivered — with a pair of pennants during his tenure.

Yet some writers were harmless. "Mother, Pat Dean, and Marion Grimm — they used to get into all kinds of trouble," Della says. "Ivey Overholt was the PR woman on Catalina. She gave a tea, and they didn't want to go. Mother said, 'I've never been to anything as innocuous as a tea.' So they raided the hotel and found lampshades to wear, and Pat put on Dizzy's golf shoes — they looked terrible! One man said, 'They don't look like they're at a tea — they look like a bunch of nuts at a cocktail party!'"

Clips for the ages

Over the years, the boys in the press car sent home some pretty magnificent writing. Here are some choice examples — the best from Catalina, alphabetized by reporter for your maximized enjoyment.

Warren Brown played for Sacramento in the Pacific Coast League, later nicknamed Red Grange "The Galloping Ghost," & wrote the Cubs history in 1946.

Chicago Herald & Examiner, 1938
Brown would dateline his 'enroute' stories with 'locations' like...

"SOMEWHERE WEST OF CLARK & ADDISON" and

"STILL GOING, Ariz. — "

<u>1940</u>
On Saturday Hartnett intends to cut the practice short so his men can go down to the dock to see the good ship Avalon arrive. This is one of the two moments of greatest excitement here daily. The other one is when the good ship Avalon sails.

The Chicago Cubs, 1946
In later years Chicago baseball writers covering the Cubs' Spring Training camp at Catalina Island were frowned upon by certain of the shopkeepers for threatening to bootleg in Avalon a brand of gum Wrigley didn't manufacture.

Ed Burns:

Chicago Tribune, 1936
AVALON, Cal. — Philip K. Wrigley, respectfully hailed on this, his so-called magic isle, as Philip I of Santa Catalina, king of Avalon, emperor of Escondido, maharajah of the Isthmus, and boss of the Chicago Cubs, arrived here by seaplane late today.

<u>1937</u>
AVALON — Mountains falling down, rain pouring out of black skies, seals, millions of seals, barking saucy reprimands at angry Neptune as he kicks the pacific to the very bedsteads of winter-soft athletes. Thus the Cubs' $35,000 meaningless training season goes on apace.

Like other teams, the Cubs issued media guides each year...so reporters could easily tell the players apart & things like that.

1937 (Exhibition game headline)

CUBS TROUNCE PIRATES, 23-14; IT'S BASEBALL (?)

(...and the Box Score headline)

Tsk! Tsk!

1940 (Covering the first intrasquad game)

Something of a World Series tenseness pervades the Island. If you think this statement is evidence of slaphappiness, make the most of it.

1941

The morning drill had been completed and the lads had retired to their clubhouse for tea and crumpets, when the heavens started giving down.

1950

Host Frankie Frisch today delayed his welcoming address...for his jolly camaraderie camp and marshmallow toast...

Ed Burns of the Chicago Tribune, *who once took another reporter's punch that was intended for Ronald Reagan. Here, Ed contemplates how the old ballyard might look when viewed from a hot-air balloon ride.*

Edward W. Cochrane:

Chicago American, 1937

AVALON, Catalina Island — Mr. Charles Grimm, the Missouri rancher, sat in the warm afternoon sun on the lawn in front of the St. Catherine fodder house. He was facing a calm sea to the east; light breakers washed lazily along the sandy beach. All was peaceful and quiet, except the mind of the manager of the Bruins.

Jimmy 'the Cork' Corcoran (who took a swing at fellow reporter Dutch Reagan):

Chicago American, 1930

Now, then, it's raining outside. We can see the raindrops running down the palm stems just outside our window. Probably they don't call them stems, but we didn't have any palm trees in our back yard in Chicago; so why get technical about it?

In his *Cork Tips* column, 1930

AVALON, Cal. — Random ramblings on a misty day on Catalina...a card table surrounded by Gabby Hartnett, Bob Lewis, Danny Cahill, and Cholly Grimm...Hornsby snoozing...Hartnett ho-hoing as usual about something...Blake looking over the clippings that someone sent him from Chicago...Misting outside...well, they say it's mist...McCarthy scowling on a huge divan...

Braven Dyer:

Los Angeles Times, 1938

Occasion of the near catastrophe was the first spring game between the regulars and rookies, won by the veterans in a photo finish, 20 to 6.

Frank Finch:

Los Angeles Times, 1951

Four ink-stained wretches from Chicago are here with the Cubs...

Gentleman Jim Gallagher became Cubs' General Manager after his writing career, then worked in the Commissioners' office:

Chicago American, 1935

Charlie Grimm was the happiest man in the world today.

Andrew Hemingway Lotshaw and Robert Lewis were the busiest.

Over in the Santa Fe's railroad yards they were prettying up the California Limited.

That could only mean one thing — the start of another Cub trip to Catalina Island, 15th to the beautiful rock in the Pacific.

Gentleman Jim Gallagher — who, like Bill Veeck, made the leap from the press box to the front office.

John C. Hoffman:

Chicago Daily Times, 1937

One of the first things Manager Grimm did upon taking off on this tour was to order a ban against poker among the players this year. This is a precedent which figures to tax the imagination of some of Herr Grimm's hands. A few of them will have to invent some new methods of getting all the money on the club. A pistol is sometimes a handy instrument, but it leaves tragic results.

Rainy 1937

One of the natives reported this morning that he saw the sun peek out from behind a cloud, but they promptly hauled him off to a psychiatrist.

What happened to that fellow is not yet clear. Some say he was hit by a boulder while passing the landslide on the only road leading from the St. Catherine Hotel to Oscar's Trocadero down in the center of Avalon, but a more reliable report said he merely had been watching Charlie Grimm and Secretary Bob Lewis do their wrestling pantomime.

1937

During our stay on Catalina Island, some of us sent out terrifying bulletins about rain, landslides, hailstorms, and the presence of Hollywood cuties. These things were supposed to have impaired the Spring Training of our Cubs, but they served nonetheless to harden the boys to life's complexities.

After rain, hailstorms, landslides, and the presence of Hollywood cuties, the White Sox will be a cinch for Manager Charlie Grimm's men.

1937

The Cubs went over to the Isthmus on Catalina Island the other day, but I didn't go along. I figured I could do the paper more good staying on the beach telling these Catalina girls...I mean fans, about the SUNDAY TIMES' new Coloroto section. Always on the job, that's me.

Edgar "the Mouse" Munzel:

Chicago Sun, 1947

"This kid reminds me of Chuck Hafey the way he levels on that ball at the plate," gurgled Grimm.

The Mouse's opinions roared — Edgar Munzel.

John C. Hoffman, sandwiched between Bob Lewis & Gabby Hartnett, cooking up burgers rather than humorous copy in the Spring of 1939.

Dutch Reagan, also a radioman at the time and later a spokesmodel for Borax and civil servant:

In his *Around the World of Sports* column in the *Des Moines Dispatch*, 1936

Heads, I tell you about my operation; tails, you get another load of Catalina, and if it stands on edge you get a break and the editor gets no column. Well, here goes... Can you imagine that? One register in the floor and I'm out two bits.

1936

In Andy Lotshaw's book a pitcher's bad day is just like our own. You know it is when you begin by dipping your tie in the coffee and end up missing the last car home.

1937, aboard the train in California

I'm quitting right here because the scenery is getting good. (Outside the car I mean.)

1937, after spending most of the column describing a goat hunt into the mountains on horseback

Now where did I lose that ball club? I've got to find 'em before this gets in print or I'll wait in vain for an expense check. Wait a minute — here comes trainer Andy Lotshaw.

1937

The Cubs are slapping apples in the grapefruit circuit, my carpet bag is on the shelf, and my favorite operation story is being second-billed... which is a break for you.

I've got enough for my column now. Let's go fishing.

"Now you're talking," Charlie Root says. "Get Klein and English."

Here you are boss — I'll be seeing you next week.

This is the press box at Wrigley Field on Catalina, about 2 Springs before that upstart radio kid from Iowa, Reagan, spread his stuff out all over the place.

I.E. Sanborn:

Chicago Tribune, 1920

This morning some of the boys who forgot to set their watches back walked into the diner at 5:30 and were surprised to find all the writers sleeping.

Overtown to the Other Wrigley Field

Before Anybody Found a Diamond at Chavez Ravine, a Beautiful Ballpark (or Two) Graced Los Angeles

"L.A. was a five-and-rollin' city — that was the '30s, man!"

Lefty Carnett

There's uptown, downtown, midtown, and cross-town (as in rivals). Yet there's one more that you may not have heard before. The locals on Catalina coined a new word to describe heading toward the big city on the mainland:

Overtown.

As in, "I'm going Overtown to see an Angels game." It's what you do when you hop the ferry to do something you can't do on the Island.

After they finished their Spring rituals on Catalina each season, the Cubs would hop Overtown on the next leg of their journey. That usually meant a few exhibition games in Los Angeles, followed by either a brief Northward leg to San Francisco or a direct move Eastward, to Arizona.

Keep in mind: Mr. Wrigley also owned the Pacific Coast League franchise, the Los Angeles Angels, in those days. During most of those years, the Coast League also had teams in Hollywood (the Stars played at Gilmore Field, now a parking lot for CBS), San Diego (the Padres, natch), San Francisco (the Seals), Oakland (the Oaks), and Sacramento (the Solons), among others. Please do not ask what a Solon is — but rest assured, Catalina Cub Dick Bartell went on to become one. (Come to think of it, Dutch Reagan became a solon, too — a Sacramento solon, no less, whilst governor of California!) In the '20s, there was even a team called the Vernon Tigers, in a now-lost

The scorecard says Wrigley Field — but it ain't Chicago.

L.A. suburb that's merely a freeway exit. Vernon was owned by silent-film star Fatty Arbuckle, who, 60 seasons before O.J., was accused of a similar heinous crime. Fatty, too, was acquitted.

The Coast League provided fertile Springtime soil for exhibition games, while other teams that trained Overtown (like the White Sox, often at Brookside Park in Pasadena — next to the Rose Bowl — and the St. Louis Browns, in Burbank) also helped with the big-league game faces.

A sampling of other California Spring Training sites, before Arizona's Cactus League was officially in place:

* The Cubs trained in Los Angeles (1903 & 1904) & Santa Monica (1905)...& for an odd brief year in Long Beach (1966)

* The White Sox trained in San Francisco, 1909-10

* The Red Sox came cross-country to train in Redondo Beach in 1911

* For reasons no one can fathom, the Detroit Tigers chose Palo Alto (a S.F. suburb) for a single season, 1932

* And the Pirates held camp in places like Pasadena & Paso Robles over the years

Old-timers may recall that there was actually *another* Wrigley Field, besides the one in Chicago. Yep, home of the P.C.L. Los Angeles Angels. It looked a lot like the Cubs' home field...and in fact, you've probably seen it used as a backdrop on some old movies and TV shows (like *It Happens Every Spring* and an episode of *The Munsters*, where Herman got a tryout with the Dodgers). In the late '50s, there was a TV show called "Home Run Derby" filmed there — where Hank Aaron, Willie Mays, Mickey Mantle, & Duke Snider took turns teeing off...long before today's pre-All-Star-Game ritual. Of all places, it was located at the corner of 42nd & Avalon.

It was kinda small. Sluggers loved it, pitchers didn't. Cal McLish says, "Hollywood was a good park to pitch in, after being in L.A. You didn't have to worry as much about home runs — it was a nice change of scenery from Wrigley Field."

Trivia: After they moved West from Ebbets Field, where did the freshly-minted Los Angeles Dodgers play their home games?

That's right — the Cubs aren't the only team who can claim their local stadium was Wrigley Field, because the Dodgers called the L.A. version home in 1958.

Quite a few interesting things happened at Wrigley/L.A. Chuck Connors displayed plenty of his pre-acting talents on the field there — like cartwheeling around the basepaths after swatting a home run — and long-time Angel Billy Schuster (who did enjoy a brief wartime stint with the Cubs) climbed batting cages and charged opposing pitchers on easy grounders, and occasionally might slide into the dugout after popping out. ("I guess you'd call Bill Schuster right comical," says Howard Auman. "He got thrown out at 1st one time — the stands were close, and he ran up into the stands and sat down there!")

Two of a kind: This is what Wrigley Field in Los Angeles looked like, before some wrecking balls ran into it in 1966.

Movie star Gail Patrick (she made 62 films) co-owned the Hollywood Stars with hubby Bob Cobb. They'd occasionally hop to Catalina from Overtown to talk baseball with Charlie Grimm & the other Cubs. Later, as Gail Patrick Jackson, she was executive producer of the Perry Mason TV series.

More Trivia: When the Los Angeles (then California, now Anaheim) Angels joined the American League in 1961, where did they play their home games?

Say, you're getting pretty good at this. Yep, during their rookie year, the Angels played their home games at Wrigley Field, too. So the trivial truth is, 3 current major league teams played their home games at a facility named Wrigley Field.*

There were perks to playing Overtown. "Every day, movie stars sat back of the dugout," Lloyd Lowe recalls. "One day, Bing Crosby came out. I see this old fella, bald-headed, smoking his pipe in the stands. And Red Barrett says, 'That's Bing Crosby over there.'

"And I say, 'No it's not.'

"And he says, 'Go look real close. He hasn't got his hairpiece on.' I didn't want to embarrass anybody, but I went over there and by golly, it was him!"

Bing remembered to wear his toupee while sitting for this portrait; Silvers & Durocher did not.

The hockey-like brawls between the cross-town Overtown rival Angels and Stars are legend, too. Yet surely those young men found more to do than baseball. A few of the guys were known to watch the ponies run at the local tracks (if they didn't leave L.A. altogether for the track south of the border). Mr. Wrigley often took the entire team to prizefights — in fact, Wrigley Field even hosted boxing from time to time. They'd go to banquets, where stars like Abbott & Costello, Jimmy Durante, and Roy Rogers would entertain. At one 1946 benefit, none other than movie actor Ronald Reagan was the emcee.

Once Overtown, the Cubs stayed at the now-restored Biltmore in downtown L.A. Mr. Wrigley owned this one, like he owned the one in Phoenix (further Overtown). Before Mr. Wrigley's purchase decision, in the roaring '20s, the team stayed elsewhere — generally the Mayfair Hotel. And there were other arrangements available, too. "In L.A., I rented Novikoff's house in 1942 — out in South Gate," says Ken Raffensberger. And Della Root Arnold, Charlie's daughter, points out that "We lived a couple blocks from the old Washington Park in Los Angeles — he walked to work." Washington Park pre-dates Wrigley Field, of course, since Charlie pitched there in the early-to-mid '20s, and Wrigley/L.A. was completed in 1925.

* *We say 'current' because the Chicago Whales of the defunct Federal League also played at the one in Chicago, before it was even owned by Mr. Wrigley, let alone named after him.*

Southern California native Bobby Sturgeon makes the tough grab... *...so undoubtedly, the crowd goes wild.*

Local talent makes good

While Overtown was a long way from Chicago, plenty of Cubbies were home-grown Southern California boys. "Bobby Sturgeon, Peanuts Lowery, Gene Mauch, Metkovich — we grew up together," says Lou Stringer. "There were 8 of us who'd played in high school." Hub Kittle and Yosh Kawano grew up in Los Angeles. And some who weren't from Southern Cal...became local faves, through their on-the-field heroics:

* Cal McLish spent 6 years in the Pacific Coast League with Los Angeles & San Diego, and he won 20 games for the Angels in 1950.

* Johnny Klippstein pitched 2 scoreless innings in the 1959 World Series for the Los Angeles Dodgers.

* Al Epperly went 170-71 pitching for the L. A. Angels, San Francisco Seals, & numerous other teams over a stellar 17-year minor-league career.

Between his Catalina Cub playing career & his Catalina Cub coaching career, Charlie Root pitched & managed Overtown for the Hollywood Stars. Before all that, he'd also pitched Overtown for the L.A. Angels.

* Ed Chandler pitched for the Los Angeles Angels & San Francisco Seals in the P.C.L. until 1957. He was a batting practice pitcher for Dodgers for several seasons after that. Then, he stayed. "I went into the stock brokerage business in Los Angeles, and did that for more than 20 years. I was a member of the Wilshire Country Club in Los Angeles for 35 years. That was major league living — in baseball, I only made $5,000 a year for a couple years!"

Dizzy Dean, feelin' right at home with Gene Autry — that croonin' cowpoke who owned the Overtown Angels years later.

* Red Adams was the pitching coach for the Dodgers from 1969-1980.

* And Gene Mauch was a perennial All-Star in the Pacific Coast League for the L.A. Angels...before managing the California Angels from 1981-1987. He made it to the League Championship Series with the Angels, in 1982 and again in 1986.

Roy Hobbs: The Greatest Hitter There Ever Wasn't

An Iowa Farm Kid Missed His Tryout With the Cubs... But Came Back to Bust Up the Wrigley Field Scoreboard With the New York Knights

Roy said, "I'm going to Chicago, where the Cubs are."

Bernard Malamud, quoting Roy Hobbs in *The Natural*

Hey, if Dutch Reagan could play '20s Cub pitcher Grover Alexander, why shouldn't Robert Redford play prospective '20s Cub pitcher Roy Hobbs?*

Most people remember Hobbs as a New York Knight outfielder, because of his batting fireworks in the 1939 playoffs against Pittsburgh (then managed by Sibby Sisti). But few recall that 16 years earlier, Roy set off from the farm for a tryout with the Chicago Cubs — as a hurler. Legend has it that he whiffed Babe Ruth (on 3 pitches) during a whistlestop, somewhere in the Midwest.

The year was 1923, so Roy surely was headed to Catalina.

Unfortunately, Roy was a bit of a greenhorn in those days — so he didn't understand big-city gals. Like the one who shot him.

This is Roy Hobbs' rookie card, unless you count the one from the 1933-36 Zeenut set of Pacific Coast League stars (which also contains Joe DiMaggio's pre-rookie card).

Writer Bernard Malamud wrote this account in 1952, filled with references from recent sports-page headlines — like the fact that a crazed lady had taken a few shots at ex-Catalina Cub Eddie Waitkus in a Chicago hotel in 1949.

Even fans who know that story may not realize another Cub — Billy Jurges — was also shot by a lady admirer, also in a Chicago hotel, in 1932.

Both fellas recovered fully, fortunately: Waitkus played for 6 more seasons (collecting 4 hits in the 1950 World Series) and Jurges (playing in only his 2nd year when the incident took place), completed 15 more big-league seasons before going on to manage the A.L. version of the Cubs, the Boston Red Sox.**

* *This in no way serves as an endorsement of Robert Redford for president.*

** *It has been predicted that the Apocalypse will come when the Cubs & Red Sox make it to the World Series...game 7... 9th inning...tie score. I believe it was Nostradamus who made this prediction.*

Strange-but-true stat: Joe DiMaggio never did get a base hit off Roy while playing in the Coast League.

Of course, after Mr. Hobbs re-emerged as an outfielder in 1939, he exploded out of his slump at Wrigley Field, against the Cubs — shattering the scoreboard to pieces with a Ruthian blast, right after a lady in a white hat stood up in the grandstand. The record does not indicate that Roy pointed to the scoreboard beforehand, nor that Charlie Root was pitching. Perhaps it was Snipe Hansen on the mound, or Hub Kittle. (It is unlikely that Johnny Hutchings was the pitcher, because he was probably in Mexico by then.) Please send cards, letters, wires, cables, and telegrams to the publisher to fill us in.

A creepy fact: They were Cub teammates. (Both guys played on the 1946 and 1947 squads.)

A creepier fact: In February of 1946 (3 years before the Waitkus incident), the *Chicago Tribune* printed this dispatch from Catalina:

> *Waitkus, who will get a shot at Cavarretta's first base job, weighed in at 178...*

By 1960, Billy Jurges was sufficiently recovered from his 1932 incident to undergo another painful experience: managing the Boston Red Sox!

Phil Cavarretta instructs Eddie Waitkus in the skill of jumping out of the way.

The folks at Wheaties had some fun with their 1935 back-of-the-box card set. Featured here is Jack Armstrong, All-American — the 2nd-greatest hitter who ever wasn't. (Some say that Jack, like Roy, never existed, either...)

And later, in a maternity ward in New York, Roy quoted Ted Williams' line about wanting to walk down the street and have people point at him and identify him as the greatest hitter who ever lived.

(Gosh, this stuff is stranger than fiction.)

Of course, some of you might feel the need to point out that this stuff *is indeed* fiction — that Malamud made Roy Hobbs up, that there were no New York Knights, and that there was no lady in white.

Aw, sure — next thing you'll be saying is that Hack Wilson, Bill Veeck, and Jolly Cholly Grimm were fairy tales, too.

To which I humbly reply, '*Fap.*' Roy Hobbs (and his Catalina-era Cub history) certainly should be in my scrapbook. Look: I got pictures!

Here's a good action shot of Roy Hobbs at his Catalina tryout. It's really a nice likeness — looks just like him, don't you think?

Another non-existent Cub: Rube Appleberry was a cartoon character, invented by former Cub pitcher Al Demaree. The Rube went on to become a radio show, too...& for publicity purposes, he'd show up at Wrigley Field from time to time.

Billy Jurges gets plugged — oh, no, not again!

Trivia: Who served up Charlie Brown's 1st home run?

Royanne Hobbs, Roy's great-granddaughter, who was quite smitten with good ol' Chuck... on April Fool's Day, 1993. (Thanks to the late great Charles M. Schulz for the research!)

HEY, KID! WAIT A MINUTE! I DON'T KNOW YOUR NAME!

ROY HOBBS WAS MY GREAT-GRANDFATHER.. WHEN YOU HIT THAT HOME RUN YESTERDAY, YOU RUINED MY LIFE!

I JUST MET THE GREAT-GRANDDAUGHTER OF ROY HOBBS!

I NEVER KNOW WHAT YOU'RE TALKING ABOUT..

PEANUTS reprinted by permission of United Feature Syndicate, Inc.

Marcelino, Lolo, & Lots of Other Locals

Hang Around the Avalon Barbershop Long Enough, & You'll Hear Plenty of Baseball Tales That're Sure to Curl Your Hair

"Chuck Connors owes me money! We were having a refreshment at the soda fountain at the Island Pharmacy. He walked in, ordered something...then as he's leaving, he says, "Charge it to Marse," then walked out!"

1951 Avalon High ballplayer Marcelino Saucedo

Catalina has pretty much always had 2 alternate universes going on at the same time.

The 1st one, the tourists, is obvious: They shop the shops, take the tours, board the boats. Yet you have to work a little to find the other — the community of people who live and work there. Keep in mind, Avalon is a small town in America... with all the dynamics that come with other little places of about 3,000 residents. Visitors seldom see this side of the Island, but it's very real and very vibrant — populated by a cast of characters as vivid as the ballplayers who dropped by every year.

The epicenter of this seldom-seen Catalina is Lolo's Barber Shop, right in the heart of the village. Lolo Saldaña and his brother, Frank, have been running the shop for about a hundred and twenty years; every fact, every tidbit, every event, every bit of information, every morsel of gossip ever laid down on the Island has come through the shop's doors at one time or another.

A lot of the old-timers, like the brothers Saldaña, remember the Cub camps as though they were yesterday. Some remained on the Island — in fact, a couple of 'em became Mayors of Avalon — and others went Overtown for successful careers. There's a U.S. Superior Court Judge...the Bishop of Monterey...and others.

Yet in the Cub days, they were just kids with big-league dreams. Hero worship? You bet. The kids on Catalina got to know the ballplayers, up close and personal...and they cherish those memories today.

Gabby Hartnett & Charlie Grimm take a minute from their busy 1935 schedules to indoctrinate the youth of Avalon with the fine points of the game. Say, isn't that Theodore 'Beaver' Cleaver directly in front of Grimm?

293

Islander Sam Simpson demonstrates his unique skills for Gabby, in hopes it will land him a position shagging fouls for the Cubs in 1933.

"The Islanders prize the autographs they have gleaned from the various players," Jimmy the Cork Corcoran wrote in the *Chicago American* in 1936. "The boys have signed everything from a baseball down to a soda cracker."

"The Cubs would come in, and they'd all get acquainted with the local people," says Marcelino Saucedo, who played baseball for Avalon High School. "Their playing field was our training field. They loved that field. In the spring, they'd practice from 9 to 1, then the high school team got on the field from 2 to 5 — but there were always 4 or 5 guys who'd stay around. We got to be friends with them. I used to talk to all of them."

"The local people were all so nice, always glad to see us," Phil Cavarretta recalls. "They'd always greet us with a band. They only had 1 high school, and they'd bring in those kids 2 or 3 times, before or after our workout. We'd take a little batting practice with 'em, and the pitchers would go down to the bullpen and work with the pitching instructor. We'd try and teach them something."

"Times were different," Eddie Carnett observes. "People were pretty friendly. It was hard to get into trouble in those days — though the ballplayers had a pretty tough reputation. Times have changed."

Some of the ballplayers became friends with the grownups, too. "They were nice people out there," Ken Raffensberger says. "I got to know a dentist who got me into the wild boar hunting — he had heads all over his office."

"We'd set around the lobby, went fishin'," Bill Voiselle recalls. "The mayor took a bunch of us out to Seal Island."

Pat Malone tries out the latest idea in 1934 batting donuts, in the form of Islander Ernest Chellberg — age 3.

TAYLOR'S CATALINA DEPT. STORE

Welcome, Chicago Cubs!

An ad from the Catalina Islander *in 1947. In that same issue, Mr. Taylor (also the Mayor) issued an official proclamation that Feb. 16th was* Chicago Cub Day.

Teams of local ballplayers liked to challenge the Cubs — even as early as the 1st year out, 1921. "The island boys played as if their life depended on it," the *Los Angeles Times* reported.

"The interest that Catalina folks show in the team gives our boys a real boost," Charlie Grimm told the *Catalina Islander* in 1947.

One of the Cubs was so enamored with the Island...and its residents...that he became a local himself: Roy "Hard Rock" Johnson lived in Avalon for years, and raised his family there.

Close the schools, shut down the shops, let's get the gang, let's have a parade: Our Cubs are back in town!

Ken O'Dea & Clay Bryant enjoy the local flavor.

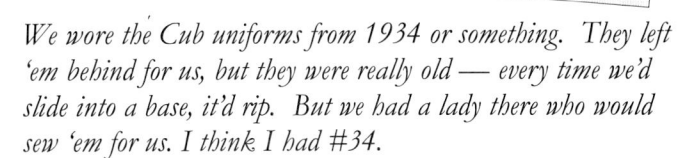

We wore the Cub uniforms from 1934 or something. They left 'em behind for us, but they were really old — every time we'd slide into a base, it'd rip. But we had a lady there who would sew 'em for us. I think I had #34.

Andy Lotshaw and I were good friends. He'd let me sit on the sides, and keep an eye on me so I wouldn't get into anything I wasn't supposed to.

Mickey Ahern, who was the PR man, he came by the school, and asked if I wanted to have my picture taken with Dizzy. I was sort of a typical tow-haired boy. I helped him out — that's how he got famous! They gave me an old dirty baseball as my pay.

"Inhabitants of this beautiful island in the Pacific are all astir over the arrival of the Cubs...It is not often the whole town turns out, but that is what it did yesterday when the boat docked."

Chicago Daily News, 1922

Let's meet the Catalina kids from the '30s, '40s, and '50s:

Scooter Hansen

Today: Runs a bunch of websites from his home in Sulphur, Oklahoma

Then: Played for Avalon High '51, Catcher/3rd base

Islander Scooter Hansen showed Dizzy Dean a few tricks in 1941. Then, after he got Dizzy straightened out, Scooter proceeded with his own illustrious career at Avalon High.

295

In 1947, they let Lolo Saldaña wear Hack Wilson's old uniform when Lolo played for Avalon High.

Lolo Saldaña sliding into home (which we doubt Hack Wilson ever did in that uniform), hustling to beat Pat Carter's toss to Don Nason.

Lolo Saldaña

Today: World-famous Avalon barber

Then: Lettered in golf, track, and baseball (all during the same time of year)...and basketball...at Avalon High School, '48...Charlie Grimm offered him a tryout in 1947...he played collegiate golf at Cal Poly San Luis Obispo

The Cubs left us their uniforms to wear. I had Hack Wilson's, 'cuz we were both stocky. Oh, I wish I'd have kept it!

They all used to mingle in town — they were very friendly. You could get real close to them. We used to have fun — we used to steal baseballs from them. We needed those balls to play with! We had relays set up, where we'd have kids all along the foul lines. If they'd hit one, we'd relay it away, and the last kid would run off with the ball! They'd be chasing us and cussing at us, but it was all in fun.

How Hack Wilson could play centerfield with those little gloves, I'll never know. He was such a great player, but he was such a drunk. They loved their booze, and those guys loved to fish.

Cavarretta was a chatterbox, always talkin'. He was a real ballplayer — I always liked to be around him.

I liked Gabby, because he was always with the kids. In batting practice, he'd be catching, he could throw the runner out at 2nd without coming out of his crouch — his arm was that good. A few years ago, his daughter was here.

They had dinners and drawings, around St. Patrick's Day one year, one of the players won a ham — Bill Serena, a shortstop. Well, he gave it to Frank, and he said, "Here, take this to your family." But my parents didn't believe him, they thought he stole it! They told him to take it back. But he finally convinced them how he'd gotten it.

Frank Saldaña

Today: Co-world-famous Avalon barber

Then: Still holds the single-season batting record (.667) at Avalon High School (Shortstop, '53)...the Phillies offered him a tryout, but he declined because he was getting married

Later: Helped start little league and softball leagues on Catalina

I caddied for Bill Serena. In the wintertime, in those days, we used to play bingo, and those guys would play. And all of a sudden, Bill Serena won this ham. He turned it over to me — I was watching, and I yelled "Yay!" when he won — and he says, "Here, take this home to your mother, son."

They were so nice to us — I was so glad they were around.

Gabby Hartnett's daughter came to the island one time. I met her riding in a taxicab. We got to talking, and I told here Lolo had some pictures, so I took her to the barbershop. She sent us a Hall of Fame deal, a nice picture.

> "Wrigley's Island Kingdom is governed by a board of trustees, the chairman of which is regarded as the Mayor. His salary is $2 a week. His honor is the town photographer, else he would have a hard time trying to live on his political salary."
>
> *Chicago American, 1925*

LOLO'S Barber Shop

" You Grow It — We'll Mow It"
SERVING YOUR BARBERING NEEDS
FOR 36 YEARS

Lolo and Frank Saldaña

Lolo & Frank will give you a shave & a trim...before inviting you up the hill to watch one of their little league teams play a ballgame.

"Hey, kid!" Bill Serena is undoubtedly yelling, "Bring back my ham!"

Harvey Cowell

Then: Entered Air Force after high school graduation, '32

Later: Two-time Mayor of Avalon (1952-1956 & 1969-1972)...Hosted President Richard Nixon in Avalon in 1971.

I remember them practicing. We had the drugstore, the Island Pharmacy, and after practice a few of them would come in — Stan Hack, Phil Cavarretta, and a few others — and they'd get a malted milk.

Mr. Wrigley would put on a program — a dinner-dance at the Hotel St. Catherine. They'd invite the Cubs and anybody in town who'd want to partake. And of course, the parade — Mr. Wrigley got out the old stagecoach — he and his children would parade with him and the Cubs.

Jack Cowell

Then: Left Avalon in 1938, hitchhiked to Chicago... stayed with Tony Lazzeri for a while, worked at Cub games in Wrigley Field

Later: Worked at aircraft plants, joined the Air Force (served in Europe), spent 21 years on LAPD

Roy Johnson was one of the coaches. He lived across the street — so 2 weeks before the team came, he'd ask me to play catch with him. So I'd go down to the field and shag balls. Every year, he'd ask me to warm him up, so he'd be broken in.

Gabby Hartnett and I played catch. He threw that ball so hard, it'd sting like crazy — but I wouldn't let him know.

They left their shoes and gloves and bats — I think I furnished the whole school with bats. I played baseball at Avalon High School, but I wasn't very good — I just played anywhere I could. I had some autographed balls, but I think we used 'em!

I hitchhiked to Chicago one year. It took me 3 days. I had 7 1/2 dollars, and I had to sleep under an overpass in Barstow 1 night. When I got to Chicago, I went to the rear gate — the players' entrance — and I saw Roy Johnson. Everybody called me Spec, because I was so freckle-faced. He said, "Spec, what the heck are you doin' here?" He took me in, and I shared Roy Johnson's locker, which was right next to Tony Lazzeri's. The year before, he'd been with the New York Yankees, and he had this big white Buick — so here I am, riding to the hotel on the Chicago lakefront in this nice new car, after hitchhiking all the way there! I couldn't get over that. I stayed there the whole summer. When Lazzeri said I could stay with him, I was surprised. Roy got me a job selling Cokes at the ballpark.

At this big hotel in Chicago, every day, the 1st thing they'd do was high-tail it to Lazzeri's room on the 12th floor...and all there was in the kitchen, in this big ice-box, was Miller High Life. They drank a lot. And they'd play poker. They treated me real good. Augie Galan was real nice, I liked him. He'd come up to the house for dinner. And Billy Jurges came, too. Gabby gave me his glove — they might have a new one, but they all liked the old one. They all treated me royally. Andy Lotshaw wrote a real nice letter of reference for me — he and Gabby.

A few of the Cubs signed this 1938 Catalina photo for their buddy Jack Cowell.

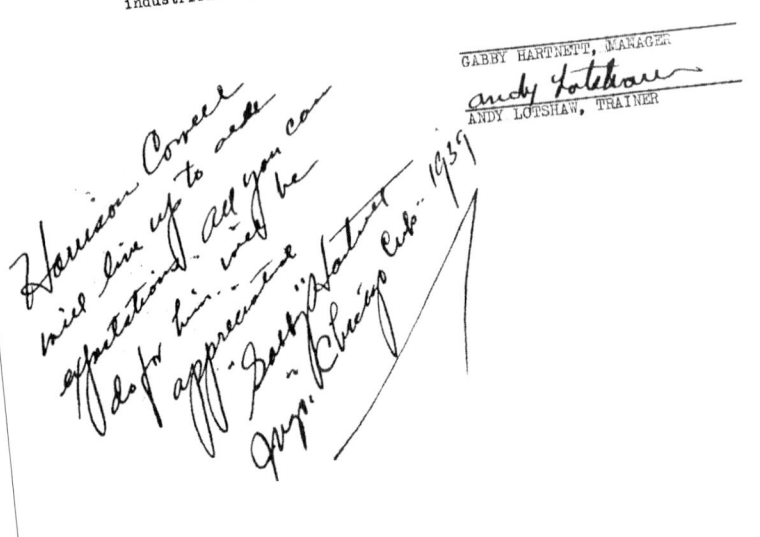

Islander Jack Cowell worked so hard for the Cubs when he got to Chicago . . . that Andy Lotshaw & Gabby Hartnett wrote a nifty letter of recommendation for him.

I knew Phil Cavarretta pretty well — he was like a young kid when I was there — he was just a year older than me! I got to know all the ballplayers well. When they came to Catalina, they'd buy steaks at the market and brought them to the house...and we'd cook for 'em. I played catch with them. They had this batting-practice pitcher from Hawaii, Clarence Kumalae. I drove back with him.

When they filmed Mutiny on the Bounty *there, they had a school picnic, and I played ping-pong with Clark Gable and Charles Laughton. I had some pictures of them.*

The guy who was the nicest person, Gabby Hartnett, would ask me to warm him up. Billy Jurges gave me a glove. It had a soft spot in the center. He and Augie Galan were pals — they ran around together, but I don't know what they did.

Roy Johnson's daughter, we went to school together — Joan Johnson. She went off to some private all-girls' college in Mill Valley.

We were always there, as a gang. We got foul balls — we'd shag 'em. Stan Hack would toss 'em to us over the fence. He was the 3rd baseman — that's where we'd gather, because in the stands, you were further away from Phil Cavarretta at 1st base.

The ballpark was just gorgeous. They used it for a parade grounds, too. And the high school team got to play there.

The Hon. Edgar Taylor, before he was quite as honorable, manning the bag in 1946.

Augie 'Goo Goo' Galan, a favorite of the locals.

The Hon. Edgar Taylor

Today: U.S. Superior Court Judge, Santa Clara County, California

Then: Went to Avalon High for 2 years, then to private school on the mainland, where he played baseball...then Stanford, then law school at New Mexico University

William Sanford White

Today: Author of **Santa Catalina Island**: *Its Magic, People, and History* — the definitive book about the Island — and another title about Catalina during World War II

Then: Son of Wilbur White, who greeted the Cubs as Mayor of Avalon from 1939-1942

I was in the grandstand every time I could, after school.

I remember when Hornsby first came out, when I was 6 or 7 — that would've been 1928 or 1929.

Stan Hack, the 3rd-baseman, he was very young when he came up as a rookie. He trained with Sacramento, and my Grandfather, Orrin Carter, had played professional ball with his manager, Buddy Ryan. Buddy called and asked us to keep an eye on him. He sorta became a part of our family every Spring — he'd have dinner with us, and bring some of the other Cubs to the house. I still have the glove he gave me, and the baseball that's signed by several of the players.

Dad was prominent on the Island. He had a Model A roadster with pigskin upholstery, and he'd pick up Stan and some of the other ballplayers after practice and take them to the Country Club and the Hotel St. Catherine.

Lon Warneke was a great friend of Stan's — he'd come for dinner sometimes. Kiki Cuyler was really a fine man; he'd visit the house, and Riggs Stephenson would have dinner with us, too. And Gilly Campbell, the back-up catcher for Gabby Hartnett, would stop by.

Lon Warneke, warming up for supper.

Doug Bombard

Today: Runs Catalina Express boat service and Two Harbors resort area

Then: Son of Mayor Al Bombard, who welcomed the Cubs back in 1946

I went into the service and was stationed in Scatfield, Illinois in 1945, when the Cubs won the pennant. They'd let us go down to St. Louis when the Cubs were in town, out at the ballpark, I called out to 'em; they came over and we chatted.

They were a good bunch of guys. My dad was mayor part of the time — he used to take them fishing. I went out with them several times. Charlie Root, Phil Cavaretta, Gabby, Jimmie Wilson, Larry French — I have some pictures of Wilson with a big string of fish. That time of year, they probably caught rock bass. The kids all went down to try and meet them — I guess I had an edge, because my dad took them out fishing.

Doug Bombard's dad (Al the Mayor) took some of the guys (like Larry French) fishin' in the late '30s. Little Doug didn't get into this photo, but he did get into the boat.

We used to give them the key to the city when they came over on the steamer to the camp. They had barbecues, too. I got in on a few at Rancho Escondido.

I remember going up there and watching — I got to know some of them fairly well. They were a bunch of cut-ups. I met Dizzy Dean when he joined the Cubs, when he was trying to make a comeback. It was a thrill. They sent me an autographed ball 1 year — I was just a kid — my dad caught me playing ball with it!

Roger Upton

Today: Creates and sells novelties on the Island

Then: Played baseball at Avalon High, '43...then went into the service

When I was 14 or 15, I got to work out with the team. I came over in 1931 for the first time — I was 6 — then every year. We stayed in band row, Las Casitas, where some of the lower class ballplayers had to stay.

I chased balls, and I got to play catch with them. I knew a lot of 'em — Stan Hack, Charlie Grimm — Lennie Merullo

paid the most attention to me. He used to take his time, talk to me when I was 12 or 13, about what I wanted to do, about playing baseball.

I got the first glove I ever got from Charlie Grimm, when I was 8, hanging over the fence, he handed it to me. One of those old-time gloves, with the short fingers — I kept it for years, I might still have it.

Absolutely, we got to go onto the field. I got to play 2nd base! I was about 16 at the time, I'd get out there. I got a break, I got to play with them. I think their regular 2nd baseman wasn't there, and Lennie Merullo was playing short, and they let me in. Bill Lee, he was their ace pitcher, I got to do a little batting practice with him. He threw me an easy one, and I hit it right back to him.

Roy Johnson saw me work out when I was a little older, in high school. He gave me a chance to go to Tulsa. "When you get out of school," he said, "we'll get you a shot down there." But I went into the service, and I hurt my arm, so I never went.

Bud Smith

Today: Mayor of Avalon

Then: Played baseball at Avalon High, '42

Later: Flew B-25s in the Army Air Corps, then worked for United Air Lines

I played ball at the high school. Whatever position we played, there would be a day set aside, a couple of times while the Cubs were here, where we would go down to the field, and if I played first base, and Phil Cavaretta was the first baseman, he'd take me on the field and give some instruction — here's how to move your feet, here's how to stretch, here's how to throw the ball, be alert, think ahead of the ball, think ahead of the play.

The biggest percentage of them went to the same church I did, St. Catherine's Catholic Church, and we'd go to the same mass. We just idolized them, and they associated with us quite a bit, and they'd spend as much time with us as they could. At the parish, we'd have a St. Patrick's Day fundraiser, they were the guests of honor. We'd have a parade, a band when they came to town, open buses, old horse-drawn carriages.

One year, I think it was 1937, there was a lot of rain, and they were staying at the Hotel St. Catherine — about a mile outside of town. It was rainy a little bit, and they'd hang around Sportland, bowling, playing pool, badminton, and the kids would hang out.

During the regular season, anytime they'd win, there'd be a blue flag with the Cubs' insignia on it that the harbormaster would fly. They'd put up a red flag if they lost — we didn't like to see that.

Marse the Pirate: Islander Marcelino Saucedo was a coach for the Pittsburgh Pirates' Rookie League team in 1969... on the same staff as Harvey Haddix & Danny Murtaugh.

Marcelino Saucedo

Today: College guidance counselor in Los Angeles

Then: Avalon High School, '53, 2nd baseman/pitcher

Later: Played baseball at East Los Angeles College, Long Beach City College, and Cal State Long Beach...teacher & head basketball coach/assistant baseball coach at La Mirada High School...worked for Pittsburgh Pirates minor league system (1969) & the Major League Baseball Scouting Bureau (7 seasons)

I had Stan Hack's uniform — his name was sewn in there. Stan Hack would tell stories, like how they'd put a hole in the glove, in the old days, so it would close around the ball. There wasn't much leather there in the 1st place.

Chuck Connors owes me money! We were having a refreshment at the soda fountain at the Island Pharmacy. He walked in, ordered something...then as he's leaving, he says, "Charge it to Marse," then walked out! I was only 17, and my sister was working at the fountain. It was only 50 cents, but I kept kidding him about it.

Walt Dubiel went to the Angels. He sent me postcards. One time, his wife came over, and he sent her to meet me — but I was away in college. My family told me he'd brought his wife to meet me, and I was shocked. He let me in on the insights of the game, he talked to me like more of a friend.

Monk Dubiel sent this postcard to his Island pal after the Cubs sent him to L.A.

Harry Chiti was this big, 18 year-old kid — but he couldn't throw the ball back to the pitcher. I guess he learned how! I remember asking Johnny Vander Meer about his no-hitters. He was a good human being. Wayne Terwilliger was one of my favorites. Mickey Owen, he was funny — he could foul tip the ball a hundred times. He was famous for that. They used to get pissed off at him.

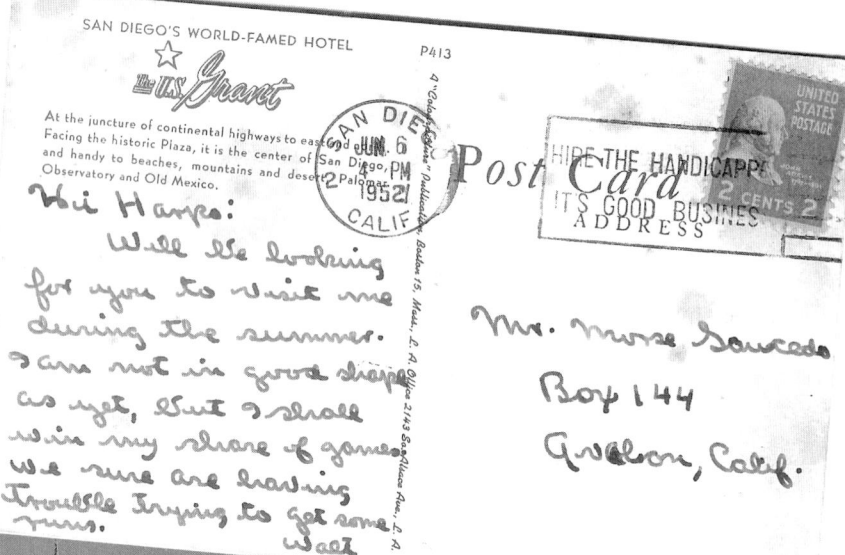

Smoky Burgess was very quiet, nice, but not outgoing. Cavarretta, he was quite famous. I never got autographs. A lot of 'em did, but I never wanted to. We respected their privacy. The only way we got to have a relationship was on the field, as ballplayers.

I used to caddy for a lot of these guys — Marv Rickert, the centerfielder, Sauer, Frankie Baumholtz, a lot of 'em. They weren't good golfers, none of 'em were good tippers. They hit the heck out of the ball, but they were narrow fairways.

Smalley was one of the ones who'd go a month in advance and work out, he and Don Carlsen, the pitcher. We used to go watch them. They couldn't wear their uniforms because it was too early, so they'd just work out in their sweats.

We played a team from San Dieguito — they came over. The coach, John Huettner, was an islander — he'd grown up in Avalon. The game went 11 innings. He'd asked Roy Johnson to look at this 1 pitcher he had. After the game, he went down and asked, "What do you think of my boy?" And Johnson, in that Southern drawl he had, he said, "Oh, he did a good job — but there were 2 local guys I was looking at." He liked Foxie Saucedo and George Dasnaw. George at 6'2" played shortstop with good range and Foxie pitched 11 innings and hit the ball over the left fielder's head to win the game 7-6.

The Monk, suffering under Frisch's reign.

Joe "Foxie" Saucedo

Then: Played baseball at Avalon High '51, pitcher/shortstop...got his nickname because of his base-stealing prowess

Later: Worked for the City of San Diego — at the Padres' ballpark once, he rescued a Dave Winfield jersey from being discarded (which he got to give to his grandson)

The Phillies sent me a letter offering a tryout, but I was getting married. Lolo got an infield tryout — he was nervous. Conrad Lopez would catch for Bob Rush. He told me, "I've never been so nervous in all my life." I don't know if anybody besides Feller threw 100 miles an hour in those days, but he sure threw hard.

I had Charlie Root's uniform — they had his name inside. They were heavy! Can you imagine a 5-foot-7, hundred-and-35-pound kid wearing a heavy flannel uniform? We had 'em for years.

Emil Verban broke his bat. It was a hairline crack. Roy Johnson was looking at the bat — he used to call everybody, "Partner," and he says to me, "Hey, Partner, you want this?" So I got a bunch of nails and tape and wrapped it all up. That thing was heavy! The following week, we were playing against a high school from San Diego, and I got 4 hits. We went into extra innings, and in the bottom of the 11th or 12th I hit a long fly ball over the leftfielder, a homer, and knocked in the game-winning run. I came back to the plate, but the bat was broken — so I threw it away.

The players would work with the high school team. I was a shortstop, so I worked with Roy Smalley. He was a heck of a nice guy, real easy to get along with — he showed me a few things, like how to get a ground ball, how to throw to 2nd, fundamentals.

Monk Dubiel loved kids, he used to tell us jokes and stories, and laugh with us. He'd buy us ice cream — he was just a big old kid himself. Ol' 96, Bill Voiselle, he was real nice. He'd show me some pitching tips.

Foxie Saucedo takes a breather from base-stealing to pose for the 1953 Avalon High team photo.

Jolly Cholly — he was a good old guy, real friendly. Frisch was kinda grouchy, but he'd talk to us. The players would give us baseballs, some would come watch our games. Dubiel was always there. Chuck Connors liked to kid around.

After he was out on Catalina, Lee Anthony would let us come to the ballgames free in L.A. — once, he came out and he saw a bunch of us kids there, and he told them to let us in.

I caddied for Grimm & Roy Johnson; most of 'em played golf.

Michael Reyes

Then: Born in 1912, worked in the pro shop

Later: Set the Island 9-hole course record in 1954 — he shot a 26 — still unbroken, even though Tiger Woods played there as a teen

I used to go up, like a batboy, and play catch with Helmsley, the catcher. I was playing catch with this one fellow, he was throwing like a bullet, just warming up. I didn't realize how hard it was coming. I said, "Hold the boat" — it was just natural to them!

You'd seem 'em around, playing golf. You'd see 'em on the links. Hank Sauer was a good golfer, and so was Stan Hack. Being athletes, they could hit a long ball.

The Most Reverend Sylvester Ryan, Bishop of Monterey, California

Today: The #1-Ranked Priest in his California seaside community

Then: Played baseball at Avalon High, '48, catcher...son of Spud Ryan (Avalon cop & semi-pro ballplayer who sometimes caught & scouted for the Cubs)

Marse was 1 year below me. I was the catcher, & Marse was the pitcher. He had 3 pitches: slow, slower, & slower than that. I spent the whole game on my stomach, in the dirt, chasing balls. I'd finish the game covered in dirt. I'd go out to the mound and say, "Marse, can't you throw any harder than that?" I was always eatin' dirt when Marse pitched.

I've gotta confession to make: I wish I could've seen Sylvester Ryan play ball for Avalon High in 1947...

My dad would have me catch since I was high enough — he was a catcher, so it fell on me to be a catcher. Early on, he told me, "This is not gonna be your career."

Dad was playing at Salt Lake in 1929 when he met and married my mother. He was invited by the Cubs to Avalon for Spring practice in 1930, and settled there. He became a policeman. He stayed playing semi-pro ball, for the Catalina Cubs, as a catcher. He had a great arm. He'd say, "I hate the big guys — they swing bad and still hit." It was exciting ball.

Nobody else wanted to catch, so it was me. We got to wear the old Cubs uniforms, but by my senior year they were so threadbare. They lived at the old St. Catherine Hotel and dressed at the Country Club. The food was kinda standard, so some of 'em came to the house to eat, since they knew dad. Stan Hack, Gabby Hartnett, Charlie Grimm, and some of the others — they would come chuckin' into the house, and my mother would cook for them. Sometimes they were invited, sometimes they weren't. They'd eat a lot.

We'd go down to the field — we'd get out of school early and watch 'em play. I remember thinking, "How can you get paid to play baseball?"

Stan Hack was wonderful to watch, Phil Cavarretta was wonderful to watch. One time, somebody hit a line drive that hit once on the ground in front of Stan Hack. He was playing deep, behind 3rd base, and went to the right and caught it with his bare hand and threw it to 1st. I can see that like it was yesterday.

Stan Hack, graceful in the field.

Bishop Ryan's dad, Spud, caught for the Cubs on Catalina... when he wasn't on duty as one of the Island's 2 policemen.

"Manager Grimm today cleared up the mystery of John Doe, the name he consistently has given for the right fielder on the Yannigans. Officer Spud Ryan, night policeman of Avalon, known in the village as John Law, will serve as John Doe not only in the games here but will be taken to the mainland as a member of the squad — providing the Cubs can get permission from the board of safety."

Chicago Tribune, 1936

A 1936 Catalina team photo: "My mother and I are sitting in the seats behind them," Bishop Ryan points out.

I saw the pennant they brought over in 1946; that was a real thrill! I recall walking around the ballfield. Dad, he'd go up and work with the pitchers. Having another catcher around was good.

They were fun people — the stories they could tell! Lots of stories about the minor leagues. Dad would say, "We had to get out and push the doggone bus!"

There was a pathway beneath the grandstand, and a little locker room there. I remember the floor must have been made of tile, because I could always hear the clicking of their cleats as they walked through there.

Other Avalon locals you may know

Gosh, Beaver — didn't you know that Tony Dow (Leave it to him to have played Wally on a famous '60s sitcom) grew up on Catalina? So did Gregory Harrison (best known for TV roles like *Falcon Crest* and *Trapper John, MD*). So did General George S. Patton. Silent movie star Tom Mix had a home in Avalon, and so did novelists Zane Grey and Gene Stratton Porter. Locals, all.

A local bear cub greets Cubs Dizzy Dean & Gabby Hartnett, 1939.

*Island Ranchmaster Jack White gives a lift to Andy Lotshaw (riding shotgun), Bob Lewis,
Hard Rock Johnson, 1947 Parade Queen Barbara Marriott, & Charlie Grimm.*

For some inexplicable reason, 'Donkey Baseball' was once a big fad in Southern Cal. In 1948, the craze made it over to the Island; we hope Lotshaw didn't have to clean up the droppings.

The 1947 Avalon High battery: Pat Carter & Don Nason.

Where Have You Gone, Conrad Lopez?

A Catalina Kid Had All the Tools — But Would He Ever Make It To The Show With His Beloved Cubbies?

"Other teams used to be in awe of Conrad."

Marcelino Saucedo

Every kid in America dreams of playing in the big leagues. And in Catalina, you can imagine how the dreams took on a new dimension... since the ballplayers were so close, so real, so down-to-earth. The kids who played ball at Avalon High — often wearing hand-me-down Cub uniforms and gloves — could easily envision growing up into one of their semi-hometown heroes. After all, they played catch with 'em, slurped shakes with 'em, kidded around with 'em...

Back in the late '40s, there was one particular youngster on Avalon who had more than just dreams.

He had the *talent*.

His name was Conrad Lopez, and everybody knew he'd be playing for the Cubs some day. It was the story of the day in Avalon, but today...it's become a bittersweet mystery.

"Conrad Lopez was a special player. Dad recommended him," says Sylvester Ryan, now the Bishop of Monterey, then the son of a local semi-pro catcher who also acted as a roving scout for the Cubs. "I was so thrilled, because he was a classmate — I'd

Conrad Lopez, as seen in his 1946 high school annual.

gone to school with him, known him since the 1st grade, and here he was signing a pro contract with the Cubs! He was truly gifted — a remarkable player."

"Conrad was a fine player," says Del Walker, who was Conrad's baseball & basketball coach at Avalon High. "He had all the skills — he could hit, hit with power, run, field, and throw."

"I used to go work out with Conrad," Marcelino Saucedo recalls. "He was kinda quiet, very humble. He was a phenomenal 3rd baseman, a natural, but he could play every position. Several people would tell Roy Johnson, 'Conrad's a heck of a ballplayer.' But Conrad would never go until Roy invited him personally. So one day, when Conrad was there and Roy was there, I introduced them — and Roy asked him to try out."

307

Marse was amazed during Conrad's Cub tryout. "Conrad was at bat. My brother and I were behind the cage, and Bob Rush was pitching to him. He was throwing about 100 miles per hour, and we winced. But Conrad did okay, and they assigned him to Bisbee in Arizona."

Catalina barber Lolo Saldaña got a tryout that day, too — but his didn't go as well:

"I had a tryout with the Cubs in 1947. I was a golfer, too, playing in the City Championship. I was a junior in high school. Coming past 16 and 17, into the 18th, I was playing the defending champion. At the 1st hole we were even. I birdied the last one to beat him. Grimm comes up to me and he says to me, 'Hey, kid.'

"I says, 'What?' — Here's Charlie Grimm, come talk to me!

"So Grimm says, 'I like what I see. I'm having a tryout for a young man this afternoon. I understand you play baseball too.'

"I told him, 'I'm not that caliber.'

"He says, 'That's okay, I like your style.' So I go out, and he hit me about 6 balls. He hit 'em hard! I was just a kid, and I was so nervous — 3 or 4 went right under my legs, and I bobbled the others. Eddie Waitkus was over on 1st base, and the ones I bobbled I managed to throw to him, after I bobbled 'em 2 or 3 times. I was still all shook up from the tournament — it was nervous time. Well, he came over and patted me on the back and said, 'Kid, I'll see ya next year — I'm coming back.' But they didn't come back the next year. And when they did come back, the Cubs had fired him and Frankie Frisch was the manager."

Marse's brother, Foxie Saucedo remembers those wonder years, too. "The Phillies sent me a letter offering a tryout, but I was getting married," Foxie says. "Lolo got an infield tryout — he was nervous. Conrad would catch for Bob Rush. He told me, 'I've never been so nervous in all my life.' I don't know if anybody besides Feller threw 100 miles an hour in those days, but he sure threw hard."

"When he finally got his tryout," Marse says, "Conrad didn't look like a rookie. He'd always been very self-disciplined; the coach would let him into the gym at 7 a.m. so he could work out on his own. I'd go along sometimes."

Foxie says the Islanders beamed with pride when their boyhood pal turned pro. "Conrad went to Bisbee, then they promoted him up to Visalia, in the old California League — but he got pneumonia in mid-season, around 1949 or 1950, and he missed the rest of the season and came home. Then he got drafted and went to Korea, and I don't think he played after that."

Marse adds, "He got really sick, and took 4-5 weeks to recover, so they sent him home." From there, Marse says Conrad went into the service and did recon in Korea — along with his brother, Gilbert. Yet the locals kept their Conrad dreams stoked, since most ballplayers in that era simply did their military hitch...and went back to the game.

"But it didn't work out for Conrad," Bishop Ryan says, "and I remember Dad being really mad about it, since he'd recommended him so highly."

Lolo (2nd from right) enlisted his buddies to help him train for his Cubs tryout. From left: Buddy Pyle, Sylvester Ryan, Coach Robert Moore, Tyke Furey, the Barber himself, & Herb Kirk. Unfortunately for Lolo, the misguided group apparently gave him field-goal-kicking tips rather than baseball instruction.

Why didn't Conrad give baseball another shot? No one knows. But no problem, finding Conrad, to ask him, to hear his take on his Avalon tryout...to learn how he felt when he went Overtown and arrived in camp...to see how he finally realized it was over. After all, the small-town charm of Avalon means it's a tight-knit group; locals stay in touch (whether they've stayed on the Island or not), and everybody's pretty much up-to-speed on what everybody else is doing.

Except for Conrad Lopez.

Conrad, it seems, has vanished. He's not in Catalina. He's not where he used to be, in Northern California. He's not where he used to be in Southern California, either.

Gone. Disappeared. *Poof* — not there any more, like a Bob Rush fastball that must've become a phantom and gone straight through the bat.

Marse heard that Conrad occasionally likes to visit Los Alamitos to watch horse races...so he stopped by one evening. "Conrad was nowhere to be found," Marse reports — but while looking around during the 6th race, he put 10 bucks down on 'Lady with Rhythm'...and won $24 & change. "I'll try my luck again with Conrad, or the ponies, or both!" he grins.

So the mystery thickens. Nobody knows what short-circuited Conrad's career. And nobody knows where he went — the guy who everybody *thought* would go straight into all the recordbooks. "I keep asking around — I know I'll find him," Marse promises.

But until Marse's sleuthing can come across anything solid, Conrad remains a phantom. A memory. The kid who *coulda* made it...

Fortunately, Conrad's legacy lives on: his grand nephew, Phil Lopez, was the star pitcher on the divison-champion Avalon High School baseball team a couple of seasons ago.

And the memories remain; locals still get chills when they describe the pop of Conrad's quick bat, the *whoosh!* of his flaming throws across the infield.

(Besides Conrad, other Catalina baseball mysteries remain, too. Of the 60-or-so living players who practiced there with the Cubs, about half a dozen couldn't be found. So, there's hope that more tall tales and legends are tucked away in attics and fading memories from Illinois to the Isthmus, waiting to be told...)

Large crowds would gather to watch Conrad's heroics. Here, Dean Davis, Bob Jordan, Frank Hernandez, Sylvester Ryan (up), & Don Lasagne (down) catch the action.

"No one can tell me where he is," says Lolo.

"I've asked over at the Island," Coach Walker shrugs, "but nobody knows what happened to him."

"I think he lives in Compton now," Marse says, "but I don't know for sure. I've talked to a lot of his relatives — and even they don't know where he is."

Conrad's grand nephew, Phil, added some familiar chills to the Avalon diamond recently.

The next Conrad Lopez?

Yet Avalon's hopes of sending a ballplayer to the bigs remain alive. For instance, the Detroit Tigers drafted pitcher John-Eric Hernandez 2 seasons back...

"I see fear in my opponents' eyes," he told the school paper in Chico. "It's fun to make people feel stupid when I pitch."

But arm trouble sidelined the pro career. If time heals the arm, of course, there's always hope for a comeback...

And of course, there may be a kid out on the Catalina diamond right now, shagging flies and popping homers at the tender age of 10 or 12... who may end up on a bubblegum card near you in a few short seasons...

Avalon's own John-Eric Hernandez — an All-American up the Coast at Chico State.

At Cal State Chico, near Sacramento, John-Eric was named MVP of the Division II College World Series in 1999. He led the nation in wins. His college coach called him "the best pitcher I've ever had."

An Islander through-and-through, his teammates call him Gilly — short for 'Gilligan.'

John-Eric's dad, Richard Hernandez — nephew to Marcelino and Foxie Saucedo — is the baseball coach at Avalon High (and a local fireman), by the way. Apparently Dad taught him well; John-Eric has an advanced bagful of stuff for his stage — moving fastball, change-up, and slider, with pinpoint control — and a very easy, fluid motion.

Conrad (on the right) contemplates the curveball while chilling with pals Dado Unzueta & Martín Saldaña (who seemed to remember spending some quality time with Norma Jeane Dougherty) in 1947.

Great Trades (In the Cub Tradition)

Some Catalina Cub Alums Made Baseball History (& Legend) By Taking Part In Some of the Most Notable Swaps of All Time

"It seems to me, if you're in 3rd place coming down the stretch, wouldn't you want to get a front-line pitcher? I don't know. They had a losing club, but they were still filling the grandstands — why should they spend the money or trade? And they wouldn't. They'd get 45,000 on weekdays, standing-room-only on Saturdays & Sundays — why spend the money?"

Carmen Mauro

Even for the Cubs, the Billy Herman trade was a bit of a stretch.

Whether you were a rookie or a grizzled veteran, your thoughts weren't usually centered on being traded away during Catalinatime. In the Spring, all you cared about was making the team.

In fact, there generally weren't too many trades during Spring Training. There might be a Winter deal or two — so if any ballplayers hadn't read the papers, they'd get a surprise at train-boarding time when they saw a few fellas they *thought* were supposed to be playing for Boston or St. Louis. And of course, there was the occasional late-season trade to help out with a heated pennant race.

Yet when the Cubs did trade, they did it with *gusto*. In fact, a few Cubbie trades rank as the most...uhm... *interesting* of all time. And occasionally (like in the semi-recent case of Greg Maddux), they skipped the trade route altogether...and lost a player to free-agency, getting nothing at all in return.

Some of these trades weren't what they seemed... or what they were supposed to be. In 1941, for instance, manager Jimmie Wilson made a classic Cubbie deal — swapping Billy Herman (a future Hall-of-Famer) for either

* 2 pair of used sweatsocks
* 1 pair of used sweatsocks
or * Something less valuable

...because Wilson saw Herman as a threat to *his* job.

(Other great post-Catalina Cubbie examples include dealing a young Lou Brock for a broken fungo bat...rookie Joe Carter for a hot dog and a Coke...and aforementioned already-emerging Greg Maddux for *less* than a hot dog and a Coke, since they let him go for free.)

Lefty O'Doul met a similar fate in 1926, being swapped from Catalina to the minor leagues for a bottle of Andy Lotshaw rub. And others are lost to the ages. Back in 1940, for instance, long-forgotten outfielder Gee Gee Gleeson swatted .313 in his 2nd season for the Cubs. He was promptly traded to Cincinnati for shortstop Billy Myers — who proceeded to hit a meager .222 in a mere 24 games for Chicago the next year, which was all he ever did with the Cubs.

In June of 1951, Mr. Wrigley traded a large chunk of his ballclub for a smaller chunk of the Dodgers — right in the midst of a weekend series at Wrigley. "I went from a first-place ballclub to a second-division ballclub," lamented Eddie Miksis.

Of course, it worked the other way, too: Randy Jackson says, "I got a phone call in December of 1955, and it was a sportswriter asking if I knew I'd been traded. No, I didn't. I asked who — Pittsburgh? He told me it was the Dodgers, and I didn't believe him. You've gotta be teasing. They had just won the World Series. This was fantastic — I was going from a 6th or 7th-place team to a winner."

In fact, a trade was often a Cub's ticket to the World Series. Ex-Catalina Cubs who made it to the Fall Classic...only after *departing* Chicago...included

* Jackson played in 3 games of the 1956 series for Brooklyn, just 1 year after his surprise trade

* Turk Lown pitched in 3 games in the 1959 World Series for the White Sox, and didn't give up a run

During practice sessions, Billy Myers gave it the ol' hustle — inspiring the staff to believe they'd made a smart swap. Alas, during the regular season...Billy had to try and hit the curve ball.

Out on Crescent Street, a couple of the rookies ask Jim 'Gee Gee' Gleeson if he'd be willing to trade girlfriend Dorothy Harris for a glove, a bat, & a fresh pair of sweatsocks. Jimmy smartly declines, but is himself soon dealt to Cincinnati so he will not be confused with 'Goo Goo' Galan.

* Bill Baker played in 3 games for the Reds in the 1940 World Series

* Lonny Frey played in 3 post-Cub World Series: 1939 & 1940 (Reds) and 1947 (Yankees)

* Paul Schramka played in the GI World Series (1951-52)

* Bob Rush pitched in the 1958 World Series for Milwaukee

* Andy Pafko played in 3 World Series after Chicago dealt him: 1952 (Brooklyn), & 1957-58 (Milwaukee)...but Andy did actually get to play in a Series for Chicago, too, in their final 1945 appearance

* Hub Kittle coached on the World Champion St. Louis Cardinals of 1982

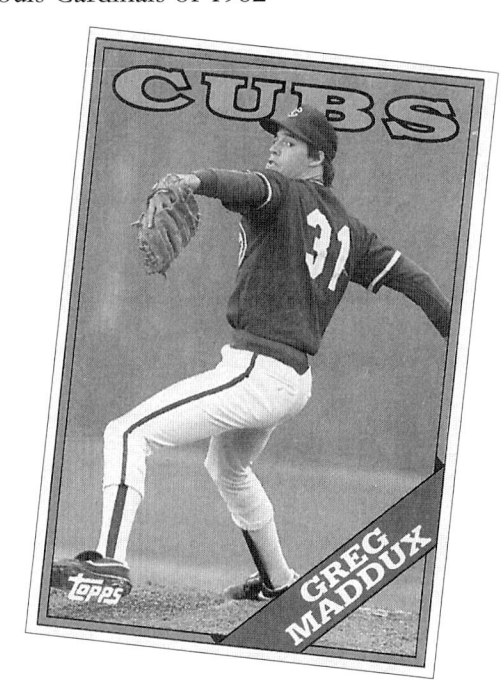

In 1988, Topps thought Greg Maddux pitched for the Cubs.

* Johnny Klippstein pitched 2 scoreless innings in the 1959 World Series for Los Angeles, & he also pitched 2 2/3 scoreless innings in the 1965 World Series for the Twins — "You have to be in the right place, at the right time," Johnny says

* Wayne Terwilliger won 2 World Series rings (1987 & 1991) while coaching for the Twins

Yet there was more to trades than World Series potential. Better teams meant tougher lineups to break into, as Carmen Mauro discovered after being dealt to the Dodgers. "Who's my competition?" Carmen asks rhetorically. "Duke Snider in center, and Carl Furillo, in the prime of their careers!"

Of course, mere trade *talk* could impact a guy's playing time, too. Bob Borkowski says manager Phil Cavarretta wouldn't play him, since the trade winds were blowing. "I got along with him," Bob says, "but he knew the front office was going to trade me — so he didn't have any reason to put me in."

And the lack of a trade could permanently sidetrack an entire career. Cy Block, who boasts a lifetime major league average of .302, bore the misfortune of being a 3rd-baseman behind perennial All-Star Stan Hack. "Cy led the league in batting in 1942 — he hit .364!" recalls his wife, Harriet. "But there was no free agency then, and they wouldn't trade him. Charlie Grimm wouldn't play him."

Bad news, good news. Depends who you ask:

Preston Ward: "I hated for the trade to go to Pittsburgh."

Lonny Frey: "I didn't fit in with that bunch, I didn't enjoy that bunch. It was cliquey, hard for a newcomer to break in, so I was glad when they traded me to Cincinnati."

And there were off-the-field ramifications, too. All the wheeling-and-dealing meant Roy Smalley never seemed to know who he was bunking with. "Dick Culler was my 1st roommate. After Don Carlsen, it was Gene Mauch. On the road, Terwilliger. Don and I roomed in Chicago; after he was traded, it was Bob Rush."

And sometime it just plain hurt, right there in your gut. After several All-Star performances in Wrigley, Andy Pafko got hit by a stunner:

When I found out I'd been traded, I felt terrible. I really felt bad — I was an established player, and it all happened so fast. We were playing the Dodgers in Wrigley Field. It was the 2nd game of a 3-game series, and at batting practice, some of the Dodger players came out of the dugout and were talking about it. Don Newcombe yells over, 'Hey, you're gonna be a Dodger tomorrow.' There hadn't been any rumors in Chicago, but they were all over New York. When the game ended, I went home and was sitting down to dinner when the phone rang. It was Wid Matthews, and he told me the news. My wife started to cry — she was a Chicago girl. So I was playing against my former teammates the next day! I hit a home run, I recall. Bruce Edwards, the catcher who was also in the trade, hit one too. And I packed my bag, because after the 3rd game the Dodgers were leaving town. It was kinda upsetting, because I hadn't any inkling!

The press wasn't always kind, either. When the Cubs swapped Dick Bartell for Billy Rogell, one paper reported: "Worn-Out Rogell Traded for Bartell — Bad Back, Lame Ankle, and Scatter Arm."

And now, for 3 really bizarre trades...

Bizarre Trade 1: "Ladies and gentlemen, your attention...*please!* Would the Cubs' manager please come up to the radio booth in the press box — immediately?"

In 1960, after pleading with Charlie Grimm to return (as manager) and fix all that had happened in the '50s (or what *hadn't* happened in the '50s, actually)...

...PK Wrigley realized Mr. Grimm was, er, past his prime. So he traded him to Cleveland.

Now, it's odd enough for a manager to be traded. But this one gets really interesting when you consider the fact that he traded Jolly Cholly for Indians *broadcaster* Lou Boudreau. Going, going, gone.

Bizarre Trade 2: "Hey, where's my locker?"

Double-header, Cubs hosting the Cards, May 30, 1922. In game 1, Max Flack started in the outfield for the Cubs...while Cliff Heathcote patrolled the outfield for St. Louis. Both went hitless. Flack, who lived a few blocks from the park, went home for a late lunch. Heathcote took a nap in the visitors' clubhouse. But while they relaxed, their bosses were hard at work... wheeling and dealing.

Specifically, these guys were traded for each other, right between games — the only time it's happened, before or since, in baseball history.

"I was asleep on a trunk," Heathcote said. His manager — Branch Rickey — woke him up and told him he was in the wrong uniform, in the wrong clubhouse. This confused Heathcote, whose nickname was 'Rubberhead' — due to an unfotunate ball-bouncing-off-the-noggin incident as a rookie, when the lad misplayed an easy fly in the sun.

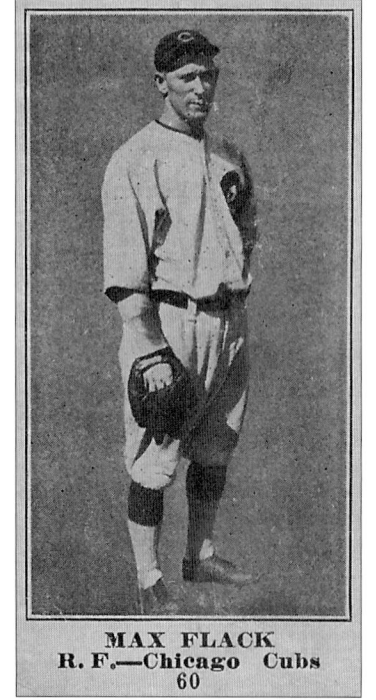

Across the way, Flack was returning — the record does not indicate whether he had a sandwich, a salad, moo goo gai pan, or perhaps some frozen sand dabs shipped over from Catalina — when skipper Bill Killefer told him that he, too, was in the wrong clubhouse.

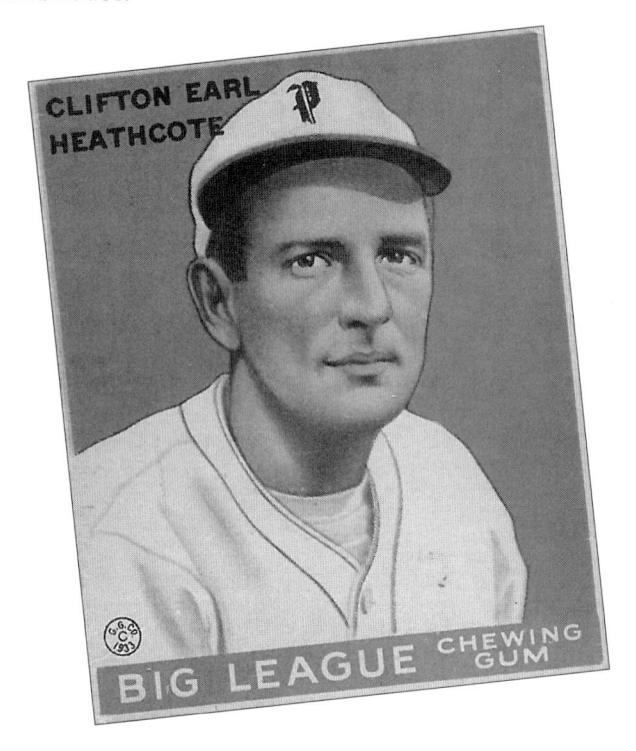

Here's Max Flack, wondering what's for lunch...& which team he'll be playing for this afternoon.

For good reason, the artist had trouble placing a team logo on Cliff's cap in this image. (It doesn't get much better on the back of the card — which dutifully reports, 'He doesn't break down any fences with his wallops, but he's a pretty dependable fellow to have on a ball club...")

Flack responded by getting a base hit for the Cards; Heathcote chalked up 2 for Chicago. The Cubs won both games, by the way. (We must wonder if anybody stole any signals in the nightcap!)

Anyhow, Cliff stayed with the Cubs for several more seasons, including 1925 — when, in Spring Training, he dared to appear in camp sporting a mustache. This was five decades before Charlie Finley bribed his A's to wear facial hair (thus, the Rollie Fingers look), so it simply wasn't kosher. The *Chicago Tribune* reported,

Cliff Heathcote, snappy outfielder, is in mourning. The gang seized him in the clubhouse before the initial workout, and trainer Andy Lotshaw wielded a razor on his upper lip. Cliff's cute little mustache was the sacrifice. The town barber, who was also addicted to the same, happened to be near. He also was seized and given an enforced shave.

They were still talking about the great mid-game trade at Catalina in 1930, nearly a full decade later — not long after Hack Wilson lost a ball in the sun to blow a game in the '29 World Series. 'Jimmy the Cork' reported on the ribbing in the *Chicago American*:

Much has been said of Cliff Heathcote's feat of playing with two teams within one day. This was okay until Hack Wilson refreshed our memory. He said he performed with the Cubs and A's the same Saturday afternoon last October.

And of course, my own personal favorite.
Bizarre Trade 3:
"They got *who* for me?"

Harry Chiti was the kid in Catalina camp when he started out — literally just a teenager. He bounced around near the end of his career, and was one of Casey Stengel's original 1962 Mets.

On a particularly hot summer's day in 1962, the Indians traded Harry to New York for 'a player to be named later.' After they'd had a cool drink, though, the Mets realized they didn't need Mr. Chiti after all — so they named *him* as the 'player to be named later,' and shipped him back where he came from.

In other words, Harry Chiti was traded for himself.

"Dubiel and some of the other players told us they'd rather play for Chicago than any of the other teams. They had a lot of trades with the Brooklyn Dodgers, and they all said they'd rather be with the Cubs because the Dodgers were so cheap! The Wrigleys treated them real well."

Marcelino Saucedo

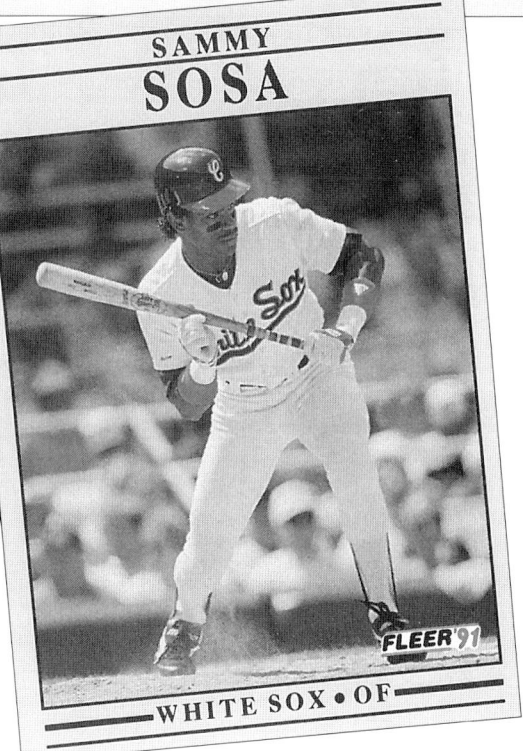

Judging from the look on his face, this photo was taken right after Harry received the news.

Of course, once every blue moon... some really dumb trades work out pretty well for the Cubbies!

On to Mesa

A Great Thing Comes to an End

"In Mesa, there was a dog track close by...and a lot of the players would go watch the races. When we were there, they'd name dogs after us. I bet on Randy Jackson a couple of times, but I'd always lose."

Randy Jackson

Things were a little too quiet out on Catalina in March of 1952 — because no Cubs were prowling around.

Yet at the time, Islanders didn't know the silence was permanent. After all, the last decadeful of Cub sightings had been checkered: from '43 through '45, they trained in the Midwest, because of wartime travel restrictions...and in '48 and '49, a large part of the squad practiced Overtown, in L.A. (where their Pacific Coast League partner team, the Angels, played).

So it didn't seem totally unnatural to be Cubless. The locals simply figured they'd come back after their brief hibernation.

But they never did.

Why the move? Several reasons — but money was pretty much the root of all thinking. After all, most teams were clustering to Arizona or Florida by the '50s, so exhibition seasons (and the accompanying ticket sales and concessions) were more important than ever.

"Spring Training changed from Catalina to Mesa," Lefty Minner explains. "We had teams to play — none ever came over to Catalina. It was better to play different clubs."

On the 1st day of ex-Catalina practice — Feb. 19, 1952, a day which will live in infamy — skipper Phil Cavarretta advises owner PK Wrigley to wake up and come to his senses.

Johnny Klippstein agrees that Catalina's remote location posed a problem. "Mesa and Catalina were very similar," he says. "They both had a nice ballpark to train in. The only thing wrong with Catalina was we had to travel everywhere else to play ballgames against other teams. You had to take the boat, then the bus to wherever you were going to play. Today, there are a lot more teams around to play against."

Of course, a few years of finicky weather didn't help. The facilities on Catalina required some hiking. The trip across to Los Angeles, through Los Angeles, and finally across the channel wasn't the most convenient on earth. And the crusty old reporters had soured on Avalon, so the once-grand PR from the Magic Isle...had degraded into a grump-fest in the Chicago papers.

"Mesa was a lot better — there were no facilities in Catalina," Yosh Kawano admits. "We had to dress in the country club, and the bath house before that."

"Mesa was darned good," says Bob Kelly. "The traveling wasn't as bad. Catalina was interesting and beautiful in the evenings, but you were pretty much stuck out there. It was on the edge of a golf course, converted to a ballfield — I thought that was pretty strange."

Truth be told, the Cubs had already been playing in Mesa for several seasons after breaking camp on Catalina — the Phoenix area was one of the 1st stops on the train trip back to Chicago. And the Oakland Oaks of the P.C.L. had camped right in Mesa for years already. Not to mention the fact that Phil Wrigley owned a regal Biltmore Hotel near the Mesa facilities (as well as a mansion in nearby Phoenix, although he hadn't set foot there in 6 years)...

...and it all came together when Mesa officials offered a sweet financial deal.

So, off the Cubs went.

"I don't blame them — they offered them 5 fields."

Lolo Saldaña

The Cubbies trained in Mesa from 1952 through 1965. Then, in 1966, the moved their camp to Long Beach — not far from the port that led back to Catalina. Hope? Nah. New manager Leo Durocher, freshly-plucked from his broadcasting career and several years coaching the Los Angeles Dodgers, could enjoy the commuting convenience to Blair Field. The next season, after Leo had found himself some new digs in Chicago, the team began a 12-year run back in Arizona — in Scottsdale — before returning to Mesa, apparently for good, in 1979.

HoHoKam Park, where Cubs go today...instead of Catalina.

The start in the desert was inauspicious enough. In the Feb. 19, 1952 *Chicago Tribune*, Irving Vaughn wrote that opening day was "disturbed slightly by a chilly wind that caused the Mesa Chamber of Commerce considerable embarrassment."

Not to be overzealously prejudiced toward Catalina or anything, and certainly not to be petty, but...may we say...*Ha ha!*

Just add water

While Mesa's part of the sprawling Valley of the Sunbelt today (believe it or not, *Mesa* is the *46th* largest city in the U.S., sandwiched between Oakland and Minneapolis!) it wasn't a whole lot more developed than Catalina 50 years ago.

"I loved Mesa, too," Turk Lown says. "They only had 1 golf course then, but they've built it up a lot."

Phil Cavarretta knows about the growth all too well. His buddy Yosh would occasionally drive Phil a few minutes out from the ballpark to view the scrubby scenery, suggesting Phil invest in some of the non-beachfront property. Phil declined, while Yosh bought...and make a few zillion dollars as a result. Sweet revenge for Yoshi, who'd spent much of the war in an internment camp in Arizona — not far down the road from that very spot.

Randy Jackson recalls the rugged local amenities in the early '50s, too:

"A guy had bought some land years earlier and drilled for water. It was kinda sparse, but he hit hot water — really hot. I mean boiling. So he turned it into a spa. The first 2 or 3 days, you could hardly get outa bed — so we'd go to the spa. It was just a couple dollars, and that water was 103 or 104 degrees. Man, you felt good. Those aches and pains were gone. But a few hours later, it was still hard to go up those stairs."

"I go back to Mesa now, and I can't believe it — it's so built up," agrees Klippstein.

Yet even then, "Mesa was laid out pretty good," Hal Jeffcoat remembers. "We used to go to the races."

Uh-oh. Races. Thus, the manager's dilemma: more distractions for the boys to find. Cavarretta, the 1st Cubs manager in Mesa, points out that Catalina offered little opportunity for a ballplayer to get into trouble. Still, while Mesa provided more nightlife than Avalon, it was hardly the big city in those days — so everything *was* close by. "In Mesa, you could walk right from the hotel to the ballpark," says Cal McLish, "and I liked that."

"We stayed at the Biltmore there," Jackson adds. "Mr. Wrigley owned it. It was really fantastic." Randy made the most of his change of scenery:

"One day, we played the Yankees in Phoenix. I hit a ball over Joe DiMaggio's head for a triple. That same day, I was on deck when the batter hit it to right field. But Yogi took off his mask and ran down the 3rd base line. He was really giving it to himself when he realized where the ball went. He said to me, 'I thought I saw the ball, but it was a butterfly.'"

And life went on...beyond the ballpark, too. Bob Rush recalls fondly: "Our daughter was born during Spring Training in 1952 — the 1st year we were in Mesa."

These days...

The Cubs play at HoHoKam Park now, where they've practiced since 1997. It seats 12,575, and it's named after a local Indian tribe (rather than serving as a tribute to Santa's jolly laugh). Actually, truth be told, *Ho Ho Kam* means '*the people who have gone*,' because the entire tribe suddenly vanished about 600 years ago. Archaeologists suspect it had something to do with the fact that they didn't figure out how to build dams or dig wells — but since Arizona is near New Mexico, the real reason probably has more to do with Elvis and radon and UFOs. But that's another book.

Compared to the handful of schoolkids and Overtown groupies who used to show up on Catalina, about 150,000 paying guests attend more than 30 Cubs exhibition games each spring now. The 48½-acre complex also includes 4 batting tunnels, bi-level bullpens, and a clubhouse that's nearly a third of an acre, all by itself. There are 3,000 parking spots.

Okay, it's a *little* better than the Catalina facility...

If you're interested in taking a field trip next March, here's the scoop:

* The address is 1235 N. Center, Mesa, AZ 85201. It's about 15 miles southeast of Phoenix, 6 miles due east of Tempe.

* The phone number is 480-668-0500.

* If you want to order tickets in advance, call 1-800-905-3315...or order on-line at *www.tickets.com*

* For info on lodging and such, call the Mesa Convention & Visitors Bureau (1-800-283-MESA)... or surf your way to *www.mesacvb.com*

Bob Rush, always the team guy, quickly adapted to the Arizona thing.

Although the grandstand was small — it offered 300 seats at the most, maybe — it's hard to imagine how it fit between the first-base line and the steep hillside. Yes, indeed, chunks of the old concrete foundation remain to prove the past — but there just doesn't look like there was enough room. Apparently, it was another great achievement of William Wrigley's engineering geniuses.

* Avalon High School, of course, and the visiting teams that enjoy the unusual road-trip boat ride from Overtown — which sure beats the heck out of a yellow-orange school busride down the smoggy, gridlocked 405!

* Local American Legion teams, local Little Leaguers, and the local softball league.

Hard to believe, but true: That big green grandstand used to fit right here. Notice a small slab of the original concrete foundation, still resting comfortably in the shade. (On the right: the same spot in 1942, manned by Bob Scheffing.)

So while the ghosts toil daily on the practice field — grab a seat beneath the line of fragrant eucalyptus, and you can almost hear them grunt their way back into shape — a question arises. Is there still any baseball on Catalina?

There's actually quite a bit. In fact, there are 2 other diamonds nearby to handle the load. Just up from the old Cub grounds is Avalon High School — home of the Lancers. Behind the quaint little campus is a well-kept ballfield. Further up into the hills is Joe Machado Memorial Park, named after a local who devoted countless hours to youth programs.

Actually, Joe Machado Memorial Park boasts rather interesting origins: In the late '70s, a developer sought permission to build a resort where Las Casitas stand. (The plan also included a resurrected version of the long-since-razed Hotel St. Catherine at Descanso Canyon, a mile or so down the hill.) The plan included eliminating the old Cubs' ballfield — so, Island officials said before they'd okay the plan, the developer had to build a new field for the community to use. Which he did. Yet after several years of planning and wrangling, the developer gave up — but not before adding a new diamond to the Catalina landscape. (And, fortunately, leaving this verdant patch of history undisturbed.)

You might wonder who's using all these great fields. Lots of groups, it seems:

Go, Lancers!

Avalon High's baseball teams are perennial league champs — and in 2001, they even won their division championship. The coach, Richard Hernandez, is an alum who went on to play collegiate ball in Long Beach. Richard's son, John-Eric, went on to pitch in the Detroit Tigers' organization (after leading the nation in wins for NCAA Division II schools, at Cal State Chico). And it's all in the family: Richard's uncle is Marcelino Saucedo, who coached and scouted in the Pittsburgh Pirates system in the '60s and '70s.

* *Just Softball* offers summer camps for kids on Catalina...while *The All-American Baseball Academy* based in Cypress (an L.A. suburb) & *Mister Baseball* (Long Beach) also offer summer camps on the Isle.

* And weekend warriors who can scare up a few bats, balls, gloves, friends & relatives around town.

"Benny Lefebvre, who's (former L.A. Dodger) Jim's son, ran a camp on Catalina; I helped with housing," says Lolo Saldaña. "He gave me one of Don Drysdale's bats — it was big and heavy."

> "I was involved with the little league for 37 years. In the '60s, I worked in the Recreation Department, and started the slow-pitch softball program so everybody could play. *Sports help people get along.*"
>
> Frank Saldaña

Yet the old Cubs ballfield is an equal-sports site. Kids have been known to play a little soccer there, and in 2001 Avalon High won a *football* game on the very same spot (30-0, no less!)...when construction work on their campus temporarily closed their home field. They've even had rugby invitationals there; imagine what Hornsby would think!

So on behalf of the Catalina Chamber of Commerce and Convention and Visitors' Bureau, I must humbly apologize for the lack of professional baseball on the island. But the amateur variety is still a heck of a lot of fun on a Saturday afternoon...

Lolo & Frank Saldaña go over the ground rules with umpire Hickey Rohlik in 1973.

In 2001 (the Golden Anniversary of the Cubs' final appearance on Catalina Island), the Avalon High School Lancers won the CIF Southern Section Division VI Championship...Overtown in Long Beach. By the way, they're at Blair Field — where the Cubs spring-trained in 1966!

The 2003 squad.

The Cubs Today

The Flannels & the Colorful Characters Are All Gone Now...or Are They?

"I only see the Cubs on TV occasionally now. It's the same old thing. They don't win. I don't know why they don't win now. I played 6 years and we had some idiots up in the front office. They would automatically trade for any ballplayer that Brooklyn was ready to get rid of."

Randy Jackson, in *Banks to Sandberg to Grace*

Hack Miller has uprooted his last tree. Johnny Hutchings discovered that he was indeed *not* in Mexico. Snipe Hansen finally trudged back to the Hotel St. Catherine. Dutch Reagan found himself a few other careers. No rookie ever managed to locate the bowling alley aboard the steamer. And Jolly Cholly Grimm belongs to the ages.

Alas, the great olde colorful Cubbies are just a memory now. Yet the team endures — albeit Wrigleylessly. Can today's group match the charm of our beloved Catalina ragamuffins?

Sure, why not? After all, the ballpark on Addison is still pretty much the same (assuming one attends only day games and refuses to acknowledge the presence of the lights.) Consider who's been wearing the red-white-n-blue down at the Friendly Confines more recently:

* There's Swingin' Sammy Sosa, with that weird little kiss-throwing thing that his mother surely loves as she watches from a thatched hut (with a satellite dish) in the Caribbean.

* There's Tarzan Wallis, so-monikered in the '70s because of his penchant for diving off rocky cliffs during spring training in Arizona.

* There's Flash Gordon, the only Cub in team history to both be named after a cartoon character *and* to have a Stephen King novel named after him.*

* And of course, there's Kerry Wood...whose rookie heroics (he set a big-league record in 1998 by whiffing 20 Astros in his 5th-ever start) have caused Cub faithfuls to wonder:

   1. How good can he become?
   2. How long until Chicago trades him for a bag of whiffle bats and a class-AA backup catcher to be named later?

Yeah, the game is different now. We have the juiced balls, bats, and batters...the short porches... and way-too-many minor-league pitchers in the bigs. Should Paul Schramka, at age 74, decide to suit up for this season...he'd probably whack a good 20 dingers.

* Granted, the novel was written when he played for the Boston Red Sox, and it used his less-colorful name (the book was called, *The Girl Who Loved Tom Gordon*), but hey — it's still quite a notable honor.

But...does *different* necessarily mean *better*? The flannels are gone, the grass at super-modern stadiums is made from petroleum distillates purchased from the Crown Prince of Saudi Arabia, and a team that won the World Series recently did it wearing uniforms that were purple and teal.

Teal!

Andy Pafko, who never would have worn purple or teal onto a ballfield, was glad he got to play when he did. Andy says, "We used to have a lot of fun in the old days. I played in a good era."

Yet there is, fortunately, one constant between that wonderfully good era and these modern times. One baseball truism that endures. A single bastion of stability in a sport gone mad:

The Cubs suck.

Yeah, we love 'em. Yep, we'll argue their relative merits (particularly against the Southside Sox) well into the night. And if anybody wearing a Cincinnati or St. Louis cap at a Northside pub were to say, "The Cubs suck," the aftermath wouldn't be pretty. But since we're family, *we* can say it. We can admit it. We can tell it like it is.

Yessir, our Cubbies suck. They will not win the N.L. Central this season. Or perhaps even this new century. But we still love 'em. Because, like our odd cousin or that nice worn-in pair of sweatsocks that we refuse to throw away, they're a part of us. They're our team. They're the good guys.

So while the standings remain frozen in the world PK Wrigley created, we must wonder: Are the players themselves any different?

Lennie Merullo, who's stayed in the game through scouting and watching his grandson play for the crosstown interleague rival, says: "The older ballplayers, they were a different breed. Not too many of 'em were educated — they were rough-and-ready guys, from tough towns. They played hard and lived hard."

Lennie, who stood at the same Catalina-altitude-adjusted sub-6-foot 5-11 as roomie Phil Cavarretta, personified that old-fashioned toughness — playing through a painful back condition. A lot of those scrappy old guys weren't big — just big hearted. Today, though, they're growing 'em taller...and with larger neck sizes, acquired in the year-round weight room.

"Today's ballplayers are overall much better — bigger and stronger, more mature," explains Fuzzy Richards. "In those days, there might've been a couple of big guys." Fuzz, for the record, towered over most of his mates at a now-not-so-noteworthy 6-1½.

Swingin' Sammy does his inimitable kiss/wave to ma routine, in the midst of uncorking more home runs each season than entire Cubs teams of the past.

The upshot from today's musclebound game, of course, is all those home runs. "To me," Cy Block told Harrington E. Crissey for *Teenagers, Graybeards and 4-F's*, "present-day baseball has lost the thrill of baseball in my day...as everything is centered around the long ball. The hit-and-run and squeeze plays are a lost art." Block blames this shift on poor training in the minors. Pafko has a slightly different take. "Today, they get better instruction — but they rush them up too quickly," Andy says. "Today, they make so many fundamental mistakes; they rush pitchers to the big leagues. They're much stronger, but..."

Kerry Wood whiffs another hapless hitter, bringing himself another K closer to being traded — the destiny of all stars who come up with the Cubs.

It must be the Wheaties

* The 2002 Cubs averaged just over 6-1¼ and just under 209 pounds. Yet the *biggest* guy on the 1929 N.L. champ Cubs was 6-1, 200 — smaller than today's *average* ballplayer! The average then was 5-11, 178. So while the height increased a little (2¼"), the weight soared by 31 pounds.

* Did the bulk help? Apparently so: In 2002, the team belted 199 home runs, compared to 139 in 1929.

* The average Cub made $2,396,882 in 2002 (slightly Sammy-skewed, of course). The entire team payroll in 1929 was less than a tenth of that. Even if you index for inflation, today's players make more than 25 *times* as much now — and that doesn't count their share of licensing rights, broadcasting rights, baseball card fees, TV commercials for local car dealers, and selling autographs.

"The Cubs take care of me, and I appreciate it."

Andy Pafko

Andy's 1950 Bowman card, where he is pictured contemplating how well the Cubs would take care of him in future years.

And so it goes. Baseball has entered its new century, and the watch may begin: The Cubs last won a World Series in 1908. We are mercilessly approaching *2008*. So the question must inevitably arise: Can the Cubs celebrate a full century without taking the big prize again?

We'll have to wait. But in the meantime, pop on the cable and find WGN, kick your feet up, grab a handful of pretzels, and watch today's happenings at the ballpark. Between innings, or if Mark Bellhorn happens to be fouling off a few 3-2 offerings in a row and your mind gets to meandering, let your thoughts settle on a sunny afternoon, somewhere around the mid 1930s, on a charming little island off the California coast. Short, stocky guys in scratchy grey wool jerseys are shagging flies in tiny leather mitts, scurrying along freshly-mowed green grass, squinting against the bright blue afternoon, not particularly noticing the fact that they can see palm trees as they make their catch, while kids from the local high school watch in unmitigated adoration...with more than a few stars in their eyes.

Aah, can't you smell the sweet gentle sea breeze now...

Appendix
Statistics & Such

"Look it up."

Stengel

Casey, encouraging one and all to look it up.

This is the appendix. We're pleased you've stopped by to visit the appendix.

The appendix is supposed to be page after page of stuff that looks like this:

Schramka, Paul Edward ("The Undertaker")
Born: Thursday, March 22, 1928, Milwaukee, WI
BL, TL, 6', 185 lbs.   Uniform #: 14 (Retired, 1972)

Batting Statistics

Year	Team	League	G	AB	R	H	2B	3B	HR	RBI	BA
1953	Chicago	NL	2	0	0	0	0	0	0	0	.000
Lifetime batting statistics			2	0	0	0	0	0	0	0	.000

World Series Batting Statistics

	G	AB	R	H	2B	3B	HR	RBI	BA
Lifetime statistics	0	0	0	0	0	0	0	0	.000

All-Star Game Batting Statistics

	G	AB	R	H	2B	3B	HR	RBI	BA
Lifetime statistics	0	0	0	0	0	0	0	0	.000

Pitching statistics

Year	Team	League	G	IP	W	L	SO	BB	SHO	SVS	ERA
1953	Chicago	NL	0	0	0	0	0	0	0	0	0.00[a,b]
Lifetime pitching statistics			0	0	0	0	0	0	0	0	0.00[a,b]

World Series Pitching Statistics

	G	IP	W	L	SO	BB	SHO	SVS	ERA
Lifetime statistics	0	0	0	0	0	0	0	0	0.00[a,b]

All-Star Game Pitching Statistics

	G	IP	W	L	SO	BB	SHO	SVS	ERA
Lifetime statistics	0	0	0	0	0	0	0	0	0.00[a,b]

Fielding Statistics

Year	Team	League	G	TC	PO	A	E	DP	FA
1953	Chicago	NL	2	0	0	0	0	0	.000
Lifetime batting statistics			2	0	0	0	0	0	.000

World Series Fielding Statistics

	G	TC	PO	A	E	DP	FA
Lifetime statistics	0	0	0	0	0	0	.000

All-Star Game Fielding Statistics

	G	TC	PO	A	E	DP	FA
Lifetime statistics	0	0	0	0	0	0	.000

[a] National-league record — tie.
[b] Major-league record — tie.

I must admit, I was tempted to put together an appendix that looked like this — because I fell in love with baseball stats in 1969, peering at the pink-n-black backs of my Topps bubblegum cards. At the tender age of 8, I would ask my older and larger brother things like, "What's 'RBI' stand for, big brother?"

He would answer, "Shut up, or I will break your face."

"Thank you, older brother," I would reply, sprinting from the room — my San Francisco Giants' Dave Marshall rookie card clutched close to my person.

But better judgment has prevailed, and this appendix will contain no such information. There are 2 reasons for this editorial decision. Here they are:

1. Casey Stengel said, "You can look it up."† *The Baseball Encyclopedia* lists all these statistics, and while I am not smart enough to have negotiated a kickback with Macmillan, the encyclopedic publisher, for frustrating my readers into buying their own copy because they simply cannot stand not knowing Ox Miller's ERA with the Cubs in 1947‡ — it seems sensible that you could go there if you really, really gotta know.

2. As I have aged, I have realized that most fans really couldn't care less what Ox Miller's ERA was with the Cubs in 1947‡ — and the small group of fans who *do* care...well, not only do you SABR guys already *know* his ERA, you could also tell me that Ox batted .429 that season, going 3-for-7 at the plate, including belting a home run. In other words, most of you don't care; the few of you who do, you either know it by heart...or ya certainly don't mind finding out.

So, this section will include a sprinkling of observations that generally aren't compiled in this fashion. Even the most detail-challenged fans might just appreciate entries like these:

Post-war pitching prowess

Year	N.L. Losses Leader	Team	Number of Losses
1947	Johnny Schmitz	Chicago Cubs	18
1950	Bob Rush*	Chicago Cubs	20
1951	Paul Minner	Chicago Cubs	17
1953	Warren Hacker**	Chicago Cubs	19
1955	Sad Sam Jones***	Chicago Cubs	20

Conventional wisdom suggests that to be a 20-game loser, a pitcher must be pretty good...but stuck with a bad team.

Looks like the Cubbies had some really good pitchers in those days.

1953 was the banner year for the Chicago staff. Besides Warren Hacker's league-leading 19, the N.L.-losses Bottom 10 also included Paul Minner (tie, 8th), and Bob Rush (tie, 9th). Interesting to note: Rush was tied with Redleg Ken Raffensberger, who had gone winless in 10 appearances for the 1940 Cubs (before he'd led the N.L. with 20 losses in 1944, while at Philly).

Besides Raffensberger, other Catalina alums went on to hit the loss list for Cincy. Hal Jeffcoat, who'd been an infielder with the Cubs on Catalina before becoming a Reds' pitcher, tied for the 8th spot in 1957.

Warren Hacker (despite the joy of practicing on Catalina) was probably wishing he could be at the Yankees' Spring Training camp instead.

Overall, the Cubs tore up this category during their post-war Lousy Era; in 11 seasons (from 1946 to 1956), the Cubs didn't fail to have at least 1 pitcher on the list every single season. In all, the Cubbies managed to condemn their pitchers to the Bottom 10 an impressive 16 times — more than any other ballclub. (This figure does not include Cub *alums*, losing for other teams — such as Raffensberger and the positionally-confused Hall Jeffcoat.)

E-6

In 1950, Roy Smalley led the National League with 51 errors.

Smalley, fielding at will.

This would be logical, given some of the things people have said about Roy's fielding prowess in these pages.

In all fairness, however, he also paced the circuit with 332 putouts, 541 assists, and 115 double plays. Like the good pitchers on bad teams who lose 20 games, Roy simply handled the ball a lot — cuz all those good pitchers got 'em to hit it on the ground, which is what they're supposed to do.

Notice that the ball is sailing past, rather than into, Ripper Collins' glove in this 1938 candid. E-3. (By the way, why is Otis Shepard, a graphic artist, standing behind Rip...dressed like an umpire?)

Call 'em Rabbit & Road-Runner?

In 1947, Lennie Merullo & Andy Pafko tied for leading the Cubs in stolen bases.

With blazing speed and apparent Jackie-Robinson-like harassment of N.L. pitchers, the boys *each* managed to swipe a whopping *4* bases that season. As a whole, the squad snatched 22 — don't you feel better, knowing the level of *consistency* — compared to Jackie's 29.

Bear Tracks, indeed

If you thought Johnny Schmitz got the nickname *Bear Tracks* because of his Wisconsin outdoorsman heritage, chalk that one up as an error. According to the record books, his shoe size was (and is, at presstime) a solid 14 — the same number of complete games he pitched for the Cubbies in 1946. Mere coincidence? You be the judge...

K, K

Emil Verban came to the plate 351 times in 1949. He struck out *twice*.

Thus, unlike former teammate Bill Nicholson, he was not nicknamed *Swish*.

Don't you guys know you're playing at Wrigley Field?

Speaking of Swish Nicholson...in 1946, Phil Cavarretta tied Swish for the team lead in home-run bashing.

They each blasted *8*, pacing the squad to a total of 56 — the same number Hack Wilson hit in 1930.

Keep in mind, Sammy Sosa — playing in the same crackerbox park — has hit more than 60, all by himself, 3 times.

Swish!!

Three years earlier, in 1943, the Cubs blasted 52 home runs. Within that power display, Swish Nicholson paced the squad. To wit:

Year	Player	Dingers
1943	Swish Nicholson	29
1943	The other 24 guys	23

Yes, your hand-held calculator is correct: besides Big Bill's efforts, the other ballplayers on the team averaged less than 1 home run apiece for the season. In fact, the Cubbies took a full 32 games to hit their first homer that year (Nicholson, naturally) — 1,120 at-bats.

All this perhaps explains today's modern tradition of Wrigley Field Bleacher Bums throwing home-run balls back onto the field: they have absolutely no idea what to do with 'em, having seen so few in years past!

5 kids, 1 hero, 1935: Johnny Patrickson, Lalo Carrera, Neal 'Corky' Kirk, Remo LaFranchi, Bob Smith . . . & Gabby.

Cavy, not hitting a home run in 1940.

Swish, Swish: Bill Nicholson.

2. In interviewing a ballplayer, you mention his manager's name and wait for a reaction. If the reaction is something like, "Frankie Frisch walked on water, I named my firstborn after Frankie Frisch, I have set up a shrine to Frankie Frisch in my cellar, where I keep candles lit day and night," that would possibly qualify as a **Liked Manager** answer.

Conversely, if the reaction more closely resembles, "Frankie Frisch — why, that dirty-rotten pond-scum #!%*!@^&#*! lazy lying 2-bit #!%*!@^&#*! no-good, didn't know #!%*!@^&#*! about baseball, kicked small dogs and baby ducks and #!%*!@#^&#*! every #!%*!@^&#*! %~#!%*!@^&#*! — I still burn that #!%*!@^&#*! in effigy at least once a week, that low-down low-life gravy-sucking #!%*!@&*! jerk loser bum," then you may wish to chalk that one up as **Dis-Liked Manager**.

The beloved Frisch.

Speaking of potent offense...

In 1950, Wayne Terwilliger pulled a double-double for the Cubs: He bashed 10 home runs and led the team with 13 steals. In doing so, he was the only double-double man on the squad.

A new stat category: The S/LM-DNS/DLM ratio

On behalf of Cub fans everywhere, I humbly propose a new statistical category: the S/LM-DNS/DLM ratio. For the uninitiated, this stands for:

*Started/Liked Manager -
Did Not Start/Dis-Liked Manager*

Here's how it works:

1. Check a player's statistics for a particular season, or series of seasons. Look at the number of games played. If it looks like the player played in most games (or, for pitchers, made the regular rotation), this counts as a player who **Started**.

If, on the other hand, a ballplayer played in, say, 4 games that season, we might want to count him as one who **Did Not Start**.

Statistics, statistics. How many baseballs can a rookie stuff into a ball-bag on Catalina?

333

Here's an hypothetical example:

Player	Manager	Starter?	Liked/Disliked Mgr.	S/LM-DNS/DLM Ratio
Lefty Sample	Anson	Y	L	1.000 %
Hack Mims	Anson	Y	D	0.000 %
Wilson S/LM Subtotal		**2**	**1**	**0.500 %**

As you can see, in this sample example, half the starters liked Manager Anson, resulting in Cap garnering a S/LM ratio of .500 — which isn't really all that great. After all, common sense dictates that most of your guys who get to play will think you're a pretty keen judge of baseball talent.

Got it?

As a public service to our readers, we have already assembled all this data, and placed it conveniently into the charts below for your betterment:

Player	Manager	Starter?	Liked/Disliked Mgr.	S/LM-DNS/DLM Ratio
Pafko	Wilson	Y	L	1.000 %
Passeau	Wilson	Y	L	1.000 %
Wilson S/LM Subtotal		**2**	**2**	**1.000 %**
Raffensberger	Wilson	N	D	1.000 %
Storey	Wilson	N	D	1.000 %
Wilson DNS/DLM Subtotal		**2**	**2**	**1.000 %**
Wilson S/LM-DNS/DLM Total		**4**	**4**	**1.000 %**

As you can see again, the Cubs racked up a perfect 4-for-4 regarding Jimmie Wilson. Jimbo's batting a thousand. Well done, Jim. Now, let's apply the stats to a larger sample, and check out the Frisch Factor:

Player	Manager	Starter?	Liked/Disliked Mgr.	S/LM-DNS/DLM Ratio
McLish	Frisch	Y	L	1.000 %
Lown	Frisch	Y	L	1.000 %
Ward	Frisch	Y	L	1.000 %
Jeffcoat	Frisch	Y	L	1.000 %
Smalley	Frisch	Y	L	1.000 %
Rush	Frisch	Y	L	1.000 %
Minner	Frisch	Y	L	1.000 %
Klippstein	Frisch	Y	L	1.000 %
Terwilliger	Frisch	Y	L	1.000 %
Frisch S/LM Subtotal		**9**	**9**	**1.000 %**
Voiselle	Frisch	N	D	1.000 %
Borkowski	Frisch	N	D	1.000 %
Schramka	Frisch	N	D	1.000 %
Chambers	Frisch	N	D	1.000 %
Mauro	Frisch	N	D	1.000 %
Van Dyke	Frisch	N	D	1.000 %
Chandler	Frisch	N	D	1.000 %
Mauch	Frisch	N	D	1.000 %
Kowalski	Frisch	N	D	1.000 %
Frisch DNS/DLM Subtotal		**9**	**9**	**1.000 %**
Frisch S/LM-DNS/DLM Total		**18**	**18**	**1.000 %**

As any moron can plainly see, Manager Frisch is the quintessential example of S/LM-DNS/DLM perfection. He not only bats 1,000 among Starters, he also achieves a 1,000 average among Did-Not Starters — going a perfect 18-of-18 among those players polled. Go, Old Flash!

(We trust this statistical abstract has been enlightening.)

Manager Frisch is seen here executing the S/LM-DNS/DLM theory, by allowing a row of S/LMs to stand directly in front of a line of DNS-DLMs.

Numbers-crunchers: How many Cubs can fit in a Catalina cart?

335

So now, as the appendix ends, a quote from Brendan C. Boyd and Fred Harris' masterpiece, *The Great American Baseball Card Flipping, Trading, and Bubblegum Book*:

Do not, whatever else you might do, take any of it too seriously.

Please do not write...long letters...complaining how we maligned your favorite ballplayer, belittled baseball, befouled the very air you breathe. We know only too well that we could not have played baseball half as well as even the most inept players mentioned herein. We know that much better than you, in fact. We tried.

Yes, folks, I tried. I hope you liked looking at my scrapbook. I sure enjoyed cutting-n-pasting it together.

Hope to see ya out on Catalina...

William 'Dutch' Seebold, 1933. Major league games caught: 0. Fish caught: 1.

*How many spots **are** there on a leopard, anyway?*

Fay Gillis Wells & Snooks, out in right field, 1937.

† If you don't believe Casey really said this, you can look it up.

‡ It was 10.13. If you had your own copy of *The Baseball Encyclopedia*, you could've looked it up.

* Bob Rush managed to dominate the Bottom 10 (for N.L. losses) in the Cubs' post-war Lousy Era, placing 6 of 10 seasons from 1949-57 — including his 1st-place finish in 1950, which followed his debut at #2 in 1949. He also sported a 3-consecutive-season streak (1952-54).

** Warren Hacker bettered teammate Rush in 1 consistency category — he appeared on the Bottom 10 list for a whopping 4 *straight* seasons, from 1953-56.

*** Did not practice losing on Catalina — he 1st joined the team in Mesa. It should be noted that in his league-topping season of 20 losses, Sad Sam did achieve a milestone of redemption: 1 of his 14 *wins* was the 1st no-hitter twirled at Wrigley Field since Hippo Vaughn's 1917 effort.

Author's Afterthoughts

Randomized Musings, Now That the Game Is Over

"Thanks, everybody!"

Noted author Jim Vitti

My wife and I first visited Catalina in January of 1984. While hiking up the hill, we came upon the field...and the marker...and I remember expressing surprise that the Cubs had trained there.

What a joy to finally write it all down.

But first, there was some research to do. About 30 years' worth. Talk about fun — I had to go to Catalina, to Los Angeles, to Chicago — and do an interview in the clubhouse at Wrigley Field.

Most people would consider a week in a library to be about as fun as being pummeled with a stick. Me? It's like having a melty Milky Way Midnight and a cold mugful of chocolate milk, watching a Joe Garagiola highlight reel.

And I got to chat with a few dozen former major leaguers, a movie star, and some of the best baseball fans on earth. The actual tallies:

* Interviews with 55 Catalina Cubs, 9 wives, 11 kids, and 3 grandchildren

* Interviews with 24 Avalon locals...and 34 other people...for a grand total of 136 interviews

* Visits to 10 libraries and museums, with help from 11 more

* Information culled from 25 newspapers and magazines...and 48 books

(Just don't tell my publisher I'd have done it for free!)

I'm particularly grateful to the brilliant writer and master motivator, Mike Russell, who encouraged me to move the long-percolating project from the back burner to the front.

It took a cast of dozens to make this book happen. Thanks to all — I'm your biggest fan.

Charlie Grimm takes a flight of fancy in the '20s.

Sit back, pour yourself a cool drink (as Chuck Klein & Babe Herman are demonstrating here), & enjoy the credits.

The California State Library in Sacramento.
The Los Angeles Public Library.
The Catalina Public Library in Avalon.
The Chicago Public Library: Tyneshia Thomas and Kathy Krajicek, who repeatedly spared me from the evil attacks of the demon-possessed card readers in the microfilm room.

Gayle Camarda, WebRef Department, St. Louis Public Library, for a dizzying level of research.
Sandy Dixon of the Iowa State Library.
Bradley Cook, Reference Specialist & Photograph Curator, Indiana University Archives.
Heather Briston & Sharla Davis, University of Oregon Archives.
Colin Toenjes of the University of Texas at Arlington Special Collections Division.
Daisy Taube at the University of Southern California.
Bob Gibler at the Lee County Historical Society in Illinois.
The Lee County Genealogical Society.
Sheila Herrn of the *Dixon Telegraph* in Illinois.
Norman Wymbs, Chairman, Ronald Reagan Boyhood Home Restoration Foundation, Dixon, IL.
Sandy Jones, Ronald Reagan Boyhood Home, Dixon, IL.
Duke Blackwood and the off-the-charts-fast-and-efficient Mike Duggan of The Ronald Reagan Presidential Library (for digging into Nelle Reagan's scrapbook about her son Dutch from the 1930s), Simi Valley, California.
Michael Reagan.
Nancy Reagan and Joanne Drake, Chief of Staff to the Reagans.
Parker Hamilton of the White House Press Office.
Army Archerd, columnist for *Variety*.
Edmund and Sylvia Morris, for so graciously providing Mr. Morris' *Chronology Raisonnée of Ronald Reagan's First Visits to California*.
Liz Fogarty of Random House.
Debbi Kuzik of the City of Mesa Parks & Recreation Division in Arizona.
Marques Thomey of the Detroit Metro Airport Authority.
Vinit Bharara of the Topps Co., Inc.
Josh Perlman of Fleer/Skybox International.
The Calvin Coolidge Memorial Foundation, Plymouth Notch, Vermont.
Teresa Clements of the Cal-State Chico Athletic Dept.
Betty Whitehead of Sagebrush Entertainment.
Jenny Vitti of UCSB, for creating the Index.
Bob Broeg (Legendary St. Louis Sportswriter).
Harrington Crissey (Pennsylvania Author).
Author Mark Stang.

> Jeannine Pedersen, Stacey Otte, & Kristi Burroughs of the Catalina Island Museum.
> Gail Hodge & Audry Paradisi of the Santa Catalina Island Company.
> Bill Loughman.

Gwen Bronson of the Catalina Island Chamber of Commerce & Visitors Bureau.
Barbara Crow, Publisher & Editor of the *Avalon Bay News*.
Sherri Walker, former Publisher & Editor of the *Catalina Islander*.
Samantha Newby of the Chicago Cubs.
Ed Hartig, Chicago Cubs historian extraordinaire.
Ernie Banks.
Salty Saltwell.
Tim Mead of the Anaheim Angels.
Mark Langill of the Los Angeles Dodgers.
Dan Hart of the Pittsburgh Pirates.
Melody Yount of the St. Louis Cardinals.
Howard Starkman of the Toronto Blue Jays.
Chuck Stevens.
Gus Zernial.
AAGPBL All-Star June 'Pep' Peppas.
Anne Carman of Spalding Sports Worldwide.

Nah, Gabby's not really throwing the ball at the baby's head...

Bill Burdick of the National Baseball Hall of Fame & Museum, Inc., Cooperstown, New York.
Michael Salmon of the Amateur Athletic Foundation, L.A.
Dick Beverage of the Pacific Coast League Historical Society.
SABR (The Society for American Baseball Research) — particularly Steve Roney of the L.A. Chapter.

Avalon High School.

Linda Hanrath, Corporate Librarian, the William Wrigley Co., Chicago.

Mrs. Blanny Wrigley Schreiner & daughter Blanny.

Miss Grace Bradley Boyd.

Mrs. Fay Gillis Wells.

Avalon natives & residents:

Blanche Belky.
Doug Bombard.
Harvey Cowell.
Jack Cowell & grandson Tim Cowell.
Florence Johnson Hamlin.
Scooter Hansen.
Bob Hoyt.
Chuck Liddell.
R. Franklin Pyke of R. Franklin Pyke Books.
Michael Reyes.
Helen Ross.
The Most Rev. Sylvester Ryan.
Lolo Saldaña.
Frank Saldaña.
Marcelino Saucedo.
Joe "Foxie" and/or "Foxy" Saucedo.
Mayor Bud Smith & Mrs. Marie Smith.
Hon. Edgar Taylor.
Roger Upton.
Del Walker, former Avalon High baseball coach.
William Sanford White.

Manager McCarthy asks boss William Wrigley if perhaps he ought to feel a bit embarrassed, being dressed in public like that.

And the Cubs of Catalina:

Red Adams & daughter, Lila Bourbon.
Lee Anthony.
Della Root Arnold, Charlie's daughter.
Howard Auman.
Bill Baker.
Cy & Harriet Block.
Bob Borkowski.
Margaret Burgess, Smoky's widow, & son Larry Burgess.
Don & Gwen Carlsen.
Eddie Carnett.
Phil Cavarretta.
Cliff Chambers.
Ed Chandler.
Joan Cherry (Irving 'Gus' Cherry's daughter), Joan's husband John Cara, & Gus's nephew Jamie Yeretsky.
Don Dunker.
Al Epperly.
Paul Erickson.
Joe Fondy, Dee's son.
Lonny Frey.
Jim Gleeson's son Jim.
Warren & Olinda Hacker & daughter Pam.
Buddy Hartnett & Sheila Hartnett Hornof (Gabby's kids) & Buddy's kids (Steve, Joanne, & Donna).
Ruth Hirsch, Crazy Legs' wife.
Ed Jabb.
Randy Jackson.
Hal & Valma Jeffcoat.
Yosh Kawano.
Bob Kelly.
Jim Kirby.
Hub Kittle.
Johnny Klippstein.
Eddie Kowalski.
Lloyd Lowe.
Turk & Violet Lown.
Bobby Mattick.
Gene Mauch.
Carmen Mauro.
Calvin Coolidge Julius Caesar Tuskahoma "Buster" McLish.
Lennie Merullo & son Boots Merullo.
Ox Miller.
Paul Minner.
Charlie Owen, Mickey's son.
Andy Pafko.
Claude & Bernyce "BUM" Passeau.
Ken Raffensberger.
Fred Richards.
Billy Rogell.
Bob Rush.
Bob Scheffing, son of Bob Scheffing.
Johnny Schmitz.
Paul Schramka.
Dwain Sloat.
Roy Smalley, Jr.
Elvin "Stub" Stabelfeld.
Harvey Storey.
Lou Stringer.
Wayne Terwilliger.
Gordon Van Dyke.
Bill "96" Voiselle & Mrs. V.
Ben Wade.
Preston Ward.
Ken Weafer.

Newspapers & Magazines:

The Avalon Bay News.
The Catalina Islander.
The Chicago American.
The Chicago Daily News.
The Chicago Examiner.
The Chicago Herald.
The Chicago Herald & Examiner.
The Chicago Post.
The Chicago Sun.
The Chicago Sun-Times.
The Chicago Times.
The Chicago Tribune.
The Des Moines Dispatch.
The Dixon Evening Telegraph.
The Los Angeles Herald-Examiner.
The Los Angeles Times.
The Metropolis Daily Planet (just seeing if you're still with me).
The New York Times.
The Rancho Cordova Grapevine.
The San Francisco Chronicle.
The San Francisco Examiner.

Catalina Island Visitor's Guide.
Spring Training magazine/SpringTraining.com.

Islandball at its finest: Klein hits, O'Dea catches, Lotshaw umps.

Books:

A Ball Player's Career, reprint by Amereon House, Adrian Anson, Mattituck, New York, 1994.

Banks to Sandberg to Grace: Five Decades of Love and Frustration with the Chicago Cubs, Carrie Muskat, Contemporary Books (a division of McGraw-Hill), Chicago, 2001.

Baseball Between the Wars: Memories of the Game By the Men Who Played It, Eugene Murdock, Meckler Publishing, Westport, Connecticut, 1992.

The Baseball Encyclopedia, Tenth Edition, Macmillan/a Simon & Schuster Macmillan Company, New York, 1996.

Baseball's Great Dynasties: The Cubs, Thomas G. Aylesworth, Gallery Books/W.H. Smith Publishers, New York, 1990.

Blood on the Moon: The Autobiography of Linton Wells, Houghton Mifflin Co./The Riverside Press, Cambridge, Massachusetts, 1937.

The Chicago Cubs, Warren Brown (*With a New Foreward by Jerome Holtzman*), Southern Illinois University Press, Carbondale, Illinois, 2001 (Originally published by G.P. Putnam's Sons, 1946).

Chuck Connors: The Man Behind the Rifle, David Fury, Artist's Press, Minneapolis, 1997.

The Cubbies: Quotations on the Chicago Cubs, Bob Chieger, Atheneum Books, New York, 1987.

Cubs Collection: 100 Years of Chicago Cubs Images, Mark Stang, Orange Frazer Press, Wilmington, Ohio, 2001.

Dutch: A Memoir of Ronald Reagan, Edmund Morris, Random House, New York, 1999.

Essential Cubs: Facts, Feats, & Firsts — from the Batter's Box to the Bullpen to the Bleachers, Doug Myers, NTC/Contemporary Books, Lincolnwood, Illinois, 1999.

The Films of Ronald Reagan, Tony Thomas, Citadel Press, Secaucus, New York, 1980.

Fouled Away: The Baseball Tragedy of Hack Wilson, Clifton Blue Parker, McFarland & Co., Jefferson, North Carolina, 2000.

Frank Frisch, the Fordham Flash, Frank Frisch as told to J. Roy Stockton, Doubleday & Co., Garden City, New York, 1962.

The Game is Never Over: An Appreciative History of the Chicago Cubs, Jim Langford, Icarus Press, South Bend, Indiana, 1980.

The Golden Era Cubs 1876-1940, Eddie Gold & Art Ahrens, Bonus Books, Chicago, 1985.

The Great American Baseball Card Flipping, Trading, & Bubblegum Book, Brendan C. Boyd and Fred Harris, Warner Paperback Library, New York, 1975.

The High Hard One, Kirby Higbe with Martin Quigley, Viking, New York, 1967.

Jolly Cholly's Story: Baseball, I Love You!, Charlie Grimm with Ed Prell, Henry Regnery Co., Chicago, 1968.

Life With Charlie, Della Root Arnold, Self-published, 1973.

A Little Piece of Paradise, James Alan Vitti, Thos. Nelson/Word, Nashville, TN, 1996.

The Marilyn Encyclopedia, Adam Victor, Overlook Press, Woodstock, NY, 1999.

Minor League Baseball Stars, Vol. III, the Society for American Baseball Research, Cleveland, Ohio, 1992.

My Early Life (or *Where's the Rest of Me?*), Ronald Reagan with Richard G. Hubler, Sidgwick & Jackson, London, 1965.

The Natural, Bernard Malamud, New York, 1952.

The New Era Cubs 1941-85, Eddie Gold & Art Ahrens, Bonus Books, Chicago, 1985.

The Old Man and the Sea, Ernest Hemingway, Charles Scribner's Sons, Manhattan Island, New York, 1952.

Pacific Coast League Stars: One Hundred of the Best, 1903 to 1957, John E. Spalding, Ag Press, Manhattan, Kansas, 1994.

Pacific Coast League Stars: Ninety Who Made it In The Majors, 1903 to 1957, Volume II, John E. Spalding, Ag Press, Manhattan, Kansas, 1997.

Reagan, Lou Cannon, G.P. Putnam's Sons, New York, 1982.

Rogers Hornsby: A Biography, Charles C. Alexander, Henry Holt & Co., New York, 1995.

Ronald Reagan, Kenneth T. Walsh, a Balliet & Fitzgerald Book/Park Lane Press, New York, 1997.

Ronald Reagan: His Life and Rise to the Presidency, Bill Boyarsky, Random House, New York, 1981.

Ronald Reagan in Hollywood: Movies and Politics, Stephen Vaughn, Cambridge University Press, Cambridge, Massachusetts, 1994.

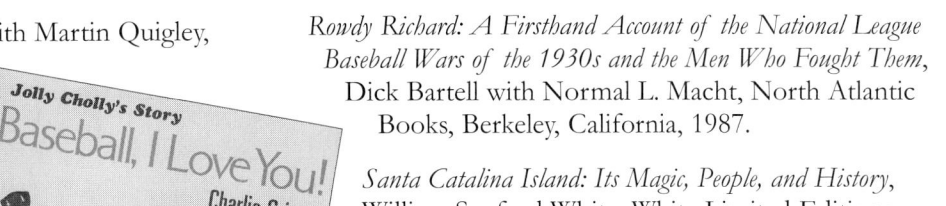

Rowdy Richard: A Firsthand Account of the National League Baseball Wars of the 1930s and the Men Who Fought Them, Dick Bartell with Normal L. Macht, North Atlantic Books, Berkeley, California, 1987.

Santa Catalina Island: Its Magic, People, and History, William Sanford White, White Limited Editions, Glendora, California, 1997.

So You Want to Be a Major Leaguer?, Cy Block, Audio Scholar Audiobooks, Mendocino, California, 1999.

Take Me Out to the Cubs Game: 35 Former Ballplayers Speak of Losing at Wrigley, John C. Skipper, McFarland & Co., Jefferson, NC, 2000.

Teenagers, Graybeards and 4-F's: An Informal History of Major League Baseball During the Second World War, as Told by the Participants, Volume 1 (The National League) and *Volume 2 (The American League)*, Harrington E. Crissey, Jr., Philadelphia, 1981/1982.

To Norma Jeane with Love, Jimmy, Jim Dougherty with LC Van Savage, Beach House Books, Chesterfield, MO, 2000.

2002 Chicago Cubs Information Guide, Chuck Wasserstrom, Chicago Nat'l. League Baseball Club, Inc., Chicago, 2002.

Veeck as in Wreck, Bill Veeck, with Ed Linn, University of Chicago Press, 1962.

We Played the Game: 65 Players Remember Baseball's Greatest Era, 1947-1964, Danny Peary, Hyperion, New York, 1994.

Philip K. Wrigley: Memoir of a Modest Man, Paul M. Angle, Rand McNally & Co., Chicago, 1975.

Wrigleyville: A Magical History Tour of the Chicago Cubs, Peter Golenbock, St. Martin's Press, New York, 1999.

You're Missin' a Great Game, Whitey Herzog & Jonathan Pitts, Simon & Schuster, New York, 1999.

342

Credits for Photos & Other Images:

All photos/illustrations courtesy of the Catalina Island Museum and the Catalina Island Company, unless noted otherwise. Many were taken by the late Alma Overholt, who handled public relations on the Island for the Wrigley family. Some of the Museum photos are from the Bill Loughman Collection.

All baseball cards, postcards, & other memorabilia courtesy of Jim Allyn. Topps and Bowman cards are reproduced with permission from the Topps Co., Inc. The Donruss card is reproduced with permission from Donruss Playoff, LP. TSN cards reproduced with permission from TSN. Fleer cards reproduced with permission from Fleer/Skybox International LP.

Additional photo/image credits:

Red Adams: 108 (bottom), 159 (right)
Amateur Athletic Foundation: 197
AP/WideWorld: 36 (bottom), 203, 263 (left),
    316 (Thanks to Kevin O'Sullivan)
Howard Auman: 56, 110 (left)
Avalon High School: 309 (bottom),
    325 (middle & bottom)
Cy & Harriet Block: 242
Mary Brace/George Brace Photos: 89,
    109 (bottom), 110 (right), 140 (right),
    143 (bottom), 171, 204 (left), 228, 281 (top)
Don & Gwen Carlsen: 105, 111 (bottom),
    381 (bottom)
California State University, Chico: 310 (left)
Lefty Carnett: 95 (top), 129
Catalina Island Chamber of Commerce &
    Visitors Bureau: 15 (middle), 248 (right)
Joan Cherry: 247 (right)
The Chicago Tribune: 76 (top), 99 (top),
    104 (bottom), 270, 353
Corbis: 44 (bottom), 118, 381 (top)
    (Thanks to Craig Prince)
Jack & Tim Cowell: 298 (both)
Barbara Crow: Dust Jacket/Inside Back Sleeve
The Detroit Metro Airport Authority
    (Marques Thomy Photos): 137, 243 (top)
James Dougherty: 116, 175 (bottom left, right)
    (Thanks to Thomas Peters, esq.)
The Hacker Family: 50, 64, 93 (bottom left), 102,
    111 (top 3), 169 (bottom 2), 260 (top), 267 (bottom left)
The Hartnett Family: 202 (left), 285 (bottom), 322 (bottom)
The Hobbs Family: 292 (top)
Kathy Jewett of KJewett & Associates: 293 (top)
Jim Kirby: 170 (right)
Hub Kittle: 61
Lee County (Illinois) Genealogical Society: 119
Lloyd Lowe: 69
The City of Mesa, Arizona: 317
Ox Miller: 62
June "Pep" Peppas: 267 (bottom right)
Nancy Reagan: 121

The Ronald Reagan Library: 123, 124 (left), 125 (left),
    126 (top), 127, 186
Ron Riesterer: 124 (right)
Thomas Rockwell: 185
Bob Rush: 151 (left)
The Most Rev. Sylvester Ryan: 87, 304 (left), 305 (top)
Sagebrush Entertainment (Hopalong Cassidy): 179
St. Louis Cardinals, Steven Goldstein Photo: 60
Frank & Lolo Saldaña: 34, 296 (both), 297 (top),
    299 (top), 303 (right), 306 (bottom right), 307,
    308 (both), 309 (top), 310 (right)
Marcelino Saucedo: 301, 302 (top 2)
Paul Schramka: 52, 53, 206 (right), 240, 335 (top)
Spalding Sports Worldwide, Inc.: 17 (top)
United Media: 292 (bottom) (Thanks to Maura Peters)

William Wrigley, still in knickers rather than long pants, watches Johnny Schulte, 1930.

USC Regional History Collection: 43 (middle)
Jim Vitti: 20, 235 (bottom), 266 (bottom), 274 (left), 320,
    321 (top), 322 (top), 323 (all), 324 (left), 343 (bottom)
Bill Voiselle: 65
Michael J. Watts: 325 (top)
Ken Weafer: 26, 165 (bottom)
Fay Gillis Wells: 185
The White House: 125

Sponsors
Avalon's Favorite Merchants & Fans

"You grow it, we'll mow it."

Legendary Island Barbers Lolo & Frank Saldaña

**Catalina Island
It's Closer Than You Think...
On Catalina Express**

Fast, smooth, one-hour boat ride to Catalina Island. Go for the day or an overnight stay!

Call for Reservations
CATALINA EXPRESS
(310) 519-1212
www.CatalinaExpress.com

Your library is incomplete without these two outstanding books about Catalina!

This is truly a book for those who love the island. With over 350 rare and historically significant photos, this well-researched 250-page book has become the definitive chronicle of charming Santa Catalina Island. $39.95 list price.

A WWII Book about Catalina Island. Features 190 captivating photos never before published. Read about US Ships torpedoed in Catalina Channel...how the US Coast Guard protected the West Coast...how the USO and stars like Marilyn Monroe aided the cause. $25 list price.

Visit www.whitelimitededitions.com

White Limited Editions, P.O. Box 126, Glendora, CA 91740   Phone or Fax 626.335.3507

Enjoy Lunch, Dinner and
Pub Specials at

The Chicago Cubs' Original
Spring Training Facilities

**FROM CASUAL TO ELEGANT
YOU'RE WELCOME AT THE**

Catalina Country Club

⌒ OPEN TO THE PUBLIC ⌒

**THREE EXQUISITE SETTINGS:
ELEGANT DINING ROOM, OUTDOOR PATIO
AND CLUBHOUSE PUB
SERVING LUNCH & DINNER DAILY
APPETIZERS & EXTENSIVE WINE LIST
BANQUET AND PRIVATE PARTY FACILITIES**

**FOR RESERVATIONS OR INFORMATION,
CALL: (310) 510-7404.**

Gabby Hartnett, Chicago Cubs' manager and the 1939 team
standing outside their clubhouse on Catalina Island.

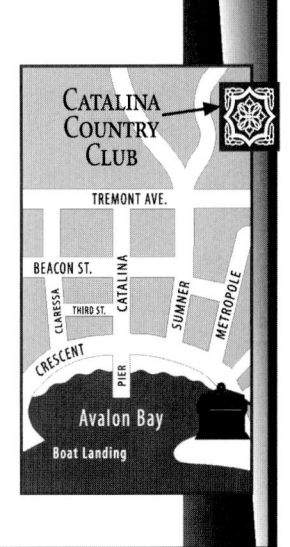

CATALINA ISLAND Museum

History's never been this much fun!

From the Native Americans to the Chicago Cubs and beyond, discover 7,000 years of history!

Come see our exciting exhibits on:
- Chicago Cubs Spring Training
- Big Bands
- The Casino Building
- Catalina's Steamers
- Communication
- Catalina Pottery and Tile
- The Island's First Inhabitants
- Sportfishing

and much more!

History's Never Been This Much Fun!

Catalina Island Museum
Casino Building
PO Box 366
Avalon, CA 90704
310.510.2414
catalinaislmuseum@catalinaisp.com

Hours: 10 - 4 daily
Closed Christmas

The Catalina Island Museum is a private, nonprofit organization, founded in 1953. Our mission is to preserve and share Catalina's 7,000 years of history.

Santa Catalina Island Company,

former owners of the Pacific Coast League Los Angeles Angels which became the Chicago Cubs' Triple A farm team,

salutes this endeavor to memorialize the Cubs' years here on Santa Catalina Island.

The Avalon Bay News

Congratulates Jim for writing such a great book about the Chicago Cubs' Spring Training on Catalina Island.

Get all the current Catalina Island news by subscribing to The Avalon Bay News:

Call (310) 510-1500 or
email: abn@catalinas.net

**SERVING CATALINA ISLAND
FROM AVALON TO TWO HARBORS
SINCE 1990.**

LOLO's Barber Shop

Serving your barbering needs for 47 years

Victor Piltch, Sylvester Ryan, Bob Thomas, & Lolo Saldaña, 1947.

A few haircuts later (1990).

You grow it and we'll mow it...

A Touch of Heaven

P.O. Box 1436
Avalon, CA 90704

310.510.1633

www.atouchofheavendayspa.com

Ristorante Villa Portofino

For the Finest in Italian Cuisine

Take your taste buds on a culinary adventure

Dinner 5:00 P.M.

Fresh Seafood · Steaks · Pasta · Veal · Chicken · Lamb
Children's Menu · Major Credit Cards Accepted

(310) 510-2009

101 Crescent Avenue
Avalon
Santa Catalina Island

Phil Cavarretta wishes they'd stop throwing all those balls at him, so he could get to a top-notch ristorante for a delicious dish of pasta. "Mangia, mangia!"

Armstrong's

**Fish Market & Seafood Restaurant
Catalina Island**
est. 1983

OPEN DAILY

Retail Fish Market

Crab Cakes & Ceviche

Avalon's First Name in Seafood Dining

Specializing in Delicious Fresh Seafood, Steaks & Chicken from the Mesquite Wood Broiler, Sashimi, Clams, Oysters & Mussels, Full Bar, Cocktails & Fine Wines

**(310) 510-0113
306 Crescent Avenue · Avalon**
Located Over the Water on Avalon Bay

I was reared in the lap of summer

and I slept in the bed of autumn...

As I embrace slumber

the eyes of night watch over me,

and as I awaken I stare at the sun,

which is the only eye of the day.

—Kahlil Gibran

HOTEL METROPOLE

Catalina's Finest Hotel

www.hotel-metropole.com

For reservations: 1.800.300.8528 (IN CALIFORNIA),
1.800.541.8528 (NATIONWIDE) OR 310.510.1884

CATALINA CLOTHING CO.

Surfwear and Accessories

310-510-2010
205 Crescent Avenue
#104-105 Metropole Market Place
Avalon, California 90704

Find us at catalinaclothingcompany.com

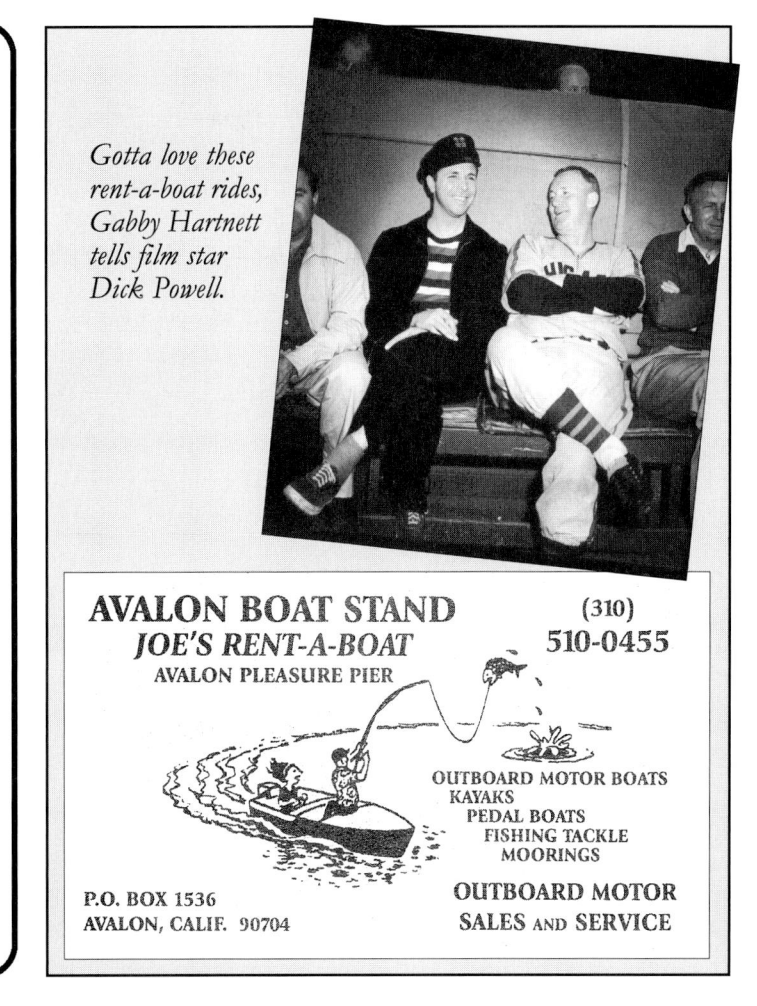

Gotta love these rent-a-boat rides, Gabby Hartnett tells film star Dick Powell.

AVALON BOAT STAND (310)
JOE'S RENT-A-BOAT 510-0455
AVALON PLEASURE PIER

OUTBOARD MOTOR BOATS
KAYAKS
PEDAL BOATS
FISHING TACKLE
MOORINGS

P.O. BOX 1536
AVALON, CALIF. 90704

OUTBOARD MOTOR SALES AND SERVICE

Bud Teachout, Woody English, & Clyde Beck... all dressed up in front of the Hotel St. Catherine, ready to head into town for a great steak.

Steve's Steakhouse
BAR & GRILLE
Fine Steaks & Fresh Seafood
UPSTAIRS HARBOR VIEW DINING
417 Crescent Avenue
Reservations (310) 510-0333

Cerritos College
Marcelino Saucedo
Bilingual Educational Counselor

- ◆ Academic
- ◆ Career Development
- ◆ Personal
- ◆ Educational Foundation
- ◆ Access First program *(for first-time offenders)*

11110 Alondra Blvd., Norwalk, CA 90650
Phone #: (562) 860-2451
Fax #: (562) 467-5040

Cliff Heathcote & Fred Fussell (seen here hanging out with Hack Miller) felt their mate had the strength to make a fine portable welder.

Shop 510-9476
H&H Portable WELDING
Catalina Island
510-9464

BOBBY HERNANDEZ
P.O. Box 1639
Avalon CA 90704
510-0965   Fax (310) 510-2399

PHILIP HERNANDEZ
P.O. Box 743
Avalon CA 90704
510-2890

Queen of Romantic Catalina

Amoroso's

Historic Glenmore Plaza Hotel

Known for its beauty, charm, and quaintness of a bygone era, with today's modern amenities

Est. 1891

Cubs Fans Forever!

P.O. Box 155
Avalon, CA 90704
Ph: 310.510.0017
Toll free: 1.800.422.8254

Glenmore Plaza Hotel: approx. 1911

THE SANDTRAP
RESTAURANT
Avalon, Catalina Island, CA
(310) 510-2505

- ★ HOT DOGS / CORN DOGS
- ★ HAMBURGERS
- ★ FRENCH FRIES
- ★ CHILICHEESE FRIES
- ★ NACHOS
- ★ CARNE ASADA
- ★ BURRITOS
- ★ TACOS
- ★ TORTAS
- ★ QUESADILLAS

104 CLARESSA ST. AVALON CA, 90704
TEL. (310) 510-0545

PICNIC FRY
CATALINA ISLAND

STAN HACK manager CHICAGO CUBS

Stan Hack, about to be beaned by a package of Wilson Weiners on this unusual 1954 card. At presstime, the editors were unable to determine if either the SANDTRAP or PICNIC FRY restaurants use Wilson Weiners . . . or the other leading brand.

Gabby Hartnett & Tuck Stainback, lookin' like they're goin' on vacation.

Catalina Island
Vacation Rentals Inc.

The largest selection of houses, cottages, condos and Hamilton Cove villas on the island!

119 Sumner Ave.
P.O. Box 426
Avalon, CA 90704-0426

(800) 631-5280

www.catalinavacations.com

Rosie & Earl Cadman

Avalon Seafood
On The Green Pleasure Pier
since 1967

P.O. Box 1073
Avalon, CA 90704

(310) 510-0197

Red Lynn, Eddie Hanyzewski, & Heinz Becker find they're unable to catch fresher fish than Rosie can.

Coyote Joe's Restaurant & Bar
Santa Catalina Island

- Music
- Specialty Drinks
- Dine-In or Take-Out

Delicious, Authentic Mexican & American Food

30 Steps from the Green Pier
113 Catalina Street
Avalon, CA 90704

(310) 510-1176

Little League Coach
Semi-retired
Member VFW

Frank Saldaña
Avalon, Catalina Island

Home: 310-510-1824
Work: 310-510-0920

The Paper Trail

Joe Felis
P.O. Box 1129
Avalon, Ca. 90704
(310) 291-5751

7 day / daily / Sunday only

CRAZY DAISY COIFFEURS AND BOUTIQUE

110 SUMNER AVE.
AVALON, CA 90704
PH 310-510-0444
FAX 310-510-1087

LINN CAMERON

Claude Passeau & Skipper Jimmie Wilson trade shopping tips about their favorite Avalon merchants.

ARROYO INSURANCE SERVICES

James W. Simonds

1414 Fair Oaks Avenue Suite 3 South Pasadena, CA 91030
(626) 799-9532 • FAX: (626) 799-1964 • License# 0735912
Web Site: www.arroyoinsurance.com • Email: jims@arroyoins.com

---

Upton's CATALINA House of Wood
CRAFT ORIGINALS MADE ON THE ISLAND

P.O. BOX 152 • AVALON, CA • (310) 510-0125

Had Charlie & Dorothy Root met a good insurance man on Catalina in 1929, they could've provided solid coverage for Della & Charlie Jr. — as well as peace of mind for themselves.

Dolphin EMPORIUM
Catalina Island

www.dolphinemporium.com

205 Crescent Avenue
Post Office Box 38
Avalon, CA 90704

Pat Hernandez
Owner
(310) 510-0786

Braving the elements on the steamship ride to Avalon, Cub catcher Gabby Hartnett scans the horizon to see if he might be able to catch a good dolphin sighting . . .

Pancake Cottage

Lou & Muriel Wilhite

118 Catalina Ave.
Avalon, CA 90704
Catalina Island

Business: (310) 510-0726
Residence: (310) 510-0494
Fax: (310) 510-2790

R FRANKLIN PYKE
BOOKSELLER

FINE OLD BOOKS
MAPS AND PRINTS

CUSTOM PICTURE FRAMING

Specializing in Santa Catalina Island Books, Pottery, Tile and Ephemera

228 Metropole Ave. P.O. Box 514 Avalon, CA 90704
e-mail: pykebook@catalinas.net   Ph. (310) 510-2588

Jaime D. Montano

CATALINA ISLAND PLUMBING
510-0969

Fifth-Generation Californian

State Licensing No. 557464

P.O. Box 1930 • Avalon, California 90704

The LANDING
BAR & GRILL

Harbor View Dining

Steak • Seafood • Pasta

Gourmet Pizzas

Enjoy lunch or dinner, indoor by the fireplace or outside on the patio overlooking the Avalon Harbor
all year round!

Banquet Facilities

Wedding Ceremony/Reception
Company Events • Birthday Parties
Up to 200 guests!

The Landing Bar and Grill
Phone: 310-510-1474   Fax: 310-510-0486
www.catalina.com/landing.html

Manager Charlie Grimm asks Chicago superfan Danny Cahill if he knows of a good plumber on the Island.

Catalina
Souvenir Shop
Established 1947

Santa Catalina Island
P. O. Box 1504 • 413 Crescent • Avalon, CA 90704

(310) 510-0061

Manager McCarthy waits expectantly, hoping that some of the boys chipped in to get him a nice Island souvenir.

1-310-510-0523
Avalon's Plaza Cafe
128 D. Sumner ave, Avalon, Ca. 90704
Owner: **Ricardo Leyva, Jr. (Rico)**
We Deliver & cater parties!

Charlie Flowers, Johnny Hutchings, Lonnie Warneke, Clauson Vines, & Hal Sueme play paper-scissors-rock to see who will pick up the lunch tab.

Individual Islander Sponsors

Michael Alegria	Dr. Rod Muller
Jeanne Brazil	Sue Muller
Ken Buck	Judy Perez
Al Casillas	Leo Perez
Tom Hall	The Walt Puffer Family
Brad Henry	Oscar Quixotic
Richard Hernandez	Paul Romo
Harvey Hyde	Bruce Rusin
Linda Hyde	Richard Saldaña
Ed Jordan	Frank Saucedo
Steve Jordan	Gaylin Schultz
Bob Johnson	Marlene Schultz
The Fred Lauro Family	Bark Tree
Memo Lopez	Dee Wells
JoJo Machado	Jim Yorke
Mike Mellinger	Mary Yorke

Newt Kimball, Al Epperly, Clay Bryant, Lefty Logan, Tarzan Parmelee, Lefty Shoun, & Cholly Grimm discuss how much they appreciate the locals, 1938.

Islander Family Sponsors

The Joe & Terri Hernandez Family
Joe Jr., Justin, & Maui

The Lipe & Maui Hernandez Family
Sons, Daughters, & Grandchildren

The Raul & Marie Hernandez Family
Jack & Siobahn

The Don & Roberta McLeish Family
Tyler & Ashlee

The Lucy McLeish Family
Donald & Buddy

The Saldaña Family
Joe, Trudy, Gina, Joey, & Ryan

In Memory of Joe "Che" Saucedo
Vera, Xavier, Lupe, Xavier Jr., & Stephanie

The Foxie & Noni Saucedo Family
Daughter Priscilla & Grandson Ricky

The Joe & Susie Saucedo Family
Debbie, Irene, Diana, & Abigail

Pete & Cathy Savage
Carly

The Pat Smith Family
Ray, Jim, & Donna

The Joe & Tina Voci Family
Gilbert & Nose

Just one big happy family, 1929.

Index
An Alphabetical List of Players & Places

" 'Garagiola' goes before 'Garbark,' right?"

Rookie intern at the publishing house

This'll probably be about the longest Index you've ever seen, unless you happen to read medical textbooks that contain lots of information about guts with lengthy Latin names and stuff like that.

That's because we had a few dozen really cool old photos that we just weren't able to stuff into any other nooks as we assembled the book, and we couldn't bear to leave 'em on the cutting room floor.

So, without further gabbing, we are pleased to present our 20-odd-page Index:

A

Aaron, Hank, 51, 227, 254, 287
Abbott & Costello, 123, 288
Adams, Lila, *108*, 130
Adams, Red, 19, 58, 63, 66, 81, *95*, *108*, 123, 152, *159*, 159, 182, 233, *246*, 246, 273, 282, 289
Adams, Earl "Sparky," *35*, 104, 224
Ahern, Mickey, 295
A Little Piece of Paradise, 251
Alderson, Dale, *273*
Alexander, Aimee, *123*, *167*, *377*
Alexander, Grover Cleveland, 7, 22, 32, 45, 89, 91, *114*, *123*, 124, 127, 140, 142, *167*, 167-168, 170, 195, 221, 241, 243, 276, 290, *358, 359*

Bob Garbark, 1938.

Allyn, Jim, 45
Alou, Matty, 56
Alston, Walter, 65, 139
Anson, Cap, 17, *21*, 21, 194, 334
Anthony, Lee, 30, *83*, 83, 91, *110*, 110, *158*, 158, 159, 244, 303
Antonelli, Johnny, 55
The Apartment, 182, 246
Appleberry, Rube, *292*
Arbuckle, Fatty, 287
Arlen, Richard, 178, 276
Armstrong, Jack, *291*

Arnold, Della Root, 13, 14, 31, 40, 41, 42, 48, 67, 69, 85, 88-89, 104, 105, 108-109, 118, 119, 120, 125, 134, 149, 164, 177, *178*, 183, 187, 188-190, 203, 213, *214*, 214, 219, 222, 236, 239, 282, 288, *353*
Asbell, Jim, 79
Astaire, Fred, 103
Auman, Howard, 38, *56*, 56, 147, 246, 274, 287
Autry, Gene, 123, 182

Hall-of-Fame hurler Grover Alexander knew his way around the batter's box, too: Ol' Pete smacked 378 base hits (including 11 homers) during his career.

B

The Babe Ruth Story, *151*, *182*, 182, 209, *210*
Bacall, Lauren, 115
Baecht, Ed, 28
Bailey, Abe, 22
Bailey, Pearl, 182
Baker, Bill, *20*, *217*, 217, 242, 263, 275, 313
Banks, Ernie, 18, *19*, *53*, 53, 58, 59, 235
Banks to Sandberg to Grace, 19, 58, 71, 114, 150, 228, 229, 233, 235, 326
Barber, Red, 219
Barrett, Red, 70, 288
Barrymore, John, 103
Bartell, Dick, *149*, 149, 150, 202, 237, 279-280, *280*, 286, 313
The Baseball Encyclopedia, 206, 330, 336
Baseball magazine, 21
Basie, Count, 25, 182
Bass, Dick, 79, *85*

Bauers, Russ, *108*
Baumholtz, Frank, *20*, 234, 302
The Beach Boys, 14
Beck, Clyde, *239*, *350*
Beck, Tiny, *239*, 239
Becker, Heinz, 269, *277*, *352*
Bellhorn, Mark, 328
Bench, John, 204
Bendix, William, *151*, *152*, *182*, 209-210, *210*
Bergen, Candice, 180
Bergen, Edgar, *180*, 180
Bernie, Ben, 182
Berra, Yogi, 152, 153, 204, 218, 318
Berry, Charlie, 189
Bertram, Clarence, *28*, *99*
The Big Country, 182, 233, 246
Bilko, Steve, 130, 144
Billboard, 14
Bird Park, *8*, *17*, *98*, 107, 108, 256
Birney, Ben, 178
Bithorn, Hi, 168
Blair, Footsie, 168
Blake, Sheriff, 39, 93, 168, *218*, *229*, 283
Block, Cy, 28, *71*, 71, 107, *108*, 201, *242*, 242, 254, 274, 313, 327
Block, Harriet, 28, 71, 100, 107, 201, 233, 242, 259, 274
Biltmore Hotel, 188, 288, 317, 318
Bogart, Humphrey, 115
Bombard, Al, *300*, 300
Bombard, Doug, 133, *300*, 300
Bonds, Barry, 240, 249, 254
Bonetti, Julio, *42*
Borkowski, Bob, *102*, 137, *138*, 138, 206, 231, 275, 313, 334
Borowy, Hank, *151*, 151-152, *152*, 182, 259, *277*
Bosio, Chris, 146
Boudreau, Lou, 198, 314
Bowman, Bob, 269
Boyd, Brendan C., 336
Boyd, Grace Bradley, 12, 110, 178, *179*, 180, 276
Brady, King, 22
Branca, Ralph, 71
Branded, 181, 230
Brickhouse, Jack, 122, 228
Brillheart, Jim, *35*
Brock, Lou, 18, 311
Broeg, Bob, 137
Brooks, Doc, 86, 115, 212

Brown, Jerry "Moonbeam," 125
Brown, Joe E., 83, 182
Brown, Parke, 276
Brown, Warren, 14, 17, 19, 33-34, 35-36, 43, 45, 63, 65, 74, 78, 79, 104, 121, 132, 133, 136, 140, 155-156, 168, 169, 171, 179, 180, 184, 211, 221, 223, 227, 233, 242, 263, 264, 265, 271, 280, *281*, 281, 282
Bryant, Clay, *90*, 98, 109, 116, 135, 162, *178*, 178, *179*, 179, 210, *295*, *356*, *362*
Buckner, Bill, 130, *157*
Burgess, Larry, 42, 56, 233, 238, 302
Burgess, Margaret, 56, 108, 321
Burgess, Smoky, 20, 53, *56*, 56, 78, 108, 233
Burke, Jimmy, 21-22, 77, 141, 196
Burns, Ed, 26, 27, 28, 33, 34, 38, 39, 44, 48, 64, 65, 75, 77, 79, 83, 84, 91, 93, 94, 97, 101, 118, 121, 133, 134, 135, 141, 143, 154, 155, 163, 166, 180, 184, 191, 192, 193, 202, 205, 209, 216, 223, 264, 265, 268, 269, 271, 278, 279-280, 282-283, *283*
Bush, Guy, *35*, *38*, 93, 94, *163*, 163-164, 191, 203, 213, *218*, 225, *228*, *243*

Ripper Collins, 1939.

C

Cahill, Danny, *91*, 122, *219*, *236*, 236, *237*, *283*, *354*
Califano, Frank, 87
Calvey, Jack, 237
Campbell, Gilly, 300
Campbell, Ray, *99*
Cannon, Ralph, 279

Cantor, Eddie, 176
Capone, Al, *239*
Caray, Chip, 122
Caray, Harry, 122, *126*, 126, 235, 262
Carey, Max, 216
Carleton, Tex, *27*, 42, *101*, 162, *168*, 168, 216, 224
Carlsen, Don, 42, *102*, *105*, *111*, 111, 113, 114, 123, 150, 151, *161*, 161, 215, 248, 274, 302, 313
Carnett, Lefty, *34*, 60, 61, *95*, 95, 109, 128, *129*, 129-130, 131, 136, 203, 246, 275, 286, 294
Carrera, Lalo, *332*
Carter, Joe, 122, 312
Carter, Orren, 300
Carter, Pat, *296*, *306*
Casey, Hugh, 130
The Casino, *12*, *15*, *25*, 30, 31, 49, 60, 100, *103*, 103, 104, 109, 113, *115*, 115, 116, 129, 139, 165, 176, 178, 182, 321
Cassidy, Hopalong, 12, 178, *179*, 179
Casto, Fidel, 254
The Catalina Islander, 12, 14, 32, 85, 295
Cat's Paw, 178
Cavarretta, Phil, 10, 12, 28, 31, 44, 58, 59, 61, 66, 72, 75, 82, 85, 95, 97, 100, 103, *110*, 110, 116, 118, 119, 120, 121, 132, 133, 134, 137, 140, 147, 150, 170, *176*, 176-177, *177*, 178, 182, 184, *186*, 197, 198, 200, *208*, 208-210, *209*, *210*, 213, 220, 221, 228, 231, 233, 236, 237, 238, 262, 266, 268, *279*, 279, *291*, 291, 294, 296, 297, 299, 300, 301, 302, 304, 313, *316*, 318, 327, 332, *348, 365, 376*
Chambers, Lefty, 127, 128, *130*, 130, 199, 206, 233, 240, 243, 259, 262, 273, 275, 334
Chance, Frank, 194
Chandler, Ed, 49, 64-65, *65*, 84, 96, 97, 100, 206, 223, 246, 254, 274, 289, 334
Chaplin, Charlie, 25, 181
Chase, Chevy, 31
Cherry, Irving, 225, *247*, 247
Cherry, Joan, 247
Cheeves, Virgil, *90*, 90, 97
The Chicago Cubs book, 221, 227
Chicago Cubs News, 127, 150, 154, 211, 216, 247, 282
The Chicago Daily News, 36, 40, 49, 74, 77, 79, 85, 90, 91, 92, 94, 95 96, 98, 103, 104, 105, 135, 164, *179*, 200, 221, 225, 226, 295

The Chicago Daily Times, *36*, 38, 39, 47, 48, 76, 77, 78, 79, 90, 91, 95, 99, 122, 135, 137, 152, 155, 163, 165, 166, 191, 199, 202, 220, 222, 225, 242, 265, 278, 281, 284

The Chicago Evening American, 12, 14, 21, 26, 32, 33, 36, 38, 39, 40, 42, 43, 44, 47, 69, 76, 77, 82, 83, 84, 89, 90, 92, 93, 97, 98, 103, 105, 122, 126, 163, 164, 167, 168, 170, 172, 173, 188, 189, 190, 192, 193, 194, 196, 209, 211, 222, 223, 224, 243, 244, 254, 258, 262, 278, 279, 281, 283, 284, 294, 315

The Chicago Evening Post, 32

The Chicago Herald-American, 33, 45, 78, 171

The Chicago Herald & Examiner, 32, 35, 37, 40, 65, 76, 98, 104, 105, 133, 179, 180, 184, 196, 222, 223, 224, 225, 233, 234, 236, 242, 257, 264, 281, 282

The Chicago News, 46, 142, 167

The Chicago Sun, 20, 34, 59, 63, 71, 78, 81, 82, 92, 95, 96, 101, 140, 159, 161, 168, 215, 219, 220, 222, 226, 265, 266, 271, 272, 284

The Chicago Sun-Times, 34, 228

The Chicago Tribune, 14, 21, 22, 25, 27, 28, 32, 33, 34, 36, 38, 39, 44, 46, 48, 52, 61, 63, 64, 65, 75, *76*, 76, 77, 79, 83, 84, 91, 92, 93, 94, 97, 101, *104*, 105, 133, 134, 135, 138, 141, 142, 143, 154, 158, 168, 171, 180, 183, 184, 191, 192, 202, 204, 205, 208, 209, 211, 216, 222, 223, 225, 226, 241, 243, 258, 264, 265, 268, 269, *270*, 271, 276, 278, 280, 281, 282, *283*, 285, 291, 304, 314, 318

Chipman, Bob, 95, *108*

Chiti, Harry, 157-158, *158*, 302, *315*, 315

Chuck Connors: The Man Behind the Rifle, 231

Churchill, Winston, 25, 181

Cobb, Bob, *288*

Cobb, Ty, 134, 165, 196

Cochrane, Edward, 14, 33, 122, 173, 193, 258, *279*, 279, 283

Cohn, Harry, 182

Colbert, Claudette, 181

Collins, Bob, *379*

Collins, Rip, 37, *73*, *114*, 169, 216, *331*, 331, *360*

Come On Marines, 178, 276

Como, Perry, 182

Connors, Chuck, 8, 42, 55, 65, 70-71, *71*, 108, 115, 139, 144, 159, 181, 182, *230*, 230-234, *231*, *232*, *233*, 241, 246, 276, 287, 302, 303, 323

Coolidge, Calvin, 25, 78, 126-127, *127*, 256

Cooper, Walker, 79, 275

Cooper, Wilbur, 105

Corcoran, Jimmy, 12, 26, 33, 36, 38, 39, 42, 43, 44, 47, 49, 69, 83, 89, 97, 98, 118, 121, 122, 126, 163, 164, 172, 190, 192, 194, 196, 244, 277, 280, 283, 294, 315

Corriden, Jr., John, 216

Corriden, Red, 37, 80, 170, 179, *216*, 216

Cosell, Howard, 281

Cowell, Harvey, 44, *127*, 127, 181, 226, 276, 278, 297

Cowell, Jack, 84, 171, 180, 181, 182, 183, 202, 212, 258, *276*, 297-299, *298*

Crawford, Joan, 49, 103, 178, 181

Crissey, Harrington, 271, 327

Crissey, Kit, 204

Critz, Hughie, 192

Crosby, Bing, 86, 115, 182, *288*, 288

The Cubs R Cookin' by Cub Wives for Family Rescue, 228

KiKi Cuyler, 1931.

Culler, Dick, 313

Culp, Benny, 212

Cusick, Jackie, 169, 234

Cuyler, KiKi, *17*, 62, *98*, *186*, 215, 244, *261*, 300, *361*

D

Dahlgren, Babe, *365*

Dallessandro, Dim-Dom, *72*, 72, 103, 276, *365*

Daniel, Daniel, 21

Dasnaw, George, 302

Davis, Curt, *372*

Davis, Dean, *309*

Davis, Nancy, 123

Davis, Jr., Sammy, 182

Davis, Spud, *20*, 137, *216*, 216

Day, Doris, *123*, 124, *167*
Day, Pea Ridge, *141*, 141
de Havilland, Olivia, 8, *177*, 177-178
Dean, Paul "Daffy," 130, 132, 137
Dean, Dizzy, 7, *9*, *45*, 59, 63, 94, 96, 100, 103, 109, *113*, 130, *132*, 132-136, *133*, *134*, *135*, 137, 178, 184, *213*, 216, 221, 245, *261*, 280, *289*, *295*, 300, *305, 362*
Dean, Pat, 282

Dizzy Dean & Clay Bryant, 1941.

Demaree, Al, *292*
Demaree, Frank, *18*, 169
DeMille, Cecil B., 25, 181
Derringer, Paul, 169, 271
The Des Moines Dispatch, 37, 69, 92, 94, 109, 118, 157, 163, 179, 198, 202, 285
Dickson, Murray, 139
DiMaggio, Dom, 72
DiMaggio, Joltin' Joe, 52, 67, *124*, 125, 132, 165, 174, 196, 217, 227, 253, *290*, *291*, 318, 319
DiMaggio, Vince, 67
Dittmer, Jack, 79
The Dixon Evening Telegraph, 122
Dobson, Joe, *176*
Dollar, Joe, 42
Dorsey, Jimmy, 25, 182
Dorsey, Tommy, 103, 178
Doubleday, Alexander, 55
Dougherty, Jim, 174, 269
Dougherty, Norma Jeane, *116*, 116, 132, *174*, 174-176, *175*, 180, *186*, 269 (See *Monroe, Marilyn*)
Doyle, Jack, 14, *97*, 97, 98, 144, 179, *217*, 217
Dow, Tony, 305
Drake, Charles, 129, 135, 279
Drysdale, Don, 324
Dubiel, Monk, 109, *169*, 169, 206, *302*, 302, 303, 315

Dugey, Oscar, 14, 92, 105
Dunker, Don, *41*, 41, 45, 78, 104, 105, 115, *161*, 161, 162, 245, 258, 274
Dunkley, Charles, 91
Durante, Jimmy, 123, 288
Durocher, Leo, 34, 130, 140, 144, 147, 168, 201, *211*, 211, 216, 228, 253, *288*, 317
Dyer, Braven, 82, 162, 202, 283

E

Earhart, Amelia, 184, *268*
Easter, Luke, 51
Eaves, Vallie, 169
Edwards, Bruce, 313
Edwards, Hank, *20*
Eichelberger, Hulda, *224*
Eisenhower, Dwight, 127
Elliott, Ace, 76, 91
English, Woody, 12, 24, 39, *68*, 68-69, 88-89, *91*, 95, 109, 188, *238*, 280, 285, *350, 362*
Epperly, Al, *13*, *34*, 35, *37*, 37, 79, 80, 95, *99*, 100, *101*, 104, 108, 114, 119, *162*, 162, 178, 202, 212, 215, 222, *254*, 264, *268*, 282, 289, *356, 363*
Epperly, Harold, *268*
Erickson, Paul, *63*, 63, 64, 96, 116, 234, 243
Erskine, Carl, 115
Essential Cubs, 150
Evers, Jack, 39
Evers, Johnny, 13, 32, 39, 74, 76, *194*, 194

Woody English, 1936.

Al Epperly, 1938.

F

Falcon Crest, 305
Feeling, Gene, 244
Feller, Bob, 130, 150, 275
Fibber McGee & Molly, *182*, 182
Fifty Years of Spring Training, 21
Finch, Frank, 158, 283
Finley, Charlie, 314
Fishman, Duke, *180*, 180
Flack, Max, 46-47, *314*, 314
Fleming, Bill, 95
Flowers, Charlie, 128, *355*
Flynn, Errol, 25
Fondy, Dee, 70-71, *71*, 233
Fonesca, Lew, 189
Ford, Whitney, 54
Four Preps, 14
Foxx, Jimmy, 215
Frawley, William, 123
Frazee, Jane, *135*
Freigau, Howard, *35*, 94
French, Larry, *5*, *18*, *19*, *31*, 40, *41*, 42, 67, 95, *98*, 98, *106*, *107*, *113*, 128, 148, *149*, 149, 162, *184*, 184, 248, 275, *300*, 300, *363*
French, Jr., Larry, *5*, *19*, *107*, *149*
French, Thelma, *106*

Frey, Lonny, 13, 17, *67*, 67-68, *68*, 101, 202, 216, 223, *250*, 250, 275, 313
Friberg, Barney, 104
Frick, Ford, 257
Frisch, Ada, 205
Frisch, Frankie, 14, 34, *20*, 43, 45, 52, 65, *74*, 75, 77, 78, 83, 100, 138, 139, 151, 160, 170, 194, *205*, 205-208, *206*, *207*, 216, 217, 228, 233, *249*, 283, *302*, 308, *333*, 333, 334, *335*
Furillo, Carl, 139, 313
Furey, Tyke, *308*
Fussell, Fred, *350*

G

Gable, Clark, 181, 299
Gaedel, Eddie, 262
Galan, Augie, *39*, 39, *67*, 67, 97, 116, *121*, 121, 129, *134*, 298, *299*, 311, 377
Galehouse, Denny, 275
Gallagher, Jim, 32, 36, 81, 90, 97, 140, 155, 184, 188, 191, 193, 209, 223, 227, 229, 262-263, *262*, 264, 268, 277, *284*, 284
Gallagher, Timmy, 184
The Game is Never Over, 262
Garagiola, Joe, 130, 358
Garbark, Bob, 135, *216*, *236*, *242*, 242, 358, *358*
Garber, Jan, 103, 182
Gehrig, Lou, 121, *166*, *190*, 217, 227, 254, 279
Geiger, Edward, 281

Larry French, 1940.

George, Greek, *145*, 145
Gibson, George, 195
Gibson, Jimmy, *34*
Gibson, Mary, *115*
Gilbert, Barbara Ann, *108*
Gilbert, Charlie, *108*, *365*
Gildner, Allison, *113*
Gilliam, Junior, 139
The Girl Who Loved Tom Gordon, 326
The Glass-Bottom Boat, 124
Gleeson, Jim, *106*, *169*, 169, 311, *312*, 312

Goddard, Paulette, 181
Golenbock, Peter, 236, 262, 263
Gone with the Wind, 177
Gonzalez, Mike, 170, *254*, 254
Goodman, Benny, 25, 104, 182
Gordon, Flash, 326
Grable, Betty, 8, 25, 122, *176*, 176-177, *177*, 178
Grampp, Hank, *35*
Grange, Red, 218, *227*, 282
Grant, Duncan, *13*
The Great American Baseball Card Flipping, Trading, and Bubblegum Book, 336
Great Depression, 7, 27
Grey, Zane, 25, *183*, 183, 305
Grimes, Burleigh, 170, 191, 219

Charlie Grimm at Fenway Park in 1946, when he managed the N.L. All-Star squad.

Grimm, Charlie, 7, 9, 11, 14, *17*, *18*, *19*, 19, 20, 28, *29*, 31, 32, 34, *36*, 36, 39, 42, 43, 46, 55, 61, 62, 66, 69, 71, *73*, 74, 75, 76, 77-78, 80, 81, *82*, 82, 87, 88-89, 90, 92, *93*, 96-97, *98*, 101, *104*, 104, *108*, 109, *115*, *117*, 118, 119, 121, 122, 123, *128*, 132, 138, 139, 143, 150, 151, 152, 156, 157, 159, 163, 180, *182*, 182, 183, 185, 188, 190, 191, 192, *193*, 193, 194, 195, 196, *197*, 197-201, *198*, *199*, *200*, *201*, 202, 204, 205, *206*, 207, 208, 209, 210, 211, 212, *213*, 213, 214, *215*, 215-216, 220, 221, 222, *234*, 243, 247, 258, *263*, 264, 266, 271, 272, *277*, 277, *279*, 279, 280, 283, 284, *288*, 292, *293*, 295, 296, 300-301, 303, 304, *306*, 308, 313, 314, 326, *337*, *341*, *354*, *356*, *364*, *377*, *378*, *380*
Grimm, Marion, 191, 282
Gwynn, Tony, 254

H

Haas, Mule, 189
Hack, Stan, 12, 45, 46, 48-49, *49*, *71*, 71, 95, *99*, 103, *119*, 134, 156, 162, 163, 165, 168, 169, 178, 204, *210*, 210, *237*, 238, 245, 297, 299, 300, 301, 303, *304*, 304, 313, *322*, *351*, *365*, *376*
Hacker, Olinda, 50, 92, 260
Hacker, Pam, 50
Hacker, Warren, 46, *50*, 50, 57, *102*, 102, 109, *111*, 244, *260*, 260, *330*, 330, 336
Haddix, Harvey, 56, *301*
Hafey, Chuck, 284
Hal Grayson Band, 25
Halas, George, 218, *227*
Haley, Dan, 116, 237
Hamlin, Florence Johnson, 116
Handley, Gene, 215
Hannah, Truck, 86
Hansen, Scooter, 175, *295*, 295, 326
Hansen, Snipe, *35*, *88*, 88-89, *89*, 93, 261, 291
Hanyzewski, Eddie, *352*
Harding, Warren, 27, *126*, 126, *127*, 256
Harlow, Jean, 181
Harrell, Ray, *34*, *92*
Harris, Dorothy, *106*, 169, 312
Harris, Fred, 336
Harris, Nancy, *113*
Harrison, Gregory, 305
Harry James Orchestra, 177
Harry the Monk, 180
Hartig, Ed, 21
Hartnett, Buddy, 31, *109*, 189, 203, *204*, 204
Hartnett, Charles Leo "Gabby," 7, 9, 13-14, 16, *19*, *27*, 33, *35*, 36, 37, 39, 40, *41*, 42, *43*, 68, *73*, 75, 76, 77, *78*, 79, *82*, 82, 84, *85*, 88-89, 90, 91, 92, 97, *99*, 107, *109*, *113*, 129, 133, 135, 145, 157, *162*, 162, 163, 168, 170, 172, *181*, 181, 182, *189*, 189, 190, *193*, 194, *201*, 201-204, *202*, *204*, 216, 222, 223, 235, 239, 243, *261*, 264, 280, 282, 283, *284*, 293, *294*, 296, 297, *298*, 298, 300, 304, *305*, *332*, *338*, *345*, *349*, *351*, *353*, *379*
Hartnett, Martha, *189*, 189, *202*, 203, 203, 236, *237*
Hartnett, Sheila (See *Hornof, Sheila Hartnett*)
Hayworth, Rita, 182
Heathcote, Cliff, *35*, *104*, 104, 200, *218*, 228, *314*, 314-315, *350*
Helmsley, Rollie, 303
Hemingway, Ernest, 29, 253
Henry, Bill, 200, 224
Henshaw, Roy, 40, 42, 79, 128

Stan Hack, Babe Dahlgren, Lou Novikoff, Swish Nicholson, Dom Dallessandro, Charlie Gilbert, & Phil Cavarretta, 1942.

Hepburn, Katherine, 231
Herman, Babe, 170, *337*
Herman, Billy, 17, 37, 61, *82*, 82, 88, *91*, *94*, *99*, *109*, *113*, 129, *137*, 137, 170, *191*, 191, 204, 210, 275, *311*, 311, *368, 376*
Herman, Jr., Billy, *109*
Herman, Woody, 25, 182
Hernandez, Frank, *309*
Hernandez, John-Eric, *310*, 310, 324
Hernandez, Richard, 310, 324
Herzog, Whitey, *60*, 60
Heston, Charleton, 182, 231, 246
Higbe, Kirby, 13, *34*, 35-36, *36*, 63, 76, 100, 170, 176, 202, 223
Higgins, Pinky, 275
Hiller, Frank, 243
Hirsch, Elroy "Crazy Legs," *234*, 234
Hirsch, Ruth, 234
Hoak, Don, 139
Hobbs, Roy, 69, 79, 160, *290*, 290-292, *291*, *292*
Hochstadter, Harry, 32, 46, 278
Hodges, Joy, 122, 123

Hoffman, John, 78, 95, 122, 165-166, 225, 279, *284*, 284
HoHoKam Park, *317*, 319
Hoover, Herbert, 25, 126, 181, 238, 256
Hope, Bob, 123
Hornof, Sheila Hartnett, 189, 203, 321
Hornsby, Rogers, *17*, 24, 44, 48, 49, 68, 69, 76, 80, 85, 88, 96, 103, 124, 137, *196*, 196-197, *197*, 204-205, *256*, 281, 283, 300, 325
Hotel Atwater, *106*, *111*, 139
Hotel St. Catherine, 12, 14, *15*, *31*, 31, 46, 67, 84, 88-89, 90, 103, 105, *106*, 107, 108, 112, *113*, 148, 154, 162, 167, 176, *177*, 182, 192, 194, 212, *226*, 236, 258, 268, *269*, 283, 284, 297, 300, 301, 304, 321, 324, 326, *350*
Hoyle, Edmond, 38
Hoyt, Bob, 29
Hubbell, Carl, 29, 130
Hudson, Rochelle, *181*, 181
Huettner, John, 302
Hughes, Pat, 122
Hughes, Roy, 204
Hutchings, Johnny, *11*, 11, *26*, 170, *241*, 291, 326, *355*

I

I Love Lucy, 123, 319
Ichiro, 254
Imitation of Life, 181
Inside Sports, 120
It Happens Every Spring, 287
Ives, Burl, 182, 246

HANDY RANDY! . . . The presence of Ransom Jackson at third base is one of the reasons Cub fans believe their favorites will surprise this year. Jackson, with only one full year of major league experience, is developing into one of baseball's standout third basemen.

J

Jabb, Ed, 45, 155, 170, 201, 242, 253, 273
The Jackie Robinson Story, 182
Jackson, Randy, 18, 19, *20*, 30, 40, 45, 52, *57*, 57-58, 64, 75, 80, *102*, 104, 114, 146, 197, 207, 214, 228, *232*, 232, 235, 238, 239, 258, 276, 281, 311, 316, 318, 326, *366*
Jackson, Reggie, 160
Jeffcoat, George, 138
Jeffcoat, Hal, 7, 101, 108, *138*, 138, 139, 211, 233, 274, 318, 330-331, 334
Jeffcoat, Valma, 138, 233
Jenkins, Ferguson, 18
John, Tommy, 159

Johnson, Don, 170, 271
Johnson, Roy "Hard Rock," *20*, 55, 60, 70, 80, *94*, 207, *211*, 211-212, *212*, *213*, 241, 248, 264, 295, 298, 301, 302, 303, *306*, 307
Johnson, Harold, 21, 76, 281
Johnson, Joanne, 103, *113*, *115*, 212, 299
Johnson, Walter, 136, 179
Joiner, Pop, *106*
Jolly Cholly's Story, 226
Jones, Percy Lee, 90, 93, 241
Jones, Sad Sam, 238, 330, 336
Jordan, Bob, *309*
Judge, Arline, *181*, 181
Jurges, Billy, 39, 44, *69*, 69, 91, *210*, 210, 290-291, *291*, *292*, 298

K

Karloff, Boris, 181
Kaufmann, Tony, 82, 94, 170
Kawano, Nobe, 177, 229
Kawano, Yosh, 19, 38, 61, 67, 103, 116, 119, 134, 177, 212, 218, 220, 221, 226, *227*, 227-229, *228*, *229*, 259, 264, 275, 289, 317, 318
Kaye, Danny, 123
Kearns, James, 96, 135, 279
Kelleher, Frankie, 71
Kelly, Bill, 70
Kelly, Bob, 12, 40, 42, 51, *52*, 52, 65, 75, 79, 80, 92, 95, *102*, 108, 110, 209, 215, 232, 275, 317
Kelly, Joe, 105
Kennedy, Bob, *258*
Kenton, Stan, 175, 182
Killefer, Bill, 19, 22, 32, 45, 46, 74-75, 92, 104, *105*, 124, 167, *195*, 195, 197, 224, 314
Killefer, Jane, *105*, 105
Killefer, Margaret, 124

Pepper, 1920s.

Kimball, Newt, *34, 356*
Kiner, Ralph, 58
King, Stephen, 326
King, Wayne, 103, 178
Kirby, Jim, 147, 170, 240, 273
Kirk, Herb, *308*
Kirk, Neal "Corky," *332*
Kittle, Hub, *60*, 60-61, *61*, 62, 81, 86, *87*, 103, *115*, 115, 116, 119, 129, 146, 148, 171, 174, 180, 182, 212, 244, 259, 289, 291, 313
Klein, Chuck, *91*, *166*, 166, 170, 221, 285, *337, 340*
Klippstein, Johnny, 12, 27, 42, 45, *53*, 53-54, *54*, 56, *74*, 84, 100, *113*, 113, 114, 147, 207, 209, 213, 223, 228, 232, 244, 260, 275, 289, 313, 316, 318, 334
Knickerbocker Hotel, 238
Koosman, Jerry, 173
Kowalik, Fabian, 79, 170
Kowalski, Eddie, 50, 206, 334
Krug, Marty, 87, 141
Kumalae, Clarence, 87, *171*, 171, 254, 299
Kush, Emil, 171
Kyser, Kay, 182

L

Lade, Doyle, 171, 199
LaFranchi, Remo, *332*
Langford, Jim, 262
Larsen, Don, 152
Lasagne, Don, *309*
Lasorda, Tommy, 139, *179*, 179, 229, 231
Laughton, Charles, 181, 299
Laurel & Hardy, 25
Lazzeri, Tony, *100*, *166*, 166, 167, *213*, 298
Lee, Bill, *26, 31, 41*, 42, *106*, 152, *153*, 153-154, *154*, 181, 301
Lefebvre, Benny, 324
Leiber, Hank, 171, 226, 265
Lelivelt, Jack "Hoss," 86, 148
Lemmon, Jack, 182, 246
Lemon, Bob, 124
Leonard, Dutch, 54, *55*, 55, 56
Leslie, Sam, *378*
Lewis, Bob, 33, 34, 36, 40, 45, 69, 90, 92, 104, 122, 123, 156, 168, 191, *218*, 225, *228*, *264*, 264-265, *265*, *266*, 266, 278, 279, 283, *284*, 284, *306*
Lillard, Gene, *26, 34*, 95, *98*, 98, *156*, 156, 157

Lingbergh, Charles, 184
Lindstrom, Fat Freddie, 171
Litwhiler, Danny, 130
Livingstone, Mickey, 95
Lloyd, Harold, 178
Logan, Lefty, 98, *115, 128*, 128, *356, 380*
Lopez, Conrad, 198, 303, *307*, 307-310, *309, 310*
Lopez, Phil, *309*, 309
The Loretta Young Show, 182, 246
The Los Angeles Times, 13, 27, 28, 32, 44, 48, 49, 52, 55, 82, 83, 89, 90, 93, 96, 143, 154, 155, 157, 158, 162, 163, 166, 167, 183, 184, 192, 194, 195, 199, 200, 202, 203, 224, 225, 226, 241, 248, 253, 256, 265, 268, 269, 278, 283, 294
Lotshaw, Andy, *35*, 38, 43, 62, 65, 70, 76, *78*, *82*, 91, 92, 96, 103, 121, *140*, 154, 165, *167*, 191, 199, 213, *218*, 218-227, *219, 220, 221, 223, 224, 225, 226, 227*, 234, 236, *238*, *262*, 264, *266*, 266, 270, 271, *276*, 285, 295, *298*, 298, *306*, 311, 314, 321, *340*
Lotshaw, Laura, 191, 218, 219, 221, *226*, 284
Louise, Anita, 176, *177*, 177
Lowe, Lloyd, 28, 37, 69-70, 80, 198, 232, 241, 254, 259, 274, 275, 288
Lown, Turk, 12, 52, *104*, *144*, 144, 207, 232, 233, 245, 253, 311, 318, 334
Lown, Violet, 144
Lowrey, Peanuts, 66, 72, 124, 139, *140*, 140, 147, 170, 182, 238, 241, 259, 289
Lynn, Red, *352*

M

Mack, Connie, 67, 201, 211
Mack, Ray, 234
MacLaine, Shirley, 246
MacMurray, Fred, 182
Maddern, Clarence, *76*
Maddux, Greg, 311, 312, *313*
Majeski, Hank, *115*, *176*, 225, *380*
Malamud, Bernard, 290, 292
Malone, Pat, 82, *94*, *107*, 134, 171, *197*, 219, *223*, 225, *281*, 281
Malone, Patsy, 108, 191
Mann, Les, 22

Bobby Mattick hurries to beat the throw to Billy Herman...but seems to miss the bag, 1940.
(No matter, though; Herman's foot seems to have slipped off the base, as well.)

Mantle, Mickey, *51*, 67, 147, 227, 287, 319
Maranville, Rabbit, 195
Marshall, Dave, 330
Maris, Roger, 68, 147
Marriott, Barbara, *306*
Martin, Pepper, 146
Marty, Joe, *18*, *99*, *165*, 165, *378*
Mason, Neil, *34*
Matthews, Wid, 34, 45, 52, 65, 83, 208, *263*, 263-264
Mattick, Bobby, *10*, 42, 60, 135, 140, 147, *148*, 148, 210, 215, 219, 228, 244-245, 262, 264, 280, *368*
Mattick, Chick, 148
Mauch, Gene, 66, 72, 80, 110, 114, 124, *146*, 146-147, 148, 150, 153, 182, 200-201, 206, *210*, 210, 215, 218, 228, 232, 241, 245, *245*, 245-246, 259, 289, 313, 334
Mauro, Carmen, 13, 18, 38, 50, 64, 84, 94, 101, *102*, 138, 139, 140, 150, 158, 207, 215, 223, 233, 238, 242, 263-264, 281, 311, 313, 334
May, Jackie, 28, 74
Mays, Willie, 130, 227, 250, 287, 319
McCall, Dutch, 138, 171
McCarthy, Charlie, *180*, 180
McCarthy, Joe, 26, 39, 43, 47, 76, 82, 83, 85, 132, 141, 193, *196*, 196, 201, *202*, 215, 254, 283, *339*, 355

McCartney, Paul, 231
McCullough, Clyde, 152, *153*, 153, 244, *379*
McGraw, John, 29, 205, *253*, 253, 257
McKenzie, Peggy, *113*
McLish, C. C. J. C. T., 27, 30, 51, 53, 61, 84, 92, 96, 105, 110, 116, 127, 130, *145*, 145-146, *146*, 212, 245, 252, 253, 273, 287, 289, 318, 334
McPartland, Johnny, 82, *221*
Meers, Russ, 161
Meiklejohn, Bill, 122
Merullo, Boots, 42, 58, *59*, 59, 232, 238, 239, 321
Merullo, Lennie, *16*, 16, 37, 42, 43, 48, 57, *58*, 58-59, *59*, 66, 72, *80*, 95, 107, *108*, *110*, 110, 134, 137, 160, 200, 212, 215, 238, 239, 245, 262, 300-301, 327, 331
Merullo, Matt, 245
Mesner, Steve, 61-62, *62*, 78, 80, 98, 259
Metkovich, George, 72, 124, 289
The Metropolis Daily Planet, 277
Michaels, Al, 187
Miksis, Eddie, 58, 71, 150, 233, 311
Miller, Freddie, *99*
Miller, Hack, *46*, 46-47, 75, 91, 104, 326, *350*
Miller, Ox, 9, 37, *62*, 62-63, 238, 242, 243, 275, 282, 330
Miller, Mrs. Shorty, 63

Milstead, Lefty, 128
Minoso, Minnie, 51
Minner, Lefty, 128, *131*, 131, 209, 233, 316, 330, 334
Miracle on 34th Street, 84, 276
Mitchell, Fred, *23*, 23, 194, 276
Mix, Tom, 25, 182, 305
Mize, Johnny, 202
Monroe, Marilyn, 8, 116, 174-176, *175*, *176*
  (See *Dougherty, Norma Jeane*)
Moore, Johnny, *79*, 79
Moore, Robert, *308*
Mooty, Jake, *42*
Morris, Edmund, 121
Moss, Mal, *116*, 116
Munson, Joe, *164*, 164, 165
The Munsters, 287
Munzel, Edgar, 20, 34, 71, 81, 92, 95, 96, 101, 159, 161, 215-216, 219, 220, 222, 226, 228, 234, 265, 266, 271, 272, *284*, 284
Murtaugh, Danny, *301*
Murray, Bill, 262
Musial, Stan, 139, 227
Muskat, Carrie, 19, 71, 150, 228, 233, 235
Mutiny on the Bounty, 181, 299
My Early Life, 121
Myers, Billy, *312*, 312, *376*

Brothers Vern & Barney Olsen, 1941.

N

Nagurski, Bronco, 218, *227*
Nason, Don, *296*, *306*
The Natural, 160, 290
Neily, Harry, 12, 278, 282
Nelson, Line Drive, *244*, 244
The New Era Clubs, 124
The New York Herald-Tribune, 185
The New York Times, 201
Newcombe, Don, 313
Newsome, Buck, *189*, 189, 191
Nicholson, Swish, 63, *66*, 66, 67, 77, 81, 95, 147, 154, 160, 165, 220, 238, 271, 331-332, *333*, *365*
Nixon, Richard, *127*, 127, 184
Nixon, Tricia, *127*, 127
Noren, Irv, 124
Northey, Ron, 243
Novikoff, Lou, 81, 154, *155*, 155-156, *156*, *237*, 237, 288, *365*
Novotney, Rube, 70

O

O'Dea, Ken, 36, *157*, 157, *295*, *340*, *372*
O'Doul, Lefty, 79, 128, 131-132, *132*, 311
Oh, Sadaharu, *254*, 254
Olaf V, King, 25, 181
The Old Man and the Sea, 29, 253
Olsen, Barney, 58, *369*
Olsen, Jimmy, 277
Olsen, Vern, *78*, *369*
O'Neill, Tip, 125
Osteen, Claude, 159
Ott, Mel, *11*, 29, 170
Otto, Wayne, 104, 277, 281
Overholt, Ivey, 282
Owen, Charlie, 12, 157, 239
Owen, Mickey, 12, 96, *157*, 157, 244, 302

More pepper, 1939.

P

Pafko, Andy, *51*, 51-52, *52*, 66, 71, 79, 80, 103, 107, 110, 117, 139, 199, 200, 212, 215, 221, 228, 238, 259, 270, 279, 281, 313, 327, 328, 331, 334
Pafko, Ellen, 107
Paige, Satchell, 54
Parker, Ace, 234
Parker, Clifton Blue, 47, 48
Parmelee, Tarzan, *162*, 162-163, 242, *356*
Partee, Roy, 86
Passeau, BUM, 28, 107, 152, 238
Passeau, Claude, 28, 76, 107, *152*, 152-153, 215, 238, 242, 334, *352*
Pat & Mike, 231
Patrick, Gail, *288*
Patrickson, Johnny, *332*
Patton, George S., 25, 305
Pawelek, Ted, 244
Payne, John, 84, 176, *180*, 180, 276
Peck, Gregory, 182, 231, 246
Phelps, Babe, *92*, 171, *173, 370*

Babe Phelps, 1934.

370

Phillips, Roy, 226
Pierce, Raymond "Lefty," 104, 128
Piltch, Victor, *346*
Poiter, Sidney, 182
Porgy and the Bess, 182, 246
Porter, Gene Stratton, 25, 305
Posedel, Bill, 130
Post, Wiley, 184
Potts, Molly, 130
Powell, Dick, *349*
Priddy, Jerry, 72, 124
Pride of the Yankees, 140
Prim, Ray, *108*
Prince Oama, *171*
Prince, Frank, 178
The Public Defender, 181
Pyle, Buddy, *308*

Q

The Quest, 92
Quiesser, Art, *35*, 105
Quinn, Wimpy, *140*, 140-141, 234

R

Raddick, Rob, *34*
Raffensberger, Ken, 40, *42*, 66, 99, 105, *154*, 154, *192*, 192, 203, 204, 253, 258, 269, 275, 288, 294, 330-331, 334, *371*
Raft, George, 178
Ramazzotti, Bob, *74*, 243

The Rancho Cordova Grapevine, 184
Ray, Bob, 13, 27, 44, 200, 203
Reagan, Dutch, 37, 55, 60, 64, 69, 84, 92, 94, 109, *118*, 118-127, *119*, *121*, *122*, *123*, *124*, *125*, *126*, 140, 142, 157, 160, 163, *167*, 167, 170, 176, 178, 179, 182, *186*, 195, 197, 198, 202, 203, *214*, 214-215, 230, 241, 280, *283*, *285*, 285, 286, 288, 290, 326, *371, 377, 381*
Reagan, Michael, 124
Reagan, Nancy Davis, 123
Reagan, Nelle, 120

SELLING DES MOINES
To The ENTIRE NATION!

For seventeen hours a day, listeners in every state in the nation and dozens of foreign countries are hearing the name of the Capital City of Iowa. They hear Des Moines through

WOC - WHO

This super-powered radio station is "selling" your city to the world constantly. Affiliated with the Red Network of NBC, it brings you the cream of the air's crop of programs.

Leading the Middlewest in sports coverage, WOC-WHO features its daily baseball broadcasts of Chicago games, and its twice-daily sports reviews.

'DUTCH' REAGAN
WOC-WHO
Sports Announcer

WOC - WHO
IOWA'S 50,000 WATT RADIO STATION!

Rebozo, Bebe, *127*, 127
Redford, Robert, 290
Reichow, Oscar, 46, 74, 90, 142, 167, 278
Reyes, Michael, 303
Reyes, Pete, 28
Reynolds, Carl, *18*, *81*, *172*, 172, *213*
Rice, Del, 139
Richards, Fuzzy, *20*, 49, *70*, 70, *77*, 109, 207, 232, 233, 327
Rickert, Marv, 172, 302
Rickey, Branch, 115, 232, 263, 264, 314
The Rifleman, 230
Roberts, Howard, 77, 98, 221
Roberts, Robin, 50
Robinson, Jackie, 54, 252, 331
Rockwell, Norman, 63, 110, 150, *185*, 185-186, 197, 205
Rodgers, Joe, 155
Rogell, Billy, 12, 101, 107, *136*, 136-137, 149, 203, 216, 243, 313

Ken Raffensberger, 1941.

Rogers, Buddy, 182
Rogers, Roy, 123, 288
Roosevelt, Franklin, 126, 190, 192, 238
Roosevelt, Theodore, 25
Root, Charlie, *15*, *18*, 31, 40, 41, 49, 67, 69, 80, 85, 92, 93, 94, 95, 97, 99, 105, *107*, 109, 118, 121, 125, *149*, 149, 152, 159, 162, 165, 183, *188*, 188-190, *213*, 213-215, *214*, 219, 222, 239, 245, 264, 282, 285, *289*, 291, 300, 303, *353, 372*
Root, Jr., Charlie, 42, 85, 105, 108, *214*, 214, 239, *353*
Root, Della (See *Arnold, Della Root*)
Root, Dorothy, *15*, 67, 189, *214*, 214, 282, *353*

Curt Davis, Charlie Root, & Ken O'Dea, 1938.

Roots, 230
Rose, Pete, 137
Ross, Helen, 116
Rowland, Pants, 265
Roy, Luther, *35*
Royko, Mike, 158
Ruether, Dutch, 159
Ruggles, Wesley, 181
Rush, Bob, 50, 54, *79*, 79, 80, 96, 103, 107, 110, 146, 150-151, *151*, *152*, 161, 185-186, 207, 212, 213, 236, 243, 258, 273, 303, *308*, 308, 313, 318, *319*, 330, 334, 336
Russell, Rip, *93*, *172*, 172, *212*
Ruth, Babe, 52, 77, 121, 131, 163, 166, *190*, 194, 196, 209, 213-214, 217, 219-220, 227, 235, 238, 254, 279, 290

Ryan, Buddy, 300
Ryan, Nolan, 173
Ryan, Spud, *87*, 87, *166*, 303-304, *304*, 307, 308
Ryan, Sylvester, *303*, 303-305, *304*, *305*, 307, *308*, 308, *309, 346*

S

S.S. Avalon, 41-42, *42*, *43*, 43, 272, 321
S.S. Catalina, *41*, 41-42, 321,
Saldaña, Frank, 115, 203, 293, 296-297, *297*, 321, 324, *325*, 325
Saldaña, Lolo, 47, 49, 81, 113, 115, 169, 198, 201, 202, 203, 208, *266*, 293, *296*, 296, *297*, 303, *308*, 308, 309, 317, *325*, *346*
Saldaña, Martín, *310*
Saltwell, Salty, 198
Sandborn, I. E., 21, 285
Santa Catalina Island: Its Magic, People, and History, 299
Santo, Ron, 122
Sargent, Edward, 84
Sarnoff, David, 185
The Saturday Evening Post, 63, 150, 185-186
Saucedo, Foxie, 66, 81, 100, 116, 150, 198, 212, 226, 302, *303*, 303, 308, 310
Saucedo, Marcelino, 48, 64, 81, 117, 150, 158, 172, 175, 180, 206, 222, 233, 293-294, *301*, 301-302, 303, 307-308, *308*, 309, 310, 315, 324
Saucedo, Tina, 116-117
Sauer, Hank, 53, 58, *64*, 64, *76*, 81, 96, 124, 139, 152, 182, 206, 241, 302, 303, 319
Sawatski, Carl, 52, 110, 172
Scheffing, Bob, *19*, 55, 77, *108*, *147*, 147, 199, *324*
Scheffing, Jr., Bobby, *108*, 108, *147*, 206, 212, 243
Schelberg, Ernie, *34*
Schmitz, Johnny, *63*, 63, 64, *83*, 83, 96, 107, 110, 161, 185-186, 243, 330, 331
Schramka, Paul, 18, 30, 40, 49, *52*, 52-53, *53*, 73, *74*, 80, 101, 150, 172, 184, 199, 207, 208, 228, 232, *240*, 240, 244, 259, 275, 313, 329, 334
Schreiner, Blanny Wrigley, *44*, 44, 123, 258, 276
Schulte, Johnny, *43*, 43, 85, 172, *343*
Schultz, Bob, 172
Schultz, Tony, 22
Schuster, Bill, 172, 287
Seaver, Tom, 173
Sedgewich, Red, 225

Seebold, William "Dutch," *92, 173, 336*
Selkirk, Twinkletoes, *244,* 244
Serena, Bill, *20,* 64, 81, 172, 208, 296-297, *297, 373*

Bill Serena, 1950.

Seys, John, 265
Shea, Merv, 216
Shepard, Otis, 101, *266,* 266, *267,* 331
Sheridan, Ann, 203
Shoun, Lefty, 42, 128, *213, 356*
Silvers, Phil, *288*
Simmons, Al, 189
Simons, Herbert, 36, 39, 90, 135, 137, 152, 155, 163, 191, 199
Simpson, Sam, *294*
Sisti, Sibby, 290
Skipper, John, 50, 199
Sloat, Lefty, 110, 128, *131,* 131, 201, 274
Smalley, Jolene, 110, 114
Smalley, Jr., Roy, *20,* 42, 70-71, 107, 110, *111,* 111, 112, 113-114, *150,* 150, 151, 160, 161, 200, 206, 208, 230, 236, 247-249, *248, 249,* 274, 302, 303, 313, 320, 321, *331,* 331, 334
Smalley, III, Roy, 150
Smith, Bob, *332*
Smith, Bud, 44, 116, 192, 276, 301
Smith, Ed, 93
Smith, Marie, 116

Smith, Red, *215,* 215-216
Snider, Duke, 139, 287, 313
Sosa, Sammy, *259, 319,* 326, *327,* 328, 332
Southworth, Billy, 147
Soylent Green, 230
Spahn, Warren, 65
Spalding, Al, *17,* 17, 194
The Sporting News, 220
Stabelfeld, Stub, 79
Stainback, Tuck, *99,* 103, 134, *144,* 144, 157, 178, *198, 226,* 226, *351, 373*
Statz, Jigger, *142,* 142, 182, 216
Stengel, Casey, 68, 147, *156, 196,* 247, 315, *329,* 329, 330
Stephenson, Riggs, *35,* 121, *164,* 164, *188,* 188, 190, 300, *378*
Steube, Clarence, 87
Stevens, Chuck, 86
Stock, Milt, 216
Storey, Harvey, 30, 40, 80, 91, 110, 133, 155, *165,* 165, *204,* 204, 334
The Stratton Story, 140
Stringer, Lou, 61, 71-72, *72,* 110, 116, 182, 219, 271, 275, 289, 321
Stueland, George, 167
Sturgeon, Bobby, 72, *85,* 110, *289,* 289

Tuck Stainback, 1937.

373

Sueme, Hal, *101*, 173, *241, 355,* 374
Sunday, Billy, 21
Sutton, Don, 159, 246

T

Taft, Charles, 126
Taft, William Howard, 126, 127
Take Me Out to the Cubs Game, 19, 50, 199
Tales from the Dodger Dugout, 115
Taupin, Bernie, 174
Taylor, Edgar, 49, 78, 256, 294, *299*, 299
Taylor, Roy, *294*
Taylor, Zack, 173, *190*, 190, *374*
Teachout, Bud, *350*
Teenagers, Graybeards and 4-F's, 204, 327
Temple, Shirley, *181*
Terry, Bill, *29*, 29, 190, 191, 250-251
Terwilliger, Wayne, *20*, *30*, 30, *54*, 54-55, *55*, 64, 76, 80, *104*, 127, 150, 172, 177, 179, 197, 212, 215, 216, 223, 232, 245, 259, 265, 302, 313, 333, 334

Hal Sueme, wishing they'd invented sunglasses in 1937.

That's My Boy, 181
Thomas, Bob, *346*
Thomson, Bobby, 54, 173, 320
Thorpe, Jim, 142
Tierney, Jim, 190, 191
Tinker, Joe , 194
Tinker-to-Evers-to-Chance, 17, 194
Tinning, Bud, *92, 173,* 173
Todd, Al, 79, 244
Todd, Kay, *114*
Tolson, Chick, *35, 143,* 143
Toney, Fred, 142
Too Many Husbands, 181
Totten, Hal, 222
Touchstone, Clay, 105
Tracy, Spencer, 231
Training Camp Gossip, 27
Trapper John, MD, 305
Triplett, Coaker, 142-143, *143, 243,* 243
Trocadero, Oscar, 284
Truman, Harry, 243
Tubb, Julian, *77,* 77, *99*
Turner, Ted, 22
Tyler, Lefty, 128

Zack Taylor in the '30s — long before that perplexing midget episode.

U

Uhle, George, 81
Unzueta, Dado, *310*
USA Today, 245
Upton, Roger, 154, 198-199, 300-301

Vaughn, Jim, *22*, 22, *142*, 142
Veeck as in Wreck, 222, 262
Veeck, Sr., Bill, 141, 144, 188, *190*, *261*, 261-262, 281, 282, *284*
Veeck, Jr., Bill, 47, 132, 145, 173, *190*, 195, 197, 213, 219, 221, 222, 236, 258, 261-262, *262*, 292
Veeck, Mike, 262

Avalon, California, 90704, from on high.

V

Valentine, Bobby, 254
Valenzuela, Fernando, 159
Vallee, Rudy, *25*, 25, 182
Vanderburg, Hy, *94*
Vander Meer, Johnny, 53, 54, 55, 173, 302
Van Dyke, Corky, *50*, 50-51, 65, 75, *102*, 105, 110, *111*, 115, 127, 183, 199, 206, 214, 238, 244, 259, *267*, 275, 282, 334
Van Dyke, Dick, 51, 183
Van Dyke, Jerry, 183
Vaughn, Irving, 34, 61, 75, 141, 163, 225, 226, 271, 282, 318

Verban, Emil, *160*, 160, 212, 303, 331
Vines, Clauson, 128, *355*
Vitti, Jimmie "Rabbit," *274*
Voelkel, Tommy, *34*
Vogel, Otto, 104, 244
Voiselle, Bill, 12, 65-66, 75, 96, 100, 199, 206, 236, 242, 251, 280, 294, 303, 334

W

Wade, Ben, 13, 45, *65*, 65, 100, 215, 245, 274
Wagner, Honus, *51*
Waitkus, Eddie, 58, 160, 234, 290-291, *291*, 308

Lon Warneke & friend, 1936.

Walker, Del, 96, 182, 307, 309
Walker, Harry, 147
Walker, Rube, 107, 110, 173, 185
Wallace, Bobby, *14*, 14
Wallis, Tarzan, 163, 326
Walston, Ray, 182
Waner, Paul, 146
Ward, Arch, 208
Ward, George, 122
Ward, Ole, 217
Ward, Preston, *20*, 42, *74*, 80, 100, *106*, *160*, 160, 161, 215, 234, 260, 275, 313, 334
Warneke, Lon, 33, *39*, 39, 42, 82, *94*, 162, *163*, 163, 190, 191, 223, *236*, *241*, 243, *249*, *300*, 300, *355, 376*
Warren, Bennie, *275*, 276
Warren, Earl, 97
Watkins, Don, *102*
Wayne, John, 25, *180*, 180, 231

Skipper Jimmie Wilson tries to avoid injury as Stan Hack, Billy Herman, Billy Myers, & Phil Cavarretta go for the ball, 1941.

Weafer, Ken, *26*, 49, 115, *165*, 165, 181
Weaver, Earl, 53
Webb, Earl, *35*, 241
Weber, Boots, 199, 245
Weems, Ted, 182
Weinert, Lefty, 128
Weisel, Maxine, *115*
Weismuller, Johnny, 25, 182
Welch, John, 103
Wells, Fay Gillis, 184-185, *184*, *185*, *336*
Wells, Linton, 184-185
Wells, Snooks, 184-185, *184*, *377*
Westnedge, Lefty, 128, 222
White, Jack, 247-249, *249*, *306*
White, JoJo, 156
White, Wilbur, 299, 300
White, William Sanford, 299-300, 344
Wilder, Billy, 246
Wilhelm, Hoyt, *18*, 18
Williams, Billy, 18
Williams, Dewey, *100*, 100, 225, 242
Williams, Esther, 123
Williams, Harry, 13, 32, 49, 278
Williams, Ted, 52, 62, 127, 227, 292
Wilson, Bert, 107, 122
Wilson, Bobby, 16, *48*, 48
Wilson, Brian, 14
Wilson, Hack, 16, *17*, *35*, 39, 46, *47*, 47-48, *48*, 72, 77, 82, 115, 171, 220, 222, *223*, *281*, 281, 292, *296*, 296, 315, 319, 331
Wilson, Jimmie, 19, 71, 80, *113*, 140, 155, 165, 171, *204*, 204-205, *205*, *212*, 300, 311, 334, *352, 376*
Wing, Toby, 203
Wings, 231
The Wining Team, 124, 140, 142, 167, 182, 197, 241

*Snooks Wells, legendary Ethiopian beast, enjoys the moment after assuring Manager Grimm that she indeed did **not** eat Galan, 1937.*

Wolf, Al, 27, 52, 192, 268, 269
Wood, Kerry, 326, *327*
Wood, Natalie, 181
World War II, 7, 14, 18, 25, 27, 31, 41, 57, 63, 72, 87, 104, 140, 141, 150, 151, *155*, 159, 165, 185, 192, 254, 268-276
Wotus, Ron, 254
Wrigley, Ada, 107, 256, *259*
Wrigley, Blanny (See *Schreiner, Blanny Wrigley*)
Wrigley, DeeDee, *44*, 259
Wrigley, Helen, 258-259, *259*, 260
Wrigley, PK, *18*, 18, 32, *44*, 44, *64*, 64, 69, 78, *93*, 97, 101, 130, 135, 136, 146, *169*, 193, *208*, 208, 210, 211, 245, 247, 255, 257-260, *258*, *260*, 263-264, 266, *267*, 276, 282, 314, *316*, 317, 318, 323, 327, *380*
Wrigley, William, 7, 9, 11-14, 18, 21, 22, *23*, 23, 25, 30, 32, 33, 34, 41, 46, 51, 68, 78, *83*, 83, 85, *86*, 86, 88, 99, 101, *102*, *105*, 126, 127, 129, 131, 132, 136, 138, 139, 157, 158, 192, 194, 195, 196, *197*, 199, 200, *201*, 228-229, 231, *255*, 255-257, *256*, *257*, 277, 282, 286, 288, 297, 311, *323*, 323, 324, *339*, 343

Film star Ronald Reagan thinks he can convince Aimee Alexander that he really is her husband, but she's not buying it.

377

Wrigleyville, 225, 236, 269, 271
Wyman, Jane, 122
Wymbs, Norman, 119
Wyse, Hank, 95, 173, 200, 269

X

(You were expecting something here?)

Y

Young, Loretta, 176

Z

Zane Grey Theater, 124
Zarilla, Al, 124
Zernial, Gus, *176,* 176

Riggs Stephenson legs it out against the New York Giants in 1932, but the ball has already escaped Sam Leslie's grasp.

Joe Marty, practicing highly-developed balancing-the-ball-on-the-bat skills on a Spring morning in the late 1930s.

Think we could get away with calling him 'the matchless Charlie Grimm'?

Bob Collins, Clyde McCullough, & Gabby Hartnett awaiting The 2nd Coming, 1940.*

Smile — you might end up on the front page of a Chicago paper's sports section.

* *It did not come to pass in 1940. Stay tuned...*

Lefty Logan, 1938.

Hank Majeski, 1937.

Mr. PK Wrigley & Charlie Grimm discuss lunchtime plans.

You never know for sure who's gonna show up at Wrigley Field. On this particular afternoon in 1988, it was the President of the United States, a Mr. Reagan.

The Spring of 1949.

Don't worry. We'll get 'em next year. 1940.